RELIGIONS OF CHINA IN PRACTICE

PRINCETON READINGS IN RELIGIONS

———

Donald S. Lopez, Jr., Editor

TITLES IN THE SERIES

———

Religions of India in Practice edited by Donald S. Lopez, Jr.

Buddhism in Practice edited by Donald S. Lopez, Jr.

Religions of China in Practice edited by Donald S. Lopez, Jr.

RELIGIONS OF
CHINA
IN PRACTICE

Donald S. Lopez, Jr., Editor

PRINCETON READINGS IN RELIGIONS

PRINCETON UNIVERSITY PRESS

PRINCETON, NEW JERSEY

Library of Congress Cataloging-in-Publication Data

Religions of China in practice / Donald S. Lopez, Jr., editor.
p.   cm. — (Princeton readings in religions)
Includes bibliographical references and index.
ISBN 0-691-02144-9 (cl : alk. paper). — ISBN 0-691-02143-0 (pb : alk. paper)
1. China—Religion.   I. Lopez, Donald S., 1952–   . II. Series.
BL1802.R43   1996   95-41332

This book has been composed in Berkeley

PRINCETON READINGS

IN RELIGIONS

———

Princeton Readings in Religions is a new series of anthologies on the religions of the world, representing the significant advances that have been made in the study of religions in the last thirty years. The sourcebooks used by previous generations of students placed a heavy emphasis on philosophy and on the religious expressions of elite groups in what were deemed "classical civilizations," especially of Asia and the Middle East. Princeton Readings in Religions provides a different configuration of texts in an attempt better to represent the range of religious practices, placing particular emphasis on the ways in which texts are used in diverse contexts. The series therefore includes ritual manuals, hagiographical and autobiographical works, and folktales, as well as some ethnographic material. Many works are drawn from vernacular sources. The readings in the series are new in two senses. First, very few of the works contained in the volumes have ever been translated into a Western language before. Second, each volume provides new ways to read and understand the religions of the world, breaking down the sometimes misleading stereotypes inherited from the past in an effort to provide both more expansive and more focused perspectives on the richness and diversity of religious expressions. The series is designed for use by a wide range of readers, with key terms translated and technical notes omitted. Each volume also contains a lengthy general introduction by a distinguished scholar in which the histories of the traditions are outlined and the significance of each of the works is explored.

Religions of China in Practice is the third volume of Princeton Readings in Religions. The thirty contributors include leading scholars of the religious traditions of China, each of whom has provided one or more translations of key works, most of which are translated here for the first time. The works translated derive from ancient oracle bones and contemporary ethnographies, from ritual texts and accounts of visions, and are drawn from regions throughout the Chinese cultural sphere, including communities designated by the current government as "minorities." Each chapter begins with a substantial introduction in which the translator discusses the history and influence of the work, identifying points of particular difficulty or interest. Stephen Teiser provides a general introduction in which the major themes and categories of the religions of China are described and analyzed.

Like the other volumes in the series, *Religions of China in Practice* is arranged thematically. As in any categorization, there are inevitable points of overlap among the categories; some chapters could easily fit under more than one section. Within each of the four thematic categories, works are ordered chronologically; in a few instances a chronological sequence has been reversed in order to maintain the proximity of related works. Two additional tables of contents are provided. The first organizes the works by tradition: the familiar categories of Daoism, Buddhism, state religion, popular religion, and minority (non-Han) religions. The second table organizes the works chronologically according to the date when the source translated was first committed to writing, not necessarily when it first circulated orally.

In addition to acknowledging the cooperation and patience of the contributors to *Religions of China in Practice*, I would like especially to thank Stephen Bokenkamp and Catherine Bell for their respective counsel at the beginning and at the end of this long project.

Religions of Japan in Practice is currently in press. Volumes nearing completion or in progress are devoted to Islam in Asia, Islamic mysticism, the religions of Tibet, the religions of Latin America, and early Christianity. Several future volumes are being planned for Judaism and later periods of Christianity.

Donald S. Lopez, Jr.
Series Editor

NOTE ON

TRANSLITERATION

All Chinese terms are rendered in pinyin, and we have attempted to make these renderings consistent through the book. Although there are no universally accepted standards for the English translation of the titles of many Chinese texts, we have attempted to be consistent in the translation of titles. In some cases, however, the preferences of individual translators have been followed. In the first occurrence of a title within a chapter, the title appears in English translation, followed by the Chinese romanization in parentheses. Subsequent occurrences of the title within the chapter are by English title. Technical terms, such as *qi,* whose meanings are open to wide interpretation, have been rendered in English according to the interpretation of each translator. The Chinese romanization of technical terms is provided in parentheses when possible. In the translations, words added to clarify the English appear in brackets. Additional information provided by the translator is provided in parentheses.

CONTENTS

Rituals of the Seen and Unseen Worlds

Earthly Conduct

CONTENTS BY TRADITION

One of the purposes of this volume is to demonstrate that the "three religions" of China, Confucianism, Daoism, and Buddhism (with a fourth, popular religion, sometimes added), are not discrete, mutually exclusive traditions, but instead overlap and interact with each other through a variety of confluences and conflicts. Another purpose of the volume is to suggest that the religions of China are not only the products of Han culture; non-Han or "minority" cultures have also influenced and been influenced by the religions of central China. The general table of contents has been organized thematically in order to suggest the continuities and shared concerns that are evident, through the juxtaposition of Confucian, Daoist, Buddhist, "popular," and minority texts. The works in the volume are listed below, somewhat tentatively, under such categories. As in the general table of contents, a work listed in one category could easily be placed under another. For example, "The Scripture on Perfect Wisdom for Humane Kings Who Wish to Protect Their States," listed here as a Buddhist work, could also be considered a work on state religion, while "Daoist Ritual in Contemporary Southeast China," listed here under popular religion, could also be listed under Daoism.

CONTENTS BY CHRONOLOGY

CONTRIBUTORS

Catherine Bell teaches in the Department of Religious Studies at Santa Clara University.

Mark Bender teaches in the Department of East Asian Languages and Literatures at the Ohio State University.

Alan J. Berkowitz teaches in the Department of Modern Languages and Literatures at Swarthmore College.

Stephen Bokenkamp teaches in the Department of East Asian Languages at Indiana University.

Cynthia Brokaw teaches in the Department of History at the University of Oregon.

Robert Ford Campany teaches in the Department of Religious Studies at Indiana University.

Kenneth Dean teaches in the Department of East Asian Languages at McGill University.

Jean DeBernardi teaches in the Department of Anthropology at the University of Edmonton.

Robert Eno teaches in the Department of East Asian Languages at Indiana University.

Daniel Gardner teaches in the Department of History at Smith College.

Peter N. Gregory teaches in the Program in Religious Studies at the University of Illinois.

Valerie Hansen teaches in the History Department at Yale University.

Donald Harper teaches in Department of East Asian Studies at the University of Arizona.

James L. Hevia teaches in the Department of History at North Carolina A & T University.

Terry F. Kleeman teaches in the Department of East Asian Languages and Literatures at the University of Minnesota.

Livia Kohn teaches in the Department of Theology and Religious Studies at Boston University.

Paul W. Kroll teaches in the Department of Oriental Languages at the University of Colorado.

Donald S. Lopez, Jr., teaches in the Department of Asian Languages and Cultures at the University of Michigan.

Victor H. Mair teaches in the Department of Asian and Middle Eastern Studies at the University of Pennsylvania.

Ellen Neskar teaches in the Department of History at Stanford University.

Peter Nickerson teaches in the Department of Religion at Duke University.

Charles Orzech teaches in the Department of Religious Studies at the University of North Carolina at Greensboro.

Harold D. Roth teaches in the Department of Religious Studies at Brown University.

Robert H. Sharf teaches in the Department of Asian Languages and Cultures at the University of Michigan.

Shi Kun teaches in the Department of Anthropology at the Ohio State University.

Daniel Stevenson teaches in the Department of Religious Studies at the University of Kansas.

Stephen F. Teiser teaches in the Department of Religion at Princeton University.

Anthony R. Walker teaches in the Department of Anthropology at the Ohio State University.

Albert Welter teaches in the Department of History and Religion at North Central College.

Chün-fang Yü teaches in the Department of Religion at Rutgers University.

Angela Zito teaches in the Department of Religion at Barnard College.

RELIGIONS OF CHINA IN PRACTICE

———

The Spirits of Chinese Religion

Stephen F. Teiser

Acknowledging the wisdom of Chinese proverbs, most anthologies of Chinese religion are organized by the logic of the three teachings (*sanjiao*) of Confucianism, Daoism, and Buddhism. Historical precedent and popular parlance attest to the importance of this threefold division for understanding Chinese culture. One of the earliest references to the trinitarian idea is attributed to Li Shiqian, a prominent scholar of the sixth century, who wrote that "Buddhism is the sun, Daoism the moon, and Confucianism the five planets."[1] Li likens the three traditions to significant heavenly bodies, suggesting that although they remain separate, they also coexist as equally indispensable phenomena of the natural world. Other opinions stress the essential unity of the three religious systems. One popular proverb opens by listing the symbols that distinguish the religions from each other, but closes with the assertion that they are fundamentally the same: "The three teachings—the gold and cinnabar of Daoism, the relics of Buddhist figures, as well as the Confucian virtues of humanity and righteousness—are basically one tradition."[2] Stating the point more bluntly, some phrases have been put to use by writers in the long, complicated history of what Western authors have called "syncretism." Such mottoes include "the three teachings are one teaching"; "the three teachings return to the one"; "the three teachings share one body"; and "the three teachings merge into one."[3]

What sense does it make to subsume several thousand years of religious experience under these three (or three-in-one) categories? And why is this anthology organized differently? To answer these questions, we need first to understand what the three teachings are and how they came into existence.

There is a certain risk in beginning this introduction with an archaeology of the three teachings. The danger is that rather than fixing in the reader's mind the most significant forms of Chinese religion—the practices and ideas associated with ancestors, the measures taken to protect against ghosts, or the veneration of gods, topics which are highlighted by the selections in this anthology—emphasis will instead be placed on precisely those terms the anthology seeks to avoid. Or, as one friendly critic stated in a review of an earlier draft of this introduction, why must "the tired old category of the three teachings be inflicted on yet another generation of students?" Indeed, why does this introduction begin on a negative note, as it were, analyzing the problems with subsuming Chinese religion under the three teachings, and insert a positive appraisal of what constitutes Chinese religion only at the end? Why not begin with "popular religion," the gods of China, and kinship and bureaucracy and then, only after those categories are established, proceed to discuss the explicit categories by which Chinese people have ordered their religious world? The answer has to do with the fact that Chinese religion does not come to us purely, or without mediation. The three teachings are a powerful and inescapable part of Chinese religion. Whether they are eventually accepted, rejected, or reformulated, the terms of the past can only be understood by examining how they came to assume their current status. Even the seemingly pristine translations of texts deemed "primary" are products of their time; the materials here have been selected by the translators and the editor according to the concerns of the particular series in which this book is published. This volume, in other words, is as much a product of Chinese religion as it is a tool enabling access to that field. And because Chinese religion has for so long been dominated by the idea of the three teachings, it is essential to understand where those traditions come from, who constructed them and how, as well as what forms of religious life are omitted or denied by constructing such a picture in the first place.

Confucianism

The myth of origins told by proponents of Confucianism (and by plenty of modern historians) begins with Confucius, whose Chinese name was Kong Qiu and who lived from 551 to 479 B.C.E. Judging from the little direct evidence that still survives, however, it appears that Kong Qiu did not view himself as the founder of a school of thought, much less as the originator of anything. What does emerge from the earliest layers of the written record is that Kong Qiu sought a revival of the ideas and institutions of a past golden age. Employed in a minor government position as a specialist in the governmental and family rituals of his native state, Kong Qiu hoped to disseminate knowledge of the rites and inspire their universal performance. That kind of broad-scale transformation could take place, he thought, only with the active encouragement of responsible rulers. The ideal ruler, as exemplified by the legendary sage-kings Yao and Shun or the adviser to the Zhou rulers, the Duke of Zhou, exercises ethical suasion, the ability to influence others by the power of his moral example. To the virtues of the ruler correspond values that each individual is supposed to cultivate: benevolence toward others, a general sense of doing what is right, loyalty and diligence in serving one's superiors. Universal moral ideals are necessary but not sufficient conditions for the restoration of civilization. Society also needs what Kong Qiu calls *li*, roughly translated as "ritual." Although people are supposed to develop propriety or the ability to act appropriately in any given social situation (another sense of the same word, li), still the specific rituals people are supposed to perform (also li) vary considerably, depending on age, social status, gender, and context. In family ritual, for instance, rites of mourning depend on one's kinship relation to the deceased. In international affairs, degrees of pomp, as measured by ornateness of dress and opulence of gifts, depend on the rank of the foreign emissary. Offerings to the gods are also highly regulated: the sacrifices of each social class are restricted to specific classes of deities, and a clear hierarchy prevails. The few explicit statements attributed to Kong Qiu about the problem of history or tradition all portray him as one who "transmits but does not create."[4] Such a claim can, of course, serve the ends of innovation or revolution. But in this case it is clear that Kong Qiu transmitted not only specific rituals and values but also a hierarchical social structure and the weight of the past.

The portrayal of Kong Qiu as originary and the coalescence of a self-conscious identity among people tracing their heritage back to him took place long after his death. Two important scholar-teachers, both of whom aspired to serve as close advisers to a ruler whom they could convince to institute a Confucian style of government, were Meng Ke (or Mengzi, ca. 371–289 B.C.E.) and Xun Qing (or Xunzi, d. 215 B.C.E.). Mengzi viewed himself as a follower of Kong Qiu's example. His doctrines offered a program for perfecting the individual. Sageliness could be achieved through a gentle process of cultivating the innate tendencies toward the good. Xunzi professed the same goal but argued that the means to achieve it required stronger measures. To be civilized, according to Xunzi, people need to restrain their base instincts and have their behavior modified by a system of ritual built into social institutions.

It was only with the founding of the Han dynasty (202 B.C.E.–220 C.E.), however, that Confucianism became Confucianism, that the ideas associated with Kong Qiu's name received state support and were disseminated generally throughout upper-class society. The creation of Confucianism was neither simple nor sudden, as three examples will make clear. In the year 136 B.C.E. the classical writings touted by Confucian scholars were made the foundation of the official system of education and scholarship, to the exclusion of titles supported by other philosophers. The five classics (or five scriptures, wujing) were the Classic of Poetry (Shijing), Classic of History (Shujing), Classic of Changes (Yijing), Record of Rites (Liji), and Chronicles of the Spring and Autumn Period (Chunqiu) with the Zuo Commentary (Zuozhuan), most of which had existed prior to the time of Kong Qiu. (The word jing denotes the warp threads in a piece of cloth. Once adopted as a generic term for the authoritative texts of Han-dynasty Confucianism, it was applied by other traditions to their sacred books. It is translated variously as book, classic, scripture, and sūtra.) Although Kong Qiu was commonly believed to have written or edited some of the five classics, his own statements (collected in the Analects [Lunyu]) and the writings of his closest followers were not yet admitted into the canon. Kong Qiu's name was implicated more directly in the second example of the Confucian system, the state-sponsored cult that erected temples in his honor throughout the empire and that provided monetary support for turning his ancestral home into a national shrine. Members of the literate elite visited such temples, paying formalized respect and enacting rituals in front of spirit tablets of the master and his disciples. The third example is the corpus of writing left by the scholar Dong Zhongshu (ca. 179–104 B.C.E.), who was instrumental in promoting Confucian ideas and books in official circles. Dong was recognized by the government as the leading spokesman for the scholarly elite. His theories provided an overarching cosmological framework for Kong Qiu's ideals, sometimes adding ideas unknown in Kong Qiu's time, sometimes making more explicit or providing a particular interpretation of what was already stated in Kong Qiu's work. Dong drew heavily on concepts of earlier thinkers—few of whom were self-avowed Confucians—to explain the workings of the cosmos. He used the concepts of yin and yang to explain how change followed a knowable pattern, and he elaborated on the role of the ruler as one who connected the realms of Heaven, Earth, and humans. The social hierarchy implicit in Kong Qiu's ideal world was coterminous, thought Dong, with a division of all natural relationships into a superior and inferior member. Dong's theories proved determinative for the political culture of Confucianism during the Han and later dynasties.

What in all of this, we need to ask, was Confucian? Or, more precisely, what kind of thing is the "Confucianism" in each of these examples? In the first, that of the five classics, "Confucianism" amounts to a set of books that were mostly written before Kong Qiu lived but that later tradition associates with his name. It is a curriculum instituted by the emperor for use in the most prestigious institutions of learning. In the second example, "Confucianism" is a complex ritual apparatus, an empire-wide network of shrines patronized by government authorities. It depends upon the ability of the government to maintain religious institutions throughout the empire and upon the willingness of state officials to engage regularly in worship. In the third example, the work of Dong Zhongshu, "Confucianism" is a conceptual scheme, a fluid synthesis of some of Kong Qiu's ideals and the various cosmologies popular well after Kong Qiu lived. Rather than being an updating of something universally acknowledged as Kong Qiu's philosophy, it is a conscious systematizing, under the symbol of Kong Qiu, of ideas current in the Han dynasty.

If even during the Han dynasty the term "Confucianism" covers so many different sorts of things—books, a ritual apparatus, a conceptual scheme—one might well wonder why we persist in using one single word to cover such a broad range of phenomena. Sorting out the pieces of that puzzle is now one of the most pressing tasks in the study of Chinese history, which is already beginning to replace the wooden division of the Chinese intellectual world into the three teachings—each in turn marked by phases called "proto-," "neo-," or "revival of"—with a more critical and nuanced understanding of how traditions are made and sustained. For our more limited purposes here, it is instructive to observe how the word "Confucianism" came to be applied to all of these things and more.[5]

As a word, "Confucianism" is tied to the Latin name, "Confucius," which originated not with Chinese philosophers but with European missionaries in the sixteenth century. Committed to winning over the top echelons of Chinese society, Jesuits and other Catholic orders subscribed to the version of Chinese religious history supplied to them by the educated elite. The story they told was that their teaching began with Kong Qiu, who was referred to as Kongfuzi, rendered into Latin as "Confucius." It was elaborated by Mengzi (rendered as "Mencius") and Xunzi and was given official recognition—as if it had existed as the same entity, unmodified for several hundred years—under the Han dynasty. The teaching changed to the status of an unachieved metaphysical principle during the centuries that Buddhism was believed to have been dominant and was resuscitated— still basically unchanged—only with the teachings of Zhou Dunyi (1017–1073), Zhang Zai (1020), Cheng Hao (1032–1085), and Cheng Yi (1033–1107), and the commentaries authored by Zhu Xi (1130–1200). As a genealogy crucial to the self-definition of modern Confucianism, that myth of origins is both misleading and instructive. It lumps together heterogeneous ideas, books that predate Kong Qiu, and a state-supported cult under the same heading. It denies the diversity of names by which members of a supposedly unitary tradition chose to call themselves, including *ru* (the early meaning of which remains disputed, usually translated as "scholars" or "Confucians"), *daoxue* (study of the Way), *lixue* (study of principle), and *xinxue* (study of the mind). It ignores the long history of contention over interpreting Kong Qiu and overlooks the debt owed by later thinkers like Zhu Xi and Wang Yangming (1472–1529) to Buddhist notions of the mind and practices of meditation and to Daoist ideas of change. And it passes over in silence the role played by non-Chinese regimes in making Confucianism into an orthodoxy, as in the year 1315, when the Mongol government required that the writings of Kong Qiu and his early followers, redacted and interpreted through the commentaries of Zhu Xi, become the basis for the national civil service examination. At the same time, Confucianism's story about itself reveals much. It names the figures, books, and slogans of the past that recent Confucians have found most inspiring. As a string of ideals, it illuminates what its proponents wish it to be. As a lineage, it imagines a line of descent kept pure from the traditions of Daoism and Buddhism. The construction of the latter two teachings involves a similar process. Their histories, as will be seen below, do not simply move from the past to the present; they are also projected backward from specific presents to significant pasts.

Daoism

Most Daoists have argued that the meaningful past is the period that preceded, chronologically and metaphysically, the past in which the legendary sages of Confucianism lived. In the Daoist golden age the empire had not yet been reclaimed out of chaos. Society lacked distinctions based on class, and human beings lived

happily in what resembled primitive, small-scale agricultural collectives. The lines
between different nation-states, between different occupations, even between humans and animals were not clearly drawn. The world knew nothing of the Confucian state, which depended on the carving up of an undifferentiated whole into
social ranks, the imposition of artificially ritualized modes of behavior, and a
campaign for conservative values like loyalty, obeying one's parents, and mod-
eration. Historically speaking, this Daoist vision was first articulated shortly after
the time of Kong Qiu, and we should probably regard the Daoist nostalgia for a
simpler, untrammeled time as roughly contemporary with the development of a
Confucian view of origins. In Daoist mythology whenever a wise man encounters
a representative of Confucianism, be it Kong Qiu himself or an envoy seeking
advice for an emperor, the hermit escapes to a world untainted by civilization.

For Daoists the philosophical equivalent to the pre-imperial primordium is a
state of chaotic wholeness, sometimes called *hundun*, roughly translated as
"chaos." In that state, imagined as an uncarved block or as the beginning of life
in the womb, nothing is lacking. Everything exists, everything is possible: before
a stone is carved there is no limit to the designs that may be cut, and before the
fetus develops the embryo can, in an organic worldview, develop into male or
female. There is not yet any division into parts, any name to distinguish one thing
from another. Prior to birth there is no distinction, from the Daoist standpoint,
between life and death. Once birth happens—once the stone is cut—however,
the world descends into a state of imperfection. Rather than a mythological sin
on the part of the first human beings or an ontological separation of God from
humanity, the Daoist version of the Fall involves division into parts, the assigning
of names, and the leveling of judgments injurious to life. *The Classic on the Way
and Its Power* (*Dao de jing*) describes how the original whole, the *dao* (here meaning
the "Way" above all other ways), was broken up: "The Dao gave birth to the One,
the One gave birth to the Two, the Two gave birth to the Three, and the Three
gave birth to the Ten Thousand Things."[6] That decline-through-differentiation
also offers the model for regaining wholeness. The spirit may be restored by
reversing the process of aging, by reverting from multiplicity to the One. By
understanding the road or path (the same word, dao, in another sense) that the
great Dao followed in its decline, one can return to the root and endure forever.

Practitioners and scholars alike have often succumbed to the beauty and power
of the language of Daoism and proclaimed another version of the Daoist myth of
origins. Many people seem to move from a description of the Daoist faith-stance
(the Dao embraces all things) to active Daoist proselytization masquerading as
historical description (Daoism embraces all forms of Chinese religion). As with
the term "Confucianism," it is important to consider not just what the term
"Daoism" covers, but also where it comes from, who uses it, and what words
Daoists have used over the years to refer to themselves.

The most prominent early writings associated with Daoism are two texts, *The
Classic on the Way and Its Power*, attributed to a mythological figure named Lao
Dan or Laozi who is presumed to have lived during the sixth century B.C.E., and

the *Zhuangzi*, named for its putative author, Zhuang Zhou or Zhuangzi (ca. 370–301 B.C.E.). The books are quite different in language and style. *The Classic on the Way and Its Power* is composed largely of short bits of aphoristic verse, leaving its interpretation and application radically indeterminate. Perhaps because of that openness of meaning, the book has been translated into Western languages more often than any other Chinese text. It has been read as a utopian tract advocating a primitive society as well as a compendium of advice for a fierce, engaged ruler. Its author has been described as a relativist, skeptic, or poet by some, and by others as a committed rationalist who believes in the ability of words to name a reality that exists independently of them. The *Zhuangzi* is a much longer work composed of relatively discrete chapters written largely in prose, each of which brings sustained attention to a particular set of topics. Some portions have been compared to Wittgenstein's *Philosophical Investigations*. Others develop a story at some length or invoke mythological figures from the past. The *Zhuangzi* refers to Laozi by name and quotes some passages from the *Classic on the Way and Its Power*, but the text as we know it includes contributions written over a long span of time. Textual analysis reveals at least four layers, probably more, that may be attributed to different authors and different times, with interests as varied as logic, primitivism, syncretism, and egotism. The word "Daoism" in English (corresponding to Daojia, "the School [or Philosophy] of the Dao") is often used to refer to these and other books or to a free-floating outlook on life inspired by but in no way limited to them.

    "Daoism" is also invoked as the name for religious movements that began to develop in the late second century C.E.; Chinese usage typically refers to their texts as Daojiao, "Teachings of the Dao" or "Religion of the Dao." One of those movements, called the Way of the Celestial Masters (Tianshi dao), possessed mythology and rituals and established a set of social institutions that would be maintained by all later Daoist groups. The Way of the Celestial Masters claims its origin in a revelation dispensed in the year 142 by the Most High Lord Lao (Taishang Laojun), a deified form of Laozi, to a man named Zhang Daoling. Laozi explained teachings to Zhang and bestowed on him the title of "Celestial Master" (Tianshi), indicating his exalted position in a system of ranking that placed those who had achieved immortality at the top and humans who were working their way toward that goal at the bottom. Zhang was active in the part of western China now corresponding to the province of Sichuan, and his descendants continued to build a local infrastructure. The movement divided itself into a number of parishes, to which each member-household was required to pay an annual tax of five pecks of rice—hence the other common name for the movement in its early years, the Way of the Five Pecks of Rice (Wudoumi dao). The administrative structure and some of the political functions of the organization are thought to have been modeled in part on secular government administration. After the Wei dynasty was founded in 220, the government extended recognition to the Way of the Celestial Masters, giving official approval to the form of local social administration it had developed and claiming at the same time that the new emperor's right to rule was guaranteed by the authority of the current Celestial Master.

Several continuing traits are apparent in the first few centuries of the Way of the Celestial Masters. The movement represented itself as having begun with divine-human contact: a god reveals a teaching and bestows a rank on a person. Later Daoist groups received revelations from successively more exalted deities. Even before receiving official recognition, the movement was never divorced from politics. Later Daoist groups too followed that general pattern, sometimes in the form of millenarian movements promising to replace the secular government, sometimes in the form of an established church providing services complementary to those of the state. The local communities of the Way of the Celestial Masters were formed around priests who possessed secret knowledge and held rank in the divine-human bureaucracy. Knowledge and position were interdependent: knowledge of the proper ritual forms and the authority to petition the gods and spirits were guaranteed by the priest's position in the hierarchy, while his rank was confirmed to his community by his expertise in a ritual repertoire. Nearly all types of rituals performed by Daoist masters through the ages are evident in the early years of the Way of the Celestial Masters. Surviving sources describe the curing of illness, often through confession; the exorcism of malevolent spirits; rites of passage in the life of the individual; and the holding of regular communal feasts.

While earlier generations (both Chinese bibliographers and scholars of Chinese religion) have emphasized the distinction between the allegedly pristine philosophy of the "School of the Dao" and the corrupt religion of the "Teachings of the Dao," recent scholarship instead emphasizes the complex continuities between them. Many selections in this anthology focus on the beginnings of organized Daoism and the liturgical and social history of Daoist movements through the fifth century. The history of Daoism can be read, in part, as a succession of revelations, each of which includes but remains superior to the earlier ones. In South China around the year 320 the author Ge Hong wrote *He Who Embraces Simplicity* (*Baopuzi*), which outlines different methods for achieving elevation to that realm of the immortals known as "Great Purity" (Taiqing). Most methods explain how, after the observance of moral codes and rules of abstinence, one needs to gather precious substances for use in complex chemical experiments. Followed properly, the experiments succeed in producing a sacred substance, "gold elixir" (*jindan*), the eating of which leads to immortality. In the second half of the fourth century new scriptures were revealed to a man named Yang Xi, who shared them with a family named Xu. Those texts give their possessors access to an even higher realm of Heaven, that of "Highest Clarity" (Shangqing). The scriptures contain legends about the level of gods residing in the Heaven of Highest Clarity. Imbued with a messianic spirit, the books foretell an apocalypse for which the wise should begin to prepare now. By gaining initiation into the textual tradition of Highest Clarity and following its program for cultivating immortality, adepts are assured of a high rank in the divine bureaucracy and can survive into the new age. The fifth century saw the canonization of a new set of texts, titled "Numinous Treasure" (Lingbao). Most of them are presented as sermons of a still higher level of deities, the Celestial Worthies (Tianzun), who are the most immediate personified manifestations of the Dao. The books instruct followers how to worship the gods supplicated in a wide variety of rituals. Called "retreats" (zhai, a word connoting both "fast" and "feast"), those rites are performed for the salvation of the dead, the bestowal of boons on the living, and the repentance of sins.

As noted in the discussion of the beginnings of the Way of the Celestial Masters, Daoist and imperial interests often intersected. The founder of the Tang dynasty (618–907), Li Yuan (lived 566–635, reigned 618–626, known as Gaozu), for instance, claimed to be a descendant of Laozi's. At various points during the reign of the Li family during the Tang dynasty, prospective candidates for government service were tested for their knowledge of specific Daoist scriptures. Imperial authorities recognized and sometimes paid for ecclesiastical centers where Daoist priests were trained and ordained, and the surviving sources on Chinese history are filled with examples of state sponsorship of specific Daoist ceremonies and the activities of individual priests. Later governments continued to extend official support to the Daoist church, and vice-versa. Many accounts portray the twelfth century as a particularly innovative period: it saw the development of sects named "Supreme Unity" (Taiyi), "Perfect and Great Dao" (Zhenda dao), and "Complete Perfection" (Quanzhen). In the early part of the fifteenth century, the forty-third Celestial Master took charge of compiling and editing Daoist ritual texts, resulting in the promulgation of a Daoist canon that contemporary Daoists still consider authoritative.

Possessing a history of some two thousand years and appealing to people from all walks of life, Daoism appears to the modern student to be a complex and hardly unitary tradition. That diversity is important to keep in mind, especially in light of the claim made by different Daoist groups to maintain a form of the teaching that in its essence has remained the same over the millennia. The very notion of immortality is one way of grounding that claim. The greatest immortals, after all, are still alive. Having conquered death, they have achieved the original state of the uncarved block and are believed to reside in the heavens. The highest gods are personified forms of the Dao, the unchanging Way. They are concretized in the form of stars and other heavenly bodies and can manifest themselves to advanced Daoist practitioners following proper visualization exercises. The transcendents (xianren, often translated as "immortals") began life as humans and returned to the ideal embryonic condition through a variety of means. Some followed a regimen of gymnastics and observed a form of macrobiotic diet that simultaneously built up the pure elements and minimized the coarser ones. Others practiced the art of alchemy, assembling secret ingredients and using laboratory techniques to roll back time. Sometimes the elixir was prepared in real crucibles; sometimes the refining process was carried out eidetically by imagining the interior of the body to function like the test tubes and burners of the lab.

Personalized rites of curing and communal feasts alike can be seen as small steps toward recovering the state of health and wholeness that obtains at the beginning (also the infinite ending) of time. Daoism has always stressed morality. Whether expressed through specific injunctions against stealing, lying, and taking life, through more abstract discussions of virtue, or through exemplary figures who transgress moral codes, ethics was an important element of Daoist practice. Nor should we forget the claim to continuity implied by the institution of priestly investiture. By possessing revealed texts and the secret registers listing the members of the divine hierarchy, the Daoist priest took his place in a structure that appeared to be unchanging.

Another way that Daoists have represented their tradition is by asserting that their activities are different from other religious practices. Daoism is constructed, in part, by projecting a non-Daoist tradition, picking out ideas and actions and assigning them a name that symbolizes "the other."[7] The most common others in the history of Daoism have been the rituals practiced by the less institutionalized, more poorly educated religious specialists at the local level and any phenomenon connected with China's other organized church, Buddhism. Whatever the very real congruences in belief and practice among Daoism, Buddhism, and popular practice, it has been essential to Daoists to assert a fundamental difference. In this perspective the Daoist gods differ in kind from the profane spirits of the popular tradition: the former partake of the pure and impersonal Dao, while the latter demand the sacrifice of meat and threaten their benighted worshippers with illness and other curses. With their hereditary office, complex rituals, and use of the classical Chinese language, modern Daoist masters view themselves as utterly distinct from exorcists and mediums, who utilize only the language of everyday speech and whose possession by spirits appears uncontrolled. Similarly, anti-Buddhist rhetoric (as well as anti-Daoist rhetoric from the Buddhist side) has been severe over the centuries, often resulting in the temporary suppression of books and statues and the purging of the priesthood. All of those attempts to enforce difference, however, must be viewed alongside the equally real overlap, sometimes identity, between Daoism and other traditions. Records compiled by the state detailing the official titles bestowed on gods prove that the gods of the popular tradition and the gods of Daoism often supported each other and coalesced or, at other times, competed in ways that the Daoist church could not control. Ethnographies about modern village life show how all the various religious personnel cooperate to allow for coexistence; in some celebrations they forge an arrangement that allows Daoist priests to officiate at the esoteric rituals performed in the interior of the temple, while mediums enter into trance among the crowds in the outer courtyard. In imperial times the highest echelons of the Daoist and Buddhist priesthoods were capable of viewing their roles as complementary to each other and as necessarily subservient to the state. The government mandated the establishment in each province of temples belonging to both religions; it exercised the right to accept or reject the definition of each religion's canon of sacred books; and it sponsored ceremonial debates between leading exponents of the two churches in which victory most often led to coexistence with, rather than the destruction of, the losing party.

Buddhism

The very name given to Buddhism offers important clues about the way that the tradition has come to be defined in China. Buddhism is often called Fojiao, literally meaning "the teaching (jiao) of the Buddha (Fo)." Buddhism thus appears to be a member of the same class as Confucianism and Daoism: the three teachings are Rujiao ("teaching of the scholars" or Confucianism), Daojiao ("teaching of the Dao" or Daoism), and Fojiao ("teaching of the Buddha" or Buddhism). But there is an interesting difference here, one that requires close attention to language. As semantic units in Chinese, the words Ru and Dao work differently than does Fo. The word Ru refers to a group of people and the word Dao refers to a concept, but the word Fo does not make literal sense in Chinese. Instead it represents a sound, a word with no semantic value that in the ancient language was pronounced as "bud," like the beginning of the Sanskrit word "buddha."[8] The meaning of the Chinese term derives from the fact that it refers to a foreign sound. In Sanskrit the word "buddha" means "one who has achieved enlightenment," one who has "awakened" to the true nature of human existence. Rather than using any of the Chinese words that mean "enlightened one," Buddhists in China have chosen to use a foreign word to name their teaching, much as native speakers of English refer to the religion that began in India not as "the religion of the enlightened one," but rather as "Buddhism," often without knowing precisely what the word "Buddha" means. Referring to Buddhism in China as Fojiao involves the recognition that this teaching, unlike the other two, originated in a foreign land. Its strangeness, its non-native origin, its power are all bound up in its name.

Considered from another angle, the word buddha (fo) also accentuates the ways in which Buddhism in its Chinese context defines a distinctive attitude toward experience. Buddhas—enlightened ones—are unusual because they differ from other, unenlightened individuals and because of the truths to which they have awakened. Most people live in profound ignorance, which causes immense suffering. Buddhas, by contrast, see the true nature of reality. Such propositions, of course, were not advanced in a vacuum. They were articulated originally in the context of traditional Indian cosmology in the first several centuries B.C.E., and as Buddhism began to trickle haphazardly into China in the first centuries of the common era, Buddhist teachers were faced with a dilemma. To make their teachings about the Buddha understood to a non-Indian audience, they often began by explaining the understanding of human existence—the problem, as it were—to which Buddhism provided the answer. Those basic elements of the early Indian worldview are worth reviewing here. In that conception, all human beings are destined to be reborn in other forms, human and nonhuman, over vast stretches of space and time. While time in its most abstract sense does follow a pattern of decline, then renovation, followed by a new decline, and so on, still the process of reincarnation is without beginning or end. Life takes six forms: at the top are gods, demigods, and human beings, while animals, hungry ghosts, and hell beings occupy the lower rungs of the hierarchy. Like the gods of ancient Greece, the gods of Buddhism reside in the heavens and lead lives of immense worldly pleasure. Unlike their Greek counterparts, however, they are without exception mortal, and at the end of a very long life they are invariably reborn lower in the cosmic scale. Hungry ghosts wander in search of food and water yet are unable to eat or drink, and the denizens of the various hells suffer a battery of tortures, but they will all eventually die and be reborn again. The logic that determines where one will be reborn is the idea of *karma*. Strictly speaking the Sanskrit word karma means "deed" or "action." In its relevant sense here it means that every deed has a result: morally good acts lead to good consequences, and the commission of evil has a bad result. Applied to the life of the individual, the law of karma means that the circumstances an individual faces are the result of prior actions. Karma is the regulating idea of a wide range of good works and other Buddhist practices.

The wisdom to which buddhas awaken is to see that this cycle of existence (*saṃsāra* in Sanskrit, comprising birth, death, and rebirth) is marked by impermanence, unsatisfactoriness, and lack of a permanent self. It is impermanent because all things, whether physical objects, psychological states, or philosophical ideas, undergo change; they are brought into existence by preceding conditions at a particular point in time, and they eventually will become extinct. It is unsatisfactory in the sense that not only do sentient beings experience physical pain, they also face continual disappointment when the people and things they wish to maintain invariably change. The third characteristic of sentient existence, lack of a permanent self, has a long and complicated history of exegesis in Buddhism. In China the idea of "no-self" (Sanskrit: *anātman*) was often placed in creative tension with the concept of repeated rebirth. On the one hand, Buddhist teachers tried to convince their audience that human existence did not end simply with a funeral service or memorial to the ancestors, that humans were reborn in another bodily form and could thus be related not only to other human beings but to animals, ghosts, and other species among the six modes of rebirth. To support that argument for rebirth, it was helpful to draw on metaphors of continuity, like a flame passed from one candle to the next and a spirit that moves from one lifetime to the next. On the other hand, the truth of impermanence entailed the argument that no permanent ego could possibly underlie the process of rebirth. What migrated from one lifetime to the next were not eternal elements of personhood but rather temporary aspects of psychophysical life that might endure for a few lifetimes—or a few thousand—but would eventually cease to exist. The Buddha provided an analysis of the ills of human existence and a prescription for curing them. Those ills were caused by the tendency of sentient beings to grasp, to cling to evanescent things in the vain hope that they remain permanent. In this view, the very act of clinging contributes to the perpetuation of desires from one incarnation to the next. Grasping, then, is both a cause and a result of being committed to a permanent self.

The wisdom of buddhas is neither intellectual nor individualistic. It was always believed to be a soteriological knowledge that was expressed in the compassionate activity of teaching others how to achieve liberation from suffering. Traditional formulations of Buddhist practice describe a path to salvation that begins with the observance of morality. Lay followers pledged to abstain from the taking of life, stealing, lying, drinking intoxicating beverages, and engaging in sexual relations outside of marriage. Further injunctions applied to householders who could observe a more demanding life-style of purity, and the lives of monks and nuns were regulated in even greater detail. With morality as a basis, the ideal path also included the cultivation of pure states of mind through the practice of meditation and the achieving of wisdom rivaling that of a buddha.

The discussion so far has concerned the importance of the foreign component in the ideal of the buddha and the actual content to which buddhas are believed to awaken. It is also important to consider what kind of a religious figure a buddha is thought to be. We can distinguish two separate but related understandings of what a buddha is. In the first understanding the Buddha (represented in English with a capital B) was an unusual human born into a royal family in ancient India in the sixth or fifth century B.C.E. He renounced his birthright, followed established religious teachers, and then achieved enlightenment after striking out on his own. He gathered lay and monastic disciples around him and preached throughout the Indian subcontinent for almost fifty years, and he achieved final "extinction" (the root meaning of the Sanskrit word *nirvāṇa*) from the woes of existence. This unique being was called Gautama (family name) Siddhārtha (personal name) during his lifetime, and later tradition refers to him with a variety of names, including Śākyamuni (literally "Sage of the Śākya clan") and Tathāgata ("Thus-Come One"). Followers living after his death lack direct access to him because, as the word "extinction" implies, his release was permanent and complete. His influence can be felt, though, through his traces—through gods who encountered him and are still alive, through long-lived disciples, through the places he touched that can be visited by pilgrims, and through his physical remains and the shrines (*stūpa*) erected over them. In the second understanding a buddha (with a lowercase b) is a generic label for any enlightened being, of whom Śākyamuni was simply one among many. Other buddhas preceded Śākyamuni's appearance in the world, and others will follow him, notably Maitreya (Chinese: Mile), who is thought to reside now in a heavenly realm close to the surface of the Earth. Buddhas are also dispersed over space: they exist in all directions, and one in particular, Amitāyus (or Amitābha, Chinese: Amituo), presides over a land of happiness in the West. Related to this second genre of buddha is another kind of figure, a bodhisattva (literally "one who is intent on enlightenment," Chinese: *pusa*). Bodhisattvas are found in most forms of Buddhism, but their role was particularly emphasized in the many traditions claiming the polemical title of Mahāyāna ("Greater Vehicle," in opposition to Hīnayāna, "Smaller Vehicle") that began to develop in the first century B.C.E. Technically speaking, bodhisattvas are not as advanced as buddhas on the path to enlightenment. Bodhisattvas particularly popular in China include Avalokiteśvara (Chinese: Guanyin, Guanshiyin, or Guanzizai), Bhaiṣajyaguru (Chinese: Yaoshiwang), Kṣitigarbha (Chinese: Dizang), Mañjuśrī (Wenshu), and Samantabhadra (Puxian). While buddhas appear to some followers as remote and all-powerful, bodhisattvas often serve as mediating figures whose compassionate involvement in the impurities of this world makes them more approachable. Like buddhas in the second sense of any enlightened being, they function both as models for followers to emulate and as saviors who intervene actively in the lives of their devotees.

In addition to the word "Buddhism" (Fojiao), Chinese Buddhists have represented the tradition by the formulation of the "three jewels" (Sanskrit: triratna, Chinese: sanbao). Coined in India, the three terms carried both a traditional sense as well as a more worldly reference that is clear in Chinese sources.[9] The first jewel is Buddha, the traditional meaning of which has been discussed above. In China the term refers not only to enlightened beings, but also to the materials through which buddhas are made present, including statues, the buildings that house statues, relics and their containers, and all the finances needed to build and sustain devotion to buddha images.

The second jewel is the dharma (Chinese: fa), meaning "truth" or "law." The dharma includes the doctrines taught by the Buddha and passed down in oral and written form, thought to be equivalent to the universal cosmic law. Many of the teachings are expressed in numerical form, like the three marks of existence (impermanence, unsatisfactoriness, and no-self, discussed above), the four noble truths (unsatisfactoriness, cause, cessation, path), and so on. As a literary tradition the dharma also comprises many different genres, the most important of which is called sūtra in Sanskrit. The Sanskrit word refers to the warp thread of a piece of cloth, the regulating or primary part of the doctrine (compare its Proto-Indo-European root, *syū, which appears in the English words suture, sew, and seam). The earliest Chinese translators of Buddhist Sanskrit texts chose a related loaded term to render the idea in Chinese: jing, which denotes the warp threads in the same manner as the Sanskrit, but which also has the virtue of being the generic name given to the classics of the Confucian and Taoist traditions. Sūtras usually begin with the words "Thus have I heard. Once, when the Buddha dwelled at. . . ." That phrase is attributed to the Buddha's closest disciple, Ānanda, who according to tradition was able to recite all of the Buddha's sermons from memory at the first convocation of monks held after the Buddha died. In its material sense the dharma referred to all media for the Buddha's law in China, including sermons and the platforms on which sermons were delivered, Buddhist rituals that included preaching, and the thousands of books—first handwritten scrolls, then booklets printed with wooden blocks—in which the truth was inscribed.

The third jewel is saṅgha (Chinese: sengqie or zhong), meaning "assembly." Some sources offer a broad interpretation of the term, which comprises the four sub-orders of monks, nuns, lay men, and lay women. Other sources use the term in a stricter sense to include only monks and nuns, that is, those who have left home, renounced family life, accepted vows of celibacy, and undertaken other austerities to devote themselves full-time to the practice of religion. The differences and interdependencies between householders and monastics were rarely absent in any Buddhist civilization. In China those differences found expression in both the spiritual powers popularly attributed to monks and nuns and the hostility sometimes voiced toward their way of life, which seemed to threaten the core values of the Chinese family system. The interdependent nature of the relationship between lay people and the professionally religious is seen in such phenomena as the use of kinship terminology—an attempt to re-create family—among monks and nuns and the collaboration between lay donors and monastic officiants in a wide range of rituals designed to bring comfort to the ancestors. "Saṅgha" in China also referred to all of the phenomena considered to belong to the Buddhist establishment. Everything and everyone needed to sustain monastic life, in a very concrete sense, was included: the living quarters of monks; the lands deeded to temples for occupancy and profit; the tenant families and slaves who worked on the farm land and served the saṅgha; and even the animals attached to the monastery farms.

Standard treatments of the history of Chinese Buddhism tend to emphasize the place of Buddhism in Chinese dynastic history, the translation of Buddhist texts, and the development of schools or sects within Buddhism. While these research agenda are important for our understanding of Chinese Buddhism, many of the contributors to this anthology have chosen to ask rather different questions, and it is worthwhile explaining why.

Many overviews of Chinese Buddhist history are organized by the template of Chinese dynasties. In this perspective, Buddhism began to enter China as a religion of non-Chinese merchants in the later years of the Han dynasty. It was during the following four centuries of disunion, including a division between non-Chinese rulers in the north and native ("Han") governments in the south as well as warfare and social upheaval, that Buddhism allegedly took root in China. Magic and meditation ostensibly appealed to the "barbarian" rulers in the north, while the dominant style of religion pursued by the southerners was philosophical. During the period of disunion, the general consensus suggests, Buddhist translators wrestled with the problem of conveying Indian ideas in a language their Chinese audience could understand; after many false starts Chinese philosophers were finally able to comprehend common Buddhist terms as well as the complexities of the doctrine of emptiness. During the Tang dynasty Buddhism was finally "Sinicized" or made fully Chinese. Most textbooks treat the Tang dynasty as the apogee or mature period of Buddhism in China. The Tang saw unprecedented numbers of ordinations into the ranks of the Buddhist order; the flourishing of new, allegedly "Chinese" schools of thought; and lavish support from the state. After the Tang, it is thought, Buddhism entered into a thousand-year period of decline. Some monks were able to break free of tradition and write

innovative commentaries on older texts or reshape received liturgies, some patrons managed to build significant temples or sponsor the printing of the Buddhist
canon on a large scale, and the occasional highly placed monk found a way to
purge debased monks and nuns from the ranks of the saṅgha and revive moral
vigor, but on the whole the stretch of dynasties after the Tang is treated as a long
slide into intellectual, ethical, and material poverty. Stated in this caricatured a
fashion, the shortcomings of this approach are not hard to discern. This approach
accentuates those episodes in the history of Buddhism that intersect with important moments in a political chronology, the validity of which scholars in Chinese
studies increasingly doubt. The problem is not so much that the older, dynastic-
driven history of China is wrong as that it is limited and one-sided. While traditional history tends to have been written from the top down, more recent attempts argue from the bottom up. Historians in the past forty years have begun
to discern otherwise unseen patterns in the development of Chinese economy,
society, and political institutions. Their conclusions, which increasingly take Buddhism into account, suggest that cycles of rise and fall in population shifts, economy, family fortunes, and the like often have little to do with dynastic history—
the implication being that the history of Buddhism and other Chinese traditions
can no longer be pegged simply to a particular dynasty. Similarly, closer scrutiny
of the documents and a greater appreciation of their biases and gaps have shown
how little we know of what really transpired in the process of the control of
Buddhism by the state. The Buddhist church was always, it seems, dependent on
the support of the landowning classes in medieval China. And it appears that the
condition of Buddhist institutions was tied closely to the occasional, decentralized
support of the lower classes, which is even harder to document than support by
the gentry. The very notion of rise and fall is a teleological, often theological, one,
and it has often been linked to an obsession with one particular criterion—accurate translation of texts, or correct understanding of doctrine—to the exclusion
of all others.

The translation of Buddhist texts from Sanskrit and other Indic and Central
Asian languages into Chinese constitutes a large area of study. Although written
largely in classical Chinese in the context of a premodern civilization in which
relatively few people could read, Buddhist sūtras were known far and wide in
China. The seemingly magical spell (Sanskrit: dhāraṇī) from the Heart Sūtra was
known by many; stories from the Lotus Sūtra were painted on the walls of popular
temples; religious preachers, popular storytellers, and low-class dramatists alike
drew on the rich trove of mythology provided by Buddhist narrative. Scholars of
Buddhism have tended to focus on the chronology and accuracy of translation.
Since so many texts were translated (one eighth-century count of the extant number of canonical works is 1,124),[10] and the languages of Sanskrit and literary
Chinese are so distant, the results of that study are foundational to the field. To
understand the history of Chinese Buddhism it is indispensable to know what
texts were available when, how they were translated and by whom, how they

were inscribed on paper and stone, approved or not approved, disseminated, and argued about. On the other hand, within Buddhist studies scholars have only recently begun to view the act of translation as a conflict-ridden process of negotiation, the results of which were Chinese texts whose meanings were never closed. Older studies, for instance, sometimes distinguish between three different translation styles. One emerged with the earliest known translators, a Parthian given the Chinese name An Shigao (fl. 148–170) and an Indoscythian named Lokakṣema (fl. 167–186), who themselves knew little classical Chinese but who worked with teams of Chinese assistants who peppered the resulting translations with words drawn from the spoken language. The second style was defined by the Kuchean translator Kumārajīva (350–409), who retained some elements of the vernacular in a basic framework of literary Chinese that was more polished, consistent, and acceptable to contemporary Chinese tastes. It is that style—which some have dubbed a "church" language of Buddhist Chinese, by analogy with the cultural history of medieval Latin—that proved most enduring and popular. The third style is exemplified in the work of Xuanzang (ca. 596–664), the seventh-century Chinese monk, philosopher, pilgrim, and translator. Xuanzang was one of the few translators who not only spoke Chinese and knew Sanskrit, but also knew the Chinese literary language well, and it is hardly accidental that Chinese Buddhists and modern scholars alike regard his translations as the most accurate and technically precise. At the same time, there is an irony in Xuanzang's situation that forces us to view the process of translation in a wider context. Xuanzang's is probably the most popular Buddhist image in Chinese folklore: he is the hero of the story *Journey to the West (Xiyou ji)*, known to all classes as the most prolific translator in Chinese history and as an indefatigable, sometimes overly serious and literal, pilgrim who embarked on a sacred mission to recover original texts from India. Though the mythological character is well known, the surviving writings of the seventh-century translator are not. They are, in fact, rarely read, because their grammar and style smack more of Sanskrit than of literary Chinese. What mattered to Chinese audiences—both the larger audience for the novels and dramas about the pilgrim and the much smaller one capable of reading his translations—was that the Chinese texts were based on a valid foreign original, made even more authentic by Xuanzang's personal experiences in the Buddhist homeland.

The projection of categories derived from European, American, and modern Japanese religious experience onto the quite different world of traditional Chinese religion is perhaps most apparent in the tendency of traditional scholarship to treat Chinese Buddhism primarily as a matter of distinct schools or sects. Monks and other literati did indeed make sense of their history by classifying the overwhelming number of texts and teachings they inherited under distinctive trends, and some members of the Buddhist elite claimed allegiance to certain ideals at the expense of others. But any clear-cut criterion of belief, like the Nicene Creed, or a declaration of faith like Martin Luther's, is lacking in the history of Chinese

Buddhism. It may have been only in the fourteenth century that there developed any social reality even approximating Ernst Troeltsch's definition of a sect as a voluntary religious association that people consciously choose to join and that excludes participation in other religious activities—and even then, the type of sect that developed, the Teaching of the White Lotus (Bailian jiao), was only tenuously connected to the "schools" of Chinese Buddhist thought on which scholars usually focus. Trends of thought and clearly identified philosophical issues are part of Chinese Buddhist history from the early centuries, and in the sixth through eighth centuries some figures identified themselves as concerned with one particular scripture: authors in the Tiantai school (named after Mount Tiantai) focused on the *Lotus Sūtra*, and figures of the Huayan school emphasized the comprehensive nature of the *Huayan* ("Flower Garland") *Sūtra*. But the founders of these schools—identified as such only by later generations—and their followers never stopped reading broadly in a wide range of Buddhist texts. Certain emphases also developed in Chinese Buddhist practice and Buddhology, foremost among them the invocation of the name of Amitāyus Buddha (*nianfo*, "keeping the Buddha in mind"), whose powers to assist those who chanted his name and whose resplendent paradise are described at length in scriptures affiliated with the Pure Land (Jingtu) school. In China, however—in contrast to late medieval Japan—dedication to Amitāyus Buddha was rarely viewed as a substitute for other forms of practice. Esoteric forms of Buddhism, characterized by restricting the circulation of knowledge about rituals to a small circle of initiates who perform rituals for those who lack the expertise, were also a strong force in Chinese Buddhism. But here too, even as they performed rites on behalf of individuals or to benefit the state, the monks of the Zhenyan (Sanskrit: Mantra, "True Word") school participated in other forms of Buddhist thought and practice as well. Even the school of Chan ("Meditation"), known in Japanese as Zen, which claimed to be founded on an unbroken transmission from Śākyamuni through twenty-eight Indian disciples to the first Chinese disciple in the late fifth century, was far less exclusive than its rhetoric seems to allow. Claims about transmission, the naming of founders, and the identification of crucial figures in the drama of Chan history were always executed retroactively. The tradition, which claimed its own content to be a non-content, was not so much handed down from past to present as it was imagined in the present, a willful projection into the future, against the reality of a heterogeneous past. As a "school" in the sense of an establishment for teaching and learning with monastery buildings, daily schedule, and administrative structure, Chan came into existence only in the twelfth and thirteenth centuries, and even then the social institution identified as "Chan" was nearly identical to institutions affiliated with other schools. At any rate, English translations of primary sources about Chan and other schools of Chinese Buddhism are readily available elsewhere. The selections in this volume do not ignore sectarian history, but tend to concentrate on practices and ideas shared by larger and less exclusive segments of the Chinese Buddhist community and on schools less well represented in other anthologies.

The Problem of Popular Religion

The brief history of the three teachings offered above provides, it is hoped, a general idea of what they are and how their proponents have come to claim for them the status of a tradition. It is also important to consider what is not named in the formulation of the three teachings. To define Chinese religion primarily in terms of the three traditions is to exclude from serious consideration the ideas and practices that do not fit easily under any of the three labels. Such common rituals as offering incense to the ancestors, conducting funerals, exorcising ghosts, and consulting fortunetellers; belief in the patterned interaction between light and dark forces or in the ruler's influence on the natural world; the tendency to construe gods as government officials; the preference for balancing tranquility and movement—all belong as much to none of the three traditions as they do to one or three. These forms of religion, introduced in more detail below, are the subject of numerous selections in this anthology.

The focus on the three teachings is another way of privileging precisely the varieties of Chinese religious life that have been maintained largely through the support of literate and often powerful representatives. The debate over the unity of the three teachings, even when it is resolved in favor of toleration or harmony— a move toward the one rather than the three—drowns out voices that talk about Chinese religion as neither one nor three. Another problem with the model of the three teachings is that it equalizes what are in fact three radically incommensurable things. Confucianism often functioned as a political ideology and a system of values; Daoism has been compared, inconsistently, to both an outlook on life and a system of gods and magic; and Buddhism offered, according to some analysts, a proper soteriology, an array of techniques and deities enabling one to achieve salvation in the other world. Calling all three traditions by the same unproblematic term, "teaching," perpetuates confusion about how the realms of life that we tend to take for granted (like politics, ethics, ritual, religion) were in fact configured differently in traditional China.

Another way of studying Chinese religion is to focus on those aspects of religious life that are shared by most people, regardless of their affiliation or lack of affiliation with the three teachings. Such forms of popular religion as those named above (offering incense, conducting funerals, and so on) are important to address, although the category of "popular religion" entails its own set of problems.

We can begin by distinguishing two senses of the term "popular religion." The first refers to the forms of religion practiced by almost all Chinese people, regardless of social and economic standing, level of literacy, region, or explicit religious identification. Popular religion in this first sense is the religion shared by people in general, across all social boundaries. Three examples, all of which can be dated as early as the first century of the common era, help us gain some understanding of what counts as popular religion in the first sense. The first example is a typical Chinese funeral and memorial service. Following the death of a family member and the unsuccessful attempt to reclaim his or her spirit, the corpse is prepared for burial. Family members are invited for the first stage of mourning, with higher-ranking families entitled to invite more distant relatives. Rituals of wailing and the wearing of coarse, undyed cloth are practiced in the home of the deceased. After some days the coffin is carried in a procession to the grave. After burial the attention of the living shifts toward caring for the spirit of the dead. In later segments of the funerary rites the spirit is spatially fixed—installed—in a rectangular wooden tablet, kept at first in the home and perhaps later in a clan hall. The family continues to come together as a corporate group on behalf of the deceased; they say prayers and send sustenance, in the form of food, mock money, and documents addressed to the gods who oversee the realm of the dead. The second example of popular or common religion is the New Year's festival, which marks a passage not just in the life of the individual and the family, but in the yearly cycle of the cosmos. As in most civilizations, most festivals in China follow a lunar calendar, which is divided into twelve numbered months of thirty days apiece, divided in half at the full moon (fifteenth night) and new moon (thirtieth night); every several years an additional (or intercalary) month is added to synchronize the passage of time in lunar and solar cycles. Families typically begin to celebrate the New Year's festival ten or so days before the end of the twelfth month. On the twenty-third day, family members dispatch the God of the Hearth (Zaojun), who watches over all that transpires in the home from his throne in the kitchen, to report to the highest god of Heaven, the Jade Emperor (Yuhuang dadi). For the last day or two before the end of the year, the doors to the house are sealed and people worship in front of the images of the various gods kept in the house and the ancestor tablets. After a lavish meal rife with the symbolism of wholeness, longevity, and good fortune, each junior member of the family pros-trates himself and herself before the head of the family and his wife. The next day, the first day of the first month, the doors are opened and the family enjoys a vacation of resting and visiting with friends. The New Year season concludes on the fifteenth night (the full moon) of the first month, typically marked by a lantern celebration.

The third example of popular religion is the ritual of consulting a spirit medium in the home or in a small temple. Clients request the help of mediums (sometimes called "shamans" in Western-language scholarship; in Chinese they are known by many different terms) to solve problems like sickness in the family, nightmares, possession by a ghost or errant spirit, or some other misfortune. During the séance the medium usually enters a trance and incarnates a tutelary deity. The divinity speaks through the medium, sometimes in an altered but comprehensible voice, sometimes in sounds, through movements, or by writing characters in sand that require deciphering by the medium's manager or interpreter. The deity often identifies the problem and prescribes one among a wide range of possible cures. For an illness a particular herbal medicine or offering to a particular spirit may be recommended, while for more serious cases the deity himself, as dramatized in the person of the medium, does battle with the demon causing the difficulty.

The entire drama unfolds in front of an audience composed of family members and nearby residents of the community. Mediums themselves often come from marginal groups (unmarried older women, youths prone to sickness), yet the deities who speak through them are typically part of mainstream religion, and their message tends to affirm rather than question traditional morality.

Some sense of what is at stake in defining "popular religion" in this manner can be gained by considering when, where, and by whom these three different examples are performed. Funerals and memorial services are carried out by most families, even poor ones; they take place in homes, cemeteries, and halls belonging to kinship corporations; and they follow two schedules, one linked to the death date of particular members (every seven days after death, 100 days after death, etc.) and one linked to the passage of nonindividualized calendar time (once per year). From a sociological perspective, the institutions active in the rite are the family, a complex organization stretching back many generations to a common male ancestor, and secondarily the community, which is to some extent protected from the baleful influences of death. The family too is the primary group involved in the New Year's celebration, although there is some validity in attributing a trans-social dimension to the festival in that a cosmic passage is marked by the occasion. Other social spheres are evident in the consultation of a medium: although it is cured through a social drama, sickness is also individuating; and some mediumistic rituals involve the members of a cult dedicated to the particular deity, membership being determined by personal choice.

These answers are significant for the contrast they suggest between traditional Chinese popular religion and the forms of religion characteristic of modern or secularized societies, in which religion is identified largely with doctrine, belief about god, and a large, clearly discernible church. None of the examples of Chinese popular religion is defined primarily by beliefs that necessarily exclude others. People take part in funerals without any necessary commitment to the existence of particular spirits, and belief in the reality of any particular tutelary deity does not preclude worship of other gods. Nor are these forms of religion marked by rigidly drawn lines of affiliation; in brief; there are families, temples, and shrines, but no church. Even the "community" supporting the temple dedicated to a local god is shifting, depending on those who choose to offer incense or make other offerings there on a monthly basis. There are specialists involved in these examples of Chinese popular religion, but their sacerdotal jobs are usually not full-time and seldom involve the theorizing about a higher calling typical of organized religion. Rather, their forte is considered to be knowledge or abilities of a technical sort. Local temples are administered by a standing committee, but the chairmanship of the committee usually rotates among the heads of the dominant families in the particular locale.

Like other categories, "popular religion" in the sense of shared religion obscures as much as it clarifies. Chosen for its difference from the unspoken reality of the academic interpreter (religion in modern Europe and America), popular religion as a category functions more as a contrastive notion than as a constitutive one; it tells us what much of Chinese religion is not like, rather than spelling out a positive content. It is too broad a category to be of much help to detailed understanding—which indeed is why many scholars in the field avoid the term, preferring to deal with more discrete and meaningful units like family religion, mortuary ritual, seasonal festivals, divination, curing, and mythology. "Popular religion" in the sense of common religion also hides potentially significant variation: witness the number of times words like "typical," "standard," "traditional," "often," and "usually" recur in the preceding paragraphs, without specifying particular people, times, and places, or naming particular understandings of orthodoxy. In addition to being static and timeless, the category prejudices the case against seeing popular religion as a conflict-ridden attempt to impose one particular standard on contending groups. Several of the contributions to this volume, for instance, are works from non-Han cultures. Their inclusion suggests that we view China not as a unitary Han culture peppered with "minorities," but as a complex region in which a diversity of cultures are interacting. To place all of them under the heading of "popular religion" is to obscure a fascinating conflict of cultures.

We may expect a similar mix of insight and erasure in the second sense of "popular religion," which refers to the religion of the lower classes as opposed to that of the elite. The bifurcation of society into two tiers is hardly a new idea. It began with some of the earliest Chinese theorists of religion. Xunzi, for instance, discusses the emotional, social, and cosmic benefits of carrying out memorial rites. In his opinion, mortuary ritual allows people to balance sadness and longing and to express grief, and it restores the natural order to the world. Different social classes, writes Xunzi, interpret sacrifices differently: "Among gentlemen [junzi], they are taken as the way of humans; among common people [baixing], they are taken as matters involving ghosts."[11] For Xunzi, "gentlemen" are those who have achieved nobility because of their virtue, not their birth; they consciously dedicate themselves to following and thinking about a course of action explicitly identified as moral. The common people, by contrast, are not so much amoral or immoral as they are unreflective. Without making a conscious decision, they believe that in the rites addressed to gods or the spirits of the dead, the objects of the sacrifice—the spirits themselves—actually exist. The true member of the upper class, however, adopts something like the attitude of the secular social theorist: bracketing the existence of spirits, what is important about death ritual is the effect it has on society. Both classes engage in the same activity, but they have radically different interpretations of it.

Dividing what is clearly too broad a category (Chinese religion or ritual) into two discrete classes (elite and folk) is not without advantages. It is a helpful pedagogical tool for throwing into question some of the egalitarian presuppositions frequently encountered in introductory courses on religion: that, for instance, everyone's religious options are or should be the same, or that other people's religious life can be understood (or tried out) without reference to social status. Treating Chinese religion as fundamentally affected by social position also helps scholars to focus on differences in styles of religious practice and interpretation. One way to formulate this view is to say that while all inhabitants of a certain community might take part in a religious procession, their style—both their pattern of practice and their understanding of their actions—will differ according to social position. Well-educated elites tend to view gods in abstract, impersonal terms and to demonstrate restrained respect, but the uneducated tend to view gods as concrete, personal beings before whom fear is appropriate.

In the social sciences and humanities in general there has been a clear move in the past forty years away from studies of the elite, and scholarship on Chinese religion is beginning to catch up with that trend. More and more studies focus on the religion of the lower classes and on the problems involved in studying the culture of the illiterati in a complex civilization. Many of the contributors to this anthology reflect a concern not only with the "folk" as opposed to the "elite," but with how to integrate our knowledge of those two strata and how our understanding of Chinese religion, determined unreflectively for many years by accepting an elite viewpoint, has begun to change. In all of this, questions of social class (Who participates? Who believes?) and questions of audience (Who writes or performs? For what kind of people?) are paramount.

At the same time, treating "popular religion" as the religion of the folk can easily perpetuate confusion. Some modern Chinese intellectuals, for instance, are committed to an agenda of modernizing and reviving Chinese spiritual life in a way that both accords with Western secularism and does not reject all of traditional Chinese religion. The prominent twentieth-century Confucian and interpreter of Chinese culture Wing-tsit Chan, for instance, distinguishes between "the level of the masses" and "the level of the enlightened." The masses worship idols, objects of nature, and nearly any deity, while the enlightened confine their worship to Heaven, ancestors, moral exemplars, and historical persons. The former believe in heavens and hells and indulge in astrology and dream interpretation, but the latter "are seldom contaminated by these diseases."[12] For authors like Chan, both those who lived during the upheavals of the last century in China and those in Chinese diaspora communities, Chinese intellectuals still bear the responsibility to lead their civilization away from superstition and toward enlightenment. In that worldview there is no doubt where the religion of the masses belongs. From that position it can be a short step—one frequently taken by scholars of Chinese religion—to treating Chinese popular religion in a dismissive spirit. Modern anthologies of Chinese tradition can still be found that describe Chinese popular religion as "grosser forms of superstition," capable only of "facile syncretism" and resulting in "a rather shapeless tradition."

Kinship and Bureaucracy

It is often said that Chinese civilization has been fundamentally shaped by two enduring structures, the Chinese family system and the Chinese form of bureaucracy. Given the embeddedness of religion in Chinese social life, it would indeed be surprising if Chinese religion were devoid of such regulating concepts. The discussion below is not confined to delineating what might be considered the "hard" social structures of the family and the state, the effects of which might be seen in the "softer" realms of religion and values. The reach of kinship and bureaucracy is too great, their reproduction and representation far richer than could be conveyed by treating them as simple, given realities. Instead we will explain them also as metaphors and strategies.

Early Christian missionaries to China were fascinated with the religious aspects of the Chinese kinship system, which they dubbed "ancestor worship." Recently anthropologists have changed the wording to "the cult of the dead" because the concept of worship implies a supernatural or transcendent object of veneration, which the ancestors clearly are not. The newer term, however, is not much better, because "the dead" are hardly lifeless. As one modern observer remarks, the ancestral cult "is not primarily a matter of belief. . . . The cult of ancestors is more nearly a matter of plain everyday behavior. . . . No question of belief ever arises. The ancestors . . . literally live among their descendants, not only biologically, but also socially and psychologically."[13] The significance of the ancestors is partly explained by the structure of the traditional Chinese family: in marriages women are sent to other surname groups (exogamy); newly married couples tend to live with the husband's family (virilocality); and descent—deciding to which family one ultimately belongs—is traced back in time through the husband's male ancestors (patrilineage). A family in the normative sense includes many generations, past, present, and future, all of whom trace their ancestry through their father (if male) or their husband's father (if female) to an originating male ancestor. For young men the ideal is to grow up "under the ancestors' shadow" (in Hsu's felicitous phrase), by bringing in a wife from another family, begetting sons and growing prosperous, showering honor on the ancestors through material success, cooperating with brothers in sharing family property, and receiving respect during life and veneration after death from succeeding generations. For young women the avowed goal is to marry into a prosperous family with a kind mother-in-law, give birth to sons who will perpetuate the family line, depend upon one's children for immediate emotional support, and reap the benefits of old age as the wife of the primary man of the household.

Early philosophers assigned a specific term to the value of upholding the ideal family: they called it xiao, usually translated as "filial piety" or "filiality." The written character is composed of the graph for "elder" placed above the graph for "son," an apt visual reminder of the interdependence of the generations and the subordination of sons. If the system works well, then the younger generations support the senior ones, and the ancestors bestow fortune, longevity, and the birth of sons upon the living. As each son fulfills his duty, he progresses up the family scale, eventually assuming his status as revered ancestor. The attitude toward the dead (or rather the significant and, it is hoped, benevolent dead—one's ancestors) is simply a continuation of one's attitude toward one's parents while they were living. In all cases, the theory goes, one treats them with respect and veneration by fulfilling their personal wishes and acting according to the dictates of ritual tradition.

Like any significant social category, kinship in China is not without tension and self-contradiction. One already alluded to is gender: personhood as a function of the family system is different for men and women. Sons are typically born into their lineage and hope to remain under the same roof from childhood into old age and ancestorhood. By contrast, daughters are brought up by a family that is not ultimately theirs; at marriage they move into a new home; as young brides without children they are not yet inalienable members of their husband's lineage; and even after they have children they may still have serious conflicts with the de facto head of the household, their husband's mother. Women may gain more security from their living children than from the prospect of being a venerated ancestor. In the afterlife, in fact, they are punished for having polluted the natural world with the blood of parturition; the same virtue that the kinship system requires of them as producers of sons it also defines as a sin. There is also in the ideal of filiality a thinly veiled pretense to universality and equal access that also serves to rationalize the *status inaequalis*. Lavish funerals and the withdrawal from employment by the chief mourner for three years following his parents' death are the ideal. In the Confucian tradition such examples of conspicuous expenditure are interpreted as expressions of the highest devotion, rather than as a waste of resources and blatant unproductivity in which only the leisure class is free to indulge. And the ideals of respect of younger generations for older ones and cooperation among brothers often conflict with reality.

Many aspects of Chinese religion are informed by the metaphor of kinship. The kinship system is significant not only for the path of security it defines but also because of the religious discomfort attributed to all those who fall short of the ideal. It can be argued that the vagaries of life in any period of Chinese history provide as many counterexamples as fulfillments of the process of becoming an ancestor. Babies and children die young, before becoming accepted members of any family; men remain unmarried, without sons to carry on their name or memory; women are not successfully matched with a mate, thus lacking any mooring in the afterlife; individuals die in unsettling ways or come back from the dead as ghosts carrying grudges deemed fatal to the living. There are plenty of people, in other words, who are not caught by the safety net of the Chinese kinship system. They may be more prone than others to possession by spirits, or their anomalous position may not be manifest until after they die. In either case they are religiously significant because they abrogate an ideal of proper kinship relations.

Patrilineage exercises its influence as a regulating concept even in religious organizations where normal kinship—men and women marrying, having children, and tracing their lineage through the husband's father—is impossible. The Buddhist monkhood is a prime example;[14] sororities of unmarried women, adoption of children, and the creation of other "fictive" kinship ties are others. One of the defining features of being a Buddhist monk in China is called "leaving the family" (*chujia*, a translation of the Sanskrit *pravrajya*). Being homeless means not only that the boy has left the family in which he grew up and has taken up domicile in a monastery, but also that he has vowed to abstain from any sexual relations. Monks commit themselves to having no children. The defining feature of monasticism in China is its denial, its interruption of the patrilineage. At the same time, monks create for themselves a home—or a family—away from home; the Buddhist order adopts some of the important characteristics of the Chinese kinship system. One part of the ordination ceremony is the adoption of a religious name, both a new family name and a new personal name, by which one will henceforth be known. The family name for all Chinese monks, at least since the beginning of the fifth century, is the same surname attributed to the historical Buddha (Shi in Chinese, which is a shortened transliteration of the first part of Śākyamuni). For personal names, monks are usually assigned a two-character name by their teacher. Many teachers follow a practice common in the bestowal of secular personal names: the first character for all monks in a particular generation is the same, and the second character is different, bestowing individuality. "Brothers" of the same generation can be picked out because one element of their name is the same; as far as their names are concerned, their relationship to each other is the same as that between secular brothers. Not only do monks construct names and sibling relations modeled on those of Chinese kinship, they also construe themselves as Buddhist sons and descendants of Buddhist fathers and ancestors. Monks of the past are not only called "ancestors," they are also treated as secular ancestors are treated. The portraits and statues of past members are installed, in order, in special ancestral halls where they receive offerings and obeisance from current generations.

Another domain of Chinese religion that bears the imprint of Chinese kinship is hagiography, written accounts of gods and saints. Biographies of secular figures have long been part of the Chinese written tradition. Scholarly opinion usually cites the biographies contained in the first-century B.C.E. *Records of the Historian* (*Shiji*) as the paradigm for later biographical writing. Such accounts typically begin not with the birth of the protagonist, but rather with his or her family background. They narrate the individual's precocious abilities, posts held in government, actions deemed particularly virtuous or vile, and posthumous fate, including titles awarded by the government and the disposition of the corpse or grave. They are written in polished classical prose, and, like the writing of Chinese history, they are designed to cast their subjects as either models for emulation or unfortunate examples to be avoided. Many of the same features can be found in the hagiographies contained in this anthology. Gods who are bureaucrats, goddesses, incarnations of bodhisattvas, even immortals like Laozi and deities of the stars are all conceived through the lens of the Chinese family.

The logic of Chinese kinship can also be seen in a wide range of rituals, many of which take place outside the family and bear no overt relationship to kinship. The basic premise of many such rites is a family banquet, a feast to which members of the oldest generation of the family (the highest ancestors) are invited as honored guests. Placement of individuals and the sequence of action often follow seniority, with older generations coming before younger ones. Such principles can be observed even in Buddhist rites and the community celebrations enacted by groups defined by locale rather than kinship.

What about the other organizing force in Chinese civilization, the bureaucratic form of government used to rule the empire? It too has exerted tremendous influence on Chinese religious life. Before discussing bureaucracy proper, it is helpful to introduce some of the other defining features of Chinese government.

Chinese political culture has, at least since the later years of the Shang dynasty (ca. 1600–1028 B.C.E.), been conceived of as a dynastic system. A dynasty is defined by a founder whose virtue makes clear to all—both common people and other factions vying for control—that he and his family are fit to take over from a previous, corrupt ruler. Shortly after assuming the position of emperor, the new ruler chooses a name for the dynasty: Shang, for instance, means to increase or prosper. Other cosmically significant actions follow. The new emperor installs his family's ancestral tablets in the imperial ancestral hall; he performs the sacrifices to Heaven and Earth that are the emperor's duty; he announces new names of offices and institutes a reorganization of government; and the office of history and astronomy in the government keeps careful watch over any unusual phenomena (the appearance of freakish animals, unusual flora, comets, eclipses, etc.) that might indicate the pleasure or displeasure of Heaven at the change in rule. All activities that take place leading up to and during the reign of the first emperor in a new dynasty appear to be based on the idea that the ruler is one whose power is justified because of his virtue and abilities. When the new emperor dies and one of his sons succeeds to the throne, however, another principle of sovereignty is invoked: the second emperor is deemed fit to rule because he is the highest-ranking son in the ruling family. First emperors legitimate their rule by virtue; second and later emperors validate their rule by family connections. The latter rationale is invoked until the end of the dynasty, when another family asserts that its moral rectitude justifies a change. Thus, the dynastic system makes use of two theories of legitimation, one based on virtue and one based on birth.

Another important principle of Chinese politics, at least since the early years of the Zhou dynasty, is summarized by the slogan "the mandate of Heaven" (Tianming). In this conception, the emperor and his family carry out the commands of Heaven, the latter conceived as a divine, semi-natural, semi-personal force. Heaven demonstrates its approval of an emperor by vouchsafing plentiful harvests, social order, and portents of nature that are interpreted positively. Heaven manifests its displeasure with an emperor and hints at a change in dynasty by sending down famine, drought, widespread sickness, political turmoil, or other portents. It is important to note that the notion of the mandate of Heaven can serve to justify revolution as well as continuity. Rebellions in Chinese history, both those that have failed and those that have succeeded, usually claim that Heaven has proclaimed its displeasure with the ruling house and is transferring its mandate to a new group. The judgment of whether the mandate has indeed shifted is in principle always open to debate. It furnishes a compelling rationale for all current regimes at the same time that it holds open the possibility of revolution on divine grounds.

The dynastic system and the mandate of Heaven were joined to a third basic idea, that of bureaucracy. A bureaucratic form of government is not, of course, unique to China. What is important for our purposes is the particular shape and function of the bureaucracy and its reach into nearly all spheres of Chinese life, including religion.

Max Weber's listing of the characteristics of bureaucracy offers a helpful starting point for discussing the Chinese case. According to Weber, bureaucracy includes: (1) the principle of official jurisdictional areas, so that the duties and powers of each office are clearly stipulated; (2) the principle of hierarchy, which makes clear who ranks above and who ranks below, with all subordinates following their superiors; (3) the keeping of written records or files and a class of scribes whose duty is to make copies; (4) training of officials for their specific tasks; (5) full-time employment of the highest officials; and (6) the following of general rules.[15] Virtually all of these principles can be found in one form or another in the Chinese bureaucracy, the roots of which some scholars trace to the religion of the second millennium B.C.E. The only consistent qualification that needs to be made (as Weber himself points out[16]) concerns the fourth point. Aspirants to government service were admitted to the job, in theory at least, only after passing a series of examinations, but the examination system rewarded a general course of learning in arts and letters rather than the technical skills demanded in some posts like engineering, forensic medicine, and so on.

The central government was also local; the chief government official responsible for a county was a magistrate, selected from a central pool on the basis of his performance in the examinations and assigned to a specific county where he had no prior family connections. He was responsible for employing lower-level functionaries in the county like scribes, clerks, sheriffs, and jailers; for collecting taxes; for keeping the peace; and, looking upward in the hierarchy, for reporting to his superiors and following their instructions. He performed a number of overtly religious functions. He made offerings at a variety of officially recognized temples, like those dedicated to the God of Walls and Moats (the so-called "City God," Chenghuang shen) and to local deified heroes; he gave lectures to the local residents about morality; and he kept close watch over all religious activities, especially those involving voluntary organizations of people outside of family and locality groups, whose actions might threaten the sovereignty and religious prerogative of the state. He was promoted on the basis of seniority and past performance, hoping to be named to higher posts with larger areas of jurisdiction or to a position in the central administration resident in the capital city. In his official capacity his interactions with others were highly formalized and impersonal.

One of the most obvious areas influenced by the bureaucratic metaphor is the Chinese pantheon. For many years it has been a truism that the Chinese conception of gods is based on the Chinese bureaucracy, that the social organization of the human government is the essential model that Chinese people use when imagining the gods. At the apex of the divine bureaucracy stands the Jade Emperor (Yuhuang dadi) in Heaven, corresponding to the human Son of Heaven (Tianzi, another name for emperor) who rules over Earth. The Jade Emperor is in charge of an administration divided into bureaus. Each bureaucrat-god takes responsibility for a clearly defined domain or discrete function. The local officials of the celestial administration are the Gods of Walls and Moats, and below them are the Gods of the Hearth, one per family, who generate a never-ending flow of reports on the people under their jurisdiction. They are assisted in turn by gods believed to dwell inside each person's body, who accompany people through life and into death, carrying with them the records of good and evil deeds committed by their charges. The very lowest officers are those who administer punishment to deceased spirits passing through the purgatorial chambers of the underworld. They too have reports to fill out, citizens to keep track of, and jails to manage. Recent scholarship has begun to criticize the generalization that most Chinese gods are bureaucratic, raising questions about the way in which the relation between the human realm and the divine realm should be conceptualized. Should the two realms be viewed as two essentially different orders, with one taking priority over the other? Should the two bureaucracies be seen as an expression in two spheres of a more unitary conceptualization of power? Is the attempt to separate a presumably concrete social system from an allegedly idealized projection wrong in the first place? Other studies (and the discussion in the next section) suggest that some of the more significant deities of Chinese religion are not approached in bureaucratic terms at all.

An important characteristic of any developed bureaucratic system, earthly or celestial, is that it is wrapped in an aura of permanence and freedom from blame. Office-holders are distinct from the office they fill. Individual magistrates and gods come and go, but the functions they serve and the system that assigns them their duties do not change. Government officials always seem capable of corruption, and specific individuals may be blameworthy, but in a sprawling and principled bureaucracy, the blame attaches only to the individuals currently occupying the office, and wholesale questioning of the structure as a whole is easily deferred. Graft may be everywhere—local magistrates and the jailers of the other world are equally susceptible to bribes—but the injustice of the bureaucracy in general is seldom broached. When revolutionary groups have succeeded or threatened to succeed in overthrowing the government, their alternative visions are, as often as not, couched not in utopian or apolitical terms, but as a new version of the old kingdom, the bureaucracy of which is staffed only by the pure.

Bureaucratic logic is also a striking part of Chinese iconography, temple architecture, and ritual structure. For peasants who could not read in traditional times, the bureaucratic nature of the gods was an apodictic matter of appearance: gods were dressed as government officials. Their temples are laid out like imperial palaces, which include audience halls where one approaches the god with the proper deportment. Many rituals involving the gods follow bureaucratic procedures. Just as one communicates with a government official through his staff, utilizing proper written forms, so too common people depend on literate scribes to write out their prayers, in the correct literary form, which are often communicated to the other world by fire.

The Spirits of Chinese Religion

Up to this point the discussion has touched frequently on the subject of gods without explaining what gods are and how they are believed to be related to other kinds of beings. To understand Chinese theology (literally "discourse about gods"), we need to explore theories about human existence, and before that we need to review some of the basic concepts of Chinese cosmology.

What is the Chinese conception of the cosmos? Any simple answer to that question, of course, merely confirms the biases assumed but not articulated by the question—that there is only one such authentically Chinese view, and that the cosmos as such, present unproblematically to all people, was a coherent topic of discussion in traditional China. Nevertheless, the answer to that question offered by one scholar of China, Joseph Needham, provides a helpful starting point for the analysis. In Needham's opinion, the dominant strand of ancient Chinese thought is remarkable for the way it contrasts with European ideas. While the latter approach the world religiously as created by a transcendent deity or as a battleground between spirit and matter, or scientifically as a mechanism consisting of objects and their attributes, ancient Chinese thinkers viewed the world as a complete and complex "organism." "Things behaved in particular ways," writes Needham, "not necessarily because of prior actions or impulsions of other things, but because their position in the ever-moving cyclical universe was such that they were endowed with intrinsic natures which made that behaviour inevitable for them."[17] Rather than being created out of nothing, the world evolved into its current condition of complexity out of a prior state of simplicity and undifferentiation. The cosmos continues to change, but there is a consistent pattern to that change discernible to human beings. Observation of the seasons and celestial realms, and methods like plastromancy and scapulimancy (divination using tortoise shells and shoulder blades), dream divination, and manipulating the hexagrams of the *Classic of Changes* allow people to understand the pattern of the universe as a whole by focusing on the changes taking place in one of its meaningful parts.

The basic stuff out of which all things are made is called *qi*. Everything that ever existed, at all times, is made of qi, including inanimate matter, humans and animals, the sky, ideas and emotions, demons and ghosts, the undifferentiated state of wholeness, and the world when it is teeming with different beings. As an axiomatic concept with a wide range of meaning, the word qi has over the years been translated in numerous ways. Even in this anthology, different translators render it into English in three different ways. Because it involves phenomena we would consider both psychological—connected to human thoughts and feel-ings—and physical, it can be translated as "psychophysical stuff." The translation "pneuma" draws on one early etymology of the word as vapor, steam, or breath. "Vital energy" accentuates the potential for life inherent to the more ethereal forms of qi. These meanings of qi hold for most schools of thought in early Chinese religion; it is only with the renaissance of Confucian traditions undertaken by Zhu Xi and others that qi is interpreted not as a single thing, part-matter and part-energy, pervading everything, but as one of two basic metaphysical building blocks. According to Zhu Xi, all things partake of both qi and li (homophonous to but different from the li meaning "ritual" or "propriety"), the latter understood as the reason a thing is what it is and its underlying "principle" or "reason."

While traditional cosmology remained monistic, in the sense that qi as the most basic constituent of the universe was a single thing rather than a duality or plu-rality of things, still qi was thought to move or to operate according to a pattern that did conform to two basic modes. The Chinese words for those two modalities are yin and yang; I shall attempt to explain them here but shall leave them un-translated. Yin and yang are best understood in terms of symbolism. When the sun shines on a mountain at some time other than midday, the mountain has one shady side and one sunny side. Yin is the emblem for the shady side and its characteristics; yang is the emblem for the sunny side and its qualities. Since the sun has not yet warmed the yin side, it is dark, cool, and moist; plants are con-tracted and dormant; and water in the form of dew moves downward. The yang side of the mountain is the opposite. It is bright, warm, and dry; plants open up and extend their stalks to catch the sun; and water in the form of fog moves upward as it evaporates. This basic symbolism was extended to include a host of other oppositions. Yin is female, yang is male. Yin occupies the lower position, yang the higher. Any situation in the human or natural world can be analyzed within this framework; yin and yang can be used to understand the modulations of qi on a mountainside as well as the relationships within the family. The social hierarchies of gender and age, for instance—the duty of the wife to honor her husband, and of younger generations to obey older ones—were interpreted as the natural subordination of yin to yang. The same reasoning can be applied to any two members of a pair. Yin-yang symbolism simultaneously places them on an equal footing and ranks them hierarchically. On the one hand, all processes are marked by change, making it inevitable that yin and yang alternate and imperative that humans seek a harmonious balance between the two. On the other hand, the system as a whole attaches greater value to the ascendant member of the pair, the yang. Such are the philosophical possibilities of the conceptual scheme. Some interpreters of yin and yang choose to emphasize the nondualistic, harmonious nature of the relationship, while others emphasize the imbalance, hierarchy, and conflict built into the idea.

How is human life analyzed in terms of the yin and yang modes of "material energy" (yet another rendering of qi)? Health for the individual consists in the harmonious balancing of yin and yang. When the two modes depart from their natural course, sickness and death result. Sleep, which is dark and therefore yin, needs to be balanced by wakefulness, which is yang. Salty tastes (yin) should be matched by bitter ones (yang); inactivity should alternate with movement; and so on. Normally the material energy that constitutes a person, though constantly shifting, is unitary enough to sustain a healthy life. When the material energy is blocked, follows improper patterns, or is invaded by pathogens, then the imbalance between yin and yang threatens to pull the person apart, the coarser forms of material energy (which are yin) remaining attached to the body or near the corpse, the more ethereal forms of material energy (which are yang) tending to float up and away. Dream-states and minor sicknesses are simply gentler forms of the personal dissociation—the radical conflict between yin and yang—that comes with spirit-possession, serious illness, and death. At death the material force composing the person dissipates, and even that dissipation follows a pattern analyzable in terms of yin and yang. The yin parts of the person—collectively called "earthly souls" (po)—move downward, constituting the flesh of the corpse, perhaps also returning as a ghost to haunt the living. Since they are more like energy than matter, the yang parts of the person—collectively called "heavenly souls" (hun)—float upward. They—notice that there is more than one of each kind of "soul," making a unique soul or even a dualism of the spirit impossible in principle—are thought to be reborn in Heaven or as another being, to be resident in the ancestral tablets, to be associated more amorphously with the ancestors stretching back seven generations, or to be in all three places at once.

Above I claimed that a knowledge of Chinese cosmology and anthropology was essential to understanding what place gods occupy in the Chinese conceptual world. That is because the complicated term "god," in the sense either of a being believed to be perfect in power, wisdom, and goodness or a superhuman figure worthy of worship, does not correspond straightforwardly to a single Chinese term with a similar range of meanings. Instead, there are general areas of overlap, as well as concepts that have no correspondence, between the things we would consider "gods" and specific Chinese terms. Rather than pursuing this question from the side of modern English usage, however, we will begin with the important Chinese terms and explain their range of meanings.

One of the terms crucial to understanding Chinese religion is *shen*, which in this introduction I translate with different versions of the English word "spirit." Below these three words are analyzed separately as consisting of three distinct spheres of meaning, but one should keep in mind that the three senses are all rooted in a single Chinese word. They differ only in degree or realm of application, not in kind.

The first meaning of shen is confined to the domain of the individual human being: it may be translated as "spirit" in the sense of "human spirit" or "psyche." It is the basic power or agency within humans that accounts for life. To extend life to full potential the spirit must be cultivated, resulting in ever clearer, more luminous states of being. In physiological terms "spirit" is a general term for the "heavenly souls," in contrast to the yin elements of the person.

The second meaning of shen may be rendered in English as "spirits" or "gods," the latter written in lowercase because Chinese spirits and gods need not be seen as all-powerful, transcendent, or creators of the world. They are intimately involved in the affairs of the world, generally lacking a perch or time frame completely beyond the human realm. An early Chinese dictionary explains: "Shen are the spirits of Heaven. They draw out the ten thousand things."[18] As the spirits associated with objects like stars, mountains, and streams, they exercise a direct influence on things in this world, making phenomena appear and causing things to extend themselves. In this sense of "spirits," shen are yang and opposed to the yin class of things known in Chinese as gui, "ghosts" or "demons." The two words put together, as in the combined form guishen ("ghosts and spirits"), cover all manner of spiritual beings in the largest sense, those benevolent and malevolent, lucky and unlucky. In this view, spirits are manifestations of the yang material force, and ghosts are manifestations of the yin material force. The nineteenth-century Dutch scholar Jan J. M. de Groot emphasized this aspect of the Chinese worldview, claiming that "animism" was an apt characterization of Chinese religion because all parts of the universe—rocks, trees, planets, animals, humans—could be animated by spirits, good or bad. As support for that thesis he quotes a disciple of Zhu Xi's: "Between Heaven and Earth there is no thing that does not consist of yin and yang, and there is no place where yin and yang are not found. Therefore there is no place where gods and spirits do not exist."[19]

Shen in its third meaning can be translated as "spiritual." An entity is "spiritual" in the sense of inspiring awe or wonder because it combines categories usually kept separate, or it cannot be comprehended through normal concepts. The Classic of Changes states, " 'Spiritual' means not measured by yin and yang."[20] Things that are numinous cross categories. They cannot be fathomed as either yin or yang, and they possess the power to disrupt the entire system of yin and yang. A related synonym, one that emphasizes the power of such spiritual things, is ling, meaning "numinous" or possessing unusual spiritual characteristics. Examples that are considered shen in the sense of "spiritual" include albino members of a species; beings that are part-animal, part-human; women who die before marriage and turn into ghosts receiving no care; people who die in unusual ways like suicide or on battlefields far from home; and people whose bodies fail to decompose or emit strange signs after death.

The fact that these three fields of meaning ("spirit," "spirits," and "spiritual") can be traced to a single word has important implications for analyzing Chinese religion. Perhaps most importantly, it indicates that there is no unbridgeable gap separating humans from gods or, for that matter, separating good spirits from demons. All are composed of the same basic stuff, qi, and there is no ontological distinction between them. Humans are born with the capacity to transform their spirit into one of the gods of the Chinese pantheon. The hagiographies included in this anthology offer details about how some people succeed in becoming gods and how godlike exemplars and saints inspire people to follow their example.

The broad range of meaning for the word shen is related to the coexistence, sometimes harmonious, sometimes not, of a number of different idioms for talking about Chinese gods. An earlier section quoted Xunzi's comment that distinguishes between a naive fear of gods on the part of the uneducated and a pragmatic, agnostic attitude on the part of the literati. Although they share common practices and might use the same words to talk about them, those words mean different things. Similarly, in one of the translations in this volume ("Zhu Xi on Spirit Beings"), Zhu Xi uses homonyms and etymology to abstract—to disembody—the usual meaning of spirits and ghosts. Spirits (*shen*), he says, are nothing but the "extension" (*shen*, pronounced the same but in fact a different word) of material energy, and ghosts (*gui*) amount to the "returning" (*gui*, also homophonous but a different word) of material energy.

Chinese gods have been understood—experienced, spoken to, dreamed about, written down, carved, painted—according to a number of different models. The bureaucratic model (viewing gods as office-holders, not individuals, with all the duties and rights appropriate to the specific rank) is probably the most common but by no means the only one. Spirits are also addressed as stern fathers or compassionate mothers. Some are thought to be more pure than others, because they are manifestations of astral bodies or because they willingly dirty themselves with birth and death in order to bring people salvation. Others are held up as paragons of the common values thought to define social life, like obedience to parents, loyalty to superiors, sincerity, or trustworthiness. Still others possess power, and sometimes entertainment value, because they flaunt standard mores and conventional distinctions.

Books on Chinese religion can still be found that attempt to portray the spirit—understood in the singular, in the theoretical sense of essential principle—of Chinese tradition. That kind of book treats the subject of gods, if it raises the question at all, as an interesting but ultimately illogical concern of the superstitious. The primary texts translated in this anthology represent an attempt to move from a monolithic and abstract conception of the Chinese spirit to a picture, or an occasionally contentious series of pictures, of the many spirits of Chinese religion.

Notes

I am grateful to several kind spirits who offered helpful comments on early drafts of this essay. They include the anonymous readers of the book manuscript, Donald S. Lopez, Jr., Yang Lu, Susan Naquin, Daniel L. Overmyer, and Robert H. Sharf.

1. Li's formulation is quoted in *Beishi*, Li Yanshou (seventh century), Bona ed. (Beijing: Zhonghua shuju, 1974), p. 1234. Unless otherwise noted, all translations from Chinese are mine.

2. The proverb, originally appearing in the sixteenth-century novel *Investiture of the Gods* (*Fengshen yanyi*), is quoted in Clifford H. Plopper, *Chinese Religion Seen through the Proverb* (Shanghai: The China Press, 1926), p. 16.

3. The first three are quoted in Plopper, *Chinese Religion*, p. 15. The last is quoted in Judith Berling, *The Syncretic Religion of Lin Chao-en* (New York: Columbia University Press, 1980), p. 8. See also Timothy Brook, "Rethinking Syncretism: The Unity of the Three Teachings and Their Joint Worship in Late-Imperial China," *Journal of Chinese Religions* 21 (Fall 1993):13–44.

4. The phrase is *shu er bu zuo*, quoted from the *Analects, Lunyu zhengyi*, annot. Liu Baonan (1791–1855), in *Zhuzi jicheng* (Shanghai: Shijie shuju, 1936), 2:134.

5. For further details, see Lionel M. Jensen, "The Invention of 'Confucius' and His Chinese Other, 'Kong Fuzi,'" *Positions: East Asia Cultures Critique* 1.2 (Fall 1993): 414–59; and Thomas A. Wilson, *Geneaology of the Way: The Construction and Uses of the Confucian Tradition in Late Imperial China* (Stanford: Stanford University Press, 1995).

6. *Laozi dao de jing*, ch. 42, *Zhuzi jicheng* (Shanghai: Shijie shuju, 1936), 3:26.

7. For three views on the subject, see Kristofer Schipper, "Purity and Strangers: Shifting Boundaries in Medieval Taoism," *T'oung Pao* 80 (1994): 61–81; Rolf A. Stein, "Religious Taoism and Popular Religion from the Second to Seventh Centuries," in *Facets of Taoism*, ed. Holmes Welch and Anna Seidel (New Haven: Yale University Press, 1979), pp. 53–81; and Michel Strickmann, "History, Anthropology, and Chinese Religion," *Harvard Journal of Asiatic Studies* 40.1 (June 1980): 201–48.

8. In fact the linguistic situation is more complex. Some scholars suggest that Fo is a transliteration not from Sanskrit but from Tocharian; see, for instance, Ji Xianlin, "Futu yu Fo," *Guoli zhongyang yanjiuyuan Lishi yuyan yanjisuo jikan* 20.1 (1948): 93–105.

9. On the extended meaning of the three jewels in Chinese sources, see Jacques Gernet, *Buddhism in Chinese Society: An Economic History from the Fifth to the Tenth Centuries*, trans. Franciscus Verellen (New York: Columbia University Press, 1995), p. 67.

10. *Kaiyuan shijiao lu*, Zhisheng (669–740), T 2154, 55:572b.

11. *Xunzi jijie*, ed. Wang Xianqian, in *Zhuzi jicheng* (Shanghai: Shijie shuju, 1935), 2:250.

12. Wing-tsit Chan, *Religious Trends in Modern China* (New York: Columbia University Press, 1953), pp. 141, 142.

13. Francis L. K. Hsu, *Under the Ancestors' Shadow: Kinship, Personality, and Social Mobility in China*, 2d ed. (Stanford: Stanford University Press, 1971), p. 246.

14. See John Jorgensen, "The 'Imperial' Lineage of Ch'an Buddhism: The Role of Confucian Ritual and Ancestor Worship in Ch'an's Search for Legitimation in the Mid-T'ang Dynasty," *Papers on Far Eastern History* 35 (March 1987): 89–134.

15. Max Weber, *Economy and Society: An Outline of Interpretive Sociology*, ed. Guenther Roth and Claus Wittich, trans. Ephraim Fischoff et al., 2 vols. (Berkeley: University of California Press, 1978), pp. 956–58.

16. Ibid., p. 1049.

17. Joseph Needham, with the research assistance of Wang Ling, *Science and Civilisation in China*, vol. 2: *History of Scientific Thought* (Cambridge: Cambridge University Press, 1956), p. 281.

18. *Shuowen jiezi*, Xu Shen (d. 120), in *Shuowen jiezi gulin zhengbu hebian*, ed. Duan Yucai (1735–1815) and Ding Fubao, 12 vols. (Taibei: Dingwen shuju, 1977), 2:86a.

19. Jan J. M. de Groot, *The Religious System of China: Its Ancient Forms, Evolution, History and Present Aspect, Manners, Customs and Social Institutions Connected Therewith*, 6 vols. (Leiden: E.J. Brill, 1892–1910), 4:51. My translation differs slightly from de Groot's.

20. *Zhouyi yinde*, Harvard-Yenching Institute Sinological Index Series, Supplement no. 10 (reprint ed., Taibei: Ch'eng-wen Publishing Co., 1966), p. 41a.

The Unseen World

1

Deities and Ancestors in Early Oracle Inscriptions

Robert Eno

When we ask questions about the oldest forms of religious practice in China, the earliest data that we find are ritual objects from China's Neolithic era: objects excavated by archaeologists in graves dating from as early as 7000 B.C.E. Such ritual vessels, weapons, ornaments, and figures, and the organization of the grave and village sites where they are found, give us a great deal of information about early Chinese religion. However, our understanding of Neolithic religion in China is tentative, and the religious imagination of the period is a closed book to us because the evidence of this preliterate era does not "speak."

The earliest written records of religious practice in China are known as the "oracle texts" or "oracle bone inscriptions." They date from the period of the Shang dynasty, a ruling house that presided over an early form of the Chinese polity from the middle of the first millennium to about 1028 B.C.E. The Shang ruling house may not have been the first dynastic line in Chinese history: many scholars believe in the existence of a prior ruling house known as the Xia. But it was during the Shang period that China entered the Bronze Age and developed the written ideographic script that is the ancestor of modern Chinese. When we examine the evidence that archaeologists have unearthed from the distant past, the first voice that we hear is that of the Shang people.

The written records left by the Shang are all religious in nature (unlike the earliest written records of Mesopotamian civilization, which are primarily commercial). During the latter centuries of the Shang period, the Shang kings established a royal ritual center on the banks of the Huan River, near the site of the present-day city of Anyang in North Central China. At this place, surrounded by royal palaces and graves, a small group of diviners in the service of the king employed specialized techniques to communicate with a complex world of spirits. The oracle texts, discovered by archaeologists only within the past century, are the records of these communications.

The Shang diviners were specialists in the art of pyromancy, the use of fire to foretell the future. Shang diviners would carefully drill hollows in turtle shells and ox shoulder blades and then, by applying red-hot pokers to these hollows, cause these shells and bones to crack. As they applied the pokers, they would call out questions or statements to spirits that had presumably been summoned by preparatory rituals. The cracking of the bones represented the responses of the spirits, and the diviners were trained to interpret the meanings of the cracks.

The subjects of royal divination were diverse. The success of the harvest, the outcomes of battles, the schedule of ritual sacrifices, even the cause of a royal toothache—all were objects of divination.

After the divination was complete, the diviners or their scribes carefully etched beside the cracks, in the earliest form of Chinese script known, the words that they had uttered to the spirits, along with, in many cases, the name of the diviner and the date on which the bone or shell was cracked. These dates were recorded according to a cyclical calendar of sixty days. Each day was named by combining in regular sequence one sign from each of two ordinal sets, the first with ten elements and the second with twelve elements (one trip through the first set constituted the Shang ten-day week). A typical inscription might begin:

> On the day jia-zi (the first day of the sixty-day calendar cycle), cracks were made; So-and-so divined . . .

with the specific question recorded next. Occasionally the diviner was the Shang king himself.

In some instances the inscriptions include a phrase prognosticating the future on the basis of the cracks, and some also record the outcome of events. In these cases, the predictions are attributed to the Shang king. When outcomes are indicated, the king's prediction is never shown to have been in error. This record of perfection indicates that the king's personal powers of spiritual interpretation may have been a central facet of his prestige and political legitimacy. (We may assume that the absence of recorded errors by the king does not reflect his perfect prescience, but rather a respectful silence concerning his failures.)

It is largely this meticulous record keeping that has allowed us to begin to understand Shang culture and religion. Although the primitive form of the inscribed characters makes them difficult to decipher, traditions of Shang culture preserved in later historical texts have provided us with the contextual clues we need to learn to read the oracle inscriptions. Nevertheless, the oracle bones came to light less than a century ago, and we are far from fully understanding the inscriptions. New information and new interpretive ideas regularly force us to reexamine our readings for individual texts.

A very large portion of the inscriptions concern the performance of ritual sacrifices to royal ancestors and other spirits. Few oracle texts have been discovered outside the ritual center at Anyang, and the divinations should be viewed as one portion of a greater sphere of religious activity focused there. The Shang kings nourished their forebears with a variety of sacrificial offerings on a regular schedule. As ancestors proliferated over time, the schedule became packed: by the end of the dynasty, major sacrificial ceremonies were mounted to individual ancestors every day of the year. Each ancestor received scheduled sacrifices on a specific day of the ten-day week, and ancestors were generally denoted according to the cyclical day on which they were regularly honored. In addition, sacrifices were offered on occasions where the undertaking of important royal activities led the king to seek ancestral goodwill, or where unforeseen disasters suggested the need to propitiate ancestors. The oracle texts suggest that it was obligatory to seek spirit approval prior to mounting any significant sacrificial ritual. Here is an example of a typical divination concerning ritual plans:

1. On the day bing-wu, cracks were made; Xing divined: On the coming day ding-wei, if we sacrifice to Father Ding will there be no misfortune? (*Lin [Kikkō]* 1.21.5)

"Father Ding" was an ancestral king. His posthumous name, Ding, denotes the day of the Shang week on which he received regular sacrifices. In this case, Diviner Xing is checking to make sure that the sacrifice due to Father Ding on the next ding-day will be well received.

The sacrificial activities of the Shang represent an area of religious practice distinct from divination per se. Sacrifices to spirits were directed by figures we refer to loosely as "priests" or "shamans," and it is not clear to what degree these people were distinct from the diviners. The Shang texts themselves say little about these figures. Some inscriptions seem to refer to a ritual practice of burning a shamaness, but our understanding of these inscriptions is not yet clear.

The oracle texts reveal that sacrificial rituals could be extremely complex. They could involve music and dance performances or offerings to a series of spirits, and they often called for the slaughter of large numbers of animals or even human beings, as the following texts indicate:

2. Shall we perform a rain dance to the [Yellow] River and to Yue Peak? (*Cuibian* 51)

3. Shall we pray for rain by offering up one ram each to the ten royal spirits: High Ancestor Shang-jia, Great Ancestors Yi, Ding, Geng, and Wu, Middle Ancestor Ding, and Grandfathers Yi, Xin, and Ding? (*Yicun* 986)

4. Shall we sacrifice one hundred Qiang people (a nomadic enemy tribe) and one hundred sets of sheep and pigs to [High King] Tang, Great Ancestors Jian and Ding, and Grandfather Yi? (*Yicun* 873)

5. Shall we sacrifice two elders of the Qiang tribe to Grandfather Ding and Father Jia? (*Jingjin* 4034)

In many cases, the inscriptions are terse and seem routine, as if the diviners were merely going through empty rituals of spiritual consultation required before ritual events. For example, a great number of oracle texts from the last years of the Shang do little more than announce the impending performance of scheduled sacrifices to royal ancestors. This has suggested to some scholars that the last Shang rulers had ceased to view divination as an effective means of spirit communication. But detailed divinations from earlier generations clearly show the seriousness of divinatory prognostication.

> 6. On the day gui-si, cracks were made; Que divined: In the coming week will there be no disaster? The king prognosticated, saying, "There shall be misfortune." It was as he said. The next day the king went rhinoceros hunting. The horse and chariot of Petty Minister Cai toppled over, and the king's son Yang, who was driving the king's chariot, also fell. (*Jinghua* 1)

This detailed inscription was undoubtedly recorded to demonstrate the divinatory powers of the king, but it is also of interest because it records the Shang king attentively reviewing what would appear to be a routine divination.

Many aspects of Shang society are revealed to us only through the bone records, but none so completely as religious practice. Every divination record, regardless of subject, enhances our understanding of Shang religion, either because it names deities, because it specifies rituals associated with religious practice, or simply because it tells us which events the Shang people believed fell under the control of the spirits.

One aspect of Shang religion revealed with great directness by the oracle texts is the Shang pantheon. Although the texts that have survived are not adequate to provide a complete picture, the central membership of the pantheon emerges clearly. The spirits with whom the royal diviners communicated seem to have belonged to four types. Most numerous are the spirits of the royal ancestors: the father and mother, uncles and aunts, grandparents and remote forebears of the ruling king. Because the royal ancestors were, in many cases, the former rulers of the state and their consorts, we can see in the communication with these spirits not only the centrality of ancestral spirit action to living members of a clan—the basis of ancestor worship, the most widespread form of religious practice in traditional China—but also the political importance of the spirit world to the well-being of the state. When the king's ancestors influenced the course of worldly events, all of Shang China felt the result.

A second, less prominent, group of spirits seems to be composed of a diverse variety of "culture heroes," legendary or semilegendary figures who played a role in tales of the distant past. Some of these spirits may have belonged to predynastic Shang ancestors; others may have been deities worshipped by smaller tribal groups that joined the Shang polity in the course of its political expansion. Incorporation of the tribe within the Shang state may have been linked to incorporation of its leading deities in the Shang pantheon.

A third group of spirits is composed of nature deities, such as river, mountain, or weather spirits. While nature deities play a minor role in the inscriptions, their very presence signals for us the complexity of Shang religious thought and may suggest an earlier, pantheistic phase of religious practice.

Finally, a single spirit of great power and abstractness seems to function as the apex of the Shang pantheon. This spirit is referred to by the name "Di" or "Shang Di" ("Di Above," sometimes translated as "Lord on High"—the word Shang is not the same as the dynastic title). The specific qualities of Di are difficult to ascertain. Modern scholars argue whether Di was conceived as a particular high ancestor, as a collective body of high ancestors, as a single force of nature, or as Nature itself. Unlike other spirits, Di received no sacrificial offerings, yet no other spirit could match the range and force of its powers. We do not even know whether the word *di* meant god or was the name of a god. The Chinese character itself is of uncertain origin. It also appears in the oracle texts as a generic title for some deceased kings and perhaps also for some nature spirits, as in passage 27 below. Later, after the Shang house was conquered by the Zhou people, the highest spirit power was referred to both as Di and as "Tian," a term that also denoted the sky and which is sometimes translated as "Heaven." We do not know whether Tian represented a non-Shang high deity whom the Zhou introduced as an equivalent of the Shang deity Di, but most interpreters agree that Tian does not appear in the oracle texts.

It is always important to bear in mind that the oracle texts, while touching on many aspects of Shang life, can only represent the concerns of the royal house and the religious skills of the pyromantic diviners. The Shang was a rich society that may have included many types of religious practice about which no literary record remains. It is, for example, very difficult to see the relationship between our oracle texts and the shamanic artistry embellishing another major relic of Shang religious practice: the bronze vessels employed in ceremonies of sacrifice. Although the examples below let us listen to the voices of China's religious past, we must bear in mind that we hear only the words of a select few.

The selection of texts that follows here represents only a tiny fraction of the thousands that have been recovered. They raise many questions, some of which can be answered through a fuller exploration of the oracle inscriptions. Other questions remain beyond our ability to answer. The selection begins with a group of inscriptions that concern the deity Di. These texts are followed by smaller groups concerning natural and ancestral deities. Last, there is a group of texts selected to illustrate the diverse concerns of Shang divination and the range of cultural features seen as relevant to the world of spirits. For simplicity, all texts are rendered as questions, and introductory dating formulas and diviner names are generally omitted. Undecipherable proper names are noted by an X.

All references in parentheses are to standard oracle text collections. Abbreviations follow Shima Kunio, *Inkyo bokuji sōrui* (Tokyo, 1967), with bracketed alternative abbreviations in some cases.

Further Readings

Kwang-chih Chang, *Art, Myth, and Ritual: The Path to Political Authority in Ancient China* (Cambridge: Harvard University Press, 1983), is a readable collection of adventuresome essays on Shang religion and society. Chang employs the dramatic iconography of ritual bronzes to explore Shang shamanism. His methodology shows how we may go beyond oracle text evidence to enrich our portrait of Shang religion. Many of Chang's ideas remain speculative rather than firmly demonstrated, but they are always informed by his extraordinary scholarship. His *Shang Civilization* (New Haven: Yale University Press, 1980) is the most complete cultural account of the Shang people and the best English-language resource for viewing Shang religion in social context. Chang pays due attention to the nature of archaeological and textual sources and problems of interpretation. David N. Keightley, "The Religious Commitment: Shang Theology and the Genesis of Chinese Political Culture," *History of Religions* 17.3–4 (February–May 1978): 211–25, offers a clear account of the Shang pantheon that attempts to show how it may reveal continuities between the political cultures of the Shang and later Chinese eras. Keightley is the foremost Western specialist on oracle inscriptions. Even beginners will find it exciting to survey the text and illustrations of his technical handbook, *Sources of Shang History* (Berkeley: University of California Press, 1978).

THE POWERS OF DI

7. Will Di perhaps send down drought upon us? (*Qianbian* 3.24.4)

Shang society was agricultural. No subject concerned the king more than the success of the crops.

8. Will Di order rain sufficient for harvest? Will Di not order rain sufficient for the harvest? (*Qianbian* 1.50.1)

Many texts are paired, one positive and one negative. Diviners seem to have prompted the spirits by adding the word "perhaps" to the less preferred option.

9. Will Di bring disaster to our harvest? Will Di not bring disaster to our harvest? The king prognosticated, saying, "Di shall not bring disaster." (*Yibian* 7456)

10. Will Di order rain in the fourth month? Will Di perhaps not order rain in the fourth month? The king prognosticated, saying, "It will rain on the coming ding-day and probably not on the coming xin-day." On the day ding-you it did, in fact, rain. (*Yibian* 3090)

11. Will Di perhaps, upon reaching the [intercalary] thirteenth lunar month, order a thunderstorm? (*Yibian* 3282)

12. It has not rained [for a long time]. Is Di harming this city [at Anyang]; does Di not approve [of our actions]? The king prognosticated saying, "It is Di who is harming the city; [Di] does not approve." (*Yizhu* 620)

13. Will Di perhaps order wind? (*Hebian* 195)

14. As for attacking the Qiong tribe, will Di provide us support? (*Lin [Kikkō]* 1.11.13)

The Shang polity was surrounded and pitted with tribes unfriendly to the Shang king and his allies. Warfare and military tours of inspection were a central part of royal life and spirit influence.

15. If the king surveys the border lands this spring, will Di provide him with support (protection)?' (*Xubian* 5.14.4)

16. If the king joined with Guo of Zhi (a military ally) in attacking the (non-Shang) tribe of X, would Di provide support? (*Yibian* 3787)

17. The outer tribes attack and destroy: has Di ordered that disaster be inflicted upon us? (*Jinzhang* 496)

18. Will Di perhaps bring an end to this city? (*Bingbian* 66)

Some interpreters have argued that the fact that Di could conceivably bring an end to the Shang ritual center in this way proves that Di was not conceived as a Shang ancestor. For a spirit to so destroy its own descendants would be to cut itself off from all further reverence and sustenance provided through sacrificial offerings.

19. If the king establishes a walled town, will Di show approval? (*Bingbian* 86)

20. Will Di not harm the king? (*Yibian* 4525)

21. Will Di perhaps not bless the king? (*Tieyun* 191.4)

22. [If we sacrifice] to Di's minister, will there be rain? (*Jiabian* 779)

Bureaucratic structures are so pervasive in later Chinese images of the spirit world that interpreters have searched the oracle texts for signs of such imagery. Texts 22–24 are among a small group that seem to support the notion of the Shang pantheon as possessing some bureaucratic features.

23. Shall we sacrifice two hounds to Di's envoy Wind? (*Yizhu* 935)

The winds were of interest to Shang diviners, although their precise role is unclear. One oracle text is simply a record of the winds of the four directions, each wind designated by a proper name.

24. Shall we, in autumn, [sacrifice] to Di's Five Meritorious Ministers? [We made these divination] cracks in the temple of Grandfather Yi. (*Cuibian* 12)

25. Shall [High King] Cheng be a guest to Di? Shall Great Ancestor Jia be a guest to Cheng? (*Bingbian* 36)

This text, which is part of a larger set on a single bone fragment, seems to refer to a ritual performance in which one spirit is worshipped in the shrine of another. In this set, Di acts only in the role of "host"; all the others mentioned are Shang ancestral kings.

NATURAL DEITIES

26. Shall we call for Que to sacrifice a sheep and a goat to the rising sun and the setting sun? (*Hebian* 178)   .

The grammar of the oracle inscriptions often fails to make clear whether offerings are being made to anthropomorphically conceived nature deities or simply in the direction of astral, meteorological, or geographical features.

27. Shall we make a burnt offering to Cloud Di? (*Xubian* 2.4.11)

This text appears to use "Di" as a generic title, applied here to a nature spirit.

28. Shall we call upon Que to sacrifice a hound by fire to Cloud? (*Yibian* 5317)

29. If we, perhaps, perform a fire sacrifice to Snow, will there will be a great rain? (*Jinzhang* 189)

30. On the day bing-shen, cracks were made; Que divined: On yi-si [nine days from now] should we offer wine libations to [royal ancestor] the Latter Yi? The king prognosticated, saying, "When we offer the libation there will be misfortune. There will perhaps be thunder." On yi-si day we offered wine libations. In the early morning it rained. After the sacrifice was performed the rain ceased. At the sacrifice to Xian it also rained. We offered two sacrifices to the Bird Star. That evening it thundered in the west. (*Yibian* 6664)

This intriguing inscription, recorded on the front and back of a single turtle shell, places sacrifices to the Bird Star, important in traditional Chinese astrology, in series with sacrifices to ancestral figures: the Latter Yi, the twelfth Shang king, and Xian, tentatively identified as the first Shang king. Does the series imply a linkage among these ancestral and nonancestral figures?

31. The king prognosticated, saying, "There shall be misfortune." On the eighth day, clouds in the form of a face covered the sun; a rainbow appeared and drank from the Yellow River. (*Jinghua* 4)

Rainbows were considered inauspicious. The inscribed graph seems to picture a two-headed, snakelike creature.

32. Shall we pray for harvest to [the Yellow] River? (*Yicun* 376)

33. Will the [Yellow] River not order rain? The king prognosticated, saying, "The River will order rain." (*Yibian* 3121)

34. Shall we pray for harvest to Yue Peak with a burnt offering of three sheep and three pigs and the decapitation of three oxen? (*Nanming* [*Nanbei*] 457)

35. Shall we, by means of an offering of wine, pray for harvest to Yue Peak, [the Yellow] River, and Kui? (*Qianbian* 7.5.2)

The third object of this sacrifice is not the spirit of a géographical feature, as the first two are, but a distant ancestor or culture hero. Some interpreters take him to be the founder of the Shang lineage.

36. Will the Huan River not bring disaster to this city? (*Xubian* 4.28.4)

37. Is it the [Yellow] River that is harming the king? (*Yibian* 5265)

ANCESTRAL SPIRITS

38. Does this eclipse of the sun mean not disaster but approval? Should we report this eclipse of the sun to the [Yellow] River? Should we perhaps report this eclipse of the sun to Father Ding, sacrificing nine oxen? (*Cuibian* 55)

Although the patterns of sacrifice are in many ways different, the functions of ancestral and nature deities overlap, as the diviner's questions here indicate.

39. Shall we pray for a good harvest to Wang-hai (a predynastic Shang ruler) by offering up a hound, a sheep, a pig, with a burnt offering of three sets of sheep and pig, and the slaughtering of nine oxen, three piglets, and three Qiang people? (*Jing* [*Jinbun*] 609)

40. Is it High Ancestor Shang-jia who is hindering the rain? (*Yibian* 6299)

41. Should we protect the king's eyes against Grandmother Ji? (*Yibian* 4720)

42. Is it Father Yi who is hurting the king's tooth? (*Yibian* 7183)

43. Has Prince Yu encountered disaster on account of Mother Geng? (*Kufang* 481)

44. Should we perhaps pray for a child to High Grandmother Bing? (*Qianbian* 1.33.3)

Childbirth was a central issue for the royal clan. The Shang throne generally passed from elder to younger brothers, and then ideally to the male children of the eldest brother of the preceding generation. The birth of male heirs was crucial, and Shang royalty practiced a form of polygamy to ensure that the succession would proceed. The inscriptions reveal the close connection between the spirit world and childbirth.

45. When Yu, the consort of the king's son Shang, gives birth, shall it not be fortunate (a boy)? (*Cuibian* 1239)

46. When Fu Hao gives birth, shall it not be fortunate? (*Hebian* 405)

Fu Hao was a powerful consort of the twenty-first Shang king, Wuding, whose forceful reign can be dated circa 1200 B.C.E. While most royal consorts may have served primarily to provide heirs, the oracle texts reveal that Fu Hao acted as a military leader, and her grave, excavated in 1976, was appointed with a lavishness rivaling those of the Shang kings. The following inscriptions reveal the royal diviners' concern for her welfare, both in childbirth and otherwise.

47. Shall Fu Hao have a fortunate birth? The king prognosticated, saying, "If she gives birth on a jia day there will be misfortune." (*Xubian* 4.29.3)

48. Shall Fu Hao have a fortunate birth? The king prognosticated, saying, "If she gives birth on a ding day it shall be fortunate; if on a geng day, it shall be greatly auspicious." On the thirty-third day thereafter, on jia-yin, Fu Hao gave birth. It was not fortunate; it was a girl. (*Yibian* 7731)

49. Should Fu Hao follow Guo of Zhi and attack the X tribe, with the king attacking Zhonglu from the east toward the place where Fu Hao shall be? (*Yibian* 2948)

50. If the king does not order Fu Hao to follow Guo of Zhi and attack the X tribe, will we not perhaps receive support? (*Yibian* 961)

51. Fu Hao is ill; is there some evil influence? (*Yibian* 4098)

52. Should we perform a sacrifice to Father Yi on behalf of Fu Hao, and sacrifice a lamb, decapitate a boar, and sacrifice ten sets of sheep and pig? (*Yibian* 3383)

MILITARY AFFAIRS, HUNTING, AGRICULTURE, AND THE KING'S RITUAL LEADERSHIP

53. The king made cracks and divined: Should we perform a sacrifice and, on the following sacrifice day, follow the Lord X and campaign against the Ren tribe? Will the ancestors above and below provide support and not visit disaster upon us? Will we report at the Great City Shang [that there has been] no disaster? The king prognosticated, saying, "It is greatly auspicious." (*Tongcuan* 592)

54. Que divined: These ten days shall there be no disaster? The king prognosticated, saying, "There shall be misfortune; there will perhaps come ill news thrice over." On the fifth day thereafter there did indeed come ill news from the west. Guo of Zhi reported saying, "The Tu tribe has attacked my eastern territories; they have ruined two walled towns; also, the X tribe has overrun the fields of my western territories." (*Jinghua* 4)

55. The king made cracks and divined: We shall hunt at Ji; coming and going there shall be no disaster. The king prognosticated, saying, "It is extremely auspicious." Acting on this we captured forty-one foxes and eight hornless deer. (*Qianbian* 2.27.1)

56. If the king issues a great order to the multitudes saying, "Cultivate the fields," shall we receive a harvest? (*Xubian* 2.28.5)

57. The king shall go and lead the multitudes in planting grain at Qiong. (*Qianbian* 5.20.5)

During later periods of Chinese history, the planting season was initiated by the king, who would ceremonially plough the first furrow so as to bring his virtue to bear on the success of the harvest. Texts such as these reveal the early origins of the ritual.

2

Laozi: Ancient Philosopher, Master of Immortality, and God

Livia Kohn

Traditionally Daoism is described as having developed in two major phases: there was first the so-called philosophical Daoism, the quietistic and mystical philosophy of the ancient thinkers Laozi and Zhuangzi. This began around 500 B.C.E., was the dominant form of Daoism for several hundred years, and since then has continued, as one among many schools of Chinese thought, well into the present day. The second form of Daoism is known as religious Daoism. It began in the second century C.E. with the revelation of the Dao to Zhang Daoling, who became the first Celestial Master or representative of the Dao on Earth. This was an organized religion, with doctrines, rituals, gods, and the ultimate goal of ascension to the heavens of the immortals. It, too, has continued as one among many other forms of Daoism until today.

While this picture is basically correct, the reality is slightly more complex. Not only are there various schools in both kinds of Daoism, but the transition between the two main streams, during the Han dynasty (202 B.C.E.–220 C.E.), also contains elements of religious doctrine and practice that influence both. These are notably the doctrines of the so-called Huang-Lao school and the practices of the immortality seekers and magico-technicians (*fangshi*—fortune-tellers, astrologers, medical practitioners), who were then wandering throughout the country.

Despite their differences, all these forms of Daoism have several things in common. The most obvious among these is their reverence for Laozi, the "Old Master." In philosophical Daoism, he is venerated as the first thinker of the school, the author of the *Classic on the Way and Its Power* (*Dao de jing*), a text that has been translated into English well over a hundred times. Historically speaking, no single person wrote the text, nor does it go back to 500 B.C.E., the alleged lifetime of Laozi. Rather, the work was put together on the basis of aphorisms from various sources in the Warring States period, around 250 B.C.E. It definitely existed at the beginning of the Han dynasty, as two copies of the text in the tomb at Mawangdui of 168 B.C.E. show.

Laozi, the philosopher, is similarly elusive. The account of his life in the *Records of the Historian* (*Shiji*) of the year 104 B.C.E. includes information on four distinct people, none of whom is properly identified as the Daoist philosopher. There is first a person called Li from the south of China; then, there is a historian by the name of Dan who served in the Zhou archives; third, there is a ritual master who met and taught Confucius; and fourth, there is a saint by the name of Laolaizi who wrote a Daoist book in fifteen sections. Any one of these people might have been the Old Master of the Daoists, yet none of them is a truly historical figure.

In religious Daoism, in its first documents of the second century C.E., Laozi is worshiped as the personification of the eternal Dao, the "Way," the ultimate power that makes the universe exist and causes beings to be alive. Known then as the god Taishang Laojun, the Most High Lord Lao, he is believed to reside in the center of Heaven and at the beginning of time. He is the origin and vital power of all-that-is. Like the universe at large, he changes and transforms in rhythmic harmony. As the original ancestor of yin and yang, he appears and disappears continually, serving in every age as the inspired divine adviser to the ruler and guiding the world to truer harmony with the Dao.

Laozi here is regarded as the savior of humanity who has appeared over and over again in the course of history, revealing the Dao to the sagely rulers of old as well as to the inspired religious leaders of the Han. Laozi is said to have made a pact with the first Celestial Master Zhang Daoling that allowed him and his descendants to represent the Dao on Earth and guaranteed the believers of this sect to survive all cosmic disasters and be saved as immortals.

The magico-technicians and Huang-Lao Daoists of the Han, finally, saw Laozi as an inspired leader of their own kinds of practices. He was a teacher of the right way to govern the country while at the same time cultivating oneself and extending one's life. He was, for them, not yet a god and yet no longer a mere thinker, reclusive official, or master of ritual. Laozi of the immortality seekers is himself a practitioner of longevity techniques, one who has lived for several hundred years, maintained his vigor, and attained the magic of the immortals. He has full control over life and death, foresees the future, and knows all about the patterns of the heavenly bodies. He can order demons about at will, and he wields talismans and spells as if he were born to it.

The text translated below contains traces of all three visions of Laozi. It is his biography from the *Biography of Spirit Immortals* (*Shenxian zhuan*), written by Ge Hong (283–343), an aristocrat and scholar of the early fourth century, who had a lively interest in all things Daoist and researched them with great acumen. Ge Hong lived in South China, where he wandered around the country to find ancient manuscripts and learned masters, then came home to write down his findings. In his autobiography—the first of its kind in Chinese literature—he describes how he eschewed all official positions and even avoided social interaction with his equals, because his one aim in life was to become immortal. For Ge Hong, immortality was not to be reached through religious observances such as prayers and rituals, although he certainly believed in the magical efficacy of talismans and spells; he believed that the desired state could be attained first and foremost through the practice of longevity techniques such as gymnastics, breathing exercises, special diets, meditations, and—most of all—alchemy.

Accordingly his main remaining work, *He Who Embraces Simplicity* (*Baopuzi*), which he named after his pen name, is a vast compendium of the techniques and practices of the immortals. It details the protective measures one has to take to keep the demons and evil spirits at bay. It describes how to reach alignment with the yin and yang energies of the universe; how to absorb the energies of the sun and the moon; how to use various herbs and minerals to improve one's health and extend one's life; how to attain magical qualities such as being in several places at once, becoming invisible, and flying in the air; how to prepare various kinds of elixirs or "cinnabars" that will have the power of instantaneously transforming one into an immortal or at least bestow very long life on Earth and power over life and death; and many many more.

The Laozi that Ge Hong presents in his collection of immortals' biographies is a Laozi in transition. The beginnings of Daoism as an organized religion under the Celestial Masters had taken place about 150 years earlier, but in an entirely different part of the country. Ge Hong himself was not familiar with the movement and had only heard rumors that some people claimed Laozi was the Dao itself, a kind of god and spiritual being who came to Earth again and again.

For him, Laozi was first of all a historical figure, an ancient philosopher who had had profound insights—insights based on his particular intellect or, as the Chinese of the time would say, on his inherent spirit, his nature-given energy. In addition to this, Ge Hong saw Laozi as a successful practitioner of immortality, as a famous and inspiring example for all practitioners. His own desire to prove that one could learn and practice to become immortal—live very long, acquire magical powers, and eventually ascend to heaven in broad daylight—required that he cast Laozi in this role. He had no interest in stylizing him as the Dao, as the religious follower did, and explicitly counters any suggestions in this direction.

The text below is therefore a collection of notes on Laozi, interspersed with Ge Hong's comments to guide the reader in the desired direction. It refers to many different sources, sometimes mentioned by title, sometimes just introduced as "some say." The texts cited explicitly are all lost today, but we know that they were among the so-called apocrypha of the Han dynasty. The apocrypha or non-orthodox materials were a group of texts that interpreted the Classics of the Confucian elite in terms of the magico-technicians' arts: astrology, fortune-telling, numerology, and other esoteric speculations.

These texts tended to stylize the emperors of ancient Chinese history—mythical rulers—as semisupernatural beings. The great culture heroes of old, like Fu Xi, who invented the eight trigrams of the *Classic of Changes* (*Yijing*) and thereby made the order of the cosmos accessible to humanity, or Shennong, the Divine Agriculturist, who discovered farming and animal husbandry, in these texts were more than the powerful rulers of the historians. They had special powers and marvelous features to show their stature. Shun, for example, one of the five great Confucian rulers, had double pupils—a symbol of his extraordinary perception. Yao, another Confucian hero, was born after his mother had seen a shooting star— an indication of his Heaven-inspired rule. Many mythical rulers also had the "sun horn" and the "moon crescent," two specially shaped bones sticking out over the eyebrows. They are so named because, in Chinese body mythology, the left eye is the sun and the right eye is the moon. Some rulers also had more sense openings than ordinary people did, and others had strange signs in the lines on their hands and feet—all features that in due course were also attributed to Laozi.

In addition to Han dynasty apocrypha and "miscellaneous records," some of which are obviously influenced by the religious movement, Ge Hong relied on historical sources. He cites the Laozi biography in the *Records of the Historian* and retells many stories contained in the *Zhuangzi*. In all these, Laozi appears as a philosopher—a reclusive and withdrawn person with uncanny powers of insight, who puts the great Confucius to shame. He immediately identifies Confucius's disciple and tells him so; he stuns the master with his dragonlike mind; he advises him on the futility of his efforts to perfect benevolence and righteousness; and so on. This more historical Laozi, too, is a stylized figure. Used in polemics among the various philosophical schools, he appears as the superior contemporary and counterpart of Confucius. Expounding a philosophy of withdrawal and serenity, Laozi is depicted as the one who has all the answers but cannot teach them, since the Dao can only come to those who are ready to receive it.

The key episode of Laozi's philosophical life is at the same time the pivot of the religion: his transmission of *The Way and Its Power* in five thousand words to Yin Xi, the guardian of the pass. The story goes back to the *Records of the Historian*. It says,

> Laozi lived under the Zhou for a long time. When he saw that the dynasty was declining, he decided to leave. He reached the pass [on the western frontier]. There Yin Xi, the guardian of the pass, told him: "You are about to withdraw completely. Would you please write down your ideas for me?" Thereupon Laozi wrote a work in two sections to explain the Dao and its Power. It had more than five thousand words. Then he left. Nobody knows what became of him. (chap. 63)

This is later taken up by all biographies and hagiographies of Laozi and becomes the standard motif of Laozi pictures: the old man sitting on his ox cheerfully leaving his homeland. Still, the story ends differently in different versions. While the historical account ends the description of Laozi's life with the transmission of *The Way and Its Power,* Ge Hong implies that he pursued his goal of immortality and ascended to Mount Kunlun, both a mountain range in Central Asia and an immortals' paradise of Chinese mythology. He then emphasizes that Yin Xi, inspired by Laozi and following the instructions of *The Way and Its Power,* became an immortal himself and in the following illustrates the power and efficacy of the sacred scripture.

In later sources, on the other hand, Laozi is said to have continued his way over the pass and wandered through Central Asia until he reached India. Everywhere he went, he converted the local population, the "barbarians," to Daoism. Adapting its ways to their primitive state, he set up particularly strict rules for them and called himself the Buddha. This version is known as the "conversion of the barbarians," a theory that led to much debate with the Buddhists and caused, more than once, the prohibition and persecution of religious Daoism.

Ge Hong exploits the scene on the pass in a set different way. Describing how Laozi controlled the life and death of his servant Xu Jia with a special talisman, he shows the ancient philosopher effectively as a master of magic and the powers of the immortals. His suggestion, of course, is that by studying the words of this sagely person and following the methods he revealed—the list includes all the longevity, immortality, and demon-fighting techniques of the Dao—one can become such a master oneself. Indeed, the scripture Laozi revealed must contain some of his essence and therefore can bestow certain powers and benefits. No wonder, then, that the recluses and aspiring immortals of Ge Hong's day all had the greatest veneration for the Old Master.

From *Shenxian zhuan* (Biographies of Spirit Immortals), chap. 1, pp. 1b–3b (ed. *Daozang jinghua* 5.11). Other editions: *Taiping guangji* 1; *Han Wei congshu* 1; *Yiwen leiju* 78. For a complete translation of the entire *Shenxian zhuan,* see Gertrud Güntsch, *Das Shen-hsien-chuan und das Erscheinungsbild eines Hsien* (Frankfurt: Peter Lang, 1988).

Further Reading

Judith Boltz, "Lao-tzu," in *Encyclopedia of Religion,* ed. Mircea Eliade (New York: Macmillan, 1987), 8:454–59; A. C. Graham, "The Origins of the Legend of Lao Tan," in *Studies in Chinese Philosophy and Philosophical Literature,* ed. A. C. Graham (Albany: State University of New York Press, 1981, 1990), pp. 111–24; Livia Kohn, "The Mother of the Tao," *Taoist Resources* 1.2 (1989): 37–113; Jay Sailey, *The Master Who Embraces Simplicity: A Study of the Philosophy of Ko Hung (A.D. 283–343)* (San Francisco: Chinese Materials Center, 1978); Kenneth J. DeWoskin, *Doctors, Diviners, and Magicians of Ancient China* (New York: Columbia University Press, 1983); Livia Kohn, ed., *Taoist Meditation and Longevity Techniques* (Ann Arbor: University of Michigan, Center for Chinese Studies, 1989).

Biography of Laozi

Laozi was called Chong'er (Double Ear) or Boyang (Lord of Yang). He came from Quren Village in Hu County in the state of Chu (modern Luyi District in Henan Province).

His mother had become pregnant when she was touched by a huge meteor. Although Laozi had therefore received his basic energy directly from Heaven, he yet appeared in the Li family and took Li as his surname.

Some say that Laozi has existed since before Heaven and Earth. Others say that he is the essential soul of Heaven, a spiritual and wonderful being. Then again some claim that his mother remained pregnant for seventy-two years and only then gave birth. At birth, he split open his mother's left armpit and emerged. Being just born, he already had white hair—which is why he was called Laozi, "Old Child." Others maintain that his mother had been unmarried [at the time of his birth] so that Laozi adopted her family name. Then there are those who insist that his mother had just come to stand under a plum tree when he was born. As soon as he was born, he was able to speak. He pointed to the plum tree (li) and said: "I shall take this [Li] to be my surname."

Other sources, moreover, state that Laozi, in the time of the ancient Three Sovereigns (mythical rulers in the early stages of the universe), was [their teacher under the name] Preceptor of the Mysterious Center. In the time of the later Three Sovereigns, he was the Imperial Lord Goldtower. Under Fu Xi [the Prostrate Sacrificer and first ruler], he was the Master of Luxuriant Florescence. Under Shennong [the Divine Farmer], he was the Old Master of Ninefold Numen. Under Zhurong [the Lord Firedrill], he was the Master of Vast Longevity. Under Huangdi [the Yellow Emperor], he was the Master of Vast Perfection. Under Emperor Zhuanxu [a mythical ruler], he was the Master of Red Essence. Under Emperor Ku, he was the Master of Registers and Sacred Charts. Under Emperor Yao, he was the Master of Perfected Duty. Under Emperor Shun, he was the Master of Ruling Longevity. Under Yu, the founder of the Xia dynasty, he was the Master of True Practice. Under Tang, the founder of the Shang dynasty, he was the Master of Granting Rules. Under King Wen, the first ruler of the Zhou dynasty, he was the Master of Culture and Towns.

However, some also maintain that Laozi was a mere archivist, while others say that he was [the statesman] Fan Li in [the southern state of] Yue and accordingly appeared under the name of Chi Yizi in [the eastern state of] Qi and as Dao Zhugong in [the southeastern state of] Wu.

All these are statements found in miscellaneous records but not in the authentic scriptures of divine immortals. Thus they cannot be considered reliable. I, Ge Hong, state: For my part, I think that if Laozi was a spiritual being of celestial origin, he should indeed have appeared in each successive generation, exchanging his honorable rank for a humble condition, sacrificing his ease and freedom in order to subject himself to toil. He should indeed have turned his back on the pure serenity [of the heavenly spheres] in order to immerse himself in the foulness and defilements [of the world], giving up his celestial position and accepting inferior rank in the world of humanity.

Most certainly, the arts of the Dao have existed ever since there were Heaven and Earth. The masters of these arts of the Dao—when would they not have been there, even for a short while? They have appeared and worked their arts from [the beginnings of culture under] Fu Xi to the time of the three dynasties [of the Xia, Shang, and Zhou]. They existed from generation to generation—yet why should they all have been only forms of [the single figure] Laozi? Adepts who pursue learning in their old age tend to love the marvelous and value the weird. Wishing to do great honor to Laozi, they produce such theories. In reality, as far as I am concerned, Laozi was a person who realized the deepest essence of the Dao. But he was not of an extraordinary or superhuman kind.

The *Records of the Historian* says: "The son of Laozi was named Zong. He served as a general in the army of the state of Wei and enfeoffed in Duan. Then came Zong's son Wang, Wang's son Yan, and Yan's great-grandson Xia, an official in Han. Xia's son Jie was grand tutor of the Prince of Jiaoxi and lived in [the eastern state of] Qi."

Thus the theory that Laozi was originally a spiritual and wonderful being goes back to the efforts of inexperienced Daoists who wished to see the strange and supernatural in him. They hoped that scholars of later generations would follow their ideas and never realized that such strange tales would only increase the disbelief people already had about the feasibility of prolonging life. Why is this? Well, if one says that Laozi was a man who realized the Dao, then people will be encouraged in their efforts to emulate his example. However, if one depicts him as a spiritual and wonderful being of a superhuman kind, then there is nothing to be learned.

In regard to his life, there is the following record: Laozi wished to emigrate to the west. The guardian of the border pass, a man named Yin Xi, knew that he was not an ordinary man. He therefore requested instruction in the Dao. Laozi was surprised and thought this strange, thus he merely stuck out his tongue. It was soft and rimless [like the Dao]. Because of this Laozi was also called Lao Dan, "Old Rimless."

This latter statement is not correct either. According to the *Scripture of [Laozi's] Nine Transformations (Jiubian jing)* and the *Scripture on [Laozi's] Original Birth and Twelve Transformations (Yuansheng shier hua jing)*, Laozi had the name Dan already before he ever approached Yin Xi's pass. In fact, Laozi changed his names and appellations several times—he was not just called Dan. The reason for this is that, as described in the [astrological texts] *Scripture of the [Constellation] Nine Palaces (Jiugong jing)*, *Scripture of the Three [Powers] and Five [Phases] (Sanwu jing)*, and the *Scripture of Primordial Planets (Yuanchen jing)*, all people must face difficult situations in their lives. When such a difficult time comes, one should change one's name or appellation to accommodate the transformation of primordial cosmic energy that is taking place. Doing so, one can extend the span of one's life and overcome the difficulty.

Even today in our generation, there are Daoists who practice this with enthusiasm. Laozi himself lived for over three hundred years under the Zhou.

Living for so many years, he was bound to encounter many difficult situations. Thus he has rather a lot of names.

To determine the exact dates of Laozi's birth and departure, it is best to rely mainly on historical works and factual records, but one should also take into consideration esoteric scriptures like the *Scripture of Lao the Immortal (Laoxian jing)*. Other materials, such as folklore and local stories, can be ignored as void and specious.

The *Central Essence of [Laozi's] Western Ascension (Xisheng zhongtai)*, the *Diagrams on the Restoration of Life (Fuming bao)*, and the *Esoteric Scripture in Chapters of Gold on the [Constellations] Pearl-Studded Bowcase and Jade Pivot (Zhutao yuji jinpian neijing)* all give some indication of Laozi's looks. He had a yellow-whitish complexion, beautiful eyebrows, and a broad forehead. He possessed long ears, big eyes, gaping teeth, a square mouth, and thick lips. On his forehead he had the signs of the three [powers] and five [phases]. He had the sun horn and the moon crescent sticking out above his eyebrows. His nose was broad and straight and had a double rim, while his ears had three openings. On the soles of his feet he had the signs of the two [forces yin and yang] and the five [phases]; his palms contained the character for the number ten.

Under King Wen of the Zhou (1150–1133 B.C.E.), he served as an archivist. Under King Wu (1133–1116), he was a historian. The common people of the time noticed that he lived very long and thus called him Laozi, "Old Master." By destiny he was endowed with a penetrating spirit and far-reaching foresight. The energy he had received at birth was unlike that of ordinary people. All this caused him to become a master of the Dao. It was because of this unusual quality that the divine powers of Heaven supported him and the host of immortals followed him.

> Thus he came to reveal various methods of going beyond the world:
> the [alchemy of the] nine cinnabars and eight minerals;
> the [dietetics of] metallic wine and the golden fluid;
> the visualization of mysterious simplicity and of guarding the One;
> the recollection of spirit and penetration of the hidden;
> the guiding of energy and refinement of the body;
> the dispelling of disasters and exorcism of evil;
> the control over demons and the nourishing of inner nature;
> the abstention from grain and the many ways of transforming the body;
> the serenity of a life in accordance with the teaching and the precepts;
> the overcoming and control of demons and malevolent specters.

These methods fill 930 scrolls of texts as well as 70 scrolls of talismans. They are all recorded in the *Essential Chapters on Laozi's Origins and Deeds (Laozi benqi zhongpian)*, as is already evident in the list of contents. But beware! Anything not contained in these was only added by later Daoists, following their personal preferences. It cannot be considered part of the perfected scriptures.

Laozi was basically a man of calm and serenity. Free from desires, he pursued only the extension of life. Thus it was that he lived under the Zhou for a long time but never strove for high rank or fame. He only wished to keep his inner light in harmony with the world of dust and grime, to realize spontaneity within, and to leave once his Dao was perfected. He was indeed a true immortal.

Confucius once went to ask Laozi about the rites. But first he sent [his disciple] Zigong to see him. Zigong had hardly arrived when Laozi told him: "Your master's name is Qiu (Confucius). After you have followed him for another three years, you can both be taught."

Confucius eventually came to see Laozi himself. Laozi told him: "A good merchant fills his storehouses but appears to have nothing. A gentleman is overflowing with virtue but acts as if he was worthless. Give up your pride and haughtiness as well as your many desires and your lasciviousness. None of these is doing you any good!"

On another occasion, Confucius was studying a text. Laozi observed this and asked what he was reading.

"The *Classic of Changes*," Confucius replied. "The sages of old studied it, too."

"If the sages of old read it," Laozi commented, "so be it. But why are you reading it? What are its essential ideas?"

"Its essential ideas are benevolence and righteousness."

"Ah well," Laozi said, [then explained.] "See, it's like that. When mosquitoes and horseflies buzz around and bite your skin, you can't catch a wink of sleep the whole night long. Similarly, when benevolence and righteousness are around with their miserable nature, they only confuse people's minds. There is no greater disorder than this.

"Now, the swan is white even without taking a bath every day; the raven is black even without being dyed every day. Heaven is naturally high; Earth is naturally thick. The sun and the moon are naturally luminant; stars and planets are naturally arranged. Even trees and grasses are naturally varied.

"You, if you cultivate the Dao without delay, you will certainly reach it! But what use can benevolence and righteousness have in that? Using them would be as if you tied on a drum to search for a lost sheep! With benevolence and righteousness you only create confusion in your inner nature!"

[Another time] Laozi asked Confucius, "Have you attained the Dao yet?"

"I have pursued it for twenty-seven years," Confucius replied, "but so far I have not attained it."

"Small wonder," Laozi said, "If the Dao could be given to people, all would present it to their lord. If the Dao could be handed to people, all would hand it to their family. If the Dao could be told to people, all would tell it to their brothers. If the Dao could be passed down, all would pass it down to their sons. However, it cannot. And why? Because without a host on the inside, the Dao cannot come to reside."

"I have mastered the *Classic of Poetry*," Confucius said again, "as well as the *Classic of History*, the *Record of Rites*, the *Classic of Music*, the *Classic of Changes*, and the *Spring and Autumn Annals*. I have recited the Dao of the ancient kings and explained the deeds of [the dukes of] Shao and Zhou. I have taken my teaching to over seventy rulers, but I have never been employed. How hard it is to convince people!"

"Really," Laozi countered, "the Six Classics are only the leftover traces of the ancient kings. How could they be their real teachings, the substance behind the leftovers? What you do today is merely following these old leftover traces! Still, even traces are made from actual steps—but what a big difference between them!"

Confucius returned and did not speak for three days. Zigong [his disciple] wondered at this and finally asked him.

"When I see people using their intentions like flying birds," Confucius replied slowly, "I adapt my intention to a bow and shoot them—and never once have I failed to hit and best them. When I see people using their intentions like deer, I adapt my intention to running dogs and chase them—and never once have I failed to bite and devour them. When I see people using their intentions like deep-sea fish, I adapt my intention to a hook and throw it for them—and never once have I failed to hook and control them.

"Except one. The one animal beyond me is the dragon—riding on the energy of the clouds, wandering freely through Great Clarity. I cannot follow him. When recently I saw Laozi I knew I had met my match. He is like a dragon!

"He made my mouth gape wide, leaving me unable to shut it. He made my tongue stick out, leaving me unable to pull it back. My spirit was so amazed that I no longer knew where I was."

On another occasion [the philosopher] Yangzi was received by Laozi.

"The patterns [in the fur] of leopards and tigers," Laozi told him, "and the nimbleness of apes and monkeys only cause them to be caught and killed!"

"May I dare," Yangzi hesitated, "to ask about the rule of the enlightened kings?"

"The rule of the enlightened kings," Laozi mused. "Their merit covered all under Heaven, yet they did not think of it as issuing from themselves. Their influence reached to the myriad beings, yet they took care to keep the people independent. They had virtue, yet did not boast of their fame and position. They were impossible to figure out, wandering as they were freely around nothingness."

Laozi was about to leave [his homeland]. He therefore went westward to cross the pass, from there to ascend to Mount Kunlun. Yin Xi, the guardian of the pass, divined the winds and energies [of the world] and thus knew in advance that a divine personage would soon come past. He duly had the road swept for forty miles. When he saw Laozi approach, he knew that he was the one.

Laozi for his part had never handed down his teaching while he resided in the Middle Kingdom. However, he knew that Yin Xi was destined to realize the Dao and therefore willingly stopped on the pass.

He arrived in the company of a retainer called Xu Jia, whom he had hired as a child for a wage of one hundred [copper pieces of] cash per day. By now Laozi owed him 7,200,000 cash. When Jia saw that Laozi was about to go beyond the pass in his travels, he quickly demanded his money. Laozi did not pay him.

At this time, a servant [on the Hangu pass heard the story and] instigated Jia to file a complaint against Laozi with the guardian of the pass. But this instigator did not know that Jia had been with Laozi already for over two hundred years. He only calculated that Jia would come into a lot of money and proposed to give him his daughter in marriage. When Jia saw that the woman was fair he rejoiced.

They then went to file the complaint with Yin Xi, who was disturbed and greatly alarmed. They all went to see Laozi.

Laozi spoke to Xu Jia: "You should have died long ago! When I first hired you in the old days, you were a slave and a pauper, but I did not have a valet, so I took you on and gave you long life through the Pure Life Talisman of Great Mystery. Only thus were you able to see the present day. Why do you speak against me now? Also, I have told you that I would pay you the full amount in gold once we got to Parthia. Why can't you be patient?"

Laozi then made Jia open his mouth and told them all to look at the ground: The perfected talisman of Great Mystery was sticking upright in the earth with its cinnabar characters as good as new. In the same instant Jia collapsed into a heap of withered bones.

Yin Xi knew that Laozi was a divine personage and had the ability to restore the man to life. He therefore touched his head to the ground and begged Laozi for Jia's life. He also requested permission to provide the necessary funds to satisfy the retainer's demands.

Laozi thereupon returned the Talisman of Great Mystery to the bony remains and, lo and behold, Xu Jia immediately rose alive and well. Yin Xi duly gave him two million in cash and sent him on his way.

Later on Yin Xi served Laozi with the proper pupil's formality and received Laozi's teachings of extending life. When Yin Xi further begged him to teach him formal precepts of the Dao, Laozi told him [the scripture in] five thousand words. Yin Xi withdrew to seclusion and wrote it down faithfully. It was named *Dao de jing*. Practicing its teaching of the Dao, Yin Xi also attained immortality.

Under the Han dynasty, the Empress Dou was a great believer in the words of Laozi, and through her influence Emperor Wen (179–156 B.C.E) and all the members of the Dou family could not help but read the scripture. Reading and reciting the text, they all gained tremendous benefits. Thus the whole empire was at peace under the emperors Wen and Jing, and the empresses of the Dou family preserved their power and glory for three generations.

Also, Shu Guang, the head tutor of the crown prince, and his son and colleague deeply penetrated the meaning of the scripture. Through it they understood the relative importance [and timeliness] of worldly merit and withdrawal to seclusion. One day they decided to give up their offices and return home. There they gave money to the needy and freely distributed goodwill, yet always remained noble and pure.

This attitude was continued by numerous later recluses following the arts of Laozi. They stripped off all glory and splendor on the outside and nourished their lives to high longevity within, without ever tumbling into the perilous world of human society. Instead they were with the vast spring of the Dao, which flows long and is ever creative. Being like this, how could they not be raised on the very principles of Heaven and Earth? How could they not be masters and models for ten thousand generations? Thus all those today who follow [the model of the recluse] Zhuang Zhou (Zhuangzi) honor Laozi as their original teacher.

— 3 —

The Lives and Teachings of the Divine Lord of Zitong

Terry F. Kleeman

The Divine Lord of Zitong is a local god from a small town in northern Sichuan who came to have a national following as Wenchang, the God of Literature and patron of the civil service examinations. The three short texts translated below are part of a corpus of scriptures, ethical tracts, liturgical manuals, and divinatory works deriving from his cult. The first, *The Esoteric Biography of Qinghe (Qinghe neizhuan)*, was revealed to a medium, who transcribed the words revealed through a process called "spirit writing." This took place in the Chengdu, Sichuan, area around 1168 C.E. It is an autobiographical account of a god, from his first human incarnation at the turn of the first millenium B.C.E. to his apotheosis in the fourth century, and is the prototype for a much longer scripture about the same god, the *Book of Transformations* (HY 170). The *Esoteric Biography* was the first salvo in a fifteen-year stream of revealed documents that reshaped the god's image, claiming for him the identity of this astral deity. Qinghe, a city in Hebei Province, is the ancestral home of an important clan of the Zhang surname, a surname with which the god has been associated since the fourth century. Members of the clan controlled the temple in Zitong for at least part of the Song dynasty (960–1279), and the god at times takes on the character of a clan progenitor deity. The text tells of how even a god goes through a process of self-cultivation and merit-building before he attains his full godhood, and it suggests that gods may be abroad in the world, hidden in human form, unknown even to themselves.

The second text, *The Scripture of the Responses and Proofs of the Divine Lord of Zitong (Yuanshi tianzun shuo Zitong dijun yingyan jing)*, is a good example of a Daoist scripture with strong Buddhist influences. Like a Buddhist sūtra, it begins with an audience with the supreme deity, but here the deity is not the Buddha but a Daoist god, the Primordial Heavenly Worthy. The Divine Lord of Zitong comes forward and describes the hardships he has undergone in aeon after aeon of rebirth. Having finally escaped from rebirth through his devotion to the Heavenly Worthy, he declares, like a bodhisattva, his wish to free others from the ignorance he once suffered. The Primordial Heavenly Worthy praises him for his compassionate deeds The Divine Lord next asks how human beings can avoid disaster. In response, the Primordial Heavenly Worthy declares that people who contemplate the virtuous deeds of the Divine Lord of Zitong will be saved, especially those seeking success in the civil service examinations and an official career. Not surprisingly, the cult to the Divine Lord of Zitong was especially popular among those who sought or held positions in the government. The text is not explicitly dated, but it can probably be safely placed in the Yuan dynasty (1280–1368). In any case, it can be no earlier than 1168 and no later than 1444.

The third work, *The Tract on the Hidden Administration (Yinzhiwen)*, is a text of uncertain date, perhaps as early as the Southern Song (1127–1279), certainly no later than the late Ming (1368–1643). Like the *Esoteric Biography*, it is a spirit-writing text, that is, a work said to be the words of a god transcribed by a medium. Together with the *Tract of the Most Exalted on Action and Response (Taishang ganying pian*, see chapters 33, 34, and 35), with which it shares many characteristics, this early representative of the morality book (*shanshu*) genre is among the most widely printed, distributed, and read books in China. The "hidden administration" of the title refers to the otherworldly bureaucracy that the Chinese believed observed, noted, and reported every good and evil act. The revealing god of this text was at the apex of this bureaucracy, the cosmic guardian of the records. He speaks of exemplary actions to be emulated and evil ones to be avoided. The intended audience certainly included elite aspirants to government office but was not restricted to them; many of the moral injunctions would seem applicable to all, and some (like the warning against using inaccurate measures) are clearly directed to nonelite groups. The ethical strictures themselves range from the socially oriented (e.g., statements on the proper treatment of travelers) to the ritual centered (e.g., prohibitions on discarding paper with writing on it). Their sum can be said to reflect fairly the majority ethical views of at least the elite portion of late imperial Chinese society.

The *Esoteric Biography of Qinghe* is translated from *Qinghe neizhuan*, 1a–2b, Daozang, HY 169. *The Scripture of Responses and Proofs* is from *Yuanshi tianzun shuo Zitong dijun yingyan jing*, Daozang, HY 28. *The Tract on the Hidden Administration* is from *Yinzhiwen*, Daozang jiyao *xing* 9/36a–96a, collated by Zhu Guishi of Daxing, reedited by Jiang Yupu (Mengying) of Suiyang.

Further Reading

Cynthia Brokaw, *The Ledgers of Merit and Demerit: Social Change and Moral Order in Late Imperial China* (Princeton: Princeton University Press, 1991); R. H. van Gulik, "On the Seal Representing the God of Literature on the Title Page of Old Chinese and Japanese Popular Editions," *Monumenta Nipponica* 4 (1941): 33–52; David K. Jordan and Daniel Overmyer, *The Flying Phoenix: Aspects of Chinese Sectarianism in Taiwan* (Princeton: Princeton University Press, 1986); Terry F.

Kleeman, "Taoist Ethics," in *A Bibliographic Guide to the Comparative Study of Ethics,*
ed. John Carman and Mark Juergensmayer (Cambridge: Cambridge University
Press, 1991), 162–95; Kleeman, "The Expansion of the Wen-ch'ang Cult," in
Religion and Society in T'ang and Sung China, ed. Patricia Ebrey and Peter N. Greg-
ory (Honolulu: University of Hawaii Press, 1993), 45–73; Kleeman, *A God's Own
Tale: The Book of Transformations of Wenchang* (Albany: State University of New
York Press, 1994); Sakai Tadao, *Chūgoku zensho no kenkyū (A Study of Chinese
Morality Books)* (Tokyo: Kokusho kankōkai, 1960).

Esoteric Biography of Qinghe

I was originally a man from around Wu and Gui. Born at the beginning of the
Zhou dynasty (ca. 1027–256 B.C.E.), I subsequently underwent seventy-three
transformations, repeatedly becoming a scholar-official. Never have I mistreated the people or abused my clerks. I am ardent by nature but circumspect
in my conduct. Like the autumn frost or the bright light of day, I am not to
be disobeyed.

Later, at the end of the Western Jin dynasty (265–317), I incarnated west of
Yue and south of Sui, between the two commanderies. I was born in a *dingwei*
year on a *xinhai* day, the third day of the second lunar month. An auspicious
glow veiled my door and yellow clouds obscured the fields. The place where I
lived was low and close to the sea. A man of the village said to the elder from
Qinghe, "You are now sixty yet you have obtained a precious heir."

As a child, I did not enjoy playing games. I always longed for the mountains
and marshes, and often my words seemed to have hidden meanings. I copied
and recited all the books. At night I avoided the gangs of children, laughing
contentedly to myself. My body emitted a radiant glow. When the local people
prayed [to statues of gods] I scolded and rebuked them. Giving a long cry, I
said, "These images are of wood and clay, yet they wear the clothing of men
and eat the food of men. When you entertain them, they respond to your
wishes. When you calumnate them, they visit upon you disaster. I am a human
being, how can it be that I lack spiritual power?"

After this I had strange dreams at night. Sometimes I dreamed I was a dragon.
Sometimes I dreamed I was a king. There was a heavenly talisman saying that
I was an official of the Water Office. I thought this strange and did not really
believe it was an auspicious omen. Later drought plagued the three classes of
farmers and no enriching moisture revived the plants. The farmers danced the
Yu raindance and invoked the spirits, all to no avail. I thought, "At night I
dream that I am in charge of the Water Office. This has been going on for a
long time and by now there should be some confirmation."

That night I went to the edge of the river to throw in a memorial to the Earl
of the Sea on which I had written the name of the office which I held in my

dreams, but my heart failed me and I was too embarrassed to do it. Suddenly clouds converged swiftly from the four directions and wind and thunder roared. A clerk bowed before me, saying, "The Judge of Fates should transfer his residence." I said, "That is not me. I am the son of old Mister Zhang, named Ya. Later, because I became prominent through the Water Office, I was given the sobriquet Peifu (Deluger)." The clerk said, "I have been commanded to speed you on your way." I said, "What about the members of my family?" The clerk said, "Let us first go to your headquarters." I was confused and had not yet made up my mind. The clerk with a bow bade me mount a white donkey and I was gone. When I looked down I saw the village gate, then in the midst of the roar of wind and rain I suddenly lost sight of my native place.

I arrived at a mountain in the Knife Ridge range which supports the asterism Triaster. It was shaped like a phoenix lying faceup. There was an ancient pool that led me into a huge cave, by the entrance to which there were several stone "bamboo shoots." The clerk said, "When the people pray, if they call using these stones there is a response. They are called 'thunder pillars.'" I had just lifted the hem of my robe to enter the cave when the clerk said, "Do you recall that you were incarnated during the Zhou and have up until now transmitted hidden merit to your family through seventy-three transformations?" Suddenly I was enlightened as if waking from a dream. The clerk said, "In the rolls of Heaven you have the rank of a god, but there are few in the human world who know this. Soon there will be portents of a revival of the Jin dynasty. You should search out a place to manifest your transformation." I said, "Thank you, heavenly clerk, for having made this resounding report."

When I entered the cave, it was like dropping down a thousand-fathom ravine. Approaching the ground, my feet made no contact and it was as if my body could soar through the sky. There was a palace fit for a king and guards ringed about it. I entered and found that my entire family was there.

Later I assumed the form of a scholar and went to Xianyang to tell the story of Yao Chang. This is the *Esoteric Biography of Qinghe.* Those who worship me with incense must remember it!

The Scripture of the Responses and Proofs of the Divine Lord of Zitong

At that time the Primordial Heavenly Worthy was in the Heavenly Palace of Occluded Brilliance. Within Jade Metropolis Mountain he had formed a canopy of five-colored clouds. Leading the corps of transcendents of the various heavens, the sun, moon, and asterisms, he glistened and glowed. The gods and spirits of the mountains and streams folded their hands and sighed in amazement, "We have been born into and reside in a filthy, muddy, dusty, temporal world. We hope to meet with Heavenly compassion that will broadly enlighten us."

At that time, the Divine Lord of Zitong stepped forward, his countenance placid. Bowing twice before the Thearch [the Primordial Heavenly Worthy], he knelt down and said, "[I], your disciple has lost his original form myriad times in aeon after aeon. I was exiled to the land of Shu [modern Sichuan]. Mindful of the commoners below, I subjected myself to the kalpic disasters. At times I was born into the body of a bird or beast; at others, I dwelt among the Man and Rong barbarians. [Among these lives] there were distinctions in wealth and status, differences in poverty and meanness. I suffered the disasters of water, fire, weapons, and soldiers, endured the sufferings of the wheel of life, of birth and death. I did not know there were heaven, earth, the sun, moon, and stars. I slandered religions and did not revere the three jewels (in a Daoist context, usually the Dao, the scriptures, and the teachers), one's teacher, or father and mother. In the end, although my life was happy, I could not escape falling into the five evil tendencies and the three [evil] paths of rebirth. For aeon after aeon I cycled in the wheel of rebirth, ignorant of enlightenment, observing the various forms of retribution that such a person experiences. Now I have encountered the Heavenly Worthy presiding over this below. I wish to preach on your behalf in order to enlighten the benighted."

At that time the Primordial Heavenly Worthy revealed a single ray of his light and it illuminated ten thousand *li*. The corps of transcendents of the various heavens and the gods and spirits of streams, waterways, and sacred peaks in Heaven above and Earth below each dwelled within the crystalline five colors in order to hear the preaching of the Law.

The Primordial Heavenly Worthy said, "How rare, godling, that you, taking pity on sentient beings, have told this tale of karmic affinity. My mind has been enlightened. The transmutations of yin and yang, the movements of the sun and moon, the motions and occlusions of the stars, the rending of the earth, all are transformations from Heaven above. Whenever a person is born between Heaven and Earth, he is endowed with the breaths of yin and yang; the five agents bring him to completion, the two breaths bind him together. He does not know how difficult it is to receive a human body, how difficult it is to be born into the Middle Land. He is jealous and greedy, does not yet know to repent. When he suffers military, pestilential, water, and fire disasters, all derive from this."

The vassal [the Divine Lord of Zitong] from the front row pressed head to floor and announced to the Heavenly Worthy, "The people have suffered disaster and calamity yet no one heeds and commiserates with them. How can they gain release and absolution?"

The Heavenly Worthy, leaning on his armrest, said, "You occupy a position as aide to august Heaven and are equal in prestige to the Supreme One. Your name is loftier than the Southern Polestar, your virtue envelops the four quarters. You control the wheel of rebirth of the Chaotic Prime, administer the Cinnamon Record of public servants. You have investigated the Six Classics and the reports of all five sacred peaks. Common people who contemplate this shall be saved.

The Heavenly Worthy then made a pronouncement:

> Thereupon the Primordial Worthy,
> Seated within his crystalline [palace],
> Lamented the evils of sentient beings
> On the three evil paths following the five tendencies.
> In a daze, they do not awaken [to reality]
> Always they are like the occulted sun or moon.
> They do not know they are endowed with the five agents, that the stars
>   move on their behalf.
> At that time the Lord of Zitong
> From his seat extended compassionate love.
> Dividing his body, he performed transformations,
> With his pen he expressed samādhi.
> Absolving and exorcizing he opened a door.
> The Jade Metropolis repeatedly proclaimed his correctness.
> He observed men in the world below
> Suffering without elders.
> They did not realize it, did not know how to become enlightened.
> Now on your behalf he repents.
> Sentient beings listen as he points out their delusions,
> The five sacred peaks present no obstruction.
> On the wheel of rebirth charged with rescuing from suffering,
> In the hells he does not gallop off, abandoning them.
> Fortunate or damned, he makes sure they continue on,
> He knows the lucky and unlucky, present and past.
> Caring about sentient beings, he serves the Great Dao,
> Compassionate, he eliminates harm for them.
> Opening forever the door of transcendent teachings,
> He relies on these teachings, forever supreme.

He further intoned:

> The Cinnamon Record of emoluments, you administer,
> Documents are brought to completion by you.
> If one wishes to ascend the path to governmental service,
> They depend on you to act as balance.
> Good and evil, these are fortune and misfortune,
> Success lies in karmic affinities.
> Grasping a brush you write it out for us,
> How could prosperity and decay be accidental?
> If there are blessings, there must be retribution.
> He has no favorites, none to whom he is partial.

The Heavens proclaim this good.
How [else] can one attain promotion?

Thereupon the Primordial Heavenly Worthy concluded this scripture. He addressed the Divine Lord of Zitong, saying, "You dwell on Mount Phoenix in the western Shu region and have manifested your numinous power in the profane world, fully manifesting your accomplishments. When I examine your actions and retirements through ninety-four transformations and make manifest your metamorphoses through quadrillions of aeons, you have had charge of one office, the relief of suffering, and have administered fortune and misfortune throughout the four quarters. Hear my few words that supplement your 'inch of goodness.' I moreover grant you my reverent awe to repay your compassion."

The Tract on the Hidden Administration

The Divine Lord said: "I have assumed the identity of a scholar-official seventeen times. Never have I mistreated the people or abused my clerks. I saved people in distress, helped them through emergencies, took pity on the orphaned, and forgave humans their transgressions. Extensively have I carried out my hidden administration, extending up to the blue vault of the sky. If people can maintain a heart like mine, Heaven will certainly bestow blessings upon them."

Then he instructed the people, saying, "Long ago, when Elder Yu was in charge of the jails, he raised a gate large enough for a team of four to enter [in expectation of the reward of the hidden administration for his good deeds in administering the jails justly. Upon retirement he was given a carriage and a team of four.]. Master Dou helped others and broke five high twigs from the cinnamon tree [of fate] [as a result of which his lifespan was extended for thirty-six years and his five sons reached high office]. By [diverting a stream and] saving an ant[hill], selection for the position of valedictorian [in the civil service examinations] was won [by Song Jiao]. By [killing and] burying an [ominous two-headed] snake [when he was a young boy], a man [Shun Shu'ao of Chu] enjoyed the glory of the prime ministership.

"To expand your field of blessings, you must rely on the foundations of your heart. Respond to the needs of others again and again, creating one type after another of hidden merit. Benefit creatures and benefit man; cultivate good and cultivate blessings. Be upright and straightforward, promote moral conversion on behalf of Heaven. Be compassionate and moral; rescue people on behalf of the state. Be loyal to your ruler, filial to your parents, respectful to your elder brother, trustworthy toward your friends. At times, make offerings to the Perfected and pay court to the Dipper. Other times, bow to the Buddha and recite sūtras. Repay the Four Graces [of Heaven, Earth, lord, and parents]; broadly promulgate the Three Teachings [of Daoism, Confucianism, and Buddhism]. Help others through crises as if helping a fish in a dried wheel rut; save the imperiled as if saving a sparrow caught in a fine net. Take pity on the orphaned and sympathize with the widowed. Respect the elderly and commiserate with the poor. Prepare clothing and food to relieve the hunger and cold of travelers. Donate coffins to avoid the exposure of corpses. If your household prospers, lend a helping hand to relatives and in-laws. In years of famine, aid neighbors and friends. Weights and measures must be fair; do not underpay or over-charge. Treats slaves and servants leniently. How can you lay all blame upon them or make intemperate demands? Print copies of the scriptures; build and repair monasteries. Distribute drugs to save the afflicted; provide tea to quench thirst. On occasion, buy animals and release them alive; other times, observe a fast and renounce killing. Always look for bugs and ants when stepping. Do not burn mountain forests when fires are prohibited (i.e., spring). Light a night-lamp to illuminate the paths of men. Build riverboats to help others cross. Do not ascend mountains to net birds or beasts. Do not poison fish or shrimp in the rivers. Do not slaughter plowing oxen. Do not throw away paper with writing on it. Do not scheme to take the wealth of others. Do not envy others' abilities. Do not sexually defile the wives or daughters of others. Do not incite others to litigation. Do not destroy the reputation of others. Do not wreck others' marriages. Do not sow dissension among brothers for the sake of a private feud. Do not cause discord between father and son for the sake of a small profit. Do not, relying upon power and position, humiliate the virtuous. Do not, depending on wealth and influence, cheat those in straitened circum-stances. If there is a good person, then draw near to him, thus supporting virtuous conduct within yourself. If there is an evil person, then avoid him, thus forestalling disaster at the eyebrows and eyelashes. Always you must hide evil and herald good. You must not condone with your mouth while con-demning with your heart. Cut the thorns and underbrush that obstruct the roads; remove tiles and stones on the paths. Rebuild roads that will wind cir-cuitously for hundreds of years; erect bridges that tens of millions will cross. Leave behind teachings to deter the evil actions of others; donate your wealth to facilitate their good deeds. Actions must comply with heavenly principles; words must accord with the hearts of men. Observe former sages even while they are supping or sitting on walls [as Shun observed Yao]; be circumspect even in actions known only to yourself and your quilt or shadow. If you do not practice evil, but serve good, then never will a baleful star shadow you; always auspicious spirits will protect you. When immediate retribution is ex-acted upon yourself and long-term retribution is visited upon your sons and grandson, or when a hundred blessings arrive together and a thousand auspi-cious omens gather like clouds, how could these not derive from hidden ad-ministration?"

4

City Gods and Their Magistrates

Angela Zito

Because most of the people who lived in late imperial China could neither read nor write and left no written testimony, modern social and cultural historians of this period must wonder at the nature of the people's relationship with the imperial officials who ruled them and often spoke for them in texts. District magistrates were the most obvious and accessible representatives of the centralized state. They presided over many kinds of social events. Their presence was expected, their opinions necessary, for any community of size. However, with only roughly 400 magistrates "on the ground" to rule a population of millions, social order must have been nurtured in ways far more subtle, and stable, than fear of brute force.

Popular religious cults, such as that of the God of Walls and Moats (Chenghuang shen) or City God, provide rich ground for understanding how people shaped their social world, a world that combined the family, the imperial domain, and the cosmos into an interactive whole. The City God worked in partnership with the district magistrate of the locale: the god ruled in the invisible (*you*) world as the magistrate worked in the visible (*ming*) one. The district magistrate was like a one-person government combining duties of tax collector, administrator of justice, educator, and ritualist. He occupied the lowest level of officialdom directly appointed by the throne and served as a sort of miniature emperor in his district. Every major locality had a City God temple inhabited by a god who held a heavenly bureaucratic rank equivalent to his earthly counterpart. The temple mimicked the magistrate's headquarters in its layout; the god rode in the same kind of sedan chair as the magistrate and had similar sorts of attendants.

As sociologist Maurice Freedman tells us, no easy or fixed boundary existed between "elite" and "popular" practice. Religion did not merely mirror a social landscape; it also provided a means for people to create their social world, with all its divisions and particular perspectives. City gods were not, then, purely the creations of the state. They represent an urban ethos, a sacralization of place in the universe. Communities often took the initiative and proposed likely deceased candidates for the post of City God, men who had served the local people particularly well. In the City God, the powers of the invisible world were made visible as the spirit of the historical memory of place and people.

Officials and people alike thought both the visible and invisible realms necessary to what we might term the social and natural order of the cosmos. When he took up a new post, the magistrate visited the City God to enlist his help in governing the people of the district. The City God's yearly festival and procession (usually held on his birthday) were noisy, crowded, colorful events. In case of natural disaster, both the people and the magistrate turned to the god for aid. The cult of the City God, shared between imperial official ritualists and popular practitioners, was claimed in different ways by each because its focus was this juncture of parallel worlds. People could also contend for its authority. The magistrate often asked for the god's help in adjudicating difficult legal cases, but common people accused of crimes could also go before the City God, seeking a sign of innocence. And they could appeal his decision up the spiritual administrative ranks.

The sources from the period rarely express such competing claims upon the City God directly. Whether legend, local history, handbook for magistrates, imperial pronouncement, or ritual prescription, they proceed from a consensus about the constitution of both nature and society. Sometimes they seem to agree, sometimes to disagree, but they are always in dialogue with one another about how gods and humans should conduct themselves in their respective worlds. Perhaps the most systematic explanation of presuppositions about a cosmos that contained within it a hierarchically ordered humanity lies in the concept of ritual (li).

From the fourth century B.C.E., but especially from the Han dynasty (202 B.C.E.– 220 C.E.), ritual had been thought of as a set of principles for order and connection that was both cosmically dictated (natural) and humanly maintained (social). The emperor and his officialdom were duty-bound to perform an intricate round of simultaneous ritual tasks such as twice yearly sacrifices to the God of Soil and Grain; to Confucius; to the gods of wind, clouds, thunder, rain, mountains, and streams, and to city gods. Once yearly, sacrifices were performed for local worthy people: chaste widows, loyal fighters, filial brothers and sons. Ghosts were propitiated three times yearly, and the emperor also sacrificed alone to Heaven and Earth twice yearly.

The four texts below focus on the cult of the City God as a locus of mediation between the visible and invisible worlds, between order and disorder, and between levels of society. They provide different views of the cult that emphasize aspects relevant to the writers' own positions in imperial society. They also describe different possibilities for how human beings can take action in this cosmos.

One very important sort of action is mediation: the ability to see two sides of a question, to resolve contradiction or opposition, seems to have been particularly powerful. We can see how this mediation would be necessary in a cosmos structured by the logic of yin-yang polarity. Rather than one element of an opposition overcoming the other completely (even violently), the point is to encompass the contradiction by creating a total situation that contains them both: often described in Chinese moral teaching as "harmony." Control of creating the social effect of this harmony, symbolized most effectively by people's relationship with their invisible gods and ancestors, was not an abstract matter. Who mediates and how become important questions for these texts.

Further Reading

Angela R. Zito, "City Gods, Hegemony and Filiality in Late Imperial China," *Modern China* 13.3 (July 1987): 333–71; C. K. Yang, *Religion in Chinese Society* (Berkeley: University of California Press, 1961); Maurice Freedman, "On the Sociological Study of Chinese Religion," in *Religion and Ritual in Chinese Society*, ed. A. Wolf (Stanford: Stanford University Press, 1974); Stephan Feuschtwang, "School Temple and City God," in *The City in Late Imperial China*, ed. G. W. Skinner (Stanford: Stanford University Press, 1977).

The following legend was collected by Jiang Xiaomei in his *Taiwan Stories (Taiwan gushi)*, vol. 2 (Taibei, 1955). The cast of characters and their relationships are particularly interesting because we see the roles of district magistrate, City God, and imperial son laid side-by-side for comparison. We can also see the realms of the Chinese world, visible and invisible, interact. The imperial son disappeared in a storm and was given up for dead and only reclaimed through the offices of the City God and his magistrate, partners in governance. In the following I have used "imperial son" instead of "prince" to translate a Chinese term whose two characters literally mean "great son," for two reasons: to highlight the importance of sonship in sacrificial mediation of gods and humans, and to preserve the sense, present in the Chinese original, that *all* sons serve this function, not only princes.

The City God of Xinzhu, Taiwan

The City God of Xinzhu possesses much magical power (*linghun*), and countless numbers of people have come from north and south to burn incense, kneel, and bow. Here is the story of how the Xinzhu City God received his titles from a Qing dynasty (1644–1911) emperor.

Once, when the emperor's son was at the seaside with his wet nurse, he was fascinated by the fishing boats and leapt about upon them. When waves washed in and the boats bobbed higher, he was even more delighted. Suddenly a great wind came up and bore the boat containing the imperial son and his wet nurse to a far-off sea. When they discovered that their son was lost, the emperor and empress were worried and sent people to search, but they found nothing.

The boat in which the wet nurse and the imperial son sat floated to a lonely island in the southern sea. The island's chief kindly saved them, and when he saw that the imperial son was talented, and since he did not have a son himself, he kept him as his own and raised him. The wet nurse, having been at sea so long, got sick after arriving on the island and died. The imperial son grew bigger day by day. He practiced spear-throwing and archery daily, sometimes going into the mountains to hunt or to the sea to fish. He happily passed his days.

Time passed as "brightness and shade passed like arrows; the sun and moon shifted." The imperial son had grown to adulthood. Although the island chief loved him dearly, the son daily thought of his old land and his father and mother. He thought that if he had the chance, he would return there.

Once he announced he wished to fish in a far sea, prepared provisions, and left the chief's lonely island, going north in a small boat. Days later he came to Fragrant Hill, on Xinzhu's coast in Taiwan. After coming ashore, he went to stay at the hostel of Mazu's Temple (patroness of fishermen and the most popular deity on Taiwan).

That night Xinzhu's district magistrate dreamt that Xinzhu's City God came to him, saying: "The imperial son is in the temple on Fragrant Hill. Go quickly to greet him." The next day the district magistrate took a great palanquin to Fragrant Hill Temple to check, and in the Mazu Temple he discovered a stalwart youth of extraordinary power. The magistrate hastened to kneel and say humbly: "The imperial son is under our eaves, brightening this poor place. This petty official was slow in coming to greet you respectfully. Please forgive him."

The imperial son did not realize the fellow's true intentions and dared not reveal his real status. He said: "I am not the imperial son. Who are you?"

The magistrate answered: "I am Xinzhu's district magistrate. Last night in a dream I received the City God's command and only then did I know the imperial son was 'lighting up the neighborhood.' Please take this palanquin, come into the city, and relax."

When the imperial son heard the story his heart eased, and he admitted he was the emperor's son. He went with the magistrate to his residence and received his hospitality. A few days later the magistrate escorted the imperial son to the capital to report. Because his son had been lost for over ten years, the emperor thought he was already dead and never imagined seeing him again. Brush and ink cannot describe his happiness. The Xinzhu magistrate's worthy service deserved the favor and grace of the emperor and he was immediately promoted. Xinzhu's City God likewise received the emperor's entitlement: "Awesome and Magical Duke, City God of Xinzhu."

Huang Liuhong, the author of the following text, was born in 1633 and lived until at least 1694, the date of the preface to his woodblock print handbook for district magistrates, *A Complete Book Concerning Happiness and Benevolence (Fuhui quanshu).* He served twice in that capacity in the 1670s. His thirty-two-chapter book of advice covers matters as diverse as tax collection, the proper etiquette for an arriving magistrate, controlling the secretarial staff, administering justice, community self-help organization, famine relief, and education. Chapter 24 discusses "Rites and Ceremonies." Besides four sections on the City God (two of which are translated below), Huang also details proper protocols for audience with the emperor, spring and autumn sacrifices to Confucius, receiving imperial edicts, the civil service examination, local banquets, and honoring chaste women and filial sons. Huang's entire book has been translated by Djang Chu as *A Complete Book Concerning Happiness and Benevolence* (Tucson: University of Arizona Press, 1984).

Worshiping the City God

The district magistrate governs the visible, or manifest, world and the City God the invisible. Generating benefit and warding off harm for the people are the duties of the magistrate. Bringing down blessings and warding off natural disasters are the duties of the City God. The magical power (*ling*) of gods depends upon their connection with people. Sacrifice, through integrity (*cheng,* the feeling of integration of self and cosmos), leads to wisdom (*ge,* the knowledge of the ethical relationships that structure the world). The invisible becomes apparent through effort in this manifest world. People of cities must pay their respects to the gods and the gods will respond. They must be reverent in their sacrifice and then it will be accepted. They must exert themselves in doing their duties in this world so they can enter into communication (*tong*) with the invisible world.

If there is a response from the god, then that magical power that depends upon the actions of the people through their magistrate (the word *ren* includes both) is present. Wisdom comes with acceptance of the sacrifice, a wisdom that grows from integrity. The manifestation of the invisible world shows that we have entered into communication, and achieving this manifestation depends upon action in the visible world.

If there is no such action, even if there are gods, they will not respond. Even if there are sacrifices, they will not be accepted. Even if there is an invisible world, there will be no communication with it. Thus the governance of this world and the invisible one will be at odds and there will be no mutual trust between them. In such circumstances, even if magistrates and gods have the power to encourage prosperity and ward off harm, it may happen that there will be neither prosperity nor preservation from harm. Why?

When magistrates have intentions that they cannot fulfill, they ask the gods who then silently probe the petitioners. If sincere intentions are lacking, there cannot be a sincere request. Without a sincere request, then the governance of the visible and invisible worlds will be at odds.

Conversely, if the intentions of the petitioner are intimately concerned with the ills of the people, if he is truly anxious on their behalf, then he will take as fundamental the task of ridding them of suffering and plan for their happiness and prosperity. I, however, am fearfully deficient and my power as an exemplar (de) is too weak to move Heaven. Because the gods' governance of the invisible world approaches closely and enters into communication with the Lord on High (Di), they can replace magistrates to emanate concern to the people below, beseeching fate to ward off disaster and bring luck down upon the people. When luck falls upon the people, prosperity is generated. When calamity has been warded off, harm is avoided. What magistrates and people want, the gods will give them. Serve the gods on behalf of the people; do your duty because of the gods. In considering the people's happiness and the uprightness of duty, who would dare not respect the gods?

I am currently the magistrate of Tancheng. Being ashamed of my own weak inadequacy, I must call upon the City God for luck in order to obtain abundance and health for the people. I have renovated his temple, replaced his sacrificial vessels, refurbished the temple guardian statues, and augmented his festivals. Because these things were done with integrity and respect, when locusts came, our crops were unharmed; when hail struck causing calamity, the winds ceased immediately. When I prayed for sun, it rose in the sky; when I prayed for rain, sufficient sweet drops fell. In innumerable instances, my requests never went unanswered.

We must realize that the City God is also an official in charge of protecting the locale. Being attached to an area expressly to govern it he, of all the gods, is the quickest to respond. If the magistrate will rely upon three things—the people (as those he represents, ren), his own integrity (cheng), and the care and performance of duties in this world—he will know that my claims are not exaggerated. I append a sample of requests.

PETITIONING THE CITY GOD TO DELIVER US FROM LOCUSTS

On [fill in date] during the Kangxi reign, this official dares to petition the City God of the district, addressing him thus:

"The spirit and the official each has duties. In this locale, we ward off natural disaster and hinder human evils."

At this time, as the peasants are in the fields with the grain not yet harvested, the locust eggs from last season are being hatched in the earth. Already half of the second cycle of wheat has been contaminated. Ten days ago, locusts came from the southwest, fluttering their wings and crawling over our fields. The people rushed around, wailing as though at a funeral, or at the end of the world.

I humbly prayed to the god, but the god has not yet rendered judgment. Can this heavenly disaster be so difficult to salvage? Can the approach of the Grave-Sweeping Festival in the spring have anything to do with it? Or is it that I have been so rude in carrying out my duties that my essential integrity cannot lead to correct wisdom? When the people cannot prevent disaster, they implore the magistrate. When the magistrate cannot prevent disaster on their behalf, he prays to the gods. The god is awesome and dwells above; can it not carry petitions made by officials and the people to the Lord on High?

We comprehend the inevitable nature of disasters like the locusts, which can completely blanket a thousand *li* of land. Tancheng County, a little pill of a place, a tiny mole, cannot escape. This is all to say that we humans have exhausted our means to save ourselves. But you do not think this way. Unlike us, you can perceive such disasters before people or their officials.

God—you govern the invisible world. Do not allow our grain to suffer; do not allow the locusts to lay eggs in our fields, so that we might have an autumn harvest. Only by your grace, your magical power, do we dare to beseech you.

Local gentry compiled and edited gazetteers about their villages, towns, or counties. They included geographies, maps, descriptions of local sights and temples, tales of special customs or foods, and biographies of worthy people. When temples were renovated, commemorative texts, such as the two imperial messages below, were inscribed in stone and often included in the gazetteer. The inscription of the Yongzheng emperor (r. 1723–1735) can be found in a woodblock edition of the *Gazetteer of the Department of Shuntian (Shuntian fuzhi)* (1886), j. 6:19b–20a. Shuntian was the administrative unit, slightly larger than a county, that contained the imperial capital city of Beijing.

In this stone stele inscription, the Yongzheng emperor describes the classic cosmos of orthodox Neo-Confucian philosophy, with references to the harmony of yin and yang. Employing the language of agriculture, he discusses the cosmos of "self-so-ness" or "natural necessity" of the Dao. He emphasizes the actual sacrificial rituals of officialdom and uses many metaphors from its domain. One important question that this text poses is: Where is the king and how does he rule in a cosmos of self-regulatory resonance?

The Text of the Stone Tablet Written by the Yongzheng Emperor for the Beijing City God Temple

The Domainal Family has received the mandate of Heaven to rule. Of the many gods it gently enfolds there are none in the sacrificial canon that are not treated with seriousness and respect. How much more shall it be for those gods of the environs of the Imperial City, within the hub of the emperor's chariot? From the harmony of yin and yang, for correct wind and seasonal rain, for a dense population, for a proliferation and luxuriance of growing things, for a glowing, a flowing, a growing, a showing, and for help toward a lush begetting, one turns finally to the protection of the gods.

In the past, the capital had a god who was sacrificed to in the City God Temple. Officials for the Ministry of Rites would sacrifice at appropriate times for the enjoyment of the god. I do worry that the appearance of the temple is not solemn and that we thus we lack the means to show our respect.

In the first month of 1726, money was especially sent from the public treasury and officials ordered to restore the temple. The work was completed by the fifth month. The wood carving and clay modeling, the decorativeness of pillars painted in precious cinnabar, the expansion meant the temple looked even better than before—good enough to show fitting thanks for the splendor of the gods and to add to the beauty of the city. Officials of the Ministry of Rites built a pavilion, polished a stone, and requested bestowal of this text.

I think that the "Six Sacrifices of Request" in the ancient classic *The Rites of Zhou (Zhouli)* and the text of "Complete Order" in the *Book of Documents (Shangshu)* both beg for luck for the people by means of beseeching and thanksgiving for the merits of the gods. At present, all within the seas is at peace and the ten thousand of the world have attained their proper place and function. An abundance extends, happiness is great. Our well-being has been safe for a long time. The state of the kingdom can be compared to a perfect sacrifice: Our wine is sweet and our ox-victim whole; our vessels are clean and all is prepared.

Only when the gods have taken up our offerings and been thus infused with life do we have a sense of wisdom (*ge*). The way to feeling this sense of wisdom lies through integrity (*cheng*). With integrity one can enter into communication (*tong*). This communication allows us to know "rising and falling, the high and low" (that is, the relations between people and gods, the visible and invisible worlds) and the bestowing of luck upon the people. As such, it is sufficient to achieve the unhindered success of the yearly harvest, the happiness of the villages at work, and an increase of benefits day by day. There is nothing inappropriate about using this power to the fullest extent.

I now wish, together with the people, to rely happily upon this power. Today the temple's appearance is new: the time is commemorated. Let those temple officials who have duties in this temple courtyard chant the words inscribed on this stone that they should learn how to fix their integrity within and show composure without. Let the ritual vessels be laid out precisely and the sweeping of the temple be pristine that the far-reaching aroma of sacrifice may be sweet in accordance with my thinking on the respectful performance of sacrifice to Heaven and Earth.

The following inscription was also collected into the *Gazetteer of the Department of Shuntian* (1886), j. 6:20.b–21.a). In it, the Qianlong emperor appears less interested in metaphysics than in history. His overt depiction of the importance of imperial action and intervention contrasts with the views of his father, the Yongzheng emperor, in the previous text.

During Another Renovation Carried Out in the 28th Year of the Reign of the Qianlong Emperor (1763) an Imperial Stone Stele Was Erected

The emperor says: Mention of the "Walls and Moats" first appears in the *Classic of Changes (Yijing)*. The usage of the terms in any detail discusses them as a sacrifice to the walls and moats of a city, one of the eight Imperial Thanksgiving sacrifices under King Yao. In the classic text the *Spring and Autumn Annals* (covers events from 721 to 481 B.C.E.), thought to have been edited by Confucius, the country of Zheng beseeches the four walls and the country of Song offers horses, but these accounts are incomplete. From that time on, the official histories make no mention of the cult of the City God. In his *Collection of Old Accounts (Jigu lu)*, Ouyang Xiu (1007–1072 C.E.) of the Song dynasty (960–1279) selects Tang dynasty (618–907) writer Li Yanbing's "Record of the Gods of Walls and Moats" and comments, "The sacrificial canon does not contain this."

Let us further examine Song writer Wang Yinglin's (1223–1296) *Record of Perplexing Studies (Kunxue jiwen)*, which cites: "In northern Ji in the sixth century, Mu Rong sacrificed at the temple of the city in Yan in Hubei Province." Therefore we can see that there are citations of "temple feasting" for pre-Tang times.

Today in the realm under Heaven, from the county, through department and prefecture, all the way to the province, at all administrative levels, no one has failed to found temples. The capital City God temple is especially looked upon as a standard by all under Heaven. None are its equal.

City gods are often titled and given imperial rank according to the differential system of relations between directors and subordinates. As the gods prevent disaster and ward off evils, so the domain respects their merits.

However, we hear of the common people performing exorcisms, crowding in on each other's toes, and babbling away. They take a person as the god and call upon him as a proxy (*shi* literally means "corpse" and denoted the son who impersonated the dead ancestor of his father at ancestor veneration ceremonies). For example: "Our prior administrator, Loyal Gan of the Yu family." Or "Loyal Min of the Yang family." Putting it like that is nearly correct, like Bao Zhi's records of the Nanyang Department in which he takes the man Xiao of Xiangguo as the City God. Unfortunately, the people do not think of the Yus and Gans as loyal officials of the Ming period (they forget why these men were elevated to that position and lose sense of their historical and actual connection to the throne).

This temple has been standing since the Jin (1115–1234) and Yuan (1206–1333) dynasties. So what is its genealogy? Actually ever since the area northwest of Peking and Hebei provinces were formed, there have been cities and thus their guardian gods. So what were their genealogies?

Within the past few years, we have ordered officials of the Board of Works to mend the walls and dredge the moats in order to fulfill the protection and safety of the inhabitants. We have ordered them to penetrate to the depths with a diffusion of moist beneficence. Our motto is: Perfect the people and then expend effort on the gods. Only in this way will there be, in the end, a concrete result. Thus our efforts will not consist in merely hauling dirt and raising beams.

I have deferentially availed myself of the Grand Bestowal from Blue Heaven above, which extends to the entirety of the social and natural cosmos, to beyond the wilds. The various kingdoms and settlements of the western border are under our military control: they are called "nomadic kingdoms." Even those who have never heretofore had the protection of walls and moats have already arranged themselves in fortifications and started plowing. Raising walls that link up and extend, damming up a waterway that surrounds and entwines, they not only wall the cities as with golden teeth, they have moats full of rushes as well.

There is a desire to lead (*feng*) the masses of people in faraway, out-of-sight, out-of-hearing places. There is not one who goes unjudged and unpardoned by "the Gentleman in the Capital." Why should not places with only one wall and one moat share in the fortune of the capital City God temple? And how much more should this be the case for the populous, crowded areas in provinces, prefectures, departments, and counties?

Restoration (*xiu*) was carried out in the fourth year of the Yongzheng reign (1726). As the years passed the temple started to crumble. Now in the twenty-eighth year of the present reign (1763), the first lunar month, we have gathered the planners from the Board of Works and used funds from the Inner House to renovate (*xin*) thoroughly. From the bedchamber, main hall, the eastern and western inner walls, the kitchen and bathhouse to the outer wall and ceremonial archway, the temple is now enlarged and sturdy and accords completely with standards for such things.

One oddity we did not change: the statues of the city gods from the provinces, which are lined up to the right and left of the side gate, each holding insignia of office. Although investigation showed that such an arrangement has no canonical reality, we do not think it was a mistake to let them stand there. Since the tableau resembles the coming and going of district magistrates, departmental and prefectural officials, as well as city governors who have come to the capital for audience, we left it standing and did not disturb it.

How auspicious that the work was finished in the twelfth month, just in time for feeding the spirits of the Hungry Ghosts Festival. We therefore went in person to watch the rites and when they were finished composed a hymn to commemorate the occasion, ordering it to be cut into the stele. The sacrificing officials were ordered to have it set to music and use it at the sacrifice.

Each year during the autumn months choose an auspicious time and send officials to sacrifice. Carry out the usual sacrificial rites.

5

The Earliest Tales of the Bodhisattva Guanshiyin

Robert Ford Campany

One of the most influential of early Mahāyāna sūtras is the *Sūtra of the Lotus Blossom of the Fine Dharma* (*Saddharmapundarīkasūtra,* Chinese: *Miaofa lianhua jing*), often called simply the *Lotus Sūtra*. It is known to have been translated from Sanskrit into Chinese as early as 255 C.E. It was retranslated at least five times by the year 601, including the version produced in 406 by the government-sponsored translation bureau headed by one of the greatest of Buddhist translators in China, the Indo-Iranian missionary Kumārajīva (ca. 350–409). Kumārajīva's translation soon became, and still remains, the most popular of the Chinese texts of the sūtra.

The twenty-fifth chapter of this translation (twenty-fourth in some translations), entitled Universal Gateway [to Salvation] of the Bodhisattva He Who Observes the Sounds of the World (*Guanshiyin pusa pumenpin*), was also circulated as an independent scripture under the title *Sūtra of He Who Observes the Sounds of the World* (*Guanshiyin Sūtra*). In it, Śākyamuni Buddha promises that if people in extreme difficulty call upon the name of the Bodhisattva He Who Observes the Sounds of the World, they will be swiftly and miraculously rescued from danger by the bodhisattva's great power and compassion. He utters this promise in response to a question by another bodhisattva:

> At that time the Bodhisattva Inexhaustible Mind . . . straightway rose from his seat and, baring his right shoulder and facing the Buddha with palms joined, said: "O World-Honored One! For what reason is the Bodhisattva He Who Observes the Sounds of the World (Avalokiteśvara) called Observer of the Sounds of the World?" The Buddha declared to the Bodhisattva Inexhaustible Mind, "Good man, if incalculable hundreds of thousands of myriads of millions of living beings, suffering pain and torment, hear of this Bodhisattva He Who Observes the Sounds of the World and single-mindedly call upon his name, the Bodhisattva He Who Observes the Sounds of the World shall straightway heed their voices, and all shall gain deliverance." (Hurvitz translation, p. 311)

The Buddha then enumerates the types of dangerous situations from which the compassionate bodhisattva rescues those who call upon him: burning, drowning, becoming lost at sea, being murdered, being attacked by demons, being jailed, falling off a cliff while traveling, and so on. We also read that the bodhisattva grants happiness, boundless merit, and the birth of children to men and women who call on and worship him. Finally, the Buddha describes how the bodhisattva appears in a multitude of different bodies—from that of a buddha to that of a boy or girl, that of a god to that of a demon—according to the needs and capacities of those who call on him. Out of compassion he displays to particular beings whatever bodily form is most apt to convey them to deliverance.

This chapter of the *Lotus Sūtra* is only one of several Buddhist texts translated or written in China before the seventh century that make such claims about the Bodhisattva He Who Observes the Sounds of the World, or Guanshiyin, as he is referred to below. Some early texts give his name as "Guangshiyin," *guang* being the character for "light" or "radiance"; this usage was soon abandoned. In such cases, I have silently altered the spelling to "Guanshiyin."

Thanks to multiple translations, monastic copying of texts, and popular sermons, the teachings contained in the *Lotus Sūtra* and other scriptures concerning Guanshiyin were spread throughout many regions of China from the third to the seventh century. How did the Chinese of that era respond to these teachings? Fortunately we have a valuable body of evidence that affords us a window onto the modes of piety these scriptures inspired. From the late fourth century, a handful of Chinese people, both monks and laypersons, began to write down and collect tales that they had heard or read illustrating the fulfillment of these sūtras' promises on Chinese soil, and some of these tales have come down to us today.

Other evidence of devotion to Guanshiyin during this period was found at the turn of the century in a sealed cave at Dunhuang in extreme northwestern China. On the walls were paintings depicting Guanshiyin saving people from various types of distress, and among the 42,000 written documents there were hanging banners depicting the same, as well as some 1,048 copies of the *Lotus Sūtra* (by far the greatest number of copies of any sūtra found in the cave) and almost 200 separate copies of the *Guanshiyin Sūtra*. These figures represent only the documents that exist today in collections outside the People's Republic of China; many more are doubtless preserved in Chinese collections.

Chinese of the fourth through the sixth centuries knew the world to be a violent, dangerous, and chaotic place. Non-Chinese nomadic groups, often collectively and derisively termed "caitiffs" (base and despicable people) in the stories to follow, invaded from the north. They seized power in the ancient cradle of Chinese civilization and pushed many Chinese aristocrats and peasants south into the Yangzi River valley, where they set up a new capital near today's Nanjing. Those Chinese who remained in the north found themselves living under an unusually harsh regime. The devastating impact of these events on the Chinese cultural imagination has been likened to the effect on Westerners of the sack of "eternal Rome" by the Visigoths about a century afterward.

The movement of certain nomadic Central Asian peoples southward and westward into the Mediterranean rim and eastern Europe was in fact caused, in part, by the southward push by other Central Asian peoples into China. Moreover, during these centuries a series of disastrous floods occurred, contributing to widespread famine and plague. Several destructive popular rebellions broke out. Meanwhile, a small group of elite families contended for power in the southern capital, creating political instability so great that over a period of slightly more than two and a half centuries five dynasties—the Eastern Jin, Song, Qi, Liang, and Chen—succeeded one another until the reunification of China under the Sui dynasty in 589. Given this combination of massive military, political, social, and natural cataclysms, it is no wonder than many Buddhist and Daoist writers of the period predicted the imminent end of the world.

It is also no wonder that devotion to Guanshiyin became so popular in this context. Here was a being who was powerful, responsive, and compassionate, whose very name implied his attentiveness to his devoted, and who specialized in extricating them from desperate, hopeless situations. One needed no special gifts or vision to invoke him; one did not have to be a monk, a male, or a literate person to receive his help. Living according to Buddhist precepts, though helpful, was in no way a necessary condition for asking Guanshiyin to intervene. In a moment of crisis—when, to cite the language of tale after tale, "death seemed certain," "when there seemed to be no way out," "when escape was impossible"—one acknowledged one's own helplessness and implored the compassionate bodhisattva for aid.

This call for help is described in both sūtras and tales as an act of extreme concentration of mind, utmost sincerity of will, and sustained or repeated exertion of body and indeed of one's total being. The person in peril is said to call on the bodhisattva "with a perfect mind" (zhixin) or "single-mindedly" (yixin) and to think on him "with utter concentration" (zhinian), "exclusively" (weinian), or "purely" (chunnian). He or she does so with "utmost sincerity" (zhicheng). The invocation often involves sustaining such states of concentration for days on end, though in emergency situations (such as the sudden threat of fire or drowning) Guanshiyin is depicted as responding immediately. And some bodily activity is usually essential: the making of an image of Guanshiyin, presentation of offerings to him, prostration of oneself before his image, or, most commonly, the repeated and continuous oral recitation of his name, of the Guanshiyin Sūtra, or even of the entire Lotus Sūtra.

The tales translated below are examples of those written to document Guanshiyin's saving responses to Chinese people in danger. In crisp, concise prose, each tale portrays a particular person in a moment of dire need who calls on Guanshiyin and is miraculously saved. These tales of Guanshiyin form a subset of a larger genre of Buddhist miracle tales. The miracle tales vary in content, but they all describe some extraordinary event, impossible or highly unlikely under normal circumstances, related to the power or authority of a Buddhist personage (such as a monk), devotional act (such as an offering to an image of the Buddha), or idea (such as karmic retribution for misdeeds). The unusual event—often characterized as an "anomaly" (*yi*) or a "divine response" (*lingyan, lingying, yingyan,* etc.)—was understood to demonstrate, as no verbal argument could do, the truth of Buddhism; and so the miracle tales constitute a narrative mode of apologetics.

This genre was closely related, both in subject matter and in literary form, to Buddhist hagiographies, or collections of life-accounts (often including miraculous events) of exemplary monks, nuns, and laypersons. The Buddhist miracle tale has continued in China down to the present day (along with counterparts in the Daoist tradition, which borrowed it as an apologetic medium), and it was also carried to Japan, where it flourished.

The authors of the earliest tale collections that survive were laypersons. They derived their news of miraculous "responses" to Buddhists' devotion from three sources: previous records written by others, hearsay from a trusted acquaintance or relative (many of the persons mentioned as sources of stories are monks), and personal experience.

Why did these authors record tales of Guanshiyin's responses to cries for help? First, recording and spreading these tales was itself an act of merit, for it encouraged others to join in devotion to Guanshiyin. (Similarly, the *Lotus Sūtra* is filled with promises of great rewards to readers and hearers who copy and spread it.) Second, the authors seem to have wanted to authenticate the fulfillment of the sūtras' promises in order to show that the sūtras were true and that the practices they enjoined were efficacious. This is suggested most clearly by the fact that the authors sometimes directly quoted a passage from the *Guanshiyin Sūtra* (or some other sūtra concerning Guanshiyin) that seemed directly relevant to a particular miraculous event. This authentication of the sūtras relates to a third function of the tales: to argue the truth of Buddhism against its detractors and to show its superiority over the competing religion of Daoism as well as the old cults of local gods. Finally, the tales were one medium used in the larger Chinese effort to domesticate Buddhism. In showing how a powerful being of foreign origin, first known to the Chinese through a translated text, responded to specific, named, historical individuals at particular places at times in China, the tales helped to weave more Buddhist strands into the fabric of Chinese religion and culture while also giving the bodhisattva an increasingly Chinese face.

Thus began the process that would culminate, during the late Tang and especially the Song (960–1279), in the feminization of the earlier masculine figure and her thorough incorporation as a goddess into Chinese religion and folklore, in which she has occupied an important place ever since.

Finally, a word on the current state of the tale collections is in order. The approximately 470 Buddhist miracle tales that survive from before the seventh century now exist in various forms. Some of the earliest were found in this century in a Japanese monastery, in a document apparently dating from the twelfth century. The majority of extant tales, however, were preserved not in their original sequences but under topical headings in encyclopedic collections such as the seventh-century Buddhist work *A Grove of Pearls from the Garden of the Dharma*

(*Fayuan zhulin*) by the monk Daoshi or later encyclopedias such as the tenth-century *Broad-ranging Records Compiled in the Era of Great Peace* (*Taiping guangji*). A great many of these tales have in turn been reassembled under their original titles by the twentieth-century scholar and author Lu Xun in his *Gleanings of Ancient Tales* (*Gu xiaoshuo gouchen*). The following translations draw on all these sources.

Further Reading

On the artistic evidence, see Miyeko Murase, "Kuan-yin as Saviour of Men: Illustration of the Twenty-fifth Chapter of the Lotus Sutra in Chinese Painting," *Artibus Asiae* 33 (1971):39–74, and Cornelius P. Chang, "Kuan-yin Paintings from Tun-huang: Water-Moon Kuan-yin," *Journal of Oriental Studies* (Hong Kong) 15.2 (1977): 140–60. The best survey of the early miracle-tale genre in China is still Donald E. Gjertson, "The Early Chinese Buddhist Miracle Tale: A Preliminary Survey," *Journal of the American Oriental Society* 101.3 (1981): 287–301. For discussion of miracle tales associated with particular sūtra texts and translations of examples, see Robert F. Campany, "Notes on the Devotional Uses and Symbolic Functions of Sūtra Texts as Depicted in Early Chinese Buddhist Miracle Tales and Hagiographies," *Journal of the International Association of Buddhist Studies* 14.1 (1991). On the emergence of the female Guanyin see, most recently, Chün-fang Yü, "Feminine Images of Kuan-yin in Post-T'ang China," *Journal of Chinese Religions* 18 (1990):61–89.

TALE 1

XiGSY 20 (*RKKO* 34). This tale was also anthologized in slightly more elaborate form in the monk Sengxiang's seventh-century collection, *Tales of the Lotus Blossom* (*Sūtra*) (*Fahua zhuanji*, T 2068, v. 51), j. 5 (71a).

There was a widow surnamed Li who lived in Liang Province (modern Gansu). Her family had long been Buddhist; they faithfully kept every fast day and attended meetings. Each time she would listen to sūtra readings; as soon as they were over, she could recite the sūtra herself. Later, a [Chinese] woman who had been made a princess among the caitiffs (the northern non-Chinese peoples who conquered much of China north of the Yangzi valley) suddenly [showed up and] sought refuge in Li's home. It was a moonless night, and Li could not bear to send her away. Soon officials came to register Li [on the population list], and their report stated that she was harboring a rebellious female slave. Once this register was submitted [to the authorities], Li was jailed.

Then with a perfect mind she recited the *Guanshiyin Sūtra* and was able to keep reciting it continuously for over ten days.

Suddenly in the middle of the day she saw Guanshiyin. He asked her why she did not leave [her cell]; she replied that it was impossible. He then said: "Just get up." On doing so she found that her shackles were already unfastened, and then she quickly found herself back at home. The warden and the guards were all completely unaware of her departure. Later when the caitiffs learned of her escape, they sent someone to question her and find out how she had managed to return home. She told them everything that had happened. She was not rearrested.

TALE 2

XYJ 6 (*LX* 437), based on *BZL* 7 (sec. 8, 539b–c note); cf. *TPGJ* 110.

Che Mu was involved in the Prince of Luling's Song-era disaster at Blue Mud and was captured by the caitiffs and held in their camp. His mother had long been a devout Buddhist. She now lit seven lamps before a Buddhist image (probably of Guanshiyin) and during the night concentrated with a striving mind on Guanshiyin, asking that her son be freed. After she did this for an entire year, her son suddenly [was able to] escape and make his way home. He walked alone for seven days and nights, heading south. Often at night he would lose his way, unable to tell east from west; but then in the distance he would see seven points of firelight, and so he would head toward those lights. It would always seem as if he was about to reach a village, but he never found one.

After seven nights of this he suddenly found himself at his home. He saw his mother still prostrated on the ground before the Buddhist image; then, seeing the seven lamps, he suddenly realized [what the firelight had actually been]. The mother and son discussed what had happened and knew it must be due to the Buddha's power. From that time on they both made earnest prayers [of thanksgiving] and scrupulously performed acts of mercy and kindness.

TALE 3

XuGSY 4 (*RKKO* 21); apparently unattested elsewhere. Sun En's rebellion (399–400 C.E.) was Daoist in ideology and recruited masses of disaffected peasants from the coastal provinces of Zhejiang and Fujian. My translation of the phrase "fled the destruction" is tentative.

Formerly, when the bandit Sun [En] stirred up rebellion, many people living near the coast, both aristocrats and commoners, fled the destruction. A group of a dozen or so people were about to be executed in the eastern marketplace. Only one among them respected the dharma, and this man began chanting [the name of] Guanshiyin with perfect sincerity. Another man who was sitting with him asked him what he was doing. He replied: "I have heard that the scriptures of the Buddha's dharma mention a bodhisattva Guanshiyin who saves people from distress. So I am taking refuge in him." The other man then followed his example. When the hour of execution arrived, the official list [of those to be executed] was found to be lacking just the names of these two people. This created shock and panic in the crowd, and everyone fled in different directions. These two men followed the crowd and were thus able to escape execution.

TALE 4

MXJ 69 (*LX* 498); cf. *FYZL* 17 (410b), *TPGJ* 110.

Sun Daode, who lived during the Song, was a Daoist and a libationer (that is, a leader in communal affairs and liturgies of the Daoist Celestial Master lineage). He still had no son even after passing the age of fifty. In the year 423 a [Buddhist] monk who lived in a monastery nearby told Daode: "If you are determined to have a son, you must respectfully and with a perfect mind recite the *Guanshiyin Sūtra*. You may then hope for success." Daode then gave up serving the Dao; with single-minded sincerity he took refuge in Guanshiyin. Within a few days he had a dream-response. His wife was indeed pregnant, and subsequently she gave birth to a boy.

TALE 5

XiGSY 53 (*RKKO* 48–49); cf. *GSZ* (371c).

The dharma-master Shi Daowang was a native of Changle in northern Jizhou (Hebei Province); his lay surname was Fan. He resided at Dragon Gorge Monastery in Yizhou (the area around Chengdu, capital of modern Sichuan Province), where he attracted many disciples. My own grandfather Jianzi, while stationed in Yizhou on official assignment, greatly respected him. Daowang was once returning from Liangzhou (in today's Shaanxi Province) along the road to Shu (that is, to Sichuan, a notoriously difficult route) when he ran into an area controlled by a group of Qiang (Tibetan) rebels who had cut off the road and killed countless people. He had several dozen disciples with him, and they in turn were part of a group of over three hundred travelers. When they met this trouble they had no idea what to do next. Daowang then single-mindedly fixed his thoughts on Guanshiyin, and he had his disciples call out

[Guanshiyin's] name. They then walked almost a hundred miles through the hostile area, but all the while they remained concealed and so escaped harm.

Another group of a dozen or so had split off and taken another route. They were to meet [Daowang's group] at a certain point, but they missed the spot. So they turned back along the road, and as they approached the appointed place they saw Daowang pass by. But between them were several hundred bandits who had cut off access to the road, so that they were unable to rejoin his group. That day the bandits were particularly numerous, but Daowang and the others walked right along beside them without being seen, nor did Daowang and his group see the bandits. This was a great deed accomplished by divine power. All the followers [in the other group] were astonished [to see it].

TALE 6

XiGSY 45 (*RKKO* 45); cf. *MXJ* 49 (*LX* 486), *FYZL* 17 (410a), *TPGJ* 110. *XiGSY* gives "knowing this person must be a deity" instead of *FYZL*'s "knowing that his prayers had met with a response." *FYZL* omits his being picked up by the ship.

The monk Lin Daoxian of Shangding was a disciple of Master [Dao]wang. He was one of the disciples traveling with him that day, and it is he who recounted this event to me. Luan Gou venerated the Buddha. He once served as magistrate of Fuping. Before this he was in a campaign against the caitiffs and was involved in a mishap. His boat was hit by fire bolts, and when these were extinguished the caitiffs were [seen to be] pressing toward them. They were just in the middle of the river, with high wind and waves. Gou thought fearfully that his death was near, but he nevertheless meditated on Guanshiyin. Soon he saw a person coming toward him through the water; the water came up only to his waist. Knowing that his prayers had been met with a response, Gou jumped into the water to meet him. His body did not sink; it was as though his feet were treading on solid ground. Then when a large transport ship came along to rescue survivors, he was the first one to be spotted. Now, Gou was so fat and heavy that his body could not be hauled up over the ship rail. He then saw four men shove him from below up into the ship. As soon as he had managed to climb aboard he looked back down at the water. No one was there.

TALE 7

XuGSY 10 (*RKKO* 24); apparently unattested elsewhere.

Han Dang, a native of Pingyuan (in today's Shandong Province), was once crossing the Hutuo River when the boat he was riding on sank in midstream.

He called out the name of Guanshiyin. Then he saw a white creature, shaped like a dragon, in the water. The current stopped and the wind subsided. The water reached only up to his knees, so he was able shortly to reach the sandy bank and was thus saved.

TALE 8

MXJ 32 (*LX* 474–75); cf. *GSY* 7 (*RKKO* 18), *FYZL* 95 (988b) and 17 (409b), *TPGJ* 110. The reference to the *Lotus* is probably to some such passage as this one in Kumārajīva's translation: "To those who can be conveyed to deliverance by the body of bhikṣu, bhikṣuṇī, upāsaka, or upāsikā (i.e., monk, nun, layman, or lay-woman), he (Guanshiyin) preaches dharma by displaying the body of bhikṣu, bhikṣuṇī, upāsaka, or upāsikā" (quoted from Hurvitz, *Scripture of the Lotus Blossom of the Fine Dharma,* 314–15).

During the years 363–366 there flourished the monk Zhu Fayi, who dwelled in the mountains and was fond of study. He lived in the Bao Mountains in Shining (probably in today's Yunnan Province). In his travels he learned many scriptures and especially excelled in the *Lotus Sūtra,* and he attracted many disciples—most of the time more than a hundred sat under him. In 372 he suddenly felt an illness localized in the region of his heart. For a long time he tried various preparations and techniques, but none cured him. After many attempts he gave up trying to heal himself and devoted himself exclusively to taking sincere refuge in Guanshiyin. After several days of devotional acts he fell asleep and saw, in a dream, a monk who came to attend him in his illness. To cure him, this monk cut him open, extracted his stomach and intestines, and washed them. He saw that there had been many impure objects inside him. After thoroughly cleansing them, the monk replaced the organs and told Fayi: "Your sickness is now expelled." When Fayi woke up, all his symptoms were gone, and he soon felt like his old self again. It is said in the *[Lotus] Sūtra* that sometimes he (Guanshiyin) appears in the form of a monk or brahmacarin (Buddhist ascetic). Perhaps Fayi's dream was an instance of this.

TALE 9

XiGSY 68 (*RKKO* 57–58); apparently unattested elsewhere. "Both his arms" is a speculation; the text's *pi* (spleen) makes no sense here but is nearly homophonous with *bi* (arms). The lay precepts Wang vowed to keep would have included an injunction against killing living beings.

Wang Tao came from the Zhaodu district of the capital. He was by nature violent and cruel, and in his youth he was leader of a band of young toughs.

After reaching the age of thirty he settled down in a forest. Once he encountered a tiger eating its captured prey. He drew his bow and shot it, and it fled,
injured; but there was another tiger that chased him down and crushed both
his arms with its fangs, and still would not let him go. Tao suddenly remem-
bered having once heard a monk speak of Guanshiyin, so he now took refuge
in and meditated on [the bodhisattva] with a perfect mind. The tiger at once
let him go, and he was able to get up. But it was still angry and resentful,
roaring as it circled around him. Tao once more tempered his heart and perfected his thoughts. The tiger then finally went away. Tao returned home and
swore that if he did not die from his wounds he would revere the Buddha and
undertake the [lay] precepts. He soon recovered and so in the end became a
devout man.

TALE 10

GSY 1 (*RKKO* 14); cf. *MXJ* 12 (*LX* 461–62), *MXJ* 128 (*LX* 533), *FYZL* 23 (459a–
b), *BZL* 7 (sec. 8, 537c note).

Zhu Changshu's forebears were Westerners (that is, Indians). They had accumulated property over several generations and were wealthy. In the 290s they
lived in Luoyang. Changshu was fervent in his reverence for the Buddha, and
he especially loved to chant the *Guanshiyin Sūtra*. Once a fire broke out in the
adjacent house. Changshu's family's house was made of thatch, and it lay directly downwind. As the fire drew ever closer, they continued to remove their
belongings, but it looked as though it would be impossible to remove them all.
Now, the *Guanshiyin Sūtra* says that when faced with a fire, one should chant
and meditate single-mindedly. So [Changshu] urged his family to stop carrying
out objects and not to try to extinguish the fire with water, but only to chant
the sūtra with perfect minds. Soon the fire had completely burned the neighboring house, but it never touched Changshu's; and then suddenly the wind
reversed itself, and the fire went out when it met [his] house. Everyone present
at that time thought that this was a divinely efficacious response (*lingying*).

In the same district there lived four or five young ruffians who bragged to
each other that the wind had just happened to shift and that there was nothing
divine about the event. They agreed to torch the house and burn it down on
the next hot, dry evening, and they said scoffingly that anyone who could
command the fire not to burn should do so. Sometime later the weather grew
very hot and dry, and the wind also picked up. The youths secretly prepared
bundles of burning sticks and threw them up onto the roof. Three times they
launched their bundles; three times the flames went out. At this they became
shocked and terrified, and each ran home to his own house.

The next morning they went to Changshu's house and told him of the previous evening's events, bowing their heads in apology. Changshu replied: "It
is not that I myself have any sort of divinity. It must have been the divine aid

of an awesome spiritual power, brought about by my chanting [of scriptures] and meditating on Guanshiyin. You lads should cleanse your hearts and believe in him." Everyone in the surrounding neighborhood was shocked by the news.

TALE 11

XiGSY 62 (*RKKO* 54–55); cf. *Fahua zhuanji* (cited above), 78a. I have read "cultivating" (*geng*) instead of the unattested characters in both of these texts, each of which resembles *geng*. "When they saw each other they were overwhelmed" is my best guess at the meaning of a difficult phrase.

Han Muzhi was a native of Pengcheng (in modern Sichuan). In 462 Pengcheng fell to the caitiffs. Muzhi fled and, in the confusion and disorder, lost his son, who was kidnapped. Now, Muzhi had long been a fervent Buddhist; so now he recited the *Guanshiyin Sūtra* with a perfect mind, thinking to win back his son by reciting it ten thousand times. In addition, at every increment of a thousand recitations he invited monks to a vegetarian feast. When he had continued thus for six or seven thousand recitations without receiving any response, he sighed and said: "How could the holy personage (that is, the bodhisattva) fail to respond to a living being? It must be that my mind is not yet perfect." With this he began reciting every single day and night, no longer counting the number of repetitions. He vowed to himself that he would keep it up until he received some sign of a response. Meanwhile his son had indeed been resold to someone in Yizhou (the area of Chengdu, capital of Sichuan Province) as a slave and was being used as a laborer. One day he was alone cultivating a wild field when he suddenly saw a monk approach him and ask: "You are Han Muzhi's son, are you not?" He surprisedly answered, "I am." "Would you like to see your father?" the monk asked. "How is this possible?" responded the boy. The monk said, "Your father has been pressing me with his extreme persistence. I am taking you back." The boy did not realize that this was a divine personage, so he politely refused. The monk then said, "Do not worry. Just hold onto the corner of my cassock." The boy tried this, and immediately had the vague sensation of being lifted and carried off by someone. Soon they came to rest outside the gate of a house. This was the new residence into which the Han family had moved; the boy of course did not recognize that it was his father's dwelling. The monk did not go in, but only sent in the boy to see if anyone was home. On entering, the boy saw the owner of the house seated reading aloud from a sūtra. It was his father. When they saw each other they were overwhelmed with mingled grief and joy. The boy could only manage to say, "Outside the gate is a divine personage." His father then ran out, but [the monk] had already left and was nowhere in sight. All the townspeople, both monks and laity, were shocked and amazed when they heard of this event.

The monk Shi Daobao, son of Wang Shu, the governor of Jian'an, had Jin as his original given name. He had advanced through the official ranks, taken a wife, and had children. Later he had an awakening and left home [to become a monk], adhering to all the most austere regulations. It is he who told me of this event. Many other monks have spoken of it [to me] as well.

TALE 12

XiGSY 65 (RKKO 56–57); apparently unattested elsewhere.

The monk Daoyu told the following story: There was a man who contracted leprosy. His family wanted to send him away; he pleaded with them to wait a short time. Before [an image of] the Buddha (or perhaps before a stūpa; literally, "before the Buddha") he prostrated himself on the ground and focused his thoughts entirely on Guanshiyin. For an entire day he did not arise; he remained utterly motionless except for his breathing. Then suddenly he stood up and said, "My sickness is healed." Immediately he looked different [from when ill], and within ten days he was completely recovered.

TALE 13

XiGSY 66 (RKKO 57); apparently unattested elsewhere.

In the country of Yueshi (that is, Tokharestan, during this period a Buddhist kingdom in the Kashmir region) there was a man who contracted white leprosy. All remedies proved ineffective. So he went before an image of Guanshiyin, bowed his head to the ground, and pleaded for mercy with the utmost feeling and in utter desperation. The image then extended its arm and rubbed his sores. At once he was healed. His body moreover gave off a radiance and appeared different from its old form. The image's arm remained extended and did not return to its former position.

TALE 14

XYJ 21 (LX 442); cf. BZL 7 (sec. 8, 537c note).

The Rongyang native Mao Dezu, when he was trying to get to the area south of the Yangzi [during attacks by non-Chinese peoples in the north], was traveling in secret and hiding. Pursued at one point by a group of caitiff horsemen, he hid in some underbrush by the side of the road. But the brush was short and sparse, and half of his body was still visible. He prepared to meet his death.

Along with the rest of his family he silently meditated on Guanshiyin. In a moment clouds formed and a downpour arrived. They were thus able to escape.

TALE 15

GSY 4 (*RKKO* 16–17); cf. *MXJ* 27 (*LX* 471–72), *FYZL* 17 (410b–c).

Dou Zhuan was a native of Henei (in modern Henan Province). During the period 345–356 [the government officials] Gao Chang and Lu Hu were each maneuvering for power and did not get along. Zhuan was employed by [Gao] Chang as a senior official. When [Lu] Hu sent cavalry to attack, Zhuan was captured along with six or seven colleagues. They were thrown into the same prison cell under heavy locks and fetters and were to be executed within a very limited number of days.

Now, at that time the monk Zhi Daoshan was in the same camp, and he was a former acquaintance of Zhuan's. When he heard of Zhuan's imprisonment, he went to the cell to see him, and they spoke through the window. Zhuan told Daoshan, "I am entrapped in a deadly situation, and my life span has become a matter of hours. How can I be saved?" Daoshan said, "The method for your salvation is not to be found among humans. Only the bodhisattva Guanshiyin can save us from mortal danger. If you can invoke and take refuge in him with a perfect mind, there will be a sudden response." Zhuan had already heard of Guanshiyin. When he heard what Daoshan had to say, he focused his mind on meditation.

For three days and nights he took refuge [in Guanshiyin] with perfect sincerity. As he did so he noticed that his fetters seemed to be gradually loosening in a strange sort of way. When he tried pushing them, they easily separated from his body. He then resumed his [state of] perfect mind and said, "Now I have received divine help in my distress; you have caused my shackles to loosen by themselves. But I still have several comrades here, and I cannot bear to leave them behind and escape alone. Since you, Guanshiyin, have the divine power to save all universally, please let us all escape." When he had finished speaking, he tugged on the [fetters of] his cellmates. One by one they were all freed, as though their chains had been cut. So they opened the cell door and ran out. Even though they fled past numerous guards, none noticed their presence. They scaled the city wall and kept moving. By this time it was approaching dawn. They walked a couple of miles, but they were afraid to travel any farther in daylight, so they hid in some brush. Meanwhile their escape was discovered, and horsemen were dispatched in all directions to look for them, torching the underbrush in the area and cutting down groves, leaving no hiding place unsearched. The small area around Zhuan [and his comrades] was the only one that the horsemen did not enter. In this way they managed to escape and return home. From that time on the reverence and faith [of these men] were extraordinary, and they all became stout upholders of the Buddha and his dharma. When [the monk] Daoshan later crossed the Yangzi, he told this story in detail to Xie (i.e., Xie Fu, author of the earliest tale collection of which fragments survive).

TALE 16

XiGSY 32 (RKKO 39–40); cf. the accounts of these events in the dynastic histories (Songshu, j. 48; Nanshi, j. 16). During the Eastern Jin the commandery mentioned in this tale was located in Jiangsu; in the Han, however, it had been located in today's Anhui Province.

Zhu Lingshi was a native of Pei [in Jiangsu or Anhui Province]. He was a meritorious official under the first Song emperor [Emperor Wu, acceded 420]. [Before this,] early in the Jin era of Flourishing Righteousness [405–418 C.E.], he served as magistrate of Wukang [City] in Wuxing [in today's Zhejiang Province]. At that time there was some disorder in his district, to which he responded by executing a good many perpetrators. The court sent Zhang Chongzhi to investigate the incident, and Zhu was arrested, thrown into prison, and given the death sentence. His final appeal had yet to be decided on. Now, there was a monk named Shi Huinan who was an old acquaintance of Zhu's. This monk went to the prison to see Zhu, telling him to meditate on Guanshiyin. He also left with Zhu a small image [of Guanshiyin] to which he could pay devotion. Zhu, who had long been a devout Buddhist, now in this perilous circumstance focused his thoughts into single-mindedness and thus continuously meditated for seven days. At that point his shackles fell off by themselves. The jailkeeper was astonished and reported this event to Zhang Chongzhi. Zhang surmised that Zhu had been able to slip out of his shackles because of his emaciated condition brought on by his worry and suffering. He ordered the jailkeeper to go back to put Zhu's shackles on him again, this time fastening them more tightly so that he could not slip out again. But within several days it had happened three more times. Zhang then sent up a report that a miracle (yi) had occurred. At that time, after a discussion of his case in the capital, Zhu's appeal had just been denied; but when Zhang's report arrived, Zhu was [exonerated and hence] returned to his district post. Zhu was thus able to live out his years. He and his brother both [later] attained distinction.

Abbreviations

BZL *Bianzheng lun (Essays on the Discernment of Right)*, polemical treatise compiled ca. 627 by Falin. *T* 2110, v. 52. Cited by chapter (*juan*) number followed in parentheses by section (*pian*) and page numbers.

FYZL   *Fayuan zhulin* (*A Grove of Pearls from the Garden of the Dharma*), Buddhist encyclopedia compiled ca. 668 by Daoshi. *T* 2122, v. 53.

GSY   *Guangshiyin yingyan ji* (*A Record of Avalokiteśvara's Responsive Manifestations*), originally written before 399 by Xie Fu but lost in that year; partially reconstructed by Fu Lian (374–426). 7 tales, preface. *RKKO* ed.

GSZ   *Gaoseng zhuan* (*Lives of Eminent Monks*), written by Huijiao ca. 531. *T* 2059, v. 50.

LX   Lu Xun, ed., *Gu xiaoshuo gouchen*, in *Lu Xun sanshinian ji* (*Gleanings of Ancient Tales*) (n.p.: Lu Xun quanji chubanshe, 1941). Citations give the serial order of the tale in the particular collection in which it appears, followed by the page numbers in this edition.

MXJ   *Mingxiang ji* (*Signs from the Obscure Realm*), compiled by Wang Yan between 485 and 501. 131 tales, preface. *LX* ed.

RKKO   Makita Tairyō, ed., *Rikuchō koitsu Kanzeon ōkenki no kenkyū* (*A Study of Tales of Avalokiteśvara's Responsive Manifestations Surviving from the Six Dynasties*) (Kyoto: Hyōrakuji shoten, 1970); citations of tales first give the serial number of the tale in its particular collection, then the page number(s) in parentheses.

T   *Taishō shinshū daizōkyō* (*The [Buddhist] Canon, Newly Prepared in the Taishō Era*) (Tokyo, 1924–1934). Number following *T* is the number assigned to the title in this edition of the Chinese Buddhist canon; volume number is given next in some cases, followed by page numbers.

TPGJ   *Taiping guangji* (*Broad-Ranging Records Compiled in the Era of Great Peace*) (Shanghai, 1930). Cited by *juan* number.

XiGSY   *Xi Guanshiyin yingyan ji* (*More Records of Avalokiteśvara's Responsive Manifestations*), compiled by Lu Gao in 501. 69 tales, preface. *RKKO* ed.

XuGSY   *Xu Guangshiyin yingyan ji* (*Continued Records of Avalokiteśvara's Responsive Manifestations*), written by Zhang Yan in mid-fifth century. 10 tales, preface. *RKKO* ed.

XYJ   *Xuanyan ji* (*Records in Proclamation of [Miraculous] Manifestations*), attributed to Liu Yiqing (403–444). 35 tales. *LX* ed.

— 6 —

A Sūtra Promoting the White-robed Guanyin as Giver of Sons

Chün-fang Yü

Ever since the fourth century C.E., a few hundred years after the introduction of Buddhism into China, Guanyin has been one of the most beloved Buddhist deities in China. By the tenth century, Guanyin began to assume feminine characteristics. The sexual transformation became complete by the sixteenth century, and the Jesuit missionaries could thus nickname her the "Goddess of Mercy." In the development of the cult of Guanyin in China, the bodhisattva appeared in several forms. Among them, the "White-robed (*baiyi*) Guanyin" is the one most familiar to her devotees.

White-robed Guanyin began to appear in sculpture, paintings, poetry, accounts of the founding of monasteries, miracle tales, and pilgrims' visions from the tenth century on. The deity is clearly feminine. She wears a long, flowing white cape, whose hood sometimes covers her head and even arms and hands. The conventional view in Buddhological scholarship traces her to tantric female deities such as White Tārā or Pāṇḍaravāsinī, the consort of Avalokiteśvara and one of the chief deities of the World of Womb Treasury Maṇḍala (*garbhakośadhātu, taicangjie*). The received wisdom in art historical circles has, on the other hand, identified this figure as a typical subject of the so-called Zen paintings, symbolizing the serenity and wisdom of Chan meditative states.

It is now time to reconsider the above interpretations. The popularity of White-robed Guanyin was not due simply to promotion by Chan monks and literati painters. Moreover, instead of being traced to tantric Buddhism, the origin of this deity may lie with a group of indigenous scriptures that portray her primarily as a fertility goddess. Although Guanyin's power of granting children is already mentioned in the *Lotus Sūtra,* these indigenous scriptures are noteworthy on two accounts: they emphasize Guanyin's power to grant sons, and they also call attention to her protection of pregnant women and assurance of safe childbirths.

These texts also provide the basis for the iconography of "Child-giving (*songzi*) Guanyin," which is indeed a variant of the White-robed Guanyin.

Indigenous scriptures celebrating Guanyin have had of course a long history in China. Since 1970, chiefly through the work of Makita Tairyō, we have known that there were a number of such scriptures composed during the Six Dynasties (420–581) and later. Although their titles remain in various catalogs, many did not survive. Of those that did, Makita extensively studied two: *Guanshiyin Samādhi Sūtra as Spoken by the Buddha* (*Foshuo Guanshiyin sanmeijing*) and *Guanshiyin Sūtra [Promoted by] King Gao* (*Gao Wang Guanshiyin jing*). Instead of dismissing these scriptures as forged, Makita regarded them as valuable documents revealing contemporary understandings of Buddhism. His sympathetic attitude has elicited similar responses in scholars in recent years. Studying similar apocryphal scriptures in other Buddhist traditions, they also see these scriptures as creative attempts to synthesize Buddhist teachings and adapt them to native cultural milieu.

One indigenous scripture bearing the title *The Dhāraṇī Sūtra of the Five Mudrās of the Great Compassionate White-robed One* (*Baiyi Dabei wuyinxin tuoluoni jing*) enjoyed particular popularity among the Chinese people in late imperial China who hoped to have sons. Although the exact date of its composition cannot be established, there is clear indication that it was already being circulated by the eleventh century at the latest. A stele dated 1082 with the White-robed Guanyin holding a baby and the text of this sūtra penned by Qin Guan (1049–1100) has survived. This scripture is not included in any existing editions of the Buddhist canon, but its existence came to light as a result of happy coincidences. I first came across a handwritten copy of this text in the rare book collection of the Palace Museum in Taipei, Taiwan, in the summer of 1986. It was written by the famous Ming dynasty calligrapher Dong Qichang in 1558 and bore seals of both emperors Qianlong and Jiaqing. A few months afterward, while I was doing research in the rare book section of the Library of Chinese Buddhist Cultural Artifacts located at the Fayuan Monastery in Beijing, I found thirty-five copies of this scripture. They were all printed during the Ming, the earliest one in 1428 and the majority during the Wanli period, around the 1600s.

Literati living in the late Ming, during the sixteenth century, appeared to have given the cult of the White-robed Guanyin a new boost. Yuan Huang (1533–1606), the literatus who promoted morality books, was forty but had no son. He started to chant this scripture and became the father of a son in 1580. When he compiled a collection of texts to help people in obtaining heirs, entitled, *True Instructions for Praying for an Heir* (*Qisi zhenquan*), he put this text at the very beginning. He also identified the dhāraṇī contained in the scripture as the *Dhāraṇī Conforming to the Heart's Desire* (*Suixin tuoluoni*), the same dhāraṇī the great pilgrim Tripiṭaka relied on in crossing the perilous desert on his way to India. The dhāraṇī, according to Huang, was therefore a translation from Sanskrit and was contained in the Buddhist canon, even though the scripture as it now stood could not be found there. Qu Ruji (1548–1610) and his friend Yan Daoche, two scholars responsible for the compilation of an important Chan chronicle, the *Record of Pointing to the Moon* (*Zhiyue lu*), were also faithful chanters of this dhāraṇī.

The copies of this scripture that I saw in Beijing were printed and distributed free of charge by donors who wanted to bear witness to White-robed Guanyin's efficacy and promote her cult. Depending on the economic ability of the donors, who ranged from members of the royal family, literati-officials, and merchants all the way down to obscure men and women, the quality and quantity of the printing varied greatly. But in all cases the donors provided accounts of miracles witnessed by others or by the donors themselves. The former, which sometimes are several pages in length, are appended immediately after the scripture, while the latter, which are usually no more than a few lines, are enclosed within a dedicatory plaque. A dedicatory plaque dated 1599, for instance, recorded the following:

> Mrs. Zhao, née Shen, prayed for a male heir a few years ago and made a vow promising the printing of the "White-robed Guanyin Sūtra." Thanks to divine protection, twin boys Fengguo and Fengjue were born to me on the twelfth day of the ninth month, 1597. Now I have finished printing one canon [yicong, e.g., 5,048 copies] of this scripture and donate them to fulfill my earlier vow. I pray that the two boys will continue to receive blessings without end. Donated on the New Year's Day, 1599.

A great number of miracles accumulated around this text. The chanting of the dhāraṇī of the White-robed Guanyin was believed to lead to the miraculous arrival of a long-awaited baby boy who would be born doubly wrapped in white placenta (baiyi chongbao), which indicated that he was a gift from White-robed Guanyin. The earliest testimony of this was traced to the Tang, and miracles attributed to this scripture were reported during the six hundred years between the twelfth and the seventeenth centuries.

In the following, a translation of the entire text of the sūtra printed in 1609 is given. Since the miracles appended at the end of the text are more numerous than in other copies, I have selected only the ones with historical dates. I have also translated the postscripts written by the Ming literati mentioned above. They provide an explanation of the origin of this scripture, the author's understanding of the correct attitude in keeping the dhāraṇī, and other interesting autobiographical details about the author's own experiences with this text.

Further Reading

Robert Buswell, *Chinese Buddhist Apocrypha* (Honolulu: University of Hawaii Press, 1990).

The Dhāraṇī Sūtra of Five Mudrās of the Great Compassionate White-Robed One

> The mantra which purifies the karma of the mouth: An-xiu-li, xin-li, mo-ke-xiu-li, xiu-xiu-li, suo-po-ke [svāhā].

The mantra which pacifies the earth: Nan-wu-san-man-duo, mo-tuo-nan, an-du-lu-du-lu-di-wei, suo-po-ke.

The sūtra-opening gāthā:

> The subtle and wondrous dharma of utmost profundity
> Is difficult to encounter during millions, nay, billions of kalpas.
> Now that I have heard it [with my own ears], I will take it securely to
>   heart
> And hope I can understand the true meaning of the Tathāgata.

Invocation:

> Bowing my head to the Great Compassionate One, Po-lu-jie-di
> Practicing meditation with the sense of hearing, [the bodhisattva]
>   entered samādhi
> Raising the sound of the tide of the ocean,
> Responding to the needs of the world.
> No matter what one wishes to obtain
> [She] will unfailingly grant its fulfillment.

> Homage to the Original Teacher Śākyamuni Buddha
> Homage to the Original Teacher Amitābha Buddha
> Homage to the Bao-yue-zhi-yan-guang-yin-zi-zai-wang (Lord Iśvara Buddha
>   of Precious-Moon Wisdom-Splendor-Light-Sound)
> Homage to Great Compassionate Guanshiyin Bodhisattva
> Homage to White-robed Guanshihyin Bodhisattva
> Front mudrā, back mudrā, mudrā of subduing demons, mind mudrā, body
>   mudrā.

Dhāraṇī. I now recite the divine mantra. I beseech the Compassionate One to descend and protect my thought. Here then is the mantra:

> Nan-wu he-la-da-na, shao-la-ye-ye, nan-wu a-li-ye, po-lu-jie-ti, shao-bo-la-ye, pu-ti-sa-duo-po-ye, mo-ke-jie-lu-ni-jia-ye, an-duo-li, duo-li, du-duo-li, du-du-duo-li, suo-po-ke.

When you ask someone else to chant the dhāraṇī, the effect is the same as when you chant it yourself.

EVIDENCE ATTESTING TO THE MIRACULOUS RESPONSES OF THE WHITE-ROBED
GUANSHIYIN BODHISATTVA

Formerly a scholar of Hengyang (in present Hunan Province) was already advanced in age but still had no son. He prayed everywhere for an heir. One day he met an old monk who handed him this sūtra, saying, "The Buddha preached this sūtra. If a person is capable of keeping it, he will receive responses in accordance with his wish and obtain unlimited blessing. If he desires to have a son, a boy of wisdom will be born to him. The baby will show the wonder of being wrapped in a white placenta." The man and his wife chanted this sūtra with utmost sincerity for one *canon* (5,048 times), and within several years they had three sons who were all born wrapped in white placenta. The governer saw these events with his own eyes and ordered the printing and distributing of this sūtra. He also obtained a son before the year was over.

A scholar named Wang Xin and his wife named Zhao of Jiangning (in present Jiangsu Province) had the misfortune of losing several children. In the spring of 1147 they obtained this sūtra and chanted it with faith everyday. On the second day of the fourth month in 1148 a son was born to them.

Zheng Zhili of Pujiang, Mao District (province unspecified), was forty years old and still had no heir. In 1207 he decided to print 5,048 copies of this sūtra and distribute the copies for free. On the seventh day of the eighth month in 1208 a son was born to him.

Yu Muzhai and his wife Wang of Danyang Village in Maoyuan County (province unspecified) decided to have one thousand copies of this sūtra printed and distributed free. In the eighth month of 1250 when the work of distributing was only half completed, a son arrived.

Fangyan and wife Wang of Yungfeng Village, She County (in present Anhui Province) decided to chant this sūtra 5,048 times and print one thousand copies for free distribution in the spring of 1254. They had a son in 1255 and named him Wanggu.

Wang Yinlin, who lived in the 6th ward in Chongle City, south of Hui District (in present Anhui Province), had five hundred copies of this sūtra printed and distributed. A son was born to him in the hour of *mou* on the twenty-first day of the fifth month in 1269 and was given the name Yinsun. A pious woman named Zheng who lived in the third ward of the north side of Shangbei City of the same district became seriously ill in the first month of 1274 when she was a young girl. She burned incense and promised to have one thousand copies of the sūtra printed and distributed free. At night she dreamt of two monks who came to protect her. She recovered from the illness.

Wang Yuyu lived in Daning ward in Nanjing and was forty years old but still had no son. He prayed to various gods but had no success. One day in the latter half of the tenth month in 1265 he received this sūtra from his friend Ma, who kept it enshrined in front of the Guanyin image on his family altar. Wang chanted it every day without interruption. On the night of the fourteenth day in the fourth month, 1267, his wife née Liu dreamt of a person in white who, wearing a golden crown and accompanied by a boy, said to her, "I am delivering to you a holy slave (*shengnu*)." Liu accepted the boy, and upon waking up the next morning she gave birth to a baby boy who was handsome and wrapped in white placenta. They named him Slave of Holy Monk (Sheng-sengnu).

Wang Mengbai, a metropolitan graduate from Qingjiang (in present Jiangxi Province) was born because his parents faithfully chanted this sūtra. When he was born, he had the manifestation of the "white robe." He himself also chanted the sūtra and in 1214 had a "white-robed son (baiyizi)" whom he named Further Manifestation (Gengxian).

Xie Congning, a native of Guangyang (Daxing, the capital) who served as a staffer in the Central Drafting Office, came from a family which had only one son for the past five generations. In 1579 he and his wife, née Gao, started to chant the sūtra, which they had also printed and distributed for free. In 1582 they had a son whom they named Gu, in 1585 another son whom they named Lu, and in 1586 twin boys Qu and Ying. All were born with double white placentas.

Ding Xian of Yibin, Nanyang (in present Henan Province), was fifty years old and had no son. So he decided to print this sūtra and distribute it for free. He also had a thousand catties of iron melted down in the south garden of the city to make a gilded image of Guangyin. It stood over six feet. At the same time, in order to seek for a son, Xing Jian, the grand commandant, had a shrine dedicated to the White-robed Guanyin erected in the northern part of the city. So the image was moved there to be worshiped. The local official set aside several thousand acres of good farmland to provide for the shrine's upkeep so that people could continue to offer incense in future generations. Not long after this, one night Ding dreamt of a woman who presented him with a white carp. On the next morning, a son was born wrapped in a white placenta. That was the fourth day of the twelfth month, 1583. Earlier, when the image was moved to the White-robed Guanyin Shrine, the gardener had a dream in which the bodhisattva appeared to him looking rather unhappy. When he told Ding about his dream, Ding had another image cast that looked exactly like the first one in the south garden. He invited a monk of repute to stay in the temple to take care of it. He subsequently dreamt of an old man wearing a white gown who came to visit him. The day after he had this dream, while he was relating it to his friend, a man suddenly came to the house seeking to sell the woodblocks of this sūtra. Ding bought them and printed a thousand copies for distribution. He also hired a skilled painter to paint several hundred paintings of the White-robed Guanyin to give to the faithful as gifts. In the fourth month of 1586, he had another son. By then, Xing Jian, the grand commandant, had also had a son and a daughter born to him and his wife.

Zhao Yungxian, the son of a grandee of the Tenth Order (the eleventh highest of twenty titles of honorary nobility conferred on meritorious subjects), was a native of Changshu (in Jiangsu Province). His wife née Chen chanted this sūtra with great sincerity. On the sixteenth day of the seventh month in 1586, a daughter was born. She was covered with a piece of cloth as white as snow on her face, head, chest, and back. When the midwife peeled it away, the baby's eyes and eyebrows could then be seen. The parents already had sons, but only this daughter had the miraculous evidence of the "white-cloth." It was for this reason that it was written down.

Yuan Huang, the metropolitan graduate who served in the Ministry of Rites, was a native of Jiashan (in Zhejiang Province). He was forty but had no son. After he chanted this sūtra, in 1580 a son was born. He named the son Yu-ansheng (Born from Universal Penetration) because he believed that the boy was a gift from Guanyin, the Universally Penetrating One. The boy had a very distinguished appearance and was unusually intelligent.

A POSTSCRIPT TO THE SŪTRA WRITTEN BY QU RUJI

I began to chant this dhāraṇī in the second month of 1580 together with my friends Li Boshu and Yan Daoche. Soon afterward Li had a son, and three years later Yan also had a son. I alone failed to experience a divine response. I often blamed myself for my deep karmic obstructions, for I could not match the two gentlemen in their piety. Then one evening in the third month of 1583 I dreamt that I entered a shrine and a monk said to me, "In chanting the dhāraṇī, there is one buddha's name you have not chanted. If you chant it, you shall have a son." Upon waking up, I could not understand what he meant by the missing buddha's name, for I had always chanted the various names of Guanyin on the different festival days of her manifestation. In the winter of 1585 I traveled north and was stuck at a government post-house because the river was frozen. On the twelfth day of the twelfth month I entered a small temple and saw this sūtra by the side of the *hou* animal mount on which Guanyin sat. It was donated by Wang Qishan, a judicial clerk. When I opened it to read and saw the name of Lord Iśvara Buddha of Precious-Moon Wisdom-Splendor-Light-Sound, a name of which I had never heard up until that time, I had a sudden realization. I knelt down and kowtowed to the seat. I started to chant the name of the buddha upon returning, and after only three days a son was born. It accorded perfectly with my dream.

In 1586 I went to the capital. Xu Wenqing, Yu Zhongpu, and other friends were all chanting the dhāraṇī in order to obtain sons. Yu's wife, furthermore, became pregnant after she had a strange dream. So we discussed plans of print-ing this sūtra to promote its circulation. I had earlier consulted the catalogues of the Northern and Southern Tripiṭakas (two collections of Buddhist scrip-tures compiled in the Ming) but did not find it listed in either one. I thought this must be a true elixir of life secretly transmitted by foreign monks. Later Yuan Huang told me that this was actually the same dhāraṇī as the *Dhāraṇī Conforming to Heart's Desire,* two versions of which were included in the Tri-piṭaka. When I learned about this, I rushed to Longhua Monastery to check the Tripiṭaka kept in the library. Although there were some variations in the sequence of sentences and the exact wordings of the mantra between the text found in the Tripiṭaka and the popular printed version, the efficacy of chanting the dhāraṇī was universally warranted. I could not help but feeling deeply moved by the wonder of Guanyin's universal responsiveness and divinity of the faithful chanters' sincere minds. The text in the Tripiṭaka did not just promise sons, but the fulfillment of many other desires in accordance with the wishes of sentient beings. According to the instruction given in the sūtra con- tained in the Tripiṭaka, this dhāraṇī should be revealed only to those who were in possession of great compassion. If given to the wrong person, disastrous results would happen, for bad karma caused by hatred might be created if the person used the dhāraṇī to subdue enemies or avenge past wrongs. Taking this warning to heart, my friend Xu and I decided that instead of reprinting the version found in the Tripiṭaka, we would print the dhāraṇī alone together with the stories about obtaining sons included in the popular versions of this text that were in circulation. After fasting and bathing, Xu wrote out the sūtra and gave it to an engraver to make the woodblocks for printing.

The term "dhāraṇī" means to keep all virtues completely. The extended meaning of the term, then, is the keeping of all virtues. For this reason, the merit of keeping the dhāraṇī is indeed limitless. With this Guanyin teaches people to do good. Therefore if the practitioners do good, when they chant the words of the dhāraṇī, blessings as numerous as the sands of the Ganges will instantly come to them. But if they do not dedicate themselves to goodness, they will lose the basis of the dhāraṇī. Even if they chant it, the benefit will be slight. I cannot claim to have realized this ideal, but I am willing to work hard toward it together with fellow practitioners. The conventional view of the world says that the ordinary people are totally different from sages and people cannot be transformed into holy persons. Because they narrow their potentiality this way, they cannot keep the dhāraṇī. On the other hand, if people fall into the other extreme of nihilism and think that in emptiness there is no law of cau- sality, they also cannot keep the dhāraṇī because of their recklessness. When one realizes that the common man and the sage possess the same mind and there is not the slightest difference at all, one has left the conventional view. When one realizes that this one mind can manifest as either ordinary or saintly and this is due to the clear working of the law of causality, one has then left the nihilistic view. Leaving behind these two erroneous views and following the one mind in teaching the world, one can then chant the dhāraṇī. Like blowing on the bellows for wind or striking the flint for fire, the effect will be unfailingly efficacious.

A POSTSCRIPT WRITTEN BY YAN DAOCHE AFTER PRINTING THE SŪTRA

The *Dhāraṇī of the White-Robed Guanyin* was not included in the Southern and Northern Tripiṭaka collections. Its miraculous efficacy in obtaining whatever one wishes, however, and more particularly sons, has been vouchsafed in the world for a long time. Is it because Indian monks such as Subhākarasiṃha and Amoghavajra (tantric masters active in the eighth century) transmitted this sūtra to gentlewomen in China who then kept it secretly, that, although it was not introduced into the canon collection, it has come down to us because of the many miracles connected with it? Or is it because Guanyin revealed her teaching in accordance with the audience and the old monk of Hengyang was actually her transformation? I do not know. I do know that originally I did not have a son, but after my wife and I chanted this sūtra for three years, in 1582 we had two sons in quick succession. That is why I am now having the sūtra printed and distributed for free in order to fulfill my earlier vow.

The keeping of the dhāraṇī is actually not limited to the vocal chanting of the dhāraṇī. To believe in the Buddha constantly, to listen to the dharma with pleasure, to serve people, to have a straight mind and a deep mind, to be vigorous in one's practice, to give donations generously, to observe strictly the precepts, to sit in meditation with unperturbed mind, to subdue all evils and cut off all passions, to be patient and gentle in adversities, and to help bad friends but draw near to good friends—all these are meant by "keeping the dhāraṇī." I am keenly aware of my own inferior qualities and cannot attain even one iota of the true way of keeping the dhāraṇī as I outlined above. Nevertheless, I am trying my best. Since I started to chant the dhāraṇī, I have insisted on observing the precept against killing. This precepts heads the list of the perfection of discipline. If you want to have a son of your own, how can you bear to take another life? When you fail to obtain any response by merely mouthing the dhāraṇī, you may begin to doubt and want to stop. This then is to commit a blasphemy against the Buddha with your body. I ask all good friends in Buddhism who want to chant this sūtra to begin by observing one precept. Gradually you can extend to all precepts. You start with one goodness and extend to all goodness. This will be the real keeping of the dhāraṇī. When this is done, not only sons but all kinds of marvelous things will be yours as you wish.

$$7$$

Zhu Xi on Spirit Beings

Daniel K. Gardner

Zhu Xi (1130–1200), scholar-philosopher of the Southern Song period, is perhaps best known as one of the principal architects of *Daoxue,* often called Neo-Confucianism. Drawing heavily on the ideas of Northern Song thinkers, Zhu crafted a philosophical system whose influence in China through the early years of the twentieth century was unsurpassed; indeed, in the Yuan dynasty (1280–1368), and thereafter until the fall of the Qing (1911), the Chinese state made Neo-Confucianism the basis of the imperial examination system. Candidates for the examinations, in answering questions about the Confucian Classics and problems of statecraft, were required to demonstrate a thorough familiarity with the interpretations and teachings of the Neo-Confucian school. Such imperial support gave Neo-Confucianism a privileged status in late imperial China; some scholars would even argue that such imperial support gave it the status of a state orthodoxy.

The following passages are from chapter 3, "Spirit Beings," of the *Conversations of Master Zhu, Arranged Topically* (*Zhuzi Yulei*), a text in 140 chapters of Zhu's conversations with his disciples and friends, recorded by his disciples, and edited and published in 1270, seventy years after Zhu's death. The sheer length of the chapter—twenty-two folio pages—and the number of conversations recorded in it—eighty-three—suggest the importance that the topic of spirit beings had for Zhu Xi and his disciples. To be sure, on occasion Zhu expresses skepticism about the existence of spirit beings, citing Confucius's well-known comments on the subject, but the preponderance of the passages in this chapter as well as those in other chapters of the *Conversations of Master Zhu* and in the *Collected Literary Works of Master Zhu* (*Hui'an xiansheng Zhu Wengong wenji*) reveal a Zhu Xi who embraces a belief in spirit beings.

For Zhu, the term "spirit beings" (*guishen*) refers to three distinct types of phenomena: (1) the expansion and contraction of yin and yang, as manifested in natural phenomena such as wind and rain, thunder and lightning, day and night;

(2) beings such as ghosts, monsters, and demons who at times appear before humankind; and (3) ancestral spirits, the recipients of ancestral sacrifice.

All three of these classes of spirit beings are discussed at length by Zhu Xi, and he explains all in terms of his influential metaphysics of principle (li) and psychophysical stuff (qi). According to Zhu, all things in the universe possess principle, which he defines as both the reason why a thing is as it is and a rule to which a thing should conform. In Zhu's view principle in the world is one; it simply has many manifestations. So although different things manifest it in different ways, the rules to which those things conform is ultimately one, as is the reason those things are as they are. Perhaps principle should be understood as something like a blueprint or pattern for the cosmos, a blueprint or pattern that underlies everything, every affair, and every person in that cosmos. Principle, for Zhu, provides coherence, even meaning, to the world around us.

Each thing, affair, and person is also endowed with "psychophysical stuff." I have adopted "psychophysical stuff" as the translation for qi, hoping that its awkwardness is offset at least to some degree by its accuracy. Psychophysical stuff, in Zhu's view, is the matter and energy of which the entire universe and all things in it, including functions and activities of the mind, are composed. The quality as well as the quantity of psychophysical stuff differ from one thing and one individual to another. Some psychophysical stuff is clearer than others, some more refined than others, some less dense than others. This endowment of psychophysical stuff gives each thing or person its peculiar form and individual characteristics. As to the relationship between principle and psychophysical stuff, Zhu is very clear: "There has never been any psychophysical stuff without principle nor any principle without psychophysical stuff." The two entities simply cannot exist independently of each other: without principle the psychophysical stuff has no ontological reason for being, and without psychophysical stuff principle has nothing in which to inhere. All three classes of spirit beings, like everything else in Zhu Xi's Neo-Confucian system, share in principle and psychophysical stuff and can be explained and made sense of by Zhu only as they relate to principle and psychophysical stuff.

It is important to note that in the following passages Zhu Xi's conversations on subjects such as exorcism, ancestral worship, divination, spirit writing, sacrifices to nature, evil spirits, and freak happenings reveal more than one man's particular views of spirit beings; they reveal a world that was generally thought by people of the day to be fully inhabited by monsters, ghosts, gods, and spirits. It was a world with no clear boundaries between elite and folk, as these spirit beings played an active role in the lives of elite and folk alike.

As a record of conversations taken down by Zhu's students, the *Conversations of Master Zhu, Arranged Topically* presents certain problems. The language, of course, is highly colloquial and idiomatic, riddled with regional expressions not always as intelligible as this translator would have hoped. I have tried to put the Song colloquial of the text into a colloquial English that might convey something of the relaxed, informal style of the original—hence the liberal use of contractions

in the translation. The reader too should keep in mind that the text is a record
not of formal lectures or sustained philosophical exposition, but rather of conversations or, perhaps more accurately, of bits and pieces of conversations strung
together by an editor years after Zhu passed away; many comments thus lack the
context necessary to make full sense of them, and the referents used in them are
not always as clear to the reader as they surely were to the hearer. Moreover, in
reading Zhu Xi's remarks to his students, we do not see the gestures or hear the
inflection in the voice that gave meaning, and sometimes even life, to those remarks. Still, the *Conversations of Master Zhu, Arranged Topically* is one of the most
useful and interesting sources for Zhu Xi's thought.

The passages that follow are presented in the order that they appear in the original
text. The numbers in parentheses after each passage refer to the juan, the folio
leaf, recto or verso side of the leaf, and the line on which the translated passage
begins in the 1880 Chuan jing tang edition of the *Conversations of Master Zhu,
Arranged Topically*.

Further Reading

For analytical accounts of Zhu Xi's treatment of spirit beings, see Daniel K. Gard-
ner, "Ghosts and Spirits in the Sung Neo-Confucian World: Chu Hsi on *Kuei-
Shen*," *Journal of the American Oriental Society* 115.4 (1995); and Miura Kunio,
"Shushi kishin ronbo," *Jimbun kenkyū* 37.3 (1985): 73–91. For a deeper understanding of how Zhu Xi's views of ghosts and spirits fit into his larger philosoph-
ical system, see the general study by Daniel K. Gardner, *Learning to Be a Sage:
Selections from the* Conversations of Master Chu, Arranged Topically (Berkeley:
University of California Press, 1990). On the transmission and transformation of
popular religion in Song dynasty China, see Valerie Hansen, *Changing Gods in
Medieval China, 1127–1276* (Princeton: Princeton University Press, 1990). For
stories and legends of ghosts and spirits, see Karl S. Y. Kao, trans., *Classical Chinese
Tales of the Supernatural and the Fantastic: Selections from the Third to the Tenth
Century* (Bloomington: Indiana University Press, 1985); and Pu Songling, *Strange
Tales from Make-Do Studio*, trans. Denis C. and Victor H. Mair (Beijing: Foreign
Languages Press, 1989). For a study of ghost stories and legends, see Anthony
Yu, " 'Rest, Rest Perturbed Spirit!' Ghosts in Traditional Chinese Prose Fiction,"
Harvard Journal of Asiatic Studies 47.2 (1987): 397–434.

Conversations of Master Zhu, Arranged Topically

1. Someone asked: Do spirit beings exist or not? Zhu said: How can I quickly
explain this matter to you? And if I were to do so, how could you possibly

believe me? You must gradually come to understand the multitudinous manifestations of principle, and these doubts of yours will be resolved by themselves. [In *Analects* 6/22 we read:] "Fan Chi asked about wisdom. The Master said: 'To give one's self earnestly to the duties due to men, and, while respecting spirit beings, to keep them at a distance, may be called wisdom.'" Let men grasp the matters that should be grasped. Those that cannot be grasped, let us put aside. When the ordinary matters of daily life have been thoroughly grasped, the principle of spirit beings will become clear of its own—this then constitutes wisdom. [As for the Master's remark in *Analects* 11/12:] "While you are not able to serve man, how can you serve ghosts?" the meaning is precisely this. (3.1b2)

2. *Shen* expands; *gui* contracts. For instance, when wind, rain, thunder, and lightning first issue forth, this is the operation of the expansive cosmic force (*shen*); as the wind dies, the rain passes, the thunder stops, and the lightning ceases, this is the operation of the contractive cosmic force (*gui*). (3.1b11)

3. The contractive and expansive cosmic forces are nothing more than the waxing and waning of the yin and yang. The transforming and nourishing operations of nature and the darkening of the sky that ensues with wind and rain are all a matter of the contractive and expansive cosmic forces. In man, the essence (*jing*) is the earthly soul (*po*), and the earthly soul is the contractive cosmic force in abundance; the psychophysical stuff (*qi*) is the heavenly soul (*hun*), and the heavenly soul is the expansive cosmic force in abundance. [Based on *Li ji* (*Shisan jing zhushu* [Yiwen reprint ed.]) 47.14a.] [As the *Classic of Changes* says in the "Great Treatise," sec. 1:] "The essence and the psychophysical stuff coalesce to constitute a thing." What thing then is without the contractive and expansive cosmic forces? [As the *Classic of Changes* continues:] "The floating up of the heavenly soul constitutes a change." When the heavenly soul floats up we can be sure of the earthly soul's descent. (3.2a1)

4. The contractive and expansive cosmic forces are simply psychophysical stuff. What contracts and expands, comes and goes, is psychophysical stuff. In Heaven and Earth there's nothing that's not psychophysical stuff. The psychophysical stuff of humans and that of Heaven and Earth are everywhere interconnected. Humans don't realize this. As soon as the mind of man becomes active, it's bound to affect the psychophysical stuff; the mind and the psychophysical stuff—in their contractions and expansions, their comings and goings—mutually influence each other. Take divination, for example. Every time you divine, you're simply speaking to whatever it is that's on your mind; with such activation there's certain to be a response. (3.2a4)

5. Someone asked: Are the contractive and expansive cosmic forces simply this psychophysical stuff or not? Zhu said: They're similar to the spirit (*shenling*) within this psychophysical stuff. (3.2a8)

6. Rain and wind, dew and lightning, sun and moon, day and night, these are all traces of the contractive and expansive cosmic forces; these are the just and upright contractive and expansive cosmic forces of broad daylight. As for the so-called howlers from the rafters and butters in the chest, these then are called the unjust and depraved (guishen); they sometimes exist and sometimes don't, sometimes go and sometimes come, sometimes coalesce and sometimes disperse. In addition, there's the saying "pray to them and they will respond, pray to them and they will grant fulfillment"; these too are what we call guishen. These are all of one and the same principle. The myriad affairs of the world are all of this principle. There's only a difference in degree of refinement and size. He also said: If you take guishen to mean "efficacy" [as Cheng Yi[1] suggests in his Commentary on the Classic of Changes (Yichuan yizhuan {Sibu beiyao ed.} 1.1a)], then it'll be clear. (3.2b1)

7. They were speaking of spirits and monsters and Zhu said: When man's mind is arranged in balance things are fine; if it dallies around ghosts and monsters appear. (3.2b8)

8. They were talking about how Xie Shilong's household had seen a ghost and Zhu said: In the world those who believe in ghosts and spirits all feel that they really do exist between Heaven and Earth. Those who don't believe in them positively think there are no ghosts. Still, there are those who truly have seen them. Zheng Jingwang thus believed that what the Xies had seen was real without realizing that it was just a special type of rainbow. Bida then asked: Is a rainbow simply psychophysical stuff or does it have substance? Zhu said: Being able to sip water it must have a stomach; only when it disperses does it become nothing. It's like thunder and spirits—these are the same sorts of things. (3.4a2)

9. They were speaking of ghosts and monsters and Zhu said: The spirits of wood are the kui and the wangliang. The kui has only one foot; as for the wangliang, there was talk of such things in antiquity. If indeed there are ghosts and monsters, they must be these creatures. (3.4a7)

10. Someone asked about the principle of life and death and of contractive and expansive cosmic forces. Zhu said: The Way of Heaven flows everywhere, nourishing the ten thousand things. There's principle and later there's psychophysical stuff; they exist simultaneously, but in the end principle is thought to be the master. Humans receive them and possess life. The clear part of the psychophysical stuff becomes psychophysical stuff, the turbid part becomes solid matter. Consciousness and motion are the work of the yang [psychophysical stuff]; the body with its form and shape is the work of the yin [psychophysical stuff]. Psychophysical stuff is called the heavenly soul; the body is called the earthly soul. The Huainanzi commentary by Gao You (ca. 168–212) (Huainanzi [SBBY ed.] 7.6a) says: "The heavenly soul is the expansive cosmic force of the yang [psychophysical stuff]; the earthly soul is the expansive cosmic force of

the yin [psychophysical stuff]." What's meant by the expansive cosmic force, then, is master of the bodily form and the psychophysical stuff. Humans are born because the essence and the psychophysical stuff coalesce; but a human only has so much psychophysical stuff, which in time necessarily is exhausted. When it's exhausted [according to the "Single Victim at the Border Sacrifices" chapter of the *Record of Rites*], "the heavenly soul and the psychophysical stuff return to Heaven and the bodily form and the earthly soul return to Earth," and the person dies. When a person is about to die, the warm psychophysical stuff rises; this is the so-called heavenly soul ascending. The lower half of the body gradually cools; this is the so-called earthly soul descending. Thus if there's life, there must be death; if there's a beginning, there must be an end. What coalesces and disperses is the psychophysical stuff. As for principle, it's simply lodged in the psychophysical stuff—it's not something that at the outset congeals to become a discrete thing by itself. Merely whatever is appropriate for a human being to do is principle; principle can't be spoken of as coalescing or dispersing. Now, when a person dies, though in the end he or she returns to a state of dispersal, still he or she doesn't disperse completely at once. Thus in religious sacrifice there's the principle of influence and response (*gange*). In the case of a distant ancestor we can't know whether his psychophysical stuff exists or not, yet because those offering sacrifices to him are his descendants they necessarily are of the same psychophysical stuff; therefore there's a principle of mutual influence and penetration (*gantong*). Still, psychophysical stuff that's already dispersed does not coalesce again. The Buddhists, however, think that a person upon death becomes a ghost and that the ghost again becomes a person. If this were so then between Heaven and Earth there would always be the same number of people coming and going and still less would people be produced and reproduced by the creative process. This is absolutely absurd. As to Boyou's becoming an evil spirit,[2] [Cheng] Yichuan said [in his *Surviving Works* (*Chengshi yishu* {*SBBY* ed.} 3.6a)] that it was of a special kind of moral principle. It would seem that before his psychophysical stuff had been fully exhausted he met a violent death and so naturally was able to become an evil spirit. Zichan appointed someone to serve as his heir so that his spirit would have a place to go and hence wouldn't become an evil spirit. It can indeed be said that Zichan "understood the situation of spirit beings" (*Classic of Changes*, "Great Treatise," sec. 1). Someone asked: [Cheng] Yichuan said [in his *Commentary on the Classic of Changes* 1.7b–8a] that spiritual beings are traces of the creative process. Is it possible that these are indeed traces of the creative process? Zhu said: They are. To speak of the standard principle, it's like a tree suddenly producing blossoms and leaves—these then are traces of the creative process. It's also like lightning, thunder, wind, or rain suddenly filling the air. These are traces too. It's just that they're what people ordinarily see and so they don't think them strange. When suddenly they hear a ghost howling or see a ghost in flames, these they consider strange. They don't appreciate that these too are traces of the creative process. But since they aren't of the standard principle people regard them as strange. For instance, the *School Sayings of Confucius* (*Kongzi jiayu* [*Sibu congkan* ed.] 4.11a) says: "The monsters of the mountains are called *kui* and *wangliang;* the monsters of the water are called *long* (dragons) and *wangxiang;* and the monsters of the earth are called *fen-yang.*" All these are produced by confused and perverse psychophysical stuff and are surely not without principle—you mustn't stubbornly think that they are without principle. It's like the winter's being cold and the summer's being warm; this is the standard principle. But there are times when suddenly in the summer it turns cold and in the winter it turns warm—how can we say there isn't a principle for this! Still, because it isn't an ordinary principle we consider it strange. Confucius therefore didn't speak of such matters; students likewise need not pay them any heed. (3.4a12)

11. Yongzhi said: As human beings praying to Heaven, Earth, mountains, and rivers, we rely on what we possess to influence what they possess [i.e., psychophysical stuff]. As descendants sacrificing to ancestors, we rely on what we possess to influence what they don't. Zhu said: The psychophysical stuff of the spirits of Heaven and Earth is constantly contracting and expanding without stop. The psychophysical stuff of a human's contractive cosmic force dissipates until there's nothing left. The dissipation can take more time or less time. There are men who do not submit readily to death, and as a consequence when they die their psychophysical stuff does not disperse; they become evil beings and monsters. In the case of a person who has met a cruel death, or a Buddhist or Daoist who dies, oftentimes his or her psychophysical stuff will not disperse.[3] As for sages and worthies, they are at ease in their deaths, so how could they possibly not disperse and become apparitions or monsters? Take Huangdi, Yao, and Shun, for instance: who has ever heard that once they died they became spirits or monsters? (3.6b12)

12. Someone asked: What about a person who dies but whose psychophysical stuff doesn't disperse? Zhu said: He is one who doesn't submit readily to death. For instance, people who bring punishment or harm on themselves never submit readily to death; indeed, all the more do they concentrate their essential spirit (*jingshen*). As for those who are at ease in their deaths, their psychophysical stuff naturally is entirely exhausted. How could one ever believe that Yao or Shun became a ghost? (3.11a6)

13. To die and have the psychophysical stuff disperse—extinguished without trace—this is the norm; this is moral principle. But there are cases of rebirth wherein the psychophysical stuff that had collected, by chance, does not disperse and somehow fuses to live psychophysical stuff and returns to life. This, however, is not the norm. [Cheng] Yichuan said: "In the *Zuo Commentary* Boyou's becoming an evil spirit is of a special kind of principle." This is to say that it isn't the normal principle of life and death. (3.11a9)

14. Guangzu inquired about the Master's letter in response to Songqing, etc.: [Cheng] Yichuan also said, "Boyou's becoming an evil spirit is of a special kind of principle." What do you think? Zhu said: Of course there's this sort of principle. And, in most cases, it's that a person doesn't meet a natural death and as a result his strong psychophysical stuff doesn't disperse; yet, even it with time can't but disperse. For instance, in Zhangzhou there was a highly public matter of a wife killing her husband and secretly burying him. Afterward he became an evil spirit; only when the matter was exposed did he stop being an evil spirit. Fearing that in this matter officials would memorialize the throne to spare the wife's life [and that the evil spirit would thus reappear], the people of Zhangzhou sent a petition [calling for the punishment of the culprits] to the various officials for their endorsement. Afterward the wife was beheaded and her lover was hanged. Hence we know from this case the general principle, that if we do not render a conviction and give a life for a life, then the injustice suffered by the dead one will not be undone. (3.11b2)

15. Someone asked: What about [Cheng Yichuan's remark that] "the Boyou affair is of a special kind of principle"? Zhu said: It *is* of a special kind of principle. The reason people get sick and come to their end is that their psychophysical stuff disperses. But there are some people who meet with punishment and some who die quite suddenly; their psychophysical stuff remains coalesced and does not at first disperse. Yet, it too in the end disperses completely. Buddhists and Daoists are selfishly preoccupied with their own bodies because at death they too are simply incapable of preserving them and are quite unhappy with such an end. Those who harbor feelings of anger at the injustice of their deaths are much the same. Hence, in none of these instances does the psychophysical stuff disperse. (3.11b11)

16. Someone asked: [The *Classic of Changes* says], "The floating up of the heavenly soul constitutes a change"; and, occasionally, it becomes a monster. Why does it not disperse? Zhu said: What we mean by the character *you*, "floating up," is very gradually to disperse. In most cases, if it has become a monster, it's because it didn't die a natural death and its psychophysical stuff didn't disperse, and consequently it became melancholy and turned into a monster. In the case of a person who's frail and dies from disease, his psychophysical stuff becomes completely exhausted and he dies. How can he again turn melancholy and become a monster! Even those who do not die a natural death will disperse with time. It's as if today we were kneading dough and making paste and in the process a small clump formed of itself and didn't disperse; with time gradually it too will be able to disperse on its own. It's also like the case of Boyou, of whom it was said [in the *Zuo Commentary*], "the essence he had enjoyed had been abundant and his use of material things extensive"—he too died without dispersing. [Zhang] Hengqu (Zhang Zai [1020–1077], another of the celebrated Neo-Confucian masters of the Northern Song period)

said: "When a thing first comes into existence, the psychophysical stuff day by day infuses and nourishes it. As the thing matures and comes to its end, the psychophysical stuff day by day returns and then, floating up, disperses. The infusing is considered the expansive cosmic force—because the psychophysical stuff is expanding. The returning is considered the contractive cosmic force—because the psychophysical stuff is returning." (*Reflections on Things at Hand* [*Jinsi lu*], chap. 1) The myriad things and affairs under Heaven, from antiquity down to the present, are all simply the yin and yang waxing and waning, contracting and expanding. Hengqu, with his notions of contraction and expansion, explained it all extremely coherently. [Xie] Shangcai (Xie Liangzuo [1050–1103], one of the Cheng brothers' most prominent disciples, and one the so-called Four Masters of the Cheng School) explained it, but it seems he didn't explain it as a cyclical matter. [It says in the *Record of Rites,* "The Meaning of Sacrifices" chapter:] "Zai Wo said: 'I have heard the names *gui* and *shen,* but I do not know what they mean.' The Master said: 'As for psychophysical stuff, it is the expansive cosmic force in abundance; as for the earthly soul, it is the contractive cosmic force in abundance. It is the union of the contractive and expansive cosmic forces that constitutes our doctrine in perfection.' " The commentary to this passage [by the Han commentator Zheng Xuan (127–200)] remarks that "the breathing of the mouth and nose constitutes the psychophysical stuff, and the hearing and seeing of the ears and eyes constitute the earthly soul." The psychophysical stuff belongs to the yang and the earthly soul belongs to the yin. Nowadays there are people who say "our vision has deteriorated"; this then is the "earthly soul descending." When people today are about to die, there's a saying, "the earthly soul is deteriorating." As for the psychophysical stuff, it simply ascends and disperses. Thus it is said [in the "Single Victim at the Border Sacrifices" chapter of the *Record of Rites*]: "The heavenly soul and the psychophysical stuff return to Heaven and the bodily form and the earthly soul return to Earth." The Daoists in their method of cultivating life have a teaching, which in large measure tallies with ours here. (3.12a8)

17. Chang Hong, dead for three years, was transformed into jade. (According to one tradition, Chang Hong lived during the reign of King Ling of the Zhou and was killed by people suspicious of his personal devotion to and love for the king. With death his body was transformed into jade.) This was what is called the earthly soul, and it had the majesty of a tiger; Hong died on account of his loyalty, and his psychophysical stuff therefore congealed in this manner. (3.12b10)

18. Someone inquired: Nowadays in many households there are freak accidents. Zhu said: These are the doings of the demons of mountains and streams. In Jianzhou there was a literatus who in his travels met up with a one-footed man asking the whereabouts of a certain household. The literatus accompanied

the one-footed man and saw him enter the household in question. A few days later and that family did, in fact, suffer the death of a son. (3.13a1)

19. There was discussion about shamans' controlling of ghosts and how ghosts mimic the shamans in order to resist them, and Zhu said: When the minds of the descendants are extremely crafty, they stimulate crafty psychophysical stuff, and the ghosts produced thereby are also cunning. (3.13a6)

20. Houzhi asked: There's probably no principle for a man's dying and becoming a wild animal. But personally I've seen a son in a Yongchun family who had hog bristles and skin on his ears. What do you make of it? Zhu said: This shouldn't be considered supernatural. I've heard that a soldier employed in Jixi had hog bristles on his chest and when asleep made hog noises. This is simply because he had been endowed with the psychophysical stuff of a hog. (3.13a8)

21. Someone inquired: Human nature is principle, which can't be spoken of as coalescing and dispersing. What coalesces to be born and disperses to die is psychophysical stuff and psychophysical stuff alone. What we call the essence, the spirit, the heavenly soul, and the earthly soul and what has perception and consciousness is psychophysical stuff. Thus when it coalesces there's existence, and when it disperses there's nonexistence. As for principle, it has always existed, through antiquity and the present; it doesn't repeatedly coalesce and disperse, wax and wane. Zhu said: It's simply that this psychophysical stuff of Heaven and Earth and of yin and yang is received by the myriad things. The psychophysical stuff coalesces and constitutes a person, it disperses and constitutes a contractive cosmic force (gui). But even though this psychophysical stuff has dispersed, this principle of Heaven and Earth and yin and yang is produced and reproduced endlessly. And while the essence, the spirit, and the heavenly and earthly souls of the ancestors may have already dispersed, the essence, the spirit, and the heavenly and earthly souls of the descendants naturally have some affinity with them, and thus, if in the rituals of religious sacrifice the descendants fully exercise sincerity and reverence, they can make contact with the heavenly and earthly souls of the ancestors. Naturally this is difficult to talk about. Looking for them once they've dispersed it seems as though they absolutely don't exist, but if you are able to exercise sincerity and reverence to the utmost there will be influence and response (gange). This indeed is because principle is always simply right here. (3.13b2)

22. From the point of view of Heaven and Earth, there's just one psychophysical stuff. From the point of view of one body, my psychophysical stuff is the psychophysical stuff of my ancestors—it's just one and the same psychophysical stuff. Thus, as soon as there's influence there's bound to be a response. (3.14b1)

23. Chen Houzhi asked: The ancestors are a collective of psychophysical stuff between Heaven and Earth; thus descendants offer them sacrifices and they coalesce and disperse. Zhu said: This then is what [Xie] Shangcai meant in

commenting [in the *Records of Conversations of Shangcai (Shangcai yulu) (Cong-shu jicheng xinbian* ed., vol. 22, p. 17)], "When you want them to exist they exist, when you want them to be nonexistent they're nonexistent." It's all due to men. Spirit beings are entities with a fundamental existence. Ancestors simply share in this same psychophysical stuff, but they have an intelligence that guides them. The descendants, in their bodies, exist right here; the psychophysical stuff of the ancestors exists right here in the same place. The same blood and pulse runs through them all. The reason "spirits do not enjoy the offerings of those not of their kindred and people do not sacrifice to those not of their ancestry" [as the *Zuo Commentary* (J. Legge, *The Chinese Classics,* vol. 5, p. 157) states] is simply that their psychophysical stuff is not related. As for the Son of Heaven sacrificing to Heaven and Earth, the various lords sacrificing to the mountains and rivers, and the great officers sacrificing to the five deities [i.e., the spirits of the outer door, the inner door, the walk, the hearth, and the center of the room], though they [i.e., Heaven and Earth, the mountains and rivers, and the five deities] are not these men's ancestors, still the Son of Heaven is master of all under Heaven, the various lords are masters of the mountains and rivers, and the great officers are masters of the five deities. And because they are masters over them, the psychophysical stuff [of Heaven and Earth, the mountains and rivers, and the five deities] also presides in their bodies. This being the case, there is an affinity between them. (3.14b11)

24. Someone inquired: With a man's death I do not know whether the heavenly and earthly souls disperse or not. Zhu said: They do indeed disperse. Someone further inquired: How about the descendants' wherewithal to influence them through sacrifice? Zhu said: In the end the descendants are of the same psychophysical stuff as the ancestors, so even though the ancestors' psychophysical stuff may have dispersed, their bloodline [lit., roots] nonetheless exists right here. By fully exercising sincerity and reverence we're able to summon their psychophysical stuff so that it coalesces right here. It's the same as water and waves: the later water is not the earlier water, the later waves are not the earlier waves; and yet all of it is just the same water and waves. The relationship between the psychophysical stuff of the descendants and the psychophysical stuff of the ancestors is just like this. The ancestors' psychophysical stuff may promptly disperse of itself, yet their bloodline nonetheless exists right here. And since their bloodline exists here, the fact is we're able to induce their psychophysical stuff into coalescing right here. This matter is difficult to talk about so I simply ask that you think about it for yourselves. (3.15a7)

25. We can speak of spiritual beings as controlling powers, but we can't speak of them as things. Moreover, they're not the sorts of clay-modeled spirits we find nowadays. They're simply psychophysical stuff. Suppose you're sacrificing to them, you just have to concentrate your essential spirit if you're going to influence them. Ancestors are of the same psychophysical stuff you've inherited, consequently you can influence them. (3.17a10)

26. Someone asked about the principle of sacrificing: Is it a matter [as Fan Zuyu (1041–1098), a prominent statesman and scholar of the Northern Song, said] that "with sincerity the spirit will exist, and without sincerity there'll be no spirit"? [As quoted by Zhu Xi in Zhu's commentary on *Analect* 3/12 in *Collected Commentaries on the Analects* (*Lunyu jizhu*).] Zhu said: The principle of spirit beings is the principle of our mind. (3.17b3)

27. As for influencing the ancestral spirit through sacrificial offerings, sometimes it's sought in the yin, sometimes in the yang. And since each thing complies with its own kind, when attracted the ancestral spirit comes. It's not that there's a thing that amasses in the void out there waiting for the descendants to seek it. It's just that if the sacrificer, in projecting his allotment of the one psychophysical stuff, fully exercises sincerity and reverence, he influences the spirit so that its psychophysical stuff firmly lodges itself right here. (3.17b5)

28. Someone asked: In offering sacrifices, the descendant makes his intentions fully true in order to get the essential spirit of his ancestor to coalesce. I don't know whether this is to bring together its heavenly and earthly souls or simply to influence the psychophysical stuff of its heavenly soul. Zhu said: To burn "southernwood and offer it with fat" [as recounted in the *Classic of Poetry*] is for the purpose of repaying the ancestor's psychophysical stuff. "To offer libations of fragrant spirits" [as the *Record of Rites* suggests] is for the purpose of summoning home the heavenly soul, that is, to bring it together with the earthly soul. As it says [in the *Record of Rites*]: "It is the union of the contractive and expansive cosmic forces that constitutes our doctrine in perfection." Someone further asked: I don't know whether it's always like this or like this only at the time of sacrificial offerings. Zhu said: It's only if the psychophysical stuff of the descendant is present that the spirit of the ancestor is present. When there are no sacrificial offerings, how can you get it to coalesce? (3.17b8)

29. Someone asked: When an ancestor's essential spirit has departed, one must "for seven days fast and for three days hold vigil," "seeking it in the yang and seeking it in the yin" [as prescribed by the *Record of Rites*], and only then will one get it to coalesce. This being the case, in coalescing it does so suddenly. And as soon as the praying and sacrificing have ended and one's sincerity and reverence have dispersed, it too suddenly disperses. Zhu said: That's right. (3.18a4)

30. Someone asked: Is it the case that, in death, the psychophysical stuff of the heavenly soul disperses, and thereupon we set up a master [of ceremonies] to act as master over it; and that he has to get some of that psychophysical stuff to coalesce right here? Zhu said: The ancients, as death ensued, summoned the heavenly soul to return to the earthly soul, set up a double, and established a master; this is because they forever hoped to connect with some of the dead person's essential spirit right here. In the ancient practice of consecrating the tortoise shell [for divination] they used the blood of a sacrificial animal, and

they did so because they believed that that tortoise shell after a while no longer possessed spiritual power and so used some living psychophysical stuff to connect with [the spirits]. In the "Monograph on Divining" in the *Records of the Historian (Shiji)*, to foretell the events of spring they rubbed the tortoise shell with a hen's egg and divined; this was to take living psychophysical stuff to connect with [the spirits]. This then is the meaning of consecrating the tortoise shell. He added: The ancients set up the impersonator of the dead. This too was to take the living psychophysical stuff of a live person to connect with [the spirit of the dead]. (3.18a10)

31. Someone asked: In using animals, offerings, and wine to sacrifice to Heaven, Earth, mountains, and rivers, are we merely demonstrating the sincerity of our mind or is there really psychophysical stuff that comes in response? Zhu said: If we say that nothing comes to accept the sacrificial offerings, why sacrifice? What thing is it that is majestic above and causes people to worship and reverence it? Yet if we were to say that there truly is a cloud-chariot with attendant that comes in response, that would be absurd. (3.18b4)

32. Someone asked: There are spirits in the world deserving of deification and temple sacrifices for several hundred years running. What is the principle here? Zhu said: Gradually, with time, those spirits too are able to disperse. Formerly when I was serving as prefect in Nankang, because of a sustained drought they were praying to spirits everywhere. I happened upon a certain temple, which had but three ramshackle buildings, in total chaos. The man there said that thirty to fifty years ago the efficacy of [that temple's] spirit was just like an echo; consequently people would come and, from behind a hanging screen, the spirit would speak with them. In the past, the spirit's efficacy was powerful like that; now, the spirit's efficacy is like this. This you can see for yourselves. (3.20b10)

33. It's customary these days to revere ghosts. For instance, in Xin'an and elsewhere, morning and evening it's like being in a den of ghosts. Once I returned to my native village [in Wuyuan County] where the so-called Five Transmitters Temple is located. It's extremely powerful and mysterious, and everybody holds it dear, believing that fortune and misfortune manifest themselves right there on the spot. The locals, in traveling away from home, take slips of paper [in the shape of money, houses, animals, etc.] to the temple, offer prayer there, and only afterward begin their journey. Literati passing through present their name cards and declare, "Disciple So-and-So is paying a visit to the temple." When I first returned to my native place kinsmen urgently bid me to go, but I did not. That night they assembled the clan members together for a banquet and went to the government office to buy wine—which had gotten old. I drank it and thereupon had a severe stomachache all night long; furthermore, the next day, by chance, there appeared a snake at the side of the stairs. Everyone, in a great uproar, thought the reason was that I hadn't

paid a visit to the temple. I told them: "I got sick because my stomach didn't digest the food; it had nothing to do with the temple. Do not be daunted by the spirit of the Five Transmitters." Among the family members there was a certain man, one bent on studying, who likewise came to encourage me to go to the temple, saying "this is the common practice." I told him, "Why should it be a common practice? It's surprising that even you would speak this way. I've had the good fortune to return here [to my native village] and am extremely close to my ancestral graves. If the spirit is able to bring misfortune and fortune may he please bury me immediately at the side of the ancestral graves—it would be extremely convenient." Zhu further said: In serving as a local official, one must do away with cults to licentious deities. But if they be temples with plaques from the emperor, one can't easily do away with them. (3.21a2)

34. They were talking about the affair in which the Purple Maiden Goddess (i.e., the goddess of spirit writing) had been invited to recite some verse, and Zhu said: When they invited her to come forth in person, a little girl from that household appeared—we don't know what to make of this. Just as in Quzhou, a man worshiping a certain spirit simply recorded a list of inquiries on a piece of paper and sealed it in an envelope in front of the spirit's temple. In a little while he opened up the sealed list and on the paper, of their own, were the answers to the inquiries. We don't know what to make of this. (3.22a10)

35. Someone asked: Somebody once asked about the Purple Maiden Goddess, etc. Zhu said: It's because it's in our own mind that she's able to respond; when she's unable to respond it's that our mind doesn't know the ins and outs of the matter. (3.22b2)

36. Someone asked: There's the standard moral principle and there's the depraved moral principle; there's the right one and there's the wrong one. The matter of spirit beings is much the same. In the world there are depraved spirit beings, but we can't say there is not a principle for them. Zhu said: Laozi remarked (D. C. Lau, trans., *Lao Tzu, Tao Te Ching,* chap. 60), "When the empire is ruled in accordance with the way, the spirits lose their potencies." That is, if the kingly Way were cultivated and illumined, this sort of depraved psychophysical stuff would completely dissipate. (3.22b4)

Notes

1. The great Neo-Confucian master of the Northern Song, Cheng Yi (*hao* Yichuan) (1033–1107), brother of Cheng Hao (1032–1085); though Zhu Xi, of course, never had the opportunity to study under him, Zhu regarded Cheng Yi as his spiritual master.

2. The *Zuo Commentary* (*Zuo zhuan*) (James Legge, *The Chinese Classics,* vol. 5, pp. 551, 557, 618) tells of Boyou of the state of Zheng being killed in the sheep market by Zishi and his men-at-arms and years later appearing as a ghost to wreak vengeance.

3. An interlinear note in the text explains: "Buddhists and Daoists devote themselves to nurturing their essential spirit, which thereby congeals and does not disperse."

Communicating with the Unseen

— 8 —

The Inner Cultivation Tradition of Early Daoism

Harold D. Roth

We can speak of early Daoism in terms of three distinct phases, each represented by extant texts, that can be arranged in a rough chronological order. The first, datable to about the middle of the fourth century B.C.E. and represented textually by Zhuang Zhou's "Inner Chapters" of the *Zhuangzi* and the *Guanzi* essay "Inward Training" ("Neiye"), which is translated in part below, is exclusively concerned with cosmology and the inner transformation of the individual leading to the attainment of "mystical gnosis." Perhaps originating among disenchanted followers of the individualistic philosopher Yang Zhu (fl. fourth century B.C.E.) and/or the early "esoteric masters" (*fangshi*) from the coastal states of Qi and Yan and the shamans of the southern state of Chu, this can be called the "Individualist" phase because of its almost total absence of social and political thought.

The second phase is represented textually by the *Laozi* and what A. C. Graham has called the "Primitivist" voice in the *Zhuangzi* because of its advocacy of a vision of a simple society and politic. The cosmology and self-transformation of the prior phase are present here, but to them is added a political and social philosophy that recommends the return to a more primitive and simple life-style associated with small agrarian communities.

The third and final phase of early Daoist philosophy is the "Syncretist" phase (again following Graham), and it is richly represented by surviving texts, such as the Huang-Lao manuscripts from Mawangdui, at least several essays from the *Guanzi* (see below), the Syncretist voice in the *Zhuangzi*, and the *Huainanzi*. The hallmarks of this phase are the presence of the same cosmology and philosophy of self-transformation as in the other phases, now commended to the ruler as an arcanum of government; the emphasis on the precise coordination of the political and cosmic orders by the thus-enlightened ruler; and a syncretic social and political philosophy that borrows relevant ideas from earlier schools such as the Legalist and the Confucian while retaining the Daoist cosmological context. It is this phase that receives the label of the "Daoist school" from the famous historian

Sima Tan (d. 110 B.C.E.), while some conclude that it can be further identified with his Huang-Lao school.

The common thread that ties these three phases of early Daoism together and differentiates them from the other early philosophical schools is their shared vocabulary of cosmology and self-transformation. Indeed, it is precisely these elements of early Daoism that carry over into the later Daoist religion and help us to see a significant aspect of continuity in an otherwise heterogeneous tradition. The early Daoist texts that appear below from the Individualist and Syncretist phases center on this common thread. They are important in the tradition as the earliest statements of methods of self-transformation and their philosophical bases, and they provide the intellectual context for the few specific references to inner cultivation that are found in the *Laozi* and *Zhuangzi*. The selections are taken from two works, the *Guanzi* and the *Huainanzi*.

The *Guanzi* is a very large collection of essays in seventy-six chapters that deal mostly with various aspects of social and political thought. Traditionally attributed to the famous prime minister from Qi, Guan Zhong (seventh century B.C.E.), like the *Zhuangzi* it was gradually compiled over about two hundred years from the mid-fourth to mid-second centuries B.C.E. Initially classified as a Daoist work by second-century bibliographers, it was several centuries later classified as Legalist and thenceforth generally overlooked as a source of early Daoism. The two inner cultivation essays translated in part below, "Inward Training" and "Techniques of the Mind, Part 1" ("Xinshu, shang"), were written by different authors who were separated by perhaps a century in time but clearly share a common vocabulary of inner cultivation. The former, datable to the earliest stratum of the *Guanzi* (mid-fourth century B.C.E.) and written in rhymed verse, is from the Individualist phase of early Daoism. The latter, divided into a core text in rhymed verse probably written toward the end of the third century B.C.E. and a prose commentary on it written perhaps fifty or so years later, is from the Syncretist phase. The selections below generally eschew political philosophy in favor of inner cultivation theory, although the last passages from "Xinshu, shang" begin to discuss the political application of inner cultivation theory. As is common for the period, there were probably no section divisions in the original texts of either essay (true too of the Mawangdui manuscripts of *The Classic on Way and Its Power* [*Dao de jing*]), but I have broken them into sections based on semantic and syntactical considerations. In addition, I have arranged the *Guanzi* selections under topical headings and have not followed the order of the original text.

The *Huainanzi* is a work of twenty-one essays on topics ranging from cosmology and astronomy to politics and inner cultivation. It was originally conceived as a compendium of all the knowledge the Daoistically inspired ruler needed for governing by its sponsor and editor (and the probable author of a few of its essays), Liu An (180?–122 B.C.E.), the second king of the state of Huainan in the old Chu region, and was presented by Liu to his nephew, Han emperor Wu, in 139 B.C.E. Initially classified as an "eclectic" work (and thenceforth also overlooked as a source of early Daoist philosophy), it has recently been reexamined in light of the discoveries and scholarship of the past two decades and is now seen by many as the final surviving statement of Syncretic or Huang-Lao Daoism. The selections below include shorter passages on psychology and inner cultivation from chapters 1, 2, and 14, and more detailed discussions of the physiology of inner cultivation and its ultimate benefits as seen in the paradigm of the Genuine Man, which represent about one-third of the chapter entitled "The Numinous Essence" ("Jing-shen"). I have chosen to present the highly patterned parallel prose of the *Huai-nanzi* in an English verse format (with actual rhymes and citations further distinguished) because the logic of argumentation is intimately connected to the prose style. This simply cannot be seen in a straight prose translation. As with the *Guanzi* essays, the location of the translated passages in the original Chinese texts of the *Sibu congkan* edition is given after each passage.

Technical Terminology

The material on inner cultivation takes us into two very thorny areas in the history of Western philosophy, those involving the tenuous distinctions between energy and matter and between mind and body. Without engaging these problems in detail, suffice it to say that in the early Chinese worldview reflected in these writings, such distinctions were not made with the same degree of certitude often found in the West.

The conceptually distinct line between energy and matter is blurred in the traditional Chinese notion of *qi*, which I have chosen to translate as "vital energy." In the very earliest texts *qi* is the vapor or steam that arises from the heating of water and watery substances and subsequently appears as the actual air that we breathe. By the time of the *Huainanzi*, *qi* is the universal energy/matter/fluid out of which all phenomena in the universe are constructed, both the physical and the psychological. One can almost see here a grand cosmic continuum in which the heaviest and most turbid *qi* is found in the most solid and dense matter, such as mountains and rock, and the most ethereal *qi* is found in what one would call psychological and spiritual phenomena, such as the most profound inner experiences of tranquility, mystical gnosis, and in ghosts and spirits as agential entities. However, this notion of a continuum fails to catch the association of *qi* with life and vitality, for in these early Chinese contexts the more ethereal *qi* is found in the vitalizing fluids associated with all living things. Human beings are made up, then, of systems constituted of varying densities of *qi*, such as the skeletal structure; the skin, flesh, and musculature; the breath; the Five Viscera (*wuzang*) of *qi* that form our inner physiology and include the physical organs of lungs, kidneys, liver, gall bladder, and spleen; and the various psychological states that make up our constantly changing continuum of experience, from rage and lust to complete tranquility.

The most concentrated and yet, paradoxically, refined and ethereal *qi* in these sources is called *jing,* which I have translated as "vital essence." It is one of the central concepts of the earlier sources from the *Guanzi* and therein appears as both the life-giving essence contained in the seeds of all living things and the physiological substrate associated with profound tranquility in the sage leading directly to sagacity. It is spoken of with awe and can truly be understood as the concrete manifestation of the Way's power to generate the living. As the source of the vital energy in human beings, it is the basis of our health, vitality, and psychological well-being.

The term *xin* (literally, "heart") is, for the early Chinese, the locus of the entire range of conscious experience, including perception, thought, emotion, desire, and intuition. It is another of those key philosophical terms that spans the definitive split between mind and body and so is alternately translated as "heart" or "mind" or some combination thereof. Just as the Five Viscera or pathways of vital energy are more inclusive than just the physical organs included in them and from which each takes its name, the *xin* means not just the physical heart but the entire sphere of vital energy that flows through and includes it.

The *shen,* which, following Willard Peterson, I translate as "numen" (from the Latin word for spirit), is the basic conscious agent or power within human beings. It is another concept that bridges accustomed notions of mind and body in a way analogous to that in which the term *qi* bridges ideas of energy and matter. The Chinese concept includes parts of the ranges of meanings of the English terms commonly used to translate it—spirit, soul, psyche—but none of these can fully capture its range of meanings in Chinese. For the ancient Chinese it is ultimately unfathomable (see the "Great Appendix" section of the *Classic of Changes* [*Yijing*]), yet it provides humans with metaphysical knowledge such as precognition (e.g., see *Guanzi* selection XII and *Huainanzi* selection VII) and is the locus of the mystical intuition called *shenming,* which I translate as "numinous light." As a most profound level of consciousness, it is experienced only fleetingly, and according to "Inward Training" (*Guanzi* selection VII), one must take determined steps to still one's normal consciousness in order to retain it within one's experience. In *Guanzi* selection XII and in associated works like the *Huainanzi,* it is said to reside in the mind and to have a "physiological substrate" in the vital essence (*jing*).

Finally, a word on the concept of Dao, the "Way" things are in all early Chinese schools of thought. For the Daoists, whose name was taken by Sima Tan from their understanding of this term, this Way is the ultimate power in the cosmos, paradoxically transcendent yet immanent. As a unitive principle beyond the grasp of any specific thing in the cosmos (and sometimes referred to simply as "The One" or by such metaphors as the "unhewn" [*pu*] and the "simple" [*su*]), the Dao mysteriously operates within the cosmos to facilitate the generation of all phenomena and to serve as the inner guiding force throughout every moment of life. Although it is ineffable and so cannot be known as an object, the early Daoist sources maintain that it can be merged with, accorded with, or directly experienced. Such an experience occurs only after the arduous practices referred to, sometimes metaphorically, in the selections below, and it sometimes involves total self-transcendance.

General Techniques of Self-Cultivation

The practices of inward discipline followed by the early Daoists are essentially apophatic—that is, they involve a systematic process of negating, forgetting, or emptying out the contents of consciousness found in ordinary experience that is based in the ego-self. These include the removal of such basic elements of self-consciousness as perceptions, emotions, desires, and thoughts. This systematic emptying leads to increasingly profound states of tranquility until the adept experiences a fully concentrated inner consciousness of unity, which is filled with light and clarity and which is not tied to an individual self.

Some sources imply further that this condition of unitary consciousness is temporary and that upon returning from it to normal differentiating consciousness the concerns of the self that had previously characterized one's conscious experience are no longer present. Therefore the sage thus transformed becomes self-less, impartial, unmoved by common passions and prejudices, and singularly able to respond spontaneously and harmoniously to any situation that arises. It is no wonder that the idea of the fruits of these practices became so desirable to those who governed. It promised a sagely, almost divine clarity and the attendant wisdom not only to govern efficaciously but also to achieve total personal fulfillment. Along these lines selections XXII and XXIII, from the *Guanzi,* and VI and X, from the *Huainanzi,* are the most relevant.

The culturally unique characteristics of this system of praxis involve the particular ways the early Daoists conceived of this process. Systematic breath-control practices, often while sitting in a stable position (e.g., *Guanzi* selections VIII, X, and XII), involved for them the circulating and refining of the *qi,* the vital energy of the cosmos, producing an increasingly rarefied and concentrated form of it called the *jing* (vital essence), which is the "material" counterpart of the psychological experience of tranquility, as well as the essential generative element in the material world. Since *jing* is expended in such daily activities as perception and the *jingshen* (numinous essence) is expended through desires and emotions, inner cultivation theory urges that these activities be kept to a minimum. By emptying the mind of these common experiences and cultivating tranquility, one will attain both the physical vitality and psychological well-being that comes from having the entire human organism function spontaneously according to its inherent patterns or "natural guidelines" (*li*). At ultimate levels these sources speak of an intuitive awareness arising that is clairvoyant and noetic and is associated with the numen. This is the above-mentioned numinous light (*shen ming*).

Our earliest sources ("Inward Training" and "Techniques of the Mind") speak metaphorically of this process as making a lodging place for the numen by thoroughly sweeping out its abode (the mind) (*Guanzi* selections VII, XX, XXI). In other passages these sources speak of emptying the mind to make a lodging place for the Way and conceive of this apophatic process as developing "inner power" (*de*) (e.g., *Guanzi* I, IX, and XVII; *Huainanzi* I, V, and IX). Uncovering the Way within is thus linked to developing increasing tranquility, which itself is the inner power that is the manifestation of the Way in mankind. This inner power can be thought of as a psychological condition of focused and balanced awareness from which the adept is able to respond spontaneously and harmoniously to whatever arises.

As the oldest surviving texts of inner cultivation theory, these sources contain a number of the earliest instances of certain important techniques of self-transformation. In this regard, note the "Inward Training" passages on systematic breath-control meditation (*Guanzi* XI) and proper posture for meditation (*Guanzi* VIII, IX, X), and on the meditative technique called "guarding the One" (*shouyi*) that was so influential in later Daoist and Buddhist meditation (*Guanzi* XIV). Also worthy of note are the passages on the progressive stages of meditative trance in "Techniques of the Mind" (*Guanzi* XX) and in the "Numinous Essence" essay of the *Huainanzi* (VII).

The translated passages have been rearranged topically and do not follow the order of the original texts. They have been numbered consecutively using Roman numerals. The location in the original Chinese text from the *Sibu congkan* edition is given in parentheses following each passage.

Further Reading

Roger Ames and D. C. Lau, *Tracing Tao to Its Source (and Other Essays from Han Dynasty Taoism)* (Princeton: Princeton University Press, forthcoming); A. C. Graham, *Chuang Tzu: The Inner Chapters* (London: Allen and Unwin, 1981); Donald Harper, "The Sexual Arts of Ancient China as Described in a Manuscript of the Second Century BCE" *Harvard Journal of Asiatic Studies* 47.2 (December 1987):539–93; Robert Henricks, *Lao Tzu, Te Tao Ching* (New York: Ballantine Books, 1989); Livia Kohn, *Taoist Meditation and Longevity Techniques,* Michigan Monographs in Chinese Studies 61 (Ann Arbor: University of Michigan Center for Chinese Studies, 1989); Kohn, *Early Chinese Mysticism* (Princeton: Princeton University Press, 1991); Allyn Rickett, *Guanzi: Political, Economic, and Philosophical Essays from Early China,* vol. 1 (Princeton: Princeton University Press, 1985); vol. 2 (forthcoming); Harold D. Roth, "Psychology and Self-Cultivation in Early Taoistic Thought," *Harvard Journal of Asiatic Studies* 51.2 (December 1991): 599–650; Roth, "Who Compiled the *Chuang Tzu?*" in *Chinese Texts and Philosophical Contexts: Essays Dedicated to Angus C. Graham,* Henry Rosemont Jr., ed. (LaSalle, Ill.: Open Court Press, 1991), pp. 79–128; Roth, *Inward Training: The First Daoist Text on Self-Cultivation* (New York: Ballantine Books, forthcoming).

GUANZI SELECTIONS

FROM "INWARD TRAINING" ("NEIYE")

The Vital Essence

I

The vital essence of all things:

Generates the five grains below and becomes the constellated stars above.

When flowing within Heaven and Earth we call it daemonic and numinous.

When stored within the chest of a man we call him a sage.

Therefore this vital energy is

Bright!—as if ascending to Heaven; dark!—as if entering an abyss.

Vast!—as if filling an ocean; lofty!—as if residing on a mountain peak.

Therefore this vital energy

Cannot be stopped by force, yet can be secured by inner power (*de*).

Cannot be summoned by speech, yet can be welcomed by the awareness.

Diligently hold onto it and do not lose it: this is called "developing inner power."

When inner power develops and wisdom emerges the myriad things will to the last one be grasped. (16/1a5–10)

II

When the vital essence is present it vitalizes on its own,

And on the outside there is a healthy manifestation.

Stored within, we take it to be the wellspring.

Floodlike (*haoran*), it harmonizes and equalizes and we take it to be the source of the vital energy.

When the source is not dried up, the four limbs are firm.

When the wellspring is not drained, it (the vital energy) freely circulates through the nine apertures.

One can then exhaust Heaven and Earth and spread over the four seas.

When one internally has no false awareness, externally there will be no disasters.

One who internally keeps his mind unimpaired, and externally keeps his body unimpaired,

Who does not encounter Heaven's disasters nor meet with harm at the hands of other men:

Call him a sage. (16/3a8–b1)

The Way

III

Clear! as though right by one's side.

Vague! as though one is not going to get it.

Indiscernible! as though beyond the limitless.

The test of this is not far off: daily we make use of its inner power.

The Way is what infuses the structures [of the mind], yet men are
    unable to secure it.

It goes forth but does not return, it comes back but does not stay.

Silent! none can hear its sound.

Sudden! so it rests in the mind.

Obscure! one cannot see its form.

Surging! it arises along with me.

We cannot see its form, we cannot hear its sound, yet we can put a
    sequence to its development.

Call it "Way." (16/1b2–9)

IV

The Way has no fixed position; the good mind, in its calmness, gives it
    a location.

When the mind is tranquil and the vital energy is structured, the Way
    can thereby be stopped.

That Way is not distant; the people get it for sustenance.

That Way is not separate; the people follow it for harmony.

Intense! as though one could be roped together with it.

Indiscernible! as though beyond the positionless.

The true state of that Way: how could it include ideas and
    pronouncements?

Cultivate your mind, make your awareness tranquil, and the Way can
    thereby be grasped. (16/1b10–2a2)

V

The Way is what the mouth cannot speak of

The eyes cannot look at

And the ears cannot listen to.

It is that by which we cultivate the mind and align the body.

It is what a person loses and thereby dies, what a person gains and is
    thereby born.

When undertakings lose it they fail; when they get it they succeed.

The Way never has a root or a trunk, leaves or flowers.

The myriad things are born by means of it and by means of it
    develop.

We name it "Way." (16/2a2–4)

The Numen

VI

The numen: no one knows its limit.
It intuitively knows the myriad things.
Hold it within your core, do not let it waver.
Do not let external things disrupt your senses,
Do not let the senses disrupt your mind.
This is called "grasping it in your core." (16/2b8–9)

VII

There is a numen residing on its own [within]:
One moment it goes, the next it comes,
And no one is able to conceive of it.
If you lose it you are inevitably disordered;
If you attain it you are inevitably well-ordered.
Diligently clean out its lodging place [the mind]
And [its] vital essence will come on its own.
Still your attempts to imagine and conceive of it.
Relax your efforts to reflect on and control it.
Be reverent and diligent and [its] vital essence will stabilize on its own.
Grasp it and do not let go
Then the eyes and ears will not overflow
And the mind will have no image apart from it.
When a properly aligned mind resides in your core,
The myriad things will be seen in their proper context. (16/2b9–3a1)

The Practice of Self-Cultivation

VIII

If you can be aligned and be tranquil, only then can you be stable.
With a stable mind at your core, with the eyes and ears perceiving
    clearly,
And with the four limbs firm and fixed
You can thereby make a lodging place for the vital essence.
The vital essence: it is the essence of the vital energy.
When the vital energy circulates freely it is generated, but when it is
    generated there is thought,
When there is thought, there is knowledge, and when there is
    knowledge there is a cessation.
When the structures of the mind are filled with knowledge, one loses
    the ability to generate it. (16/2a5–b1)

IX

When the physical form is not aligned, inner power will not come.
When in your core you are not tranquil, the mind will not be well
    ordered.
Align the body, carefully reach for inner power,
And then flowingly it will arrive on its own. (16/2b6–8)

X

If you can be aligned and tranquil,
Your flesh will be relaxed, your eyes and ears will perceive clearly,
Your muscles will be supple, and your bones will be strong.
You will then be able to hold up the Great Circle [of Heaven] and
    tread over the Great Square [of Earth].
You will thus reflect the ultimately transparent and contemplate the
    ultimately luminous.
Diligently be aware; do not waver, and you will daily renew your inner
    power,
Thoroughly understand the world, and exhaust the Four Directions.
To bring forth diligently that which fills you (vital energy): this is
    called "grasping it within."
If you do this but fail to return, this will cause a wavering of your
    vitality. (16/3b1–5)

XI

In this Way [of breathing]:
You must coil, you must contract, you must uncoil, you must expand,
You must be firm, you must be regular [in this practice].
Hold fast to this excellent [practice]; do not let go of it.
Chase away the excessive [in sense perception]; abandon the trivial [in
    thought].
And when you reach the ultimate limit [of this practice]
You will return to the Way and its inner power. (16/3b6–7)

XII

By concentrating your vital energy as if numinous, the myriad things
    will all be contained within you.
Can you concentrate? can you unify [your awareness]?
Can you know good and bad fortune without resorting to divination?
Can you stop? can you halt?
Can you not seek it without, but attain it within?
You think and think and think further about this.
You think, yet still cannot penetrate it.
The daemonic and numinous in you will penetrate it.
It is not due to the inherent power of the daemonic and numinous,

But rather to the utmost refinement of your essential vital energy.
When the four limbs are correctly adjusted and the blood and vital
energy are tranquil,
Unify your awareness, concentrate your mind and the eyes and ears
will not be overstimulated.
Then even the farthest will be like the nearest. (16/4a2-7)

The One

XIII

One who can transform while seeing the unity in things, we call
"numinous";
One who can alter while seeing the unity in events, we call "wise."
To transform without changing your vital energy; to alter without
changing your wisdom:
Only the noble person who holds fast to the One is able to do this.
Hold fast to the One; do not lose it and you will be able to master the
myriad things.
The noble person employs things, and is not employed by them:
The noble person grasps the pattern of the One. (16/2b1-3)

XIV

When you broaden the mind and relax it, expand the vital energy and
extend it,
And when your physical form is calm and unmoving,
You can guard the One and discard the myriad vexations.
You will not be lured by profit nor will you be frightened by harm.
While extremely empathetic and humane, when alone you delight in
your own person.
This is called "revolving the vital energy": your thoughts and deeds
resemble Heaven's. (16/4b7-5a4)

Conclusion

XV

The vitality of all people inevitably comes from their peace of mind.
When anxious, one loses this guiding thread; when angry, one loses
this basic point.
When one is anxious or sad, pleased or angry, the Way has no place to
settle.
Love and desire: still them! Folly and disturbance: correct them!

Do not push it! do not pull it! And its blessings will return on their own.

And that Way will come to you on its own to rely on and take counsel with.

If you are tranquil then you will attain it; if you are agitated you will lose it.

That mysterious vital energy within the mind, one moment it arrives, the next it departs.

So fine nothing can be contained within it, so vast nothing can be outside it.

The reason we lose it is because of the harm caused by agitation.

When the mind can adhere to tranquility, the Way will become stabilized on its own.

The person who has attained the Way:

The pores are permeated by it; the hair is saturated by it.

Within the chest, is unvanquished.

[Follow] this Way of restricting sense-desires and the myriad things will not harm you. (16/5a4–9)

FROM "TECHNIQUES OF THE MIND PART I" ("XINSHU, SHANG")

The Way

XVI
The Way is not far off but it is hard to reach its limit.

It rests together with human beings, but it is hard to grasp. (13/1a10–11)

The Way lies within Heaven and Earth. So great there is nothing beyond it; so small there is nothing within it. Therefore the text says it "is not far off but it is hard to reach its limit." Rest in it and there will be no gap between the Way and human beings. Only the sage is able to rest in the Way. Therefore the statement says it "rests together with human beings but is hard to grasp." (13/2b5–8)

XVII
That which is empty and formless, we call it the Way.

That which transforms and nourishes the myriad things, we call inner power. (13/1b2)

The Way of Heaven is empty and formless. Empty, then it does not submit. Formless, then it is nowhere obstructed. It is nowhere obstructed and so it universally flows through the myriad things and does not alter.

Inner power is the lodging place of the Way. Things attain it and are thereby generated. Human awareness attains it and thereby directs the vital essence of the Way. Therefore inner power means "to attain." "To attain" means to attain the means by which it is so.

To act without effort, this characterizes the Way. To lodge it, this characterizes inner power. Therefore there is no gap between the Way and inner power. Thus to speak of them is not to differentiate them. That there is no gap between them is the reason why the Way lodges in inner power. (13/3a2–8)

XVIII
The Way can be secured but cannot be explained. (1b6–7)

The Way: it moves, but we do not see its form; it bestows, but we do not see its inner power. The myriad things by means of it get to be so. No one knows its zenith. Therefore the statement says it "can be secured but cannot be explained." (13/3b1–2)

Self Cultivation

XIX
The position of the mind in the body is analogous to that of the ruler [in the state]. The functioning of the nine apertures is analogous to the responsibilities of the officials.

When the mind rests in its Way,
The nine apertures will comply with natural guidelines.
When lusts and desires fill the mind to overflowing,
The eyes do not see colors, the ears do not hear sounds.
When the one above departs from the Way,
The ones below will be mistaken in their duties.
Therefore we say, "the techniques of the mind are to take no action
    and yet control the apertures." (13/1a5–8)

"The position of the mind in the body is analogous to that of the ruler [in the state]. The functioning of the nine apertures is analogous to the responsibilities of the officials."

The eyes and ears are the organs of seeing and hearing. When the mind does not interfere with the work of seeing and hearing, the organs will be able to fulfill their duties. When the mind has desires, things pass by and the eyes do not see them; sounds are there but the ears do not hear them. Therefore the statement says: "When the one above departs from the Way, the ones below will be mistaken in their duties." Therefore the statement calls the mind "ruler." (13/2a7–2b1)

XX
Empty out your desires and the numen will enter its abode.
If the abode is not thoroughly swept clean, the numen will not reside
    there. (13/1a11–12)

That which the sage directs is his [inner] concentration. Relinquish desire and
you[r body and breathing] will become aligned. When you are aligned you will
become tranquil. When you are tranquil you will become concentrated. When
you are concentrated you will become solitary. When you are solitary you will
become illumined. When you are illumined you will become numinous. The
numen is the most honored. Thus when the abode is not cleaned out, the
honored one will not dwell in it. Therefore the statement says, "if it is not
thoroughly swept clean, the numen will not reside there." (13/2b8–10)

XXI
Heaven is said to be empty,
Earth is said to be tranquil.
And so they do not waver.
Clean out its dwelling,
Open its doors,
Relinquish selfishness,
Avoid speaking.
Then the numinous light will be as if present.
When one is confused it (the mind) seems chaotic.
Still it and it will naturally become ordered.
Strength on its own cannot stand up everywhere;
Wisdom cannot plan for everything. (13/1b8–11)

The Way of Heaven is empty; the Way of Earth is tranquil. Empty, and so it
does not submit; tranquil, and so it does not alter. It does not alter and so it
does not err. Therefore, the statement says "they do not waver."
    "Clean out its dwelling, open its doors." Its "dwelling" refers to the mind.
The mind is the lodging place of wisdom. Therefore when the statement says
"the dwelling, clean it out," [it means] one must relinquish all personal preferences. The "doors" refers to the eyes and ears. They are the means by which
we see and hear. (13/3b8–9)

The Sage

XXII
The words of the Genuine are not measured and not partial.
They do not emerge from their mouths,
They are not visible on their countenances.

Among those people within the Four Seas, who can understand this
   principle? (13/1b7–9)

The words of the Genuine are effective. Not measured, their words are immediately responsive. Responsiveness is not something that one can deliberately establish. Therefore the statement says "not measured." Not partial, their
words are spontaneously adaptive. Adaptation is not something that one can
deliberately choose. Therefore the statement says "not partial." (13/3b2–4)

> XXIII
> Therefore Noble Persons are not enticed by likes
> Nor oppressed by dislikes.
> Calm and tranquil, they take no action,
> And they discard wisdom and precedent.
> Their responses are not contrived.
> Their movements are not deliberately chosen.
> The mistake here lies in intervening directly oneself.
> The fault here lies in altering and transforming things [instead of
>   adapting to them].
> Therefore Noble Persons who have the Way:
> At rest seem to be guileless,
> In response to things seem to fit together with them.
> This is the Way of stillness and adaptation. (13/2a3–7)

Most people are so burdened by their dislikes that they miss out on what they
like. They are so enticed by what they like that they forget what they dislike.
This is not the Way. Therefore the statement says "They are not enticed by
likes nor oppressed by dislikes." The Noble Person's dislikes do not fail to
adhere to natural guidelines. Their desires do not exceed what is essential to
them. Therefore the statement says "Calm and tranquil, Noble Persons take no
action, and they discard wisdom and precedent." Therefore this says that they
are empty and pure. "Their responses are not contrived, their movements are
not deliberately chosen." This says that they are adaptable. To be adaptable is
to relinquish the self and take other things as models. To respond only when
stimulated is not something contrived. To move according to natural guidelines
is not something you deliberately choose. "The mistake here lies in intervening
directly oneself. The fault lies in altering and transforming things." To intervene directly oneself is to not be empty. One is not empty and so one bumps
up against other things. One alters and transforms things and so one artificially
generates them. One artificially generates them and so there is chaos. Therefore
the Way esteems adaptation. Adaptation is to adapt to the talents [of others].
This speaks of how Noble Persons employ others. "Noble Persons at rest seem
to be guileless, in response to things seem to fit together with them." This
speaks of their fitting with the times. It is like the shadow's imaging the shape,

the echo's responding to the sound. Therefore, when things arrive they immediately respond. When things pass by, they just let them go. This says that they [always] return to being empty. (13/4a6–4b3)

HUAINANZI SELECTIONS

"GETTING TO THE SOURCE OF THE WAY" ("YUAN DAO")

I

Happiness and anger are aberrations of the Way.
Worry and sadness are lapses of inner power.
Likes and dislikes are excesses of the mind.
Lusts and desires are the fetters of one's nature.
In a human being:

> Great anger damages the yin.
> Great joy collapses the yang.
> Weak vital energy causes dumbness.
> Shock and fright bring about madness.
> When worry, sadness, and rage abound,
> Illnesses develop.
> When likes and dislikes abound,
> Misfortunes follow one another.

Thus

> When the mind does not worry or rejoice,
> This is the perfection of inner power.
> When it is absorbed and does not alter,
> This is the perfection of stillness.
> When lusts and desires do not fill it up,
> This is the perfection of emptiness.
> When there is nothing liked or disliked,
> This is the perfection of equanimity.
> When it is not confused by external things,
> This is the perfection of purity.

Those who are able to practice these five will be absorbed in the numinous light. Those who are absorbed in the numinous light are those who actualize what is within them. (1/12b6–13a2)

II

Now why is it:

> That people are able to see clearly and hear acutely,
> That the body is able to support weight
> And the hundred joints can bend and stretch,
> That one's discrimination can determine white from black,

Discern ugliness from beauty,
And perception can distinguish similarities and differences
And distinguish this from that?
Because the vital energy infuses these activities
And the numen directs them.
How do I know this is so?
If people's attention focuses on something and their numen is thus tied up in it, then even if they stumble over tree roots or bumps into tree limbs, they remain unaware of what has happened.

If you wave to them they cannot see you;
If you call to them they cannot hear you.

It is not that their eyes and ears have left them. So what is the reason that they cannot respond?
Because their numen has lost its hold.

So when it focuses on the small
It forgets the great;
When it focuses on the inner
It forgets the outer;
When it focuses on the upper
It forgets the lower;
When it focuses on the left
It forgets the right.

When there is nowhere [the vital energy] does not infuse,
There is nothing on which the numen does not focus.
Therefore those who value emptiness take the tip of an autumn hair as their abode. (1/17a1–6)

III
That which is tranquil from our birth
Is our heavenly nature.
Activity only after it is stimulated
Causes impairment of this nature.
When external things arrive and the numen responds,
This is the activity of perception.
When perception comes in contact with external things,
Preferences arise from that.
When preferences are formed,
Perception is enticed by externals,
One cannot return to the self,
And the natural guidelines are destroyed.
Thus those who penetrate the Way
Do not use the human to replace the heavenly.
They outwardly transform together with things
And inwardly do not lose their true state. (1/5a6–11)

"THE PRIMEVAL REALITY" ("CHUZHEN")

IV

    The nature of water is clear,
    But soil muddies it.
    The nature of human beings is calm and tranquil,
    But lusts and desires disrupt it.
What humanity receives from Heaven is:
    The relationship between the ears and eyes and sounds and colors,
    The relationship between the nose and mouth and tastes and fragrances,
    The relationship between the skin and flesh and cold and heat.
Their essentials are the same in everyone.
So why is it that some people attain the numinous light
While others are nothing more than fools?
It is because the ways in which they control them are different.
Hence
    The numen is the fount of knowledge.
    When the numen is clear, knowledge is illumined.
    Knowledge is the storehouse of the mind.
    When knowledge is impartial, the mind is balanced.
Human beings never mirror themselves in surging water,
They mirror themselves in still water,
Because it is tranquil.
No one sees their form in cast iron,
They see it in the burnished iron of a mirror,
Because its surface is even.
Only the even and tranquil
Can reflect the true nature of things.
When looked at from this viewpoint,
Utility depends on what has no use.
Therefore
    The Empty Chamber generates brightness
    And the lucky and auspicious will stop therein.
    So when the mirror is bright
    Dust cannot sully it.
    When the numen is clear
    Passions cannot disrupt it. (2/10a9–b4)

V

Stillness and quietude, placidity and tranquility,
Are the means by which we nourish our nature.
Harmony and serenity, emptiness and nothingness,
Are the means by which we nourish inner power.
When the external does not confuse the internal,

Then our nature will attain what is suitable to it.
When one's nature does not move from this harmony,
Then inner power secures its position.
To nourish the nature and thereby pass through one's generation,
To embrace inner power and thereby last out one's years,
Can be called "being able to embody the Way."
If you act in this manner,
The blood flowing through the arteries will not be stifled,
And the Five Viscera will not have a profusion of vital energy.
Bad and good fortune will not confound you,
And praise and blame cannot soil you. (2/11b8–12a1)

"INQUIRING WORDS" ("QUANYAN")

VI

The foundation of creating order [in the state]
Lies in making the people content.
The foundation of making the people content
Lies in giving them sufficient use [of their time for farming].
The foundation of giving them sufficient use
Lies in not stealing their time [for state matters].
The foundation of not stealing their time
Lies in restricting the state's demands on them.
The foundation of restricting the state's demands on them
Lies in limiting the desires [of the ruler].
The foundation of limiting the desires [of the ruler]
Lies in his returning to his innate nature.
The foundation of returning to one's nature
Lies in removing what fills the mind.
When one removes what fills the mind, one is empty.
When one is empty, one experiences equanimity.
Equanimity is the simplicity of the Way.
Emptiness is the abode of the Way.
Those who are able to be in possession of the empire
Certainly do not neglect their states.
Those who are able to be in possession of their states
Certainly do not lose their families.
Those who are able to regulate their families
Certainly do not neglect their persons.
Those who are able to cultivate their persons
Certainly do not forget their minds.
Those who are able to reach the source of their minds
Certainly do not impair their natures.
Those who are able to keep their natures whole

Certainly have no doubts about the Way.
Therefore [the Yellow Emperor's inner cultivation teacher] Guang
   Chengzi said:
Diligently guard what is within you;
Fully prevent it from being externalized.
Excessive knowledge is harmful.
Do not look! Do not listen!
Embrace the numen by being still
And the body will be naturally aligned.

There have never been people who were able to understand other things without first attaining it within themselves. Thus the *Classic of Changes* says: "Tie
it up in a bag. No blame. No praise." (14/2b4–11)

"THE NUMINOUS ESSENCE" ("JINGSHEN")

VII

Now the Way of Heaven and Earth is immense and grand, yet it must still
restrict its brilliance and conserve its numinous light.

The ears and eyes of people,
How can one expect them to toil for long periods without rest?
The numinous essence,
How can one expect it to course [through the body] for long periods
   without respite?

Therefore the blood and vital energy
Are the flowerings of humanity
And the Five Viscera [of energy flow through the body]
Are the essences of humanity.

Now if the blood and vital energy are concentrated within the Five Viscera
and do not flow out:

Then the chest and belly are replete
And lusts and desires are eliminated.
When the chest and belly are replete
And lusts and desires are eliminated
Then the ears and eyes are clear
And hearing and vision are acute.
When the ears and eyes are clear
And hearing and vision are acute,
We call this "illumination."

When the Five Viscera [and their associated emotions] can be assimilated by
the mind and their functioning is without error:

Then wandering attention will be done away with
And the circulation [of the vital energy] will not be awry.
When wandering attention is done away with
And the circulation [of the vital energy] is not awry,

Then the numinous essence is abundant
And the vital energy is not dissipated.
When the numinous essence is abundant
And the vital energy is not dissipated,
Then one is functioning according to natural guidelines.
When one functions according to natural guidelines,
One attains equanimity.
When one attains equanimity
One develops penetrating awareness.
When one develops penetrating awareness
One becomes numinous.
When one is numinous then:
      With vision there is nothing unseen,
      With hearing there is nothing unheard,
      And with actions there is nothing incomplete.
For this reason
Anxiety and worry cannot enter
And aberrant vital energy cannot seep in.
Thus
There are certain things that one seeks outside the Four Seas
Yet never encounters.
And others that one holds within the bodily frame
Yet never sees.
Thus
      The more you seek,
      The less you attain.
      The greater you see,
      The less you understand. (7/2a11–b10)

VIII
Now the sense apertures
Are the portals of the numinous essence
And the vital energy and attention
Are the servants of the Five Viscera (because they are affected by the
    emotions associated with the Viscera).
When the eyes and ears
Are enticed by the pleasures of sound and color,
Then the Five Viscera oscillate and are not stable.
When the Five Viscera oscillate and are not stable,
Then the blood and vital energy are agitated and not at rest.
When the blood and vital energy are agitated and not at rest,
Then the numinous essence courses out [through the eyes and ears] and is
    not preserved.

When the numinous essence courses out and is not preserved,
Then when either good fortune or misfortune arrives,
Although it be the size of hills and mountains,
You have no way to recognize it.
But if you make:

> Your ears and eyes totally clear and profoundly penetrating
> And you do not let them be enticed by external things;
> Your vital energy and attention empty, tranquil, still, and serene,
> And you eliminate lusts and desires;
> Your Five Viscera stable, reposed, replete, and full,
> And you do not let their vital energies leak out;
> Your numinous essence stay within your bodily frame,
> And you do not let it flow out:

Then you will be able to gaze before past generations
And to see beyond future events.
If you still think this an inadequate accomplishment, then how much less
worth doing is it to worry about good and bad fortune? Thus it is said:

> The farther you go,
> The less you know.

This says that the numinous essence cannot be allowed to be enticed by
external things.
Therefore:

> The five colors disrupt the eyes
> And cause them to be unclear;
> The five sounds confuse the ears
> And cause them to not be acute;
> The five tastes disrupt the mouth
> And cause it lose the ability to taste;
> Preferences confuse the mind
> And cause it to fly about [from one thing to the next].

These four things are how the people of this world commonly nourish their
vitality. However they are all human attachments. Thus it is said:

> Lusts and desires
> Dissipate a person's vital energy,
> And likes and dislikes
> Belabor a person's mind.

If you do not quickly eliminate them, then the attention and vital energy will
diminish daily. Now why is it that common people are not able to complete
the full course of their lives and along the way die prematurely by
execution?

> It is because they set too much store in living.
> If you can avoid making life your preoccupation
> You will be able to attain long life. (7/2b10–3b2)

IX

> Sadness and joy
> Are aberrations of the power,
> Pleasure and anger
> Are excesses of the Way,
> And likes and dislikes
> Are the fetters of the mind.

Thus it is said that [sages]:

> In life, act in accord with Heaven;
> In death, transform with other things;
> In tranquility, share the power of the yin;
> In activity, share the surge of the yang.

Their numinous essence, being calm and limitless,
Is not dissipated amidst external things.
And the world naturally submits to them.
Thus
The mind
Is the ruler of the physical form
And the numen
Is the treasure of the mind.
When the physical form
Toils without rest then it collapses;
When the vital essence
Is used unceasingly then it runs out.
Hence sages honor and esteem it
And do not dare to allow it to seep out.
Now the owner of the jade disk of Xiahou stores it in a box because it is
supremely precious. The preciousness of the numinous essence is not merely
that of the jade disk of Xiahou.
Hence sages:

> Based in Nothing respond to Something
> And invariably access the natural guidelines.
> Based in the Empty accept the Full
> And invariably fathom the nodal points.
> Calm and still, empty and tranquil,
> By this they fulfill their destiny.

Hence there is nothing from which they are too distant
And nothing with which they are too intimate.
Embracing inner power and blending with the harmonious,
They accord with Heaven.
They make the Way their boundary and inner power their neighbor.
They will not, to gain good fortune, take the first step.
They will not, to avoid misfortune, make the first move.

Their anima and animus rest in their dwelling,
And their numinous essence is preserved in its root.
Death and life do not alter their inner self.
Thus it is said that they are supremely numinous. (7/4b2–5a1)

X

Those we call the Genuine are people whose natures are united with the
Way. Therefore:
> They possess it but appear to have nothing,
> They are filled by it but appear to be empty.
They rest in this unity
And know not duality.
They concentrate on what is inside
And pay no attention to what is outside.
They illuminate the great simplicity
And, without acting, revert to the unhewn.
They embody the foundation and embrace the numen
And so roam freely through the turmoil of Heaven and Earth.
Untrammeled,
They ramble outside this dusty world
And wander amidst effortless activity.
Unfettered and unhindered,
They harbor no contrived cleverness in their minds.
Hence death and life are great indeed, but they do not alter them. Although
Heaven and Earth support and nourish, they take in nothing from them.
They discern the flawless and do not get mixed up with things. While seeing
the chaos of affairs, they are able to preserve their source.
Such beings as this:
Forget emotions
And cast aside perception.
Their mental attention is concentrated internally
And penetrate through to be a companion with the One.
At rest they know not what they are doing;
In motion they know not what they have done.
> Abruptly they come;
> Suddenly they go.
> Form like withered wood,
> Mind like dead ashes.
> They forget their Five Viscera,
> Throw off their physical frame,
> Know without studying,
> See without looking.
> They complete without acting

And they discern without ordering.
When stimulated they respond,
When pressed, they move,
When it is unavoidable, they go forth,
Like the brilliant glow of a flame,
Like the mimicry of a shadow.
Taking the Way as their guiding thread,
They await things and respond spontaneously to them.
Embracing the foundation of Great Purity, they accept nothing and things cannot disturb them. Vast and empty, they are tranquil and without worry.

Great swamps may catch fire,
But they cannot burn them.
Great rivers may freeze over,
But they cannot chill them.
Great thunder may shake the mountains,
But it cannot startle them.
Great storms may darken the Sun,
But they cannot harm them.

Hence
When they see precious jewels,
To them they are like gravel.
When they see the emperor's favorites,
To them they are like passing travelers.
When they see [the beauties] Mao Qiang and Xi Shi,
To them they are like clay statues.
They take life and death to be a single transformation
And the myriad things to be of a single class.
They merge their vital essence with the foundation of great purity
And roam freely beyond the boundless.
They do not [recklessly] expend their vital essence
Nor [thoughtlessly] use up their numinous [essence].
They tally with the jumbled unhewn
And stand amidst the supremely pure.

Hence, their sleep is without dreams.
Their wisdom is without traces.
Their anima does not sink.
Their animus does not soar.

They repeatedly return from end to beginning, and they do not know the start and the finish.
They peer into the dwelling of total darkness
And awaken to the lodging of total brightness.
They rest in the territory of the vast
And roam in the land of the boundless.

At rest, they have no contents.
In place they have no location.
In movement they have no form.
In stillness they have no body.
They are present yet seem to be absent.
They are alive yet seem to be dead.
Emerging from and entering the continuous,
They command ghosts and spirits.
Plunging into the fathomless,
They enter where nothing exists.
Because their dissimilar forms succeed each other,
They continually cycle from end to beginning,
And no one is able to categorize them.
This is how their numinous essence is able to ascend to the Way. This is the
roaming of the Genuine. (7/5a2–6a9)

9

Body Gods and Inner Vision: The Scripture
of the Yellow Court

Paul W. Kroll

The *Scripture of the Yellow Court,* or *Huangting jing,* is one of the cardinal scriptures of medieval Daoism. A text by this name is mentioned by Ge Hong (283–343), author of *He Who Embraces Simplicity* (*Baopuzi*) and collector of the occult traditions of South China, but that version—if it was indeed seen by Ge Hong— no longer exists. The *Scripture of the Yellow Court* that was known from the mid-fourth century on, and which became a fundamental and hugely popular text, shows clear signs of being influenced by or adapted to the new, Shangqing revelations (see chapters 11 and 12).

There are in fact two redactions of the *Scripture of the Yellow Court,* an "inner" (*nei*) scripture and an "outer" (*wai*) one. Both are composed in verse of heptasyllabic lines—the longer inner scripture consisting of 435 verses, divided into 36 stanzas, and the shorter outer scripture made up of a single run of 99 verses. Generally speaking, the inner scripture is a more difficult and grammatically troublesome text to read, perhaps bearing out the suggestion that "inner" connotes esoteric, as opposed to the "exoteric" teachings of the "outer" scripture. However, scholars are divided over the question of which version is primary—that is, whether the inner scripture represents an intricate elaboration of the outer scripture, or whether the latter is a summary in simpler language of the former.

In any event, the focus of the *Scripture of the Yellow Court* is on the corporeal divinities believed to reside in one's physical form and on the means by which they may be cultivated, so as to ensure the production within and ultimate escape from one's mortal frame of a refined and purified embryo, an etherealized self. Central to this goal is the practice of "inner vision," by which the adept is able to turn his gaze within and fix distinctly and sensibly the gods of his body, whose appearance and attributes are closely described in the scripture. This process of visualization or, to render the Chinese term literally, "actualization" (*cun*) further reveals that the indwelling spirits of one's body are identical with their counterparts in the macrocosm; indeed the somatic landscape is a perfect, complete microcosm.

Prominent among the body spirits are the Five Viscera—liver, heart, spleen, lungs, and kidneys—which are fundamentally involved with the traditional system of the Five Phases (*wuxing*) and thus coordinated symbolically with the five directions, five colors, five flavors, five sacred peaks, and so forth. It is in fact the spleen, symbolizing the center and known by the esoteric name "Yellow Court," that invests the scripture with its title. In addition to the viscera, each with its individual powers referred to in detail in the text, there is much allusion to the three "cinnabar-fields" (*dan tian*) situated in the brain, near the heart, and below the navel, which control the three major divisions of the body, and also to the two-tiered "nine palaces" (*jiu gong*) of the brain—all of these points with their own presiding spirits and complex of connections linking the body with the universe. Conduction and circulation of the vital breath through the somatic passages, along with the swallowing of saliva and channeling of other bodily humors—the one a yang action, the other a yin—are critical practices for the nourishing and harmonizing of these inner organs and spirits.

But the *Scripture of the Yellow Court* is less a manual than an aide-mémoire. The rhythmic gait of the verses, with jingling end-rhyme on every line (instead of on every other line, as in classical poetry), betokens the oral/aural nature of the text and its basically mnemonic function. It is to be recited in order to render one's body fit for meditation and ultimate etherealization. In one of the scripture's prefaces we are given instructions for the proper method of recitation, requiring the burning of incense, the ritual purging and purifying of oneself. Ten thousand recitals, we are told, will enable one to "see one's five viscera, one's entrails and stomach, and also to see the spectres and spirits of the whole world and put them in one's own service." The therapeutic powers of the scripture are such that if one can recite it when at the point of death, one will be made whole again.

The imagery of the *Scripture of the Yellow Court* is often puzzling, and sometimes seemingly incomprehensible, when considered literally. But the adept will have learned, through private training with his teacher, the true reference and secret significance of the lines—the reality behind the words. Thus, as with Laozi's *Classic on the Way and Its Power* (*Dao de jing*), that often cryptic scripture that stands at the head of the Daoist tradition, commentators occasionally differ radically in their interpretation of specific terms and lines. The *Scripture of the Yellow Court* is not, in this regard, a text for reading—it is a script pointing primarily beyond itself, to action.

The selection below features the first four stanzas of the inner scripture. The translation is as close as possible to the original and aims to suggest the metrical—sometimes mesmerizing—pulse of the verses. The prose paraphrase following each stanza then unpacks the meaning in plainer words, relying mainly on the explications offered by medieval commentators.

Further Readings

There is at present no English translation of either version of the *Scripture of the Yellow Court*. Studies in Western languages include Rolf Homann, *Die wichtigsten Korpergottheiten im Huang-t'ing ching* (Goppingen: Verlag Alfred Kümmerle, 1971); Isabelle Robinet, "The Book of the Yellow Court," in Robinet, *Taoist Meditation: The Mao Shan Tradition of Great Purity,* trans. Julian F. Pas and Norman J. Girardot (Albany: State University of New York Press, 1993); K. M. Schipper, *Concordance du Houang-t'ing ching nei-king et wai-king* (Paris: Ecole Française d'Extrême-Orient, 1975).

First Stanza

In the purple aurora of Highest Clarity, before the Resplendent One of the Void,
The Most High, Great Dao Lord of the Jade Source of Light,
Dwelling at ease in the Stamen-Pearl Palace, composed verses of seven words,
4   Dispersing and transforming the five shapes of being, permutating the myriad spirits:
This is deemed the *Yellow Court,* known as the *Inner Book.*
The triple reprise of a concinnate heart will set the embryo's transcendents dancing;
Glinting and luminous, the nine vital breaths emerge amidst the empyrean;
8   The young lads under the Divine Canopy will bring forth a purple haze.
This is known as the *Jade Writ,* which may be sifted to its essence—
Chant it over ten thousand times, and ascend to the Three Heavens;
The thousand calamities will thereby be dispelled, the hundred ailments healed;
12   You will not then shrink from the fell ravagings of tiger or of wolf,
And also thereby you will hold off age, your years extended forever.

First Stanza—Paraphrase

In the light of perpetual morning, in the Shangqing heaven, in the realm of the cosmocrat who puts all of space in order,

The great deity whose seat is in the ultimate illumination of dawn,
Who resides in a palace symbolic of perigynous jewels, wrote a poem
    in seven-word lines,
4   Having the power to affect all entities, from fish, birds, men, mammals,
    and invertebrates to the multitudinous gods.
That poem was this very text, the *Inner Scripture of the Yellow Court.*
Once the three "cinnabar fields" are brought into harmony through it,
    the spirits of one's immortal embryo will respond with delight,
And the pneumata of the Nine Heavens, conducted through the three
    "cinnabar fields," will shine forth from the chambers of one's brain,
8   As the deities of one's eyes, beneath the eyebrows' arch, emit a
    vaporous aura of supernatural purple.
This text, also called the *Jade Writ,* deserves the closest study,
For, after ten thousand recitations of it, one may be translated to the
    highest heavens,
Immune to earthly misfortune, impervious to disease,
12   Proof against attacks from savage beasts,
And able to enjoy perpetual life.

Second Stanza

Above there are ethereal souls, below is the junction's origin;
Left serves as lesser yang, the right as greatest yin;
Behind there is the Secret Door, before is the Gate of Life.
4   With emergent sun and retreating moon, exhale, inhale, actualizing
    them.
Where the Four Breaths are well blended, the arrayed mansions will be
    distinct;
Let the purple haze rise and fall, with the clouds of the Three
    Immaculates.
Irrigate and spray the Five Flowers, and plant the Numinous Root.
8   Let the channeled course of the Seven Liquors rush into the span of
    the hut;
Circulate the purple, embrace the yellow, that they enter the Cinnabar
    Field;
Make the Shrouded Room bright within, illuminating the Gate of Yang.

Second Stanza—Paraphrase

The spirits of the liver, lungs, and spleen are above, representing
    Heaven, as contrasted with the navel (or, alternatively, a spot three

inches below the navel), representing the underworld of matter and generation.

The left and right kidneys are yang and yin.

The Secret Door of the kidneys is at the back of one's body, while the Gate of Life, located below the navel (equivalent either to the lower cinnabar field or to the "junction's origin" where semen is stored), is in front.

4 Sun and moon, imaged in one's left and right eyes, respectively, are to be made sensibly present in concentrated visualization, so that they will shed their light on one's internal organs, while one conducts the breath carefully through the body.

Bringing together the pneumata of the four seasons in oneself will render distinct the astral lodgings and somatic dwellings of sun, moon, and Dipper.

As the purple vapor of the divinities of the eyes infuses one's body, it is joined by clouds of purple, yellow, and white, symbolic of the Primal Mistresses of the Three Immaculates—goddesses who preside over the three major divisions of the body and the twenty-four major corporeal divinities.

One should swallow the saliva that nourishes one's internal organs, especially the essential "flowers" of the five viscera, taking care to cultivate the "Numinous Root" of the tongue, which activates and gathers in the saliva.

8 The humoral juices of the the body's seven orifices are channeled throughout the body and into the bridge of the nose, the "hut" between the eyebrows.

The spreading purple vapor from the eyes and the rising yellow pneuma from the spleen are brought into the upper cinnabar field located three inches behind the sinciput,

While, below, the "Shrouded Room" of the kidneys is bathed in light, as is the Gate of Yang (the Gate of Life) in front.

Third Stanza

The mouth is the Jade Pool, the Officer of Greatest Accord.

Rinse with and gulp down the numinous liquor—calamities will not encroach;

One's body will engender a lighted florescence, breath redolent as orchid;

4 One turns back, extinguishes the hundred malignities—one's features refined in jade.

With practice and attention, cultivate this, climbing to the Palace of Ample Cold.

Not sleeping either day or night, you will achieve then full perfection;
When thunder sounds and lightning spurts, your spirits are placid,
   impassive.

Third Stanza—Paraphrase

The mouth is the reservoir of the jade liquor of saliva, controlling in
   this capacity the nourishing and harmonizing of the body's organs.
Drinking down the spiritually potent saliva and circulating it in
   prescribed fashion will enable you to avoid misfortune;
Your body will be lit from within like a luminous flower, and your
   breath will acquire a sweet fragrance;
4   All debilitating influences will be opposed, and your skin will become
      pure as snow, white as jade.
Through repeated exercises you will become expert in this practice and
   be able to ascend to the celestial palace where the white moon itself
   is bathed when at apogee, at the winter solstice.
Unstinting concentration will lead to complete spiritual realization,
Such that your corporeal spirits will remain serenely fixed when
   confronted by any outer startlements.

Fourth Stanza

The person within the Yellow Court wears a polychrome-damask
   jacket,
A volant skirt of purple flowering, in gossamer of cloudy vapors,
Vermilion and azure, with green withes, numinous boughs of halcyon-
   blue.
4   With the jade cotter of the Seven Panicles, shut tight the two door-
      leaves;
Let the golden bar of the layered panels keep snug the door-post and
   catch.
The shrouded barrier of the murky freshets will be lofty, tall and
   towering;
In the midst of the Three Fields, essence and breath will become more
   subtle.
8   The Delicate Girl, winsome but withdrawn, screens the empyrean's
      radiance;
The tiered hall, shiningly iridescent, illumines the Eight Daunters.
From the celestial court to the earthly barrier, arrayed be the axes and
   bills;
With the numinous terrace hardy and firm, forever one will not
   weaken.

Fourth Stanza—Paraphrase

The "Mother of the Dao," one of the spleen's indwelling divinities, is
    clothed in a rich coat with the symbolic colors of all Five Viscera;
Her buoyant skirt, made of the silky gauze of cloud-breaths, is
    decorated in the purple hues of the deepest heavens and the celestial
    pole,
With tints of red, green, and blue, in sylvan designs, embellishing her
    other garments.
4   One must keep one's gaze focused within, concentrating on the interior
    gods, oblivious of the outside world, letting nothing escape through
    the doors of one's eyes, turning the key of one's seven orifices.
Barring the exits at all bodily levels, keeping the portals shut fast.
Then the shrouded barrier of the kidneys, source of bodily juices, will
    grow in strength;
Elemental essence and vital breath will become rarefied, less carnal,
    within the three "cinnabar fields."
8   The shy divinity of the ears turns away from the brilliant lights of the
    heavens,
While the layered chamber of the throat—passageway for the saliva—
    now gleams with a splendor that shines out to the divinities of the
    eight directions.
All the inner spirits are stalwart as arrayed weapons, from the celestial
    hall between the eyebrows to the earthly barrier of the feet,
And the sacred estrade of the heart will prove an everlastingly
    impregnable structure.

—10—

An Early Poem of Mystical Excursion

Paul W. Kroll

Many ancient and medieval Daoist texts took the form of poetry—as in large portions of the *Laozi*—or lyrical prose—as in the *Zhuangzi*. The earliest substantial poem to be constructed on identifiably Daoist themes was "Far Roaming" ("Yuan-you"), included in the famous anthology of Yangzi-area songs known as the *Lyrics of Chu (Chuci)*, which contains poems dating from the early third century B.C.E. to the early second century C.E. as edited by the Han dynasty scholar Wang Yi (d. ca. 158). "Far Roaming," in 178 lines, is modeled on the first and most famous poem of the *Chuci*, "Encountering Sorrow" ("Li sao") by the exiled Chu courtier Qu Yuan (trad. dates 343–290 B.C.E.). However, whereas Qu Yuan's versified flight from the corrupt world and fantastic celestial journey revolves ultimately around politics and ends in despair and disillusionment, the mystical progress of the "Far Roaming" poet terminates—following a peregrination to the four corners of the heavens and the territories of various mythical divinities—in triumphant arrival at the domain of "Tai chu," that is, "Grand Antecedence," the primordial realm of space and time existent before the differentiation of physical phenomena. It thus celebrates the return to that original state of "formlessness" so often yearned for in Daoist writings; but it does so through an exhaustive, airborne passage through the cosmos.

Much of the terminology of the poem, as will be apparent in the notes appended to this translation, draws on earlier Daoist notions of self-cultivation. In turn, some of the phrasings in "Far Roaming" later influenced the development and naming of certain medieval Daoist practices—just as the poem itself may be viewed as the forerunner of the *you xian* or "Roaming to Transcendence" poems so well known in Six Dynasties and Tang literature.

Traditional Chinese scholarship credits Qu Yuan with the authorship of "Far Roaming" (as, indeed, most of the *Chuci* poems), but this is clearly impossible. Numerous verbal similarities with Sima Xiangru's (179–117 B.C.E.) "Rhapsody on the Great Man" ("Daren fu") have long been recognized, prompting some scholars to see it as either an early draft or a later revision of that composition. But this too is doubtful; the author of "Far Roaming," whose name we are unlikely ever to know, was far more conversant with Han dynasty Daoist concepts and techniques than is evident in any of Sima Xiangru's extant writings. A plausible speculation is that the author may have been one of the many *littérateurs* who gathered during the 130s B.C.E. at the court of Liu An, the prince of Huainan, responsible for the compilation of the Daoist classic *Huainanzi* as well as an early edition of some of the poems later to be collected by Wang Yi as the *Chuci*.

Until now the standard English translation of the "Far Roaming," and the entire *Chuci*, was that published in 1959 by David Hawkes (*Ch'u Tz'u: The Songs of the South*; slightly revised in 1985 as *The Songs of the South: An Anthology of Ancient Chinese Poems by Qu Yuan and Other Poets*). However, Hawkes's rendering, fluent as it is, is often a mere paraphrase of the text or, worse, a translation of the commentary instead of the text, thus obscuring much of the poem's expressive imagery and blunting the verbal and conceptual exactness of the piece that is so crucial for students of religion and literature. The present translation aims to uncover more of the poem's original wording and implications, while still approximating the rhythmical force of the original Chinese. The thirteen sections into which I have divided the poem reflect major shifts of topic or action (there are no such divisions indicated in the Chinese text); different indentations mirror the varying line-lengths of the original.

Further Reading

The influence of the *Chuci* on Daoist poetry has yet to be satisfactorily explored. There are some preliminary observations in Isabelle Robinet, *Histoire du taoïsme, des origines au XIVᵉ siècle* (Paris: Cerf, 1991), pp. 42–43, "*Les Chuci* et les randonnées extatiques."

The translation of *Chuci* by David Hawkes, mentioned above, is now outdated in many respects.

Far Roaming

I

Grieving at the pressing constraints of the age's vulgarity—
I wish to rise up lightly, to roam far off.
For this body frail and lowly, there is no way to do so—
4   How may I compel it to mount up, to be borne above?

Encountering squalor and filth on sinking into the mire—
Alone, knotted in gloom, with whom can I talk?

At night, fitful and restive, I can get no sleep—
8   My soul afluster and agitated, even until dawnglow.

If Heaven and Earth verily be inexhaustible,
Pity the prolonged toils, then, of human life.
      Those who have gone, I cannot catch up to—
12   And those who are to come, I hear nothing of.

With steps halting, hesitant, my longings are far-stretched—
In despair, fazed and fretted, musings are made to veer.
Dazed and distracted in thought, adrift and unsettled—
16   Saddened and sore at heart, I grieve all the more.

II
Spirit now flicks forth in a flash, not to turn back again—
While physical form, withered and dessicate, will remain alone.
What is inward I examine, indeed, with discipline most firm—
20   And seek that which is the source of True Vitality.

Silently, by attenuation and stillness, I find pleasure and
      contentment—
In tranquility doing nothing, become self-possessed.
Having heard of Red Pine's clearing away the worldly dust—
24   I wish to receive the influence of the example he bequeathed.

Esteeming the ideal Potency of the Realized persons—
I admire their ascent to transcendence in ages past.
Sharing in transformation, they departed, no more to be seen—
28   Their name and renown, made evident, increases every day.

I wondered at Fu Yue's assumption into the constellated stars—
      And envied Han Zhong's attaining to unity.
      With forms spruce and smug, they seeped into the distance—
32   Disengaging from the human throng, withdrawing and evading.

Adapting to Vitality's permutations, then they even rose up—
      As spirits darting away of a sudden, or spectres uncanny.
      At times it somewhat seems that they are sighted afar—
36   Quintessences candidly shining in their comings and goings.

Severed from the fumes and grime, they made good their faults—
Never turning back in the end to their seats of old.
Eluding the host of troubles, they were not fainthearted—
40   And none in the world knew whither they had gone.

III
I fear the chronic sequences of Heaven's seasons—
As the radiant Geist travels westward in a gleam.

When the faint frost descends, saturating all below—
44   I sorrow for the early blighting of the scented plants.
  Would that I might stroll astray, footloose and fancy-free—
  But ever, through the years, I am without accomplishment.
Together with whom may I share these scents left behind?—
48   Facing into the wind at morning, I unloose my feelings.
      Gaoyang is now remote, far away—
      How shall I take to his route?

    IV
    Springs and autumns pass speedily, they do not tarry—
52 Why should I remain in these my olden haunts?
    Xuanyuan may not be caught up and held on to—
I shall follow, then, Wang Qiao for my pleasure and amusement;
Sup on the Six Pneumas and quaff the cold-night damps—
56 Rinse my mouth with True Solarity and imbibe the aurora of dawn;
    Conserve the limpid clarity of the divine and illuminated—
As Essence and Vitality enter in, and pollution and filth are expelled.

    I comply with the triumphal wind, to follow its roamings—
60   And arrive at Nanchao in but a single breathing.
  On seeing the Royal Scion, I sojourned there with him—
  To study the consonant Power of Unifying Vitality.

    He said, "The Dao may be received—
64   It may not be taught.
    Its smallness admits of no inward—
    Its greatness admits of no bounds.
    Let your soul not be confounded—
68   And *That* shall be just as it is.
    Unify your vitality, make your spirit acute—
    Preserve it even in the midst of the night.
    Be attenuate, to abide things thereby—
72   Let the priority be Doing Nothing.
    All the sorts are thus brought to completion—
    This is the Gateway of Power."

    V
    When I had heard the Most Esteemed One, I then proceeded—
76   Oblivious of whither I would be going.
  I continued on to the Feathered Persons at the Hill of Cinnabar—
  Loitered in the long-standing land where death is not;
  At dawn washed my hair in the Vale of Sunlight—
80 And at dusk dried myself in the realm of Ninefold Solarity;
  I sucked in the tenuous liquor of the Flying Springs—

Took to heart the floriate blooms of gorgeous gemstones.
The suffusion of a jade sheen therewith imbued my features—
84   My essence, becoming whole and unmixed, now took on strength.
As body, weakening and wasting, turned tender and listless—
Spirit, growing fine and subtle, was released, unrestrained.

VI
Honoring the fiery Potency of the lands to the south—
88   I thought lovely the brumal burgeoning of cinnamon trees.
The mountains, drear and cheerless, held no beasts—
The wilds, still and null, appeared to have no people.
Settling my troubled sentient-soul, to ascend the auroras—
92   I gather up a floating cloud, and journey above.

I commanded Heaven's Warder that he open the barrier—
Pushing back the portal's folds, he gazed upon me.
I summoned Feng Long, sent him ahead as Way-shower—
96   Inquired where was the seat of Grand Tenuity;
I perched on the layered *yang*, and entered the Thearch's palace—
Advanced to the Conceiver of Weeks, and observed the City of Clarity.
At dawn I loosed the skids at the Court of Grand Observances—
100 And at dusk looked out from over Mount Wuweilü.

VII
I marshalled my carriages, a myriad in number—
Massed and amply adrift, they raced on together.
Directing the flowing fluency of the eight dragons—
104 I carried along the rippling flutter of the cloud banners.

I set up the motley flag of the virile rainbow—
All five colors loosely mixed, in dazzling coruscation.
The shaft-horses hunched and twisted, stooping and rearing—
108 The trace-horses swerved and stretched, peremptory in proudness.

Riding in intricate tangle, with riotous welter—
Our company sprawled widely, moving en masse.
Holding the reins myself and wielding the whip—
112 I led us onward to visit Gou Mang.

VIII
Then, passing on from Greatest Radiance, we turned toward the
    right—
And I sent Fei Lian in front, to open the route.
With the sun's force beginning to brighten the unlit spots—
116 I surmounted heaven and earth by the straightest passage.

The Patrarch of the Wind acted as forerunner for me—
As the fumes and grime withdrew, all was cool and clear.
Phoenixes winged their way, taking our banners forward—
120   And I came then to Ru Shou, in Xi Huang's realm.

IX
I grasped a sweeper-star to use as my ensign—
Hefted the Dipper's handle to use for my standard.
Separating in scattered dispersal, we ascended and descended—
124   And wandered then the coursing waves of a besetting fog.

At an hour eclipsed and clouded, dull in its duskiness—
I summoned the Dark Warrior for a hastening escort.
I put Wen Chang behind, to take the retinue in charge—
128   To group and dispose the host of spirits, with wheel-hub next to
        wheel-hub.

The road grew long and longer, as it stretched into the distance—
I slowed and slackened our pace, edging higher up.
On the left the Rain Master was bid to attend me on the path—
132   To the right the Lord of Thunder served as my paladin.

X
Wanting to pass beyond the world, thoughtless of returning—
Indulging my mind's wish, I was poised high to rise.
Inwardly joyed and joyful, myself well-content—
136   For a while's delight and diversion, I would take my own pleasure.

I traversed the clouds in the blue, roaming in smoothest flow—
Of a sudden glanced down, and discerned my homeland of old.
My coachman grew wistful, my own heart was grieved—
140   The flank horses looked back and would not go on.

Thinking on olden friends and times, pictured in imagination—
I sighed long and greatly, then wiped the tears aside.
Gliding with effortless ease, I was rising far-removed—
144   But I curbed my will a while and slackened the pace.

XI
Pointed toward the Daemon of Fire, racing straight ahead—
Now I shall fare onward to the Mount of Uncertainties in the
        south.
Scanning the indistinct maze of the land beyond the limits—
148   Awash in shapeless seemingness, I am borne along.

But, as Zhu Rong admonished me, I turned the yoke about—
Then passed instructions to a *luan* bird to invite Consort Fu.
I bid the Numen of the Xiang to play upon her cithern—
152   And commanded Hai Ruo to dance with Ping Yi.

The "All-Encompassing Pool" was set forth, "Receiving the Clouds"
    performed—
The Two Maidens orchestrated the songs of the Ninefold
    Hymnody.
A dark wyverne and a wriggling fay emerged together and
    advanced—
156   Their forms coiling and curling, writhing and winding round.

The feminine sunbow curved and vaulted, arching all the more—
Luan birds wafted loftily, hovering in flight.
The strains of music spread everywhere, boundless, endless—
160   Upon which I then rushed away, in aimless meander.

XII
Now I unreined my team's pace, raced on in full gallop—
Asunder to the farthest periphery, at the Gate of Cold.
I outran the fierce wind, to the Fount of Clarity—
164   And followed Zhuan Xu to the layered ice.

Passing on from Dark Tenebrity by way of a swerving route—
I mounted the interspaced Ties, and looked back round.
I summoned Qian Ying, to let himself be seen—
168   Going before, he made the road level for me.

XIII
    Now I ranged and roamed the Four Wastes—
    Sweeping in circuit to the Six Silences.
    I ascended even to the shattering cracks—
172   Descended to view the Great Strath.

In the sheer steepness below, Earth was no more—
In unending infinity above, Heaven was no more.
As I beheld the flickering instant, there was nothing to be seen—
176   Giving ear to the humming hush, there was nothing to be heard.
Gone beyond Doing Nothing, and into utmost Purity—
Sharing in the Grand Antecedence, I now became its neighbor.

Notes

Line 8: "Soul" is *hun*, literally "cloud-soul"—i.e., the ethereal, heaven-aspiring soul, as distinct from
the carnal or sentient-soul, *po*, earth-bound and heavy.

Line 17: "Spirit" is *shen,* the nonphysical, actualizing force that causes bodily functions to operate and allows for interaction with Nature and other beings.

Line 20: "True Vitality" is *zhengqi,* the inspiriting pneuma or breath whose presence maintains life in the vital fusion of soul, spirit, and body.

Line 21: "Attenuation and stillness" are qualities of *wuwei,* "doing nothing," in the following line—the nonpurposive or, better, naturally centered mindfulness so often talked of in the *Laozi* and other Daoist texts. Cf. *Zhuangzi,* chap. 13: "With attenuation and stillness one reaches out to Heaven and Earth, has complete access to the Myriad Things."

Line 23: Red Pine (Chi Song), elsewhere Master Red Pine (Chi Song Zi), according to legend a "rain-master" in the time of the culture-hero Shen Nong, was one of the most often invoked "transcendents" (*xian*) in Han times.

Line 25: "Potency" is *de,* inner power or spiritually radiating force (often translated, with etymological correctness but all the wrong connotations, as "Virtue"). The "Realized persons" (*zhenren;* sometimes translated "Perfected" or "Genuine") are those who have sloughed off all remnants of their corporeal state and perfected their spiritual destiny.

Line 29: According to tradition, Fu Yue became minister to King Wu Ding of the Shang dynasty in the late fourteenth century B.C., after appearing to the latter in a dream. One legend, referred to in *Zhuangzi,* chap. 6, has Fu Yue taking a postmortem place among the stars, where he can be seen in sidereal form "astride Winnower and Tail" (i.e., constellations in our Scorpio and Sagittarius).

Line 30: Han Zhong is known as a man from the state of Qi in the Warring States period, said to have consumed a gleaning of herbal drugs after his king refused to take them; he thereby became a transcendent, "attaining to unity" (the phrase is from *Zhuangzi,* chap. 6, and *Laozi,* chap. 39). In medieval times Han Zhong's name was attached to a formula for a cinnabar elixir.

Line 42: The "radiant Geist" (*yao ling*) is the sun.

Line 49: Gaoyang is an appellation of Zhuan Xu, second of the five legendary "thearchs" or emperors (*di*) of antiquity, who was able to bring the whole world under his control by, among other methods, "channeling his pneuma, thereby to transform [the people] in his teachings" (*zhiqi yi jiaohua*).

Line 53: Xuanyuan is a designation of Huangdi, the Yellow Emperor, first of the five great monarchs of early times and, for Daoists, a paragon of enlightened rule.

Line 54: Wang Qiao (sometimes Wangzi Qiao) was, along with Master Red Pine with whom he is often paired, one of the most familiar transcendents in Han literature. Royal scion (see line 61) of the Chunqiu era state of Jin, Wang Qiao reputedly ascended on high on the back of a crane, after mastering the techniques of spiritual perfection. In the following lines he becomes the poet's teacher.

Lines 55–56: The four extraordinary actions of these lines, the last of which was even developed as a detailed practice in medieval Daoism, indicate the poet's new, rarefied diet, which will conduce to shedding the carnal husk of his physical body in lines 83–86.

Line 58: "Essence and Vitality" (*jing* and *qi,* respectively) or, more literally, "seminal fluid and breath," now increase in health and fullness, driving out the seeds of corporeal corruption.

Line 59: The "triumphal wind" (*kai feng*) is a southerly wind that carries the poet to Nanchao, near the Lu River in present-day Anhui, the area in which was located Mount Jinting, Wangzi Qiao's sacred domain in Daoist geography.

Lines 63–74: Wang Qiao's teaching is accomplished in cryptic, seemingly paradoxical couplets, reminiscent of the *Laozi*—on which text several of the lines are indeed based.

Lines 75–86: Following his encounter with Wang Qiao, the poet starts off on his unbounded, seemingly free-blown, tour of Earth and the heavens. In this section of the poem he visits places from early mythology—the Hill of Cinnabar (Danqiu) in the south with its immortal, angelic denizens (akin to *xian*), the Vale of Sunlight (Yang gu) near where the sun rises beyond the eastern ocean, Ninefold Solarity (Jiuyang) where the sun sets, and the Flying Springs (Feiquan) of Kunlun, the cosmic mountain in the west. Essence and spirit become infused with glowing incorruptibility and his body slips away.

Lines 87–92: As a native of the south, the poet appreciates the sun-stained lands beyond the Yangzi, but now their barrenness upsets him and he wishes to rise away to the heavens, to put down finally his carnal- or sentient-soul (the phrase *zai ying po*, beginning line 91, is taken from a famous passage in *Laozi*, chap. 10).

Lines 93–94: The poet is given free access to the celestial realms. This is a conscious, sharp contrast with a similar passage in the "Li sao," where Qu Yuan is turned away from the gates of Heaven; there, instead of "pushing back the portal's folds," the porter simply "leans upon" them, refusing to open them.

Line 95: Feng Long is a god of the clouds and thunder.

Line 96: Grand Tenuity (Taiwei) is a constellation on the ecliptic, between our Virgo and Leo, representing the celestial thearch's southern palace.

Line 98: Conceiver of Weeks (Xunshi) and City of Clarity (Qingdu) are starry seats of the gods, as is the next line's Court of Grand Observances (Taiyi).

Line 100: Wuweilù is identified as a "jade mountain in the Eastern Quarter." Some commentators read a different Weilù here, referring to the great gulf far beyond the Eastern Sea into which all the world's waters are said to drain. Either interpretation is fitting.

Lines 112–113: Gou Mang is the attendant spirit of the east and springtime; Tai Hao (the next line's "Greatest Radiance") is that direction's and season's tutelary spirit. These names, as those of other gods in the poem, are also toponymic of the divinities' domains.

Line 113: After visiting the east, the poet intends to journey to the west—"turning to the right" means turning westward in the Chinese south-focused orientation.

Line 114: Fei Lian is the traditional "Patrarch of the Wind" (Feng bo, line 117).

Line 120: Ru Shou is the attendant spirit of the west and autumn. Xi Huang is the presiding thearch of that direction.

Line 121: A "sweeper-star" (or "broom-star") is a perihelial comet. Wielding comet and grasping the Dipper (most important of all constellations to the Daoists), the poet is comfortable in this cosmic environment.

Line 125: With darkness coming on in the west, the poet turns northward, commanding the emblematic symbol of the north (the "Dark Warrior," Xuan Wu) to escort him.

Line 127: Wen Chang is one of the important northern constellations, made up of six stars located in front of the Dipper's bowl.

Lines 133–144: Having now quartered the heavens, the poet wishes to "pass beyond the world." In the midst of his heavenly ramble, he catches sight of his old home below, which saddens him momentarily. But he shakes off his earth-bound memories, staying above mundane ties. This is direct counterpoint to the close of the "Li sao," where Qu Yuan is unable to go any farther on his spirit-journey when he glimpses his old home and his thoughts are suddenly recaptured by human concerns.

Line 145: The poet chooses to fare south again. The "Daemon of Fire" (Yan shen) is the God of Fire (Yan Di), tutelary thearch of the south and summer.

Line 146: The Mount of Uncertainties (Yi Shan, more normally Jiuyi Shan, "Mount of Nine Uncertainties"), in present-day Hunan, was said to be the burial place of the legendary sage-king Shun.

Line 149: Zhu Rong is the attendant spirit of the south, paired with the thearch Yan Di (line 145). He apparently warns the poet back, so as not simply to make again the same directional circuit he has already traversed.

Line 150: In the rest of this section the poet amuses himself by calling forth various divinities to enjoy a musical interlude with him. The *luan* bird is a phoenix of the second rank, sometimes translated as "simurgh." Consort Fu (Fu fei) is the goddess of the Luo River; in the "Li sao" she proved fickle and untrustworthy when Qu Yuan met her, but our poet has better luck.

Line 151: The Numen of the Xiang (Xiang ling) is the goddess of the Xiang River.

Line 152: Hai Ruo is the god of the North Sea; Ping Yi is the patrarch of the Yellow River.

Line 153: The music of the "All-Encompassing Pool" ("Xianchi") is traditionally identified with the sage-king Yao, that called "Receiving the Clouds" ("Cheng yun") with the Yellow Emperor.

Line 154: The "Two Maidens" are Yao's daughters, Ehuang and Nüying, wives to Shun. The music they perform, the "Ninefold Hymnody" ("Jiu shao"), is the canonical music of Shun.

Line 162: The Gate of Cold (Hanmen) is the gateway of the extreme north, wherein lies the Fount of Clarity (Qingyuan).

Line 164: Zhuan Xu, whom the poet lamented in line 49 he could not follow, is here made a companion, appearing in his symbolic role as tutelary thearch of the north and winter.

Line 165: Dark Tenebrity (Xuan ming) is the attendant spirit of the north—and the realm itself.

Line 166: The "interspaced Ties" (jian wei) are the mainbraces, usually numbering four or eight, that hold in place the network of the heavens.

Line 167: Qian Ying is a rather mysterious and rarely referred to figure, identified as a creator-spirit. The semantic content of the name, "Dusky Plenitude," points to his productive nature and association with the north.

Line 169: The Four Wastes are the barren zones at the utter extremes of the four directions. From here to the end of the poem, the poet moves out into abstract space and time.

Line 170: The Six Silences are the still, lifeless voids at the edges of the four directions plus those of height and depth—i.e., the "Four Wastes" made three-dimensional.

Line 171: The "shattering cracks" are the rifts in the sky-dome whence lightning flashes.

Line 172: The "Great Strath" (Da huo) is the bottomless gulf beyond the Eastern Sea into which all the world's waters ultimately pour.

Lines 177–178: The poet passes on beyond even such concepts as "Doing Nothing" (wuwei) and "utmost Purity" (zhiqing), into the primordial space-time continuum of Grand Antecedence (Tai chu), thus returning to the very origin of being.

—— 11 ——

Declarations of the Perfected

Stephen Bokenkamp

In the late fourth century C.E. a new Daoist movement emerged to redefine and eventually overshadow the main religious Daoist organization of the time, which was known as "the Way of the Celestial Masters." The Way of the Celestial Masters had begun in the second century in what is now Sichuan Province with revelations presented by the deified Laozi to Zhang Daoling. For some sixty years, a period that coincided with the decline of the central Han ruling house, the Celestial Masters existed as a developing theocratic kingdom, though one severely limited in size and influence. After 215 C.E., when Zhang Daoling's grandson, then head of the organization, swore his allegiance to a new claimant to the imperial throne of the Central Kingdom, the religion began its spread out of the Sichuan basin and throughout North China. After 316 C.E., when the capital Chang'an fell to "barbarian" invaders, Celestial Master Daoism moved south of the Yangzi River in force with the waves of northern immigrants who came to occupy the new capital in present-day Nanjing.

This brief history of the Celestial Masters is necessary to understand the emergence of the new Daoist movement we will consider here, for the new way was in large part the result of social upheavals resulting from the emigration described above. For the émigré northerners not only established their old administrative units in the south, supplanting the southern aristocracy, they also imposed upon the southerners their social mores, including Celestial Master Daoism. In fact, Daoism now became perhaps even more important than it had been in the northern homeland, for the émigrés found it desirable to suppress southern ecstatic religion and cultic practices that might provide a focal point for organized resistance. For this purpose, Celestial Master Daoism, with its animus toward "profane gods," proved the ideal weapon.

The southern response to this infringement was a "new" Daoism, claiming access to yet higher heavens and more exalted deities than those known to the Celestial Masters, while at the same time incorporating much Celestial Master belief. This response began quietly. During the years 364 to 370, Yang Xi, a medium employed by a southern gentry family, began to receive visits from a group of deities descended from the Heaven of Highest Clarity (Shangqing). In addition to instructing him in ways more advanced than those known to the Celestial Masters, these deities ministered to the spiritual needs of the southern family that Yang served, answering such questions as: "What is the fate of my ancestors in the spirit world?" "Which deities are to be trusted?" "What must I do to better both my worldly and my posthumous destiny?" Before long, other aristocratic families came to address their own questions to Yang.

Thanks to Yang's literary skill and to the satisfying answers he provided, a corpus of the poetic and prose transcripts of his visions and many of the scriptures he received from the deities came to be treasured by a group of the newly "marginalized" southern families. This scriptural legacy in fact eventually served its purpose, integrating a number of these gentry families into the higher strata of society once again and winning over the former northerners. Among the beneficiaries was Tao Hongjing (452–536), a member of a prominent southern lineage who came to serve the emperor as spiritual master and scholar. It was Tao who collected the fragments of Yang Xi's writings into the *Declarations of the Perfected* (*Zhengao*), upon which the following translation is based.

The "Perfected" or "True Ones" (*zhenren*) of the title refers to the class of deity that appeared to Yang. These deities, of the Heaven of Highest Clarity, distinguished themselves sharply from the Transcendents (*xian*, a term sometimes erroneously translated "immortal" though, as Yang Xi's visitors made clear, all such beings would eventually perish) of earlier Daoism. The term *zhenren*, which finds its source in the *Zhuangzi* and other texts, denotes that these are fully realized beings, possessed of incorruptible and immortal bodies, while the Transcendents were held to populate lower heavens or even inaccessible mountain peaks. Some of the Transcendents have, as the Perfected are fond of pronouncing, "not even achieved escape from death." A large number of the Perfected, on the other hand, far from having to worry about death, had never been human. These Perfected were stellar deities or perhaps female inhabitants of the mythical Kunlun Mountain in the west, where they served in the court of the Queen Mother. Other Perfected had once been human. Their careers are carefully mapped out in the text for the edification of those who might aspire to this status.

One sign of the elevated status of the Perfected is that, unlike the Transcendents of earlier scripture, these beings might not normally come into physical contact with the mundane world, even to the slight extent of handing on a writing or charm. In a portion of the text preceding that translated below, Yang is told that the deities who descend to him may not express themselves in debased human writing. He is thus to act as an intermediary, writing out their words in his own excellent calligraphy. At the same time, the Perfected women are particularly careful that he transcribes their words correctly. After each transmission they look over what he has written and then "present" it to him as if they had written it themselves.

The section of the *Declarations* translated below is valuable in that it provides insights into Yang Xi's adaptation of both the southern shamanic tradition and Celestial Master belief. It contains Yang Xi's record of his own betrothal and "marriage" to one of the celestial Perfected, the Consort An, who traces her lineage to the mythical Kunlun Mountain. It is thus a "spirit-marriage" reminiscent of those recorded in the poems of the *Lyrics of Chu* (*Chuci*) (see chapter 10 in this volume) where shamans, both male and female, describe their meetings, celestial travels, and intercourse with nature spirits and recount their longings once the spirit has gone.

At the same time, the passage is an explicit renunciation of the sexual rites of marriage between human partners performed by the Celestial Masters of Yang's day. The Celestial Master rite, called here "the Way of the Yellow and the Red" (both to represent the female and male who were conjoined and as a description of the books containing this method, which were written in red on paper with yellow borders), featured a method of sexual intercourse involving various massages and *coitus reservatus* to preserve the vital essences of both the male and the female. More than this, though, the rites of the Yellow and the Red were meant to join the pneumas, or "breaths," of the protective spirits inhabiting the bodies of the two adepts into a perfect whole. Thus, the initial sexual act of an initiated couple was to be performed ritually, with the elders present, to ensure that the union would not drain the bodily spirits and vital essences of the two participants.

The Shangqing "spirit-marriage" in which Yang Xi is invited to participate also involves the merging of corporeal spirits, but, as his mate is celestial, all traces of the human sexual act are absent. The emphasis that the Perfected who arrange this union repeatedly place on this fact testifies to the importance of such visionary and meditational experiences in the Shangqing texts. We might compare Yang's vision of union with the divine to the ecstatic visions of St. Teresa, St. Bernard, and other Christian mystics, for, while human sexual congress is specifically denied, Yang's poetic imagery contains more of the erotic than even explicit descriptions of the Celestial Master marriage rite. At the same time, this restructuring of the Way of the Yellow and the Red represents for Daoism the first step toward a celibate priesthood.

While the Celestial Masters urged abstention from sex only after one's reproductive duties had been fulfilled, the Shangqing deities warn against any depletion of the body's vital essences. Yang Xi, in the passage translated here, is explicitly informed that his spirit-marriage is to allay the Perfected's "worries that [he] will injure or deplete [his] spiritual forces." Later Daoists would see celibacy as a necessary precondition to the process of perfecting the body. For some later traditions, one could not conduct the highest Daoist rites without such preparation.

The sort of spiritual union that Yang envisions is distinguished by the name "mating of the effulgent spirits" (*oujing*) rather than the Celestial Master "joining of the pneumas" (*heqi*). The "breaths" or "pneumas" (*qi*) of the latter term refer to the vital emanations of the two adepts' corporeal spirits. These spirits were believed to be formed of remnants of the single "primal pneuma" (*yuanqi*) that emerged from the Dao at creation to vivify all things. The Shangqing term is more explicit, since each human being was potentially possessed of twenty-four "efful-gent spirits," divided into groups of eight situated in the "three primes," the three parts of the body: upper (the head), middle (the chest), and lower (just below the navel). These spirits became glowing orbs of light when properly charged by the adept through various meditation procedures. Of course the adept must al-ready be fairly advanced in these practices to merge with a celestial being, whose body was completely rarified and "effulgent."

As can be seen by these brief representations, the poems presented to Yang Xi by the Perfected in the following passage shimmer with arcane references to the meditations of the Shangqing scriptures. A large number of these meditations involve envisioning the light of celestial bodies (the sun, moon, and stars), in the form of either radiant deities or glowing pneumas, and conducting these energies into one's body to recharge the depleted spirits within.

What for mortals restores a degraded body to its pristine perfection continues to serve as "food" for celestial beings. For example, when the Perfected Consort writes, "Looking down, I rinse my mouth with liquid from a cloudvase; looking up, I pluck a deep-blue blossom from a crabapple tree," she is taking astral sus-tenance before descending into the human world. The original referents for such delightful images are not always explained in the scriptures, so the translation of them that follows, while literal enough, is often conjectural. They would perhaps not have been any clearer to those Yang Xi entrusted with his writings than they are to us today.

While the spiritual composition of the human body in Daoism is extremely complex, it is important for the following account to know that the body, in addition to the "eight effulgent spirits of the three-primes" also contained two different sorts of "soul": three yang "cloud-souls" and seven yin "white-souls." The former are effervescent and tend to fly from the body, both in dream and at death, while the latter, more dense of composition, are associated with carnal desires and sensory experience.

The marriage Yang describes is undeniably a spirit-marriage, accomplished only in the locked chambers of his imagination, yet it does bear a certain resemblance to the aristocratic wedding ceremonies of the time. In the aristocratic marriages of fourth-century China, both parties commonly had some say in choosing their partner—at least more so than in later periods of Chinese history when virtually all marriages were arranged. Women of this period were considerably freer of social restraint than their later sisters. In some cases high-born women might even pick among suitors. Still, the fact that Consort An actually proposes marriage to Yang Xi is something that rarely, if ever, occurred in human societies. In fact, as we will see, Yang Xi is gendered "feminine" in his relationship to the goddesses.

Despite whatever freedom sons and daughters may have had with regard to choice of their future spouse, marriage in this period still was less a joining of persons than a joining of families. We will see below that both Yang Xi's Perfected instructor, the Lady of South Mount, and Consort An's mother must approve this match. Such arrangements, including the initial meeting of the couple, were handled by a go-between; in this case, the Lady Wang of Purple Tenuity. (Purple Tenuity is the name of a constellation which, in Chinese astronomy, was envisioned as the palace of the celestial deity, who might be observed in the pole star.)

Given the lineages of the participants, the match Lady Wang arranges was indeed an appropriate one. Yang Xi was connected through his divine teachers with Mount Mao, just south of present-day Nanjing in the east of China, while Consort An traced her antecedents as well as her education back to Kunlun Mountain and the Queen Mother of the West. For example, the divine fruits Consort An presents to Yang as a token of her intent at their betrothal find their counterpart in the sacred peaches of the Queen Mother. This cosmic joining of the west and east is expressed in Chinese mythology in the meeting of the stars Weaving Maid and Oxherd. In this respect, the positions on the bed platform assumed by Yang Xi and Consort An at their initial meeting is symbolic.

Further aspects of mundane marriage figure in the scenes that follow. In Yang Xi's day, wedding ceremonies customarily ended with an event known as "creating a commotion in the bridal chamber" or "teasing the bride." The guests at the wedding feast would, once they were all more than a little tipsy, escort the young couple into the bedchamber and tease them by asking embarrassing questions. Here, the assembled Perfected do nothing of the sort, but they do end the wedding gathering with a series of poems directed not at the "bride" but at Yang Xi, urging him to forget mundane sex and to apply himself to the pursuit of perfection. Thus while the "bride and groom" are sometimes here referred to by the traditional terms "inner and outer," denoting usually that the woman's place was inside the home and the man's outside, there is no question that "inner" takes on a new meaning in this text. The Perfected Consort is fully "within the Dao." Yang Xi, while a promising student and destined for great things through this match, is still an outsider.

There are other, subtle ways in which Yang takes on the feminine role with respect to his goddess. She takes the initiative, visiting him in his meditation chamber, bringing betrothal gifts, and touching his hand at their first meeting (given that the Perfected handle nothing mundane, this gesture is highly significant). He is bashful, coy, and tongue-tied as she pursues her match. Even the term here translated as "betrothal" was, in mundane marriages, usually initiated by the male rather than the female. Finally, though, the telling point is that the desired outcome is not that she come to live with him, as we would expect of a marriage in that society and time, but that he be borne off in a cloudy carriage to her home among the stars. Before the austere goddesses of Shangqing Daoism, Yang Xi becomes the blushing bride.

Further Reading

Stephen R. Bokenkamp, *Traces of Transcendence* (Berkeley: University of California Press, 1996); Isabelle Robinet, *Taoist Meditation: The Mao-Shan Tradition of Great Purity*, trans. Julian F. Pas and Norman J. Girardot (Albany: State University of New York Press, 1993); Edward H. Schafer, *Mao Shan in T'ang Times* (Boulder: Society for the Study of Chinese Religions Monograph 1, 1960); Michel Strickmann, "The Mao-shan Revelations: Taoism and the Aristocracy," *T'oung-pao* 63.1 (1977): 1–64.

Betrothal

On the night of the twenty-fifth day of the sixth month (July 26, 365), Lady Wang of Purple Tenuity descended to me. A divine woman came along with her. This goddess was wearing a blouse of cloud-brocade and outer garments of cinnabar red above and blue below with multicolor patterns that glistened brightly. At her waist was a green embroidered belt from which were suspended more than ten tiny bells. These bells were green or yellow and hung irregularly spaced around the belt. To the left of her belt hung a jade pendant just like those of our world, but a bit smaller.

Her garments flashed with light, illumining the room. Looking at her was like trying to discern the shape of a flake of mica as it reflects the sun. Her billowing hair, black and long at the temples, was arranged exquisitely. It was done up in a topknot on the crown of her head, so that the remaining strands fell almost to her waist. There were golden rings on her fingers and jade circlets on her arms. Judging by her appearance, she must have been about thirteen or fourteen.

To her left and right were two maids. One of these wore a vermilion robe and carried slung on a sash a bag with blue insignia. In her hand, she held another brocade bag about eleven or twelve inches in length and filled with some ten scrolls. A white jade tag closed the mouth of the bag. I saw inscribed upon the tag the words: "Cinnabar Seal of Purple Primordiality for the Jade Clarity Heaven *Divine Tiger Text of Inner Perfection.*"

The other maid was dressed in blue and held in both her hands a white casket bound with a scarlet sash. The casket appeared to be made of ivory. The two maids seemed to be about seventeen or eighteen years of age. The decorations of their clothing were quite out of the ordinary.

Both the divine maiden and her maids had complexions as bright and as freshly translucent as jade. Their five-fragrance perfume filled the room with a delightful scent as if I had lit incense. When they first entered the room, they followed behind Lady Wang of Purple Tenuity. Just as she entered the door, the Lady said to me: "Today an honored guest has come to see you. She wishes to form a relationship with you."

At this, I immediately rose to my feet. The Lady said: "O but you need not arise. You may sit facing each other to make your courtesies." She then sat in the position of master, facing south. On that night I had previously taken up a position on the lower end of the bed platform, facing west. The divine maiden, noticing this, sat down beside me on the bed platform facing east. Each of us then made our greeting to one another with our left hands.

When we had finished, Lady Wang of Purple Tenuity said: "This is the youngest daughter of the Upper-Perfected Primal Sovereign of the Grand Void, Lady Li of Golden Terrace. Long ago the Primal Sovereign sent her to Tortoise Mountain to study the Way of Highest Clarity. Once she had achieved the Way, she received the writ of the Most High appointing her as Perfected Consort Nine Blossoms of the Upper Palaces of Purple Clarity. She was given the surname An, the name Yubin (Densecloud Dame) and the byname Lingxiao (Spirit Syrinx)."

Lady Wang of Purple Tenuity also asked me whether I had ever seen such a person as this in the world. I responded: "She is numinous! Illustrious! Exalted! Outstanding! I have nothing with which to compare her!"

Hearing this, the Lady laughed out loud and said: "And how do you feel about her?"

I did not venture any further response.

The Perfected Consort sat for a long time without saying anything. In her hands she held three jujubes—at least they looked like dried jujubes, but they were larger, had no pits, and did not taste like jujube, but like pear. First she gave one to me, then one to Lady Wang, keeping one for herself, and said we should eat them. After we had eaten, some more time passed in silence.

After a while the Perfected Consort asked me my age and in what month I was born. I immediately answered: "I am thirty-six. I was born in the *gengyin* year (330 C.E.), ninth month."

The Perfected Consort then said: "Your master is that Perfected Lady of the South Mount (Wei Huacun) who holds power as the Director of Destinies. Her Way is exalted and wondrously complete. In truth, yours is a lineage of great virtue. I have long heard of your own virtues, but I never expected that one day I would be able to discuss with you our predestined affinities. I take delight in the fact that the conjunction of our hidden destinies in fact betokens the intertwining intimacy of kudzu and pine."

Then, using my name for the first time,[1] I responded, saying: "Sunken in this inferior baseness, dust staining my substance, I regard you as distant as the clouds. There is no affinity that would allow me to receive your respect; in fact, I fear for my deficiencies whenever the spirits descend. Now I leap in joy, forgetting my limitations, in the hope that you might instruct me and dispel my ignorance, thereby saving this human, Yang Xi. This is my only wish, night after night."

The Perfected Consort said: "My lord should not speak deferentially. Deferential speech is really not appropriate to this occasion."

There was another long pause. Then the Perfected Consort commanded me, saying: "I wish to present you with a page of writing, so I must trouble you to take up the brush to convey my humble sentiments. Is this possible?"

"I obey your commands," I responded. Forthwith, I smoothed out a sheet of paper, dipped my brush, and copied verbatim the following poem:

> A Cloud-swathed gate stands above in the emptiness;
> Then red-gem tower rises into the densecloud Net.
> The Purple Palace rides on green phosphors,
> Its spirit-observatories shadowed among jagged peaks.
> Within vermilion chambers roofed in malachite,
> Upper potencies flash their scarlet auroras.
> Looking down, I rinse my mouth with liquid from a cloudvase;
> Looking up, I pluck a deep-blue blossom from a crabapple tree.
> Bathing my feet in heaven's jade pool (stars in our Sagittarius),
> Striking oars in the ox-herder's river (the Milky Way),
> I urge on the carriage of effulgent clouds (exteriorized spirits of my
>   own body)
> And rein in the descending dragons on the Slopes of Mystery.
> Shaking out my garments on the borders of this world of dust and
>   dregs,
> I lift my skirts and stride over the turbid waves.
> My desire is to make a bond between mountain and marsh,
> To let the rigid and the yielding conform to one another in harmony.
> Hand in hand, paired in matched purity:
> Our Way of supreme perfection will not be depraved.
> In Purple Tenuity we have met a fine matchmaker.
> I sing that we may receive blessings in abundance.

When I had finished writing, she took the paper and looked it over, then said: "I present this to you to reveal the sincerity of my intentions. You need utter no thanks. If there is something that you do not understand, please just ask."

Lady Wang of Purple Tenuity then said: "I would also like you to transcribe a text to ensure that you understand and to set forth this auspicious event." So I again spread out paper and wet my brush. Then the Lady bestowed upon me the following poem:

> Two images—one inside, one outside—melt together;
> Like the primal breath which indeed split in two.
> This mystic union requires no wedding carriage,

It only awaits your elevation to perfection.
[Lady] of the South Mount has smelt forth shining gold—
Her wondrous perceptions fill your book-bag.
Now your fine virtue reflects into the flying auroras
And, as a result, you have moved a person of the holy heavens.
Riding whirlwinds, companions in quilt-wrapped repose;
When you match her in durability, she will lead you into the crimson
    clouds.
Enlightened, you protest the barriers between Heaven and humanity,
But the fated numbers already hold your predestined affinities.
The Highest Way, in truth, is not depraved;
It is something unheard of in the world of dust.
Now, with mortal eye, you observe the signs betokening eternal union;
I sing forth boldly—this is your fate!

Once I had finished writing, Lady Wang of Purple Tenuity took it and looked
it over. When she was finished, she said: "I present this to you. Today it has
fallen to me to act both as overseer of your predestined relationship and as the
matchmaker who sings your unspoken intentions."

She also said: "Tomorrow, Lady of the South Mount is to return from her
journey. The Perfected Consort and I should go to greet her at Cloud-kiln. If
we do not return tomorrow, it will be several days before you see us again."

After a long interval, Lady Wang announced: "I am leaving. The Perfected
Consort and I should be able to come and see you tomorrow after all."

I sensed her descending from the bed platform, but she had already disappeared. The Perfected Consort remained behind for a moment and said to me:
"You have not expressed your deepest sentiments, but I have not failed to notice
your intentions. I wish you would give voice to all you feel. Tomorrow I will
come again." With these words, she took my hand and pressed it. Then she
descended from the bed platform. She had not even reached the door when
suddenly I could no longer see her.

Marriage

On the night of the twenty-sixth of the third month [July 27], a host of Perfected came as listed below:

> Lady Wang of Purple Tenuity;
> The Perfected Consort Nine Blossoms of the Upper Palaces of Purple
>   Clarity;
> My Teacher, Lady of the South Mount, Director of Destinies of the
>   Upper Perfected;
> The Perfected One of Purple Solarity;

The Middle Lord of Mount Mao;
The Perfected One of Pure Holiness;
The Younger Lord of Mount Mao;
[and a youth I learned was Wang Ziqiao, the Perfected of Mount
   Tongbo.]

After each had been seated for a long while, the Perfected Consort of Purple Clarity said: "I wish again to tire your hand in writing out a matter that I might clear my mind and forget speech."

I spread out paper and awaited her transmission. The Perfected Consort then spoke, slowly and in a soft voice: "I am the youngest daughter of the Primal Sovereign; the beloved child of Lady Li of the Grand Void. Long ago I began my study of transcendence at Tortoise Terrace [on Kunlun Mountain] and received my jade insignia from the Most High [Lord Lao]. I accepted the Tiger spirit-registers from the Purple Sovereign and the rose-gem halberd from the Thearch of Heaven. Having received documentation as a Consort of the Highest Perfected, I traveled the heavens of Jade Clarity. Frequently I

Opened the gates into the Nine Nets with my own hands,
Tread with my own feet the chambers of mystery.
Taking celestial form in that holy Void,
I raised my head to sip from the solar root,
Joined in feasts at the Seven Watchtowers,
Emerging to rein on my cloudy chariot.
Controlling the three celestial timekeepers (sun, moon, and stars) I
   ascended with them,
Dispersing the effulgent spirits of my own body as rosy mists to serve
   as my flying conveyance.
It is not that I am unable
To pick and choose among the highest chambers,
Search among the scarlet lads,
Seek a fine match in the palaces of kings,
Or mate myself to some exalted spirit.
I could touch the mysterious and draw out a counterpart;
I could befriend some gentleman in the court of the Thearch.

"It is just that I grasp the crux of things and so seized this rare opportunity, thereby responding to cosmic rhythms and numerological fate. In lowering my effulgent corporeal spirits into the dust and evanescence of your world, I have harnessed them as dragons to plunge below. This was done expressly to summon to me the male who pursues the mysterious and to pursue with him an association wherein I might gain a suitable counterpart. We came together because of predestination. As a result

Our records were compared, our names verified;
Our immaculate tallies joined in the jewelled realms—

Our dual felicity has been arranged:
We will travel as wild geese supporting one another.
We will share sips from a single gourd-goblet,
Toasting the nuptial quilt and knotting our lower garments.
When you look to your mate for the food she will prepare—
It is the Perfected drugs she holds inside herself. . . .

"If, from this moment wherein we achieve the Way, we fasten the inner and the outer as securely as metal or stone, intertwining our emotions in shared affection and joining our hearts within the bed curtains, then what need is there to embrace beneath the quilts? If we were to engage in such meaningless contact, would not it only defile your corporeal spirits, bring to grief your cloud-souls, and give free rein to your white-souls?

"It is I who have come to seek familial ties with you, noble lord. There is nothing depraved in what I propose.

"Now it can be said that we have achieved our dearest ambitions. Our true feelings are already one. We are about to

Yoke our team together in the gemmy Void,
To travel together in the dark mysteries.
We will together pluck scarlet fruit in the groves of jade;
Together pick cinnabar blossoms in Wildwind Garden;
Share with each other the waters of Vermilion Stream;
Side-by-side bathe on the banks of the Cyan River.
Clothed in feather capes with purple flowers,
You in solar cap, I in Lotus crown,
We will roam carefree the Heaven of Highest Clarity,
Together joining in audience the Three Primes.
The eight effulgent-spirits of our bodies will then emerge,
Bearing us through phoenix portals and cloudy gates.[2]
We will raise our heads to sup marrow of gold,
Then sing songs of jade mystery.
Floating in the emptiness, we'll sleep and feast,
And meet on high the grand dawn.
As the music of the spheres issues all around,
The incense-mother will present us with pleasing vapors.
Side-by-side, we will observe all as one,
Taking each other's sashes in our hands, binding together our skirts—

"Will this not be the highest joy? Will this not be the fulfillment of our aspirations?

"If you, noble lord, will only comply with fate and consent to this marriage, I will certainly not decline. Moreover, you should not turn your back on the true and the unseen merely to give free rein to your baser human emotions."

Once she had completed transmitting this to me, she once more took it and looked it over. Then she said: "I present this writing to you in the hopes that it will relieve your hesitations and doubts." As she finished speaking, she smiled.

After a long while, Lady Wang of Purple Tenuity said "The Perfected Consort's declaration is now complete. The predestined relationship we have discussed is now evident to all. You should no longer harbor any doubts, your mystic apportionment of fate has brought this about."

Then Lady of the South Mount, my teacher, presented writings to me that said: "You have repeatedly moved the unseen to meet with you. It is this mystic fate that brings the two of you together. In response to your destiny, I have come to betroth you and to construct for the first time this destined match. This joining of Perfected persons is a joyous event.

"Though you are announced as mates, this only establishes your respective functions as inner and outer. You must not recklessly follow the filthy practices of the world by performing with her base deeds of lewdness and impurity. You are to join with the holy consort through the meeting of your effulgent inner spirits. I betroth this daughter of a noble Perfected being to you so that, in your intimate conjoinings, there will be great benefit for your advancement and no worries that you will injure or deplete your spiritual forces. Hereafter, you may command the myriad spirits. There will be no further trials of your mystic insight. Your banner of perfection will now overcome all in its path and you may together pilot a chariot of the clouds.

"Long ago, at the suggestion of Lady Wang of Purple Tenuity, I worked out this intention for you. Now all has gone as we had hoped. I am greatly pleased.

"Be cautious that doubts do not again swell in your heart. Yesterday I met with Lady Li of Golden Terrace in the clear void. She said that you still harbor in your heart doubts concerning the correctness of all of this and that there is a trace of regret in your expression. If you go contrary to this action, you will greatly wrong us.

"The Perfected Consort possesses the precious *Divine Tiger Text of Inner Perfection* written in cinnabar and blue. This is far finer than the sort of thing you now own. If, with your fine talent, you seek to copy it, I am certain she will not keep it secret from you. But the joining of your hands in wedlock is not just a matter of texts. You two will ride your effulgent inner spirits into the gem-filled heavens. If there are further matters about which you remain unenlightened, might you not simply ask me in private?"

The Perfected Consort, observing what the Lady had written, smiled and said:

> "We will join hands at the Paired Terraces—
> All sigh in delight at this fine match!
> The twin-yoked conveyance formed of our effulgent spirits,
> With this is accomplished."

The Perfected of Pure Holiness then presented me with a writing that said: "The Way of the Yellow and the Red is a method for joining the pneumas of male and female that was taught by Zhang Ling to convert people. It is only one method of joining the Elect. It is not something that the Perfected practice. I have often seen people practice this and succeed in cutting off their seed, but I have never seen anyone sow this seed and thereby reap life. Among the millions who have practiced this way, none has succeeded in avoiding whippings and interrogations after death in the Three Bureaus.[3] If, among ten million, one person happens to achieve the Way this way, he or she still has far to go to avoid death. Zhang Ling received this practice only for the purpose of instructing mortals. He himself did not practice this method to achieve his own transformation and elevation.

"Be cautious lest you speak of this lower way which pollutes life, or you will injure the correct pneumas bestowed upon you by the perfected heavens. One whose thoughts harbor overflowing desires, whose heart preserves sexual fantasies, and who at the same time practices the higher Way will have cause to know the punishments of the Three Bureaus. This sort of behavior is as misguided as 'jumping into a fire while holding a piece of jade, in hopes that it will save you' or 'burying a dog in a golden casket.'" . . .

Lady Wang of Purple Tenuity presented me with a writing that said: "As to the joining of effulgent spirits among the Perfected, what is most important is that the mating and love occur between the effulgent spirits of the two parties. Though we call them husband and wife, they perform none of the acts of mortal husbands and wives. It is simply an accessible way to speak about the ineffable. If one harbors thoughts of the Yellow and the Red in one's heart, one will not be able to see the Perfected or join with a spiritual mate. Such a one would in vain labor at the task of self-perfection and would, moreover, be taken to task in the Three Bureaus."

When the cock crowed, Lady of the South Mount presented me with a writing that said: "Now that the cock has crowed, the marriage that we have discussed is confirmed." . . .

[The Perfected of Purple Solarity and the Middle Lord of Mount Mao were the last to offer their words of felicitation and advice. Once they were done speaking] the host of Perfected departed. The Perfected Consort remained behind for awhile. She said to me: "Again I must trouble the noble Lord with a few words." Then she bestowed upon me the following writing:

"You should dissolve your cares in fragrant purity and let your heart be bright at our joining of tallies. Only then will we enjoy constant intimacy in piety and clarity, so that our hidden potencies and flowing effulgences join appropriately. For our joyous meetings, you should arrange your hair. Bind it up high according to the proprieties. You, noble lord, are elevated and of dazzling spirituality. Clear away all further obstructions and forget the base ways of the world."

When she was done speaking, she grasped my hand and descended from the bed platform. Before even reaching the door, she suddenly disappeared.

Notes

1. In polite speech, Chinese avoid using the first-person pronoun. One might simply drop the pronoun altogether or, at a slightly more intimate level (as Yang adopts here) refer to oneself by one's given name.

2. The "Three Primes" are the three registers of the human body, centered on the head, the heart, and the area just below the navel. The "eight effulgent spirits" refer to the glowing, etherealized spirits created in each of these three areas through Shangqing meditation practice.

3. The Three Bureaus are those of Heaven, Earth, and Water. They were believed to control human destinies, both in life and after death.

— 12 —

Seduction Songs of One of the Perfected

Paul W. Kroll

During the years 364–370, Yang Xi, a visionary priest living in Jurong, southeast of the Eastern Jin capital city (present-day Nanjing), and in the employ of a court official named Xu Mi, was the recipient of a series of midnight visits by Daoist divinities identifying themselves as coming from the celestial realm of Highest Clarity (Shangqing), a heaven whose denizens had been heretofore unknown to mortals. These midnight visits, the beginning of the Shangqing revelations, mark a new and profoundly influential turn in medieval Daoism, representing a synthesis of "northern," Celestial Master (Tianshi) teachings with the native, occult traditions of the "south" (i.e., the area of the ancient states of Wu and Yue). The texts and practices to emerge from the Shangqing revelations, along with those of the Lingbao movement a few decades later, not only are important for Chinese religious history; they also had an enormous effect on Chinese literary, social, and political history for the next five hundred years.

Yang Xi's transcriptions of the communications made to him by the "Perfected" or "Realized persons" (*zhenren*) of Highest Clarity, were gathered together in definitive form a century following his death by Tao Hongjing (456–536), the great adept, scholar, alchemist, official, and systematizer of Shangqing texts. Although the document recording these communications, entitled the *Declarations of the Perfected* (*Zhengao*), is not, strictly speaking, a "scripture" (*jing*), it has long been recognized as a foundation text of medieval Daoism.

One of the most powerful features of the *Declarations of the Perfected* material is the consummate literary skill displayed in it by the Shangqing divinities. Indeed, the Perfected communicate with a verbal artistry calculated to impress and enchant the sophisticated, highly literate aristocracy of the Eastern Jin court. Among the many different sorts of documents included in this collection are some seventy poems and songs recited to Yang Xi by his divine visitors. Seen in the context of a society that put a premium on literary—especially poetic—ability, these compositions, most of which are in the pentasyllabic meter favored by the Eastern Jin literati themselves, are virtuoso efforts combining spiritual content with lyric technique.

Among the dozen or so Perfected who favored Yang Xi with poems, the most prolific was the female Perfected known by the title Lady of Right Bloom of the Palace of Cloud Forest (Yulin gong youying furen, or Lady Youying). By name Wang Meilan, cognomen Shenlin, Lady Youying was the thirteenth daughter of the great goddess Xiwangmu. Her special domain was an island in the Eastern Sea called Watchet Whitecap (Canglang), the seamount itself being nominally regarded and verbally imaged as a stabilized wave in the iron-gray ocean—part of the Encantadas of the orient sea that included the famous immortals' isle of Penglai.

The nine poems of Lady Youying that make up the following selection were meant mainly for one particular auditor—namely, Xu Mi, the noble patron of Yang Xi. Now in his fifties, Xu Mi is known by the Perfected as someone entangled in earthly, carnal desires. However, the beautiful Lady Youying is prepared—in fact, fated—to be his ethereal consort, if only he will renounce the ways of the world and turn himself to Higher Things. This is the Lady's hope—to convince Xu Mi to join her in the realm of unearthly delight. Filled with the colors, sounds, and scenes of the celestial regions that she knows so well, her poems aim to lure him on to a mystical union with her, a sacred marriage in the "unseen realm" of the heavens. The dates attached to the poems below specify the nights on which Lady Youying chanted her (untitled) verses to Yang Xi, instructing him to convey these effusions to Xu Mi.

Songs such as these are direct heirs to the Chuci's "Far Roaming" poem (translated in chapter 10). Found in abundance in the Daoist canon, and imitated in various ways by many poets in the Six Dynasties and Tang periods, they are the transcendent, expansive complement to the this-worldly, more subdued verse that we are too used to thinking of as typical of Chinese poetry.

Further Reading

On the Shangqing revelations, see Isabelle Robinet, *La Révélation du Shangqing dans l'histoire du taoïsme* esp. chap. 10, "L'Apport littéraire des textes du Shangqing au taoïsme" (Paris: Ecole Française d'Extrême-Orient, 1984); Robinet, *Taoist Meditation: The Mao Shan Tradition of Great Purity*, trans. Julian F. Pas and Norman J. Girardot (Albany: State University of New York Press, 1993); Robinet, *Histoire du taoïsme, des origines au XIVe siècle*, esp. chap. 5, "Le Shangqing" (Paris: Cerf, 1991); Michel Strickmann, "The Mao Shan Revelations: Taoism and the Aristocracy," *T'oung Pao* 63.1 (1977): 1–64; Strickmann, *Le Taoïsme du Mao Chan: Chronique d'un révélation* (Paris: Presses Universitaires de France, 1981).

English translations from Shangqing scriptures include Stephen R. Bokenkamp, *Traces of Transcendence* (Berkeley: University of California Press, 1996); Paul W. Kroll, "In the Halls of the Azure Lad," *Journal of the American Oriental Society* 105

(1985): 75–94; Kroll, "Spreading Open the Barrier of Heaven," *Etudes Asiatiques* 40 (1986): 22–39; Edward H. Schafer, "The Jade Woman of Greatest Mystery," *History of Religions* 17 (1978): 387–98.

For the influence of Shangqing texts on poets in the Tang dynasty, see Paul W. Kroll, "Li Po's Transcendent Diction," *Journal of the American Oriental Society* 106 (1986): 99–117; Kroll, "Verses From on High: The Ascent of T'ai Shan," *T'oung Pao* 69 (1983): 223–60, revised version in *The Vitality of the Lyric Voice: Shih Poetry from the Late Han to the T'ang,* ed. Lin and Owen (Princeton: Princeton University Press, 1987), pp. 167–216; Edward H. Schafer, "Wu Yün's 'Cantos on Pacing the Void,' " *Harvard Journal of Asiatic Studies* 41 (1981): 377–415; Schafer, "Wu Yün's Stanzas on 'Saunters in Sylphdom,' " *Monumenta Serica* 35 (1981–1983): 1–37; Schafer, *Mirages on the Sea of Time: The Taoist Poetry of Ts'ao T'ang* (Berkeley and Los Angeles: University of California Press, 1985).

AUGUST 21, 365

Reining in the sky-lights, I settle over Watchet Whitecap,
Cantering, prancing above the fords of the Blue Sea.
A scarlet haze casts confusion over the Greatest Yang,
As my plumed canopy turns the Nine Heavens upside-down.
5   The cloud chassis drifts in the Hollow of Space;
In a flash and a flicker—between the wind and waves:
I have come to seek my companion for the unseen realm,
Who hand-in-hand with me may serve at the thearch's dawn-source—
A regal scion who will concord with my luminous virtue;
10   With our heads aligned, we shall summon jade worthies.
Below, we'll glimpse the Palace of the Eight Buttresses;
Above, we'll rest at the summit of the Rarefield Grove.
Rinse with these oils of the Rose-gem and Purple Palace,
Then you shall realize the bitterness of the world's mire and filth.
15   —In what place will the Seemly One reside?
Devote yourself to it, and you shall gain my intimacy.

NOTES

Line 1: The Lady's carriage is fitted out with radiant celestial lights, the outer counterpart to her own inner brilliance.
Line 3: The sun.
Line 6: Passage by the *zhenren* from the celestial to the earthly plane (the region of "wind and   waves" or, elsewhere, "wind and dust") always takes place with abrupt suddenness.

Line 8: The thearch referred to here is the god-king of the rising sun.

Lines 11–12: Two paradise realms.

Line 13: The palace where the Realized Maidens of the Nine Heavens dwell.

Line 15: "Seemly One" (*jiaren*) is the title by which Lady Youying refers to Xu Mi, as it had earlier been a formulaic designation for a desired goddess, woman, or lord in the *Chuci*.

AUGUST 31, 365

The world values intercourse redolent and perfumed;
But the Dao exalts communion in the mystic empyrean.
I shake out my vestments, seek a mate for the unseen realm,
Turning the coach to the borders of the wind and dust.
5   Your goodly virtue reflects my numinous radiance;
Awn and root shine in floriate luxury.
Our private words make much of unplanned good fortune;
In accordant purity, holding high the esteem of Perfection.
Xian and *heng*—let us comply with their images,
10   And, hand in hand, we shall share coverlet and sash.
—So what are you doing, in the midst of human affairs,
Daily therein giving rise to harm and woe?

NOTES

Line 9: Hexagrams 31 ("courtship") and 32 ("marriage") in the *Classic of Changes* (*Yijing*).

OCTOBER 4, 365

Cantering, prancing, with carriage-shafts of clouds and sky-lights,
Drifting I surview space above the auroras.
My enskyed phaeton dances this way and that,
Its purple canopy at home in the numinous quarter.
5   A vermilion haze envelops its banners and ensigns;
My plumed cloak fans the scented breeze.
At my lightning's peal, savage beasts are fear-struck,
And a bellowing of thunder incites mystic dragons.
Tuned sounding-pipes mingle with resonances of the court,
10   While golden reed-organs give song to ethereal bells.
I cull divine herbs on the banks of Watchet Whitecap,
And gather flowers on the peak of Eight Abatements.

With vermeil countenance daily becoming more refreshed,
One progresses backward, even to the nonage of infancy.
15   Nourish, then, your physical form—be still on the eastern crag;
With your seven divinities freely be in communion.
The wind and the dust hold anxiety and sorrow
That may unmake this white-haired old fellow of mine.
For long in the unseen realm I have shed faraway sighs,
20   Regretting that you do not sooner extricate your tracks.

NOTES

Line 12: A paradise isle near Canglang and Penglai.
Lines 13–14: One can reverse the process of aging, if one follows proper Daoist
    practice and "etherealizes" one's body.
Lines 15: The "eastern crag" is Mount Mao, the most sacred mountain of the
    Shangqing tradition.
Line 16: These seven divinities are the corporeal gods of hair, brain, eyes, nose,
    ears, tongue, and teeth.

OCTOBER 24, 365

Rose-gold sky-lights float in the mystic dawn-source,
And the purple coach voyages, borne on the haze.
Upward, I surmount the interior of the Green Pylons;
Downward, I glimpse the enceinte of Vermilion Fire.
5   Orient auroras open out an ample radiance,
And divine light sets asparkle the Seven Numina.
Screened from the glint I drift among the Three Candles,
Coursing at will, freely composed in the unseen realm.
A wind wraps round the eaves of the Hollow of Space;
10   Aromas and tones are engendered with the touch of my staff.
Hand-in-hand I dance with the Weaver Maid,
Our lapels matched in the courtyard of the Gourd-star.
To the left I turn the blue-plumed banner,
The floriate canopy inclining in the wake of the clouds.
15   I revel in a bedchamber outside the Nine Lineaments,
Where affirmation and negation are not projected for me.
Embracing realization, I relax in the Grand Stillness,
A figure of gold becoming daily more that of a babe.
—How could *this* resemble your lapses amidst the filth,
20   The agonizing gloom—a life without relief?

NOTES

Line 6: The stars of the Dipper.
Line 7: The sun, moon, and stars.
Line 11: The Weaver Maid is the star known to us as Vega.
Line 12: A constellation made up of stars in our Delphinus.
Line 15: The Nine Heavens.
Line 16: She is beyond matters of duality.
Line 17: The Grand Stillness at the beginning of things, ultimate potentiality.
Line 18: The incorruptibility of her form will eventually return her to the state
 of an infant in the womb, a favorite Daoist image.

NOVEMBER 16, 365

My three reins pull against the purple coach,
Inclined in the clouds, by the brink of the Eastern Grove.
Ascending in the north the pylons of mystic perfection,
Hand in hand, we knot up the lofty net.
5 An aromatic haze bestrews the eight sky-lights;
A mystic wind buffets the rose-gold waves.
Upward, we surmount the ford by the *lang*-gem garden;
Downward, we glimpse the props of the empyrean's barrows.
As jade pan-pipes sing out above the clouds,
10 Phoenix calls penetrate to the nine reaches.
Borne on the pneuma, we float in Grand Emptiness—
Why bother treading over mountains and rivers?
With a staff of gold, we give orders to plumed numina;
Mustering weapons, we humble the myriad demons.
15 Together we'll tap the radiance of the Two Chronograms;
The thousand-year-old cedrela will be as but a child's tooth!
Forfeit realization—and you surrender to the House of Confusion;
If you cannot resolve this, what recourse may there be?

NOTES

Line 2: Near the source of the sun.
Line 4: That is, the starry network of the skies.
Line 5: The eight sky-lights are the running lights of her coach.
Line 6: Of the Milky Way, referred to in Daoist texts as the "Rose-gold River."
Line 15: That is, we will sup the effluvia of sun and moon.
Line 16: The longevity of the cedrela tree of the first chapter of *Zhuangzi*, for
 which a thousand years was a single spring, will seem nothing to us.

MARCH 6, 366

Reining in the sky-lights, I ascend the empyrean's dawn-source,
Rambling to revelry in the Palace of Watchet Whitecap.
Prismatic clouds wreathe the cinnabar auroras;
Numinous cumuli bestrew the Eight Hollows.
5   The Perfected Ones on high chant in rose-gem abodes;
Lofty Transcendents carol in blue-gem chambers.
Nine phoenixes sing through the vermilion sounding-pipes;
The rhythms of the void commingle in the plumed bells.
With our necks entwined, within the Golden Court,
10   I'll unite with my mate amidst the unseen realm.
Together we will tap the ichor of the jade ale—
In a flash and a flicker, are now in the nonage of infancy!
—Well then, why do you crouch athwart the worldly road,
Your lapses and maladies increasing with every day?

MAY 9, 366

Purple pylons frame the acme of the void;
Mystic hostels surge up into the steep tempest.
Sapphire and *lang*-gem spread out in the numinous park;
Flowers quicken—setting forth rose-gem and turquoise.
5   I speed the phaeton over the ford of Watchet Whitecap,
As the eight winds incite the hymnody of the clouds.
With wings unfurled—fanning the covered north;
I grasp a staff, and give voice to the golden syrinx.
Phoenix sounding-pipes accord with a thousand bells,
10   And Divine Lads of the West sing of dawn and morning.
My heart wide-flung—beyond the nullity of the void;
Ethereal sentiments—oh, what an endless expanse!
I dance whirling on the high passes of Grand Hollow,
While the Six Ethers revolve in layered opacity.
15   How could one follow up this route of mine,
Unless he were not to wither at the end?

NOTES

Line 13: That is, the vast hollow of space.
Line 14: The Six Ethers are, here, the exhalations of the original yin elements
of the cosmos.

MAY 9, 366

As darkling waves excite the watchet surf,
The whelming ford drums up a myriad currents.
Harnessing the sky-lights, I view the Six Voids,
Longing to ramble through them with the Seemly One.
5   A marvelous singing—but no one to pair with me;
The clearest tones—but given up to whom?
Amidst the clouds I speed the rose-gem wheels;
For what should one hasten amidst the world's dust?

MAY 28, 366

I unleash my heart through the fords of hollow space;
Gathering the reins, I whip up the vermilion phaeton.
Why is it that the Seemly One comes so tardily?
And when the time he'll fulfill the force of the Dao?

—13—

Answering a Summons

Stephen Bokenkamp

Master Zhou's Records of His Communications with the Unseen (*Zhoushi mingtong ji*) is a partial record of the visions of Zhou Ziliang during the years 515–516 C.E. Ziliang was a young disciple of the prominent Daoist master Tao Hongjing (452–536) and had served as Tao's assistant during the collection, copying, and ordering of the Shangqing scriptures. Partially as a result of his acquaintance with the visionary transcripts of Yang Xi (330–ca. 375 C.E.), the original recipient of the Shangqing scriptures, Ziliang himself began to entertain visits from divinities.

The first visitors were lower-level Transcendents and Perfected beings, officials of Mount Mao (near present-day Nanjing), where he resided with his master, Tao. Many of these were the same Perfected who had visited Yang Xi 150 years earlier. Their appearance now signaled that Ziliang was especially favored; he had been named to a position in the hierarchy of deities within the mountain. They informed the nineteen-year-old that, though his book of life indicated forty-six more years for him, the post to which he was called would be far grander than anything he could otherwise hope for. His name would be stricken from the ledgers of death held in Mount Tai (in modern Shandong Province) and entered in the jade registers of the Transcendents in the Palace of the Grand Bourne, near the summit of the highest heavens. The young visionary responded to this summons, committing suicide on December 6, 516, so that he might take up the office promised him.

Tao Hongjing subsequently retrieved and annotated the diary of his disciple. He appended a preface, translated below, and presented the collection to the emperor. It is not difficult to see why Tao would want to do this. The reigning emperor, Liang Wudi—a fervent patron of Buddhism—had only twelve years before begun to issue harsh proscriptions against Daoism, mandating that Daoist monks and nuns return to lay life. Tao Hongjing, as a scholar, master calligrapher, alchemist, and botanist, had managed to maintain good relations with the emperor even as his fellow believers were oppressed. This was at least in part due to the fact that the good "Buddhist" emperor hoped that Tao might complete the Daoist elixir of long life. Tao took advantage of this imperial sponsorship to

continue defending Daoism, as some of his notes to the text translated below
show.

In addition, the emperor had bestowed upon Tao Hongjing the favor of a state-
supported monastery on Mount Mao, hoping that Tao would on this holy mountain complete the divine elixir that the emperor had commissioned. This was the
Hermitage of Scarlet Solarity, completed on imperial command in 515, just as
Zhou Ziliang's visions reached a climax. It is clear that Ziliang's visions represented
on one level a celestial confirmation of the emperor's wisdom in continuing to
support Tao Hongjing, even though Tao had yet to discover the elixir. On yet
another level, they might have constituted a warning to the emperor that even
once the elixir was found a very real-seeming death awaited anyone rash enough
to attempt this method of immediate access to the world of the spirits. Through
his presentation of Zhou's diary, then, Tao is indirectly able to instruct the emperor in what to expect from Daoist elixirs.

Besides revealing Tao Hongjing's stake in this affair, the *Records* are of interest
for what they reveal concerning the life and motives of the young Daoist adept,
Zhou Ziliang. The passages of Ziliang's *Records* translated below have been selected
with a view to revealing a few of this young man's possible motives for opening
himself to these visions and for preparing the drug that would eventually translate
him to the exalted postmortem position promised him. In fascinating counterpoint, Tao's notes, translated in brackets for key passages, contain further enlightening bits of information, as well as Tao's own soul-searching concerning the
event.

Zhou Ziliang was born on February 19, 497. His father died when he was six
years old and, for what economic or psychological reasons we can only imagine,
Ziliang was sent to his Daoist aunt, the younger sister of his mother, to be raised.
Soon thereafter, as a result of Liang Wudi's suppression of Daoism in 504, Ziliang's
aunt was forced to leave the temple she served and to marry, returning to lay life.
At this time, Ziliang was sent to another temple in the mountains.

Up to this point, Zhou Ziliang's life had been one of rejection and relocation.
Finally, as Tao Hongjing relates in his preface, Ziliang met Tao and accompanied
him on the master's journey to the far south to visit the Southern Marchmount
Huo (near present Nan'an County in Fujian Province), where Yang Xi's Perfected
teacher, Lady Wei Huacun (Lady of South Mount), was believed to have her
otherworldly headquarters (see chapter 11 in this volume). The Five Marchmounts (*wuyue*) were especially holy Daoist mountains roughly situated in the
four directions and the center of China. They were believed to house exalted
deities with dominion over the gods of the mountains and rivers in the surrounding area.

When Tao brought the young Ziliang back to Mount Mao, near the capital, he
managed to have the young man's family summoned as well. Finally, after a separation of some ten years, Ziliang was reunited with his mother and with his aunt.

After this separation there were, Ziliang's *Records* show, certain stresses on the
newly united family. In particular, Ziliang's practice of Daoism had advanced far
beyond that of his aunt, who was once his mentor and who still held considerable

power over the details of his life. Under her tutelage, he had been inducted as an ordinary novice in the Celestial Master order, receiving the text of Laozi's *Dao de jing* and a protective talisman. Tao Hongjing, after their return to Mount Mao, the most holy mountain of Shangqing belief in that it was here that Yang Xi had practiced, had begun to induct Ziliang into the higher mysteries of these texts. Tao records that he bestowed on Ziliang the *Inner Texts of the Three Luminaries* (*Sanhuang neiwen*) an important text of southern Daoism, as well as the *Charts of the Five Marchmounts*, (*Wuyue tu*), which would give him access to the higher Perfected. While none of the texts of Yang Xi is mentioned by name, it is clear from his writings that at least some of these were made available to Ziliang, perhaps in his role as "copyist" (as mentioned in Tao's notes). Even a brief comparison of the way Ziliang describes the descent of the Perfected with the way similar events are described by Yang Xi in the brief passages translated here will be enough to convince the reader that Zhou Ziliang was fully cognizant of the earlier work (see chapter 11).

Ziliang is instructed by many of the same Perfected who had appeared to Yang Xi. There is first a contact by a deputy from the cavern-paradises of Mount Mao, but later such spirits as the second of the three Mao brothers who ruled over the mountain known by their name and Zhou Ziyang, whose surname matches Ziliang's, begin to appear as well. The Mao brother appearing in the excerpts translated below is Mao Gu, who held the title Certifier of Registers, revealing his control over the destinies of humans. He shows up as well at the wedding feast of Yang Xi translated in chapter 11. Zhou Ziyang, or "the Perfected (Zhou) of Purple Solarity," we also encountered at Yang Xi's wedding. He is the deity who provides Ziliang with the recipe for the elixir with which he is to end his mortal life.

As his meetings with these deities commence, Ziliang is advised to give up his plans to move his father's remains to a tomb on the mountain. His father is soon to be reborn, and, at any rate, Ziliang is now more closely tied to his Perfected patrons than to any earthly relative. At the same time, Ziliang begins to rebel against the domination of his aunt.

While these events seem to highlight eternal and apparently cross-cultural patterns of rebellious adolescent psychology, we can finally only speculate on the influences the events of his life might have had on the substance of Ziliang's visions. One thing, though, is clear. Zhou Ziliang's direct communications with the unseen powers put him in a position of power. For once, he is the director of his own destiny.

Further Reading

Isabelle Robinet, *Taoist Meditation: The Mao-Shan Tradition of Great Purity,* trans. Julian F. Pas and Norman J. Girardot (Albany: State University of New York Press, 1993); Kristofer Schipper, *The Taoist Body,* trans. Karen C. Duval (Berkeley: University of California Press, 1993); Michel Strickmann, "A Taoist Confirmation of Liang Wu Ti's Suppression of Taoism," *Journal of the American Oriental Society* 98.4 (1978): 467–75; Strickmann, "On the Alchemy of T'ao Hung-ching," *Facets of Taoism: Essays in Chinese Religion,* ed. Holmes Welch and Anna Seidel (New Haven: Yale University Press, 1979), pp. 123–92.

FROM TAO HONGJING'S PREFACE

In the seventh year of the reign-period "Celestial Confirmation" (508 C.E.), I was roaming the mountains and seas of the eastern seaboard when I was persuaded to make for Qingzhang Mountain of Yongning. [It happened in this way:]

When I came to the east, I boarded an ocean-going catamaran bound for Mount Huo of Jin'an. Just at dusk, we set sail on the Zhejiang [River], but the ocean tides swept the boat straight for a large island at the mouth of the river with such force that human strength could no longer guide it [and we ran aground]. As a result of this near catastrophe, I headed instead upriver to Dongyang, wishing to proceed from there [overland to the mountain]. While in Dongyang, I happened upon a person of Yongjia Commandery who described the mountain scenery of that area as exceedingly beautiful. I thus changed my plans.

I accompanied this person through the mountain defiles to Yongjia Commandery, where I took lodging with the prefect of Yongning, Lu Xiang. Lu personally accompanied me to stay for a while in the hall of the local Celestial Master parish which, by chance, Zhou Ziliang had just entered as a novitiate. This is how we came to know one another. Contemplating now this predestined meeting, it seems as if the gods had mandated that we be brought together. Were it not so, there is no way to explain how we both happened to come to Qingzhang Mountain.

At this time, Zhou Ziliang was still twelve years of age and was in the process of formally requesting to "enter the mountain and submit to the discipline" as a disciple [of Celestial Master Daoism]. He first received a register of personal Transcendent Powers, the five-thousand-word text of the *Laozi,* and the "Talisman of the Elder of the Western Marchmount for Interdicting Tigers and Leopards" and then devoted himself assiduously to the menial tasks assigned him of tending the incense burners and lamps in the temple. Zhou loved to practice calligraphy and paint as well as to practice other minor skills. Anything he applied himself to he was able to accomplish.

After this, he accompanied me to the Southern Marchmount Huo and later on to Muliu Island (modern Yuhuan Island), serving me day and night with the utmost respect. In the eleventh year (512), he returned with me to Mount Mao. There I bestowed on him the *Charts of the Five Marchmounts* and the

Inner Texts of the Three Luminaries, formally accepting him as my disciple. In the autumn of the next year, his family and close relations came to the mountain to live, establishing themselves together with Zhou in a temple outbuilding on the westernmost of the three peaks.

On the day of the summer solstice of the fourteenth year (June 20, 515), Zhou suddenly retired to recline in his chamber before noon. He conferred with the spirits for a long time and then emerged. His aunt did not know what he had been doing and questioned him closely about his strange behavior. Zhou told her a bit of what he had seen, as recorded below in his transcripts.

For the next forty or fifty days, Zhou was seen to act very strangely indeed. He would habitually close the curtains and bar the door to his chamber, not letting anyone enter. Alone in his room, he burned incense. Each day, he ate only a single cup-measure of honey-sweetened rice.

Now the Zhou family had originally served profane gods, so the family elders all feared that Ziliang might have been bewitched by some of these deities taking on the guise of Daoist spirits. Some family members even announced that they themselves were in danger of contamination by these perverse energies. They thus interrogated Ziliang closely. He would only answer: "It might after all be a false dream, you have no way of knowing for sure. If you are all so worried about it, you can break relations with me." At this, none of the family members could decide what to do. They determined to let the matter go for the present and wait to see how things would develop.

In the seventh month (August 515), Ziliang received a mandate from the Perfected to mingle in the affairs of the world so that people would no longer be suspicious. From this time on, Ziliang was more active than ever before, bustling about and managing temple affairs.

Several months later, he moved to the Hermitage of Scarlet Solarity, where I was in residence. When I later went in reclusion to the eastern mountain, Ziliang lived alone in the western hall of Scarlet Solarity, managing the affairs of the temple and contacts with outsiders. He entertained both Daoists and laity, all of whom loved and respected him. He was the perfect gentleman by nature, slow of speech and quick of action. It could truly be said that he aided others wordlessly, with uprightness, impartiality, and not a trace of selfishness.

Last winter, in secret accord with the Perfected's instructions, he suddenly required a separate residence. On the pretext of convenience, he requested that he be allowed to build and subsequently set up a rough, three-chambered hut. It took a long time for him to complete this structure. It was not until the tenth month of this year (November 516) that he secretly completed the door and window coverings, the bed platform and curtains.

On the nineteenth (November 28, 516), his uncle came to visit and to present him with fruits [left over from the Lower Prime rites]. The uncle noticed that Ziliang stayed in the shadows and averted his face during the visit. No one could explain the reasons for this behavior.

On the twenty-sixth (December 5), Ziliang sealed all of the doors to the western and eastern halls [of Scarlet Solarity]. In his hut, he bathed and massaged himself to circulate the pneuma within his body in preparation for meditation. Then he entrusted his ledgers and ritual implements to his assistant He Wenxing. During the evening, Ziliang carried his quilt and pillows out of his temple residence, saying that he must perform purification rituals or, to others, that he was going on a short trip.

On the morning of the next day, he was alone in his hut. When he later returned to the hermitage, his appearance and speech were as usual. No one noticed anything extraordinary. Again he bathed himself with scented water and put on clean clothes. Then he played chess with Wenxing and read, repeatedly glancing out at the sundial. When the *die* hour had passed (about 3:00 P.M.), he arose, saying, "It is time." He immediately fastened his belt, lit incense, and went to the main hall of Scarlet Solarity where he did obeisance in turn to all of the powers of the Dao. He then returned straight to his hut. Everyone thought that he was preparing to perform the purification rituals he had mentioned.

About the *bu* hour (5:00 P.M.), Ziliang's younger brother Ziping found him in the meditation chamber of his hut burning incense. Ziliang came out to the door and asked Ziping why he had come. Ziping said, "Auntie has become ill. She wants you to come and fix a medicinal broth for her."

Ziliang replied: "I am also feeling a little ill. I was just about to take some medicine. You should go back now. If she is not feeling better, you can come back again." Ziping saw that there was a half-cup measure of liquor heating in a kettle in Ziliang's hut.

Ziping hastily returned to their aunt and repeated Ziliang's message to her. She was greatly alarmed. She immediately ordered Ziping to run back to Ziliang's hut. When he reached the hut, Ziping saw Ziliang lying prone on the floor and did not dare enter. Within a few moments, Ziliang's mother and aunt reached the hut as well and, seeing Ziliang prostrate on the floor, began to wail mournfully: "What have you done? What have you done?"

Ziliang only closed his eyes, raising his hand to snap his fingers three times, and said: "Don't cry out. Don't cry out. You will ruin everything."

Ziliang's mother, in trying to raise his head, stepped on his headcloth. He rolled over, his hand still raised, and repeatedly fumbled with his headcloth, setting it straight. In a moment, his breathing ceased.

Ziliang had ignited in his censer a sliver of frankincense about the size of a cowhage bean. When he died, it had not yet stopped burning. Judging from this, we can estimate that only about half the time it takes to eat a meal had elapsed since he took the elixir. He was only twenty years old.

He had clothed himself only in his undergarments, his sleeping robes and his Daoist ritual robes, the sash of which was tightly tied. He had removed his everyday outer garments and folded them. His face and body were fresh and unblemished, as if he were still alive. Everyone who heard of the event or who saw him was shocked and dismayed.

On the twenty-ninth (December 8), Zhou Ziliang was prepared for burial and a mound was readied on the easternmost ridge. At the *die* hour (around 2:00 P.M.) on the third day of the eleventh month (December 12, 516), Ziliang's coffin was lowered into the ground and earth was carried to form his grave mound.

From this time forward Zhou Ziliang was remote from me in both voice and form—he appeared to me in neither vision nor dream. Such is the gulf of separation between humans and the spirits. But should I not await the proper moment to meet with him again?

The means by which Ziliang achieved the Dao as well as his present rank and style in the spirit world are all layed out in his records. Here I have simply summarized some of his earthly activities as well as what I observed of him to form a preface to his own records.

Four letters, their seals still damp, were found on the bookshelf in Ziliang's lodgings. One was addressed to me, one to his aunt and mother, one to his uncle, and the lengthiest one, of four sheets in length, to the Daoists of the Southern Hall and the eastern mountain. All were farewell letters dated the twenty-seventh. Judging from these facts, Ziliang probably had written them after his return from Scarlet Solarity and before he began to burn the incense. In addition, the kettle was checked. It seemed to smell only of ordinary liquor. Ziliang's earthenware basin had been washed out and was odorless. No traces of drugs were found anywhere. There was really no evidence as to which drug he had used to achieve the Dao. [Note: In Ziliang's *Records* there was a recipe for the "Ninefold Perfected Jade-Liquor Elixir." Presumably this is what he used.]

I am full of remorse about this affair. I regret that I did not earlier look into Ziliang's activities. His letter causes me to blame myself.

I sent people to inspect all of Ziliang's chests and book boxes, hoping to find any records he might have left behind, but not a scrap was ever found. He Wenxing said that on the sixteenth (November 25) Ziliang had burnt two bundles of writings—over a hundred pages—and had not heeded when Wenxing had tried to stop him. Hearing that so many of his writings had gone up in smoke, I was even more aggrieved.

On the morning of the first day of the eleventh month (December 10), I personally went to the cavern of Yankou peak to see what I could find. I saw a large sealed letter-case that had been thrown inside. Climbing to an overhanging precipice, I was able to snag and retrieve it. I then did obeisance, respectfully requesting permission [of the spirits to whom it had been entrusted] and returned with it.

When I opened it, I saw that it was indeed a record of the instructions Zhou Ziliang had received from the Perfected. For the fifth month there were only four entries dating from the summer solstice forward. The records for the sixth and seventh months were complete. From the eighth month to the end of the seventh month of this year, there were only scattered entries, briefly outlining what had occurred and what was said. I could not fathom how Zhou Ziliang could have experienced further events such as those of the sixth and seventh months and still not recorded them. But it must be that he purposely abbreviated things in this manner. As I think of these things now, I fear that we will never know more. How could we?

During those weeks when the Perfected first began descending to him, Ziliang had both leisure and quiet. Later, all was hustle and bustle for him and he was forever involved in various duties so that he could not manage to get away by himself much. As a result, when he came to write out his visions, he was only able to record brief entries. I do not think that the instructions and admonitions he received from the Perfected during that period of over ten months could really have been as sparse as this. It is a shame. Not looking into this properly was the fault of his master—my fault.

Also, from the eighth to the tenth month of this year, there is not a single entry. I even looked at the remains of those writings he had burnt, but there was nothing.

That which Ziliang confided to his aunt or to me was in fact only a few items from his records. These items were as follows: (1) On that day when everyone blamed him for sleeping during the day on the summer solstice, he could not but tell something. (2) When he was blamed for ceasing to eat meat, he was forced to state his reasons. (3) That time when he helped me to prepare incantations for summoning rain and the Perfected commanded him to write them out in black ink rather than red, he could not but tell me why he suggested this. (4) When he was told by the Perfected of the divine order canceling my summons to fill a celestial position, the Perfected instructed Ziliang to tell me.

Other than these four occasions, even when questioned he would answer briefly or evasively so as not to reveal the directives of the Perfected. Because of this, I simply stopped asking after awhile.

After we moved to Scarlet Solarity Temple, I would ask him to direct appropriate questions to the Perfected. Later I would repeatedly inquire as to whether he had received an answer and he would always say "not yet," thus keeping the words of the Perfected secret. Looking at his records now, I see that he did indeed receive answers. It must have been that he was afraid to relay responses to such questions because people would give him thank-you presents and then everyone would come to rely on him for information. Then, if he did not ask the Perfected, he would be blamed by people; but if he did ask, he would violate the instructions of the Perfected. This is why he was so secretive about the whole thing.

[Note: The *Records* contain many secret names of the Perfected and Transcendents as well as their precepts and teachings, just like scripture. Just as with scripture, it is required that one purify the scripture table on which the *Records* are placed and the cloth with which they are touched. One must bathe oneself and burn incense before reading them. If one wants to copy them for transmission to others, one must also make appropriate announcements to all of the gods and to the mysterious possessors of these texts. It is not permissible haphazardly to write out their contents.]

FROM ZHOU'S RECORDS, ANNOTATED BY TAO HONGJING

On the day of the summer solstice (June 20, 515), slightly before noon, I was sleeping on the bed on the south side of my residence. I awoke and ordered Shansheng [note: his aunt's seven-year-old brother] to lower the curtains of my bed. I had not quite fallen back asleep when I suddenly saw a man about six feet in height. His mouth and nose were small and he had sternly knit eyebrows and bushy sideburns that were speckled with white. He looked to be about forty years old. He wore a scarlet robe and a red headcloth topped with cicada-wing decorations and trailing extremely long ribbons. His purple leather belt was about seven inches wide and carried a pouch decorated with a dragon's head. On his feet were purple sandals that made a whistling sound as he walked.

There were twelve persons in attendance upon him. Two held up his trailing robes as he walked. They had their hair in double buns like those of the old women of Yongjia and wore purple blouses and green trousers under skirts. The trousers restricted their steps so that they walked extremely slowly. Three others wore purple trousers, tunics, and flat headcloths. Each bore a jade slip, but I could not make out the writing. The final seven all had white cloth trousers and tunics and white leather boots. Each carried something. One had a rolled mat under his arm, one carried a scepter and a five-colored feather fan, one carried a large scroll, one carried paper, a writing brush and a large black inkstone, another one grasped an umbrella.

This umbrella was shaped like a feather, but it seemed to be made of various colors of silk, so that it was wondrously variegated. It was round and deep, and the black handle was extremely long. After they had entered the room, this person propped the umbrella under the eaves by the door.

The other two dressed in white both carried bags that seemed to be as big as small posts and looked as if they were stuffed with writings. The person carrying the mat unrolled it and put it on my reading couch. It was white and glowing and woven of a grass like a calamus rush mat, though the weave was larger. Six of these servants first entered the room and leaned against Ziping's bed.

As soon as the head-man entered the room, he knitted his brows and said to them, "He is living too close!"

Then he sat down on the mat and leaned his forearm on my bookstand, where my brush and ruler were laid. He grabbed the brush and ruler, placed them in my brush holder, and moved the brush holder to the north side of the stand. He turned to his attendants and said "Why didn't you bring my writing table?"

"When your lordship set out, you were not planning on coming here," they replied.

That person then addressed me, saying: "I am a deputy in the administrative offices of this mountain. I came to greet you because your conduct is without flaw."

I rose and staightened my tunic but did not answer. He continued: "Today is an auspicious day. It is almost noon; have you performed the purification rituals?"

"I performed the normal morning obeisances and ate. I have not yet learned the purification rites."

"It is permissible to eat at noon on such days, but sleeping on the summer solstice is not beneficial. You should not always be such a sleepyhead," he said.

"I seem to be coming down with something and feel fatigued. I was so tired I could not help but sleep."

"Well, there's no real harm in a little rest," he said.

Just then a wind arose and was about to blow over the umbrella, so he ordered his assistants to see to it.

The youngster Chidou was playing in the courtyard. He came running by and was about to bump the umbrella, but an attendant pushed him lightly to the side with his hands. At the same time, Langshan came to fetch a cup from the shelf and, in so doing, knocked into the attendant and almost fell over, but other attendants caught him in time.

"Who was that youngster?" the deputy asked.

"His family is from Qiantang and is surnamed Yu," I said. "He was sent to this place [by his Buddhist father] to stay for a while."

"Well, do not allow him to run around naked like that or the spirits will see him," said the deputy. He also asked about Langshan.

"His family is in Yongjia. He came to live with Master Tao," I replied.

"Your Master Tao is a person of perfect aspirations. That is why others throw themselves under his protection." The deputy then turned his attentions to me: "Your father was not without minor transgressions during his life. He only resolved these matters some three years ago. For the time being he is in a place where he is no longer troubled by his past misdeeds. He told me that his tomb is in the state of Yue and, even if you were personally to urge him to move it, he would not be willing. You should fill up that trench you have been digging south of here.

"Your father wanted to come with me today but could not because the proper documents have not yet been filled out. In the spring of next year, he will be reborn into a prince's family—you see, he must reemerge into the world since his former transgressions have not been entirely redeemed."

[Note: In the *jiawu* year (514), Ziliang had wanted to fetch his father's casket, but nothing came of it. . . . I went to look and there is indeed a pit that had been filled in.]

"Now your own past lives are a source of blessing for you, so you have come to know the true doctrine. In this life as well you have lost faith with neither god nor man. According to your registers of life, you have yet another forty-six years to live. It is so that 'Just as those born as humans cling to life, those who die and become spirits cherish the mysterious and dark,' but, speaking truthfully, the 'mysterious and dark' is by far superior.

"At present, our office has an open position. We desire that you fill it. The protocols are nearly settled so there is no need for me to say more about that. You are to be summoned in the tenth month of next year. I came to notify you so that you may begin making preparations ahead of time. If you choose to disobey this order, your records will be charged over to the Three Bureaus where the fate of mortals is decided. Do not be imprudent!"

My face showed my fear. The deputy continued: "Should you remain in this world, sowing transgressions, how will you ever repay them all? On the other hand, by taking up an official position in my grotto, you will come face to face with heavenly Perfected and roam freely through the administrative centers of the sages. Just consider! There is no better spot below the heavens!"

I said, "I only desire to follow your instructions."

"It is not," he went on, "that you have been without your minor faults. You should meditate on these and repent of them, for if you do not, they may obstruct your progress. Those who practice the Dao do not go about naked or reveal their topknots. [In Chinese belief, ghosts always appeared with disheveled hair. Mediums, when possessed by the spirits of the dead, would thus loosen their hair. To distinguish their visionary practice from that of popular mediums, Daoists always wore their hair in a topknot, which was to be kept covered. Nakedness, too, was to be avoided out of fear of spirit incursion through the unprotected nether orifices of the body.] Nor are they reckless and unrestrained toward the innocent. In all of your actions, as well as in what you eat and drink, you should strictly adhere to the regulations. I will speak with you again shortly, but this is all I want to tell you now. I am returning to my post. If you have any hesitations or doubts, I will not be far. Guard my words and do not reveal them to the uninvolved—this does not, of course, include your fellow aspirants on this mountain."

With that, he arose from his mat. He had not yet gone out the door when he saw beyond the gate several children playing. At this, he turned and added: "Do not allow the children to draw near to the ritual area or the meditation chamber. The meditation chamber contains scriptures. It is positioned on the foundations of a former temple which burned down. There are spirit soldiers still guarding the spot. Your residence is too near to this area. [This is the reason for the deputy's comment ("He is living too close!") on first entering Ziliang's chamber.] Do not enter it lightly. These children are yet innocent, so their actions will be the responsibility of the family heads.

"Further, the cause of your aunt's illness is deep-rooted. Although it will not kill her, it will be difficult to heal."

"Once we seem to have healed her, the illness arises again in her stomach. How can this be removed?" I asked.

"You cannot remove it immediately. I do not know if it can be done in months or even years. If it is possible to determine the blockage in her stomach, I will tell you." The children departed and he descended the steps and disappeared.

NIGHT OF THE SIXTH MONTH, FOURTH DAY [JUNE 30, 515]

The Huayang lad came and bestowed on me the following words:

"If you wish to free your thoughts and join with the spirits, you must not mix in worldly affairs. The person constantly in your thoughts right now only desires to seek her own benefit. If you are unable to aid her, she will be displeased. Though you now serve the honored ones, she bitterly upbraids you. When you are scolded, you should envision the gods within your body. Though you hear, your heart should not receive such words, nor should your mouth respond. It should be as if she were cursing an animal or a bird. After such incidents, you should immediately bathe, since anger is a great defilement which robs the body. Once you are so defiled, the Perfected spirits will not descend to you and perverse pneuma will enter into your body.

"Of old there was one named Liu Wenchang whose master, Li Shaolian, was violent and abusive. Shaolian beat and cursed his disciple without restraint. Whenever this happened, Wenchang would verbally respond. After eleven years, the mountain spirits invaded Wenchang and put him to the test. He thereupon fell prey to perverse influences and was infected with illness. Today he is a common runner in the offices of the Guarantor of Human Destinies. He is able to serve the correct spirits solely due to his loyalty and simplicity in his former life. Li Shaolian is still in the world, where he suffers day and night and may not even see the spirits. Let this be a lesson to you. You must be cautious."

[Note: Last year I heard from members of Ziliang's family that his aunt often practiced by ingesting various talismans (a common Celestial Master practice). She always ordered Ziliang to write these talismans for her. Once Ziliang began to have communications with the spirits, he would be late in writing the talismans or slack off in other ways. His aunt would then scold him bitterly, saying such things as "when one raises a dog, it should bark and chase off rats—no one would bother to raise sand! You only write talismans and copy texts! And now you don't even work at that. What good are you?!?" Each time this happened, Ziliang would get angry. The instructions here probably are the result of these incidents. Now his aunt feared that he was slacking off in his required services to others and often punished him during that period of time. After this, Ziliang, whenever he was scolded, would always just smile contentedly and then go to bathe. Everyone, young and old, thought this very strange.

As to his relationship to his master, I never had an angry word with him or scowled at him. The comparison to Liu Wenchang and Li Shaolian must only be a metaphor for his relationship to his aunt.]

NIGHT OF THE NINTH DAY, SEVENTH MONTH (AUGUST 4, 515)

The Two Perfected Zhou and Wang of Ziyang and the Certifier of Registers, Lord Mao, appeared. Their dress was as before. About a dozen attendants accompanied them, among whom was the lad of Ziyang. They spoke together for a long time and then the Certifier of Registers said to me:

"We have been very busy lately. The affairs of Heaven are many and troublesome for us gods. On the sixth, I went to the Palace of Eastern Florescence and saw that your name was already inscribed on the green tablets. Your position is 'Overseer, Guarantor of Dawn.' You are now my underling. Is this not an exalted position? It corresponds perfectly with your hidden destiny. Though this is not your rank here in the world, you should begin to comport yourself accordingly. . . ."

Wang Ziyang said: "This is a great achievement, but I fear that the trials will be difficult."

I then made bold to ask: "How many trials will there be? No matter if the trials are great or small, I fear that this mortal may try to avoid them. How could I not be afraid?"

"There should be two small trials," Wang responded, "perhaps wolves and wild dogs, or strange noises and shapes such as would frighten a mortal. When you see such things you should merely settle your emotions and act with determination. Do not be afraid. If you do not pass these trials, it will only temporarily delay your progress."

The Certifier of Registers went on: "All of the Directors of Destiny and the gods of various localities, together with their scribes, were assembled at the Palace of Eastern Florescence to check the registers of life. Of all people in the world, not one in fifty had a praiseworthy record; not to mention achieving the status of divine Transcendent—those were only two or three in a hundred million! There were also quite a few who had achieved Transcendence and later been dropped from the ledgers. I am beginning to worry that there will be no names left on the registers of Transcendence. This is especially worrisome in that the era is fast drawing to a close and the world is increasingly troubled by calamities. Those whose names were dropped from the registers this month must be reported to the Palace of the Grand Bourne at the turn of the seasons and further have their registers of death reinstated at Mount Tai. Such as these are really pitiable! Some were dropped because they lacked diligence in their practice or because someone who preceded them in death implicated them in the practice of perverse religion. Others were diligent at first but became lax and lost all they had achieved. What a pity!

"On the other hand, there are those who are about to ascend into the cloud-filled heavens; those for whom the sun and moon do not shine in vain. The Perfected descend to such as these and bestow the teachings upon them. Some dwell deep in the mountains; others have studied the Dao for years. No one knows about them. We Perfected often descend to instruct such as you—and who now knows about you?"

"Certifier of Registers Mao is only telling you this by way of exhortation," added Lord Zhou. "Do not slack off while you are here on Earth. You are already approaching the status of a lower Transcendent. You will eventually rise to the rank of middle-level Transcendent and will be able to travel to the Grand Bourne, piloting a chariot drawn by dragons and kirin. Will that not be joyous?"

Lord Wang said: "The exhortations of the Certifier of Registers Mao and of Zhou Ziyang are profound indeed. You should take note of them. On this mountain there are three or four people who have already reached the status of lower-level Transcendent. Do you want to know who they are?"

I then inquired as to the status of my Master, Elder Tao [Hongjing]. He responded: "If you only model yourself on him, your pursuit of Transcendence will be easy. Tao long ago reached the top rank of lower-level Transcendence."

[Note: Originally Ziliang had written "middle of the middle ranks of Transcendence," but this had been crossed out in dark ink and "top rank of lower-level Transcendence" had been written in instead. I do not know the reason for this. Since it says "long ago reached," perhaps I have recently been dropped two ranks for negligence. Lord Wang said that there were four people on this mountain who had already gained Transcendence, but Ziliang did not ask who they were. I wish that he had.]

So then I asked about my aunt. He replied: "She has no major transgressions, but she must be more diligent. She might achieve Transcendence in a later life, but for this one there is nothing to report."

[Note: Ziliang's aunt was originally from Qiantang and was surnamed Zhang. When she was three, her father died and she returned with her mother to Yongjia. Her mother remarried into the Xu family and the aunt took this surname. When she was ten, she left the family and began to study the Dao with a master in Yuyao, where they set up a meditation hall. She was by nature extremely upright and so was eventually given charge over the son of her younger sister, Ziliang. When she was thirty-five, Daoist officials, in response to governmental restrictions, urged her to leave the order for the sake of convenience and to marry into the Zhu family of Shangyu. (This refers to the 504 edict of Liang Wudi, on the occasion of his conversion to Buddhism, that Daoists all return to lay life.) With this, she fell into the ways of the world (an oblique reference to the fact that she had sexual intercourse with her husband) and, out of shame and remorse, developed her stomach illness. After four years, she took her newborn son and returned to Yongjia. Still, her illness has not been cured. Now, eleven years later, she tells me "since I was young I have never harmed an ant or needlessly broken the stem of a flower. I eat only once each day. Still I regret that my disposition is too stern and that I am harsh with those under me." As Lord Wang says, there is really no grave transgression here, but she is not without her minor flaws. It is probably due to the fact that she was not able to follow the destiny she had given herself to. She has been wronged by the spirits and demons, but since her studies were broken off, how can she achieve Transcendence in this life? Perhaps in two or three more lifetimes she will be more fortunate.]

Then Lord Zhou asked me my name. I was flustered and unable to respond with the name that I had previously been bestowed. I only responded without thinking, "Zhou Ziliang."

"How could you be so negligent?" Lord Zhou angrily shouted. "You are the Daoist Zhou Taixuan (Grand Mystery), with the byname Xuling (Spirit of the Void)! Your worldly name is Ziliang. As written on the jade slips of all the celestial records, your name is Taixuan! Do not reveal this secret name to the profane."

——14——

Visions of Mañjuśrī on Mount Wutai

Daniel Stevenson

While visiting Mount Wutai in North China in 840 C.E., the Japanese pilgrim Ennin (793–864) came across a thriving cloister by the name of Bamboo Grove Monastery (Zhulin si). In addition to being a major center of Tiantai learning and practice (the tradition with which Ennin himself identified), Bamboo Grove Monastery was renowned for a particularly compelling method of intoning the name of Amitābha Buddha, known as the "five-tempo Buddha-recitation" (*wuhui nianfo*). According to local tradition, both the Bamboo Grove Monastery and the five-tempo chant were the creation of a Buddhist visionary by the name of Fazhao (d. ca. 820). Fazhao himself is said to have received inspiration for them directly from the Buddhist divinities Amitābha and Mañjuśrī while he was in a state of religious transport (*samādhi*). As described in Fazhao's (*Jingtu wuhui nianfo lue fashi yizan, Taishō daizōkyō* [T] 46.476b), the *wuhui* or five tempos (literally: "five groupings") represent five different rhythmic and tonal patterns for chanting the Buddha's name (i.e., "*na-mo A-mi-tuo-fo*"): (1) high tone, leisurely chant; (2) high and rising tone, leisurely chant; (3) neither leisurely nor fast-paced chant; (4) chant with gradually increasing pace; (5) rapid repetition of the four characters "*A-mi-tuo-fo*." Fazhao states (T 47.476b), "These five forms of chanting proceed from the leisurely to the fast-paced, during the course of which one concentrates one's thought wholly on the Buddha, dharma, and saṅgha and abandons all other thoughts. When thought becomes no-thought, it is the door of nonduality of the Buddha. When sound becomes no-sound, it is absolute truth. Hence, practicing mindful recollection of the Buddha for the rest of your days, you will always be in accord with the nature of reality."

Upon his return to Japan, Ennin instituted Fazhao's practice of five tempo recitation and contemplation of Amitābha to the community of Mount Hiei, the home complex of the Tendai order situated on the northern edge of the imperial capital of Kyoto. From there Fazhao's teaching played an influential role in the spread of devotion to Amitābha among the Japanese monastic and lay populace, eventually paving the way for the emergence of the independent Pure Land schools of Hōnen and Shinran.

Fazhao's impact was felt just as keenly in China. His distinctive style of chant drew a sizable following throughout the Wutai region (northern Shanxi) and the Tang dynasty capital at Chang'an, ultimately attracting the attention of the imperial court itself. During the reigns of Emperor Daizong (r. 762–779) and his successor, Dezong (r. 780–805), Fazhao was honored with the title of state preceptor, and his five-tempo chant was introduced to various "pure land cloisters" (*jingtu yuan*) in the major state-sponsored monasteries of the capital. From there it appears to have been disseminated to pure land cloisters in state temples throughout the provinces, all as part of a general effort to reform vinaya and liturgical practice nationwide.

Fazhao produced only two major treatises that we know of, both of which were ritual works concerned with his five-tempo Buddha-recitation. They in turn vanished from China during the persecutions of Buddhism by the Emperor Wuchang a half-century later, leaving little more of Fazhao than his memory and vestiges of his chant. And yet Fazhao must have established quite a legacy for himself in the eyes of his contemporaries. For Pure Land historiographers from the Song period to the present have consistently honored him as the third or fourth patriarch of the Chinese Pure Land movement, as well as an incarnation of the Pure Land saint Shandao.

Historical notoriety in the Chinese Buddhist tradition does not necessarily commend a person as a good subject for examining either the origins or the actualities of its religious life and institutions. Often such eminence is itself the retrospective creation of later tradition and, therefore, of little relevance to either the person or the period it purports to describe. Moreover, the standard biographies and epitaphs on which we are required to draw are typically exemplary or commemorative in character, given more to stock displays of virtue than to an individualized portrait of inner religious life. When figures become invested with a particular ideological significance—as in the case of Fazhao and other historical patriarchs of the great Chinese Buddhist schools—often their narratives are further redacted to reflect specific ideals of sectarian thought and practice. In either event, we are confronted with a highly selective portrait that may not only be anachronistic but systematically edits out the sort of complex nuances that might tell us something substantial about the individual in question and the period in which he or she lived.

As one might expect of a Pure Land patriarch, the image of Fazhao vouchsafed by Buddhist historians does indeed pay service to the usual conventions of Pure Land hagiography: He despairs over the decline of dharma and the corruption of the age, turns to Amitābha as the only viable path to salvation, evangelizes extensively among the Chinese populace, and experiences the requisite signs for confirming his rebirth in the Pure Land. And yet Fazhao's biography at the same time belies these paradigms in the most unsettling way, his "pure" devotion to Amitābha spilling over into visions of paradisial grottoes and themes of physical transmogrification that are more suggestive of religious Daoism than of the simple Pure Land doctrines of faith and rebirth with which we are familiar.

If one stands convinced of the historical applicability of normative descriptions of Pure Land piety, a logical solution to this tension might be to marginalize Fazhao as an exceptional figure, making him either a man of unusual spiritual proclivities (i.e., a hysteric who hallucinated a lot) or a syncretist whose story simply does not fit the mold. However, there may be other factors at work as well, including the possibility that these inconsistencies are themselves apparent rather than real. Could it be, for example, that they reflect differences in the literary genre and editorial bias of the Buddhist sources at our disposal, or the unrealistic nature of our own expectations of how a Pure Land Buddhist should behave?

All told there are some eight or nine biographies of Fazhao preserved in major Chinese compendia. Their narratives center around a series of visions that Fazhao experienced while dwelling on Mount Wutai during the early 770s, the contents of which they present in nearly identical form. Rather than originating from the sort of formal epitaph or commemorative testimonial that usually informs Buddhist biography, text-critical studies indicate that they are redacted from a first-hand or "veritable record" (shilu) of Fazhao's experiences compiled and circulated by Fazhao himself. This would indicate that differences in literary genre rather than personality may indeed be at work, in which case Fazhao's biography becomes an invaluable source for illumining neglected dimensions of medieval Buddhist spirituality and testing the limits of some of our assumptions about Chinese Pure Land Buddhism.

Happily, the record of Fazhao's visions on Wutai is not the only personal testimonial by Fazhao that we have. When Fazhao's chief work on the five-tempo recitation turned up among the cache of manuscripts discovered at Dunhuang in western China at the turn of this century, its middle fascicle was found to contain a vivid account of the revelatory episode during which Fazhao received the five-tempo chant from the Buddha Amitābha (*Rite for Intoning the Buddha's Name, Reciting Scripture, and Performing Meditation According to the Five Tempos of the Pure Land* [*Jingtu wuhui nianfo songjing guanxing yi*], T 85.1253b–1254a). In addition to shedding light on one of the most pivotal, yet obscure, events of Fazhao's career (due to the loss of Fazhao's works, Chinese biographers had only a dim awareness of this event), this document complements the Wutai record by expanding our glimpse into the complex world of Fazhao's religious life.

Translations of both the Wutai visions from Fazhao's biography and Fazhao's revelation of the five-tempo recitation are included below. The Wutai sequence is taken from the *Expanded Accounts of Mount Clear-and-Cool* (*Guang qingliang zhuan*), compiled in 1060 by the monk Yanyi. Although principally concerned with the history and form of the Wutai pilgrimage cult (Mount Clear-and-Cool being an alternate name for Mount Wutai), Yanyi's text contains the most detailed account of Fazhao's visions and the version thought to be closest to his original "veritable record." The Amitābha revelation (rendered in its entirety) is extracted from the Dunhuang text of Fazhao's *Rite for Intoning the Name of the Buddha, Reciting Scripture, and Performing Meditation According to the Five Tempos of the Pure Land.* Taken together, these two documents provide us with a number of fruitful areas for inquiry: As firsthand testimonials from an eminent Tang-period monk—a rare commodity in any period of Chinese Buddhist history—they allow us to survey the manifold world of medieval Buddhist religious life (and Pure Land spirituality in particular) in ways that may be more reflective of its natural syntax. Since Fazhao is regarded as one of the great patriarchs of Chinese Pure Land, they at the same time offer an instructive counterpart to prevailing norms of Pure Land hagiography and ideology, allowing us to highlight some of the limitations posed by both the sources and the strategies that we use to study Chinese Buddhism. Finally, being written testimonials of visionary or revelatory experience, they raise questions about the nature and rhetorical function of religious experience as a whole within the Chinese Buddhist tradition.

As background to these two documents, a few additional details about Fazhao's career may prove instructive. Almost nothing is known of Fazhao's secular background and early years, beyond the fact that he grew up and took ordination in Sichuan. Sometime in his early twenties Fazhao journeyed down the Yangzi River to Jiangsu and Zhejiang, the scene of a recent upsurge of interest in Tiantai teaching led by Xuanlang (673–754) and his famous successor, Zhanran (711–782). Shortly thereafter, in 765, Fazhao returned upriver to Mount Lu for the purpose of visiting sites associated with Lushan Huiyuan (334–416), the fifth-century monk hailed by later devotees as the progenitor of Chinese Pure Land Buddhism. Huiyuan is said to have made a collective vow, together with various monk and lay disciples, to seek rebirth in the Pure Land of Amitābha Buddha. For this he came to be regarded by later Chinese Pure Land advocates as one of the first Pure Land patriarchs. His Society of the White Lotus served as the primary historical model for lay and monastic Pure Land societies of the Song. An account of his life (and his Pure Land affiliations) is available in Eric Zürcher, *The Buddhist Conquest of China.* During a period of intensive practice of buddha-mindfulness meditation (*nianfo sanmei*) on Mount Lu, Fazhao experienced an ecstatic vision of Amitābha Buddha in which he was directed to seek out a monk by the name of Chengyuan in Nanyue in South China. Before the year was out, Fazhao arrived in Nanyue, located Chengyuan, and took him as his teacher.

Chengyuan (712–802) was himself a native of Chengdu in Sichuan. As a youth he studied under the Chan master Chuji (669–736), a grand-disciple of the fifth patriarch, Hongren, and proponent of a distinctive Sichuan branch of Chan that later came to be known as the Jingzhong line. Subsequent travels in quest of the dharma took him to Huizhen, an heir to the Tiantai and Vinaya lines of Yuquan Monastery (in Hubei), as well as the famous Pure Land teacher Cimin Huiri (680–746?). By the time Fazhao joined his congregation in Nanyue, Chengyuan's diversified religious training had melded into a form of exclusive devotion to Amitābha Buddha that drew together elements from Tiantai, Chan, the Lü or Vinaya school of Daoxuan, and the Pure Land teachings of Huiri.

The heart of Chengyuan's program of religious practice seems to have been the *pratyutpanna samādhi* (*banzhou sanmei*)—a form of ritualized meditation that was popular in various Tiantai and Pure Land circles. As described in Tiantai sources of the period, the pratyutpanna samādhi entailed retreat in a specially consecrated sanctuary—the so-called pratyutpanna or buddha-mindfulness sanctuary (*banzhou* or *nianfo daochang*)—for a fixed period of ninety days. During this time the practitioner continually circumambulated an altar to Amitābha Buddha, while simultaneously intoning the Buddha's name and visualizing his sublime form. Through this blend of ascetic rigor, sustained concentration, and invocation of Amitābha's grace one sought to enter a state of meditative ecstasy (*samādhi*), thereby achieving visions of the Buddha or insight into ultimate reality itself. Judging from Fazhao's writings, Chengyuan probably supplemented this regimen with methods taught by Cimin Huiri, as well as a form of meditation from the Jingzhong line of Chan known as *yinsheng nianfo* or "intoning the Buddha's name by drawing out the sound." *Yinsheng nianfo* coordinated chanting of the Buddha's name with concentration on the exhale of the breath, thereby making it a powerful blend of two venerable forms of Buddhist meditation—meditation on the breath (*ānāpāna-smṛti*) and mindful recollection of the Buddha (*buddhānusmṛti*).

Through Chengyuan's influence, the ninety-day pratyutpanna samādhi became Fazhao's chosen form of cultivation, inspiring him in 766 to vow, for the rest of his life, to dedicate the three months of the summer retreat to the practice of pratyutpanna samādhi. This resolution marked something of a culmination in Fazhao's spiritual career. For it was not long thereafter, during the first pratyutpanna retreat after Fazhao's pledge, that the Buddha Amitābha revealed the five-tempo recitation to him.

By his own testimony, two weeks into the rite Fazhao slipped into a state of deep ecstasy or samādhi, during which he was transported to the Pure Land of Sukhāvatī. There Amitābha personally entrusted him with his special method for intoning the Buddha's name. The five tempos of the practice were said to function in mystical sympathy with the exquisite music emitted by the flora and fauna of the Pure Land itself, thus making the method an effective antidote for the corrupt age of the decline of dharma (*mofa*). Though charged by Amitābha to spread this teaching, Fahzao waited for nearly eight years (774 in Taiyuan) before he expounded the practice openly.

Not long after his visitation from Amitābha, Fazhao began to experience the series of visions that ultimately beckoned him to Wutai, and it is here that the biographies by Yanyi, Zanning, and others begin their tale. The first of these experiences occurred in 767. However, it was not until three years later, in 769—after several such episodes—that Fazhao understood their significance and finally set out for Wutai.

Mount Wutai or the "five-terraced mountain" consists of a cluster of five peaks situated in northern Shanxi between the city of Pingcheng (Datong) to the north and Taiyuan to the south. In pre-Buddhist times it appears to have been revered as a place of medicinal herbs and Daoist immortals, although details of this early history remain obscure. With the steady growth of Buddhism under the Northern Wei dynasty (386–535), Wutai came to be identified with the mythic Mount Clear-and-Cool, the earthly abode of the bodhisattva Mañjuśrī described in the *Avataṃsaka Sūtra (Huayanjing)*. Its fame as a center of sacred pilgrimage became firmly established under the Tang (618–907), especially with the rising fortunes of the Huayan school and court patronage of the esoteric Buddhist master Amoghavajra (Bukong, 705–774), a personal devotee of Mañjuśrī. By the time Fazhao arrived on Wutai in 770, the mountain was home to a well-defined array of monasteries and sacred sites. Geographical details and lore of these wonders were available not only through a rich oral tradition but in the systematic textual form of Huixiang's *Old Record of Mount Clear-and-Cool (Gu qingliang zhuan)* (677) as well.

Fazhao's adventures on Wutai fall into two main episodes. The first of these centers around his journey-in-spirit to the magical Bamboo Grove Monastery and subsequent building of its earthly replica. By all indications this sort of phenomenon was not unusual for Mount Wutai. For, in addition to the Bamboo Grove, we hear of at least three other monasteries in the area that were founded under similar circumstances. The Monastery of the Golden Pavilion (Jingesi)—the earliest and most striking example of this sort of architectural revelation—was revealed in a vision to the dhyāna master Daoyi in 736. With the support of the esoteric Buddhist master Amoghavajra and the Tang imperial court, its terrestrial counterpart was finally completed in 770, the very year that Fazhao came to Wutai. Hence, Fazhao's vision of the Bamboo Grove Monastery, his decision to publicize the event, and his effort over the next thirty years to realize his vision in wood and stone would seem to fit a pattern that was already familiar to the patrons of Wutai. The first complex of buildings was completed on the site sometime between 777 and 805. By the time Ennin visited Wutai several decades later, Bamboo Grove Monastery boasted some six separate cloisters (all of splendid design) and had sufficient prestige in the eyes of the imperial court to be honored as one of the few Buddhist monasteries permitted to perform clerical ordinations.

The second episode involves a mountain cleft known as the Diamond Grotto, perhaps the most famous of Wutai's many pilgrimage sites. The earliest legends of the Diamond Grotto connect it with the mountain spirit of Wutai and describe it as an immortals' paradise similar in character to the grotto heavens (*dongtian*) of religious Daoism. With Wutai's gradually transformation into a Buddhist pilgrimage site, the Diamond Grotto came to be identified as the terrestrial abode of Mañjuśrī and his retinue of ten thousand bodhisattvas. In so doing, however, it retained many of its indigenous characteristics, thereby greatly enriching and transforming the Chinese cult of Mañjuśrī. The continuing presence of these liaisons with Daoist and popular Chinese religious lore can be seen in the tale of Fazhao's own visionary journey to the grotto (note especially his ingestion of healing elixirs). It is also evident in the lore surrounding the figures of Buddhapāli and Wuzhu, two legendary Tang period monks who appear in Fazhao's adventures at the Diamond Grotto. According to Wutai tradition, Buddhapāli was an

Indian monk who came to Wutai in 676 to search for Mañjuśrī. After several years of trial at the hands of the latter, he was finally ushered into the Diamond Grotto paradise, never to emerge again. Wuzhu, a contemporary of Fazhao, is likewise known for having made a journey-in-spirit to the Diamond Grotto. After allegedly relating his experiences in a veritable record much like Fazhao's, he is said to have retired deep into the mountains, never to be heard from again. Like the terrestrial immortals of Daoist lore, both appear to Fazhao in etherealized form during his visit to the mythical Diamond Grotto.

Although ostensibly autobiographical, Fazhao's two revelatory testimonials are no less garnished with convention and design than any other form of literary statement. The two events of the Wutai visions and the five-tempo revelation, one will recall, are separated by some five or six years and a distance of several thousand miles. However, both were committed to writing in northern Shanxi during the early 770s, at a time when Fazhao was beginning to make his way into the elite aristocratic and monastic circles of Chang'an. In terms of literary form, Fazhao's revelation from Amitābha and the veritable record of his Wutai experiences are reminiscent of two closely related types of Buddhist testimonial known as the "tale of miraculous response" and "record of [divine] origins." Both forms were well established during the Tang period and tended to lend themselves readily to the style of first-person narrative that we find in Fazhao's texts.

The "tale of miraculous response" (yingyan ji) is a form of pious testimonial concerned with remarkable manifestations of numinous power. Accounts of this sort may focus on any number of different objects, from a given deity such as Amitābha or Avalokiteśvara (Guanyin), to sacred images, relics, pilgrimage sites (such as Wutai), and the like. Although often compiled by educated clergy or laymen, they tend to privilege diffused or popular patterns of religiosity over the narrow ideological concerns of the elite traditions of monastic Buddhism.

The connection between Fazhao's visions of Mañjuśrī and the Wutai pilgrimage cult places his story comfortably within the miracle-tale genre, especially when we consider the claim that Fazhao compiled his veritable record so that "other people may hear of it and conceive the desire to come to [Mount Wutai]." The fact that Yanyi's account of Fazhao itself appears in a collection dedicated to Wutai lore—namely, his *Expanded Accounts of Mount Clear-and-Cool*—further strengthens this identification. However, at the same time that it extols the numinous powers of Mount Wutai, Fazhao's visionary record also chronicles events leading to the founding of the Bamboo Grove Monastery. In this capacity, the veritable record of Fazhao's Wutai visions (and, for that matter, his revelation of the five-tempo recitation from Amitābha as well) come closer to the "record of origins," a genre of testimonial that is similar to the miracle tale in its concern for manifestations of sacred power but directed to more specific polemical ends, such as establishing the sanctity and legitimacy of a given text, teaching, monastery, and what not. As a rule, one tends to find tracts of this sort organically attached to the object that they are intended to promote.

One will recall that Fazhao's record of the divine Bamboo Grove Monastery took shape and circulated concurrently with his efforts to raise funds for the monastery's terrestrial counterpart. When construction was completed, the narrative itself was carved on a stele at the site of the monastery as a kind of "testimony to its divine origins." In similar fashion, the tale of Fazhao's revelation from Amitābha is incorporated directly into the *Rite for Intoning the Buddha's Name, Reciting Scripture, and Performing Meditation According to the Five Tempos of the Pure Land,* Fazhao's chief treatise on the five-tempo Buddha-recitation. Indeed, it is no accident that the revelatory narrative itself appears side by side with supporting citations from the Buddhist sūtras and a lineal history connecting Fazhao's style of practice with those of exemplary Chinese saints of the Chinese past. Both of these were common means of establishing textual and spiritual legitimacy in Tang period China. (Fazhao's lineal history centers on the practice of "buddha-mindfulness samādhi" and includes the likes of Nāgārjuna and Vasubandhu, Huiyuan, Zhiyi, Tanluan, Daochuo, Shandao, Cimin Huiri, etc.; see T 85.1255b.) Thus, the circumstances surrounding the creation and dissemination of both narratives are quite typical of the record of origins.

Considerations of literary convention and extramural interest highlight the complex nature of Fazhao's testimonials, raising suspicions about its pretensions to be a simple pious confessional and compelling us to look for unstated designs and meanings beneath its surface. Bearing in mind the circumstances under which Fazhao compiled and published the veritable record of his Wutai visions and his treatise on the five-tempo Buddha-recitation, one might want to consider how these narratives and the experiences described in them contributed to Fazhao's authority as an evangelist. (Both narratives, one will recall, were created during the early 770s, the period when Fazhao was first beginning to catch the eye of the imperial court and the elite of Chang'an.) According to his own testimony, Fazhao composed his veritable record with great reluctance, only after the persistent urging of successive visits from divine beings. The same trope appears in the tale of his revelation from Amitābha as well. The stated reason for this hesitation and secrecy is Fazhao's Buddhist altruism—that is, to save unbelievers from the sin of slandering these miracles. But might this narrative ploy serve other motives than those explicitly stated, such as enhancing Fazhao's own sanctity? If so, what do the various rhetorical forms in which religious experience and revelation are presented tell us about eighth-century notions of sainthood, the conventions that define it, and the authority that it carries in society?

While this sort of hermeneutic of suspicion can tell us a lot about the unstated social and political concerns that impinge on Fazhao's narratives, we have just as much to gain from reading the text sympathetically, as a cohesive and meaningful statement of Fazhao's spiritual experiences and purpose. Indeed, Chinese Buddhists have for generations approached his testimonials with precisely this sort of affirmation and familiarity—that it is a legitimate record of the religious experiences of an acclaimed Pure Land patriarch and saint. Hence, in this manifold assemblage of symbols, motifs, and motives, we have a rare opportunity to crawl into the personal narrative of an eminent Tang period Pure Land devotee and explore, through that narrative, the complex array of values and interests that shaped religious discourse during his day.

One useful line of enquiry is to consider ways in which Fazhao's tale conforms to or deviates from familiar notions of Pure Land spirituality, whether they be the normative images of later Chinese Pure Land hagiographical and doctrinal treatises or the accepted views of secondary scholarship. How, for example, do such ideals as the bodhisattva path, intoning of the Buddha's name, and rebirth in the Pure Land figure into these two revelatory narratives? Are they moderated in any way by the presence of other, unanticipated religious themes or attitudes? What is the cosmological and soteriological relationship between Amitābha's western Pure Land and Mañjuśrī's Diamond Grotto? On several occasions in the text, Fazhao displays extreme anguish over the impurity and limitations imposed by his mortal body. Does Fazhao's attitude toward his own physicality and his reaction to the spiritual paradise vouchsafed in his visions tell us anything significant about the meaning of Buddhist "enlightenment" or rebirth in the Pure Land? How do the Wutai pilgrimage cult and quasi-Daoist elements such as grotto-heavens and transmutation of the body through elixirs of immortality figure into Fazhao's quest? In light of this complex amalgam of symbols, ideals, and themes, is it necessary to redescribe the semantic range of such labels as "Daoism," "Buddhism," and "Pure Land" in Tang period China?

The translated passages are from *Guang qingliang zhuan* and *Jingtu wuhui nianfo songjing guanxing yi, quan zhong, xia* (Pelliot collection of the Dunhaung manuscripts [Musée Guimet, Paris]), P. 2066, 2250, 2963), in *Taishō shinshū daizōkyō*, vol. 85, pp. 1253b–54a.

Further Reading

Fazhao's place in Chinese Pure Land tradition is discussed briefly by Stanley Weinstein in *Buddhism under the Tang* (Cambridge: Cambridge University Press, 1987), pp. 67–74, as well as Chün-fang Yü in *The Revival of Buddhism during the Ming*. For the classic Tiantai description of the pratyutpanna samādhi practice, see Neal Donner and Daniel B. Stevenson, *The Great Calming and Contemplation* (Honolulu: University of Hawaii Press, 1993), pp. 234–48. For further discussion of the Jingzhong line of Chan and the *yinsheng nianfo* practice, see Seizan Yanagida, "The *Li-tai fa-pao chi* and the Ch'an Doctrine of Sudden Awakening," trans. Carl Bielefeldt, in *Early Ch'an in China and Tibet*, Berkeley Buddhist Studies Series 5, ed. Lewis Lancaster and Whalen Lai (Berkeley: Asian Humanities Press, 1983), pp. 13–50. For details on Mount Wutai and its culture, see Raoul Birnbaum, "The Manifestation of a Monastery: Shen-ying's Experiences on Mount Wu-t'ai in T'ang Context," *Journal of the American Oriental Society* 106.1:119–37; also, "Secret Halls of the Mountain Lords: The Caves of Wu-t'ai Shan," *Cahiers d'Extrême-Asie* 5 (1989–1990): 116–40; "Thoughts on T'ang Buddhist Mountain Traditions and

Their Contexts," *T'ang Studies* 2 (Winter 1984): 5–23; *Studies on the Mysteries of Mañjuśrī* (Boulder: Society for the Study of Chinese Religions, 1983); Robert M. Gimello, "Chang Shang-ying on Wu-t'ai Shan," in *Pilgrims and Sacred Sites in China*, ed. Susan Naquin and Chün-fang Yü (Berkeley: University of California Press, 1992), pp. 89–149.

Fazhao's Visionary Experiences on Mount Wutai

The Buddhist monk Fazhao was a native of Nanliang (in Sichuan Province). However, further details of his secular background are not known. On the thirteenth day of the second lunar month during the second year of the *dayan* reign period of the Tang (767 C.E.), Fazhao was taking his morning gruel in the refectory of Cloud Peak Monastery, when the image of Mount Wutai suddenly appeared in his bowl. Approximately one *li* (kilometer) to the northeast of the Monastery of the Buddha's Radiance he saw a mountain slope, along the foot of which flowed an alpine stream. On the north side of this stream there was a single stone portal. Some fifteen li beyond it stood a magnificent monastery. Its name-pillar read "Bamboo Grove Monastery of the Great Sage" (Dasheng zhulin si). The vision lasted for some time, then faded away, leaving Fazhao quite astonished.

In the morning hours of the twenty-seventh day, Mount Wutai again manifested itself in his bowl. But this time Fazhao saw the mountain range in its entirety, with Huayan Monastery and the other cloisters all clearly discernible. Everywhere the ground was a shimmering gold. And every landmark—both inside and out—was fully visible, unimpeded by mountain or forest. Pools, terraces, storied buildings, and towers, all were adorned resplendently with the myriad precious gems. The Great Sage Mañjuśrī, accompanied by his retinue of ten thousand bodhisattvas, [could be seen] dwelling in its midst. [In the heavens and the terrain around the mountain] pure realms of the buddhas appeared. When the meal concluded the vision disappeared.

After this, the doubt in Fazhao's mind became even more pressing. Thus, when he returned to his cloister (*yuan*), he promptly related his experience to the other monks and asked whether anyone among them had ever been to Mount Wutai. At that point two *ācāryas*, Jiayan and Tanhui, spoke up, saying, "At such and such a time we once journeyed to Mount Wutai and passed the [summer] retreat at the Monastery of the Buddha's Radiance." Their recollections of the mountain corresponded almost exactly with what the master had seen in his bowl. Fazhao thereby found the answer to his question, but he still had not yet resolved to make pilgrimage there himself.

In the summer of the fourth year [of the *dayan* era] (769), Fazhao entered the sanctuary for buddha-mindfulness (*nianfo daochang*) in the upper story of the towered hall of Xiangdong Monastery in Hengzhou to perform the ninety-day [pratyutpanna samādhi]. During the early afternoon hours of the first or second day of the sixth month, an auspicious rainbow-hued cloud spread over the entire monastery grounds. Within the cloud multistoried towers and roofed pavilions appeared. In the pavilions several dozen divine monks, each a full ten feet tall, could be seen performing ritual circumambulation with mendicants' staffs in their hands. People everywhere throughout Hengzhou and its suburbs saw Amitābha Buddha, Mañjuśrī, Samantabhadra, and their retinue of ten thousand bodhisattvas present in the divine assembly. Their bodies were huge in scale. When the monks [of Xiangdong Monastery] saw this manifestation of the holy sages, they dropped, weeping, to the ground in prostration. The visitation lasted into the early evening hours, when it finally disappeared.

Later that same night, while Fazhao was engaged in walking meditation outside the inner sanctum, an old man of about seventy years old appeared and said to him, "Master! Once you vowed to go to Mount Wutai. How is it that you still have not gone?"

Fazhao replied, "Times are in turmoil and the journey is dangerous. If I go will I ever get there?"

The old man said, "Master, you should make haste and depart."

Fazhao promptly withdrew to the sanctuary, where he renewed his vow to travel to Mount Wutai to pay obeisance to the Holy One (Mañjuśrī) as soon as the summer [retreat] ended. That autumn, on the thirteenth day of the eighth month, he set out for Mount Wutai from Nanyue, accompanied by some ten companions. Ultimately they met with no difficulties en route.

Sometime within the first five days of the fourth month of the following year they reached the Wutai county seat. Gazing far off toward the southern expanse opposite the Monastery of the Buddha's Radiance, they saw several shafts of white light. The entire party witnessed it. On the sixth day they arrived at the Monastery of the Buddha's Radiance, where they took up residence. It turned out to be exactly like the monastery that Fazhao had seen in his bowl.

During the latter part of that very night, Fazhao happened to step out the door of his chambers. All at once a beam of white light descended down the slope of the mountain to the north and moved directly toward him, finally coming to rest in front of him. The master rushed back into the hall and asked the assembly of monks there: "What is this strange light?" They replied, "Here we frequently witness the inconceivable auroras of the great sage [Mañjuśrī]." Upon hearing this, Fazhao, with utmost solemnity, set out in pursuit of the ray of light.

Having gone about a league to the northeast of the monastery, he came to a rise, at the foot of which ran a mountain stream. On the north bank of the brook there was a stone portal. Two blue-robed youths—possibly eight or nine years old, dignified and upright in demeanor—stood to either side of the gate. One identified himself as Sudhāna; the other, Nānda. They exchanged glances of delight, bowed, then prostrated to Fazhao in greeting. "Why do you tarry so long in the cycle of birth and death and only now come to see us?" they asked. Thereupon they led him through the portal and off again toward the northeast.

After a distance of about five kilometers, they suddenly came upon a golden gate-tower. It must have been nearly one hundred feet tall, with supporting towers attached. As Fazhao proceeded through the gate, a magnificent monastery came into view, before which sprawled a great golden bridge. On a golden pillar beside it was inscribed the name "Bamboo Grove Monastery of the Great Sage." It was all just as it had appeared in Fazhao's bowl.

The precincts of the monastery covered an area of nearly twenty leagues in circumference. Within its grounds were 120 different cloisters, each magnificently adorned with jeweled pagodas. The earth itself was of pure gold. Clear brooks and flowering fruit trees filled their midst. Fazhao entered the monastery and went directly into the lecture hall. There he saw the great sage Mañjuśrī on the west and Samantabhadra on the east. Each was seated on a lion throne and engaged in preaching the dharma. Seat and body together, they towered nearly 100 feet tall. To either side of Mañjuśrī stretched a retinue of some ten thousand bodhisattvas. Samantabhadra likewise was attended by countless bodhisattvas, who circumambulated clockwise around his throne.

Arriving before the lion thrones of the two sages, Fazhao touched his forehead to the ground in obeisance and asked, "We ordinary unenlightened beings of this latter age [when the dharma is in decline] are far removed from the time of the Buddha. Our powers of wisdom grow increasingly inferior, and the obstructions of our impurities ever deeper. All manner of afflictions beshroud and bind us, so that our intrinsically enlightened buddha-nature has no possibility of manifesting. Among the vast array of Buddhist teachings, I am at a loss to tell which form of Buddhist practice is the most essential, and which will lead most easily to buddhahood and bring benefit and joy to the multitude of living beings. My sole wish is that you will strip away my net of doubt about this."

Mañjuśrī responded, "The practice of buddha-mindfulness (nianfo) that you have been using is perfectly suited to the current age. Among all the forms of Buddhist practice, none surpasses buddha-mindfulness and making of offerings to the three jewels. For accomplishing the dual cultivation of wisdom (jñāna) and merit (puṇya), [which lead to the realization of buddhahood,] it is these two methods that are the absolute essence. How so? Over countless aeons I myself practiced contemplation of the Buddha's form, invoked the Buddha's name, and made offerings [to the three jewels]. Because of these practices, I am endowed today with the omniscient wisdom of all modes (sarvākarajñatā). Thus you should know that all the teachings [of the Buddhist path]—from the perfection of wisdom (prajñāpāramitā), through manifestation of profound meditative concentrations, to the supreme perfect enlightenment realized by all the buddhas—are born from the practice of buddha-mindfulness. Mindfulness of the Buddha is the king of all teachings. Therefore, practice without cease the mindful recollection of the peerless King of Dharma!"

Fazhao again asked, "How does one perform this [buddha-]mindfulness?"

Mañjuśrī replied, "To the west of this world-realm lies a buddha-land known as Highest Bliss (Sukhāvatī), in which there resides a buddha named Amitābha. The power of that buddha's original vow is inconceivable. You should fix your mind on and carefully visualize that land. Continue this without interruption, and, when your life reaches its full term, you are certain to be born in that realm. You will then be freed forever of the fear of back-sliding. Speedily you will depart from the three realms [of cyclic birth an death] and rapidly attain to buddhahood."

Having spoken these words, the two sages each extended a golden-hued hand, massaged the crown of Fazhao's head, and gave him prediction (vyā-karaṇa) [of his future buddhahood], saying, "Because you have cultivated buddha-mindfulness, you are destined to realize supreme perfect enlighten-ment soon. For any good son or good daughter [of the Buddha] who wishes to become a buddha quickly, there is no practice that will lead more rapidly to the realization of supreme enlightenment than buddha-mindfulness. When [your life comes to its end] and you exhaust the last of this current cycle of retribution, you are certain to leave the ocean of suffering and reach the other shore [of nirvāṇa]."

The sagely one, Mañjuśrī, then spoke in verse, saying, "Those of you who long for liberation should first eliminate all thoughts of selfish pride. Envy, craving, and desire for fame and profit—all such unwholesome motives you must cast away. Concentrate solely on invoking the name of Amitābha, and you will come to abide easefully in the realm of the Buddha. When you are able to dwell easefully in the realm of the Buddha, the buddhas everywhere will always be visible. Through being able to see the buddhas at all times, you will come to know the nature of true suchness (bhūtatā). For, by speedily severing the afflictions, the nature of suchness is able to be known. Though immersed in the ocean of suffering, you will always be in bliss, just as a lotus is never encumbered by the waters [from which it grows]. Thus, with the purification of your mind you will come forth from the river of attachment and speedily gain the fruit of supreme enlightenment."

Again the bodhisattva said in verse, "The myriad dharmas are solely the product of the mind. If one realizes that mind itself is inapprehensible and always practices in accordance with this [truth], then it is known as absolute reality."

Thereupon the bodhisattva Samantabhadra also said in verse, "I admonish you and living beings everywhere: always show deference toward bhikṣus. Humble forbearance is the seed of supreme enlightenment. To forswear all anger will bring future rebirth [among the] noble and true. All who behold you will be filled with joy, and at the sight of you put forth the aspiration for peerless enlightenment. If you practice in accordance with these words, buddha-fields as numerous as grains of dust will manifest from your mind. Throughout them you will be able to realize all of your [bodhisattva] vows, freely coming to the aid of each and every type of being. Speedily you will leave the river of attachment and ascend to the other shore."

Upon hearing these words an indescribable joy welled up in Fazhao, and his net of doubts was completely cleared away. He prostrated in gratitude [to the two bodhisattvas] and humbly stood with palms joined in reverence, where-upon Mañjuśrī said to him, "You may now tour and pay reverence to the other bodhisattva cloisters."

Fazhao paid his respects to each place in succession, until he arrived at the garden containing fruit trees of the seven precious gems. Their fruits were at the peak of ripeness and as large as bowls. He picked one and tasted it. Its flavor was truly exquisite, and upon finishing the entire fruit his body and mind felt deeply tranquil. Finally he made his way back to the two sages, saluted them with prostrations, and took his leave. The two youths saw him through the gate, whereupon he prostrated again in homage. When he lifted his head from the ground, they and the monastery had vanished.

On the eighth day of the fourth month Fazhao arrived at the Prajñā Cloister of Huayan Monastery. There he took up residence on the lower floor of the western tower. At midday on the thirteenth he set out together with a party of some fifty other monks to make pilgrimage to the Diamond Grotto. Reaching the spot where the monk Wuzhu is alleged to have seen the great sage [Mañ-juśrī], Fazhao humbly prostrated and invoked the names of the thirty-five buddhas, saluting them altogether some ten times over. Suddenly the site turned to pure crystalline *vaiḍūrya* and a palatial hall of the seven precious gems appeared in its midst. Therein, gathered in one and the same assembly, Fazhao saw Mañjuśrī and Samantabhadra, with the ten thousand bodhisattvas and Buddhapāli in attendance. Fazhao was overwhelmed with joy at the sight of it [but showed no sign of this to the others]. Then the party returned to the monastery.

That night, around midnight, from the upper story of the western tower of Huayan Monastery, Fazhao saw five holy lamps appear halfway up the moun-tain slope to the east of the monastery. They were as large as bowls. He prayed, "May they multiply into one hundred lamps," whereupon the lamps became one hundred in number. Again Fazhao prayed, "May they divide into a thousand." No sooner had he said this than they multiplied again. Then they transformed into three columns, [with the lamps of each column] arranged directly opposite the others. In this fashion they covered the entire moun-tainside.

Fazhao [was so overcome that he] forgot himself (lit., forgot his body) and set off alone to find the sages whom he had seen at the Diamond Grotto. In the late hours of the night he finally reached the Diamond Grotto. There he once again venerated and invoked the names of the thirty-five buddhas ten times over. Then, using the method of the five tempos, he recited the name of Amitābha one thousand times. With tears of grief streaming down his cheeks he declared, "Due to evil deeds that I have committed since time immemorial

I have drifted through [the ocean of] birth and death, plagued by all manner of tortuous and crippling bodies."

So saying, he struck himself some thirty times. But before his blows came to a stop, a divine monk appeared. He was approximately seven feet tall and identified himself as Buddhapāli. Arriving in front of Fazhao, he said to him, "Why is the master weeping?"

Fazhao replied, "I have come from far away with the hope of seeing the great sage."

Buddhapāli asked, "Does the master really wish to see him?"

To which he responded, "I wish to see him."

Buddhapāli took off his sandals, stepped up onto the planked threshold of the cave, turned to Fazhao, and said, "Master, simply shut your eyes and follow me."

Thereupon he led Fazhao into the Diamond Grotto. All at once a single cloister came into view. Its name post of pure gold read "Monastery of Diamond Prajñā." Everywhere it was resplendently adorned with the seven precious gems. Its rooms, pavilions, multistoried halls, and towers altogether covered an expanse of some 175 bays. A copy of the Diamond Prajñā [Sūtra] (Vajra-cchedikā-prajñāpāramitā) was stored in the jeweled pavilion, together with the rest of the scriptural canon.

Arriving before the great sage, Fazhao threw himself to the ground in obeisance, joined his palms in adoration, and announced to Mañjuśrī, "The only thought in my mind is, how soon I will realize supreme enlightenment and deliver vast numbers of beings into [nirvāṇa] without remainder? When will I bring to fruition my peerless oceanlike vow?"

After hearing this entreaty, the bodhisattva Mañjuśrī said, "Excellent! Excellent!" Once again he massaged the crown [of Fazhao's] head and gave him prediction [of buddhahood], saying, "Your heart is truly set on being a bodhisattva. During such an evil age as this one, to be able to make this sublime vow to bring happiness and benefit to beings that you utter now [means that] you are certain to realize supreme enlightenment quickly. Without fail you will soon fulfill the immeasurable vows of Samantabhadra, become a teacher of gods and men, and save countless numbers of beings."

Having received this prediction, Fazhao touched his head to the ground in obeisance, then again asked: "It is still unclear to me: In the present time and in future ages, will all of my comrades of the fourfold saṅgha who practice buddha-mindfulness, persevere zealously, and renounce fame and profit definitely experience (gan) [Amitābha] Buddha coming to welcome them at the time of their death, achieve rebirth in the highest grade [of the Pure Land], and speedily depart from the stream of attachment?"

Mañjuśrī assured him, "This is certain—beyond any doubt whatsoever, except for those who seek fame and gain and whose hearts are not resolute."

When he finished speaking, he sent the lad, Nānda, to fetch tea and medicinal foods. Fazhao stopped him, saying, "I need no medicines." But the Sagely

One replied, "Just take it. There is nothing to fear," whereupon he handed him two bowls of broth. The flavor of one of the bowls was extraordinarily ambrosial. After he finished it, Mañjuśrī again gave him three more bowls, together with medicinal foods, all of which were served in vessels of precious crystalline *vaiḍūrya*. Then he instructed Buddhapāli to see the master out; but Fazhao pleaded with the sage to stay. Mañjuśrī said to him, "It is impossible. This present body of yours is fundamentally impure and profane in substance. There is no way that you can remain here. But, because your karmic connection with me has now matured, as soon as this current existence spends itself and you are reborn in the Pure Land [of Amitābha], you will be able to come to me directly [with your newly found spiritual powers].

When he finished speaking, the monastery and its inhabitants vanished and Fazhao found himself back on the threshold at the entrance of the cavern.

As dawn began to light the sky, all Fazhao saw was a lone divine monk who said to him: "Farewell. Work hard! Work hard! You must persevere boldly." Having spoken these words, he suddenly disappeared.

After a long while, Fazhao slowly began to make his way back to the monastery. His [mixed feelings of] joy and sadness did not abate. For the first time he realized just how difficult it is to fathom the great sage's compassionate vow. Even though Fazhao had personally witnessed these spiritual wonders of the great sage [Mañjuśrī], he felt that he dare not relate his experiences recklessly, for fear that he might cause others to doubt or slander [these sacred events].

During the beginning of the twelfth month—the height of winter—Fazhao entered the buddha-mindfulness sanctuary at Huayan Monastery. There he pledged to cut off all grains and prayed that he might be born in the Pure Land, attain the forbearance of the nonarising of dharmas (*anutpattika-dharma-kṣānti*), speedily transcend the sea of suffering, and bring all manner of beings to salvation.

This he kept up for seven days. Then, early one evening while in the midst of practicing buddha-mindfulness, a single divine monk entered the sanctuary. The monk told him, "What you saw in your visions was the true domain of Mount Wutai. Why don't you tell other people about it?" As soon as he spoke these words he disappeared.

As Fazhao harbored reservations about this monk, he continued to refrain from making his experiences public. The next afternoon, while right in the midst of his recitations, another divine monk appeared. He looked to be about eighty years old. His spiritual presence was solemn and stern. He said to Fazhao, "What you saw in your visions was the true domain of Mount Wutai. Why do you not make a verbatim record (*shilu*) of it and circulate it widely to people? It will cause those who see it to arouse the thought of enlightenment, cut off evil, dedicate themselves to cultivation of the good, and, ultimately, gain great benefit. Why, master, do you keep this matter secret and not speak of it to others?"

Fazhao replied, "It is not my personal intent to conceal these events. I simply fear that others may doubt and slander them and thereby fall into hell. This is why I do not speak of them."

The divine monk said to Fazhao, "Even when the great sage Mañjuśrī himself appears in this region, people still slander the event. Should any less of a response be expected for your visionary experiences? And yet, if you enable numerous people to hear of them, some will conceive the desire to come to this place. They will thereby extinguish countless sins accumulated over boundless numbers of lives, put an end to evil and cultivate the good, invoke the name of the Buddha, and achieve rebirth in the Pure Land. Certainly this is equivalent to bringing benefit to boundless numbers of sentient beings. How is it not to be considered vast? What is the point in keeping it secret simply out of worry over doubt and slander?"

Upon hearing these words, Fazhao replied, "I humbly accept your instruction and will no longer dare to keep this matter hidden."

The divine monk smiled faintly, then vanished. Fazhao, as he had been urged, made a record of all that had happened to him up to that point and related the experiences, one by one, to the assembly of monks.

Sometime during the first nine days of the first month of the sixth year of the *dayan* era, the Buddhist monk Huicong from south of the Yangzi, together with Chonghui, Mingjian, and some thirty-odd monks of the Huayan Monastery, accompanied Fazhao to the spot near the Diamond Grotto where he himself had previously encountered the Prajñā Cloister. There they erected a commemorative stele. Fazhao's party of disciples and companions gazed up at him with humble admiration, feelings of sadness and joy mingled in their hearts. Suddenly they heard from the spot the sound of a temple bell, its tone pure and bright. The entire party gasped in awe at this numinal wonder. Expressly they proclaimed to Fazhao, "What you witnessed is surely not false." At the same time they ruminated to themselves how fortunate they were to possess the karmic affinity from former lives that enabled them to travel here together with Fazhao. They wrote out the story [of their experiences] on the wall of their chamber at the hermitage, so that all might know of it, together arouse the thought of enlightenment, and together aspire to the fruit of buddhahood.

Sometime later, on the thirteenth day of the ninth month during the twelfth year of the *dayan* reign-period (777), Fazhao was visiting the Eastern Peak [of Mount Wutai] together with a party of eight junior monks and various other persons, when some ten beams of white light appeared. A black cloud gathered ominously, but soon the clouds parted and rainbow-hued rays of light [streamed down], enveloping and penetrating their bodies. Within the radiance a globe of crimson light took shape, in which the great sage Mañjuśrī appeared, seated on a blue lion. Everyone in the group saw him clearly. At that moment, a fine snow [began to] fall, whereupon rainbow-hued spheres of light [spread] over the entire mountain valley, [multiplying into] an inestimable number. The junior monks Zhunyi, Weixiu, Guizheng, and Zhiyuan, the Śrāmaṇera

Weiying, the layman Zhang Xi, the young attendant Rujing, and others all witnessed the spectacle.

Later, the great master Fazhao measured out a distance of fifteen leagues in the southernly direction from Huayan Monastery, thereby arriving at the foot of a hill in the middle of the Central Terrace [of Wutai]. There he specially constructed a monastery based on the groundplan of the Bamboo Grove Monastery of the Great Sage that he had encountered [in his vision]. He gave it the name "Bamboo Grove."

Fazhao's Vision of the Pure Land and Revelation of the Method for Intoning the Buddha's Name According to the Five Tempos

You with insight will know that this *Rite for Intoning the Buddha's Name, Reciting Scripture, and Performing Meditation According to the Five Tempos* is in fact not my own personal invention. For a long time I have kept it secret and not taught it openly to others. But now I fear that generations to come may raise doubts [about the practice], thereby falling into evil destinies [of rebirth]. The teaching of the Sage clearly states that, aside from one's immediate companions in the practice, it will bring benefit to persons with profound faith. Hence it is permissible to expound [this practice] for such individuals. Out of compassion for them, I will now give a brief explanation [of the origins of this practice].

On the fifteenth day of the fourth month during the second year of the *yongtai* reign period (766), I was staying at the Amitābha Terrace on Nanyue. At that time I pledged, for the rest of my earthly life, to spend the ninety days of the annual summer [retreat] in a sanctuary for [the practice of] buddha-mindfulness and the pratyutpanna [samādhi]. Moreover, I vowed to do this for the sole purpose of [achieving] perfect enlightenment and [bringing benefit to] all living beings, and not for any other end.

As that summer marked the commencement of my pledge, upon making this vow I entered the sanctuary [for pratyutpanna samādhi]. There I persevered with fierce resolve. On the evening of the fourteenth day into the rite I was alone in the hall, which was situated on the northeast side of the [Amitābha] Terrace. That night, during the third watch, I thought to myself, "At this very moment there are pure and marvelous buddha-lands [all around me] throughout the ten directions of the universe. The bodhisattvas who congregate there are continuously graced by the most peerless, profound, and wondrous teachings, whereby they acquire vast spiritual powers and the ability to deliver incalculable numbers of beings [from suffering]. And yet, I am unable to partake of these [marvels]. Doubtless it is the excessive gravity of my sinful obstructions that prevents me from entering the stream of saintliness and being able to save beings on a grand scale such as this."

I anguished over this thought deeply. Unaware of the tears streaming down my face, in a piteous and pleading voice I called out to the Buddha. The instant I spoke the Buddha's name a certain experience occurred. Suddenly I was no longer in the hall of the sanctuary but saw only a cloud-like pavilion of rainbow light that filled the universe about me. Within it a golden bridge appeared, which stretched out before me directly toward the land of Highest Bliss (Su-khāvatī) in the west.

In a flash I arrived in the presence of the Buddha Amitābha. With my fore-head I made obeisance to the feet of Amitābha Buddha. As I did so, Amitābha Buddha said to me with a faint smile of delight, "I know that your heart is true, and that your greatest wish is to bring benefit and joy to other beings without a single thought of profit for yourself. It is excellent, excellent indeed, that you are capable of making such a vow as this! I have a wondrous teaching—like the most priceless of gems—that I am now going to impart to you. You are to take this precious teaching, practice it, and spread it widely throughout [the continent of] Jambudvīpa, bringing benefit to gods and humans everywhere. Beings beyond reckoning will realize liberation upon coming into contact with this precious teaching."

I, Fazhao, said to the Buddha, "What is this marvelous teaching that you possess? My sole wish is that the Lord Buddha reveal it to me!"

The Buddha said, "There is a priceless method for invoking the name of the Buddha using five tempos of Brahmā-chant. It is perfectly suited to this tur-bulent and evil age and will surely flourish there. In this present era, when dharma is in its final decline, any creature whose karmic circumstances destine it to hear you perform this recitation—even if for a split instant—will without fail put forth the thought [of seeking perfect enlightenment]. [Surely you know of] the five-toned melodies emitted by the jeweled trees [of the Pure Land] as described in the *Sūtra of [the Buddha of] Immeasurable Life (Wuliangshoujing)*. This method of intoning the Buddha's name in five tempos comes from pre-cisely that! Through this causal connection, beings will be able to recite the name of the Buddha and be assured of rebirth in my land when their lives have run their course. Any being in the future who is tormented by the misery of impoverishment, upon encountering this priceless five-tempo method for rec-ollecting and reciting [the name of] the Buddha, will be delivered from all destitution. Likewise, the sick will receive medicine; the parched will receive drink; the famished, obtain food; the naked, receive clothing; those shrouded in darkness will obtain light; those in need of crossing the ocean will obtain a boat. Anyone who meets with this jewel-like treasure [of a teaching] can be assured of gaining ease and bliss. How is such a thing possible? Any being who encounters this precious teaching will thereupon be able to recite the Buddha's name. Within this very lifetime, they will rise up from the ocean of misery and ascend [toward buddhahood], never to fall back again. Speedily perfecting the six pāramitās and the omniscient wisdom of all modes (sarvākarajñatā), they will rapidly achieve buddhahood. Such sublime joy as this will be their lot!"

When [the Buddha] finished speaking these words, the entire buddha-realm, with its vast assembly of bodhisattvas and [emanation] buddhas, its streams, birds, and groves of trees, all proceeded to intone the name of the Buddha and chant Buddhist scripture in melodies of the five tempos. I managed to retain a small bit of it.

Then I said to the Buddha, "I have now been enfolded by the Buddha's sustaining grace and entrusted with this teaching. Anyone who harbors doubts about this teaching and refuses to accept it is fated to be lost [in saṃsāra] for endless aeons and denied rebirth in the Pure Land. But I am still uncertain [about one point]: Once someone has accepted this practice, will any [other] being who hears it put forth the thought of enlightenment and take up recitation of the Buddha's name or not? Will they [also] enter profound meditative concentrations, speedily realize *bodhi,* and experience [all manner of] great benefit or not?"

The Buddha Amitābha replied, "Whenever you use this technique of intoning the Buddha's name or chanting scripture according to the five tempos, the infinite melodies and song produced by the streams, birds, groves of trees, and myriad bodhisattvas in this land of mine will suffuse throughout space. Simultaneously it will harmonize with the sound of one's recitation of the Buddha's name, ensuring that you are protected from all disturbance—human as well as nonhuman—and personally effecting the conversion of each and every being that is present. Even those who merely chance to see or hear you [perform this practice], without exception, will arouse the thought of enlightenment, accept this practice in joy and faith, and take up recitation of the Buddha's name. When their lives reach their end, I will come to welcome them [into the Pure Land]. Great will be the gain. Henceforth rest assured of this!"

When the Buddha finished speaking, I suddenly found myself back in the sanctuary [on Nanyue]. Having witnessed this marvelous vision, I was overwhelmed with feelings of compassion and joy and possessed by a keen determination to practice and spread this method of reciting the Buddha's name. From that moment down to today, everything has been just as [the Buddha Amitābha] predicted. My net of doubt has been entirely eliminated. I have vowed, for the rest of this life and for all time to come, to always remain in this evil world and strive to deliver beings through this wonderful teaching, [so that] all may ascend to the Land of Highest Bliss and speedily attain buddhahood. Any of you who are fortunate enough to have a [karmic] connection that brings you into contact with this teaching, do not harbor doubts or slander it. If you do you will surely plummet to hell!

──15──

Ny Dan the Manchu Shamaness

Kun Shi

Among the different Tungus-speaking groups in northeastern China, the Manchu people are the largest by population (9.8 million in 1990) and the best known to the West because of their 267-year rule of China in the Qing dynasty, the last dynastic period, which ended in 1911. The Manchu are found in almost every corner of China, but most of them live in the three northeastern provinces of Liaoning, Jilin, and Heilongjiang. Once herders and hunters, they are now farmers and city dwellers. Thirteen Manchu autonomous counties were established in Hebei, Jilin, and Liaoning provinces between 1985 and 1989.

Unlike many minority ethnic groups in South China, the Manchu do not have any subgroups; they have a complex clan system, which remains an important socioeconomic institution in rural areas. Although they may be known to readers of English only as Manchu, they have been called *Manzu* (Man nationality) by the Chinese since 1911 and officially identified as such since the 1950s. Through history, they were variably recorded as Sushen in the Zhou dynasty (ca. 1027–256 B.C.E.), Yilou in the Han dynasty (202 B.C.E.–220 C.E.), Wuji in the Northern dynasties (386–550 C.E.), Mohe in the Sui and Tang dynasties (589–907 C.E.), and Nüzhen, or Jurchen, from the late Tang to the Ming dynasty (1368–1644). The name Jurchen was replaced by Manchu in 1635, a decade before China was conquered by the Manchu to establish the Qing dynasty (1644–1911).

The Manchu have been linguistically and culturally influenced by the people of Central China, the Han Chinese, particularly for those who migrated from former Manchuria to other parts of China. However, they are certainly not completely sinicized, as many Chinese scholars and most Western researchers have believed. Numerous publications about the Manchu and fieldwork conducted by ethnologists in rural areas in recent years suggest that the Manchu language, folkways, belief system (shamanism), and folklore have not died out; on the contrary, they are growing strongly as part of a nationalistic cultural revival. The Manchu language has become the second language in the growing number of Manchu autonomous counties; the Manchu script, designed based on Mongolian in 1599, with forty letters and written vertically from left to right, is used by some Manchu elders and shamans. The Qing-style dress, *changshan*, is still common for the elderly, especially at rituals. Genealogical practices and the worship of images are performed. Each courtyard house has a niche for making offerings to ancestors. The houses generally face south; inside heatable brick beds (*kang*) are located on the north and west side. A dying person cannot sleep on the western *kang* because the area above it is for storing genealogical records and statues of ancestors. At weddings, two poles are erected in the yard, one for making offerings to the clan deities and the other for offerings to the wild spirits. When a person dies, the coffin should be taken out through the window, so the diseased spirit may not find its way back to harm the living. *Hala* (clan) as the traditional form of social organization is still active, and the *mukunda* (clan chief) is respected and has the power of social control comparable to that of local officials. Above all, the shamanic practices of the Manchu are now so popular that the shamans are honored as living treasures and the shamanic tradition is regarded as an important element in Manchu ethnic identity. Today, young shamans are being initiated and shamanic rituals are conducted openly in a tolerant atmosphere.

Archaeological discoveries and historical records show that the Manchu ancestors practiced the archaic tradition of shamanism about three thousand years ago. But the Tungus-Manchu word *saman* for "shaman" was first recorded in Chinese by Xu Mengshen in a twelfth-century publication, *A Collection of Agreements Reached by the Three Kingdoms* [*Liao, Jin and Xixia*] (*Sanchao beimeng huibian*): "The Jurchen shamans are like *wuyu* (sorceresses). They can transform their shape and perform magic." Later the term shaman was introduced to Europe. "Shaman" in Manchu means "those who are the most knowledgeable." This coincides with the requirement that the Manchu shamans be masters of their folklore, rituals, healing techniques, and other aspects of their culture. In practice shamans are able to ascend or descend into the other worlds in ecstasy, or altered states of consciousness, to achieve and maintain well-being and healing for themselves as well as for members of their communities. Because shamanism is so interwoven with other aspects of Manchu culture, scholars argue that shamanism forms the foundation of the cultural traditions of the Manchu as well as other Tungus groups in northeastern China.

The Manchu shamans observe two forms of practices: clan ancestral worship and the more archaic form of wild-spirits worship. The former includes elaborate and standardized rituals that were favored by the Qing imperial court; whereas the latter is more spontaneous, involving such ecstatic performances as fire-walking and magical flight. But some components are essential to both forms: drums, percussion waist bells, the sacred *solo* (sky) pole, divination, ecstatic dancing, and ritual chanting all contribute to the cultivation of supernatural power and the process of healing.

Numerous volumes of Manchu folklore and ethnographic collections, most of which are related to the shamanic theme, have recently been published. One of the best-known folktales is the legend of Ny Dan ("Nü Dan" in Chinese) the shamaness. In longer versions, the same basic story appears in myth or epic forms under the title of *Nisan Shamaness.* The term "legend" is used here because *Ny Dan the Shamaness* chiefly represents legendary historical figures.

Ny Dan the Shamaness was recorded by the Manchu scholar Aisin-Gioro Wulaxichun in 1985 from an older Manchu named Ji Chunsheng. Ji was nearly eighty years old at the time of recording and lived in Sanjiazi Village, Youyi Township, Fuyu County, Heilongjiang Province. The legend was narrated in Manchu and recorded in Manchu script, phonetic symbols, and Chinese transliteration and translation, with detailed notes. Based on the content of the story, *Ny Dan the Shamaness* may be the prototype of *Nisan Shamaness,* which is circulated among all Tungus-speaking groups (the Ewenki, Hezhen, Manchu, Orochun, and Sibe) and the Daur people in northeastern China.

Apart from being a fascinating legend, *Ny Dan the Shamaness* offers several clues to the understanding of Manchu shamanism and history. First, female shamans were the most powerful and common. Manchu myths relate that the Almighty Sky Deity created Nisan (Ny Dan) and sent her down as the first shaman to teach humankind. Historical records and myths show that the Manchu once had female shamans. The reason that they now only have male shamans is probably due to the rise of patriarchal dominance. Second, shamanhood can be obtained through learning. Among the Manchu, only the intelligent young people are chosen to become shamans, and they have to spend years learning to read Manchu scriptures, to recite chants and chant songs, and to master the techniques of healing through ecstasy. Third, the drum is an important vehicle for the magical flight of the shaman(ess). Many Manchu myths describe how shamans ride their drums to the other worlds to retrieve wandering souls or to obtain healing power. The constant drumming can induce an ecstatic state. Fourth, Tibetan Buddhist monks and lamas are the opponents of shamans. Although there are traces of Tibetan Buddhist influence over shamanism, they belong to two different systems. The conflict in the legend reflects the real Tibetan Buddhist persecution of the shamans (mainly in Mongolia) from the late sixteenth to early nineteenth centuries. Fifth, shamans may earn a living as healers or soul retrievers. Shamans in traditional societies are generally nonprofessionals; they farm or herd as the common folk do. But many of the Manchu shamans did become professional during the Qing dynasty. Finally, the shaman's power is both boundless and limited. Ny Dan is so powerful that even the emperor has to ask for her help; but there is a limit to her power to retrieve the souls. Ny Dan is like a deity, capable of mobilizing the sacred eagle, but she is at the mercy of the envious Tibetan monks (called "lamas" in the story) and the ungrateful emperor. However, the shamanic power outlasts that of the emperor, and the shamaness eventually becomes an immortal. As the legend ends, Ny Dan not only is still dancing and drumming somewhere below or above but also is attracting Manchu people to carry on the shamanic tradition.

The following text was narrated by Ji Chunsheng and recorded by Aisin-Gioro Wulaxichun, Central Academy of Nationalities Beijing, China. Textual source: "Ny

Dan Saman [Ny Dan Shamaness]," in Aisin-Gioro Wulaxichun, *Manzu gu shenhua* (*Ancient Myths of the Manchu*) (Huhhot: Inner Mongolian People's Press, 1986), pp. 88–106.

Further Reading

Margaret Norwak and Stephen Durrant, *The Tale of the Nisan Shamaness: A Manchu Folk Epic* (Seattle: University of Washington Press, 1977); Giovanni Stary, *Three Unedited Manchu Scripts of the Manchu Epic "Nisan Saman-i Bithe"* (Wiesbaden: Harrassowitz, 1985).

Ny Dan, the Shamaness

Ny Dan the shamaness was twenty years old when her husband died. To support her mother-in-law, she learned the art of shamanism. After gaining the shamanic techniques, Ny Dan helped her people to heal the sick. She could even revive a deceased person soon after death by entering the lower world and bringing back the soul. As time went by, Ny Dan's shamanic power gradually increased.

One day the crown prince was seriously sick. Two lama priests were called in to the court, but they could not help. The crown prince's sickness went from bad to worse, and he finally died. The emperor wailed over his son's death. When he heard the story that Ny Dan the shamaness could retrieve souls of the dead, the emperor sent his men to ask the shamaness for help. Ny Dan the shamaness was washing clothes when the imperial wagon came, but she picked up her hand drum and set off in the wagon.

Because the emperor invited Ny Dan the shamaness, the two lama priests were furious at her. They hid behind the gate of the imperial palace and attempted to murder the shamaness. On her way, Ny Dan had a vision in which she learned of the plan of the two lama priests. So when she reached the gate of the imperial palace, Ny Dan the shamaness got off the wagon and flew into the palace on her hand drum. Thus the lama priests failed in their conspiracy.

Ny Dan the shamaness stepped down from the drum and met the emperor. Seeing that Ny Dan the shamaness flew into the imperial palace on the drum, the emperor was annoyed.

"No civil officials nor generals under Heaven can enter my palace at will; how dare a shamaness ride on a drum and fly into the palace!" the emperor thought. But anxious to save his son's life, the emperor did not pour out angry words.

The emperor said, "Go to the lower world quickly and bring back the soul of my son!"

As soon as Ny Dan reached the lower world, she met her [deceased] husband, who was boiling in a cauldron of oil. When he saw Ny Dan, he thought: "Gosh! You are also dead?" Then Ny Dan told him how she became a shamaness and learned the shamanic magic.

Ny Dan said: "The soul of the crown prince is in here and the emperor asked me to get it."

The husband said: "If you can help others to retrieve their souls, why do you not save my life?"

"You have been in the lower world too long and your flesh has decayed. I am not able to revive your soul now. Even if I took your soul back, you could not live as before."

Ny Dan's husband was very disappointed and angry. He quarreled with her and blocked her way. Ny Dan was angered and, with her magic, threw her husband's soul far away into a deep waterwell in Fengdu town. Now his soul could never be reincarnated again. It was in this matter that Ny Dan committed a sin.

Ny Dan the shamaness walked swiftly forward and finally found the soul of the crown prince playing on a thick layer of grass. She quickly caught the soul in her hand and flew back to the human world.

The emperor was very pleased with the revival of his son. He offered a grand feast and invited many people for celebration. At the feast, the emperor suddenly thought of his younger sister who died years ago; so he asked Ny Dan to retrieve her soul.

Ny Dan replied: "Your sister died three years ago and her flesh has already decomposed. Even if I could obtain her soul, she cannot be revived."

The emperor was displeased on hearing the reply. Thinking of Ny Dan once riding her drum into the imperial palace and now refusing the imperial request, the emperor became furious. At this moment, the two lama priests came to the emperor and criticized Ny Dan.

They told the emperor: "Ny Dan the shamaness can actually revive your sister's soul, but she does not intend to do it." The emperor was outraged. He ordered Ny Dan to be thrown into a deep well in the west, wrapped in a heavy iron chain. Ny Dan thus died in the well due to the false charges of the two lama priests.

After Ny Dan's death, the imperial palace was shadowed with pitch-darkness for three days. The emperor was puzzled and asked his ministers: "What is happening?"

A minister carefully observed the sky and replied: "The dark days are not because of clouds, but due to the wings of a big bird. Please ask a master archer to shoot at the sky and see what will happen."

The emperor asked one of his generals to shoot an arrow into the sky, and a piece of the Eagle Deity's tail feather fell from above. The feather was so big that a wagon could not hold it.

The minister said: "This is because Ny Dan the shamaness died of unjust treatment. It is said that she could summon the Eagle Deity for help. So the dark days are caused by her wandering soul, seeking revenge."

Hearing such words, the emperor repented and addressed [Ny Dan]: "If you really died of unjust treatment, I will order the Manchu to conduct offering rituals in honor of you while making offerings to their deities."

As soon as the emperor finished, the dark sky suddenly became clear. Since that time, the Manchu must present offerings to the Eagle Deity when they make ritual offerings to their ancestors. Ny Dan the shamaness is regarded as the creator of all shamans.

Even today, anyone passing by the well where Ny Dan was chained can hear the shamanic drumming and dancing. Some people have attempted to pull out the iron chain that held Ny Dan the shamaness, but the chain is endless.

—16—

Teachings of a Spirit Medium

Jean DeBernardi

In this chapter, the teachings of a Malaysian Chinese spirit medium are presented. They are unusual in a collection of this sort: while they have their roots in textual sources they are oral performances and as such are not designed as written texts. However, these oral narratives are significantly related to the written word, and through that word to a cultural past that is made present through performance.

In Southeast Asia, Hong Kong, and Taiwan, spirit mediums are visible and active religious practitioners. They are folk healers; more rarely they teach religious ideas, drawing on a deep tradition of popular literature and the textual works of the "three doctrines"—Buddhism, Daoism, and Confucianism. These together provide many of the exemplary heros and moral principles of popular religious culture. Indeed, some of these heros and heroines are embodied in trance performance, where they make use of an elevated moral vocabulary to explicate the Dao and exhort their followers to good behavior.

By contrast with the well-worked-out conceptual schemes and elegant ritual practices of Confucianism or Buddhism, local religious practice is eclectic and dynamic. For example, the temple fairs celebrating a god's birthday are ideally "hot and exciting": these events overwhelm the senses with gaudy reds and golds, clamorous drumming and gonging, eye-stinging clouds of incense. Spirit mediums are as likely as Daoist priests to be the ritual practitioners at these events, but instead of chanting texts they perform rites of self-mortification, walking on hot coals, playing with red-hot iron balls, "bathing" in hot oil or burning joss sticks. Scholars of religion politely describe these religious practices as "syncretic," but Chinese popular religious culture has also been described in the last century as "barbaric," "objectionable," and "pragmatic" (rather than spiritual). Many have emphasized the gulf between the "great traditions" of China and local practice, though anthropologists have persisted in insisting that the two are merely variations on a theme, or transformations rung on a shared conceptual order.

Here, Chinese local religious practice is explored as a practice that animates the textual and literary as lived performance. The sensually appealing practices of the "folk" are perhaps a world apart from the calm and controlled ritual practice of the elite, but many of the basic concepts of the world traditions live in popular discourse. In particular, they are given voice in a moral discourse on the art of "being human": indeed often it is the "god" (while possessing the body of the spirit medium) who makes the textual local and accessible through speech, bridging past and present, literary and lived realities.

Spirit Mediums

In everyday practice, spirit mediums perform a variety of services, ranging from the treatment of illness with magical charms or herbs to the provision of gambling advice and ambiguously written predictions of lottery numbers. Their worshippers are indeed pragmatic in their approach to the god, whom they regard as a savior who will aid them in their everyday life problems.

Mediums are possessed by a variety of Chinese deities. Often these are categorized as martial and literary gods, and the two are different in performance. Martial gods perform martial arts displays, often with sword, spear, or halberd, as well as performing the acts of self-mortification described above. Observers often note that these acts are convincing proof of the genuineness of the presence of the god. Literary gods by contrast are more restrained and demonstrate a scholarly learning. Often it is noted that the spirit medium's personality or manner changes dramatically when the god possesses him (or, more rarely, her), and a changing style of speech and movement is convincing proof to the audience that a god is truly present.

The identities of the gods who possess spirit mediums connect these gods to a literary archive. Many of the deities are drawn from popular literature: Guan Gong is one of the heroes of the *Three Kingdoms* (*Sanguo yanyi*); Ji Gong is from *Ji Gong's Tale* (*Jigong zhuan*); the Monkey God is from *Journey to the West* (*Xiyouji*); the Inconstant Ghost is from the hell journey books frequently distributed in temples. Many of these deities also appear in folk opera, films, even comic book renditions. In trance performance they come alive as individuals with well-defined personalities: Ji Gong, the "Mad Monk" or "Dirty Buddha," for example, is a trickster who despite his Buddhist vows eats dog meat and drinks rather than fasting and abstaining. As he possesses the god, he will call for ale, and he jokes and teases his clients. His trance performances are at times serious, though in many cases his teachings were parodies of orthodoxy rather than solemn didactic events.

It is often commented that the god speaks a literary form of the language spoken (in Malaysia, usually Southern Min), which is described as a "deep" version of that language. By contrast, contemporary Malaysian Chinese are judged to speak a form of their "dialect" (or "topolect") that is not at all deep. The god's literary Southern Min most notably excludes common borrowings from English and Malay and includes many literary terms that are not frequently encountered in spoken conversation. The god's language is often considered difficult to understand,

and a temple committee member usually stands by the god to translate his or her words into colloquial language.

"Deep" or literary Southern Min is in fact a register of Southern Min that at one time had social connotations of education and style. Before Mandarin was adopted and promoted as the national language of China, literate persons learned to read characters in the literary form of their topolect. In Southern Min, this now rarely used literary register is quite distinctive from vernacular language in both pronunciation and vocabulary. Use of the literary register continues to carry social overtones of high status and learning; in English much the same effect is carried by vocabulary (consider what is communicated by saying that you must "deliberate" on a matter instead of "think it over"). In contemporary Penang, deep Southern Min is now almost exclusively the style of the gods who possess spirit mediums.

In the practice of spirit mediumship, the use of words drawn from a literary lexicon links the present to the past and creates a unique situation of authoritative transmission. In the classical Chinese view of textual interpretation, in reading a written text one reads the written word in order to know the heart of the writer. To cite a fifth-century Chinese scholar: "None may see the actual faces of a faraway age, but by viewing their writing, one may immediately see their hearts and minds" (Stephen Owen, *Remembrances: The Experience of the Past in Classical Chinese Literature* [Cambridge: Harvard University Press, 1986], p. 59). When the "god" speaks, however, one hears the voice of that faraway age. One spirit medium—said to be an avatar of his deity—offered inspired textual exegesis of the *Classic on the Way and Its Power* (*Dao de jing*) to class of students; another offered his teachings while possessed by Laozi himself. Possessed spirit mediums offer a uniquely authoritative form of textual interpretation.

Text and Performance

The transmission of tradition through the teachings of spirit mediums may be compared with the Chinese tradition of reading and interpreting texts. "Orality" and "literacy" had a special relationship in traditional Chinese education, and while China has the world's deepest literary tradition, the transmission of that tradition has emphasized the transformation of the written into the oral. In reading classical Chinese, the approach to the written word had two important dimensions. First, the text to be studied was memorized and recited and was not considered to be known until known by heart. Second, the text was condensed, and ancient texts in particular were "terse, fragmentary, and incomplete" (Owen, p. 69). Understanding the written word involved exegesis, and later scholars built frames for understanding the author's words. For example, a text such as the *Classic of Changes* (*Yijing*) is read together with several layers of exegetical commentary.

Chinese literary critics express the view that "by means of meditating on the words of a poem, one reaches the state of wordless communication with the spirit of the poet" (James Liu, *Language—Paradox—Poetics: A Chinese Perspective* [Princeton: Princeton University Press, 1988], p. 102). Owen has characterized the condensed style of literary Chinese as "synechdochic," and he compares the process of recovering meaning to the rite in which an article of clothing is used to recall a soul (Owen, p. 2). The reader must take the text—a fragment—and use it to recall the intention of its author. Take, for example, the problem of interpreting the following two lines of poetry:

> All day long I seek but cannot find it,
> Yet at times it comes of its own accord.

But what is "it"? Poet-critic Mei Yao Chen in his commentary remarks that the poet means that "a good line of poetry is hard to get." (He corrects another [possibly facetious] interpreter who said, "This is a poem about someone's lost cat" [Liu, p. 100].)

In the process of transmission, the past is always being reread from the perspective of the present. As Liu points out (p. 104), Chinese critics accepted interpretive indeterminacy in reading the fragments of the past. Confucius's relativistic comment on this subject was that "when a humane one sees it, he calls it humane, when a wise man sees it, he calls it wise." Reading from a Confucian perspective, both the love poems and spirit invocations of the *Songs of the South* (*Chuci*) were political allegories on the often entangled relationships of ministers with their lords; in a recent lecture a well-known Chinese novelist in exile retold China's history starting with the birth of the cosmos and reinterpreted the most famous poem in *Songs of the South* to demonstrate that the love of democracy was as old as China itself. Different times, different meanings, but the same conclusion: as the Chinese author put it when questioned, history is important because China's past is its present.

It was the role of Confucian scholar-gentry to transmit the past; in the trance performance, the past is also transmitted, but it meets the present in a unique way, for here the spirit of the poet, teacher, philosopher is given voice again. The oral recitation of cosmology, the invention of poetry, and exegesis of the moral concepts handed down from the past are all basic to the authority of the god, much as mastery of Confucian texts provided educational capital for the scholar-gentry of imperial China.

Reference to the literary tradition is not always explicitly made but rather resides in the use of extraordinary vocabulary—discussion of the Dao, of the Confucian virtues of filiality and loyalty, of Buddhist ideas of merit and rebirth. The presence of the past is nowhere more fully symbolized than in the use of the literary register known as deep Southern Min, and of a moral vocabulary that links the present to the transmitted values of the past. The "orality" of the trance performance, then, cannot be simply contrasted with "literacy." The trance performance is indeed a form of transmission of ideas, a lived exegesis, a giving voice to the past.

The text that follows translates the teachings of a Chinese spirit medium and is based on interviews conducted in the course of ethnographic research in Penang, Malaysia, in 1980–81. The spirit medium worked in a remote area of Penang, in a temple hidden at the end of an unpaved road. Other spirit mediums reported that this spirit medium had once been the master at a major urban temple and had been widely famous in Singapore and Malaysia. Low attendance at a temple fair celebrating his patron deity's birthday suggests to me that his influence had waned and perhaps explains his willingness to teach me. When I went to his temple the first time, Mr. Lim was in trance, and the temple committee member who brought me there urged me to ask the god to help me write my book. With some reluctance I abandoned my observation point, stepped up to the altar where a martial artist god (the Second Commander of the Eastern Quarter) possessed the medium, and asked for help. The "god" began to lecture me on the basic tenets of the three religions—Daoism, Buddhism, and Confucianism, illustrating his points allegorically. I returned to Mr. Lim's temples several times with a male research assistant, and we interviewed Mr. Lim out of trance in these visits. Though not in trance, Mr. Lim repeated parts of his initial lecture, expanding on many points.

Further Reading

Kenneth Dean, *Taoist Ritual and Popular Cults of Southeast China* (Princeton: Princeton University Press, 1993); Jean DeBernardi, "Space and Time in Chinese Religious Culture," *History of Religions* 31.3 (1992): 247–68; David K. Jordan and Daniel Overmyer, *The Flying Phoenix: Aspects of Chinese Sectarianism in Taiwan* (Princeton: Princeton University Press, 1986); Graeme Lang and Lars Ragvald, *The Rise of a Refugee God: Hong Kong's Wong Tai Sin* (Hong Kong: Oxford University Press, 1993); Steven Sangren, *History and Magical Power in a Chinese Community* (Stanford: Stanford University Press, 1987); Arthur Wolf, ed., *Religion and Ritual in Chinese Society* (Stanford: Stanford University Press, 1974).

The Great Ultimate

The Ultimate of Nonbeing produced the Great Ultimate. The Great Ultimate opened Heaven and Earth. Heaven and Earth produced creatures, then humankind. First there were animals, then there were humans. People began to worship the gods in the Early Six Kingdoms period: they passed this on to people in the Middle Six Kingdoms. [He broke from his narrative to express his uncertainty as to our motives in wanting him to teach us.]

I must influence you, and help you. I don't know your heart in doing this,

I don't know if you are good or bad. I can tell you how to behave, how to worship, things like that, and then I can influence you.

People come, and they can return. How can they return? One way is to meditate, and to follow a vegetarian diet. . . . I will discuss *dao li* for you.

The Ultimate of Nonbeing produced the Great Ultimate. The Great Ultimate opened Heaven and Earth. Heaven and Earth produced creatures, then humankind.

What is *dao?* What is *li?* All religions are persuasive words. Religion calls people to do things in a certain way. Religion persuades and advises people. This is not the same as discussing *dao li.* Religion advises us "do not do that, you must do good, you must not do bad." This is advice, it is not *dao li. Dao li* is very deep. The Three Religions and the Nine Streams have yet to talk of *dao li.* And no race has yet explained it.

What is a race, what are the five races? Red race, white race, black race, yellow race, brown race. And there are four types of hair. This is *dao li.* Red hair, white hair, black hair, brown hair. All are the same, but their languages are different. Where is *dao li?* It is in our bodies.

The Three Religions and Nine Streams are in our bodies. What are the Nine Streams? The Nine Streams are man. . . . There are three religions: Daoism [he touches his forehead], Buddhism [he touches his left shoulder], and Confucianism [he touches his right shoulder].

In our bodies there are eight "people": Daoism, Buddhism, Confucianism, and inside there are five elements. Gold is the heart, wood is the liver, water is the stomach, fire is the lungs, and earth is the kidneys. There are five people inside. Dogs are the same, birds are the same, pigs are the same. If you kill them and look, their organs are the same. But they only have two souls.

The organs are the same, the body structure is the same. But when people speak, their speech is not the same. She speaks English, he speaks Hindi, he speaks Bengali, she speaks Malay, he speaks German: they are all different. Within the Chinese race, the yellow race, there are also differences. Within the Chinese race there are Hoq Jiu, Teo Jiu, Hong Kong, Hainan, Shanghai, Keng Hua, all are part of the yellow race. The languages they speak are not the same.

Animals have two souls. We humans have three souls. People say that when we die, the soul does not die. What are the three souls called? The yin soul, the intelligence soul, the heart soul. The first two vanish, they break, scatter, and are no more. The heart soul does not die—it goes and travels. I don't know where it wants to go. The intelligence soul and the yin soul die. They scatter, they break, they disperse. It's like ashes scattering—inside there is absolutely nothing. This heart soul can fly.

The heart soul flies. I do not know what it wants to combine with. It must go and combine. How to combine? You must have good deeds and good morals, then you will have good rewards. Then the heart soul can combine with a human womb and be reborn.

If you are not good you will go and join with the animals of Heaven, of Earth, of water, with these animals, or with worms or grass. Grass also has one soul—without a soul, there is no life.

The heart soul is flown down by Heaven, and depending on where you want to fly, where you want to go, you are flown there to join up and be born. This is what you call reincarnation. Here is the seed of rebirth: the heart soul does not die. What is the intelligence soul? The intelligence soul accompanies our consciousness. The yin soul is matter and flesh. Everything in hell, below, of the soil is called yin. Yin is the soul of below, and I speak of matter and flesh. A person's intelligence soul is aware of the three souls. The intelligence soul comes and holds together the three souls. When this happens it is called our consciousness, and it must stay if we are to endure. You must have the intelligence soul. Do you know?

You must keep the Dao. People can come to Earth, and they must return. But today, no one wants to return. People no longer meditate and go to Heaven. Why is this? It is because people today are greedy for office, greedy for sex, greedy for money, greedy for power. People cannot return—they go instead to Hell. When you are born, you come to Earth. When you die, it is not definite that you will return to Heaven. These days, everyone goes to Hell.

What is it like to return? You meditate, and you can take soul and matter and return to Heaven. If you go to Hell, your flesh and bones are lost to you. It's not that you cannot return, but you must know how to go back. . . .

When people come to be born, they have sin, and we repay our sins. We have sin, and we have desire. This word "desire" is very deep. If there were no desire, no one would come down, no one would desire the world. Heaven gives you the choice of how to make up for your sins. You decide where you want to go, and what you want to link up with. You look and say: "Wa! The world is so pretty!" and you want to be reborn in the world. Good. So Heaven lets you link up with a womb to be reborn. Once you have been reborn, you arrive in the world and know the bitterness. This is called "taking the sins." It is the same for everyone. This is called *dao li*. *Dao li* is very deep. I will tell you about it.

It makes no difference whether you are male or female, or what color you are: red race, yellow race, white race, brown race, black race. We all are the same, it's only our languages that are different. Did you know this?

You are ten months in the womb. Is this not so? I was ten months, she was ten months, the black race, Bengalis, are also ten months. No less, no more. . . . Before 300 days, a child will not be born. After 295 days it will be born (300 days is not exact). This is desire. This is *dao li*.

Those who understand these things will discuss filiality. You can follow this or not. You can chose to be filial or unfilial to your parents: you can think and decide which is right. You are born of a mother, I am also born of a mother, she is also born of a mother, am I right or not? You are carried in the womb how long? 295 days. Your mother carries you like a burden. And when you are born, how is your mother? She risks her life for you.

When you are born, this is called "crossing the sea of blood." Below you, all is blood. Your mother is swooning, as if dead, and below is blood. You must cross the sea of blood. When you are born, your eyes are open, and your hands are also open. You see the sea of blood and are frightened: your eyes close, and you clench your fists. Your mouth is plugged by blood, "dirt" blocks the mouth, and your fist clenches. When your eyes meet the blood, they close, the eyelids close, and the hands make a fist. The blood must be removed from your mouth, then you let out three cries: "Wah, wah, wah!" After crossing the sea of blood, you must cross the sea of suffering. The three cries are the sea of suffering.

People have desire, but they do not know the sorrow. If you know the sorrow, you know how to keep the Dao, and how to "be human." If you want to suffer the sins, how can you take them on? You can return to Heaven if you follow Heaven, and follow Earth. Heaven is man's grandfather, father, mother; Earth is our elder brother, elder sister, younger brother, younger sister.

When you are one, two, three, and four years old, your parents bear eight parts of your sin. You bear only two parts. When you are five, six, seven, eight, you bear four parts, and your parents bear six parts.

What sins do you have? You do not know what food is, what rice is. When you are a child, you do not understand. . . . You do not know that you can eat some things, but others you cannot. . . . Some things are good, others are bad, but the child does not understand, and he takes food and wastes it recklessly.

For him, everything is paste, and he does not understand that you must not mix excrement with things that you eat. When you are a child, you do not know these things, so you do not sin. But if your parents do not take care of you, if they fail to tend their children, then they bear eight parts of the sin, and the child only two parts, until the child has reached the age of sixteen. Once you have reached sixteen, whatever you do—murder men, set fires, be wicked, be poisonous—it's your affair. Your parents do not bear the responsibility.

This filiality is very deep. You cannot repay your parents. If men follow them and please them, then this is good. You must do things to please them, you must "follow father follow mother." You must not oppose Heaven and Earth. To "follow" you must recognize that he is big, you are small. He is the elder, and in a certain instance he is wrong. He is the one who taught you and raised you, and now clearly he is wrong. But he is still right. You must not correct him to his face. When he has passed by, then you can speak. This is called "following." People must not oppose their elders. We are small, and he is big, and she is the mother who gave us life.

A bird understands filiality. How is a bird born? From an egg, hatched from a layer of shell. We humans are born from the womb. A bird can repay his parent's love: you are human, but you do not understand how to repay the kindness of your parents.

The eggshell hatches what bird? A crow, and in three years the crow must molt. He has no feathers and cannot fly, and is in danger of starving. But when his stomach is empty he can cry "Wah, wah, wah," and his grandson will know to feed him worms until his feathers have grown back again. This is called "repaying kindness." . . . We humans do not understand how to repay the favors that our parents have done for us. Birds know how: humans are ungrateful.

Speaking of animals of the Earth, which is the most filial? Take the goat. He is born from the womb, like us. The goat's mother has tears, like us. When the kid is born, he faces Heaven and kowtows: one, two, three—then he gets to his feet. When he stands up and is hungry, he kneels on his front legs to suckle his mother's milk. The goat is born like us, and he understands filiality. . . . The kid knows how to find his mother when he is hungry, and he knows how to be a filial son. If you are human, you must know how to be a filial child.

Speaking of being bad, a tiger will attack and eat people, but you can teach tigers to be obedient. Tigers are bad and eat humans, but you can tame them. You are a human being, but no one can teach you to be good.

What is it to be faithful or grateful? People forget about gratitude and are unfaithful. They fail us in loyalty, in faithfulness, in filiality.

If you raise a dog, he cannot speak, but he is the most grateful and the most faithful creature. If today he does something wrong and the master hits him, he will not keep resentment in his heart. He does not criticize or blame the master. If you leave him and then return, he will wag his tail on seeing you. This is called "having gratitude and loyalty." A dog understands gratitude and loyalty. You must not be ungrateful and disloyal.

People don't obey. Those who are born from eggs, who are wrapped in a single membrane, can obey. You do not know how to obey. Take chickens and ducks. This house has chickens, that one has ducks. If you let them out to play, then later call for your ducks "gu gu gu," they will understand and return home to eat. Other people's chickens or ducks do not come near. A chicken or a duck will obey. You are human, and you don't obey. . . . What use are people? They're useless.

These things, dao li, are very deep, very long. If you want to study the Dao, it is very deep, very long. If you want to study the Dao, you must not covet money or power, status or women. You must take the world lightly and refuse money. You must seek perfection. You must go to the deep forest to study. After fifty years, you can become an immortal. These days, people are greedy for sex, for power, for money. They hurt people, kill people, set fires—they dare to do this sort of thing. We have this sort of thing.

People see what is good. Everyone says that they want to be filial, and that people ought to be honest. No one intends to do people in recklessly, or to hurt them by talking behind their backs.

Do you want to obey me or not? If not, I can repeat myself a hundred times, you know. If you don't want to obey, then think it over slowly. If you understand how to think about people, then you will hear me and know that I am right. You must study this yourselves. Good.

Now, I tell you not to hurt people, but you defy me. You say "No," you don't want to hear this. I say: "Don't go and steal." You say: "If I don't steal, I don't eat." But "Heaven will not starve people to death." You want to have your needs satisfied, you want your children to eat. "For every blade of grass a drop of dew." But you want to do things like that. You tell him not to, but he wants it like that. He definitely wants to be a success. These days people are like this: "Do it now, get it now, it's okay now." These people say that if you "do good," then your children get nothing. If you "do bad," then they will get something: "Be fierce, be poisonous, set fires, ride a horse." He rides a horse [enjoys high status], but there will be a day. The next generation will suffer.

No one takes notice of people who are good. But the future generations will be better off. These days you cannot find three consecutive generations rich. After two generations, the wealth is gone. If you are impatient to get, you are not thinking of the next generation. Have you no concern for your children and grandchildren? If you want to understand, it's like that.

I don't look at you and ask what religion you practice. Daoism is fine, Buddhism is fine, it doesn't bother me. I want to call you to do good.

In the world today, people do as they like. There is no distinction between men and women, and people are anarchic. No one know how to distinguish Heaven and Earth, no one understands principles. They lack reason.

Officials, those in the government, are the same. They do not, "follow the road" in their actions. Do you know what this is called? This is a "gold-money world." If you murder someone, you can fix it so that there's no trial. The money is given to you [by your fate], and in a "gold-money world," money buys a life. It is true. If you have money you can murder men. A gold-money world.

If you have money, you can talk. If you have no money, no matter what you say, it is not the truth. I call this a "glass" but you say "cup." I say that "glass" is more correct, but I don't have money. You have money, and you say that "cup" is more correct, so it's "glass" that's wrong. If you have money, everyone speaks your language. He says "glass" is right and I say "cup." I have no money, so even if I'm right, he will say I'm wrong. It's like that. Most people call this a "biscuit," but he calls it "cake," even though most people say "biscuit." If you have money, people will speak your language.

Rituals of the Seen and Unseen Worlds

— 17 —

Spellbinding

Donald Harper

Spellbinding (*Jie*) is a short account of demons and uncanny phenomena written on forty-five bamboo slips. It forms one section of a sizable bamboo-slip manuscript that treats astrological, numerological, and other occult lore. This and a second similar manuscript were discovered during excavation of Tomb 11 at Shuihudi, Hubei Province, in 1975–76; the burial is dated ca. 217 B.C.E. While we know from bibliographic records that demonological literature circulated among the elite of the Warring States (403–221 B.C.E.), Qin (221–207 B.C.E.), and Han (202 B.C.E.–220 C.E.) periods, none of this literature survived the vicissitudes of transmission down to the present. Thus *Spellbinding* is a unique example of an otherwise lost genre of ancient magico-religious literature.

Spellbinding contains seventy separate entries (numbered in the translation for convenient reference). Entry 1 is a prologue that gives the following explanation of the purpose of the text:

> The Wanghang bogy who harms the people,
> Treats the people unpropitiously.
> May the way to spellbind it be declared,
> Enabling the people to avoid the baleful and disastrous.

Wanghang is one of several cognate words (including Wangliang, Fangliang, and Panghuang) that denote a much-feared telluric bogy who preyed on people. Legend relates that when the flood hero Yu founded the Xia ruling house (in the late third millennium B.C.E., according to tradition), Yu cast nine talismanic caldrons—emblazoned with the images of all the spirits and demons of the terrestrial realm—that served magically to protect the people from the evil Wangliang and all manner of demonic harassment. *Spellbinding* fulfills the promise of the legend of Yu's caldrons in the form of a text that describes how to deal with specific varieties of demonic phenomena, from talking animals (entry 15) to revenants (entry 19) and the wolf at the door (entry 52).

The sixty-nine entries that follow the prologue are remarkable evidence of everyday beliefs of the third century B.C.E.. At that time certain naturalistic ideas had already gained currency among the elite; most notably the concept of "vapor" (*qi*) as the stuff of all existence, and the cyclical theories of Yin Yang and the Five Phases (*wuxing*) that were used to describe the operation of nature. *Spellbinding* reveals the magico-religious aspects of the beliefs of the time that coexisted with naturalistic ideas and continued to thrive in their own right. Some of the entries may appear to describe unreal situations and demons who are reminiscent of the fantastic composite creatures recorded in the *Classic of Mountains and Seas* (*Shanhai jing*), our chief source for knowledge of the early Chinese spirit world. However, *Spellbinding* shows that such creatures had real existence in the popular mind— not only did they exist, they often inhabited the immediate environment of the home and represented safety and health hazards. For example, entry 27 describes the Morphic Spirit (the name may refer to the ability of the demon to change shape as it pleases) that can occupy a house and paralyze its residents. By digging down "to the springs" (that is, to a depth that touches the subterranean level of the world), a "red pig with a horse tail and dog head" is obtained. Once caught, the Morphic Spirit is cooked and eaten, which should satisfy any doubts we might have concerning the substantiality of the creature in contemporary estimation (consumption of the offender is described in other entries as well). Even Yin and Yang are reified as demons whose mischief must be neutralized exorcistically (entries 12, 13, 32); and vapor (*qi*) is often the medium through which a demonic entity exerts its influence on its victims.

The religious viewpoint reflected in *Spellbinding* is basically animistic. Several tens of demons are named using a nomenclature that is most often descriptive: Demon of Abandoned Places (entry 3), Spirit Dog (entry 9), Demon Who Was Mourned as a Suckling (entry 49), and so forth. Most of the demons are not known from other written records, and it is difficult to know what larger religious significance they may have had outside their single occurrence in *Spellbinding*. Even given the difficulty of using *Spellbinding* to deduce the nature of popular animistic religion, the text gives us at least a glimpse of religion in action in the late Warring States period. The subsequent success of Buddhism in China and the indigenous formation of religious Daoism must be seen against the background of the popular traditions that produced *Spellbinding* several centuries earlier. Religious Daoism, in particular, regarded illness and the presence of demons as equivalent phenomena; and Daoism emphasized therapeutic measures to relieve the suffering of believers. A similar approach is evident in *Spellbinding*, which also includes many demonifuges that anticipate the exorcistic element of Daoist liturgy. Entry 42, which concerns the Hungry Demon (E Gui), bears witness to the Buddhist adaptation of popular religion. Previously it was thought that the name E Gui was invented as a translation of Buddhist *preta*, one of the lowest and most miserable of the ranks of rebirth. We now know that Buddhism did not introduce the Hungry Demon to China, but rather it adopted an indigenous demon to become the Buddhist *preta*.

While *Spellbinding* identifies many individual demons, a number of the entries concern uncanny or troubling phenomena that for lack of a better term I call quasi-demonic. Entries 18, 20, 37, and 38 provide techniques to alleviate harmful emotions. Sadness, sorrow, anxiety, and anger are not demons per se, but it is interesting that *Spellbinding* regards their effects as comparable to the actions of demons. Fear of bugs (*chong*) is also prevalent in *Spellbinding* (the category of *chong* includes snakes and other reptilian creatures). Some bugs are individual demons; for example, the Spirit Bug in entry 26 and the Conjunction Bug in entry 28. Entry 41 describes the mischief caused by the vapor (*qi*) of Bug-misfortune (*yang*). The word *yang* is used in Warring States, Qin, and Han texts. From a root meaning of misfortune caused by bugs, *yang* has the extended sense of misfortune in general (which is the meaning of *yang* in entry 70). The belief that all bugs were potential agents of misfortune is reflected in the several entries that concern household bug extermination (entries 10, 17, 54, and 66).

The exorcistic methods described in *Spellbinding* were intended to be employed by anyone. Beginning with the four exorcistic body postures listed in entry 1 (sitting like a winnowing basket is to sit with legs stretched out in front and spread open; the leaning stand is standing on one foot; linked movement may refer to a kind of shuffling movement), successive entries provide a catalogue of exorcistic magic. Before the discovery of *Spellbinding* we did not know that this kind of magic was part of common practice, and that it was not limited to the shamanic specialists or the officiants of state-sponsored rituals and cults. The very nature of *Spellbinding* as a text that teaches people to identify demonic phenomena and deal with them expeditiously broadens our perspective on magico-religious traditions before Buddhism and religious Daoism.

The translation of *Spellbinding* is made difficult by several factors. Some of the original bamboo slips are damaged and characters are missing. When it is possible to surmise what kind of word is missing, I supply a probable translation in brackets. Otherwise two dots mark one missing character. With a newly excavated manuscript, unattested vocabulary and unusual grammar represent another kind of difficulty. Continuing research on the text and the possible archaeological discovery of related texts will undoubtedly improve the translation. At several places in the translation it is necessary to add words to the text to make the English meaning clear; these words are also placed in brackets. Explanatory comments are placed in parentheses. Because it constitutes a unified concept in third-century B.C.E. thought, the word *qi* is regularly translated as "vapor," even though a functional translation might adopt a number of different translations; for example, "vitality" (entry 5), "breath" or "air" (entry 27), "essence" or "influence" (entry 13), and "taste" (entry 27). The following measure words are translated conventionally, but represent third-century B.C.E. measures: cup (*sheng*, 200 cc), inch (*cun*, 2.3 cm), and foot (*chi*, 23 cm). Entries 36–38 utilize calendrical numerology associated with the ten Celestial Stems (*tian gan*) and twelve Earthly Branches (*di zhi*), which are combined to form a set of day designations in a sixty-day cycle. Entry 38 specifies a day with the Celestial Stem *wu* in its designation and further specifies the time of midday—appropriate since *wu* is also associated with the center. The choice of sunrise on a *geng* day in entry 36 and sunset on a *gui* day in entry 37 is clearly significant, but the explanation is not obvious.

The text below is from *The Bamboo-slip Manuscripts from the Qin Tomb at Shuihudi (Shuihudi Qin mu zhu jian)* (Beijing, 1990), pp. 212–19.

Further Reading

Donald Harper, "A Chinese Demonography of the Third Century B.C.," *Harvard Journal of Asiatic Studies* 45 (1985): 459–98; Harper, "Warring States, Ch'in and Han Periods," in "Chinese Religions: The State of the Field," *Journal of Asian Studies* 54.1 (1995): 152–60; Mu-chou Poo, "Popular Religion in Pre-Imperial China: Observations on the Almanacs of Shui-hu-ti," *T'oung Pao* 79 (1993): 225–48.

Spellbinding

1. Spellbinding and casting odium on demons:

> The Wanghang bogy who harms the people,
> Treats the people unpropitiously.
> May the way to spellbind it be declared,
> Enabling the people to avoid the baleful and disastrous.

What demons detest are namely: reclining in a crouch, sitting like a winnowing basket, linked movement, and the leaning stand.

2. When without cause a demon attacks a person and does not desist—this is the Stabbing Demon. Make a bow from peach wood; make arrows from non-fruiting jujube wood, and feather them with chicken feathers. When it appears, shoot it. Then it will desist.

3. When without cause a demon lodges in a person's home—this is the Demon of Abandoned Places. Take earth from an old abandoned place, and make imitation people and dogs with it. Set them on the outside wall, one person and one dog every five paces, and encircle the home. When the demon comes, scatter ashes, strike a winnowing basket, and screech at it. Then it stops.

4. When without cause a demon deludes a person—this is the Enticing Demon who likes to sport with people. Make a staff from mulberry heartwood. When the demon comes, strike it. It will die of terror.

5. When without cause a demon takes hold of a person and becomes glued— this is the Sad Demon who is homeless and becomes the follower of the person. It causes the person to be pale in complexion and lack vapor (*qi*; *qi* deficiency

leads to loss of vitality); he enjoys observing the cleansing and purifying abstentions, and he does not drink or eat. Use a jujube-wood hammer that has a peach-wood handle to strike the person's heart. Then it does not come.

6. When without cause the people in a household all become diseased, and some die while others are sick—this is the Jujube Demon who is situated there, buried in an upright position. In the drought season the ground above it is damp; in the wet season it is dry. Dig it up and get rid of it. Then it will stop.

7. When without cause the people in a household all become diseased, most of whom suffer from nightmares and die—this is the Childbirth Demon who is buried there. There is not grass or matting above it. Dig it up and get rid of it. Then it will stop.

8. When without cause the people in a household all become diseased; some die while others are sick; and men and women have whiskers that shed, head hair that falls out, and yellow eyes—this is the fertilized egg. The kernel of the egg (the embryo in the fertilized egg) was born and became a demon. Pound one cup of selected kernels. In the same mortar, eat the egg kernels along with millet and meat. Then it will stop.

9. When a dog continually enters someone's house at night, seizes the men and sports with the women, and cannot be caught—this is the Spirit Dog who feigns being a demon. Use mulberry bark to make . . and . . it. Steam and eat it. Then it will stop.

10. When in summer during the period of Great Heat (late July) the house becomes cold without cause—young ants (*long;* it may also mean a dragon) are occupying it. Fumigate the inside of the house with nonfruiting jujube wood. The ants (or dragon) will depart.

11. When wild beasts or the six domestic animals encounter a person and speak—this is the vapor (*qi*) of the Whirling Wind. Strike it with a peach-wood staff, and take off a shoe and throw the shoe at it. Then it will desist.

12. When without cause the stove cannot cook food—the Yang Demon has taken its vapor (*qi*). Burn pig feces inside the house. Then it will stop.

13. When without cause a person's six domestic animals all die—the vapor (*qi*) of the Yin Demon has entered them. Then quickly crumble tiles and use them to encircle . . .. It will desist.

14. When cold wind enters a person's house, and he is alone without anyone else being there. Sprinkle sand. Then it will desist.

15. . . birds and beasts are able to speak—this is a prodigy. They should not speak more than thrice. If they do speak more than thrice, the person should increase the number of people around him. Then it will stop.

16. When his vapor (*qi*) is not circulating and yet the person can move. When it lasts for the whole day, there is a great matter; when it does not last for the whole day, there is a small matter.

17. When killing legged and legless bugs, they are able to rejoin after having been broken in two. Spew ashes on them. Then they will not rejoin.

18. When a person has thoughts that are sad and does not forget them. Take foxtails or cattails from an abandoned place, pick twice seven of their leaves, face the northeast and wad them, and lie down to sleep. Then it will stop.

19. When a person's wife and concubine or his friend dies and their ghost returns to him. Wait for it with an ignited [torch made of] nutgrass on a nonfruiting jujube-wood shaft. Then it will not come.

20. When a person's heart is sorrowful without cause. Take a stick of cinnamon one foot one inch long and break it in the middle. On the day of the full moon when the sun first rises, eat it. After doing that, then by late afternoon it will stop.

21. When the demon of an old abandoned place continually terrifies people and terrifies human habitations. Make straw arrows and shoot it. Then it will not terrify people.

22. When a demon continually summons a person saying, "You must die on such-and-such a month and day"—this is the Earth Demon who feigns being a rat and enters people's vinegar, fermented sauce, fermented gruel, or drink. Search for it and get rid of it. Then it will desist.

23. The dwelling place of a great spirit cannot be passed through. It likes to harm people. Make pellets from dog feces and carry them when passing through the place. On seeing the spirit throw them at it. It will not harm the person.

24. When a demon continually drums on a person's door at night, singing or wailing to be admitted by the person—this is the Malevolent Demon. Shoot it with straw arrows. Then it will not come.

25. When people or birds and beasts as well as the six domestic animals continually go into a person's home—these are spirits from above who are fond of those below and enjoy entering. Have men and women who have never entered the home (a euphemism for sexual intercourse) beat drums, ring clappered bells, and screech at them. Then they will not come.

26. When a demon continually follows men or women and goes away when it sees another person—this is the Spirit Bug who feigns being a person. Stab its neck with a good sword. Then it will not come.

27. When the people in a household all do not have vapor (*qi*) to breathe and cannot move—this is the Morphic Spirit who is situated in the house. Dig down to the springs. There is a red pig with a horse tail and dog head. When cooked and eaten, it has a fine vapor (*qi*).

28. When the people in a household all have contracting muscles—this is the Conjunction Bug who occupies the west wall of the house. Clear away the southwest corner to a depth of five feet below ground level. Strike it with an iron hammer. You must hit the bug's head. Dig it up and get rid of it. If you do not get rid of it, within three years everyone in the household has contracting muscles.

29. When a demon continually scolds a person and cannot be dismissed—this is the Violent Demon. [Stab] it with a nonfruiting jujube-wood sword. Then it will not come.

30. When a demon continually causes a person to have foul dreams, and after waking they cannot be divined—this is the Master of Diagrams. Make a mulberry-wood staff and prop it inside the doorway, and turn a cookpot upside down outside the doorway. Then it will not come.

31. When a demon continually follows a person as he travels and he cannot dismiss it. Jab it with a female writing-brush (*nü bi*; perhaps the name of a plant, or a name for a woman's hairpin). Then it will not come.

32. When a woman is not crazy or incoherent, yet sings in a high-pitched voice—this is the Yang Demon who takes pleasure in following her. Take twice seven seeds from a north-facing .. and incinerate them. [Put] the ashes into food and feed it to her. The demon leaves.

33. When without cause a demon treats a person's home as its sanctuary and cannot be made to leave—this is the Ancestral .. who is roving. Throw dog feces at it. It will not come.

34. When a demon continually enters a person's home naked—this is the Child Who Died Young and Is Unburied. Spew ashes on it. Then it will not come.

35. When a demon continually encounters a person and enters a person's home—this is the Roving Demon. Use broad cattails to make corded arrows and incinerate them. Then it will not come.

36. When a person continually gives birth to a child who dies before able to walk—this is the Blameless Demon who inhabits it. On a *geng* (the seventh Celestial Stem) day when the sun first rises, spew ashes on the gate, and after that offer sacrifices. On the tenth day collect the sacrifices, wrap them in woolly grass, and bury them in the wilderness. Then there will not be disaster.

37. When a person is anxious without cause. Make a peach-wood figurine and rub it. On a *gui* (the tenth Celestial Stem) day at sunset, throw it into the road and quickly say, "So-and-so will avoid anxiety."

38. When a person is angry without cause. On a *wu* (the fifth Celestial Stem) day at midday, eat millet in the road. Then suddenly it will stop.

39. When without cause the people in a household are all injured—this is the Gleaming Fang Demon who inhabits it. Take woolly grass and yellow soil, and sprinkle them in a ring around the house. Then it will leave.

40. When a demon enters a person's house, appears suddenly and vanishes, and does not desist. Get fermented gruel made from bran and wait for it to come. Pour [the gruel] on it. Then it will stop.

41. When without cause a person's head hair lifts up like bugs and chin or cheek whiskers—this is the vapor (*qi*) of Bug-misfortune that inhabits it. Boil grass shoes, and use them to paper [the hair]. Then it will stop.

42. Whenever a demon continually enters a person's house holding a basket and says, "Give me food"—this is the Hungry Demon. Throw a shoe at it. Then it will stop.

43. Whenever there is a great Whirling Wind that harms people. Take off [a shoe] and throw it at it. Then it will stop.

44. When a person continually loses a newborn infant—this is the Child Who Perished in Water who has taken it. Make an ash house to imprison it. Hang a scrub-brush inside. Then it will be captured. Slash it with the scrub-brush. Then it will die. If boiled and eaten, it will not be harmful.

45. Whenever a grove has been established in a land (the grove is sacred to spirits of the locality), and a demon there continually shouts in the night—this is the Ferocious Demon who seizes people and punishes them on its own. Enter with clothes undone and lapel-straps untied. The captives can be obtained.

46. When the people in a household suffer nightmares while sleeping and cannot occupy [the house]—this is the . . Demon who occupies it. Take peach-wood stakes and pound them into the four corners and center. Slash the outside walls of the home with a nonfruiting jujube-wood knife and shout at it saying, "Again quickly hurry out. If today you do not get out, your clothes will be stripped away with the nonfruiting [jujube-wood] knife." Then there will not be disaster.

47. When a large goblin continually enters a person's home and cannot be stopped. Strike it with a peach-wood figurine. Then it will stop.

48. When a demon continually summons a person to come out from the house—this is the Ferocious Demon who has no place to live. Do not respond to its summons. Throw white stones at it. Then it will stop.

49. When a demon baby continually calls to people saying, "Give me food"— this is the Demon Who Was Mourned as a Suckling. Some of its bones are on the outside. Spew yellow soil on them. Then it will desist.

50. When in a household someone who is sleeping sinks down together with the bedmat—this is the Earth Imp who occupies it. Pour plain boiling water over it and fill it with yellow soil. It will not be harmful.

51. When without cause there is a demon who joins with a person—this is the Elf Demon. Pour water on it. Then it will desist.

52. When a wolf continually shouts at a person's door saying, "Open. I am not a demon." Kill it, boil it, and eat it. It has a fine taste.

53. When there is the sound of a drum in the household and the drum is not to be seen—this is the Demon Drum. Respond to it with a handmade drum. Then it will desist.

54. When a horde of bugs covertly enters a person's house—this is wildfire that feigns being bugs. Respond to it with manmade fire. Then it will desist.

55. When a demon continually startles and reviles a person—this is the Blameless Demon. Stab it with a nonfruiting jujube-wood sword. Then it will stop.

56. When a demon continually steals a person's domestic animals—this is the Violent Demon. Shoot it with straw arrows. Then it will stop.

57. When a demon continually follows someone's woman and cohabitates saying, "The son of God-on-High descends to roam and wishes to leave [with her]." Bathe oneself in dog feces and strike it with reeds. Then it will die.

58. When a demon continually says to a person, "Give me your woman" and cannot be dismissed—this is a spirit from above who descends to take a wife. Strike it with reeds. Then it will die. If it is not expelled, after it comes five times the woman will die.

59. When Heaven fire burns a person's home and cannot be expelled. Halt it with white sand. Then it will stop. When a bolt of lightning ignites a person's [home] and cannot be stopped. Oppose it with man-made fire. Then it will desist.

60. When lightning attacks a person. Strike it with the same wood (the piece of wood struck first by the lightning). Then it will desist.

61. When cloud vapor (qi) covertly enters a person's home. Oppose it with man-made fire. Then it will stop.

62. When a person passes by an abandoned waste and a woman carrying a child chases the person. Oppose it by opening an umbrella. Then it will desist.

63. When a person is traveling and a demon stands blocking the road. Unbind the hair and rush past it. Then it will desist.

64. When birds and beasts continually make a person's house ring with noise. Burn loose head hair as well as the fur and whiskers of the six domestic animals at the places where they stop. Then it will stop.

65. When a person is sleeping and in the night a demon crouches over his head. Strike it with a bamboo whip. Then it will desist.

66. When birds, beasts, and legged or legless bugs enter a person's house in great hordes or singly. Strike them with a bamboo whip. Then it will stop.

67. When without cause the people in a household all have spreading welts—the Gibbon Mother inhabits the house. It is the size of a pestle and is red and white. In the wet season the place it occupies is dry; in the drought season it is damp. Dig to a depth of three feet inside the house and burn pig feces there. Then it will stop.

68. When the people in a household all have itching bodies—the Pestilence Demon inhabits it. Burn fresh paulownia wood inside the house. Then it will desist.

69. When the well of a household is bloody and has a putrid smell—the Earth Bug battles down below and the blood seeps upward. Dump sand in it and make a new well. Feed it mush and give it morning dew to drink. In three days it will be able to be human. If not, feed it for three months. If it is captured and is not a human, it will invariably be a dried out bone. Pick it up at dawn, enclose it in woolly grass, wrap it with hemp, and discard it at a distant spot. Then it will stop.

70. When the Whirling Wind enters a person's home and takes something from it. Throw a shoe at it. If the thing it took is recovered, place it in the center of the road. If not recovered, discard the shoe in the center of the road. Then there will be no misfortune (yang). Within one year there is invariably a misfortune in the family.

— 18 —

Record of the Feng and Shan Sacrifices

Stephen Bokenkamp

The account that follows is not a religious text, but a description of one of the most venerated and austere of the ancient imperial Confucian rituals, the Feng and Shan rites, as they were performed in 56 C.E. It was written by Ma Dibo, a minor official who participated in the rite, probably as a subordinate to the Chamberlain of State Ceremonials. Ma's specific function, as described in his account, seems to have been the inspection and readying of the stones which were to form parts of the ritual altar. Having, in his official capacity, ascended Mount Tai, where the Feng rite was to be held, ahead of the imperial party, Ma is able to describe the event from several perspectives. Through him, we learn of the setting and preparations for the rite, the performance and meaning of the ritual, the supernatural responses to the rite, and even a few comical details ignored in more sober histories. More important, Ma, by turns inspired by what he witnesses and annoyed at what he has to endure, gives us a real sense of what it must have felt like to participate in an imperial ritual.

While some early texts attempt to establish the antiquity of the Feng and Shan rites, we have verifiable accounts of only six performances in all of Chinese history. Such was the respect in which the rite was held that quite a few Chinese sovereigns, urged to perform the Feng and Shan, declined to do so on the grounds that they were unworthy or that the times were not right. In 56 C.E., Liu Xiu, posthumously known as the Thearch of Shining Martiality, deemed the times to be right. Thirty years earlier, he had reestablished the Han dynasty after a sixteen-year interregnum; now the kingdom was at peace and he could properly announce to Heaven and Earth the new beginning of the Liu-family dynasty. At the same time, through this rite he could connect in the minds of his subjects his rule with that of the most powerful of the Former Han rulers, Liu Che (posthumously styled the Martial Thearch), who had conducted the rites in 110 B.C.E., and with that of Ying Zheng, the unifier of the Central Kingdom, who called himself while living the "First Illustrious Thearch of the Qin" and who had conducted the rites in 219 B.C.E.

According to traditions established by these powerful emperors, the Feng rite to Heaven was to be conducted atop lofty Mount Tai (in modern Shandong Province), while the Shan rite to the feminine Earth spirit was held on a lesser peak, Liangfu, at the foot of Mount Tai. As this ritual program indicates, Mount Tai was regarded as an axis where the deities of Heaven and those of Earth might meet. China did not have a single *axis mundi,* however, but five—all holy mountains located roughly in the four cardinal directions and the symbolic "center" of the realm. Mount Tai was associated, in this five-phase ordered symbolic map of the kingdom, with the east, spring, and new growth. It was thus appropriate for a rite celebrating the beginning of a new dynastic line. While all of the five mountains received imperial sacrifice, Mount Tai was the sole mountain deemed suitable for the Feng and Shan.

But Mount Tai was more than the royal passage between Heaven and Earth or a symbol of cosmic beginnings. Popular belief held that the souls of the dead proceeded to an administratively organized purgatory beneath the mountain and its peaks hid caverns and springs that were the dwellings of spirits. In addition, during the Qin (221–207 B.C.E.) and Han (206 B.C.E.–220 C.E.) dynasties, Shandong was home to various schools of *fangshi* (wonderworkers and wizards), some of whom were able to win the allegiance of both Ying Zheng and Liu Che. These *fangshi* told of islands of immortality, inhabited by winged Transcendent beings, which floated just beyond sight in the eastern seas. Some held that the floating islands could sometimes be glimpsed from the summit of Mount Tai; others, arguing that specific ritual observances could cause the Transcendent beings to appear, held that the emperor could gain long life through accomplishing the Feng rite. The Feng rites of Ying Zheng and Liu Che were conducted in the strictest secrecy, in hopes of just such occurrences.

Liu Xiu's performance of the rites was somewhat different. He explicitly denied the goal of attempting to "meet with Transcendents" and organized his rites according to the instructions of his Confucian officials instead of relying on the sort of *fangshi* who had advised the previous two emperors. One token of the devout Confucian purpose of Liu Xiu's rites is recorded by Ma Dibo—the emperor visited the ancestral home of Confucius before beginning the ritual. The purpose of Liu Xiu's rite was simply to announce to Heaven and to Earth his achievements as emperor and to ask their continued blessing for his dynasty. A result of this determination was that Liu Xiu performed the Feng and Shan openly before his assembled officials, a decision that occasioned the logistical problems Ma describes so well.

Despite this, the basic elements of the rite remained the same. The term *feng* means "to seal." Liu Xiu's announcement to Heaven was to be written on stone tablets and enclosed in a stone coffer sealed with his official insignia. This coffer was further to be "sealed" within the piled earth of the ritual platform and covered with two massive stones. The earth placed around the coffer was to be of the "five colors" symbolizing the four directions and the center; that is, the entire realm. *Shan* means "to clear away" and was interpreted to mean the clearing of a ritual space on Liangfu for the rites to Earth. Ma Dibo is much less explicit concerning this lesser rite—his official duties may have prevented him from attending it— but it is likely that a stone coffer bearing an announcement to Earth was buried in the Shan rite as well.

The ultimate purpose of the Feng rite, then, was to enact the sealing of a new covenant between the emperor, one of whose titles was "child of Heaven," and Heaven, also called the "Thearch on High." The Shan rite was meant to actualize a similar covenant with the feminine divinity of Earth. Through this covenant, the position of humanity between Heaven and Earth was secured and the mediating status of a specific dynastic assured.

Acting as spirit "associates" in the conduct of the rites in 56 C.E. were the founder of the Han dynasty in the case of the Feng and his empress in the case of the Shan. This means that the spirits of these two ancestors were believed present at the rite and were charged with ensuring that the announcements were properly received in the spiritual hierarchy. The role of ancestors as intermediaries was common not only in imperial rites, but in family ritual as well. It should be noted here that what Western sources mistakenly call "ancestor worship" actually involved not "worship" of the ancestors, but the maintenance of family ties through ritual means in the hope that one's forebears might continue to aid their descendants. The imperial ancestors were, of course, believed to inhabit the summit of the celestial bureaucracy and were sometimes envisioned as dwelling in the constellations that ring the North Pole.

Imperial rites such as this were meaningful on a symbolic level, but to be regarded as truly effective they were expected to be accompanied by signs of acceptance on the part of Heaven and Earth. Ma records that the emperor Liu Xiu regarded the fine weather and lack of mishap during his performance of the rite as ample confirmation of Heaven's pleasure. The populace and presumably the history books as well required more dramatic wonders. Ma records several of these, all having to do with propitious vapors that appeared in the sky at key points during the ritual program. The Han court included officials whose job it was to scrutinize the skies for such atmospheric anomalies. Perhaps it was one of these officials who reported the white vapor that extended down to the altar at the conclusion of the rite. And why was it that all of the assembled officials failed to notice this token of Heaven's pleasure? They were inside the vapor, Ma reports, and so could not see it. Thus, despite Liu Xiu's Confucian attempts to demystify the rite, its mystery was preserved.

Further Reading

Hans Bielenstein, *The Restoration of the Han Dynasty,* vol. 4, *Bulletin of the Museum of Far Eastern Antiquities* 51 (1979): 3–300; Edouard Chavannes, *Le T'ai chan: Essai de monographie d'un culte chinois* (Paris: Annales du Musée Guimet 28, 1910); Howard J. Wechsler, *Offerings of Jade and Silk: Ritual and Symbol in the Legitimation of the T'ang Dynasty* (New Haven: Yale University Press, 1985), pp. 170–211; Arthur P. Wolf, ed., *Religion and Ritual in Chinese Society* (Stanford: Stanford University Press, 1974).

Record of the Feng and Shan Rites

In the thirty-second year of the Established Martiality reign-period (56 C.E.), the emperor went by carriage on a ritual inspection tour of the eastern lands. On the twenty-eighth of the first month (March 4, 56), he departed the palace at Luoyang, arriving in the state of Lu on the ninth day of the second month (March 14). From there he despatched the recently appointed Receptionist Guo Jianbo to lead five hundred convict laborers to repair the road to Mount Tai.

On the next day, the prince of Lu sent all of the Lius of the imperial household, together with members of the Kong clan and the Ding clan of Xiaqiu, to wish the emperor long life and to receive presents from him. Together they visited the house of Confucius (ancestral home of the Kong clan) where the emperor held for them a banquet of meats and liquors.

On the eleventh (March 16), the imperial party set out, reaching lodgings in Fenggao on the next day. On the same day, the emperor despatched the leader of the Court Gentlemen Brave as Tigers to ascend the mountain to inspect everything thoroughly. He also increased the convict labor force that was repairing the road to one thousand persons.

On the fifteenth day (March 20), purification rituals were begun. (The Confucian purification ritual [*zhai*] usually lasted for three days and was to be performed preparatory to any rite in which the spirits or ancestor were invoked. The official or emperor was to seclude himself in a special chamber for contemplation, eat only pure foods [especially highly polished rice], bathe, and in other ways prepare for the main rite to follow. For a Daoist version of this ritual, see chapter 20.) The representative of our kingdom and families went into seclusion in the residence of the Grand Protector. (The term "kingdom and families" is used metonymically throughout this text to refer to the emperor, who represents his kingdom and all of the families it contains. Hereafter, this term will be rendered simply "emperor.") The princes performed their purifications in the offices of the Grand Protectorate, while the Imperial Marquises all held theirs in the offices of the county seat. All the Chamberlains, Commandants, Generals, Grandees, Gentlemen of the Palace Gate, and other lesser officials, as well as the Duke of Song (senior heir to the Shang dynasty), the Duke of Wei (senior heir to the Zhou dynasty), the "Praising Perfection" Marquis, all of the Marquises of the eastern regions, and the Lesser Marquises of the Luoyang area conducted their purification rituals beyond the walls of Fenggao on the banks of the Wen River. The Defender-in-Chief and the Chamberlain for Ceremonials conducted their purifications at the residence of the

Supervisor for Forestry and Hunting. (These two officials are the highest rank of those mentioned here. The Defender-in-Chief was one of the "Three Dukes," the highest officials in the land, while the Chamberlain for Ceremonials was one of the "Nine Chamberlains," who reported directly to the emperor. He was not only responsible for imperial ritual, but also administered the National University. Presumably they were provided with this spot close to the mountain for their ritual seclusion so that they and their staffs could oversee preparations for the rite.)

I had earlier gone to the residence of the Supervisor for Forestry and Hunting, together with seventy others. We had inspected the altar for sacrifices to the mountain, as well as the old Hall of Light and the site where the Court Gentlemen had once carried out suburban offerings.

(The Hall of Light was a ritual building of five chambers in which the emperor was to carry out rites in accord with the seasons and the movement of the stars. The Hall of Light mentioned here was built by the Han emperor Liu Che before his performance of the Feng and Shan. It was a simple, thatched pavilion of two stories, the bottom square and the top round in shape. The suburban sacrifices were sacrifices personally conducted by the emperor on the outskirts of the capital city. Usually, at the time of the winter solstice Heaven was worshipped at an altar in the southern suburbs, and at the time of the summer solstice Earth was worshipped at an altar in the northern suburbs. Before his Feng rite, however, Liu Che had instructed his officials to carry out the suburban rite on an altar at the foot of the mountain. Presumably this is the site mentioned here.)

Entering the Supervisor's field pavilions, we inspected the stones they were preparing for the rite. Two of the stones were thin, flat, and nine feet in circumference. These were placed on the ritual platform. One of them was from a stone dating to the rites of the Martial Thearch. At that time, they had used five carts but still were unable to haul it up the mountain, so they positioned it at the foot of the mountain to form part of a building. This rock was thereafter known as the "five-cart stone."

The four massive stones for the corners of the ritual platform were twelve feet long, two feet wide, and about a foot and a half thick. The stone slats meant for the coffer were three feet long and six inches wide. [When fit together] they formed a shape like a slender box. There were ten of these. In addition, there was a stone for the stele inscription that was twelve feet tall when set upright, three feet wide, and one foot two inches thick. It had been inscribed with a text recording the meritorious activities and virtues of the emperor.

That same morning we went up the mountain on horses. Often the road became excessively steep and we were repeatedly forced to dismount and lead our horses. We spent about as much time walking as riding. When we reached Midpoint Observatory, we left our horses behind.

The Midpoint Observatory is twenty *li* from level ground. Looking to the south, one could see to the horizon and everything was plainly visible. Looking up, one could see the peak Celestial Pass. Despite the altitude, it was still like looking up to a soaring peak from the very bottom of a valley. So high was it that it was like gazing up at soaring clouds; so precipitous was it that it looked like a stone wall, steep and stark, as if no path could possibly ascend to it.

Looking up at people on the peak, I took some to be small white stones, others to be patches of snow. But when you watched long enough, these white things would pass by a tree or something and you knew them to be people.

When I really could ascend no more, I would throw myself spread-eagle on a rock. After lying still for awhile, I would revive again. I also availed myself of the liquor and dried meats that were sold at various spots along the route. At some places there was spring water, which greatly refreshed our spirits. In this way we urged one another along until we came to Celestial Pass peak.

When we arrived at this spot, I thought that we had reached the top. I asked someone along the way and he said that we still had another ten *li* to go.

From this point on, the road followed along the side of the mountain. Where it was broad, it was only eight or nine feet wide, but it sometimes narrowed to five or six feet. Looking up, I could see sheer precipices clustered darkly and pine trees a grizzled green, as if all were in the clouds. When I looked down into the stream-cut valley, there was only a roiling blue haze so dense that I could not see more than a few feet.

Then we came to a spot just below Heaven's Gate peak. This peak shadowed over us so hugely that, looking up, one felt as if one were gazing up a shaft at the sky from deep within a cave. We went straight up for a distance of seven *li,* clinging to a path that twisted and turned on itself like a sheep's entrails. This is called the "encircling path." In many places there were cables that one could grasp to ascend. My two servants supported me below the arms while the person ahead of me pulled. At such spots one saw only the heels of the one in front, while those in front could glimpse only the top of the head of the one following. It was like one of those paintings where people are depicted as if lined up one on top of the another. (Apparently Ma is referring here to the sort of Han painting [which we now know only through mortuary art] in which rows of officials are depicted without perspective so that they seem to be standing on each other's heads.) Our mode of ascent was just like what old texts call "scraping the chest along while hugging the rock"—it was harder than clawing one's way into Heaven.

When we first started out on this stretch of road, we would rest every ten steps or so. I gradually became exhausted, breathing so hard that my lips were parched. Then we rested every five or six steps—one tiny step after another before we would stop in our tracks. There was no way to avoid the mud. You might see a bit of dry ground before you, but your feet just would not go where you willed them.

We had started our ascent at breakfast time and reached Heaven's Gate after the *bu* hour (after 5:00 P.M.).

One of Guo Jianbo's men found an implement of bronze. It was shaped like an amphora with a square handle and an opening. No one recognized it. We thought that it might have been an implement used in earlier Feng and Shan rites. The person who found it was Yang Tong of Zhaoling in Runan.

We ascended to the east for another *li* or so until we came to the Mujia shrine. Mujia was a deity of the Martial Thearch's time. A little over one hundred paces to the northeast of this shrine, we reached the site where the Feng rite was to be performed. The First Illustrious Thearch of the Qin had erected a stele and a ceremonial gateway to the south; the Martial Thearch of the Han had his to the north of that. Some twenty paces beyond, to the extreme north of the area, we came to the round earthen platform to be used for our ritual. It was nine feet tall, square with rounded corners, and about thirty feet across. It had two stairways leading up to it that were forbidden to us ordinary mortals. His highness would ascend the easternmost stairway.

On top of the platform was a square altar of about twelve feet around, topped by the square stones. On the corners of the altar were the four massive stones mentioned previously, and there were four ceremonial arches on the four sides. We faced this altar and bowed repeatedly, announcing our presence.

Many people had placed offerings and money on the altar, and none of it was swept away. When the emperor eventually ascended to this altar, he encountered acrid pears and soured dates, hundreds of piles of coins, and even bolts of silk, all scattered about in disorder. When he asked the reason for this, the person in charge said: "Formerly, when the Martial Thearch was below Mount Tai preparing to ascend for the Feng and Shan rites, his officials ascended first to kneel and offer their respects. They scattered pears, dates, and money along the road, hoping to gain good fortune thereby. This is the same sort of thing."

His highness responded: "The Feng and Shan are important rites, which are to be performed only once every thousand years. Why should capped and belted officials of the kingdom act in such a fashion?" (The emperor's point is that his rite will naturally benefit all of his subjects. There is no need for anyone to seek extra blessings. Further, his officials should know better than to engage in such superstitious behavior.)

Seventy *li* up Mount Tai, we reached the summit to the southeast of Heaven's Gate, which is called "Solar Observatory." It is so named because when the cock first crows, one can see the sun just about to emerge. When the sun comes out, it seems to be about three feet across. Those looking toward the region of Qin might see as far as Chang'an; those looking toward Wu might see Mount Guiji; and those gazing toward Zhou might see as far as Qi. The Yellow River is over two hundred *li* from Mount Tai, but from the shrine it looks like a belt girdling the foot of the mountain.

To the south side of the mountain is a temple, entirely planted with one thousand cypress trees. The largest of these are fifteen or sixteen arm spans in circumference. Legend has it that these were planted by the Martial Thearch of the Han. On Lesser Heaven's Gate peak there are the "Five Grandee" pines.

When the Inaugural Illustrious Thearch of the Qin performed the Feng sacrifice on Mount Tai, he met with violent winds and rain squalls. He took shelter under these pine trees and, because they had ensured his safety, he appointed them the "Five Grandees."

To the northeast of the mountain is a stone chamber. South of the ritual platform is a jade basin with a jade tortoise inside. To the south of the mountain is the Elusive Spirits spring. Drinking of it, we found its waters to be clear and delicious. Its waters are said to be beneficial to one's health.

As the sun began to set, we descended. After we traveled down several times around the "encircling path," dusk fell and it began to drizzle. We could not see the path. We proceeded in file, sending one person out in front so that we had only to follow along by listening to his footsteps. Late in the night we reached safely the spot just below Heaven's Gate peak.

On the nineteenth (March 24), the emperor's procession reached the offices of the Supervisor of Forestry and Hunting. The emperor took up residence in a pavilion, while his officials spread themselves out in the fields. On this day, the clouds and vapors over the mountain took the form of a palace with lofty gateways. The officials all gathered to observe this.

On the evening of the twenty-first (March 26), when bullocks were sacrificed, the white, vaporous smoke, ten feet wide, rose to the southeast. It stretched as far as one could see and was extremely dense. At the time, the sky was completely clear and cloudless. According to the *Catalogue of Auspicious Signs of Heaven's Mandate (Ruiming pian),* favorable omens from Mount Tai all involve responses of the sun.

On the morning of the twenty-second, burnt offerings were presented to Heaven from the foot of Mount Tai when the sun was about twenty feet high. The smoke of these offerings went directly north.

Once these offerings were complete, all of the officials began to ascend the mountain in order. The Commandery had supplied three hundred wagons. These were to convey the most exalted officials—the Dukes, Princes, and Marquises—while the majority of the Chamberlains, Grandees, and lesser officials were to walk up the mountain. The emperor rode in the first wagon. All of the wagons were pulled up the mountain by men.

Upon reaching Midpoint Observatory, there was a brief rest before the ascent began again. It was midday when they reached the ritual site. In only a short while, all of the officials had taken up their positions. The emperor was on the ritual platform facing north. The Court Gentlemen Brave as Tigers took up positions with their halberds below the steps to the platform.

The Director of the Imperial Secretariat then presented the jade tablet and stone slats. He kneeled facing south. The Chamberlain for Ceremonials then said: "It is requested that you seal it." The Resplendent Thearch personally placed his seal on the tablet, then retreated to his original position. At this, over two thousand mounted warriors pulled open the two square stones atop the altar by pulling ropes attached to them from the spot where the Martial

Thearch's Feng rite had taken place. The Director of the Imperial Secretariat secreted the jade tablet inside and further held it in place with the stone slats. It was bound with cables of gold, sealed shut with a paste (of gold and quicksilver). Running from south to north there were two slats on each side and from east to west, three slats. Within the slats, the coffer formed by the sealing paste and the earth packed around it were green, red, white, and black—each according with the appropriate directions (east, south, west, and north, respectively).

Once this major portion of the rite had been completed, the Chamberlain for Ceremonials announced: "It is requested that you bow." At this, the Resplendent Thearch bowed repeatedly. The assembled officials all shouted "Ten thousand years!" with a sound that shook the mountain and valleys.

There was a white vapor of ten feet across that stretched from the southeast directly toward the altar. Also, from the altar, a blue vapor rose to Heaven. From a distance, the mountain peak was invisible. Those atop the peak were in the midst of this vapor and did not notice it.

A short while after the Feng ceremony was completed, the emperor ordered all the higher officials to descend in order. The emperor followed them. The several hundreds of lesser officials then began their descent, urging and pushing one another along. The ranks of officials stretched for over twenty *li*.

Since the path down had many narrow spaces, with deep valleys and cliffs of over a thousand feet high, those walking along behind would trip upon the ones in front who crawled through such dangerous spots. When those in front drew near to one of the torches [set out along the way], they would rise up. Further on, they would stop and the procession would bunch up again.

Those following along began to strike great rocks so that the rocks began to sound out noisily. But even though those making a racket with the rocks found no one to harmonize with them, they just could not control their excitement or keep silent. (Chinese court musical instruments included stone chimes, hung on racks. Ma is being sarcastic here. The music of such instruments would naturally be much more mellifluous than that produced by haphazardly striking stones, and there was certainly no court orchestra accompanying the officials' descent of the mountain.)

It was after midnight before the emperor reached the foot of the mountain. The various officials did not all arrive until the next morning. The elderly among them, when they had felt their strength give out and could no longer walk, had spent the night sleeping under the overhanging cliff faces.

Early in the morning of the following day, the Imperial Physician respectfully asked the emperor concerning his health. The emperor replied: "Yesterday we ascended and descended a mountain. When I wished to move forward, I was rushing those in front; when I wanted to rest, those behind stepped on my heels. The path was precipitous and dangerous. I was afraid that I could not pass through it, but I am unfatigued. There were those among the officials and underlings who lay exposed to the elements all night and had only water to drink, but not one of them fell, not one of them has become ill. Is this not the doing of Heaven? Mount Tai often has thunderstorms, but we have ascended and descended, offered burnt offerings, and completed the Feng rite atop the mountain, and all the while the weather has been clear and mild. Our achievements must be worthy that Heaven should respond in this fashion!"

On the next day, all the officials came to wish the emperor long life, but he ritually declined their congratulations. He curtailed the responsibilities of the hundred ranks of officials. Once this brief ceremony was concluded, he set out to spend the night at Feng gao, thirty *li* away. On the twenty-fourth (March 29), the emperor proceeded ninety *li* to Mount Liangfu, where he made offerings of cattle in the evening. On the next day, he accomplished the Shan sacrifice to Earth at the northern side of Liangfu. This is because one sacrifices to Heaven on the yang (southern side) of a mountain and to earth on the yin (northern side). In accordance with the old ritual regulations of the Inaugural Prime reign-period (86–80 B.C.E.), sacrifices were made to the High Thearch (the founder of the dynasty, Liu Bang) as an associate to Heaven; and to the High Overseer (his empress) as associate to Earth.

—19—

The Scripture on the Production of Buddha Images

Robert H. Sharf

The production and worship of Buddhist icons, whether images of buddhas such as Śākyamuni and Amitābha (Amituofo), or bodhisattvas such as Avalokiteśvara (Guanyin) and Maitreya (Mile), has been a central feature of Buddhist religious life throughout Asian history. Contrary to the views of some contemporary apologists who see the veneration of Buddhist icons as a degenerate practice proscribed by the canon or as a rueful display of "folk piety," the worship of Buddhist icons was both countenanced by the scriptures and promoted by the priesthood. Indeed, one common goal of Buddhist ascetic and meditative discipline in China was to "see the Buddha" (*jianfo*), and the wide variety of Buddhist icons found throughout the continent rendered service to this goal.

It is similarly misleading to view Buddhist icons as primarily didactic—intended merely to symbolize the virtues of buddhahood or to nurture a sense of reverence toward the Buddha and his teachings. The completion of a painted or sculpted icon in Buddhist countries involves an elaborate "eye-opening ceremony" in which the pupils of the icon are "dotted" to the accompaniment of invocation rites and offerings. Such ritual consecrations are intended to transform an inanimate image into a living deity, and both textual and ethnographic sources indicate that icons thus empowered were treated as spiritual beings possessed of apotropaic powers, to be worshiped with regular offerings of incense, flowers, food, money, and other assorted valuables. Chinese Buddhist biographies and temple records are replete with tales of miraculous occurrences associated with such images; images were known to fly through the air, to sweat, to communicate in dreams, to prophesy, and so on.

The *Scripture on the Production of Buddha Images* (*Zuo fo xingxiang jing*) is a short text that actively encourages the dissemination of Buddhist icons by enumerating the marvelous rebirths that await those who produce them. Unfortunately, we know virtually nothing of the provenance of the *Scripture on the Production of Buddha Images*: there are no extant Sanskrit or Tibetan versions, and the identity of the translator was lost at an early date. Be that as it may, an examination of the rather archaic language of the text, together with evidence provided by early Chinese Buddhist catalogues, suggest that the text was translated toward the end of the Eastern Han dynasty (25–220 C.E.) or shortly thereafter. This places the text among the earliest known Buddhist scriptures translated into Chinese.

The *Scripture on the Production of Buddha Images* can be loosely grouped together with a number of other short scriptures that detail the merit acquired through specific acts of piety. The importance placed on the ritual veneration of icons is immediately evident in the titles of many of these texts: *Scripture on Consecrating and Washing an Image of the Buddha* (*Taishō daizōkyō* [T] 695); *Scripture on the Merit Gained through Washing an Image of the Buddha* (T 697); *Scripture on the Merit Gained through the Construction of Stūpas* (T 699); *Scripture on the Merit Gained through Circumambulating a Buddha Stūpa to the Right* (T 700); and so on. There is, moreover, a later Mahāyāna version of the *Scripture on the Production of Buddha Images* that is considerably longer and more complex than the early text (the *Mahāyāna Scripture on the Merit Gained through the Production of Images* translated by Devaprajñā in 691 C.E. [T 694]).

The *Scripture on the Production of Buddha Images* is also significant in being the earliest extant work to associate the production of a Buddha image with King Udayana—the young protagonist of the scripture who is so enamored of the Buddha's beauty that he is moved to capture his likeness in a portrait. King Udayana was a historical figure who apparently ruled over the Indian kingdom of Vasta from its capital at Kauśāmbī (present-day Kosam in the district of Allahābad, Uttar Pradesh) during the time of the Buddha. While Udayana is more renowned for his military and amorous exploits than for his religious devotion, a series of apocryphal Buddhist tales transformed Udayana into the pious Buddhist benefactor responsible for the creation of the first Buddha image.

The details of the Udayana legend were greatly embellished in later accounts. The fully developed narrative found in medieval Chinese sources runs roughly as follows: the Buddha once spent a summer retreat in heaven in order to preach to his deceased mother Māyā. One of his royal patrons, King Udayana, became distraught upon learning that he would not be able to see the Buddha during the Buddha's absence. He implored Mahā Maudgalyāyana, a disciple of the Buddha famed for his supernatural powers, to transport a piece of fine sandalwood along with thirty-two skilled artisans to Heaven so that they might carve an exact likeness of the Buddha. (Each of the artisans would be responsible for carving one of the thirty-two special marks of the Buddha.) In short order the artisans completed their task and the marvelous image was brought back to earth. When Śākyamuni later returned from his sojourn in heaven the image miraculously rose to greet him. The Buddha then paid homage to the image and prophesied its later importance in spreading the religion.

There are actually several versions of this story, one of which claims that the Udayana image would eventually make its way to China. Sure enough, a number of images of Indian origin were identified in China either as the original "Udayana image" or as an equally sacred twin of the original. One fifth-century document claims that the original was brought to China in the first century C.E. by Han Emperor Ming's envoy Cai Yin along with the *Scripture in Forty-two Sections* (*Sishi'er zhang jing*). (See chapter 28 in this volume.) This legend, which links the image to the very first Buddhist missionaries in China, is but one of many that highlight the importance of icons in the transmission of Buddhism to East Asia. Another source claims that the famous Kuchean translator Kumārajīva had the Udayana image in his possession when he was brought to China in 401. Yet another contends that the image was procured in 505 at the behest of Emperor Wu of the Liang dynasty, a ruler known for his profligate patronage of Buddhism.

In the meantime, the Chinese pilgrim Xuanzang (596–664) visited Kauśāmbī on his journey through the Indian continent in the 630s. Xuanzang reports that the original image was still to be found at the site, and he goes on to say that while many tried to abscond with the image, no number of men were able to move it. Indeed, Xuanzang insists that all other images claiming to be the original sculpture made for Udayana are mere copies. Xuanzang himself had a sandalwood copy of the image in his possession (along with six other icons) when he returned to China in 645.

Images purporting to be the Udayana image became the source for popular tales attesting to the supernatural power of the icon, and one eminent monk, Zhuli (544–623), reportedly performed self-immolation before the image in part to protest its imminent removal from his temple in Jiangdu. In the Northern Song dynasty (960–1126) the Japanese Buddhist pilgrim Chōnen (938–1016) had a sandalwood copy made, which he brought back to Japan in 986. When a cavity in the rear of the image was opened for the first time in February 1954 it was found to contain a miniature set of internal organs fashioned out of silk, in addition to various valuable coins, crystals, scriptures, and historical documents relating to the history of the image. This magnificent piece of Chinese sculpture, enshrined at Seiryōji temple in Kyoto, served as the model for over a hundred replicas, thus propagating the Udayana legend in Japan. (Indeed, according to one Japanese account the sculpture brought to Japan by Chōnen was actually the original image made for Udayana—the replica commissioned by Chōnen traded places with the original just prior to Chōnen's departure!) The Seiryōji image is the only example of a Chinese Udayana image to survive to the present day.

The *Scripture on the Production of Buddha Images* was popular not only because of its connection to the famous Udayana image, but also because it was short— short texts were relatively easy to copy and thus to disseminate. At the Fengshan caves, for example, nine copies of the *Scripture on the Production of Buddha Images* dating to the Tang period have been found carved on stone. This cave site, located some seventy-five kilometers southwest of Beijing, was the center of an attempt, spanning the seventh to the twelveth centuries, to preserve the entire Buddhist canon on stone slabs. The slabs, of which some 14,620 are extant today, were then sealed in caves specially excavated for this purpose, or, as the caves filled up, buried nearby. (Attempts to preserve the Buddhist canon in stone were typically motivated by the belief that the "end of the dharma" [mofa] was at hand.) The discovery of nine copies of the *Scripture on the Production of Buddha Images* at this site suggests that the text was particularly popular in medieval times: the only scriptures that warranted more copies at Fengshan were the *Heart Sūtra* (*Banruo boluomiduo xin jing*) and the *Diamond Sūtra* (*Jingang banruo boluomi jing*).

The final line of the *Scripture on the Production of Buddha Images* refers to rebirth in Amitābha's pure land—a "Mahāyāna" theme that is quite incongruous in this otherwise "Hīnayāna" scripture. The fact that Amitābha's paradise is not mentioned elsewhere in the text despite its concern with auspicious rebirths suggests that this line is a later interpolation. The only significant difference between the early text translated here and the later version (T 693) translated in the Eastern Jin (317–420) is that the prose portion of the Eastern Jin text is followed by a set of verses that recapitulate the content of the scripture.

This translation of the *Zuo fo xingxiang jing* is based on the text found in the *Taishō daizōkyō* (T 692:16.788a–c), consulting the parallel but somewhat less obtuse translation done in the Eastern Jin (*Zaoli xingxiang fubao jing*, T 693:16.788c–790a).

Further Reading

For a full account of the various sources bearing upon the Udayana image, see especially Martha L. Carter, *The Mystery of the Udayana Buddha,* supplemento n. 64 agli Annali—vol. 50, fasc. 3 (Napoli: Istituto Universitario Orientale, 1990); and Alexander Soper, *Literary Evidence for Early Buddhist Art in China* (Ascona, Switzerland: Artibus Asiae, 1959). On Xuanzang's encounter with the image, see Samuel Beal, *Si-yu Ki, Buddhist Records of the Western World* (London, 1884), vol. 1, pp. 235–36. On Zhuli's self-immolation before the image, see Koichi Shinohara, "Dynastic Politics and Miraculous Images: The Example of Zhuli (544–623) of the Changlesi temple in Yangzhou" (forthcoming in a volume edited by Richard Davis). On the Seiryōji image, see Gregory Henderson and Leon Hurvitz, "The Buddha of Seiryōji: New Finds and New Theory," *Artibus Asiae* 19 (1956): 5–55.

The Scripture on the Production of Buddha Images

The Buddha arrived in the country of Kauśāmbī, where there was a grove belonging to Kausika. At that time the king, named Udayana, was fourteen years old. When he heard of the Buddha's arrival, the king ordered his ministers and attendants to prepare his carriage. The king then went to welcome the Buddha.

Seeing the Buddha from a distance the king's heart leapt with joy. The king immediately alighted from his carriage and proceeded on foot, taking leave of his ministers, attendants, and those who carry his parasol. The king then greeted the Buddha, touching his forehead to the Buddha's feet and circling him three times. Then, kneeling with palms joined respectfully together, he addressed the Buddha saying: "In the heavens above and on earth below there are none who compare to the Buddha. The face, eyes, and body of the Buddha now shine forth magnificently, and I never weary for a moment of gazing upon the Buddha. The Buddha is presently the teacher of all those in the heavens above and the earth below, and many are those who revere the Buddha's compassion."

The Buddha, remaining silent, did not respond.

The king addressed the Buddha further saying: "When people perform virtuous acts they gain good fortune, but where does this lead them? I dread no longer being able to look upon the Buddha after the Buddha is gone. I want to produce an image of the Buddha to venerate and bequeath to later generations. What sorts of good fortune will I obtain thereby? I ask that the Buddha take compassion upon me and explain this matter, as I earnestly desire to understand."

The Buddha said: "Young king, your question is excellent indeed. Listen to what I say, and having heard it, take it to heart." The king said: "Yes, I am ready to receive this teaching."

The Buddha said to the king: "I will teach you of the good fortune to be gained by one who produces an image of the Buddha." The king said: "I am grateful."

The Buddha said: "A person of this world who produces an image of the Buddha will, in a later life, have clear eyes and a handsome appearance; his body, hands, and feet will always be excellent. One born in heaven will also be exceptional among the gods in his purity, with exquisite eyes and countenance. Such is the fortune obtained by one who produces an image of the Buddha.

"The place in which one who produces an image of the Buddha is born is devoid of defilement; the bodies of those born there are flawless. After death he will attain birth in the seventh Brahmā Heaven. Moreover, surpassing all the other gods, his handsome appearance and beauty will be without peer, and he will be honored by all the gods. Such is the fortune obtained by one who produces an image of the Buddha.

"One who produces an image of the Buddha will be born to a noble family, with resources far surpassing those of people in this world. He will not be born a child to a poor or destitute family in a later life. Such is the fortune obtained by one who produces an image of the Buddha.

"The body of one who produces an image of the Buddha will, in a later life, always be the color of reddish gold, handsome without peer.

"One who produces an image of the Buddha will most certainly be born to a wealthy family, with money and precious jewels beyond reckoning. He will always be loved by his parents, siblings, and relatives. Such is the fortune obtained by one who produces an image of the Buddha.

"One who produces an image of the Buddha will be born in India (Jambu-dvīpa), either to the family of an emperor or a prince, or born a child to a family of great virtue. Such is the fortune obtained by one who produces an image of the Buddha.

"One who produces an image of the Buddha will, in a later life, become an emperor. He will be the most honored and celebrated among all the monarchs, the one in whom all other monarchs take refuge and pay homage. Such is the fortune obtained by one who produces an image of the Buddha.

"One who produces an image of the Buddha will, in a later life, become a wheel-turning king, able to ascend to Heaven and return at will. He will accomplish whatever he sets out to do. Such is the fortune obtained by one who produces an image of the Buddha.

"One who produces an image of the Buddha will, in a later life, be born in the seventh Brahmā Heaven. His life will span a single aeon and his wisdom will be without equal. One who produces an image of the Buddha will never again be born in one of the evil destinies after death. He will always guard his chastity, and his thoughts will always be on his desire to follow the Buddhist path. Such is the fortune obtained by one who produces an image of the Buddha.

"One who produces an image of the Buddha will, in a later life, always honor the Buddha and revere the scriptures. He will continually make offerings to the relics of the Buddha of variegated silk, fine flowers, exquisite incense, lamps, and all the precious jewels and rare objects of the world. Afterward for innumerable aeons he will practice the path to nirvāṇa. Those who aspire to present precious jewels to the Buddha are not common men; they have all practiced the Buddhist path in previous lives. Such is the fortune obtained by one who produces an image of the Buddha.

"One who produces an image of the Buddha will, in a later life, attain such wealth that there never will come a time when it will be exhausted; nor can such wealth be calculated. It is, perhaps, possible to measure the water in all the rivers and oceans of the four quarters by measuring it out by the gallon. But the wealth attained by one who produces an image of the Buddha exceeds the amount of water in the rivers and oceans of the four quarters by a factor of ten. In his future life he will be honored and protected by all. One who produces an image of the Buddha can be likened to one who, during a down-pour, has a fine shelter—he has nothing to fear.

"One who produces an image of the Buddha will, after death, never again be born in one of the evil destinies, be it hell, the animal realm, or the realm of hungry ghosts. One who sees an image of the Buddha and, with a pious heart, joins palms together and takes refuge in the Buddha's stūpa or his relics, will not, at death, reenter the realms of hell, animals, or hungry ghosts for one hundred aeons. Rather, at death he will be born in heaven, and, when his long life in heaven is complete, he will once again descend into the world as the child of a wealthy family, with immeasurable precious jewels and rare objects. Afterward he will certainly attain the path of Buddhist nirvāṇa."

The Buddha told the king: "To produce an image of the Buddha is a worthy deed, and the good fortune obtained thereby is, without exaggeration, such as I have explained." The king was pleased and bowed before the Buddha, touching his forehead to the Buddha's feet. The king and all his ministers then bowed to the Buddha and took their leave. At the end of their long lives they were all reborn in the land of Amitābha Buddha.

— 20 —

The Purification Ritual of the Luminous Perfected

Stephen Bokenkamp

Whether they describe it as hovering beyond the division between existence and nothingness, nowhere yet immanent in everything, or anthropomorphically, in the robes of an emperor and seated on a throne in the highest of heavens, Daoists conceive of the Dao as the universal organizing principle underlying existence. Because of this, Daoist ritual is, by definition, at once cosmic and concrete in conception. That is to say, Daoist ritual procedures are meant to bring humans, with their mundane concerns, into harmony with unseen and all-pervasive forces of order. We should not, then, imagine Daoist ritual to consist of "sacrifices," "prayers," or "offerings" directed to remote deities in some far-off transcendent realm. There is no such easy division between the here-and-now and the divine. While Daoists do imagine a panoply of gods, transcendent emanations of the Dao, in exquisite language and often bewildering detail, the spirit world, they believe, is both as distant as the stars and as near as your nose. This was held to be literally true, since each part of the human body, including the nose, is possessed of a spirit-administrator. As one early text puts it, the human body "includes Heaven and Earth, the sun and moon . . . mountains and streams, rivers and seas. . . . It also has its emperor, with his three Ministers, nine Chamberlains, twenty-seven Grandees. . . ." Each part of this bodily cosmos (the microcosm) corresponds to and moves in sympathy with the greater cosmos (the macrocosm).

Daoism held each of these interlocking spheres to be inhabited by spirits, concentrations of pneuma or "primal breath," which was itself but differentiated particles of the Dao. The task of salvation thus becomes a complicated bureaucratic process. One must properly preserve and administer the interior hierarchies while simultaneously looking outward to the spiritual potencies of the macrocosm in order to merge inner and outer in the harmonious whole (the primordial Dao) as it existed before its evolution into the myriad things.

Daoist ritual thus seeks not to bridge spatial distances, since the spirit-world extends without interruption from within each of us into the farthest reaches of space, but temporal distance. One longs not for a distant other, but for a prior wholeness. In one sense or another, then, all Daoist ritual functions to reconnect humanity with the primordial Dao.

But what could be done for the dead, those who had, through their transgressions in life, fallen into the earth-prisons to suffer the consequences of their deeds and eventual reassignment to a suitably humble rebirth? Surely the dead were impossibly distant from the Dao, which is life. Were one's ancestors to fall into this category, they might never be blessed with a rebirth in which they could even hear the message of salvation. Ritual provided the answer. One could, through ritual, impart one's own merit and thus the life-giving actions of the Dao to the suffering dead. This was to be accomplished through using one's own internal spirits to notify the celestial spirits of the sorry plight of the departed. In this way, the illumination of the scriptures might reach even the darkest depth of the purgatories.

The ritual instructions translated below show one way in which this might be accomplished. They come from the original Lingbao (Numinous Treasure) scriptures, which were composed around 400 C.E. Two features of these scriptures are particularly important for the history of Daoism: First, they were meant to represent a synthesis of all the important religious traditions of the time—most prominently, Celestial Master Daoism, Shangqing Daoism, and Buddhism. They are thus the first Daoist scriptures to incorporate and redefine Buddhist beliefs, practices, and even portions of Buddhist scripture. They do this quite openly, positing the temporal priority and spiritual superiority of their message against any charge of plagiarism. The very name of the scriptures (ling, "spirit-endowed," representing the heavens and yang joined to bao, "jewel," representing the Earth and yin) refers to the claim that these scriptures are translations of spirit-texts that emerged at the origin of all things when the breaths of the Dao separated into the two principles yin and yang, thus giving the Lingbao texts priority over texts composed later.

Secondly—and related to this synthesizing tendency—the Lingbao scriptures are the source for much later communal ritual in Daoism, rites that continue to be practiced right down to the present day. This success seems to be due in large part to the hermeneutical strategies employed in the texts to support their synthesis of seemingly incongruous religious ideas. Terminology and concepts appropriated from other scriptures, Buddhist and Daoist alike, are shown here to be different manifestations of a primordial unity, that of the Lingbao scriptures. For instance, the Buddhist notion that one's merit might be shared with others, even those already departed, here provides a means by which the beneficial effects of Daoist meditations on the interior gods might be shared with one's ancestors. In this way, one might hope not only to achieve primordial unity, but to share it as well. Given Chinese veneration of the ancestors, this was regarded as a significant improvement in Daoist practice.

Just as the message of the Lingbao scriptures originated in the beginnings of time, so their practices replicate the cosmogenesis, thereby constituting the best route back to that perfect primeval order, the Dao. While this claim of interpretive superiority was not always accepted, Daoists everywhere came to regard this pursuit of original unity and order as the best possible ritual scenario. As a result, Daoist ritual manuals today are nearly all called "Lingbao" and modeled on these early texts.

The initial revelation of the Lingbao scriptures in graphs of light that spread across the heavens at the genesis of the cosmos figures as a subtext in the ritual that follows: The ritual text begins with the highest god of the Lingbao pantheon, the Heavenly Worthy of Primal Origin, emitting five-colored beams that illuminate the heavens and earth-prisons of all the world-systems in the ten directions, revealing the karmic causes that have brought the inhabitants of each to their just, but miserable, rewards. This light, repeating the initial action of the scriptures in opening primordial darkness, becomes the agency by which those in the earth-prisons might become "enlightened" and so achieve favorable rebirths.

The lamps that the practitioner lights in the central courtyard of the house where the ritual is held explicitly symbolize this action. More importantly, the incantations that accompany the rite are bureaucratic documents that charge the officials of the spiritual-hierarchies in each of the ten directions to ensure that the illumination of the scriptures reaches to all. Through performing this rite, then, the petitioner personally assumes a position in the macrocosmic bureaucracy. The meritorious action of releasing souls from the earth-prisons redounds finally to the glory of the practitioner, who announces his or her own future at the close of each directional petition.

The list of days given for this ritual are explained elsewhere in the Lingbao scriptures as the specific times during which the gods of the ten directions assemble in the celestial metropolis in the highest of the heavens. At these times, they are most closely under the direction of the Heavenly Worthy and might be dispatched to accomplish the salvific actions required of them. While these deities, and the structure of the rite itself, are organized according to the "ten directions" (the four cardinal directions, their intermediate points, and both an upper and a lower central position), the rite speaks of the earth-prisons of the Nine Dark Regions of Everlasting Night. Apparently, then, the underworld was at this time envisioned as a replica of the human world, which, in Chinese belief, was divided into nine regions.

The Purification Ritual of the Luminous Perfected is the earliest example we have of the "ritual of universal salvation" (*pudu*), which is still today practiced by Daoists and Buddhists alike. While the core of the rite remains today much the same, this early version is significantly different from the elaborate forms that the *pudu* was to take in later times. First of all, the practitioner here need not to be a professional priest. Early accounts of this rite specify that it was to be performed by a "student of the Dao," that is, any Daoist adherent who had received the text. Secondly, as the instructions translated below indicate, the ritual was to be performed not in a temple, but in the central courtyard of the practitioner's own house. These particular features mark the rite as originating in the early days of the Lingbao movement, when there was not yet a widely established priesthood or temples that housed them.

Further, although the ritual is "universal" in the sense that it works for the salvation of all, even to the extent of employing the terms of Mahāyānist universalism in calling for the salvation of "all forms of life that creep or fly, that wriggle or crawl," early accounts of the ritual suggest that it was performed primarily for the salvation of the practitioner's own ancestors. This is also clear from the ritual text itself, which requires the practitioner to fill in his or her family name in each of the incantations.

The title of the ritual deserves a note of explanation. The term "Luminous Perfected" (mingzhen) refers to the perfected deities of the celestial macrocosm. They are stellar emanations and directional spirits, visualized by the practitioner as descending in formal procession as detailed in the text. The rite itself is known as a "purification" or "purgation" (zhai), a term that in Confucian and imperial ritual denoted the specific practices conducted preparatory to ritual action. During the Confucian zhai, which usually lasted for three days, the official or emperor was to seclude himself in a special chamber for contemplation, eat only pure foods, bathe, and in other ways prepare to invoke the spirits. In Daoism, zhai became a name designating the ritual invocation of the spirits itself, rather than the prefatory practices.

The Purification Ritual of the Luminous Perfected appears in the earliest catalogues of Lingbao scriptures and was probably written early in the fifth century C.E. The version of the rite translated here comes from a Daoist collection composed ca. 575.

Further Reading

Charles D. Benn, *The Cavern-Mystery Transmission: A Taoist Ordination Rite of A.D. 711* (Honolulu: University of Hawaii Press, 1991); Stephen R. Bokenkamp, *Traces of Transcendence* (Berkeley: University of California Press, 1996); Judith M. Boltz, "Opening the Gates of Purgatory: A Twelfth-Century Taoist Meditation Technique for the Salvation of Lost Souls," *Tantric and Taoist Studies,* ed. Michel Strickmann (Brussels: Institut Belge des Hautes Études Chinoises, 1983), pp. 488–510; John Lagerwey, *Taoist Ritual in Chinese Society and History,* (New York: Macmillan, 1987), esp. pp. 195–201.

The Purification Ritual of the Luminous Perfected

The Most High Lord of the Dao advanced, bowed, and said to the Heavenly Worthy: "Today, in attendance on your throne, I was privileged to see the Celestial Youths of the various heavens receive your awesome illumination which lighted not only the Halls of the Blessed of all the heavens but also the earth-prisons of the innumerable worlds. Everywhere the reward of good is joy, the reward of evil, pain. The good enjoy blessings and wander freely and limitlessly. The evil, smeared with soot, are dragged endlessly through the eight sorts of difficulty and no longer enjoy human shape.[1]

"These latter are extremely pitiful. They suffer the results of their evil karma for millions of *kalpas*, never recognizing the root cause of their fate. Is there not some act of merit that might redeem the souls of these dead from the Nine Dark Regions of Everlasting Night so that they might physically enter into the light and achieve rebirth in a fortunate family? If they receive your mercy, they will enjoy grace in life and in death. The departed will know carefree joy and flourish when they come back into the world, enjoying fortune, fame, and a longevity in years. Then, in truth, your mercy will be as clouds that shade the eight reaches of the realm and as breezes that spatter dew on fragrant orchards, so that all men and women yet to be born will come to hear the sounds of the law. I beg that you, O Heaven-honored one, might expound such a method, bestowing on us the proper explanations that all will see the light and achieve peace."

The Heavenly Worthy announced to the Most High Lord of the Dao: "Listen attentively to my words. Seal these good thoughts and right understandings in your heart and ponder them day and night so that you do not forget. I will now expound for you the wondrous sounds of the true law which you may use to redeem the souls of transgressors, releasing them from the Nine Dark Regions of Everlasting Night and the eight sorts of difficulty, eradicating from their hearts the imbedded evil to plant the roots of faith. In both life and death they will know joy. This karma will extend from generation to generation.

"This is an exalted and wondrous method that might be transmitted only once every 400,000 *kalpas*. If there is in the world one worthy and enlightened, then bind that person by oath and transmit it. If this method is kept secret, then good fortune will descend to the possessor; but if it is improperly leaked to others, then misfortune will follow. This is an injunction of wind-borne swords, announced to the Luminous Perfected.[2] One who breaks these regulations has no cause to complain to the heavens."

Thereupon, the Heavenly Worthy commanded the Heaven-soaring Spirit to recite the *Upper Chapters of Salvation through Counteracting the Sources of Blessing and Blame (Zuifu yuandui badu shangpin)*. When he recited this scripture, the sun, moon, and stars in all of the heavens shone dazzlingly into the Nine Dark Regions and the Courts of Everlasting Night in all the illimitable worlds. The bodies of the hungry ghosts and of the dead in penal servitude there were illumined so that they all saw the root causes of their various fates. At this, they were all enlightened. At once, their hearts were fixed on goodness and within them arose the desire to return to the gates of the blessed. They were released from the five sorts of suffering[3] and the three paths of unfortunate rebirth⁴ and their karmic guilt was cleansed. At this, the earth-prisons were quiet and vacant. All of the inhabitants, male and female, heard the sounds of the law. Those who responded in their hearts became divine Transcendents.

This is what the Heaven-soaring Spirit said:

According to the *Upper Chapters of Salvation through Counteracting the Sources of Blessing and Blame,* you should regularly practice this purification rite in the six odd-numbered months of each year. In those months, you should observe ten days—the 1st, the 8th, the 14th, the 15th, the 18th, the 23rd, the 24th, the 28th, the 29th, or the 30th—as well as the eight seasonal nodes (the days beginning each of the four seasons, the solstices, and the equinoxes) and the *jiazi* and the *gengshen* days (the 1st and 57th days of each sixty-day cycle).

In the central courtyard of your house, set up a large lamp with nine flames. Light them so that their luminescence will above penetrate to the halls of the blessed in all of the nine mysterious regions of the heavens and will below shine into the Nine Dark Regions of Everlasting Night.

Then, according to the old methods of the awesome rites, perform the ritual calling forth the officials of your body to communicate with and report to the officials of Heaven [in the following manner:]⁵ Face toward the east and knock your teeth three times. Then, while holding incense in your fingers, utter the following incantation:

Most High Lord Lao of the three pneumas—the mystic, the primordial, and the inaugural—of the Three Heavens, call forth from my body the merit officers of the three and the five: the official envoys of the left and right, the runners mounted on dragons of the left and right, the incense-bearing golden lads, the message-bearing jade maidens, and those directly commissioned by the Five Thearchs, thirty-two persons of each class. Issuing forth, they are to inform the Perfected officers of this area that I am now burning incense to communicate with the spirits. I vow that the correct and perfected breaths of the ten directions might enter into my body to bear all of my vows swiftly and directly to those above.

Above you should call from the myriad armed and mounted warriors of the Celestial Transcendents, the Earth-bound Transcendents, the Perfected Ones, the Flying Transcendents, the sun and moon, the planets and constellations, the Nine Palaces, the Five Thearchs, the Five Marchmounts, the Three Rivers, and the four seas, thirty-two riders of each class. Also call on the attendants of the thirty-two heavens who oversee purification rituals, the incense-bearing golden lads, the flower-strewing jade maidens, and those directly commissioned by the Five Thearchs, thirty-two persons from each class. Together with the envoys mounted on flying dragons who announce affairs, these deities should all descend en masse to oversee the purification ritual and the ritual hall. In this manner, your incense fumes and your vows will both penetrate immediately to those above. Once your practice of the Dao is complete, these spirits and powers will all return forthwith to the palaces of the heavens to report.

During the day you should burn incense and at night light the lamps, so that the fires are never extinguished.

Once the scriptures are exposed in the center of the courtyard below the nine lamps and you have circled the lamps to present incense and to deliver the above vows, you should then make nine bows to the east and say:

Now I [*fill in your name*] take refuge in the Heavenly Worthy of the Numinous Treasure, overseer of the illimitable realms of the east, in all of the great sages who have already achieved the Dao, in all of the supreme Perfected lords, in the venerable ones, in the celestial lords of the nine pneumas, and in all of the spiritual officers of the east. As a result of this bond of trust, I now perform this purification ritual, burning incense and lighting lamps that the merit of this rite will illuminate all of the heavens and universally provide salvation for the emperor and princes, rulers of our kingdom, their officials, envoys, and subjects, all Masters of the Law who have received the Dao, my father and mother and venerable ancestors, my fellow students of the Way, the members of my household, Daoists studying in reclusion in the mountains and forests, and all worthies, even unto all forms of life that creep or fly, that wriggle or crawl, and which are endowed with breath. May they all alike obtain release from the ten sorts of suffering and eight sorts of difficulty.[6] May they reside in inaction and all come to experience self-realization.

Let the brilliance also shine on the millions of ancestors of the [*insert your surname*] family whose departed souls now serve as captive laborers in the earth-prisons that they all might find release and be implanted with the roots of faith. May they depart forever from the five roads leading to suffering[7] and may their karma from previous lives be erased. In death may they enjoy extended bliss and in life blessings. May all realms below the heavens enjoy great peace! May the Way and its power flourish!

Now therefore, I burn incense, taking refuge of my own accord in the virtue of the master, the Heavenly Worthy, in the great sages, and in the highest Perfected. Once I have achieved the Way, I will rise into the formless to join in perfection with the Dao.

Having completed this vow, remove your headcloth and kowtow, knocking your forehead on the ground eighty-one times.

Next face south and bow three times, saying:

Now I [*fill in name*] take refuge in the Heavenly Worthy of the Numinous Treasure, overseer of the illimitable realms of the south, in all of the great sages who have already achieved the Dao, in all of the supreme Perfected lords, in the venerable ones, in the celestial lords of the three pneumas, and in all of the spiritual officers of the south. . . .

The rest of the vow is the same as that above. When you are finished, remove your headcloth and kowtow, knocking your forehead to the ground twenty-seven times.

Next face west and bow seven times, saying:

Now I [*fill in name*] take refuge in the Heavenly Worthy of the Numinous Treasure, overseer of the illimitable realms of the west, in all of the great sages who have already achieved the Dao, in all of the supreme Perfected lords, in the venerable ones, in the celestial lords of the seven pneumas, and in all of the spiritual officers of the west. . . .

The rest of the vow is the same as that above. When you are finished, remove your headcloth and kowtow, knocking your forehead to the ground sixty-three times.

Next face north and bow five times, saying:

Now I [*fill in name*] take refuge in the Heavenly Worthy of the Numinous Treasure, overseer of the illimitable realms of the north, in all of the great sages who have already achieved the Dao, in all of the supreme Perfected lords, in the venerable ones, in the celestial lords of the five pneumas, and in all of the spiritual officers of the north. . . .

The rest of the vow is the same as that above. When you are finished, remove your headcloth and kowtow, knocking your forehead to the ground forty-five times.

Next face northeast and bow one time, saying:

Now I [*fill in name*] take refuge in the Heavenly Worthy of the Numinous Treasure, overseer of the illimitable realms of the northeast, in all of the great sages who have already achieved the Dao, in all of the supreme Perfected lords, in the venerable ones, in the celestial lords of the Brahmā breath, and in all of the spiritual officers of the northeast. . . .

The rest of the vow is the same as that above. When you are finished, remove your headcloth and kowtow, knocking your forehead to the ground nine times.

Follow the same procedure for the southeast, the southwest, and the northwest, in that order. For all of the four corners, you should bow once and knock your head nine times. The deities in whom you take refuge for each of the four corners will all be the same as in the case of the northeast.

Next face northeast and make thirty-two bows toward the upper direction, saying:

Now I [*fill in name*] take refuge in the Heavenly Worthy of the Numinous Treasure, overseer of the illimitable realms of the thirty-two heavens, in all of the great sages who have already achieved the Dao, in all of the supreme Perfected lords, in the venerable ones, in the celestial lords of the thirty-two heavens, and in all of the Perfected Beings, jade maidens, divine Transcen-

dents, and spiritual officers of the Mystic Metropolis of the Jade Capital and
the upper palaces of Purple Tenuity. . . .

The rest of the vow is the same as that above. When you are finished, remove
your headcloth and kowtow, knocking your forehead to the ground 288 times.
    Next face toward the southeast and make twelve bows toward the lower
direction, saying:

Now I [fill in name] take refuge in the Heavenly Worthy of the Numinous
Treasure, overseer of the illimitable realms in the lower direction, in all of
the great sages who have already achieved the Dao, in all of the supreme
Perfected lords, in the venerable ones, in the high luminaries of the nine
regions of the Earth, in the four overseers, the Five Thearchs, the twelve
Transcendent superintendents, in the Perfected persons, divine Transcendents, and jade maidens of the Five Marchmounts, the Four Watercourses,
and the nine palaces, and in all of the spiritual officers of the nine realms of
Earth in the illimitable worlds.
    Now, therefore, I burn incense and light lamps that, through the merit of
these actions, I might illumine the nine stygian regions of the courts of
eternal night in the subterranean realms of the illimitable worlds. I do this
universally for the Thearch and kings, rulers of the kingdom, their officials
and subjects, all Masters of Law who have received the Dao, my father and
mother and honored ancestors, my fellow students of the Dao, those within
my gates, those Daoists studying perfection in seclusion in the mountains
and forests, and all worthies, even unto my ancestors of the millionth generation. I do this for all departed souls in the halls of eternal night; to redeem
all they have done in former lives, breaking the laws of Heaven and the
prohibitions of Earth, so that they are bound about by their transgressions
and receive the recompense of their hidden deeds at death. They return again
and again to be smeared with soot since their fated destinies cannot be broken. They are dragged through the five sorts of suffering and have no way
to depart the courts of eternal night.
    Now, through burning incense, lighting lamps, and through the forgive-
ness that comes of confession, I hereby redeem and rescue them. May the
brilliant light universally shine throughout the halls of everlasting night and
the earth-prisons of the nine stygian regions to eradicate the roots of transgression of these benighted souls and to release them from the Three Bureaus
and the nine suboffices.[8] May they not be shackled or locked up. May they
receive salvation to ascend to the halls of the blessed. Departing from the
paths of evil, may they be reborn to live forever in blessed households, in
the families of princes or nobles. May there be rejoicing at their rebirth;
peace and prosperity throughout the heavens.
    Now, therefore, I burn incense, taking refuge of my own accord in the
virtue of the master, the Heavenly Worthy, in the great sages, and in the

highest Perfected. Once I have achieved the Way, I will rise into the formless to join in perfection with the Dao.

When you have finished, kowtow, knocking your forehead to the ground 120 times.

Notes

1. The "eight sorts of difficulty" (ba 'nan) are variously enumerated in Buddhist and Daoist texts. The Lingbao explanation is that the eight hardships include the five kinds of suffering in the earth-prisons and the three paths of unhappy rebirth. The standard Buddhist gloss is that the eight sorts of difficulty are the eight conditions in which it is difficult to see a buddha or to learn the Buddhist law: (1) in the earth-prisons, (2) as a hungry ghost, (3) as an animal, (4) in a frontier region, (5) as a long-lived god, (6) as one born deaf, blind, or dumb, (7) as a worldly philosopher who adheres to heretical views, (8) in the intermediate period between a buddha and his successor.

2. The "wind-borne swords" refers, in Buddhist texts, to the approach of death. Here the expression indicates that those who break the injunction will be sternly dealt with by the righteous demons who uphold Daoist law.

3. According to the Lingbao scriptures, the "five sufferings" are the representative punishments of the earth-prisons: (1) embracing the fiery bronze pillar, (2) impalement on the mountain of swords, (3) climbing the tree of blades, (4) being boiled in a pot, and (5) swallowing coals and ashes. Buddhist explanations of the term reflect the Buddhist notion that all forms of existence lead to suffering. A standard explanation gives the five as the sufferings of (1) the earth-prisons, (2) hungry ghosts, (3) animals, (4) the demons, and (5) humans.

4. The three paths of unfortunate rebirth are (1) the road that leads to the earth-prisons, (2) the road that leads one to become a hungry ghost, and (3) the road that leads to rebirth as an animal.

5. This incantation, referred to by name in the text, occurs elsewhere in the Lingbao scriptures. It involves calling forth from one's body the spirits who reside there to report the purposes of the rite both to local deities and to their counterparts in the heavens. The exact identification of each of these spirits would require much explanation. Here it is enough to note the way in which they match, in name and function, the spirits of the macrocosm summoned.

6. The "ten sorts of suffering" include the five sufferings of the dead listed above as well as five more kinds of torment afflicting the living. These are: (1) serving as a slave and thus suffering the bitterness of separation from the family; (2) to remain in ignorance, never meeting a teacher, and thus never coming to know the Dao; (3) to be orphaned and alone; (4) being imprisoned for some offense; (5) constant illness throughout one's life.

7. The term used here is literally "the five ways," which in Buddhist texts refers to the five places of rebirth. These five were existence (1) in the hells, (2) as a hungry ghost, (3) as an animal, (4) as a human being, (5) as a god (deva). Although later Daoists adopted this meaning of the term, the context in which it is used in the Lingbao scriptures as well as early glosses indicate that the fifth-century explanation was somewhat different. This is not so remarkable since, for Daoists, rebirth as a human being or as a spirit of any kind was regarded as a desirable goal. In the Lingbao texts, the "five ways" are simply the paths of behavior that lead to the five sorts of suffering in the hells: (1) jealousy, (2) murder, (3) stealing, (4) lust, and (5) untruthfulness.

8. The Three Bureaus are those of Heaven, Earth, and Water, thought to have ultimate charge of the records of life and death of all living beings. This concept originated with Celestial Master Daoism and is continued in the Lingbao texts, though the latter's celestial bureaucracy is much more complex.

— 21 —

Saving the Burning-Mouth Hungry Ghost

Charles Orzech

The Buddha's Discourse on the Scripture of the Spell for Saving the Burning-Mouth Hungry Ghost (Fo shuo qiuba yankou egui tuoluoni jing) is one of three key texts in the development of Buddhist performances held during the Ghost Festival of the seventh month of the Chinese lunar calendar. The Ghost Festival is the second most important festival of the year and the event in which Buddhism's presence in China is most visible. Chinese rites for the dead, whether performed at funerals, at seasonal festivals, or at cyclical village renewal ceremonies (*jiao*), have all been shaped by Buddhist practice. Indeed, the rituals performed on behalf of recently dead relatives throughout the year and for the uncared-for dead during the annual festival are widely viewed as the foundation of lay Buddhism and as a key factor in the survival of Chinese Buddhism into the twentieth century.

Prior to the eighth century, Buddhist rites for the salvation of ancestors were based on the *Yulanpen Scripture* and the *Scripture for Offering Bowls to Repay Kindness (Bao'en fengpen jing)*, which recount the efforts of the Buddha's disciple Mulian (Sanskrit: Maudgalyāyana) to save his mother from the sufferings of the underworld. According to these scriptures, Mulian's magical powers are ineffective in obtaining his mother's release. Mulian in despair goes to the Buddha for aid, and the Buddha explains that offerings made to the community on behalf of the dead are the only effective means for releasing beings from the lower realms.

Plays and operas about Mulian continue to be an important part of the celebrations right up to the present. But since the eighth century, new styles of ritual, developed in the esoteric (*mijiao*) tradition of Buddhism, replaced parts of the older rites. Thus, while village performances continued to elaborate on the story of Mulian, the rituals performed by Buddhist monks and nuns since the eighth century have all been based on *The Spell for Saving the Burning-Mouth Hungry Ghost,* in which another of the Buddha's disciples, Ānanda, figures prominently.

A convenient starting point for investigating the integration of esoteric rites into the Ghost Festival is the reign of Emperor Daizong of the Tang dynasty (r. 762–

779). It was under his patronage that the esoteric school of Buddhism and its major proponent, the monk Bukong jingang (Sanskrit: Amoghavajra 705–774), rose to dominance of the court. As with other missionaries to China, the esoteric masters recognized the central importance of the dead in China and promoted their own rites as the latest and most effective means for accomplishing what the already established Ghost Festival and the prescription of the *Yulanpen Scripture* set out to do. The esoteric rites introduced by Bukong aimed simultaneously at the goals of enlightenment and the goals of healing, protection, and rainmaking. The new techniques contained in *The Spell for Saving the Burning-Mouth Hungry Ghost,* in the ritual text *Distributions of Food and Water to Hungry Ghosts* (*Shizhu egui yinshi ji shuifa,* T 1315), and in a host of other manuals concerning the salvation of suffering beings were adopted by the imperial house and quickly became standard. It was this eighth-century rite that was introduced to Japan by Kūkai in the ninth century, forming the core of Obon celebrations there.

The effective decapitation of the esoteric school and the gradual disappearance of its lineages after the persecution of Buddhism during the Huichang era (845 C.E.) draws a curtain over the ghost ritual during the Five Dynasties (907–960) and the Song (960–1279). Rites for forlorn dead proliferate in the form of "plenary masses" (*shuilu dahui*) during this time, but these rites are not the same as those of the Tang era and may have been devised as substitutes in the absence of trained esoteric school practitioners.

During the Yuan dynasty (1280–1368), perhaps under the influence of newly imported Mongol Diamond Vehicle practices, the mantras and ritual techniques of *The Spell for Saving the Burning-Mouth Hungry Ghost* reappear, now incorporated in the anonymous ritual manual, *Rites from the Essentials of the Yoga Teachings for Distributing Food to Burning Mouths* (*Yujia jiyao yankou shishi yi,* T 1320). From this time forward, the *Rites from the Essentials of the Yoga Teachings* is the text on which all subsequent versions of Buddhist ritual manuals are based, while *The Spell for Saving the Burning-Mouth Hungry Ghost* provides the canonical charter of the rites, their key mantras, and the tale of their origin. Modern ritual manuals often incorporate both texts, the ritual following that set out in the Yuan dynasty with *The Spell for Saving the Burning-Mouth Hungry Ghost* serving as a preface or an appendix, or sometimes present only in the form of a drawing of the Buddha preaching to his disciple Ānanda.

In contrast to pre-Tang and modern folk performances, the hero of *The Spell for Saving the Burning-Mouth Hungry Ghost* is the Buddha's preeminent disciple and attendant Ānanda, not Mulian, and the issue is not one of Buddhist versus non-Buddhist rites for the dead but of the comparative efficacy of esoteric and nonesoteric Buddhist ritual. The *Yulanpen Scripture* promotes the collective power of the Buddhist community to make merit for the dead as clearly superior to Mulian's spells. Conversely, the new scripture portrays the collective power of the community as ineffective, while the proper spell (*tuo-luo-ni,* Sanskrit *dhāraṇī*) is efficacious. The contrast is all the more pointed, since Mulian is traditionally regarded as foremost of the Buddha's disciples in the practice of spells. Only the efficacy of the esoteric spell can multiply the offerings to feed the unimaginable numbers of suffering beings.

Finally, *The Spell for Saving the Burning-Mouth Hungry Ghost* is typical of the many esoteric texts that gained wide popularity in China from the early eighth century onward and which, through their spread and adaptation in Daoist and folk practices, transformed the landscape of Chinese religions.

The translation below is based on *Fo shuo qiuba yankou egui tuo-luo-ni jing,* Amoghavajra's translation (T 1313 21.464b–65b).

Further Reading

For a treatment of the Ghost Festival up to the point when esoteric material is infused into it, see Stephen F. Teiser, *The Ghost Festival in Medieval China* (Princeton: Princeton University Press, 1988); for the overall integration of the festival into Chinese culture, see Robert P. Weller, *Unities and Diversities in Chinese Religion* (Seattle: University of Washington Press, 1987). For Mulian operas, see David Johnson, ed., *The Mu-lien Operas* (Berkeley: Chinese Popular Culture Project, 1989). For an outline of the esoteric rituals of the Ghost Festival, see Charles D. Orzech, "Seeing Chen-yen Buddhism: Traditional Scholarship and the Vajrayana in China," *History of Religions* 29.2 (1989): 87–114. For a full treatment of this text as well as an earlier translation, see Charles D. Orzech, "Esoteric Buddhism and the *Shishi* in China," SBS Monograph Series no. 2 (University of Copenhagen, November 1993). For comparison with Daoist esoteric rites, see Judith Boltz, "Opening the Gates of Purgatory: A Twelfth-Century Taoist Meditation Technique for the Salvation of Lost Souls, *Tantric and Taoist Studies,* Mélanges Chinois et Bouddhique 21 (1983): 487–511.

The Buddha's Discourse on the Scripture of the Spell for Saving the Burning-Mouth Hungry Ghost

At that time the World-Honored One was residing at Kapilavastu at the Banyan Monastery, with all the monks and bodhisattvas—an innumerable assembly. They surrounded him and he expounded the teaching on their behalf. At that time Ānanda was alone in a quiet place contemplating the teaching he had received. Just after the third watch of the night he saw a hungry ghost (*egui,* Sanskrit *preta*) whose name was Burning Mouth (Yankou). His appearance was repulsive, his body was emaciated. His mouth was fiery and his throat was like a needle. His hair was disheveled, his nails and teeth were long and sharp. He was very frightening. He stopped before Ānanda and said, "After three days your allotted lifespan will be exhausted and then you will be born among the hungry ghosts." At that time, when Ānanda had heard these words he became terrified and asked the hungry ghost, "If after I die I am born among the hungry ghosts, is there any skillful means (*fangbian,* Sanskrit *upāya*) which may be practiced to escape such grief?"

Then the hungry ghost told Ānanda: "Tomorrow, if you are able to distribute bushels of provisions in measure like those used in the city of Magadha, to the one hundred thousand myriads of hungry ghosts—ghosts numberless as the sands of the Ganges—and to the one hundred thousand brahmins and seers (*ṛṣis*), and so forth, and if you distribute one bushel of food and drink [to each being], and on my behalf present these offerings to the three jewels, then you will attain increased longevity and cause me to depart from the suffering of the hungry ghosts and to attain birth in Heaven."

Ānanda looked at this Burning Mouth hungry ghost; his body and appearance was withered and extremely emaciated, his mouth was fiery and his throat was like a needle. His hair was disheveled and his nails and teeth were long and sharp. Moreover, having heard such disagreeable news, he was terrified and the hair on his body stood on end. He forthwith got up from his seat and hastened to the Buddha and fell prostrate, touching his head to the Buddha's feet. His body was trembling as he said to the Buddha: "Can you save me from suffering? I was alone in a quiet place meditating on the teaching I had received when I saw Burning Mouth, a hungry ghost, who told me that 'after three days it is certain that your lifespan will be used up and you will be born among the hungry ghosts.' I then asked how I could escape such suffering, and the hungry ghost replied: 'If now you are able to distribute every sort of food and drink to one hundred thousand myriads of hungry ghosts—ghosts numberless as the sands of the Ganges—and to the one hundred thousand brahmins and seers, and so forth, you will get increased longevity.' World-Honored One, how will I be able to help so many hungry ghosts, seers, and others to food?"

Then the World-Honored One told Ānanda: "Now do not fear, I have a skillful means which will enable you to distribute every sort of food and drink to so many hundreds of thousands of hungry ghosts—ghosts numberless as the sands of the Ganges—as well as to all of the brahmins and seers and so forth. Do not worry."

The Buddha then explained to Ānanda, "I have a spell called The Wonderous Victorious Power of Unlimited Awesome Self-Existent Light. If one chants this spell, then one will be able to completely satisfy with excellent food and drink hungry ghosts as numberless as sands of the Ganges, as well as brahmins, seers, and so forth. Through its use each and every one of this throng of beings will get forty-nine 'Magadha' bushels of rice. Ānanda, in a previous existence I was a brahmin in the place of Avalokiteśvara Bodhisattva and in the world of the Self-Existent and Awesome Thus-Come One, and therefore I received this spell. [It] enables one to distribute every sort of food and drink to numberless hungry ghosts, seers, and so forth. It causes all the hungry ghosts to be liberated from their suffering bodies and to attain birth in Heaven. Ānanda, if you now receive and keep it, your blessings and lifespan all will get increased."

At that time on Ānanda's behalf the World-Honored One pronounced the spell: NAMO SARVA TATHĀGATA AVALOKITA SAMVARA SAMVARA HŪM.

The Buddha told Ānanda, "If there are good sons and good daughters who want and seek long life, merit, and prosperity, and [want] quickly to be able to fulfill the perfection of giving, then every morning—or at any time when there are no hindrances—take a clean vessel and using pure water set out a little drink and rice or various cakes and so on. Using the right hand put these in the vessel and recite the previous spell seven times. Afterward, invoke the names of the four Thus-Come Ones.

"NAMO BHAGAVATE PRABHŪTA-RATNĀYA TATHĀGATĀYA. Because of the power (jia zhi, Sanskrit adhiṣṭhāna) [generated by] invoking the name of the Thus-Come One Baosheng (Jewel-Born), one is able to smash all demons and for many lives to come mitigate evil karma and forthwith you will get your merit fulfilled.

"NAMO BHAGAVATE SURŪPĀYA TATHĀGATĀYA. Because of the power [generated by] invoking the name of the Thus-Come One Miao-si-shen (Fine-Body), one is able to smash all ghosts and demons of vile appearance and forthwith get a satisfying and pleasing countenance.

"NAMO BHAGAVATE VIPULA-GĀTRĀYA TATHĀGATĀYA. Because of the power [generated by] invoking the name of the Thus-Come One Guang-pu-shen (Expansive-Body), one is able to make the throats of all the ghosts expand so that the food that is distributed can satisfy them.

"NAMO BHAGAVATE ABHAYAM-KARĀYA TATHĀGATĀYA. Because of the power (generated by) invoking the name of the Thus-Come One Li wuwei (Fearless), one is able to cause all ghosts and every terror to be entirely eradicated and [they will] depart from the realm of the ghosts."

The Buddha told Ānanda, "When good sons and others of your clan invoke the power of the names of the four Thus-Come Ones, they should snap their fingers seven times and take the rice vessel and sprinkle rice and water on purified ground. Having done this the distribution is complete and each of the hundreds of thousands of myriads of hungry ghosts in all the four quarters—ghosts as numberless as the sands of the Ganges—will have forty-nine 'Maga-dha' bushels of rice. Having received this rice they will be completely satisfied, and all these ghosts and others will completely slough their ghost bodies and be born in Heaven. Ānanda, if monks and nuns and male and female devotees regularly use this spell with the names of the four Thus-Come Ones to em-power food and distribute it to ghosts, they will moreover get complete satis-faction and uncountable merit. It would be no different from getting the merit from offerings made to one hundred thousand myriads of Thus-Come Ones. Their lifespan will be prolonged and enhanced and the good roots will be completed. All nonhumans, demons (yakṣas), and specters (rakṣas) and all of the evil ghosts and spirits will not dare to harm them, and they will be able to attain limitless merit and long life.

"If you wish to distribute food to all of the brahmins and seers and so forth, take pure water and food and fill a vessel. Then, using the previously mentioned spell, empower [it] twice seven times and cast [the offerings] into pure flowing water, and so it is done. It may [now] be regarded as the beautiful food and drink of gods and seers and offered to the one hundred thousand myriad of brahmins and seers. Thus, all will obtain this empowered food. Through use of the spell of Majestic Virtue, each and every one will accomplish their fundamental vows and all good merit, and at the same time each and every one will issue a vow, wishing to distribute food to people so that their lifespans will be lengthened and their appearance and strength will be peaceful and joyous.

"Moreover, the spell will cause the minds of those who witness the rite to be upright, understanding, and pure. They will each completely attain the majesty of the god Brahmā and perform the acts of the god Brahmā. Moreover, the merit obtained is like the merit gotten by making offerings to one hundred thousand myriad of Thus-Come Ones; thus all sorts of injustices and enemies will be unable to afflict or harm you.

"If monks, nuns, and male and female devotees wish to make offerings to the [three] jewels—the Buddha, the teaching, and the community—they should take incense, flowers, and pure drink and food and use the power of the previously mentioned spell twenty-one times as an offering to the three jewels. These good sons and daughters then may use the heavenly delicacies so obtained as offerings to the buddhas, the teaching, and the community of the worlds of the ten directions. Furthermore, if you praise their merit, you will consequently have joy and merit. If you persevere in intently praising all the buddhas, then all of the gods and good spirits will come to protect you, and you will have fulfilled the perfection of giving.

"Ānanda, if you do as I have said and cultivate, practice, and promote this technique, you will cause all living beings everywhere to see, hear, and obtain innumerable blessings. This scripture is called the *Scripture of the Spell for Saving the Burning-Mouth Hungry Ghost and Suffering Beings*. You should respectfully hold fast to its words."

All the great assembly, Ānanda and the others, heard what the Buddha said and with wholehearted faith they reverently received it and joyfully put it into practice.

22

The Law of the Spirits

Valerie Hansen

In traditional China, as in most cultures, there was some uncertainty about what happened after death. Some Buddhist sects promised rebirth in a paradise, and Daoism, immortality to a chosen few. Still, the majority of the dead, it was thought, went to an underworld. There they retained the power to influence events on earth. If they wanted to hurt the living, they could play tricks, cause illness, provoke misfortune, or even bring death. Some of the deceased performed miracles and came to be worshiped as gods. The Chinese feared the dead, but they believed that they adhered to their own laws. The three readings below from the eleventh and twelfth centuries show how the living used the law of the spirits to protect themselves from the dangers that the dead posed.

The first document is a model tomb contract from *The New Book of Earth Patterns* (*Dili xinshu*), a government manual for siting graves initially published in 1071. Starting in the first century C.E., if not earlier, and continuing through to the twentieth century, some Chinese buried tomb contracts with the dead. Mimicking this-worldly contracts for the purchase of land, these contracts recorded the purchase of a grave plot from the earth gods. Tomb contracts were intended to ward off the dangers that resulted from penetrating deep into the earth to dig a grave. The practice seems to have peaked in the Song dynasty (960–1279), when the government paid for such contracts to be drawn up on behalf of dead officials. Just after the Song had fallen, Zhou Mi (1232–1298) said: "Today when people make tombs they always use a certificate to buy land, made out of catalpa wood, on which they write in red, saying: 'Using 99,999 strings of cash, we buy a certain plot, and so forth' " (Zhou Mi, *Guixin zashi* [Xuejin taoyuan edition], bieji xia 7a–b). Nine was an auspicious number, hence the figure 99,999. The money in these contracts was not real money, but spirit money (facsimiles of real money) that could be burnt. Not all contracts were written on catalpa wood. Hundreds of lead and stone tomb contracts have been excavated, and presumably more were written on cheaper materials, like paper or wood, that have since decayed.

The New Book of Earth Patterns was written at imperial order by a team of scholars, headed by Wang Zhu, who examined preexisting ritual manuals and then compiled this book. This manual was intended for official use, but commoners also consulted it, Wang Zhu tells us. In the section about tomb contracts, this book cites *The Spirit Code* (*Guilü*) to say that burial without using a tomb contract is tantamount to wrongful burial and very unlucky. The idea of a law code for spirits raises interesting issues: Why should spirits have a law code? Is it written down? What is its relation to human law? These questions are not easily answered, but the widespread use of tomb contracts reveals that many people believed (or hoped) that the spirits of the dead could be bound by contracts. The similarity of the contracts to this-worldly contracts also suggests that people thought the law of the spirits resembled earthly law.

Because *The New Book of Earth Patterns* spells out the many steps of an official funeral ritual, it describes the ritual context in which tomb contracts were used. The manual specifies that any official with the posthumous rank of lord or marquis and below (or any commoners paying for their own funerals) should have two iron contracts: one was to be placed in the temporary aboveground funeral structure and the other, buried in front of the coffin. Then a prayer was said. Once prayer was completed, the two copies of the contract were held together and the characters for agreement (*hetong*) were written on the seam where the two join. Borrowed from real life, this practice ensured that either the buyer or seller could check the authenticity of a contract by matching it with their copy to see if the characters met exactly. If they did, then the contract was authentic and the signatories were bound to honor it. If they did not, it was a forgery. At the end of the funeral, the participants took the iron contract in the temporary funeral structure and buried it in the ground. That was the gods' copy. The one at the foot of the coffin was for the master of the tomb, the dead official. He needed to have his copy with him in case he had a dispute in the underworld with the spirits of the dead about his ownership of his funeral plot.

The text of the model contract follows contemporary land contracts very closely. It gives the date of the transaction, here the date of the funeral, and the name of the buyer, the dead person, without naming the seller, the lord of the earth. As was true of land contracts, the dimensions of the plot are given in two ways: on a grid with the north-south and east-west axes, and by naming the neighbors, who were the animals who watched over the four directions. The price was the usual 99,999 strings of cash as well as five-colored paper offerings. The contract then specifies the consequences if the contract is violated: any spirits who return from the dead (read: to bother the deceased or his living kin) will be tied up and handed over to earl of the rivers. Like a land contract, the contract contains a clause saying it will take effect once the money and land have been exchanged, which in this case must mean when the paper money is burned at the funeral and the body interred. The contract ends with the names of the witnesses, who can serve as intermediaries should any disputes occur, and the names of the guarantors, who will make good the buyer's price should he or she fail to come up with the money. The mystical identities of the neighbors, witnesses, and guarantor mark this as a tomb contract. After the end of the contract comes an amendment specifically prohibiting the former occupants of the grave plot from approaching the dead. Only if they stay 10,000 *li* (a great distance) away can the deceased and his or her kin enjoy peace and good fortune. The contract ends by invoking the statutes and edicts of Nüqing, the emissary of the Five Emperors of the directions (north, south, east, west, and middle). These statutes and edicts are part of the spirit law code.

Of fifteen excavated contracts I have found that follow the model given in *The New Book of Earth Patterns,* eleven date to the Song. They show a surprising geographic range, which testifies to the wide circulation the manual enjoyed: to the west, from Xinjiang and Sichuan; to the north, from Shanxi and Shaanxi; in Central China, from Hebei, Henan, Hubei, and Anhui; and to the southeast, from Jiangsu, Zhejiang, Jiangxi, and Fujian. Most of these tombs contain lavish grave goods, suggesting the people who used this text were well-off.

The New Book of Earth Patterns does not explicitly mention the dangers the spirits of the dead pose to the newly dead or their living kin, but another text found in a tomb in Southeast China, in Jiangxi, does. The text is written on the eight-sided body of a cypress figure, which had a carved human head with ears, eyes, mouth, and nose. Dated 1090, the figure was found in the tomb of the eighth daughter of the Yi family, a woman from an important local family (according to her biography, which is only partially quoted in the excavation report). She was interred in a wood coffin enclosed in a stone coffin. With her were buried two pottery vases, a pottery figure, her biography carved on a stone plaque, porcelain plates, wooden combs, iron scissors, an iron knife, an iron stick, a copper mirror, a large ax, and some items of relatively high quality: a silver comb, two silver bracelets, and a pair of gold earrings. Clearly, this was an expensive burial.

This text presumes a different relationship with the spirits of the dead from that presumed in *The New Book of Earth Patterns*. Here there is no contract with the lord of the earth for the purchase of the grave. Instead a cedar figure is deputed by those who preside over the world of the dead to prevent any lawsuits against the dead woman's family. The text repeats the same phrases over and over in its list of who cannot be summoned or sued by those in the middle of the earth, that is, the spirits of the dead. It does not say what such a summons would result in, but presumably the people mentioned in the text—the dead woman's children, husband, siblings, family, and in-laws—would suffer some kind of misfortune or even death. Those in the middle of the earth also have the power to bring epidemics. And they can summon fields, silkworms, farm animals, and trees, and so cause havoc on people's farms. Because this text is designed to protect the dead and their descendants, its repetitious phrasing takes on the quality of an incantation. The cypress figure is the subterranean equivalent of a henchman whose job it is to prevent anyone from serving his mistress with a court summons.

The final text shows what happens when the underworld court issues a summons. It is an anecdote from a collection called *The Record of the Listener* (*Yijianzhi*). From 1157 to 1202 an official named Hong Mai transcribed thousands of strange and unusual tales. Many of these tales, like the one translated here, are about people who visit the netherworld and come back. The Chinese word for death, *si*, means both to faint and to lose consciousness; many people had unusual visions when they fainted, which they recounted on awakening. The events and miracles Hong Mai describes may defy belief, but these were the kind of stories circulating in twelfth-century China, and Hong Mai often, as here, gives the name of the person who told him the anecdote. This source, then, can provide insight into the beliefs of common people in the Song dynasty, people who could not afford elaborate burials like those specified in *The New Book of Earth Patterns* or like that of eighth woman in the Yi family.

The anecdote begins with the facts of the case: how the debtor Mr. Lin bribed the clerks in the local court to frame the lender, Registrar Xia. The one person willing to speak out on Registrar Xia's behalf is Liu Yuan Balang. In his eloquent refusal to be bought off by Mr. Lin's underlings, he raises the possibility of a court in the underworld where wrongs can be righted. Registrar Xia then dies, after instructing his sons to bury all the relevant documents concerning Mr. Lin's unpaid debt, because he plans to sue in the underworld court. A month later Mr. Lin's eight underlings die. And Liu Yuan Balang has a premonition that he is going to be summoned to testify. Because he is convinced of his innocence, he does not fear that he personally has to stand trial, so he assures his wife that he will return after two or three days. And he loses consciousness.

The narrative resumes when he wakes up. He has indeed been summoned to the netherworld court to serve as a witness. When Liu Yuan Balang arrives, he sees that Registrar Xia has succeeded in his suit against Mr. Lin's eight underlings, whose necks are encased in a wooden frame called a cangue. Liu's account reveals much about the workings of the netherworld court, which are similar but not identical to those of a human court; in this vision, the presiding official is the king of the netherworld, not an underworld district magistrate. As on earth, he is served by clerks, who keep records and guide the prisoners from place to place. On hearing Liu's account, he awards him an extra ten years of life.

The king sits in judgment on the dead, who await their appearances before him in a kind of purgatory that Liu visits on his way out. There Liu sees people who have committed various offenses. They tell him they "borrowed" money, rent, and possessions, but in fact they stole them with no intent to return the goods. Now that they are awaiting trial, they claim to have borrowed the items. Some ask for money. Others ask their family members for merits; this reflects the Buddhist belief that merits accrued by one person for doing good deeds can be transferred to another. The king urges Liu to tell the living about his court, and then the runner who has accompanied Liu asks for a bribe. The always righteous Liu refuses, and he wakes up in this world when the clerk in the netherworld pushes him to the ground. The proof that he did indeed journey to the netherworld is twofold: his false topknot lies dislodged on his pillow, and he lives for an extra decade past eighty. The story concludes with Hong Mai's explanation of how he heard it.

The central theme in this story is justice. Registrar Xia is unable to obtain justice in human courts, but, as Liu Yuan Balang suspects, the underworld does have a court where wrongs can be righted. Many accounts of visits to the netherworld survive, and many tell of bureaucratic incompetence, of clerks who summon someone with an identical or a similar name by mistake. These people are then allowed to return to life. Strikingly, no one is ever punished in the subterranean court for a crime he or she did not commit. What about the real villain, Mr. Lin? The account does not reveal his fate, and the reader knows only that Registrar Xia is able to sue the eight underlings. Mr. Lin may be punished after he dies when he is tried before the king. Or perhaps he has already been punished, but Liu simply does not see him because he was not party to the bribery attempt.

The story about Registrar Xia and Mr. Lin illustrates exactly what the people who used tomb contracts and the cedar figure feared. Registrar Xia may be dead, but he is still able to bring charges against the living in the underworld court. He causes not only the deaths of the eight underlings but also their continued suffering in the afterlife. Other spirits had the same power to sue in underworld courts. Digging a grave is dangerous: one could unwittingly antagonize the previous owners, who could claim title to the plot. That was why people used tomb contracts. That was not the only danger. Once someone went before the underworld court, a host of charges could be brought against the deceased and their descendants based on their previous conduct. It was in order to block those charges that the eighth woman of the Yi family buried the cypress figure in her tomb.

The legalistic vision of the afterlife so evident in these three readings is striking and suggests that they are products of people thoroughly familiar with the earthly legal system. The model tomb contract in *The New Book of Earth Patterns* is like a contract to purchase land. The cedar person is like a henchman hired to prevent the issuing of summonses. And Registrar Xia encounters a court in the netherworld very much like the one in the human world—except that justice is done there.

The model tomb contract is from Wang Zhu, *Dili xinshu* (Beijing library Jin edition), 14:13a. The text written on a cedar figure is from Peng Shifan and Tang Changpu, "Jiangxi faxian jizuo BeiSong jinian mu," *Wenwu* 5 (1980): 29 (p. 35 photo). The tale from *The Record of the Listener* is from Hong Mai, *Yijian zhi* (Beijing: Zhonghua shuju, 1981), *zhiwu* 5:1086.

Further Reading

Valerie Hansen, *Changing Gods in Medieval China* (Princeton: Princeton University Press, 1990); Valerie Hansen, *Negotiating Daily Life in Traditional China: How Or-*

dinary People Used Contracts, 600–1400 (New Haven: Yale University Press, 1995), where an earlier version of the translation below appears. I would like to thank Victor Mair, Liu Xinru, and Bao Weimin for their help with these translations, and the late Anna Seidel for her many insights into the netherworld system of justice.

A MODEL TOMB CONTRACT FROM THE
NEW BOOK OF EARTH PATTERNS

Blank year, month, and day. An official of blank title, named blank, died on blank year, month, and day. We have prognosticated and found this auspicious site, which is suitable for the grave, in this plain, in this district, in this county, and in this prefecture. We use 99,999 strings of cash as well as five-colored offerings of good faith to buy this plot of land. To the east and west, it measures so many steps, to the south and north, it measures so many steps. To the east is the green dragon's land, to the west the white tiger's, to the south the vermillion sparrow's, and to the north the dark warrior's.

The four borders are controlled by the imperial guard. The deputy of the grave mound and the earl of the tomb sealed it off by pacing the borders and the thoroughfares; the generals made orderly the paths through the fields so that for one thousand autumns and ten thousand years no spirit will return from the dead. If any dare to contravene, then the generals and neighborhood heads are ordered to tie them up and hand them to the earl of the rivers.

We have prepared meat, wine, preserved fruits, and a hundred types of sacrificial food. All these things constitute a contract of our sincerity.

When the money and land have been exchanged, the order will be given to the workers and carpenters to construct the tomb. After the deceased is peacefully buried, this will forever guarantee eternal good fortune.

The witness represents the years and months. The guarantor is the direct emissary of this day.

Bad ethers and heterodox spirits are not allowed to trespass. Those formerly living in the residence of the deceased must forever stay 10,000 *li* away. If any violate this contract, the main clerks of the earth government will be personally responsible for punishing them. The master of the tomb, and all his own kin and in-laws, whether living or dead, will enjoy peace and good fortune. Hastily, hastily, in accordance with the statutes and edicts of the emissary of the Five Directional Emperors, Nüqing.

A TEXT WRITTEN ON A CYPRESS FIGURE

On the twenty-second day of the sixth month of the fifth year of the Yuanyou reign (1090), Teacher Qiao Dongbao of the western region association of the

Five-Willow District, Pengze County, Jiang Prefecture, died and the grave of
his late wife, the eighth woman of the Yi family, was relocated. The elders of
the Haoli death precinct by Mount Tai, the envoy of the Celestial Emperor,
and the emissary of the First Emperor's True Law, aware that the spirits disturbed by the relocation of the grave might call the living, issued an enlightened
decree that one cedar person should cut off all summons and suits from the
middle of the Earth.

If the eighth woman's sons and daughters are summoned, the cypress person should block the summons. If Teacher is summoned by name, the cypress person should block the summons. If her family is summoned, the
cypress person should block the summons. If the siblings are summoned, the
cypress person should block the summons. If the in-laws are summoned to
testify, the cypress person should block the summons. If pestilence and plague
are summoned, the cypress person should block the summons. If the fields or
silkworms or the six domestic animals—horses, cattle, sheep, chickens, dogs,
and pigs—are summoned, the cypress person should block the summons. If
the first and second trees are summoned, the cypress person should block the
summons. If the summoning does not end, the cypress person should block
the summons. Quickly, quickly in accordance with the statutes and edicts.

A TALE FROM *THE RECORD OF THE LISTENER*

Registrar Xia of Ningbo and the wealthy Mr. Lin together bought a concession
to sell wine in a government store. They sold the wine wholesale to other stores,
who paid their share depending on how much wine they sold. After many
years, Mr. Lin owed Register Xia two thousand strings of cash. Registrar Xia
realized he would not get the money back so he sued Mr. Lin in the prefectural
court. The clerks took a bribe and twisted his words to reverse the story so
that Registrar Xia became the debtor. Prior to this Mr. Lin ordered eight of his
underlings to change the accounts to show that he was in the right. Registrar
Xia refused to change his story and was put in jail and beaten. Accordingly he
fell ill.

In the prefecture lived a man named Liu Yuan Balang, who was generous
and did not trouble himself over details, and who was upset by Registrar Xia's
treatment. He proclaimed to the crowd, "My district has this type of wrongful
injustice. Registrar Xia is telling the truth about the money from the wine but
is miserable in jail. What is the point of prefectural and county officials? I wish
they would call me as a witness, as I myself could tell the truth, which would
definitely cause someone else to be beaten."

Lin's eight underlings secretly heard what he said and were afraid it would
leak out and harm their case, so they sent two eloquent men who extended
their arms to invite Liu to drink with them at a flagged pavilion, where they
talked about the case and said: "Why are you concerning yourself with other

people's affairs? Have some more wine." When the wine was done, they pulled out paper money with a face value of two hundred strings and gave it to Liu saying, "We know that your household is poor, so this is a little to help you."

Liu furiously replied, "The likes of you start with unrighteous intent and then bring an unrighteous case. Now you again use unrighteous wealth to try to corrupt me. I would prefer to die of hunger. I refuse even one cash of your money. This twisting of the straight and distortion of truth is definitely not going to be resolved in this world. If there is no court in the netherworld, then let the matter rest. If there is such a court, it must have a place where wrongs can be righted." Then he called the bar owner, "How much was today's bill?"

He said, "1,800 cash."

Liu said, "Three people drank together, so I owe six hundred." He suddenly took off his coat and pawned it to pay the bill.

After a while, Registrar Xia's illness worsened, and he was released from jail to die. As he was about to die, he warned his sons: "I die a wronged man. Place in my coffin all the previous leases for the wine concessions and contracts specifying each person's share so that I can vigorously sue in the underworld."

After just one month Mr. Lin's eight underlings abruptly died one by one.

After another month, Liu was at home when he suddenly felt shaky, and everything went dark. He said to his wife, "What I see is not good. It must be that Registrar Xia's case is being heard, and I'm wanted as a witness, so I must die. But since I have led a peaceful life with no other bad deeds, I probably will return to life, so don't bury my corpse for a period of three days. After that you can decide what to do." Late that night he lost consciousness.

After two nights he sat up with a start and said, "Recently, two government clerks chased me. We went about thirty miles and reached the government office. We encountered an official wearing a green robe who came out from a room in the hall. When I looked at him, I realized it was Registrar Xia. He repeatedly apologized and said, 'I am sorry to trouble you to come. All the documents are in good order, we just want you to serve as a witness briefly. It shouldn't be too taxing.' Then I saw Lin's eight underlings, all wearing one cangue that was five meters long and had eight holes for their heads.

"Suddenly we heard that the king was in his palace, and the clerks led us to the court. The king said, 'The matter of Xia's family needn't be discussed. Only tell me everything that happened when you drank wine upstairs.'

"I testified, 'These two men sent an invitation. Then we drank five cups of wine and bought three types of soup. They wanted to give me paper money with a face value of two hundred strings of cash, but I didn't dare accept it.'

"The king looked left and right, sighed, and said, 'The world still has good people like this. They really are important. We should discuss how to reward him, so let's take a look at his allotted lifespan.'

"A clerk went out and after a moment came back and said, 'A total of seventy-nine years.'

"The king said, 'A poor man doesn't accept money, how can we not reward him? Add another decade to his lifespan.'

"He then ordered the clerk who had brought me to take me to see the jail in the earth. Then I saw many types of people and prisoners in fetters. They were all from the city or the counties of my prefecture. Some bore cangues and some were tied up; some were sentenced to be beaten. When they saw me coming, one by one they cried out and sobbed. They then told me their names and addresses and asked me to return to the world to tell their families. Some said they had borrowed somebody's money, some said they had borrowed somebody's rent, some said they had borrowed somebody's possessions, and some said they had stolen people's land and harvest. They all asked their families to return their goods so as to lessen the sentences they had to serve in the underworld. Others asked for money and others for merit to be transferred by their relatives. I couldn't bear to look at them and turned away, and I still heard ceaseless sighs.

"As I went again to the palace, the king said, 'Since you have completed your tour, when you return to life, please tell each detail to the living, and teach them about the underworld court.' I bowed and took my leave.

"As I went out the gate, the clerk seeing me off wanted money, and I steadfastly refused. He berated me, 'For two or three days I have served you. How is it that you don't even say thank you? Moreover, give me 10,000 strings.' I again refused him saying, 'I myself have nothing to eat, so where am I going to get extra money for you?' The clerk then grasped and knocked off my topknot. He pushed me on the ground, and then I regained consciousness."

He rubbed his head, which was already bald, and his topknot lay between the pillows. Sheriff Wang Yi from Jinan, Shandong, lived in Ningbo at the time and himself saw that it was as told here.

Around 1180, Liu had his eightieth birthday, and he fell ill. Sheriff Wang went to see him and was very concerned. Liu said, "Sheriff, you needn't worry. I haven't died." Afterward he turned out not to be ill. He was probably counting the additional years the king of the netherworld had given him.

When he reached ninety-one, he died. Sheriff Wang is now the administrator of public order in Raozhou, Jiangxi. This story was told by Administrator Wang.

— 23 —

Shrines to Local Former Worthies

Ellen Neskar

A common view of Confucianism regards it not as a religion, but as a rational, ethical teaching based on fundamental human relationships. Religious elements or institutions, if at all acknowledged, are most often associated with either the family or the state and are thought to serve the interests of the bureaucratic hierarchy. Thus, for example, the family altars for ancestral worship and the state-regulated temples to Confucius promoted a stable social order and supported the prevailing state ideology. However, in the Han dynasty (202 B.C.E.–220 C.E.), Confucian scholars and local administrators living in the provinces began to build sacrificial shrines honoring exemplary men of the past. During the Song dynasty (960–1279), such "local former worthies shrines" emerged as an important religious institution among elites. Belonging to neither the family nor the state, these shrines represent a new level of communal and individual religion in Confucianism.

The worthies were "former" because they were men, not gods, who lived in historical times. Although some had lived hundreds or thousands of years earlier, most belonged to the very recent past, and some were honored only months after their deaths. They were "local" both because their shrines were built by local elites and administrators for the benefit of other local elites and, more importantly, because in life they had had some connection to the places where their shrines were founded. The most common connections were birth and official service in the region, but a visit to, or retirement in, the region might also suffice. And they were "worthy" because their lives and deeds manifested certain ideal virtues: compassion, humaneness, loyalty, erudition, and wisdom.

Few rules governed worthies' shrines: the classical Confucian ritual texts did not sanction them, and the central government was little involved or concerned with their spread. Local elites and administrators made all decisions concerning the shrines. The documents that follow all date to the Song dynasty, when worthies' shrines were becoming important. Because there was little precedent or tradition, some Song men attempted to establish conventions for shrine-building, standards or criteria for enshrinement and guidelines for the functions of and activities held in the shrines. The authors of our documents were trying to control or shape a growing phenomenon in the absence of central government regulation or clear guidance from the past.

The first document is a commemorative essay written by the famous Neo-Confucian philosopher Zhu Xi (1130–1200) to mark the founding of a shrine in honor of a certain Gao Deng (fl. 1127). Similar essays commemorated all manner of other projects: the establishment or repair of government schools and private academies, Buddhist and Daoist temples, bridges and granaries, prisons and examination halls. Such essays praised the founders of the project for their service to the community, the community for producing such diligent servants, and the subject of the essay—be it a bridge or a temple—for its value to the community. Since it was customary to inscribe the essay on a large stone stele and place it at the site of the project, the praise was designed as much to inform and inspire future generations as it was to commemorate the past.

Inscriptions written for worthies' shrines dwell on the life of the former worthy and are clearly eulogistic and hagiographic in nature. Authors tend to combine formulaic praise with detailed accounts of the worthy's life and deeds. Whether or not the material included in these essays provides a historically accurate rendering of the worthies' accomplishments and contributions to society, it can be argued that it does reflect the ideal self-image of the elites who promoted the shrines.

Zhu Xi's essay for Gao Deng's shrine is particularly important, for in it Zhu discusses the kinds of men who might be honored in shrines. Former worthies were men of widely varied roles and occupations. From the Han through the early years of the Song, most of those honored in shrines had empirewide reputations as statesmen and officials, military leaders, martyrs and imperial loyalists, or poets and prose writers. In his essay Zhu Xi argues for honoring a different kind of man.

Zhu opens by quoting Mencius on the ancient sages Bo Yi and Hui of Liuxia. Although Zhu cites only snippets, his readers would have known the whole of Mencius's argument. In several different conversations, Mencius distinguishes between the qualified sageliness of Bo Yi and Hui of Liuxia and the perfect sageliness of Confucius (see *Mencius,* 2A:2.22–28, 2A:9.1–3, 5B:1.1–7, 6B:6.2, and 7B:15.). Bo Yi was the "pure sage," willing to serve only a good ruler in times of order, but Mencius questioned his inflexibility. And although Hui of Liuxia was the "accommodating sage," willing to serve any kind of ruler in both times of order and times of disorder, Mencius worried about his lack of discrimination. Mencius did not worry about Confucius, for he was the "complete concert of sagehood," the "timely sage," whose actions were always in accord with time and circumstances. Mencius may have wished to follow the example of Confucius in his own life, but nevertheless he offers the ways of these qualified sages for others to follow.

Zhu Xi uses Mencius to provide a classical Confucian provenance for enshrining men who were not famous and were less than perfect. His central message is that there were many paths to virtue. Worth was to be judged neither by a high position in the government nor by occupation, but by success in cultivating humaneness and improving society. From the mid-twelfth century on, the repertoire of worthies grew to include men who had served at best in low-level local posts or who had lived their entire lives in retirement and relative obscurity. On occasion even Buddhist monks and Daoist priests were honored as former worthies. Gao Deng is typical of the men, of small political accomplishment and even lesser fame but of great personal virtue, who came to be enshrined in this period.

Zhu Xi's praise in fact focuses precisely on Gao Deng's outspoken criticism of government policies and his subsequent exile from court: in effect, on his political failure. Gao's unsuccessful career must be understood within the context of the factional struggles that rocked the Song state. In 1126 the foreign Jurchens had conquered the northern part of China, forcing the Song court to flee south. Court officials and elites tended to divide into two factions. Those who wished to pursue a policy of accommodation to the Jurchens supported the prime minister, Qin Gui, the antagonist of Zhu's essay. Those who wished to attack the Jurchens and retake the north followed the general Li Gang, also mentioned in the essay. Many of those who, like Zhu Xi, were later to become famous for creating the new philosophy we now know as Neo-Confucianism were affiliated, directly or by descent, with the prowar faction. Qin Gui's faction won the struggle and initiated a comprehensive purge of prowar agitators from court.

Zhu Xi notes that Gao had participated in the 1127 antigovernment demonstrations held by students at the national academy. A meeting with Qin Gui led to Gao's first demotion to a low-level position in local government office. While serving there, Gao was hounded by a superior in the prefectural government who supported Qin Gui. When the superior himself suffered persecution, Gao Deng rose to the post of examination official. True to his convictions, Gao used the opportunity to pose an exam question that, although somewhat oblique, criticized Qin Gui and the government's policies. For this he was stripped of all official rank and exiled to Rongzhou Prefecture, deep in the undeveloped and unpopulated south. Until his death, Gao lived in Rongzhou as a private teacher.

Although the traditional goal for most Confucians was to serve as adviser or minister to a ruler, the topos of the persecuted, unappreciated, or disaffected Confucian had a long and venerable tradition. Local worthies' shrines institutionalized this image. Gao Deng is representative of those who ran afoul of the government but were enshrined as local worthies. Local shrines turned victims into heroes and alienated officials into brave and staunch supporters of Confucian virtues: to have been exiled by a corrupt government was for many a true sign of worth.

During the Song the typical worthy changed from being a man of power and renown in the central government to a man whose fame did not depend on political rank or might even rest on the state's rejection of him. Local worthies, then, were not necessarily representatives of the central government, nor did they promote the prevailing state ideology. If we can use the worthies as a measure of elite self-image, we must conclude that the Song elite had swung from defining themselves in terms of their success at court to seeing themselves as the neglected talents or persecuted victims of a corrupt, faction-ridden government.

The second document is a legal judgment issued by a local magistrate, Mr. Hu, concerning a shrine honoring the famous general Zhuge Liang of the third century. The text is found in the *Pure and Clear Collection of Judgments by Famous Judges* (*Minggong shupan qingming ji*), a collection of legal cases from the late thirteenth century. Magistrate Hu had at his disposal numerous sources dealing with earlier shrines, and he cites liberally from local histories and commemorative essays.

Unlike Zhu Xi's commemorative essay, Magistrate Hu's judgment is not a celebration of the virtue of a newly enshrined worthy. Rather, it addresses questions raised by a local sheriff concerning the propriety of an existing shrine. Unfortunately, the original complaint is not extant, and the exact circumstances surrounding the case remain unclear. As a result, some of the magistrate's comments on the sheriff's complaint are obscure. Yet the case is important because it raises general issues: What sort of connection must a worthy have to the place he is enshrined? Do sacrifices to former worthies comply with legal and ritual codes? How is a shrine appropriately furnished? What kind of rituals should be held in them? Who may participate in the rituals? While Magistrate Hu deals directly with these questions, he also discusses the more fundamental problem of distinguishing between licit and illicit sacrifices. And his final judgment offers a set of guidelines for establishing a proper or licit former worthy's shrine.

Magistrate Hu's definition of licit sacrifices comes from the canonical Confucian text, the *Record of Rites* (*Liji*). There it is stated that sacrifices might properly be offered by emperors and nobles to natural forces, such as the wind and rain, to geographical landmarks, such as mountains and rivers, and to various worthy men who had in some way ensured the security and peace of their country. All these were to be entered in the *Sacrificial Statutes* of the state. In late imperial times, *Sacrificial Statutes,* or lists of licit sacrifices and shrines, were compiled by both the central and local governments. Shrines not included in these lists could be considered illicit and might be subject to closure by government officials.

Local worthies' shrines were not included in the *Sacrificial Statutes* compiled during the Song dynasty. Still, central government officials took no action against them, and local elites considered them licit. Those who built shrines interpreted the line from *Record of Rites* that reads "the various nobles may sacrifice to those of their own region" to mean that local administrators and elites might offer sacrifices to various natural forces and worthy men that were in some way connected to the region in which they were enshrined.

A local connection became the only quasi-objective requirement for the enshrinement of worthies. At first even Zhu Xi, one of the most prolific shrine-builders of the twelfth century, refused to commemorate a shrine honoring the three founders of his Neo-Confucian movement. Explaining his reluctance, Zhu Xi wrote:

It is my view that the Way of the three masters is grand and marvelous. However, this county, Wuyuan, is neither their native home nor a place where they sojourned or served in office. Nor have they been given ranks in the *Sacrificial Statutes* of the prefecture. How might sacrificing to them comply with the rituals codes or be considered appropriate? (*Zhuzi daquan,* Sibu beiyao edition, 79:3a)

Magistrate Hu went to considerable lengths to verify Zhuge Liang's connection to Shaoling County, the location of the shrine at issue. According to the local histories, Shaoling had centuries ago been part of a larger territory that Zhuge had administered. Therefore, although Zhuge was not a native of the region, he had served there and might be offered sacrifices as a local worthy.

While the notion of a local connection might seem straightforward enough, it was open to various interpretations. Some even argued that especially worthy men might be honored in places to which they had no connection whatsoever. Magistrate Hu refers to one interpretation when he cites Su Shi's (1037–1101) analogy between spirits of the dead and water. Su had offered this analogy in an essay commemorating a shrine built in Chao Prefecture to honor the Tang literary figure Han Yu (768–824). Han Yu was not a native of Chao Prefecture, nor had he served in office there. He had, however, spent less than a year there in exile from the central government. The original Su Shi passage reads:

Some say: "His excellency [Han Yu] was a thousand miles from his native country, and he was here in Chao Prefecture less than a year. If he were to have consciousness after death, he would not care about Chao Prefecture." I, Su Shi, say that is not right. His excellency's spirit is in the world as water is in the ground. There is no place it does not go. . . . It is as though one were to dig a well and find water and then say, "Here is the only place that there is water." How could that be right? (*Su Shi wenji,* Zhongguo gudian wenxue jiben congshu edition [Beijing: Zhonghua shuju, 1990], 17:509)

Despite Su Shi's claim for the universal presence and mobility of spirits, few Song men were willing to enshrine worthies in regions where they were not connected. Rather, this argument led only to a looser interpretation of the local connection and was used to strengthen claims for enshrining worthies whose local connection was somewhat tenuous.

Magistrate Hu clearly accepted Zhuge Liang as a legitimate, locally connected worthy. But he argues that, however legitimate a worthy's connection may be, any shrine or sacrifice to him that smacks of popular cults was to be considered illicit. Physical condition, the quality of sacrifices, and the manner in which they are offered are as important as the local connection is in deciding the legitimacy of a shrine. Therefore, he still considered the existing shrine and the sacrifices offered Zhuge inappropriate. A visit to the shrine horrified Magistrate Hu: it was built by a busy road; the statue of Zhuge was vulgar and sat in the midst of statues to various strange ghosts and spirits; and all manner of people freely visited the shrine to offer strange sacrifices and prayers.

The magistrate is typical of Song gentlemen who were concerned about the ease with which sacrifices to Confucian worthies, popular deities, and illicit spirits could be confused. He suggests that local devotees were treating Zhuge Liang as an efficacious popular god by offering him lively and sometimes improper prayers. Claiming that the spirit of Zhuge Liang could not be pleased by all this, the magistrate decided that something had to be done. And nothing less than a new shrine in a new location would do. The entire list of orders in his final judgment ensures that Zhuge Liang would be offered sacrifices in a location and manner befitting his stature as a former worthy.

Apparently, some prefects and local elites felt they had to be constantly vigilant to maintain physical and functional boundaries between shrines to worthies and shrines to popular deities. One problem, of course, was location. In principle, local worthies' shrines could be, and were, built almost anywhere—in government-sponsored schools and private Confucian academies, in government offices and examination halls, in pavilions on mountaintops, at town gates and crossroads, in Buddhist monasteries, in the old residences or study halls of the worthies. Often the site was chosen to commemorate a specific local connection. A man who had held an administrative post might be enshrined in his government office; another might be enshrined in the rooms where he had once studied. But elites found it difficult to control the shrines placed at city gates or along busy roads.

Like Magistrate Hu, Song men increasingly thought to solve this problem by moving shrines to the precincts of the local government schools. In late imperial China, local schools were the most important and visible institution associated with Confucianism. Since the Tang dynasty (618–907), the central court had mandated and funded the establishment of temples to Confucius in each prefectural and county school. Schools were already by design the site of state-sanctioned and legitimate sacrifices to Confucian sages and worthies. Shrines established in schools came under the jurisdiction of professors, students, and local administrators. In many cases they were perceived as extensions of the official temple to Confucius, and their worthies would share in the state-mandated sacrifices to Confucius held twice a year. Shrines built at miscellaneous sites could not share in this official and Confucian protection.

Clearly, the magistrate's judgment was an attempt to replace the existing shrine to Zhuge Liang with an appropriate and dignified local worthies' shrine. By associating Zhuge's shrine with the school and with other former worthies, he ensured that Zhuge would be revered as a former Confucian worthy. And by ordering that only the educated elite officiate at sacrifices and barring practitioners of popular religion from entering the shrine, he has reclaimed the worship of Zhuge Liang as the sole prerogative of the elite.

It seems that wherever shrines to worthies were built, dignity, restraint, and order were the guidelines. Although we have no sketches or floor plans of worthies' shrines, commemorative essays and prayers suggest that the ideal shrine was bright and spacious. Near the entrance were large stone steles inscribed with commemorative essays. Inside, the atmosphere was sober, and decorative furnishings sparse. Portraits of the worthies were drawn on silk and usually accompanied by eulogistic colophons. Worthies were represented by either spirit tablets or images molded out of clay or carved from wood.

The use of images was controversial. Some felt they were more the custom of Buddhists and Daoists than of Confucians. Others, like Magistrate Hu, complained that images would be vulgar and could be confused with those of popular deities. Still others argued that images depicted the worthies in undignified postures: they were made to sit on the bare ground, they sat cross-legged (like the Buddha), and they showed the soles of their feet beneath their skirts. During ceremonies, sacrifices of cooked foods, fruits, and wines were offered to the images or spirit tablets. Both Zhu Xi and Su Shi argued that the use of an image would give the impression that the worthies had to "creep and crawl [along the ground] to eat [the offerings]" (*Zhuzi daquan,* Sibu beiyao edition, 46:7b, 68:1b–2a). To prevent such indignities, they suggested that during each sacrificial ceremony the officiants temporarily place on the altar a plain wooden spirit tablet, inscribed with the worthies' names.

Portraits, on the other hand, were treated as a matter of course. They were to capture as true a likeness as possible and were to be drawn and mounted with dignity. A prayer offered to the famous Song literatus, Ouyang Xiu, says that "a portrait of his excellency [Ouyang] was drawn and hung in the school to celebrate his loyalty, to praise his heroism, to inspire later generations, and to move those who come here to pay obeisance to and revere him. His portrait is awesome; it is as though he were alive" (Li Geng, in *Ouyang Xiu xuan shiji,* Wenyuange siku quanshu edition, 7:13b). Whereas the spirit tablet or the image was the concrete focus of sacrificial offerings, portraits were to be contemplated as a means to understanding the essence of the worthy. For inspiration and to encourage thoughts of reverence, students were urged to "gaze upon the [worthies'] countenances" or "regard their comportment."

The religious ceremonies and sacrificial rites performed in the shrines were not codified or standardized. Varying from shrine to shrine, the offerings could include live animals, cooked meats, seasonal fruits, silk and cotton, tea, wine, incense, and the performance of music, dance, and prostrations. Generally, the sacrifices were offered by the community of elites as an act of thanksgiving and recompense: worthies were not asked to bestow favors or to act as intercessors for the benefit of individual petitioners. The first prayer in the third selection is typical of the prayers and sacrificial reports that were burnt as offerings on these public occasions. Often they expressed the hope that the spirits of the worthies would approach or descend, listen to the words of the prayer, and be satisfied with the offerings. Like this prayer, which was offered to ten worthies during a ceremony celebrating the renovation of their shrine, most were solemn. They praised the men for their exercise of virtue, which was a model for others, and thanked them for their benevolence on behalf of the local people.

The second prayer, which Zhu Xi addressed to Confucius, is more typical of those offered to the worthies by individuals during private visits to shrines. Although Zhu tells Confucius about a problem he was having with one of his students, he does not ask Confucius to solve the problem or to effect a change in the student. Rather, Zhu requests guidance in perfecting his own learning and furthering his own moral cultivation. One of the primary functions of the worthies was to act as models of moral excellence that would inspire elites to behave virtuously. Worthies were enshrined so that their virtuous example might continue to teach and inspire others in death as it had in life. When a shrine was located in a local school or private academy, obeisance or sacrifices were offered daily, bimonthly, or monthly by students and teachers. In these cases ritual obeisance to the worthies was incorporated into the regular curriculum of study and was an integral part of students' education in ritual forms of behavior. Students were exhorted to study the worthies' deeds and writings, gaze upon their portraits, and use the worthies as models. The shrines were meant to encourage local elites to emulate the virtue of the worthies and to aspire to attain the stature of a worthy in their own lives.

The translations are from Hong Hua, *Panzhou wenji* (*The Collected Works of Panzhou*), Wenyuange siku quanshu edition, 71:10b–11a; *Minggong shupan qingming ji* (*Pure and Clear Collection of Judgments by Famous Judges*) (Beijing: Zhonghua shuju, 1987), pp. 542–43; and Zhu Xi, *Zhuzi daquan* (*The Complete Works of Master Zhu*), Sibu beiyao edition, 79:22a–23b; 86:1b–2a.

Further Reading

John Shryock, *The Origin and Development of the State Cult to Confucius* (New York: Paragon, 1966); Rodney Taylor, *The Way of Heaven: An Introduction to the Confucian Religious Life* (Leiden: E. J. Brill, 1986); Thomas Wilson, *Genealogy of the Way: The Construction and Uses of Confucian Tradition in Late Imperial China* (Stanford: Stanford University Press, 1995).

Essay Commemorating the Sacrificial Hall to the Master Gao Dongxi at the Prefectural School in Zhangzhou

Mencius said: A sage is the teacher of a hundred generations: this is true of Bo Yi and Hui of Liuxia. Therefore, when people hear of the character of Bo Yi, the corrupt become pure and the weak acquire determination. When they hear of the character of Hui of Liuxia, the mean become generous and the corrupt become honest. They distinguished themselves a hundred generations ago, and after a hundred generations, all those who hear of them are inspired.

Mencius's discussions of the two masters were detailed. He considered Bo Yi the "pure sage" and [Hui of Liuxia] the "accommodating sage." But he was still distressed by Bo Yi's narrow-mindedness and Hui's "insufficient respect." More-over, since their ways were different from that of Confucius, Mencius did not wish to learn from them. Then one day he understood them and wrote these discussions. Afterward, people followed them as teachers of a hundred gener-ations. Yet Confucius, in contrast, did not reach such [status]. Why?

Confucius's way was great and his virtue harmonious. Yet he left no concrete legacy. Therefore those who study to be like him try to "penetrate his doctrines" and "look up to him for their whole lives." Still it is not enough. The two masters were pure in their intentions; their conduct was eminent; and their legacy is clear. Therefore, those who admire them are suddenly moved to the point of excess. Thus, the merit of the two masters is truly not insignificant. Mencius's intentions can be understood.

In Linzhang there was a Master Dongxi, his excellency Gao. His given name was Deng and his courtesy name was Yanxian. During the Qinggang reign-period (1126) he studied at the Imperial University, where he joined his ex-cellency Chen Shaoyang in the student demonstrations [calling for war against the invading Jurchens who had captured the north]. They sent up a memorial condemning the "six bandits" (six ministers who led the propeace government faction) and asking to retain Li Gang [leader of the prowar faction]. Those in authority did not want to mobilize the troops [against the Jurchens].

At the beginning of the Shaoxing reign-period (1131–1163), Gao was sum-moned to an audience in the Administrative Chambers. His discussion with the [propeace] prime minister, Qin Gui, was not suitable. So he was removed from his office and demoted to the post of vice prefect of Gu County in Qing-jiang Prefecture, where he had an extraordinary administration. But the gov-ernor hoped to gain Qin Gui's favor, and he gathered a list of Gao's faults and turned the case over to the judiciary. It happened that the governor was himself slandered and died in jail. Subsequently, Gao Deng was released and sum-moned to examine *jinshi* degree candidates in Chaozhou. He made the students answer the policy question: Did the dreadful government policy of not listening to straightforward words cause the floods of the Min and Zhe rivers? He then gave up his commission and returned home. When Qin Gui heard of the exam question he was extremely angry. He removed Gao from office and exiled him to Rongzhou.

His excellency Gao's learning was extensive and his conduct eminent. In written essays he liberally explained [his points] and in discussions he gave illustrations. The whole day long, like a torrent, he spoke of nothing but being a filial son and loyal minister and of sacrificing one's life in favor of righteous-ness. Those who heard him were in awe; their souls were moved and their spirits lifted. When he was in Gu County, students were already fighting to come to him. And when he was here in Rongzhou, his disciples were indeed numerous. When he became ill, he wrote his own tomb inscription and summoned the students who had studied with him to give his parting words. He sat up straight, folded his arms, smoothed his whiskers, opened his eyes, and died. Alas! He can indeed be called a hero of his generation.

Gao's learning and conduct were not entirely in accord with that of Confucius. Still, the eminence of his purpose and actions indeed merit his being considered the "pure worthy." Those who hear of his character after one hundred generations will have the principles to purify the corrupt and make the weak determined. How can we speak of his merit as a teacher of the age in the same breath as we speak of those who styled themselves followers of Confucius's harmonious conduct but who tolerated everything and covered up for each other?

More than twenty years after Gao died, Mr. Tian Dan of Yanping became professor at the prefectural school. He sought out Gao's extant writings and had them carved on woodblocks. He also had a portrait of Gao made and performed sacrificial offerings to him in order to inspire and discipline the students. In the course of this he [sent a letter to me] via Mr. Wang Yu, a native of the prefecture. He wanted a piece of writing as a commemorative record. I was ill and before I got around to it, Mr. Tian left Rongzhou. When the present prefect, Mr. Lin Yuanzhong of Yongjia, arrived, he and Mr. Wang sent off another letter urging me not to put it aside. I felt that my base writings truly could not match his honor Gao's outstanding integrity and his venerable determination. For a long time I used my illness as an excuse. But they forcibly roused me to write it. Yet my words do not come up to my intentions. Mr. Lin has ventured to have it inscribed on stone and placed into the wall of the shrine.

May the students of Zhangzhou and all scholars from the four directions who come here on business read them and truly be deeply moved and inspired.

Written in the ninth month of autumn of the fourteenth year of the Qunxi reign-period (1187) by Zhu Xi of Xin'an.

Former Worthies Ought Not to Be Mixed with Weird Spirits and Cruel Ghosts

The abundant virtue of Zhuge Liang—is it Mr. Wang Tong alone who dares not forget it? Across a thousand years, what loyal minister or gentleman of determination can hear of his spirit and not be inspired? Whenever I read his two reports on his military campaign, I close the book and shed tears over it. If the underworld could rise, I would be happy even to hold the whip and drive his carriage. How could I grudge a room of one beam to offer him sacrifices for a hundred generations? Furthermore, on examining the records of the [ancient kingdom of Sichuan], I find that when Zhao Lie commanded Jingzhou, Zhuge Liang, as army supervisor and leader of Court Gentlemen, concurrently supervised the three commanderies of Lingling, Guiyang, and Changsha. At that time, Shaoling County was still attached to Lingling. His carriage wheels and horses' hoofs may well have passed often through this spot. Is this not sufficient reason to enshrine him and offer him sacrifices here?

However, today I have examined the shrine that has been set up alongside the road, all grimy amid the hustle and bustle. Is this adequate as a cottage for peaceful repose? The sculpted image is dirty and vulgar, utterly lacking [Zhuge's] heroic demeanor, his whistling and singing. Moreover, [images of] weird spirits and cruel ghosts are mixed in fore and aft [on the altar], while hayseeds and country bumpkins stand half-naked to the left and right. Even supposing the sacrificial animals were fat, the ritual vessels fine and pure, and the officiant of the rites rose up strong and tall to make the sacrifices, ghosts of mere horse-doctors and peasants of the summer fields can still come and spit on him. Can we say that Zhuge Liang would enjoy it? The county sheriff's report acknowledges one part of this but not the other. He is particularly wrong when, based on the precedent of offering Zhuge joint sacrifices [nationally] in the military schools, he argues that [separate local] sacrifices should not be offered in the region of Sichuan.

[According to the classical *Record of Rites*,] he who possess the realm [i.e., the emperor] sacrifices to the hundred spirits: from Heaven, Earth, the four directions, the famous mountains and great rivers, to all who virtuously benefited the people, died in diligent service, labored to stabilize the state, ably warded off great disasters, and forestalled great worries—these are all recorded in the *Sacrificial Statutes*. The various noble lords may sacrifice only to those of their region: those in Jin sacrificed to the Yellow River, in Lu to Mount Tai, in Chu to the Sui, Zhang, and Han rivers. To sacrifice to those one ought not sacrifice to is called illicit sacrifice and brings no fortune.

Today it is said, "whom the emperor sacrifices to, all in the realm may sacrifice to." The sacrificial ordinances of the Three Dynasties [the Xia, Shang, and Zhou], I fear, were not like this. Some say, "since his excellency's spirit is in the realm as water is in the earth, then there is no place it does not go"; and indeed one may find this in a discussion by Su Shi. At the time [Su Shi wrote this], the people of Chao Prefecture had built a new temple to the south of the prefectural city in honor of Han Yu. It took a full year to complete. One may imagine the [propriety] of its construction, from its ridge pole above to the walls below. Although [the spirits of] the wise and upright do not care about red columns and carved pillars, still such people "have become the stars and planets in Heaven and the rivers and mountains in Earth." Even if those below fast and purify themselves and don their richest clothing in order to offer them sacrifices, I still fear they would be unable to cause the spirits to approach. If the temple building and the fasting chamber are rained on from above and blown by the wind from the sides; if the sacrificial animals are lean and the sacrificial wine sour; if the ritual vessels are only temporarily placed; and if the libationer's rising and bowing does not fit the proper forms, then even though Han Yu be called a spirit of the South Sea (present-day Hainan), he would not be willing to enjoy the offerings.

Now when the county sheriff speaks of Zhuge's spirit, he is probably refer-ring to this [precedent]. But I do not know how the shrine in Shaoling com-pares to that temple in Chao. Zhuge once had a shrine in Hengyang, on the Zheng River. During the Qiandao reign-period (1165–1173), the Ever-Normal Intendant, Mr. Fan Chengxiang, went searching for its old ruins and found an abandoned building in the midst of a wild overgrowth. He then moved it to a bright and high spot and had it entirely rebuilt. Zhang Shi wrote a piece to commemorate the affair. That being so, could they have been lax in the plans for the shrine's appearance?

Now the county sheriff wishes to preserve this [building] in order to convey his reverence, but he does not understand that its unkempt condition can not be countenanced either.

Judgment: I have undertaken to tour the inner and outer precincts of the city to determine whether or not there is another shrine to Zhuge Liang. If there is not another, then I will order artisans to seek a true likeness and draw a copy using one piece of fine silk. In the second month of spring and autumn I will offer sacrifices at the shrine to the former worthies in the prefectural school. This will ensure that all those [spirits] who dwell with [Zhuge] day and night will be the highest disciples [of Confucian learning]. The class of confused and malicious spirits will not get to wreak their havoc [upon Zhuge], those who officiate at the spring and autumn sacrifices will all be noble men who wear the officials' cap and the jade belt, and the sorcerers and exorcists of strange and malicious spirits will not get to creep into [the shrine]. If we do all this, then perhaps [Zhuge's] spirit will have no cause for shame. All existing vulgar shrines are to be destroyed. I have hung a notice on the sight.

Sacrificial Prayers and Reports

A PIECE FOR THE SACRIFICE TO THE TEN WORTHIES

In the northeast corner of the Yucheng there was a building in which several columns were arrayed with the portraits of ten prefects from the Jin and Tang dynasties. All were purely upright and were good administrators. They may act as models for those to come in the future. Generation after generation ought to sacrifice to them without shame. It happened that there was a typhoon and the roof tiles flew off and the ridge pole snapped. This was contrary to the idea [in the *Classic of Poetry*]: "Do not hew the sweet pear tree [under which Prince Shao sat]." After I rebuilt the parapet, I repaired the shrine and set up portraits. On an auspicious day I set out the sacrificial animals and wine and performed repeated prostrations to please their spirits. The spirits are regarded today as they were in the past. Eternally, they protect our people. They cause those who follow in their footsteps to be without fault in their official duties. Thus, the way we repay them is ever more reverential.

SACRIFICIAL REPORT TO THE FORMER SAGE ON DISMISSING A STUDENT

I am an unworthy and ordinary man. But the students have selected me to be an official in this county. In that capacity, I have managed the school's affairs, but my behavior and ability are so meager and my governing and teaching are not to be trusted. Among the students under my direction, there is a certain Mr. X, who was put in charge of cleaning the toilets because of his bad behavior. I believe that since I have not carried out the Way myself, I have been unable to lead and hone others and have allowed matters to come to this. Moreover, as I was not able to establish proper regulations early on, I controlled him by suppression. As a result, both virtue and regulations were lax, and ultimately disobedient gentlemen had no restrictions. Therefore, I am reporting to the former sage and former teacher [Confucius] to request that I may rectify the school's rules and shame the students by making punishments clear. By raising the two rods in teaching, one receives their awe and steadfastness. The former sage and former teacher said that the way to pass laws down to later generations was through the proper running of schools. If the former sage and former teacher approaches and resides above, dare I not clasp my hands [in prayer] and knock my head to the ground?

— 24 —

Daoist Ritual in Contemporary Southeast China

Kenneth Dean

This chapter treats the relationships between local cults and Daoist and Confucian ritual traditions. The materials in this section concern a god named Guo Chongfu. He was born in 963 on the twenty-second day of the second lunar month near Shishan, in Nan'an District of Fujian Province, in the mountains above coastal Southeast China. He died a mysterious death at the age of thirteen. Ever since that time, he has reappeared in dreams and visions to fellow villagers, and later to a wide circle of worshippers. J.J.M. De Groot, who worked as an ethnographer in Southeast China for a decade in the late 1800s, remarked in his *Les fetes annuellement célébrés à Emoui (Amoy)* (1886, reprinted 1977, 1:201) that Guo Shengwang ("Saintly King Guo," otherwise known as Guangze Zunwang, the "Reverent Lord of Broad Compassion") could "without hesitation be called the tutelary saint of the province [of Fujian]. . . . [T]here he finds his place amongst the domestic gods which are venerated." De Groot also mentioned that the god was the only major local deity among the four gods worshiped on altars in every home in Amoy, the others being Guanyin, the God of Wealth, and the Stove God. He notes that festivals are held for the god on the twenty-second of the second and the eighth lunar months. The former date is the birthday of the god, the latter the date for the sacrifices at the tomb of the god's parents.

Officials of the Fujian Provincial Religious Affairs Office in Fuzhou stated in 1987 that the month-long pilgrimages to the tomb are the largest and most significant expression of popular religious activity in Fujian today. After many years of suppression during the Cultural Revolution and the reign of the Gang of Four, the tomb was rebuilt in the early 1980s by a group of a dozen young people. The ritual sacrifices have been revived as well. They are led, according to the traditional pattern, in rotation by one of the five branches of the Huang lineage that live at the base of Phoenix Mountain in Shishan. As the involvement of the young people in rebuilding the tomb of the god's parents indicates, leadership in these rituals comes not only from those high in the lineage hierarchy but also from younger activists not necessarily connected to the lineage.

The principal sources of information on the cult are the *Brief Gazetteer of Phoenix Mountain Temple* (*Fengshansi zhilue*) of Yang Jun, published in 1887, and the *Gazetteer of Guo Mountain Temple* (*Guoshan miaozhi*), compiled by Dai Fengyi, a Hanlin academician, second-rank secretary in the Chinese Documents Section of the Inner Secretariat, in 1897. These two gazetteers differ greatly in tone and offer contrasting versions of the god's legend. Both sources focus on the founding temple of the cult network, the Fengshan si, or Phoenix Mountain Temple, in Nan'an, which has recently been rebuilt.

It is interesting to note that the temple is called a *si*, meaning a Buddhist monastery. For many centuries, Buddhist monks have lived in and maintained this temple dedicated to a popular god. As we will see, however, the principal rites of the cult call for the services of a Daoist ritual specialist or a specialist in Confucian ritual. This is an example of the coexistence of the "Three Religions," or perhaps the "three ritual traditions," in popular Chinese religion.

The sources translated below on Daoist rituals performed on the birthday of the cult, ballads and songs on the god, and so forth were gathered during fieldwork in Fujian from 1985 to 1987. Most of these sources were gathered from Daoist ritual specialists during the performance of Daoist community sacrifice rituals (*jiao*) in smaller temples scattered in isolated villages around the base of Guo Mountain. I have argued elsewhere that the Daoist liturgical framework gradually restructured popular cult worship in many parts of China.

Throughout China in traditional times, and to a surprising extent still today in areas such as Southeast China, cultural activity and economic and political decision-making center around the main temple or lineage hall of the village. The Daoist or Buddhist priest performing rituals in the temple is at the center of a circle traced by the movements of the god's procession around the boundaries of his spiritual precinct. Making up the procession is every genre of popular performing arts in the regional culture. Outside the temple theatrical troupes performed for the gods and the community, while in the space between the stage and the temple, community and family representatives set out a variety of offerings in time with the ritual. Inside the temple, following the movements of the priest, are the village headsmen (*huishou*), who have sponsored much of the ritual. They have set out Lamps of Destiny on the altar to attract the attention and blessings of the gods. All these offerings, together with the texts sacrificed by the Daoist priests, represent a liturgical system that has much to reveal. The ritual, the procession, the offerings, and the theater are intimately interrelated. There is a rhythm and a flow of intensities throughout the course of the entire community performance. Each performance by the priests of a ritual text is unique. Each community brings its own desires to bear upon the selection of elements from the regional culture and ritual tradition. Unique connections between different sectors occur at each ritual, criss-crossing the structural unity.

The activities of the entire community—the setting out of different categories of offerings, the performance of ritual theater, the processions of the gods, and the worship conducted by the community representatives inside the temple—are all structured by the sequence of rituals performed by the Daoist priests. At the most obvious level, the timing of these different aspects of the festival is determined by the timing of the Daoists ritual. At a deeper level, the liturgical framework organizes distinct groups along parallel lines. Finally, at the level of cultural construction of reality, the liturgical framework generates a complex process model of spiritual power in a multifaceted interaction with local systems of power.

The funding for rituals is gathered according to two systems; on the one hand, every person in the village is expected to contribute the same small amount. Similarly, every family sends a male representative to the temple, and each one takes turns casting divination blocks. The men with the most successive affirmative casts are elected as the *huishou*. Depending on the rank they attain in this fashion, they are expected to make a major contribution to the costs of the festival. On the other hand, individuals may contribute additional amounts if they so choose, within certain limits depending on the locality. Individuals can also choose to contribute or to demonstrate their wealth and standing by sponsoring extra theatrical performances, or throwing lavish feasts.

Every family brings a table out into the courtyard before the temple and arrays a set of offerings appropriate to the rite being conducted by the Daoists. For example, in a *jiao* I attended in 1986 near Zhangzhou, when the Daoists emerged from the temple on the third day of the ritual to ascend the stage set up facing the temple across a courtyard, each family in the community had prepared an offering table in the courtyard facing northward toward the stage. This offering table contained offerings symbolically keyed to the significance of the Daoists' ritual, with offerings for the high gods. When the Daoists emerged again the next day to perform the feast for the universal deliverance of hungry ghosts (*pudu*), another set of offerings keyed to the needs of the dead was laid out by each family facing east toward the *pudu* altar.

Theater is an integral part of the liturgical framework. In a fundamental sense, theater is performed for the gods, as an offering, rather than for the spectators. Indeed, before human actors can perform, marionettes consecrate the stage and the marionette god of theater emerges at midnight to sing of the Supreme Harmony brought by song to the mortal realm. Prior to the afternoon and evening performances of the regional repertoire, short ritual plays are performed. These performances are timed to coincide with certain Daoist rites. A presentation usually takes place simultaneously with the opening rituals on the first night. Another occurs just prior to the Presentation of the Memorial. In some rituals, a concluding theatrical performance takes the form of the exorcistic dance of Zhong Kui, itself modeled on the Daoist Sealing of the Altar rite, which is performed on the evening of the last day of a ritual during the reopening of the doors of the temple.

The various groups involved in a ritual share certain structural features. The priests, the community representatives, the puppet troupe or theater group and the musicians, and the entire community follow parallel prohibitions during the course of the ritual. Most groups are marked by special clothing; the community representatives make a brave showing in traditional Qing scholars' robes while the Daoist priests are splendid in embroidered vestments. A multitude of performing arts and militia troupes dress up for the procession of the gods, which frames the ritual and reinscribes the boundary of the cult.

The community representatives follow the actions of the Daoist priests during the course of the ritual. They emerge during the inspection of the offerings at set times throughout the ritual. After the central inner rites have been completed, they follow the Daoists out and follow them up onto the stage (in some areas only the general manager, or *zongli,* ascends the stage). Here the Daoists perform the Presentation of the Memorial (*jinbiao*), a descendent of the Announcement of Merit (*yangong*) ritual of medieval Daoism. This ritual is addressed to the Jade Emperor, the high god of the popular pantheon, in full view of the entire community. Their climb to the stage platform, transformed by the ritual into the Golden Gates of Heaven, surely symbolizes the elevation of the local leaders before the gods and above the people.

At various points in the ritual, outside the temple, in traditional times and when possible nowadays, the ritual master leads spirit mediums in recitations of chants detailing the hagiographies of the local gods. Manuscripts of these chants are often written in vernacular Chinese. Occasionally the medium will go into trance and enter into the temple. This usually occurs at some point in the ritual that calls for dramatic emphasis. The rites performed by these groups are complementary to the rituals performed by Daoist priests.

Inside the temple, the local gods are invited to special "seats" on the Daoists' altar. If the cult has achieved the necessary qualitative leap in its development, the priests will recite a Daoist scripture dedicated to this god, identifying him as a Daoist astral divinity. Often the god will be identified as a transformation of the Pole Star, *Ziwei.* This god is usually pictured on the right of the Daoist altar, in the fifth place after the Three Pure Ones (Sanqing), anthropomorphic representations of the abstract Dao, and the Jade Emperor (Yuhuang shangdi), chief of the popular pantheon. The scripture, written in classical Chinese, will present the god's essential qualities and divine mission as revealed in the form of an audience with the Heavenly Worthy of Primal Origin, before the entire universal Daoist pantheon. In these ways we see illustrated the universal qualities of the Daoist liturgical framework.

At the same time, the various and sometimes contradictory representations of the god illustrate the role of contradictory elements invested by different social groups which are nevertheless absorbed into the Daoist liturgical framework. Thus we see the god represented in the trance of spirit-mediums outside the temple, in carved statues carried around the spiritual parameters of the village, in special "seats" upon the altar, and in his underlying form as the Pole Star among the highest emanations of the Dao. Daoism would also appear to be playing a contradictory role in enfeoffing the local leadership in the eyes of the local gods while at the same time claiming that these gods were part of a universal pantheon. These local leaders included the very officials who when in office had often suppressed local cult celebrations similarly structured by Daoism. Are we to interpret Daoist ritual as a symbolic affirmation of local authority, appealing to the cosmic spiritual order rather than the imperial order? In that case Daoism could be seen to serve the imperial metaphor. Or can we see a deeper level, at which Daoism refuses to be drawn into either the bureaucratic metaphor erected by the despotic signifier or the local codes of territoriality and blood ties? Perhaps Daoism served to scramble the codes, creating floating signifiers that distinct groups in Chinese society could fix upon to fashion their own interpretations of the significance of their own participation in the ritual/festival.

Recent fieldwork has shown that in many areas of Southeast China a wide range of traditional popular rites have been revived or reinvented since the end of the Cultural Revolution. In Fujian, many temples were rebuilt by the early 1980s, Daoist rituals were being performed by the mid-1980s, and large-scale processions were being openly performed by the early 1990s. Nearby areas such as northern Guangdong, Zhejiang, and Jiangxi provinces have seen a slower, more gradual recovery of these fundamental cultural forms. These developments are not unique to the southeast area. Reports from across southern China, including Anhui, Hunan, Guangxi, Guizhou, Yunnan, and Sichuan, indicate a widespread renaissance of popular religion and regional opera. This entire process is of great significance for the future of China. Research into the history and practice of northern Chinese ritual life is also under way. This research will lead to a deeper understanding of the roles of Daoist, Buddhist, and Confucian ritual within the localized popular cultures of the different regions of China. In many places, however, these popular efforts continue to meet with government bans and prohibitions. This is particularly striking in urban areas, where forces of modernization and governmental policy often combine to prevent the performance of many popular religious rituals.

The materials translated in this chapter are drawn from my book *Taoist Ritual and Popular Cults of Southeast China* (Princeton: Princeton University Press, 1993), chap. 4 and appendix 2. In that book I explain how the cult of the Reverent Lord of Broad Compassion continues to this day to reveal the role of contradictory interpretations of the god. These different understandings can be seen in the three versions of the legend of the god translated below in the section "Myths and Legends of the Cult." Version 1 is from Yang Jun's *Fengshansi zhilue* (*Brief Gazetteer of Phoenix Mountain Temple*), 1:4a–b. Version 2 is from J. J. M. De Groot, *Les fêtes annuellement célébrés à Emoui* (1977), 2:521–22. Version 3 is from Dai Fengyi's *Guoshan miaozhi* (*Gazetteer of Guo Mountain Temple*), 2:2a–b.

The next set of materials, on the "Imperial Canonization of the God," translated from Dai Fengyi's *Guoshan miaozhi*, reveals the official version of the heroic miracles of the god in response to social turmoil brought on by the Taiping Rebellion in the mid-nineteenth century. Here we see part of the process by which a local god was canonized as a saint by the state. This report resulted in new titles and honors from the court for the founding temple of the Reverent Lord of Broad Compassion.

The next section, "A Daoist Scripture Written about the God," is translated from Yang Jun's *Fengshansi zhilue*. This kind of scripture is recited as part of Daoist rituals held to commemorate the birth of the god. The scripture is followed by a popular ballad dedicated to the god, from the *Guoshan miaozhi*, and a pair of texts in the voice of the god recorded by spirit mediums, from the *Fengshansi zhilue*. All of these kinds of materials form the basis both for Confucian rites at the grave of the parents of the god, which are controlled by powerful local lineages, and for the Daoist rites on the birthday of the god held at numerous temples dedicated to the god, which unite a wider social network in the common worship of the god.

Further Reading

J. J. M. De Groot, *Les fêtes annuellement célébrés à Emoui (Amoy)* trans. C. J. Chavannes, *Annales de Musée Guimet*, vols. 11–12 (Paris, 1886; reprinted Paris: Leroux, 1977), 2 vols.; De Groot, *The Religious System of China, Its Ancient Forms, Evolution, History and Present Aspect, Manners, Customs and Social Institutions Connected Therewith* (Leyden: E. J. Brill, 1892–1910; reprinted Taipei: Southern Materials Center, 1982), 6 vols.; Kenneth Dean, *Taoist Ritual and Popular Cults of Southeast China* (Princeton: Princeton University Press, 1993); David K. Jordan, *Gods, Ghosts, and Ancestors: Folk Religion in a Taiwanese Village* (Berkeley: University of California Press, 1972); John Lagerwey, *Taoist Ritual in Chinese Society and History* (New York: Macmillan, 1987); Daniel Overmyer, *Folk Buddhist Religion: Dissenting Sects in Late Traditional China* (Cambridge: Harvard University Press, 1976); P. Steven Sangren, *History and Magical Power in a Chinese Community* (Stanford: Stanford University Press, 1987); Michael Saso, *The Teachings of Taoist Master Chuang* (New Haven: Yale University Press, 1978); Kristofer Schipper, *The Taoist Body* (Stanford: Stanford University Press, 1993); Michel Strickmann, "History, Anthropology, and Chinese Religion," *Harvard Journal of Asiatic Studies* 40 (1980): 201–48. James Watson and Evelyn S. Rawski, eds., *Death Ritual in Late Imperial China* (Berkeley: University of California, 1988); A. P. Wolf, ed., *Religion and Ritual in Chinese Society* (Stanford: Stanford University Press, 1974).

MYTHS AND LEGENDS OF THE CULT

VERSION 1

A geomancer was invited by Elder Yang to select an auspicious spot for his grave. The family mistakenly offered him a meal of a lamb that had fallen into a latrine. The geomancer was angered at its impurity. The god's mother served the geomancer assiduously in washing and combing, and washed his clothes each day. The geomancer asked her, "Have you found a good tomb for your late husband?" She replied, "I barely have time to support my family, how could I hope for such a thing?" She was very upset. The geomancer said, "Would you like to have an audience with the Son of Heaven? Receive blood sacrifices for ten thousand years?" The woman urged him to go on. Then he pointed to the sheepfold where her son tended the sheep. "That is a perfect point [zhengxue]. Tomorrow morning grind up the bones of your husband and wash and boil them and bring them here. Then I will pretend to be angered by their desecrated state and I will slap you on the face. Then you should burst into tears and spill the bones and ashes onto the ground of the stockade. Then quickly fetch your son and run off. I too will depart at that time. You and your son will escape from several battles. When you encounter a great rainshower and see a monk wearing a metal rain-hat, a cow riding its cowherd, then that will be your former residence, and you may settle down." They came upon a great downpour and saw a monk with a copper pot on his head and a cowherd taking shelter from the rain underneath a cow. The god's mother said, "This is my old home (now the site of the Longshan Temple)." When they went back to the home of Elder Yang, they learned that the ash and water had all turned into black hornets which had stung to death everyone in the house. Nowadays, [at the tomb] they first sacrifice to the Elder, so as not to forget their roots.

VERSION 2

A geomancer was invited to the house. The slave served him so well that upon leaving, the geomancer asked him what he desired. The slave said, "Offerings of incense for my descendants for ten thousand years." The geomancer then led him into the mountains and found a spot for a tomb. He told the slave to bury the bones of his father there. "Wait until you see pass by someone wearing a metal hat, and an ox riding upon a boy. At that auspicious moment bury the bones of your father, and glory and prosperity will come to your family." The slave disinterred the bones of his father and placed them in an urn and went to the assigned spot to wait for [the signs]. At that time it began to rain lightly. A peasant passing by with a metal pot in his hands happened to use it to block the falling rain, and a boy passing by with a cow took refuge under the beast. This was obviously the appointed moment, so the slave began to dig a tomb. As soon as he had placed the urn in the tomb, it closed up by itself. The slave hurried home to see what would happen next. Soon thereafter a star shone in his home and a boy was born. He was destined to become the god of the region. . . . At the age of sixteen the boy dreamed that he would become a saint. He told this to his mother, washed and combed himself, and sat down on a chair and died with his legs crossed. All of a sudden his chair rose up in the air. His mother rushed in at that instant and prevented his miraculous ascension by pulling on one of his legs. That is why one always represents this god with one leg folded and the other hanging down. Other people say, however, that he died in the mountains in a tree and that his mother, coming upon him, pulled on his leg to get him down out of the tree.

VERSION 3

As a boy the god was uncommonly virtuous and filial. He tended animals in Qinxi for Elder Yang. . . . When his father died it was difficult for them to [find the funds to] bury him. The god's heart was grieved. Although he went back to tending the animals he wept constantly. A geomancer noticed his filial piety and pointed to a mountain belonging to Elder Yang and told him, "Bury him there and it will be most auspicious." The god then kowtowed before him and thanked him profusely. He asked permission of Elder Yang and set up a tomb. Then he returned to the foot of Guo Mountain and served his mother until the end of his days. When he was sixteen, he led a cow to the top of the mountain. At the setting of the sun he sat upon an old wisteria vine and died. When his mother arrived she pulled at his left leg. . . . Later when his mother died the people of the li were so moved by the god's perfect filial piety that they decided to worship her at the tomb in Qingxi and buried her together with her husband. They carried out the ritual of joint worship of the tomb of the State of Lu.

The three versions of the origin of the tomb reveal sharply contrasting representations of the nature of the god. In version 1, the ash and ground bones turn into magical weapons of death and destruction, resulting in the defeat of Elder Yang and the takeover of the geomantic powers of his land. In version 2, the planting of the god's grandfather's bones bears fruit in the birth of the god. Here bones reap good fortune. The class tensions are brought out in the position of the slave and his enormous wish to transcend his status and achieve a lineage of his own. In version 3's tamer account, all these conflicts are neutralized by the filial piety and propriety of the god, who asks and receives permission from Elder Yang to build a tomb on his land.

As to the manner of the god's death/ascension, Ming and Qing dynasty Fujian gazetteers all state that, at the age of ten or thirteen or sixteen, the boy-god climbed Guo Mountain with a jug of wine and a cow. He sat cross-legged on an old vine. He transformed by sloughing off his body (a traditional method of leaving the world employed by Daoist adepts) and was found dead the next day by his mother. The wine was gone from the jug, and the cow had been devoured, leaving only the bones. His death/ascension took place on the twenty-second day of the eighth lunar month.

IMPERIAL CANONIZATION OF THE GOD

THE GOD'S DOSSIER AND THE MIRACLES OF GUANGZE ZUNWANG AFTER THE SUPPRESSION OF THE REBELLIONS OF THE 1850S: THE MAGISTRATE'S REPORT

The Department of Yongchun and the District of Nan'an of Quanzhou Prefecture have held a meeting to report on events. According to a report from the *shenshi* (gentry) of Yongchun and Nan'an, entitled "Report on the Divine Spirit's Manifest Responses," we humbly make the following report: We memorialize requesting an enhancement of the enfeoffment of the gods as well as the bestowal of imperial plaques, in order to repay the protection of the god. We humbly point out that these included . . . (there follows a list of the god's early miracles with citations from the various gazetteers, and from the *Filiations of Guangze Zunwang,* by the Nan'an man, Ceng Tianjue). In 1853 the Small Knives Association rose up in Xiamen, Tong'an, and other locations. This was a grave matter, the disturbances were spreading everywhere. In all four corners of Nan'an there was looting and robbing. The government troops encircled the bandits for several months, but still the flames of rebellion spread further, wreaking tremendous havoc. The officials and the gentry went to Guo Mountain and prayed to the god. That night in a dream the god pointed out that the time was right for the gathering together of village militias who should join forces with the government troops in attacking the bandits. Accordingly, the bandits were pacified. Every time the god was prayed to for rain, he responded. In the fourth month of 1853, the local bandit leader Lin Jun rounded up a band of four or five thousand men and crept into Yongchun City from Dehua. From dawn until noon the government troops battled the bandits. After they had fought for over four hours, things were at a crisis. Suddenly we saw atop Dapeng Mountain to the north of the city masses of soldiers dressed in armor. There among them were flags and banners with the name "Guo" upon them. When the gentlemen and soldiers saw this, their courage increased a hundred fold. They attacked with furious strength. The band of thieves was forced together and decimated. Countless heads were chopped off. The bandit leader Lin Jun was forced to run far away. The town and its moat were thus recovered at the hour of noon. The entire region depended on the god for bringing peace. Then, in 1864, the bandit leaders Liu Guangju, Xie Xian, and Xie Jin formed a secret society (*dang*) and called together [a rebel band] in the He Mountain stockade of Yongchun. They disturbed and harmed the people. At that very time, the hairy bandits [of the Taiping Tianguo] had sneakily taken Zhangzhou City and the surrounding countryside. The aforementioned bandits plotted to coordinate with them. After several sieges by government troops on the stockade, they finally broke off their water supply. The bandits broke out of their nest like frightened rats. The leaders Liu and Xie Jin were captured alive and punished according to law [executed on the spot]. Only Xie Xian escaped. In

1867 Xie Xian slunk to the border of Yongchun and Dehua and made alliances with bandit groups, plotting again to raise trouble. Then local civil and military officials, together with local gentry, joined forces to capture and annihilate them. They destroyed the bandit lair. Xie Xian scurried in all directions, running in flight. He would suddenly appear and then disappear; it was impossible to determine his whereabouts in order to capture him. The officials and gentry again made a visit to the Guo Mountain Temple. Within a month Xie Xian was captured and immediately received his heavy punishment. Were it not for the resplendent power of the god, how could we have annihilated these demons? Now in the entire Datian, Dehua, Yongchun, Nan'an region, all is calm; the villages and households are at peace. We felt deep thanksgiving and so composed this report. The report has been reworked into a memorial requesting the enhancement of the enfeoffment and the bestowal of imperial plaques. As for these former matters, the humble [department and district magistrates] [Weng] Xueben and [Wu] Weishu met together and examined the record of temple sacrifices. We found that this orthodox spirit was in fact able to drive away disaster and overcome adversity. He has merit with the people, and so his case merits a request in the form of a memorial for the enhancement of his title. Now Guangze Zunwang has been repeatedly enfeoffed in the Song dynasty. His deeds are detailed in the gazetteers. In 1853 when the local bandit Lin Jun was disturbing the region the awesome power of the god shone forth and protected the people. These acts accord in nature and in principle with those listed above under the driving away of disaster and the overcoming of adversity. We have met and gathered together all the documents and now send them to the provincial government for inspection.

A DAOIST SCRIPTURE WRITTEN ABOUT THE GOD

THE TRUE SCRIPTURE OF THE IMPERIALLY ENFEOFFED VENERABLE KING OF BROAD COMPASSION, PRINTED AT THE SNOWY SEAS [STUDIO] THROUGH CONTRIBUTIONS COLLECTED BY YANG JUN, OF [FUJIAN] COMMANDERY

1. Sacred Spell to Purify the Heart
2. Sacred Spell to Purify the Mouth Spirit
3. Sacred Spell to Purify the Spirits of the Body
4. Spell to Pacify the Tutelary Divinity
5. Spell to Purify Heaven and Earth
6. Spell to Express Hope via the Spirit of Incense
7. Spell to Control Demons
8. Sacred Spell of Golden Light
9. Invocation

Bowing before the Saint of Phoenix Mountain
Venerable abode of the King of Broad Compassion

His loyal heart pierces the sun and moon.
His vermilion liver illumines the *qian* and *kun* hexagrams.
His filial piety moves the heavenly vault above.
His virtue transforms the center of the nation.
His mercy extends beyond the Three Realms.
He powerfully vouchsafes the courts of the Nine Heavens.
He was given by decree the Seal of Thunder and Lightning
Which he uses especially to exterminate the five rebellious emotions.
Excising all deviant evil beings
Exorcising pestilence he subdues ghosts and goblins.
He captures the masses of demons and sprites.
He protects the Emperor and makes peaceful the altars of grain and
    harvest.
He mercifully saves the myriad people.

10. Sacred Spell to Open the Scripture

Silent, empty, quite without ancestors
Empty up and down for a myriad fathoms
Down fell the Writings of the Cavernous Mystery
Who can fathom their hidden reaches?
Once you have entered the Path of the Great Wheel (Mahāyāna)
Who can calculate the number of years and kalpas?
Unborn and yet not extinguished
Wishing to be born he followed the lotus blossom
And surpassed the pathways of the Three Realms
His merciful heart liberated from the entanglements of the world.
The Perfected Being's most high merit
[Enables him to be] an immortal for age after age.

THE MARVELOUS SCRIPTURE ON THE AWAKENING OF THE WORLD AND THE
SUBDUING OF DEMONS BY STELLAR GOD GUO, KING OF BROAD MERCY, NUMINOUS
SALVATION AND UNIVERSAL VIRTUE, WHO PRESERVES PEACE, AS PROCLAIMED BY
THE HEAVENLY VENERABLE OF NO BEGINNINGS, THE MOST HIGH EMPEROR OF
PRIMAL YANG

Formerly, the Heavenly Venerable of No Beginnings, in the Great Luo Heaven,
together with all the Imperial Lords of Heaven and the Immortal Sages of the
ten directions, assembled in the Hall of the Ninefold Radiance of the Jade Void,
on the Jade Brahmā Seven-Treasure Stage, and chanted the Cavernous Stanzas
and sang Immortal songs, gathering together the Unobstructed Marvelous Dao.
They expounded the most precious mystic Writings.

    Just at that moment there appeared a spirit in charge of inspecting trans-
gressions. He offered up a document, memorializing:

At this time people below are all being victimized by hordes of demons, all manner of monsters are being worshipped; which delude [the people's] hearts. They do not know to turn toward the good, but falsely do wrong. The variety of their crimes would be difficult to describe.

When the immortals had heard the memorial, they broke rank and [rushed] forward, memorializing: "Great is the Mercy of the Heavenly Venerable. Great is the Sageliness of the Heavenly Venerable. You are the Father of all things and the Master of the myriad spirits. Broadly dispense compassion and save the lower realm."

The Heavenly Venerable spoke:

Excellent. Excellent. This class of beings [i.e., humankind] has encountered tribulations. If one wished to subdue the demons and enlighten the masses, then the only one who could accomplish this task is the Stellar Lord Guo of Numinous Salvation and Universal Virtue. He is perfectly loyal and filial, correct, upright, and unselfish. As for the Stellar Lord, he is related to the Perfected Immortal Nan Ling. He descended and was born in the Qingxi area of Quanzhou Commandery. He served his mother with perfect filial piety. When he was thirteen years old, he sloughed off his body in the first year of the Tianfu [reign-period] of the Latter Jin dynasty. He revealed his saintliness atop an ancient vine in Nan'an.

By Jade Imperial Decree, [he was enfeoffed as] Stellar Lord Guo of Numinous Salvation and Universal Virtue, Heavenly Venerable Who Protects and Urges Good Conduct Everywhere. [His] Divine Residence is in the Palace of Jade Purity, and he has a position within the Bureau of Responsive Origins. He worships as his Master the High Emperor Red Hill. He has control over the dispensation of the Lightning and Thunder of the Southern Pole and has administrative power over the heavenly responses. In the past he has punished the deviant and the evil. Now he judges the good and the bad. He cuts up demons and sprites beneath the Dipper stars and the Mainstays of Heaven and exorcises pestilence from the center of the nation. From the Song dynasty onward, he has killed robbers and saved the August Palace from fire. At first he was enfeoffed as "Great General." [His titles] were successively improved to those of Duke and King. An edict was issued commanding the construction of a tall and imposing temple with ritual sacrifice to be held in spring and autumn. The fire of incense lasted long. In the Great Ming [dynasty] the Islander Dwarfs (Japanese pirates) were vicious and wild, and the Lu brigands ran amok. [Then the god] greatly opened forth his divine powers and swept away the masses of ghouls and annihilated all the fiends. He was enfeoffed as Venerable King of Broad Compassion, Awesome Martial Heroic Prowess, Loyal Response, and Dependable Benevolence. His cinnabar heart and vermilion liver protect the nation and preserve the people. His loyalty and sincerity transfix the sun. His meritorious acts merge with Heaven. Then the Sacred [Qing] dynasty piled up enfeoffments of kingly honors, decreeing the addition of the words "Protector of Peace." His merit supports the altars of grain and the harvest. His powers are stationed on Phoenix Mountain. He has refined himself to perfection for one thousand years. No one surpasses his virtue.

When the Immortals heard this, they were all overjoyed. Then the Heavenly Venerable ordered a golden lad to carry a talisman to Phoenix Mountain to summon him. When the Stellar Lord received the summons, he immediately returned and was granted an audience with the Heavenly Venerable. Kowtowing, he memorialized:

Your Servant resides in the Bureau of Thunder. He had been granted [the task] of garrisoning Phoenix Mountain. May I ask for what reason I have had the honor of a summons?

The Heavenly Venerable said:

I today command you to [go to] the lower realm to sweep away demons and ghosts, to save and raise up the masses of living beings, enlighten the world and save the people, protect the nation so that it will be forever pure.

The Stellar Lord repeatedly bowed, accepted his mission, and descended, transmitting the [following] order everywhere.

Now, as for the Lord who has been moved responsively by this Sacred Dynasty. He is a ruler of intelligence. How could he countenance the likes of ghouls and goblins acting viciously under the light of bright Heaven's transforming sun? I all along punished crime on behalf of Heaven, cutting down all demons. I open up my heart which probes the hidden, and open up the road to life. Now all you demons, wash your hearts and cleanse your thoughts. All listen to my words. Return to the correct, cast off evil. Quickly return to the Cavern Headquarters. Face the stone wall and refine yourselves to perfection. Turn your heads back to famous mountains and there weave baskets and become enlightened. Await perfect merit and worshipfully do your work. Then your nature will be calmed and your spirit coalesce. You will be able to prove your worth as a High Perfected and reach the stairway of the Marvelous Dao. Wherever this order reaches, the King of Demons will be tied at the neck; he will leap to take refuge in the Way. People and Heaven will all be benefited. The nation will know rising peace.

At this time the Stellar Lord again pronounced the precious stanzas and awoke the World, saying:

Now, the Great Sages of the Empire established Rites and Music, wrote the [Classic of] Poetry (Shijing) and the [Book of] Documents (Shangshu). All of these alter habits and change customs. At this time the people below have lost their original perfection. They are blind to their heavenly nature to the point that neither the ancient stanzas of former saints nor the codes and regulations of former kings can be recited or held in the heart. On the contrary, they maintain their stubborn, vulgar feelings. They consider the Dao and righteousness to be common writing. They take ghosts and spirits to be nonexistent and consider rewards and responses [from the gods] to be empty lies. They do not know that the rewards of good and evil are like a shadow following a shape. If you are good, then Heaven rewards you with good fortune. If bad, then Heaven besets you with misfortune. Therefore I pronounce the precious stanzas, universally transforming people of the world. I judge good and evil in the minutest measure. Revere ghosts and spirits in the center of the room. Never desist from doing something if it is only a little good. Nor do something because it is only a little bad. This would be as though good and evil were not diametrically opposed, and as if there were no definite good or evil. If you can give birth to a heart that follows the good and expels evil, then that is the Way of turning misfortune into good fortune. All of you multitudes, listen to my words. Refine your own bodies, push them upward. Thus you can prove to be a Saint and complete your perfection. Descend and take this [command], and do not forsake good people and superior men. Strive with sincere hearts. The Perfect Dao is before you. The precious stanzas universally transform. The myriad families are raised up and enlightened.

Thereupon he returned to the Gates of Heaven, obtained an audience and beheld the Venerable countenance, and reported back concerning the imperial command. He bowed in thanks to all the Immortals and sang out in thanks over the promise held out [by the order], which enables one to meet with the Most High Wheel of the Law. Thereupon the Heavenly Venerable sang in praise of the Stellar Lord and pronounced this *gatha*:

> The Perfect Saint, King of the Preservation of Peace Most
> High Stellar Lord Guo,
> General of the Bureau of Thunder of the Nine Heavens,
> Venerable Who Universally Transforms the Ten Directions,
> Recounting a Scripture while astride a brocade phoenix,
> Upholding the Law grasping a golden whip,
> Within his belly the Primal Mechanism is marvelous,
> Within the crucible cinnabar and lead are made.
> Capable of using the power of his wisdom
> To subdue all the demons and sprites,
> Traveling on a tour of inspection beyond the Three Realms
> He examines good and evil feelings
> Without prejudice or party.
> His responses are extremely discerning,
> He propagates the teachings of the Heavenly Venerable.
> Awakening and enlightening living beings,
> If people of the world know to carefully revere him

They will obtain blessing and increase their lifespans.
With complete sincerity bow and recite [this scripture].
The myriad nations will all be tranquil.

At this time, the Heavenly Venerable's *gatha* was concluded. He spread it about the Jade Capital. All the Heavenly Emperors and Lords, and the Immortals and Saints from the Ten Directions, were greatly delighted. They made bows and withdrew. Faithfully keep and worship: *The Marvelous Scripture on the Awakening of the World and the Subduing of Demons* by Stellar God Guo, King of Broad Mercy, Numinous Salvation and Universal Virtue, Who Preserves Peace, as Proclaimed by the Heavenly Venerable of No Beginnings, the Most High Emperor of Primal Yang. The end.

PRECIOUS APPELLATION

Great Saint of Phoenix Mountain, Orthodox Spirit of the Bureau of Thunder, Ruler of the Nine Lands and Ten Directions of the Three Realms, Controller of the Five Sacred Mountains, the Eight Poles, and the Four Mainstays, Ritual Ruler of the Orthodox One, Examiner and Inspector of the Records of Good and Evil, Ruler of the Teaching of Actionless Action, Source of Responses of Good or Bad Fortune, Subduer of Demons and Sprites, Exorciser of Pestilence. All Beings Rely upon Him. Evil Deeds are put Right by Him. Great is His Loyalty, Great is His Filial Piety, Great is His Saintliness, Great is His Mercy: Heavenly Venerable of the Protection of Peace, Great Stellar Lord Guo, of Numinous Salvation and Universal Virtue, Subduer of the Demons of the Three Realms, Southern Pole Commander of Heaven, King of Broad Compassion, Awesome Martial Heroic Prowess, Dependable Benevolence, and Loyal Response.

Precious Appellation of the Patriarch of Thunder [within] the Bureau of Response to the Origin of the Nine Heavens, [the] Most High King of Jade Purity. Transforming his Shape he fills the Ten Directions. Discussing the Dao he straddles a phoenix. Above the Thirty-six Heavens, he reads the Precious Talismans [and] examines the Rosegem Books. Prior to 1500 Kalpas, he established the orthodox and the true [and] empowered the great transformations. In his hands he holds a Scepter of Golden Light. He proclaims the Precious Scripture of the Jade Pivot. Those who are disobedient he turns to dust. The announcing of his name [brings results] as swiftly as wind and fire. Using his pure heart he expands his vast vow. Using the power of wisdom he subdues all demons. He is commander in chief of the Five Thunders. Moving his heart through the Three Realms, [he is] Father to the masses of living beings and Master of the myriad immortals. Great is his Mercy, Great is his Compassion, Great is his Vow, [the] Heavenly Venerable of Universal Transformation through the Sound of Thunder of the Response to the Origin of the Nine

Heavens, Jade Sovereign of Perfected Dao. Precious Appellation of the Jade Sovereign (omitted)

Hymn to Conclude the Scripture

Venerable King of Broad Compassion
Mystic Door to the Salvation from Distress
From the Peak of Phoenix Mountain you let shine your radiance.
All the Heavens have heard of your
Awesome Responses Delivering from Evil and Prolonging Life.
Uphold and recite [this scripture to ensure] the Preservation of Peace.

On the seventh evening of Guangxu *wuyin* (1878) in Fuzhou, Qian Taibao, who exalts and worships Phoenix Mountain Temple in his heart, reverently wrote this. He ordered that it be printed and distributed. Anyone who recites the scripture must first fast and observe prohibitions, lustrate himself, and with a sincere heart fix their breath. After this grind your teeth and pronounce the sounds and harmoniously recite it. Communicate to the spiritual powers whatever you feel, and all that you pray for will be responded to.

SONGS AND BALLADS CELEBRATING THE GOD

Beneath Poetry Mountain in Minnan in the Later Tang
Master Guo had a son but no daughters.
The boy had a lofty nature, quite uncommon.
The family was poor, there was nowhere for him to study.
At the household of Yang the Elder
They received their meals in return for looking after the livestock.
Thinking of his parents, he wept through winter and summer.
August Heaven was unkind; he lost his father.
Mother and son stood face to face deep in sadness.
Her dowry could not cover the costs of a grave site.
Leaving a relative unburied, they felt empty and sad.
Who should come along but an old man with white hair.
Stroking his beard by the side of the road he spoke to them.
Their misery and complete filial piety moved him.
He truly showed them a perfect grave site in the shape of a sleeping
    cow.
The boy went to [Yang] the Elder's home and begged for it.
"No matter how much you beg I won't give it to you."
Then he pitied this young boy of such a perfect nature.

He called him back and listened to him.
"We are in dire straits; wind and rain pierce our secluded hut.
I seek a single grave mound in which to rest the spirit of my ancestor.
When my father was alive, it was hard for me to leave home.
Now that my father is dead, my mother's life is even more difficult.
Depending on others we cannot experience good times.
We eat vegetables and drink water in the side courtyards."
From antiquity perfect sincerity could model Heaven.
The birds planting and the elephants plowing [for the filial paragon
    Shun] were no ordinary events.
How much more so such perfect conduct in one so young.
Mysteriously [his conduct] truly moved Heaven to feel pity.
The emperor said, "Ah, on the Earth below there is a filial boy."
He ordered Wu Yang [the legendary physician] to descend and
    summon him, [saying],
"Otherwise I fear he will be consumed by goblins."
In the setting sun he stood in a straw raincoat on the top of the
    mountain.
"Who is it that comes here?" [It was the] Taishen ("Great God"—
    Messenger of Heaven),
In embroidered robes riding a horse with feathered cape;
Holding jade court tablets and golden books, he proclaimed the
    emperor's words.
"I don't want to go to Heaven; I want to stay on Earth.
At home I have an old mother who relies on her only son."
But alas, how could the emperor's order be disregarded?
He sat atop an ancient vine and died with tears streaming down.
The wine was gone from the jar and the cow left only its bones.
The pain of his old mother could not be assuaged.
These strange events indeed coincide with those of antiquity.
By his side were a group of children scared half witless.
The cattle returned and pushed against the thatch fence.
His mother threw down her spinning and rushed to see what had
    happened.
His two eyes shone brilliantly and his left foot hung down.
"My son, after you are gone, how will I live on?"
She wailed and wept in the empty mountains; her tears fell like the
    rain.
The elders by the roadside knelt down and said,
"Old woman, do not feel so bitter this night.
Your son has transformed this village with his filial piety."
These events were fully recorded
See how the neighboring women and children brought her food.
Later Heaven sent down a jade casket.

Like the people of Lu, she was jointly buried [with her husband].
From this time on, the power of the King took shape.
Horses of wind and chariots of clouds came down
To express thanks to the people of the village for carrying out his
     wishes.
In his home region he drives away disaster and sweeps away adversity.
Beginning in the Tang and Song dynasties and lasting for so many
     springs and autumns,
His magnificent temple stands atop Phoenix Mountain.
He drove away plagues of insects and the demons of drought.
With his deep red banner on his white horse, he routed the rebel
     leaders.
His heavenly words are resplendent; he is worshipped in the Register
     of Sacrifices.
Living under the care of the True King, people have no worries.
His overflowing virtue and abundant deeds are difficult to recount in
     full.
Oh sir, look at the edge of the sky where calling birds return.
Crying "Zhou Qiu."

MEDIUMISTIC WRITINGS IN THE VOICE OF THE GOD

THE VENERABLE KING OF BROAD COMPASSION'S WRITING ENCOURAGING FILIAL PIETY

That which the world does not lack is the Five Relationships. That which a
person needs in life is loyalty and filial piety. If you possess loyalty, then you
put your heart into serving the nation and the people, revering the court and
bringing peace to the common people. Such a man has power and rank. As for
the word "filial piety," this is the road that every ignorant man or woman must
follow. I was born in the Tongguang reign-period of the Latter Tang dynasty
(923–925). Although young, I indeed displayed exceptional qualities. However,
at the time both my parents were impoverished. The Way of our family was
meager and simple. When I was little, my heavenly nature was wholehearted.
I took filial piety toward my parents as the basis [of my conduct]. I shepherded
sheep for people and fed cattle. I used my earnings to provide the amount
needed to feed my parents breakfast and dinner. When my father had died but
my old mother was still alive, I followed her and moved to Shishan so she
would be happy with me sitting at her side, always staying close by. When the
cultivation of filial piety was complete, my heavenly nature manifested. The
High Emperor was pleased by my loyal, sincere, filial heart. He first ordered
immortal lads and friends in the Dao to assist me to accomplish the aim of
transcending and sloughing off [the body]. When it came to the Tianfu reign-

period of the Latter Tang dynasty, I sat on an ancient vine and transformed by sloughing [off my body]. Although my buddha bones had always been intact, still it was my Way of filial piety that moved the heart of Heaven. Later I protected the nation and the people, frequently manifesting mystic experiences, so the people of the village set up a temple and worshiped in it. The court recorded my merit and enfeoffed me, and [my cult] could be said to have flourished. Now, since I was an accomplished immortal buddha, so my saintly father and saintly mother too were enfeoffed with honors. They were buried together in the old neighborhood of Qingxi. Now why is it that, year after year, people go up to their graves? This has to do with my father and mother being completely close to me, [yet] I could not live to see many days. When I was just over ten years old, I transformed by sloughing off my body, so I could not long provide the joy of staying by my parents' knees. To this day my heart is still sorrowful. Therefore I composed the Rites for Ascending to the Graves, in order to record [their] mercy which never ceases in a thousand autumns. And everyone comprehends my feelings, so people of the world follow me up to the grave. And they could be said to be very numerous. Now I had not thought that after becoming a buddha, my *hun* and *po* souls would still stay before my father and mother. That I would become an Immortal, and yet be bowing and kneeling in rites [to my parents] that have had honors repeatedly bestowed upon them. Alas, who is not someone's child? And who has no father or mother, yet can avoid strong selfishness? My protection goes only to good people. If people of the world know how to serve parents well and regularly go up to the graves [of my parents], then I will comfort them and bestow good fortune on them. Yet if there are those who do not know how to serve parents well, and do it all for fame or advantage, yet follow me up to the graves, how could they actually come with me up to the graves and not reflect on my deep feelings? If they can painfully right their former wrongs and filially revere their parents at home, loving their brothers as friends, single-heartedly with all their might follow the Five Relationships truly, sincerely without dissatisfaction, then they will become complete men between Heaven and Earth. Yesterday I received the High Emperor's command, ordering me to transmit this message to the people of the world. Now the quality of feeling in one heart can bring all forms of good fortune. That is what I look forward to with this minor expression of my intent. Thus he descended into a medium in the Zhenfu Academy on Guangxu *dingqiu* (1877).

THE PRECIOUS INSTRUCTIONS OF THE VENERABLE KING OF BROAD COMPASSION

I am the Blue Lotus Lad Spirit. Yesterday, together with some friends in the Dao, we roamed the dusty world. At times the wind made a soughing sound, deep was the color of the moon, and my heart was greatly pleased by this.

Suddenly the conversation turned to the sunken ways of the world, and the fallen weakness of human hearts. So I could not stop sighing, alas, and was endlessly sad. Thereupon I paid a respectful visit to the King of Broad Compassion on Phoenix Mountain. I begged him to send down Precious Instructions to guide the ignorant and the confused. The Venerable King said: Excellent! Excellent! I have observed the people of the world. Generally speaking they are disloyal as ministers, unfilial as children, unfriendly as older brothers, disrespectful as younger brothers, unharmonious when married, and unreliable as friends. Either they lie and act false or they are deviant and hateful. They either cheat orphans and widows or they deceive good people. Or they act licentiously with unrestrained desires, happily behaving like dogs. Or they abort fetuses and drown daughters, thoughtlessly giving in to their fierce hearts. Or with sharp tongues say what they like, and their phrases harm the harmony of Heaven and Earth. Or they use knives and brushes at this work and create sprouts of hills and mountains. Or in the name of sacrificing to spirits they carelessly slaughter livestock. Or with an eye to immediate profits, they slaughter cattle and lambs. The many kinds of their crimes I cannot bear are too numerous to describe in full. Even more despicable, a precious character of but a single brushstroke is a source of great concern to Confucian scholars, but merchants completely disregard [precious words]. Either they display brocade characters on the sides of firecrackers, which when exploded send the ashes flying into the dust and dirt, or they print "Originary Treasure" on top of gold paper, and after they burn it they cast the ashes into the mud. It has got to the point that men and women coming into the temple to offer incense also take incense and paper [spirit-money], printed with words, and casually toss them away, treading on them as they come and go. Generally no one can even point out their confused behavior. Ah! At first I would not have thought that under the sun by the rivers and streams things could come to this. Blue Lotus, since you have asked, from now on let there not be such cause for grief. From now on, proclaim this for me to the people of the world. To those who are able to reverently follow my instructions, I will bring protection, silently in the dark. [I will] change misfortune to good fortune, bestow good luck, and remove ill omens. If there still be those who dare ridicule my words and do not obey my instructions and teachings, I will come to them silently in the dark and increase my examination [of their conduct], measure the lightness or severity of their crimes, and let fall their punishments. There will not be even a moment of laxity. I have stated this so. Thereupon [the Blue Lotus Lad] kowtowed, together with his friends in the Dao, to the Venerable King. Receiving his command they withdrew, and just now I met up with this noble group of mediums, so I made a special visit to completely recount [this]. You all can sincerely and solemnly follow these Saintly Instructions, and also everywhere exhort the [people of the] realm, causing everyone to rise out of their ignorant straits and obtain immeasurable good fortune. On the date of the full

moon of the seventh lunar month, in the *jimao* year of the Guangxu period, the Blue Lotus Lad Spirit followed orders and descended into a medium in the Kuiyin Academy.
(August 25, 1879)

— 25 —

Calling on Souls and Dealing with Spirits:
Three Lahu Ritual Texts

Anthony R. Walker

The Lahu people of southwestern Yunnan Province, whose language belongs to the Yi division of the widespread (India to Vietnam) Tibeto-Burman family, had no tradition of writing until early this century. American Baptist missionaries then introduced them to a Roman script invented by missionaries working among Lahu in Burma. A few years after the founding of the People's Republic, Chinese linguists modified or "reformed" this missionary romanization. In the past, however, the only way Lahu were able to record and send simple messages was by carving notches, rubbing charcoal, and sticking chicken feathers on pieces of wood. Their ethnic wisdom, including ritual traditions, was passed from generation to generation by word of mouth. The three texts presented here—one to recall a wandering soul to its proper human abode, the second to propitiate the tutelary spirit of the house, and the third to exorcise a malicious life-threatening spirit—offer a glimpse of the oral heritage of this preliterate mountain folk.

Today there are well over half a million Lahu, most of them (411, 476 according to the 1990 Chinese national census) living in far southwestern Yunnan (mostly in the four border prefectures of Lincang, Simao, Xishuangbanna, and Honghe, and a few hundred in Yuxi Prefecture, to the north of Simao). In 1953, in pursuance of the Chinese Communist Party's policy of regional autonomy for national minority peoples, the Lancang Lahu People's Autonomous County was set up in Simao Prefecture. In the following year, the neighboring Menglian Dai, Lahu, and Va Autonomous County was set up. Much more recently, the Lahu have come to participate in two other autonomous counties: the Shuangjiang Lahu, Va, Blang, and Dai Autonomous County of Lincang Prefecture, which was set up in 1985, and the Zhenyuan Yi, Hani, and Lahu Autonomous County of Simao Prefecture, established in 1990. There are also significant Lahu populations in Myanmar (Burma) (perhaps as many as 140,000) and Thailand (60,000), and much smaller numbers in Laos (possibly 2,000) and Vietnam (around 4,000). There are even a few dozen Lahu refugees from Laos who live in southern California, where "green card" (and doubtless much else) has been added to the Lahu lexicon. Lahu populations outside of China are descendants of people who left the Middle Kingdom from the late eighteenth to early nineteenth centuries onward, to seek less crowded soils or to escape political oppression.

Traditionally a mountain-dwelling, mostly slash-and-burn dry-rice farming folk, Lahu in some areas of southern Yunnan began to learn wet-rice plow agriculture from Han immigrants beginning in the late eighteenth century, while in other areas they picked up similar skills from their long-time lowland neighbors, the Dai people. But not all Lahu live in environments where irrigated rice agriculture is a viable alternative to their traditional slash-and-burn technology.

Lahu villages (comprising anywhere from a dozen to several hundred houses) are frequently found in the high mountains, but some are located on the fringes of the valleys, where they have access both to flat land ideal for wet-rice production and to mountain land for hunting, gathering, and the cultivation of dry-land crops of various kinds. The houses may be Chinese-style brick- or mud-walled structures, built directly on the ground and with tiled roofs, or Dai-style wooden or bamboo stilt houses with grass-thatched roofs. In modern China these "natural villages," as the Chinese call them, are controlled by village committees, but traditionally there was a headman known as the "master" of the village, who was assisted, informally, by the elders of his community. Ritual specialists were frequently among the most influential of such elders. Even today, despite four decades of instruction in "scientific agriculture" and, on-and-off, in the follies of supernaturalism as well, ritual specialists still command more than passing respect in at least some Lahu communities.

Traditional Lahu ideas and practices concerning the supernatural are quite varied. This is to be expected for a people whose ethnic unity rests on neither political nor sociological but rather linguistic and ethnohistorical criteria; a people, moreover, who recognize among themselves several major cultural divisions. In some parts of Lancang County, Lahu religious ideas have been much influenced by the teachings of an eighteenth-century Chinese Mahāyāna Buddhist monk who journeyed there from his monastery near Dali to be hailed as something of a messiah in many Lahu communities. Then again, in many of the the more southerly areas of Lahu settlement, especially in Xishuangbanna Prefecture and Gengma and Menglian counties of Simao Prefecture, where the dominant cultural tradition was that of the Theravāda Buddhist Dai peoples, Theravāda ideas and local Buddhist ritual practices have permeated many a Lahu community, if not always in a thoroughly coherent manner.

If, through much diversity of belief and practice, we are to identify a "traditional" ideological core of Lahu supernaturalism, this is probably best labeled as "animo-theistic." On the one hand, there is among these Lahu people a pervading belief in "soul force," which "animates" not only humankind, but also animals, trees, waterways, pathways, rocks, rice, sun, moon, lightning, rainbows, guns, and so forth—indeed most of the objects of the natural environment to which

Lahu accord special significance. On the other hand, there is also a belief in a supreme, Heaven- and Earth-creating divinity (G'ui-sha), whom Chinese scholars like to call the Lahu "Sky God" (Tian Shen), and whom Christian missionaries have found little difficulty in identifying with the God of the Semitic tradition. For the most part, this creator-divinity is conceived as a transcendent power (although arguably of greater everyday significance to many a Lahu than is the creator-divinity of closely related minority folk such as Hani and Lisu). It is doubt-less the spirits (*ne*), rather than the creator-divinity, that are of more immediate concern to most Lahu, at least to those who have not fully endorsed either Marxist or Christian ideological positions.

Traditional Lahu explanations for sickness and misfortune, where no natural explanation is immediately evident, frequently have recourse to indigenous the-ories of spirits and soul force. Lahu call the human soul, or the spiritual "coun-terpart" of a person's physical body, the *aw-ha*. The notion of "counterpart" is obviously an important one, since they use the very same word for a photograph (the photo of a tree is a "tree counterpart," a photo of a house a "house counter-part," etc.; a map is called an "earth counterpart"). Frequently Lahu talk, sing, and pray about this counterpart as if it were a single entity. It is evident when talking to them, however, that they also conceive of it as divisible into several distinct entities (one, at least, remaining with the body until its physical death, while others depart now and then, causing the body to suffer one or another variety of sickness). Into just how many separate entities one may divide the spiritual counterpart is a matter of considerable disagreement. Dai neighbors of the Lahu frequently mention the number 32, and some Lahu follow suit; others are not so dogmatic, or else their dogma is a different one.

There is more or less general agreement that the spiritual counterpart, or one of its component entities, is susceptible to spirit attack, which may take a num-ber of different forms. The spirit may "bite" the soul (the Lahu word is exactly the same for a dog biting one's leg, or a child one's breast), it may entice the soul from the body, or it may cause unbalance between soul and body by itself taking up residence in the body of its victim, in place of, or alongside, the right-ful spiritual counterpart. In any of these situations, Lahu say, the physical body will suffer. Sometimes specific physical symptoms of illness are identified as characteristic of attack by some particular spirit. For example, a swelling of hands and feet, accompanied by an itchiness of the skin, is associated with the attack of the lightning spirit; a sharp, stabbing pain at the center of the forehead suggests the sun spirit; fever, loss of appetite and abdominal swelling are asso-ciated with the rainbow spirit. But identification of the responsible spirit may not always be so easy. Many maladies or other types of misfortune are believed to require the diagnostic skills of a specialist for positive identification of their supernatural origins. Such specialists may interpret their own dream experiences or, more frequently, engage in divination to obtain the information their clients desire. A common form of divination involves careful measurement of a piece of cloth with outstretched and opposed fingers and thumb. Having made his initial measurement, the specialist prays, "If this person has offended such-and-such a spirit, let my second measurement be greater/lesser than the first one"; he then remeasures the cloth and so obtains an answer. Once a spirit has been identified, the specialist will prepare for a short propitiatory rite or else recommend that his client seek the services of another specialist more adept at such propitiation than himself. The ritual paraphernalia for spirit propitiation rites varies considerably from one Lahu group to another but generally involves the construction of a simple altar or offering post, the latter topped by a leaf cup. Onto the altar or into the leaf cup are placed one or two simple offerings, notably grains of uncooked rice, beeswax candles, and strips of colored cloth or thread. Commonly a fowl is sacrificed as the major offering to the spirit.

If the specialist determines the sickness to be the consequence of soul-loss, then a recall ceremony is in order. Again, ritual details vary from one Lahu group to the next but seem most often to involve the use of a fowl of the opposite sex from that of the patient (some Lahu mentioned to the writer that the soul sees the fowl as a beautiful human being of the opposite sex and will be attracted to it). Sometimes the officiating specialist carves a rough replica, a few inches in length, of the ladder used to enter a Lahu stilt house. He may also ask the patient's family to assemble the family's jewelry, together with a piece of clean white cloth and some cotton threads in a cane basket. In his recall prayer the specialist requests the wandering soul to return to him following the light of the beeswax candles he has lit for the ceremony; he asks the soul to climb the house ladder, don the jewelry and clothing (symbolized by the length of cloth) that has been prepared for it, and come up to the very claws of the chicken. At the conclusion of the rite, the specialist makes the chicken's bound feet scratch at the entrance of the house, or else on the fireplace inside. This symbolizes the return of the soul to its proper place. Finally the specialist binds his patient's wrist with cotton thread to tie the returned soul into his or her body.

For an exorcism, the ritual materials are not necessarily more complex than those for a simple propitiation, although special transport—perhaps a horse and elephant roughly carved from the root of the wild banana, or a raft of banana stems and twigs of wood—may be offered, in addition to rice, beeswax candles, and items of the family's silver jewelry, or perhaps imitations thereof, made of pieces of broken pots or pans. The major difference between simple propitiation and exorcism lies in the words the specialist utters. In the first case he begs the spirit to accept the gifts and cease to harm his patient; in the second, he demands that the spirit leave, sometimes calling on a supernatural patron to assist his endeavor to banish the offending spirit.

At the conclusion of any such rite in which a chicken has been sacrificed, chicken bone divination is generally performed to determine whether the spirit has accepted the offerings, or whether the soul has returned to its proper abode. The chicken's upper leg bones (femora) are cleaned of flesh and carefully examined for the small holes (foramina), of which there are usually two on each bone. Into these the specialist inserts thin slivers of bamboo, about the size of toothpicks, and reads the oracle according to the direction in which the slivers point and whether they fit tightly or loosely into the holes.

If a client fails to recover after such a ritual, sufficient explanations are at hand to forestall skepticism about the value of such time-honored procedures. It could be that the spirit was wrongly identified. Perhaps the soul never left the body at all. Spirit or soul may have rejected the offerings. Or maybe the specialist himself lacked sufficient competency or power. New divinations may then be ordered and new rites performed. At the very least—and the psychosomatic import is not to be underestimated—the patient is made to feel that action is being taken to relieve the symptoms from which he or she is suffering.

The original Lahu language text of "The Recall of the Wandering Soul" may be found in Anthony R. Walker, "*Aw_v Ha Hku Ve*: The Lahu Nyi Rite for the Recall of a Wandering Soul," *Journal of the Royal Asiatic Society of Great Britain and Ireland,* part 1 (1972): 16–29. The original Lahu language text of "The Propitation of the Guardian Spirit of the House" may be found in Walker, "Propitiating the House Spirit among the Lahu Nyi (Red Lahu) of Northern Thailand: Three Lahu Texts with an Ethnographic Introduction," *Bulletin of the Institute of Ethnology,* Academia Sinica (Nankang, Taiwan) 44 (1977): 47–60. The original Lahu language text of "The Exorcism of Malicious Spirits of the Bad Dead" may be found in Walker, "Exorcising the *Jaw* and *Meh_v* Spirits: Three Lahu Nyi (Red Lahu) Ritual Texts from North Thailand," *Contributions to Southeast Asian Ethnography* 7 (1988): 51–94.

Further Reading

Anthony R. Walker, "Divisions of the Lahu People," *Journal of the Siam Society* 62.2 (1974): 253–68; Walker, "The Lahu People: An Introduction," in *Highlanders in Thailand,* ed. John McKinnon and Wanat Bhruksasri (Kuala Lumpur: Oxford University Press, 1983), pp. 227–37.

The Recall of a Wandering Soul

1. Ha o . . . h, Ha o . . . h! Oh chicken (the bird, with legs tightly bound, that the specialist holds as he chants the recall prayer), within the four corners of this village, put back the souls of the womenfolk into the bodies of the womenfolk, put back the souls of the menfolk into the bodies of the menfolk; do not allow them to wander away from the master of their house, do not permit them to separate from the mistress of their house.

2. Oh soul of this child, if you have become a yellow bird, if you have become a green bird [that is, any kind of bird], living on a white tree, they say you will have no happiness, they say you will have no safe place; they say you will be lost between the feet of a bird of prey, they say you will be lost between the hands of a bird of prey.

3. If you have become an animal of the forest, living between the hills and the streams, they say you will find no safe place; the safe place is at the side of the master of the house, the happy place is at the side of the mistress of the house.

4. If you live between the hills and the streams, they say you will have no safe place; they say you will be lost between the jaws of a white tiger, between the jaws of a yellow tiger; so if you have gone away this night (performing the rite at night allows the soul to return by darkness, so avoiding shame or "loss of face," the fear of which might cause it to linger away from its human owner), come back now along these silver steps (the replica house ladder that the specialist has prepared for the rite); come back to the four corners of this house and put on this silver jewelry, put on this golden jewelry.

5. Do not obey the voices of death, do not obey the voices of sickness; they say in the land of the dead the houses are made of banana leaves; they say the rice over there is the rice of death; they say in the land of the dead you may never wear gold, they say you may never wear silver; so tonight come quickly back!

6. Come back and sit down at this rice table, come back to the fireplace and put on this silver jewelry, come back and put on this golden jewelry; come back and dress in these silk clothes, come back and dress in these smooth clothes.

7. They say in the land of the dead there is nothing to drink, they say there is nothing to eat; there are hills and the hills are infertile, there are streams and the streams are infertile; they say the houses of the dead are of banana leaves, they say the rice is the rice of death; they say in the land of the dead you cannot wear silver, you cannot wear gold; so tonight come back between the feet of this chicken, between the hands of this chicken (the bird's claws which are to release the soul).

8. Tonight, if you have gone away, come back to this sieve; if you have gone away come back to this winnowing tray (common household objects that here stand for the house itself); if you have gone visiting the ancestors, come back now along this red thread; if you have gone visiting the ancestors, come back now along this white thread. (On occasion such threads are tied between two posts to represent the handrail of a symbolic bridge over which a soul or spirit is invited to pass; it is possible that a similar meaning is intended here.)

9. Ha o . . . h! Tonight, if you have gone away, come back along these silver steps, come back to this fireside, where we have prepared for you a white market with nine divisions, where we have prepared for you a yellow market with nine divisions (a great market); come eat free of cost, come drink free of cost!

10. Do not obey the voices of death, do not obey the voices of sickness; do not leave the children of this house, do not leave the master of this house.

11. Oh chicken, within the four corners of this village, put the women's souls back into the bodies of the womenfolk; put the men's souls back into the bodies of the menfolk.

12. Oh, if the women's souls live between the hills and the streams, they say they will have no safe place; if the men's souls live between the waters and the rocks, they say they will enjoy no happiness; come back, for happiness is at the side of the master of the house, happiness is at the side of the mistress of the house.

13. Ha o . . . h, ha o . . . h! Come back! Hear the sounds within the four corners of the village and come back! Hear the voice of this chicken and come back!

14. If you are visiting the ancestors, come back along this red string; if you are visiting the ancestors, come back along this white string.

15. Has the soul come back? It has returned!

The Propitiation of the Guardian Spirit of the House

1. Ha! This evening, at this place, oh blesser of this house (the tutelary house spirit), order and bestow upon us this boon, that the womenfolk and the menfolk, the big and the small, the children and the grandchildren, every person in the very same manner enjoy untroubled thoughts.

2. You four blessers of this house, you who watch over us and who shield us, within the four corners of this house, inside the house and at the entrance of the house, let there be no troubled thoughts; let men of evil intent not prevail against us, let malicious spirits not harm us.

3. Ha! Blesser of the four corners of this house, three times in one day shield and protect us, three times in one night [that is, all the time] shield and protect us.

4. This evening I order but one time, you please order nine times that all of us be separated, all of us be protected, from all house troubles. (The householder humbles himself before the greater powers of the tutelary spirit.)

5. At your side, blesser of the house, I again light these pure beeswax candles [to guide the spirit to the site of the ritual performance], I again stretch out my hand in supplication, I again offer my prayer.

6. Within the four corners of this house, oh blesser of this house, three times in one day again shield and again protect us from all house troubles, spare us all from troubled sleep.

7. This boon order upon and grant to this house, that neither the big nor the small be wracked by troubled thoughts, that none of us suffer from death nor from sickness, that we suffer no decay.

8. Blesser of the house, all-true, all-seeing blesser of the house, this boon order and grant that, within the four corners of the house, men of evil intent may not prevail against us, malicious spirits may not not harm us.

9. Three times in one day, three times in one night, ensure that the lives of the animals suffer no decay; let the animals' hairs not fall out; you who watch over all our animals, you all-true, all-seeing blesser of the house, all-true, all-precious blesser of the house, watch over all these animals; let the animals' hairs not fall out, let the animals' lives suffer no decay; this boon order and bestow upon us.

10. Oh blesser of the house, within the four corners of this house may the womenfolk and the menfolk, the big and the small, enjoy easy thoughts; let there be no troubled thoughts, either behind or in front; let men of evil intent not prevail against us, let malicious spirits not harm us; at this one corner within the four corners of the house [where the house's altar is located], I once again search for this boon.

11. Three times in one day, three times in one night, within the four corners of this house, I again stretch out my hand, I again pray to the side of the all-true, the all-powerful father up there (the creator-divinity G'ui-sha).

The Exorcism of Malicious Spirits of the Bad Dead

1. Pi-ya has great strength! Kui-ya has great strength! (two names of the same supernatural entity) Long long ago, when Mother Ai-ma created the earth (among some Lahu, Ai-ma is said to be the female counterpart to the male creator-divinity, G'ui-sha), for thirty-three years Pi-ya was supported, for thirty-three years Kui-ya was supported, each day he was fed nine full baskets of iron seed; long long ago, when the earth was created, Pi-ya projected his power against the earth, and the earth hardened; today he cuts off from the people of this household the shadow of death, he removes from them the shadow of sickness. (This passage refers to a version of the creation myth, which relates that, after earth had been created, its surface was soft and entirely

unsuitable for human habitation. To rectify this, G'ui-sha sought the help of the "great spirit" Pi-ya, whom he proceeded to keep for many years on a diet of iron. In this manner Pi-ya acquired vast power that, when he projected it against objects of the natural world, caused miraculous happenings. The first of these was to harden the surface of the earth, making it suitable for human habitation.)

2. When Pi-ya took hold of the leaves of the white pine tree and projected his power against them, the leaves became needles; when he took hold of the white tiger and projected his power against it, the white tiger became striped; when he took hold of the Great Barbet and projected his power against it, the bird's tail became red; when he took hold of the Blue-throated Barbet and projected his power against it, the bird's head became red; when he took hold of the Spotted-necked Dove and projected his power against it, the bird's neck became spotted; when he took hold of the Castanopsis tree and projected his power against it, the tree put forth many branches; when he took hold of the Lagerstroemia tree and projected his power against it, the tree put forth many branches; when he took hold of the duck and projected his power against it, the duck's feet became webbed; when Pi-ya seeks out you malicious spirits, Pi-ya is very strong; when Kui-ya seeks out you malicious spirits, Kui-ya is very strong!

3. You male death-bearing spirits, unload your spirit feet and be gone! You female death-bearing spirits, rise up on your spirit feet and be gone! (The "death-bearing spirits" are malicious supernatural entities that seek to bring human beings to violent bloody ends by gunshot, lightning strike, drowning, murder, suicide, death in childbirth, etc. Lahu particularly fear such violent ends because, so they say, the soul force of the victim may not gain access to the land of the dead but is transformed instead into a lonely, vengeful, and highly malicious spirit.)

4. When Pi-ya seeks out you malicious spirits, then Pi-ya is very strong! When Kui-ya seeks out you malicious spirits, then Kui-ya is very strong! Be gone, evil spirits, to the place where the thirty-three hills join together, where the thirty-three rivers join together (the ends of the earth). When Pi-ya seeks out you malicious spirits, then Pi-ya is very strong! When Kui-ya seeks out you malicious spirits, then Kui-ya is very strong! When Pi-ya takes hold of the *ma-sha* tree and projects his power, the tree's bark begins to bleed!

5. I make offerings to you death-dealing spirits and send you away down there, to the nine bends of the rivers, to the place where the great mountains come together, the great rivers join together; I present you with offerings and send you away to the country down there (the ends of the earth); do not forget Pi-ya's words, do not forget Kui-ya's words!

6. The womenfolk of this household are suffering from bone sickness [i.e., any sickness], so unload your spirit feet and be gone, turn around and be gone with you! These menfolk have bone sickness; they are unable to turn their heads toward the sky! Put the bone sickness of these womenfolk underneath this earth.

7. Pi-ya's hands are on the uphill side of the house, Kui-ya's hands are on the downhill side of the house [i.e., Pi-ya's hands protect the house]; it is said that when Pi-ya seeks out you malicious spirits, Pi-ya is very strong!

— 26 —

A Funeral Chant of the Yi Nationality

Mark Bender

The Yi Nationality is one of the largest officially recognized ethnic minority groups in China. It comprises over eighty subgroups, with names such as Lipo, Lolopo, and Nosu. The Yi language, which has several dialects, is in the Tibeto-Burman language family. Over five million Yi (pronounced like the Old English "ye") live in villages scattered throughout the mountainous regions of Yunnan, Sichuan, Guizhou, and Guangxi. Most Yi are farmers, raising rice, wheat, and buckwheat in the river bottomlands and in terraced fields.

The forebears of the modern Yi were probably part of the Nanzhao and Dali kingdoms, which flourished between the eighth and thirteenth centuries C.E., controlling much of Southwest China and parts of Southeast Asia. During the Ming dynasty (1368–1644), large numbers of Chinese migrated from eastern China into the southwest, particularly into Yunnan, where the Yi have been strongly influenced by Chinese customs. At present, most Yi live in specially designated autonomous prefectures or counties that are administered locally, usually by Yi officials.

Despite steady antireligious propaganda between the 1950s and 1970s, one of the traditional institutions that has resisted the forces of change in some Yi communities is that of the shaman, or *bimo*. In these areas Yi shaman are still active as bearers and interpreters of oral, and sometimes written, religious and folk traditions. The ancient Yi writings, today understood by only a few shamans, record mythic epics, legends, folksongs, divination rites, funeral chants, and geographical, astronomical, and herbal lore.

Shamans perform at weddings, house raisings, and other communal events, usually singing mythical creation epics and other narrative poems. The shaman's most important task, however, is the conducting of funerals, which in some cases may take years to complete. Each step of the funeral process is accompanied by a chant. In northern Yunnan, major steps include cleansing the corpse, closing the coffin, and directing one of the deceased's three souls on the proper road to the Tree of Forgetfulness. Once past the tree, the soul forgets everything in this world and rises within a multicolored tower of light into Paradise to dwell with his or her ancestors. The other two souls stay in the grave or family altar, one in each place. While performing the funeral chants, the shaman wears a felt-covered bamboo hat and a felt cloak, ringing a brass bell and holding a pine staff from which hangs a collection of eagle claws.

"Cleansing the Corpse" was collected by local Yi researchers in Moding County in the Chuxiong Yi Nationality Autonomous Prefecture in the early 1980s. The chant has many features common to Yi funeral discourse, including the description of the diligent search for the proper ritual materials (or, in some chants, life-saving medicine), direct address of the dead, repetitions and parallelisms in structure and imagery, and the use of a question-and-answer format to convey information. The convention of using a specific number (such as in the phrase "seventy old shamans") to indicate the concept of "many" is also common.

The first lines of "Cleansing the Corpse" act as a sort of prologue, situating the chant in the ethical and metaphysical system of the local culture. The values of diligence and persistence in activities until properly completed are illustrated by the bee and plow imagery. The busy bees constantly fly in and out of their hives (many Yi farmhouses have beehives under the eaves). In the process of plowing, the large clods are roughly turned in the furrows with one pass of the plow, but several more passes are needed to make the soil suitable for tilling. Water figures importantly in the next line, linked with images of change within the ongoing cycle of generations of human life. Finally, the images of the bamboos being eaten by the red worms suggests the inevitability of death. The next lines show that when death finally comes, a shaman is to be called and preparations made for the proper care of the corpse and souls.

An important theme in the rest of the chant is the necessity of securing the proper articles for cleansing the corpse—the vines for binding the deceased's limbs, and the water and bowl for rinsing. These articles must be "pure"; thus the vine is white, the water clear, and the basin carved from a naturally grown tree. Without these, the corpse cannot be properly purified and the soul will be hindered on its way to Paradise. A related theme is that of the importance of communicating to the dead that the proper actions are being made on her or his behalf, that the shaman and the deceased's family have gone to great lengths to secure the proper materials. Aside from being a show of respect for the dead, the funeral ritual as a whole is important because it is considered highly undesirable to have unappeased ghosts lingering around the household.

From another perspective, the chant reflects a deep sensitivity to features of the local landscape and an intimacy with the process of rice-raising and the seasonal weather cycle, which may include periods of drought. Moreover, ideas such as the existence of multiple souls, the accepting attitude toward death (at least the deaths of older people), the place of the individual in the scheme of generations, the motifs of trees, bamboos, and water dragons, and the process of a shaman guiding souls to the afterworld are widespread among ethnic groups in Southwest China.

The song was performed by Pu Xingke and recorded by Pu Qiwang. The written text is from Zhou Zhi, ed., *Yizu wenxue ziliao* (*Yi Literary Materials*) (Moding, Yunnan: Moding xian wenhua guan, n.d.). This collection of songs, printed for a small local audience, was given to the translator in 1986. All the songs were recorded in a highly colloquial Mandarin Chinese, though the original language was probably the Lolopo dialect of Yi.

Further Reading

Mark Bender, trans., "Cutting the New Year's Firewood—A Yi Folksong," *Chicago Review* 39 (1993): 256–57; Alan Y. Dessaint, *Minorities of Southwest China: An Introduction to the Yi (Lolo) and Related Peoples and an Annotated Bibliography* (New Haven: HRAF Press, 1980); Han-Yi Feng and John Knight Shryock, "The Historical Origins of the Lolo," *Harvard Journal of Asiatic Studies* 3 (1937): 103–27; Lin Yueh-hua, *The Lolo of Liang Shan (Liang-Shan i-chia)*, ed. Wu-chi Liu, trans. Ju-shu Pan (New Haven: HRAF Press, 1961); Leo J. Moser, *The Chinese Mosaic: The Peoples and Provinces of China* (Boulder: Westview Press, 1985).

Cleansing the Corpse

When the rainy season comes,
honeybees fly out of their hives.
On the twelfth day the big bees come out,
on the thirteenth day the small bees come out.
All that come out are not big bees,
all that come out are not small bees,
yet those that come out, will come out
again and again.

First the plow cuts deeply
turning up the earth in the fields.
Then shallow cuts are needed
to break the earthen clods.
The plow cuts deeply, then cuts shallow,
preparing the soil for planting.

Water lays in the rice fields along the rivers;
water flows on forever in the dragon-stirred springs.
Tree leaves change by the waterside
dropping to the water
to circle 'round and 'round.
Time flows like a mountain waterfall
passing just so fast.

Red worms eat even the tallest bamboos.
They eat them up toward the sky,
they eat them down into the earth.
When the worms eat their way to the highest point in the sky,
when the worms eat their way to the deepest point in the earth,
then seventy old shamans
will come to speak to you,
will come to talk to you,
will come to speak Yi to you,
will come to cleanse your corpse.

What will be used to cleanse it?
The corpse-cleansing vine must be used.
Now, there are myriads of vines,
but which is the right one to use?

Seventy old shamans will help you find the right one.
They will search hard for three days,
they will search hard for three nights.
If they search for three days,
they will return in only two.
If they search for two days,
they will return in only one.

It was said that the corpse-cleansing vine
grew on the mountain tops.
Searching there, the shamans spied a clump of vines,
the stems of which were red,
and the leaves round in shape.
It was said that this was the corpse-cleansing vine—
but it was not the corpse-cleansing vine.
It was just a small, red vine.

It was said that the corpse-cleansing vine
grew halfway up the mountainsides.
Searching halfway up a mountainside,
the shamans spied a clump of vines,
the stems of which were a bluish yellow,
and the leaves of which had three sharp points.
It was said that this was the corpse-cleansing vine—
but it was not the corpse-cleansing vine.
It was just a vine for making bracelets.

It was said that the corpse-cleansing vine
grew in the mountain ravines.
Searching a mountain ravine,

the shamans spied a clump of vines,
the leaves of which were a bean-leaf blue,
the stems of which were a bluish yellow.
It was said that this was the corpse-cleansing vine—
but it was not the corpse-cleansing vine.
It was just a vine used for weaving
the baskets used to carry rice and sprouts.

It was said that the corpse-cleansing vine
grew just outside the mountains.
Searching the area just outside a mountain,
the shamans spied a clump of vines,
the leaves of which were as big as bean leaves,
the stems as thick as string and
measuring thirty feet in length.
It was said that this was the corpse-cleansing vine—
but it was not the corpse-cleansing vine.
It was just the vine used to tie up broom handles.

It was said that the corpse-cleansing vine
grew in earthen caves in the hills.
Searching at a cave,
the shamans spied a clump of vines,
the leaves of which were round and soft,
the stems of which were a chalky white.
A hoe was used to dig it out;
an axe was used to chop it out.
The hoe was used to dig, the axe to chop.
Thus, the corpse-cleansing vine was brought home.

The vine is in hand, but what of the water?
There is no way to cleanse the corpse without it.

In the First Month, a dry month, the shamans searched for water.
It was said that there was corpse-cleansing water—
but there was no corpse-cleansing water to be found.
Between the first and the fifteenth of the month they searched.
but found only enough water to fill a drinking bowl.

In the Second Month they searched for water.
It was said that there was corpse-cleansing water—
but there was no corpse-cleansing water to be found.
There was only water enough for sprinkling the rice seedlings.

In the Third Month they searched for water.
It was said that there was corpse-cleansing water—

but there was no corpse-cleansing water to be found.
There was only enough water for washing the oxen's' backs.

In the Fourth Month they searched for water.
It was said that there was corpse-cleansing water—
but there was no corpse-cleansing water to be found.
There was only enough water for the oxen to wet their feet.

In the Fifth Month they searched for water.
It was said that there was corpse-cleansing water—
but there was no corpse-cleansing water to be found.
There was only enough water for watering the transplanted seedlings.

In the Sixth Month they searched for water.
It was said that there was corpse-cleansing water—
but there was no corpse-cleansing water to be found.
There was only enough water for flooding the growing stalks.

In the Seventh Month they searched for water.
It was said that there was corpse-cleansing water—
but there was no corpse-cleansing water to be found.
There was only the early autumn rain water on the fields.

In the Eighth Month they searched for water.
It was said that there was corpse-cleansing water—
but there was no corpse-cleansing water to be found.
There was only the lowered water of harvest time.

In the Ninth Month they searched for water.
It was said that there was corpse-cleansing water—
but there was no corpse-cleansing water to be found.
There was only the water of the yellow, rain-soaked fields.

In the Tenth Month they searched for water.
It was said that there was corpse-cleansing water—
but there was no corpse-cleansing water to be found.
There was only the winter field water,
which is kept for spring planting.

In the Winter Month they searched for water.
It was said that there was corpse-cleansing water—
but there was no corpse-cleansing water to be found.
There was only enough water for pounding sticky-rice cakes.

In the Year's End Month they searched for water.
It was said that there was corpse-cleansing water—
but there was no corpse-cleansing water to be found.
There was only water enough for scalding the butchered hogs.

Seventy old shamans
began searching in the First Month
and searched until the year's final month,
but not a trace of the corpse-cleansing water was found.

It rains in the mountain peaks,
but no water collects in the caves.
Yet, when the shamans dug amidst the leaves
piled at the mouth of a cave,
clear, cool water flowed forth.
This was to be the corpse-cleansing water.

After finding the corpse-cleansing vine,
after finding the corpse-cleansing water,
they still needed the corpse-cleansing basin.

To the south, in Luoji Village,
the whole town makes ceramic basins.
It was said that they were corpse-cleansing basins,
but they are not.
They are used for storing vegetables.

To the west, at Stone River Village,
the whole town makes iron basins.
It was said that they were corpse-cleansing basins,
but they are not.
They are used for boiling food.

In the mountains was a huge tree,
which when carved yielded a huge hollow.
This was to be the corpse-cleansing basin.

We are now cleansing your face.
The more your eyes are rinsed,
the brighter they become.

We are now cleansing your body.
The more your body is cleansed,
the whiter it becomes.
We are now cleansing your hands and feet.
When cleansed, they will feel so very light.

Earthly Conduct

27

Abridged Codes of Master Lu for
the Daoist Community

Peter Nickerson

Lu Xiujing during his time was the foremost Daoist cleric in southern China. Born in 406, Lu hailed from Dongqian in Wuxing Commandery (modern Huzhou in Zhejiang Province); like many of the leading Daoist priests of the period, he came from an old southern aristocratic family. He also married into one, having been made at an early age to take as his wife a woman of the Tao family. Soon thereafter, Lu felt that he had been called to the religious life; he left his home and family, eventually establishing a hermitage or abbey on Mount Lu, southeast of the southern capital of Jiankang. Later he received the favor of Liu-Song Emperor Ming (r. 465–472), who built for him another establishment, the Hermitage for the Reverence of the Void (Chong xu guan) in the northern suburbs of the capital. He died in 477.

Lu is perhaps best known as the creator of the first catalogue of Daoist scriptures, his *Catalogue of the Scriptures of the Three Caverns* (*Sandong jingshu mulu*), and for systematizing the Lingbao scriptures and their associated rituals. However, the *Abridged Codes for the Daoist Community* (*Lu xiansheng daomen ke lue*), which bears his name, addresses a different issue: the organization of the Daoist church. More than simply the set of rules the title implies, the work is also a polemic that makes an impassioned case for the reform of the social organization and ritual practice of the Daoist religion. The text as we have it today also includes a commentary. A likely supposition is that it was the same commentator, perhaps a disciple, who created this "abridgment" of Lu Xiujing's rules based on other, longer writings of the Master. (Toward the end of the text, the copyists appear to have become confused about where the main text and the commentary begin and end; it would seem that the conclusion to the essay was entirely the work of the commentator.) It is also possible that Lu himself wrote the commentary.

The plan for reform the *Abridged Codes* sets out is presented as a continuation of the institutions that had been transmitted by Taishang Laojun, the Most High

Lord Lao, to the first Celestial Master, Zhang Daoling, in 142 C.E. At that time, according to the *Codes,* China's golden age was long in the past, and the world had arrived at the historical stage of "Lower Antiquity" (*xiagu*), a degenerate time in which people worshiped demonic spirits of the realm of the dead (the "Six Heavens"), especially slain soldiers, with lavish sacrificial meals of wine and meat. Such improper worship (in fact a caricature of popular god-cults) only worsened the situation, bringing people impoverishment, illness, and early death. The Daoist religion was revealed to provide a correct religious alternative to these popular, sacrificial cults. The early Daoists prohibited most forms of sacrifice: the "Pure Bond" (*qingyue*) between the Daoists and the gods decreed that popular gods and minor spirits would no longer receive sacrificial offerings (while the Daoist priests themselves would have to forgo money payments for their ritual services). Instead, communications with the true celestial powers were to be bureaucratic, that is, written in the same manner as the memorials sent by officials to the monarch. This was the ritual of "sending up petitions" to which the text refers. For instance, when a Daoist parishioner was ill, the appropriate procedure was for a priest to write and "send" (through visualization and meditation) a petition to the Celestial Bureaus. In the petition text, the patient confessed the sins that were the root cause of his or her illness, and the priest requested the responsible celestial deities—"civil and military officials"—to descend and rectify the problem.

The Way of the Celestial Masters began as far more than an antisacrificial movement and a cult of healing. Putting the traditional date of 142 aside, the Celestial Masters emerge historically as a "rebel" movement in Sichuan and southern Shaanxi during the last decades of the second century, under the leadership of Zhang Lu, purportedly Zhang Daoling's grandson. In this guise the movement is often called the Way of the Five Pecks of Rice. As an autonomous sect with an independent territorial base, the Way of the Celestial Masters had to be concerned also with social and political organization. Thus the Daoist statelet was divided into "parishes" (*zhi*) administered by priests called "Libationers" (*jijiu*). The contributions of rice assessed to members have even been interpreted as a tax, like the annual tax in grain levied by the state, although other sources call the rice payment for the healing services of the priests. (As noted above, payments of money were in theory prohibited.) In the *Abridged Codes,* such "pledges" (*xin*) or "offerings" (*gui*) appear in both contexts: as annual imposts levied on each Daoist household, and as offerings made in connection with the healing ritual of petitioning and other rites. Ostensibly the pledge-offerings were provided to requite the efforts of the assisting Celestial Officials; practically, since they normally included vegetarian foodstuffs and items of use to the priest, such as paper and writing brushes, they were ultimately to have been distributed to the priest, recluses, and the poor, with fearsome supernatural consequences for the priest who took more than his 30 percent.

In fact, the church structure the *Abridged Codes* attributes to Zhang Daoling is substantially more complex than the organization one can suppose actually to have existed under the Way of the Celestial Masters in the late second century.

According to the *Codes,* all Daoist families must possess household registers (*zhailu*) listing each resident member of the family. The family head is to return to the parish for each of the Three Assemblies (*sanhui*) held during the year so that the records can be updated, assuring that both the parish priest and the gods themselves will have the correct information. Accurate registration of the population had been a goal of Chinese regimes since the Warring States period. Just as the population registers were seen as the basis for state administration, for example the tax and corvée labor systems, so the Daoists insisted on good record-keeping as the foundation for the effective use of their bureaucratic healing and other rituals. In addition to the Three Assemblies, the communal religious life of the Daoists was also structured around the kitchen-feasts (*chu*) that were held to formalize transitional events such as births and marriages. (Despite the relative equality of men and women in the Way of the Celestial Masters—women also could be ordained as priests and Libationers—one may see in the instructions for kitchen-feasts the perpetuation of other attitudes.)

Similar worries about regulation and the maintenance of hierarchy are evident in the great concern the *Abridged Codes* expresses for the ordination and promotion of novices and priests according to set forms and in a strict sequence. Levels in the Daoist church hierarchy were symbolized by the registers (*lu*) each individual church member was supposed to possess. (This is why the family household registers are called in the *Codes* "auxiliary registers.") The higher the rank, the greater the number of registers possessed, the higher the celestial regions to which the adept had access, and the greater the number of spiritual forces under his or her command. The Daoist novice (*lusheng*) could, based on merit (and the ability to provide the requisite pledge-offerings) progress through a series of registers, passing from command over a single spirit-general to the possession of high parish office and the ability to summon a whole panoply of supernatural forces to the aid of the faithful. That church hierarchy was to have been reflected also in a graded code of ritual vestments (*fafu*).

Although the rhetorical form is very different, our text is still very much in the spirit of Daoist codes (*ke*). The fundamental meaning of *ke* is "class" or "category"; in Daoism, *ke* also denotes the Daoist liturgical rites themselves. The purpose both of Daoist organizational codes and of Daoist liturgy was to achieve harmony and order by means of *categorization.* Thus it is easy to see how early Daoism was so pervaded by the bureaucratic spirit. In social organization, the system of registers and initiatory grades brought all members of the Daoist community into a single hierarchy represented by the graded series of parishes and registers. Daoist ritual similarly was bureaucratized, as evinced by the primacy of the healing rite of petitioning Celestial Officials.

More practically, this drive to streamline the channels of religious authority led also to the prohibition of competing religious, technical, and magical practices—not only the sacrificial cults organized around spirit mediums (*wu*), but also medicine and, especially, divination. In the *Codes,* divination and mediumism are so little distinguished that creating calendrical and geomantic taboos and avoidances (such as unlucky days or times for certain activities, or for travel in certain directions), which was the province of diviners, is named simply as a form of spirit-mediumism. Since mediums and diviners were often the first recourse of average people seeking diagnoses and cures of medical or other problems, the Daoists' prohibition of competing practices was an attempt to reserve to Daoist priests the authority to dispense the benefits of religious ritual.

The *Abridged Codes* is a marvelous written statement of Daoist social and institutional organization. But to what extent were its tenets put into practice? In addressing this question, we must confront the same types of questions as are raised by all prescriptive, normative texts: we know what their authors thought *should* be done, but not necessarily what *was* done. This is particularly so for works like the *Codes,* which is written in a self-consciously reformist mode. The essay was composed precisely because, the author felt, the Daoists of his day were not adhering to the Celestial Master tradition. In this respect, the *Codes* has much in common with other Daoist reformist tracts of the fifth century, for instance, the *Scripture of the Inner Explanations of the Three Heavens* (*Santian neijie jing,* HY 1196), also written in the south, and the *Scripture of the Precepts Chanted by Lord Lao* (*Laojun yinsong jie jing,* HY 784), written in the north by Kou Qianzhi (fl. 425–448). (Kou in fact had tried to establish a Daoist theocracy, based on his reformed Way of the Celestial Masters—and with Kou himself as the new Celestial Master—under the protection of Emperor Taiwu of the Northern Wei dynasty.)

The *Abridged Codes* may have had a fairly narrow immediate audience—Lu Xiujing's biography shows him most often in the company of rulers, imperial princes, and elite religious—and these reforms may not have been put into effect with any kind of thoroughness. Still, the *Codes,* by criticizing the ostensibly corrupt practices of some Daoists, in fact provides a suggestive picture of Daoism beyond the confines of Lu's elite confraternity. According to the *Codes,* Daoists rarely attended the Three Assemblies or contributed the proper pledge-offerings, and thus the priests' name-registers were in disarray. Those who were ambitious to advance in the Way abandoned the regular sequence of promotion and obtained from unscrupulous priests numerous registers for which they were not qualified. Priests used only incomplete, corrupt models for their ritual documents and failed to dress in the ritual vestments that were appropriate to their ranks.

The text devotes a great deal of attention to the maintenance of the Quiet Room (*jingshi, jingshe, jing*), which each Daoist household was in theory to possess. It was particularly important as the room in which all of the priest's ritual communications with the Daoist celestial authorities were to take place. People's failure to build and maintain the Quiet Room properly is taken in the text as symptomatic of the decline of the church. Venal priests abused their offices to get rich offerings and fine meals and ended up "sleeping on the Quiet Room's altar and vomiting beside the petition table."

Lu Xiujing's activities and writings did indeed provide some of the early foundations for what, in ensuing centuries, became a thriving network of Daoist abbeys (*guan*). However, as shown by the kinds of practices to which both other sources and the criticisms in the *Abridged Codes* attest, much was going on in Daoist practice beyond the narrow borders of Lu's own circle. Once outside a well-defined, small territory, the Daoists could no longer impose sectarian discipline upon their clients, and instead were thrown into competition with both Buddhist and popular practitioners, often largely on the basis merely of perceived ritual efficacy. The *Codes,* continuing an old tradition, sought to reform the present by making it conform to the (reinterpreted) models and institutions of the past; the text also, often in spite of itself, shows indications of a very different future.

A full assessment of the impact of Lu Xiujing's activities and the reforms dictated by the *Codes* will have to await further study of medieval Daoist institutions. Already the work may be appreciated for the picture it provides of the religious landscape of fifth-century China (albeit a view from a very special angle), and of the attempts of leading representatives of the Daoist religion of the time to reshape that landscape. From the *Codes* one may also gain much insight into the bureaucratic mentality of the Way of the Celestial Masters. That mentality molded the Celestial Masters' liturgy, which remained the basis for Daoist ritual and church organization from that time onward.

The *Lu Xiansheng daomen ke lue* is no. 1119 in the Harvard-Yenching (HY) index of the Daoist Canon.

Further Reading

Catherine Bell, "Ritualization of Texts and Textualization of Ritual in the Codification of Daoist Liturgy," *History of Religions* 27.4 (1988): 366–92; Masayoshi Kobayashi, "The Celestial Masters under the Eastern Jin and Liu-Song Dynasties," *Taoist Resources* 3.2 (May 1992): 17–45; Henri Maspero, *Taoism and Chinese Religion,* trans. Frank A. Kierman, Jr. (Amherst: University of Massachusetts Press, 1981), esp. books V and VII; Anna Seidel, "Early Taoist Ritual," *Cahiers d'Extrême-Asie* 4 (1988): 199–204; Rolf A. Stein, "Religious Taoism and Popular Religion from the Second to Seventh Centuries," in *Facets of Taoism: Essays in Chinese Religion,* ed. Holmes Welch and Anna Seidel (New Haven: Yale University Press, 1979); Michel Strickmann, "The Mao Shan Revelations: Taoism and the Aristocracy," *T'oung Pao* 63.1 (1977): 1–64, esp. 1–14, 31–40.

Abridged Codes of Master Lu for the Daoist Community

Now the Way is empty and quiescent, beyond forms and appearances; [but] the Greatest Sage applies his character and actions to his teachings. The Most High Lord Lao [the deified Laozi] saw that Lower Antiquity was decrepit and full of malice. The pure had become insipid and the simple broken up. The cosmic order had lost its balance, and men and demons mingled chaotically. The stale vapors of the Six Heavens took on official titles and appellations and brought together the hundred sprites and the demons of the five kinds of wounding, dead generals of defeated armies, and dead troops of scattered armies. The men called themselves "Generals"; the women called themselves "Ladies." They led demon troops, marching as armies and camping as legions, roving over Heaven and Earth. They arrogated to themselves authority and the power to dispense blessings. They took over people's temples and sought their sacrificial offerings, thus upsetting the people, who killed the three kinds of sacrificial animals [ox, sheep, and pig], used up all their prospects, cast away all their goods, and exhausted their produce. They were not blessed with good fortune but rather received disaster. Those who died unjustly or early and violently could not be counted.

The Most High was appalled that things were like this and therefore gave to the Celestial Master [that is, to Zhang Daoling, traditionally in 142] the Way of Correct Unity and the Covenant with the Powers [i.e., Daoism], with its prohibitions, vows, statutes, and codes, in order to regulate and instruct the myriad people. As for contrariness and obedience, calamities and blessings— he made them know what was good and what was evil. He set up twenty-four parishes and thirty-six chapels, with female and male priests numbering 2,400. He sent down 10,000 sets of the petitions to the 1,200 Celestial Officials, and talismans of punishment for attacking temples [of the popular religion]. He killed demons and gave life to men. He washed the universe clean and made the cosmic order bright and correct. All around Heaven and all over Earth, there were no longer any wanton (yin), wicked demons. Putting an end to the people's obsession with [divinatory and geomantic] prohibitions, he governed them with a Pure Bond (qingyue).

The spirits did not eat or drink [i.e., receive sacrificial offerings], and Daoist Masters did not accept money. The people were made to cultivate compassion and filiality within, and to practice respect and yielding without, thus aiding the times and regulating change, assisting the state and supporting its mandate. Only the Son of Heaven sacrificed to Heaven; only the Three Dukes sacrificed to the five sacred peaks; only the feudal lords sacrificed to the mountains and rivers; and the people gave cult to their ancestors only on the auspicious days of the Five La [in the first, fifth, seventh, tenth, and twelfth months] and sacrificed to the Soil God and the Stove God only in the second and the eighth months. Beyond this, no sacrifices were allowed. If one gave cult to one's ancestors other than on the auspicious days of the Five La, or sacrificed to the Soil God or the Stove God other than on the days of the Soil God in the second and eighth months, this was to commit the offense of giving excessive cult (yinsi).

The ill were not to take medicines or use the acupuncture needle or moxa. They were only to ingest talismans, drink water [into which the ashes of the burnt talismans had been mixed], and confess all their sins from their first year of life. Even all those who had committed capital crimes were pardoned, and of those whose symptoms had accumulated and were distressed by major illnesses, none was not healed. Thus those of the highest virtue attained divine transcendence; those of medium virtue doubled their lifespans; and those of the lowest virtue extended their years.

But now the people who worship the Way turn these matters upside down; in everything they rebel. I respectfully request that I might expose these maladies, as follows:

When the Celestial Master set up parishes and established offices, they were like the offices of the daylight world (*yangguan*) in the commanderies, counties, cities, and prefectures that govern the people's affairs. Those who worship the Way all list their households and are entered in the records, each having a place to which he or she belongs. Now on the seventh day of the first month, the seventh day of the seventh month, the fifth day of the tenth month—the annual Three Assemblies—each of the people assembles in his or her own parish. The Master should revise the registers—removing the dead and adding births, checking and tabulating the population figures, and correcting the roster of names. Promulgating this and ordering that, he makes the people know the Rituals (*fa*, also "Law"). On that day the Celestial Officials and the Terrestrial Spirits all assemble at the Master's parish and collate the documents. Master and people both ought to be quiet and serious; they may not drink wine, eat meat, or chatter and joke. When the Assembly is over and the people have returned home, they should instruct old and young in the codes and prohibitions and the rituals and encourage them reverently to practice them. If this sort of transformation through the Way is propagated, then there will be Great Peace (*taiping*) for family and state.

But the people who worship the Way nowadays mostly do not go to the Assemblies. Some use distance as an excuse, while some, refusing to leave home, turn their backs on their original Masters and go over to closer parishes. They only appreciate wine and meat, and they egg each other on in corruption. The bright codes and upright teachings they cast away and do not continue to spread. The canons of the Rituals and the old petitions thereupon are sunk into oblivion. Once the main net-cord has been abandoned, the myriad meshes all come loose in disorder. Not knowing the codes and constitutions, they are partial only to pledge-offerings. The people of the Way cannot tell contrariness from obedience and have a nose only for food and drink. Above and below are both lost and can no longer rely on one another. Instead, people decide things arbitrarily and stab each other in the back; once they act they are lost in conflict. They take the true as false and the false as true, right as wrong and wrong as right. A thousand branches and ten thousand strands—in what matter are they not obstreperous? Upside-down, disordered, muddled—they remain forever unaware. A Master like this will have his descendants extinguished and his seed cut off. People like this will have Heaven destroy them before their time. Although the future is all dark, once this has come to pass it will be exceedingly clear. Can the understanding, noble person afford not to reflect on this?

The household registers of the Daoist codes are the auxiliary registers of the people. The male and female population both should be entered in them. The Celestial Officials who Guard the House will take these registers as correct, and the household members, whether moving or resting, will always be protected. In each of three seasons (the Three Assemblies in Spring, Autumn, and Winter), one revises the entries in the registers; for this there is a constant rule. If the population numbers increase or decrease, the records should always be changed. If a boy is born and survives his first month he should be given a hundred sheets of paper and a pair of writing-brushes. Hold a kitchen-feast of superior quality for ten people. If a girl is born and survives her first month she should be given one each of a broom, a dustpan, and a mat. Hold a kitchen-feast of medium quality. When taking a wife, hold a kitchen-feast of superior quality for ten people. The owners of the registers [i.e., the heads of the bride's and groom's families] should take the registers of both households to their own parishes in order that [the Masters of those parishes] may exchange registers and edit the Records of Destiny [to show that the bride has joined the groom's family's household].

On the days of the Three Assemblies, the myriad spirits of the Three Offices [of Heaven, Earth, and Water, which keep records on each individual's behavior] check all their records against each other. If a new person has been added but the news is not sent up, the Celestial Bureaus will not have the name. If a person has been lost but is not removed from the record, then the roster of names will not be correct. As for the people who worship the Way nowadays, sometimes one person is converted in the beginning, and down to his grandchildren's time the registers are not revised. On the days of the Three Assemblies, they also do not make a report. Since neither root nor branch has been attended to, the original Master has no way to find out about the true situation and thus fills in his records in accordance with the previous year. Sometimes the dead bones have been scattered, and still their owner is listed. Or someone is born and lives to have a hoary head and yet still has not been registered. Sometimes someone marries a wife and does not send up the news. Sometimes a woman is given in marriage but is not removed from the records of her natal household. Thus one ends up with hundred-year-old boys and centenarian virgins. In this way present and departed are mixed up; existence and nonexistence are not genuine. Then when the day comes that one is ill, one does not go to one's original Master but instead solicits another priest. The new priest makes no inquiries about the past and simply writes a petition. The ailing person was not previously registered, yet the present petition suddenly appears. It will not be under the jurisdiction of the Celestial Officials who Guard the House, nor will the first Three Celestial Masters take charge. The Three Heavens will lack a record, and the Directorate of Destiny will not have the name. In vain one shatters one's skull on the ground [from vigorous kowtowing]—

though there be a profusion of documents, since it was not done according to the Rituals, the Way will not assist. How can one help but to give thought to a principle like this?

As for the codes for worship of the Way, the Master takes the Records of Destiny as the root, and the people take pledges (*xin*) as the chief matter. The Master sets out the pledges for them and sends the pledges up to the Three Heavens. He asks the Celestial Officials who Guard the House to protect, ward off disaster, and dispel calamities in accordance with the population records. Although there are three Assemblies in one year, the donation of pledges is entirely restricted to the fifth day of the tenth month. Once having arrived at the parish, if one's household is safe and well, one should hold a kitchen-feast of the highest quality for five people. If one's household has decreased, then one does not hold the kitchen feast but does donate the pledges as usual. If one's Destiny-Pledges (*mingxin*) do not arrive, then one's Record of Destiny is not sent up. Although one might later make bountiful offerings and gain blessings through kitchen-feasts, this cannot absolve the lack of the annual pledge. Therefore the Teachings say: "Although a thousand pieces of gold are precious, they do not compare to one's original Pledge-Destiny" (*xinming*). If a household that worships the Way does not offer its Destiny-Pledges for years repeatedly, the Three Heavens will excise their names from the records. The Officials who Guard the House will return to the Celestial Bureaus and the Emanations of the Way will no longer shade them. The injuries of demon-bandits will bring them illness and early death. These discouraged families remain forever unaware and instead blame the Master and resent the Way. Is it not pitiful!

For the household that worships the Way, the Quiet Room is a place of utmost reverence. The structure should be separate, not joined with other buildings. Inside it should be pure and empty, not cluttered with extra things. When coming and going, do not go crashing in and out recklessly. The room should be sprinkled and swept and kept immaculate and austere, like a dwelling for gods. Place in it an incense burner, an incense lamp, a petition table, and a scholar's knife—these four things only. Plain and unadorned, expenses for it should amount to just one hundred or so cash. Nowadays those who mix with the profane have altars, icons, banners, and all manner of ornament. Is there no longer a distinction between elaborate and simple, or a difference between ostentatious and plain?

Yet the people who worship the Way nowadays mostly do not even have a Quiet Room. Some mark and fence off an area and make a parish altar without even clearing it first, so that the weeds and underbrush stick up into the heavens. Or, even if they put up a building, it has no door, so that the domestic animals all wander in, and the excrement and filth piles up knee-deep. Some call it a Quiet Room but store miscellaneous household items in it. They blunder in and out, while rats and dogs take up residence there. Is not praying in such a place to the venerated and marvelous Way far from the mark?

The ritual vestments (*fafu*) of the Daoists are like the court clothing of the secular world. Lords, literati, and commoners each have rank and order: a system of five grades in order to distinguish noble and base. Therefore the *Classic of Filial Piety* (*Xiaojing*) says: "If they are not the ritual vestments of the former kings, one dare not wear them." The old ritual vestments were the single-layered robe and the lined turban, with trousers and coat for the novices. As for the pledges made when receiving a parish, a man gives a single-layered robe and a black turban, and a woman gives a deep purple robe. This clear statement should be sufficient to put confusion to rest.

The turban and the robe of coarse cloth, as well as the cape, come from the Supreme Way. When making ritual prostrations one wears the coarse cloth; when chanting scriptures one wears the cape. How could the models of the Three Caverns of Daoist scripture have anything to do with the lesser ways (*xiaodao*)? Recently, even those who merely receive the rituals of a small parish or of a novice usurp the prerogative of the robe and coarse cloth. This is already greatly mistaken. Then moreover to match a hat and coat with a skirt, or wear trousers with the cape or robe of coarse cloth—how can one even discuss this sort of muddle and disorder?

There are standards for the turban, the robe of coarse cloth, the skirt, and the cape, as well as their lengths and the numbers of stitches. This is why they are called ritual vestments [lit. also "legal/regulated clothing"]. The vestments all have powerful gods that attend on and protect them. The Perfected of the Grand Ultimate (*Taiji zhenren*) said: "If they are not made in accordance with the Rituals, then the spirits will punish the wrongdoer." Since by dressing contrary to the codes one oversteps one's bounds and indulges in excess, can one escape calamities?

The teachings of the codes say that if a person (*min*, a Daoist "commoner") has three diligences, this makes a merit. Three merits make a virtue. If a person has three virtues, then he or she becomes different from ordinary people and may be appointed with a register. After receiving the register, one must have merit in order to advance from the Register of Ten Spirit-Generals by steps to the Register of One Hundred Fifty Spirit-Generals. If among the novices (*luli*, lit. "Clerks of the Registers") there are those who are loyal and good, simple, careful, and prudent, loving the Way and surpassing in diligence, steeped in the old and knowledgeable about the present, capable in proselytizing—they may be appointed as Priests who Disperse the Emanations of the Way. If among the Dispersers of Emanations there are those who are pure in cultivation of the Way, they may be promoted to posts in Detached Parishes. If in the Detached Parishes there are those who are even more refined and sincere, they may be promoted to posts in Traveling Parishes. . . . [And so on through eight more grades.] One ought to seek offices through perspicaciously spreading merit and virtue. Neither let the person dominate the office, nor the office the person.

If one learns without a Master this becomes like a plant growing without a root. Something that grows severed from its basis is called a "rootless weed" (commentary omitted). . . . Yet people today receive registers without such

virtues and receive parishes without such talents (commentary omitted). . . .
Some are without both a teacher and documentary records.

> Such a person first worshiped the Way, but then lost his or her Master for some time
> and did not reaffiliate. Or first the person was an ordinary layperson, living alone
> away from home, fickle and false of faith. The priest did not first convert the person
> in accordance with the rituals, but instead immediately conferred a register and a
> parish. This kind of practitioner is entirely a fraud, a priest in vain. Even if the person
> additionally cultivates diligently and submits to the good, his or her name will not
> be in the records of the Three Heavens. Therefore there will be no escape from a
> premature demise. How much more dismal will things be in the case of the licentious
> and disobedient!

Some have a Master but no records (commentary omitted). . . . Some, although
they have a Master and records, are without virtues. When they receive registers, they cross over to another Master, thus neither returning to the basis
nor following the proper sequence of grades. The appointments are made recklessly without the selection of qualified people. In carrying registers these lax
Daoists care only for quantity; in receiving parishes they care only for quantity
and size. They compete to be first and struggle to be victorious, each trying to
be ascendant over the other. (More details on the parish system omitted.)

Without the Precepts and the Statutes, inferior priests do not follow the
commands of the teachings. They overstep the codes and break the Prohibitions, slight the Way and debase the Rituals.

> Now those who receive the Way keep to to the Precepts and Statutes within and hold
> to the Mighty Rituals. Observing avoidances and prohibitions in accordance with the
> Codes, they follow the commands of the teachings. Therefore the Scripture says: "If
> the priest does not receive the 180 Precepts of Lord Lao, he is without virtue." Then,
> if one is not a real priest, one does not deserve the obeisance of the common people
> and cannot control spirits. Being so obtuse, lax priests do not know that the Way
> and Virtue are venerable, and whether acting or at rest they are guilty of shortcomings,
> thus debasing their rituals and techniques.

They let free their covetous natures, drowning themselves in wine and lusting
after food.

> When they propagate the Rituals of the Way, they do not look for merit and virtue.
> When they perform healing rituals, they lack any compassionate or humane intent.
> They hope only for gain, and their thoughts are all on wine and meat. Never do they
> instruct the people in the Codes and Prohibitions. They only collect substantial of-
> ferings and seek for good food—dishes flavored with the five pungent roots, and the
> meat of the six kinds of domestic animals. The things that in the Way are most
> tabooed, they eat! Then, having violated the prohibitions themselves, they then go
> on to butcher chickens, pigs, geese, and ducks. They drink wine until they are awash
> in it, then in that condition go to send up petitions (zou wen, lit. to "memorialize" in

a communication to an emperor). Then they end up sleeping on the Quiet Room's altar and vomiting beside the petition table. There are always those of this sort.

They turn their backs on the upright teaching of the Pure Bond of the Covenant with the Powers

The Ritual Master of the Covenant with the Powers does not take money; the spirits neither eat nor drink. This is called the Pure Bond (*qingyue*). In curing illness one does not use acupuncture, moxa, or hot liquid medicines. One only ingests talismans, drinks [talismanic] water, confesses one's sins, corrects one's behavior, and sends a petition—and that is all. When choosing a site for a dwelling-place, installing a sepulcher, or moving house—when moving, coming to rest, or in all the hundred affairs—not divining for a lucky day or making inquiries concerning auspicious times, simply following one's heart, avoiding or inclining toward nothing is called the Bond [or "is called restraint," *yue*]. Casting out the thousand sprites and ten thousand numena—all the profane gods—as one takes up the worship of the Lord Lao and the first Three Celestial Masters is called the Upright Teaching.

and resort to the upside-down rites of perverse and calamitous spirit-mediumism.

Making sacrifices to demons and gods and praying for blessings is called Perverse. Weighing the words of demons and gods in order to divine auspiciousness and inauspiciousness is called Calamitous. Irresponsibly creating taboos and avoidances that are not in the codes and teaching of the Celestial Masters and Laozi is called Spirit-mediumism. As for writing charts, and thus divining the baneful geomantic influences of the sites of sepulchers and dwellings, one ought instead to send up a petition to exorcise those influences. To persist in using calendars to pick days and choose times is even more stupidly obstreperous. That which is illumined by the upright codes, they are forever unwilling to follow. That which the rituals prohibit, they compete in reverently employing. Thus turning one's back on the true and turning toward the false is called Upside-down.

They take up their scholars' knives and brushes [the basic tools for writing petitions] and travel among the villages.

The Rituals of the Way are incorrupt and retiring, responding rather than singing their own praises. Quietly one refines one's techniques on one's own, waiting for the one who will seek one out and make a sincere claim of his or her need, after which one will extend one's succor. If one goes about promoting oneself, this is prohibited by the Rituals.

When they meet up with fugitive disobedient people, inquisition weighs them down, and disasters descend upon them.

Although they are people of the Way, for long they have had no Master. The parish has no record of their Destinies, and their families have no household registers. Or they have a Master, but on the Three Auspicious Days they do not attend the Assemblies and offer their pledges. Then, when they have some emergency, they set down offerings and make vows to give kitchen-feasts, not understanding how grace is bestowed. This is called Fugitive. Although they worship the Way and its Rituals, they do not follow the prohibitions in the codes, committing excesses and killing living beings, believing in perversities and making divinatory inquiries, doing evil in a hundred ways, malefic and rebellious beyond description. This is called Disobedient. All fugitive and disobedient people will have their Reckonings (*suan*, i.e., their predetermined lifespans) shortened and their names excised from the records. The Three Offices will send out the Lords and Clerks of Summoning for Inquisition secretly to keep watch on their households, afflict their members with inquisitorial punishments, and call disasters down upon them. If their sins are heavy, then they will meet with the Six Calamities; if their sins are light, then the Five Disasters descend upon them. Thus they are made to suffer from death, disease, state officials, imprisonment, floods, fire, thieves, and bandits.

In the case of people like this, if in emergencies they wish to be instructed in the Way, the Master should always dispel the inquisition and the sin-produced affliction in accordance with the codes. If the people can be persuaded gently and will return to the good, spit out evil, and take an oath with the Three Offices, then once they confirm this faith they may be delivered following the sequence prescribed by the codes. Yet stupid, false Priests have no codes or precepts to go by and no way of distinguishing the empty from the substantial. They only have decrepit, old petitions, and talismans with parts missing. The beginnings of these documents do not fit with the ends; they cannot be used in worship. And still these priests follow their own opinions and edit the documents as they wish, recklessly making emendations. With filthy turbans, foul ink-stones, shameful paper, dirty brushes, and cursive writing with wild strokes, stinking of wine and meat, they follow their appetites and seek whatever their minds fasten on. With substanceless words and false speech, they ignore the facts. They go against the source and turn their backs on principle, offending the [otherworldly] Officials of Inquisition. Sometimes they go overboard and arrest innocent demons, or unjustly charge spirits that are causing no affliction. Sometimes they bind spirits they should loose, or promote the ones they should attack. Upside-down and jumbled, affairs thus have no standard.

When they enter the Quiet Room to memorialize the Celestial Bureaus, these inferior priests cannot tell where one sentence of the petition ends and the next begins. What they recognize, with a torrent of a voice and a roll of drums they broadcast to neighbors in all directions. What they cannot understand, they skip over—coughing, sputtering, and bellowing. The Celestial Clerks and Soldiers will not serve people such as this, and the Emanations of the Way will not descend upon them. Inquisitorial afflictions will become more urgent daily, and illnesses will keep taking turns for the worse. Vainly increasing one's rich offerings in the end produces no results. Guest and host [i.e., client and priest] are lost together and cannot see that they are wrong. This then gives rise to slander: resentment against the Way and blame toward the spirits. Sometimes things get to the point that people burn their registers, destroy their Quiet Rooms, and make over their chapels—serving demon-kind in all possible ways—and then disaster entirely destroys their families. A loss such as this!—can one afford to be unaware?

—28—

The Scripture in Forty-two Sections

Robert H. Sharf

The Scripture in Forty-two Sections (*Sishi'er zhang jing*) is a short collection of aphorisms and pithy moralistic parables traditionally regarded as the first Indian Buddhist scripture to be translated into Chinese. There are, in fact, good reasons to question the purported Indian origins of this scripture—it may well have been compiled in Central Asia or even China. Moreover, all versions of the text that have come down to us show signs of later revision at the hands of medieval Chinese editors. Nevertheless, most scholars believe that the original *Scripture in Forty-two Sections*, whatever its origins, was indeed in circulation during the earliest period of Buddhism in China.

According to tradition, the *Scripture in Forty-two Sections* was translated at the behest of Emperor Ming of the Han dynasty (r. 58–75 C.E.). The earliest surviving account of the story runs as follows: One night Emperor Ming had a dream in which he saw a spirit flying around in front of his palace. The spirit had a golden body, and the top of his head emitted rays of light. The following day the emperor asked his ministers to identify the spirit. One minister replied that he had heard of a sage in India called "Buddha" who had attained the Way and was able to fly. It seemed that the spirit observed by the emperor must have been he. Thereupon the emperor dispatched a group of envoys led by Zhang Qian who journeyed to Yuezhi (Scythia?) and returned with a copy of the *Scripture in Forty-two Sections*. The text was later deposited in a temple.

There is considerable debate among scholars concerning the date of this legend. The brief account given above is found in an early preface to the *Scripture in Forty-two Sections* that may date to the middle of the third century C.E. The story was considerably embellished in time, and at least one glaring anachronism was removed. (Zhang Qian, the leader of the envoys, was in fact a historical figure who went to Bactria in the second century B.C.E., and thus his name is omitted in later renditions.) Sources disagree as to the date of the departure (given variously as 60, 61, 64, 68 and C.E.), the return date (64 to 75 C.E.), and the destination of the envoys (some versions mention India rather than Yuezhi). While the "Preface" makes mention only of the scripture, a fifth-century source reports that the envoys managed to secure the famous Udayana image of the Buddha as well. (See chapter 19 in this volume.) In the fifth and sixth centuries we also begin to find mention of two Indian monks, Kāśyapa Mātaṅga and Dharmaratna, who return with the Chinese envoys, and by the medieval period these monks are regularly cited as cotranslators of the scripture. Finally of note is another relatively late tradition that has Emperor Ming build the first Chinese Buddhist temple—the Baimasi at Luoyang—as a residence for the two Indian translators. This temple became an important center for the translation of Buddhist texts for centuries to come.

Despite questions concerning the date and authenticity of the legend, scholars are generally agreed on two points: (1) Buddhism was introduced into China *prior* to the traditional dates given for the "dream of Emperor Ming," and (2) some form of the *Scripture in Forty-two Sections* did in fact exist in the Eastern Han dynasty (25–220 C.E.). Evidence for the first point comes from both art-historical remains and casual references in Han historical sources, while the second point can be deduced from a passage in a memorial presented to Emperor Huan by the scholar Xiang Kai in 166 C.E. In a long diatribe against the moral abuses of the court, Xiang Kai criticizes the emperor for venerating saints but failing to emulate them:

> Moreover I have heard that altars have been established for Huanglao and the Buddha within the palace. Their Way is that of purity, emptiness, and reverence for nonaction. They value life and condemn killing. . . . Since your Majesty has deviated from this teaching, how can you hope to obtain its rewards? . . . The Buddha did not pass three nights under the [same] mulberry tree; he did not wish to remain there long, for this would give rise to attachment and desire. That was the perfection of his essence. A deity sent him a beautiful maiden but the Buddha said: "This is nothing but a leather sack filled with blood," and he paid no further attention to her. His concentration was like this, and thus he was able to realize the Way.

Xiang Kai was likely referring to some early form of the *Scripture in Forty-two Sections;* compare the quote above with section 2 of the scripture: "Taking a single meal at midday, and lodging a single night under a tree, [a *śramaṇa*] takes care not to repeat either." And the anecdote concerning the gift of the maiden to the Buddha may well have been derived from section 24: "A deity presented a woman of pleasure to the Buddha, wanting to test the Buddha's will power and examine the Buddha's Way. The Buddha said: 'Why have you come here bearing this leather sack of filth? Do you think to deceive me? . . . Begone! I have no use for her.'"

In addition to evidence provided by Xiang Kai's memorial, there are stylistic and linguistic features that mark this work as one of the earliest Buddhist texts in China (notably the archaic transliterations used throughout the work). Yet the text remains somewhat of a mystery: it bears none of the characteristics of a formal sūtra, and no Sanskrit, Tibetan, or Central Asian versions are known to exist. Indeed, it seems that it was not originally considered a sūtra in the formal sense of the word at all: early Buddhist catalogues refer to it simply as "Forty-two Sections from Buddhist Scriptures," or "The Forty-two Sections of Emperor Xiao Ming." Such titles are in fact appropriate, as the text consists largely of snippets culled from longer Buddhist sūtras scattered throughout the Buddhist canon. (Parallel sections are found in the *Dīgha, Majjhima, Saṃyutta,* and *Aṅguttara Nikāyas,* as well as the *Mahāvagga.*) But while we can identify the source of many of the forty-two sections, scholars have yet to determine whether the collection was first assembled in India, Central Asia, or China.

We also know little about the role the scripture played in the propagation of early Buddhism. At first glance the *Scripture in Forty-two Sections* appears to be a sort of handbook or introduction to basic Buddhist terms and principles for the benefit of novices. Yet this view is not without its problems; one cannot help but notice, for example, the many technical terms and allusions that go unexplained in the text, such as the "nineteen heavens," the "three honored ones," the "three poisons," and the "five hindrances." This might suggest that it was intended for Buddhist adherents rather than for neophytes, or that it was meant to be used in conjunction with oral teachings (as was often the case with Chinese Buddhist texts).

In order to appreciate the place of the *Scripture in Forty-two Sections* within the Chinese Buddhist world, it might be useful to turn for a moment to the much better known Pāli compilation, the *Dhammapada (Verses on the Teachings).* Although considerably longer (423 verses), the *Dhammapada* is similar insofar as it provides a general and attractive overview of the ethical teachings of Buddhism. It too consists primarily of extracts culled from the most popular Pāli literature, and like the *Scripture in Forty-two Sections* it consists largely of short aphorisms and parables. The *Dhammapada* is widely employed as a handy summary and reminder of the Buddha's teachings, to which the pious may refer for inspiration or solace. It is also commonly used to provide themes for sermonizing. And even today, despite copious references to technical Buddhist doctrines, the *Dhammapada* is widely used as a vehicle for the dissemination of Buddhism into non-Buddhist cultures.

It is quite possible that the *Scripture in Forty-two Sections* was compiled in the early days of Chinese Buddhism with a similar range of functions in mind. In fact, it has been put to such use in this century. Shaku Sōen (1859–1919), the first Japanese Zen master to visit and teach in the West, used this scripture as the basis of a series of talks given during a tour of America in 1905–1906. And John Blofeld, a Western convert to the religion who devoted his energies to the transmission of Buddhism to the West, chose this scripture as the first to be translated in a series begun in 1947. Although the tenets of the scripture are not presented in any systematic way, the simplicity and brevity of the work make it suitable for use as an introductory text.

Whether initially compiled in India, Central Asia, or China, the version of the *Scripture in Forty-two Sections* disseminated in East Asia bears certain unmistakably

Chinese stylistic features. The most obvious Sinitic touch is the phrase "The Buddha said," which is used to introduce most sections. This peculiarity, along with the decidedly moralistic tone of the work, is strongly reminiscent of certain Confucian classics, such as the *Classic of Filial Piety* (*Xiaojing*) and the *Analects* (*Lunyu*). Both texts are similarly comprised of short moralistic maxims and illustrative anecdotes, many of which are prefaced with the phrase "the Master said."

Beyond this rather obvious stylistic adaptation there are a few passages that are most certainly interpolations by a Chinese editor. One obvious example is found in the earliest extant edition of the text, namely, that now found in the Korean Canon. The key passage is found at the end of section 9:

> Feeding one billion saints is not as good as feeding one solitary buddha (*pratyeka-buddha*). Feeding ten billion solitary buddhas is not as good as liberating one's parents in this life by means of the teaching of the three honored ones. To teach one hundred billion parents is not as good as feeding one buddha, studying with the desire to attain buddhahood, and aspiring to liberate all beings. But the merit of feeding a good man is [still] very great. It is better for a common man to be filial to his parents than for him to serve the spirits of Heaven and Earth, for one's parents are the supreme spirits.

Recent work on Indian Buddhist inscriptions has shown that filial piety was not an exclusively East Asian concern, but played an important role in Indian Buddhism as well. But the phrasing and context of the references to filial piety in this passage marks it as a Chinese insertion.

Another interesting example of the "sinification" of the work is the regular use of the word *dao* ("way" or "path") as a translation equivalent not only for *mārga*, for which it is a standard and appropriate semantic equivalent, but also for what one suspects would be *nirvāna* ("extinction") or *dharma* ("teachings" or "truth") in an Indic original. This is characteristic of early translations influenced by Daoist and "dark learning" (*xuanxue*) ideas, and it lends a distinctly Chinese "mystical" tone to what is otherwise a moralistic Hīnayānist work. I have translated *dao* as "Way" whenever possible to preserve some of the flavor of the Chinese.

One area in which this translation departs from the original Chinese is in the handling of Sanskrit terminology. In the interests of clarity I have translated most of the technical terms that are merely transliterated in the Chinese. (The one exception is the term *śramana*—used throughout the text to refer to ascetics and ordained followers of the Buddha—where I have retained the Sanskrit.) While some of the terms, such as *śramana, arhat,* and *śrotāpanna,* are briefly explained in the opening paragraphs of the text, others, including *upāsaka* and *pratyeka-buddha,* are not explained at all. It must be kept in mind that the transliteration of foreign terms is an awkward process in Chinese that often yields unwieldy and bizarre-looking polysyllabic compounds. The copious use of such transliterations, many of which go unexplained, would have lent the text a decidedly exotic character.

This translation of the *Sishi'er zhang jing* is based on the edition found in the Korean Tripiṭaka (K 778:19.865–67). The Korean text, which is reproduced with little alteration in the *Taishō daizōkyō* (T 784:17.722a–24a), is in turn based on the Shu Tripiṭaka published under the Northern Song. While the Korean version of the *Scripture in Forty-two Sections* represents an earlier recension than either the "Shousui" text compiled in the Song (the most popular version of the scripture, although it is also the most "corrupt") or the "Zhenzong" edition (the edition reproduced in the *Nanzang* Tripiṭika of the Ming and all subsequent Chinese collections), even the Korean text shows traces of later redaction when compared with early citations found in pre-Tang works. I have also consulted the commentary by Emperor Zhen Zong of the Song dynasty (r. 998–1022), the *Zhu sishi'er zhang jing* (T 1794:517a–522c), as well as the Japanese translation by Fukaura Masafumi in the *Kokuyaku issaikyō, kyōjūbu* 3, pp. 169–73. The excerpt in the introduction taken from Xiang Kai's memorial is found in fascicle 60b of the *Houhan shu*.

Further Readings

Discussions in English of the dating and significance of the *Scripture in Forty-two Sections* can be found in T'ang Yung-t'ung, "The Editions of the Ssu-shih-erh-chang-ching," *Harvard Journal of Asiatic Studies* 1 (1936): 147–55; E. Zürcher, *The Buddhist Conquest of China: The Spread and Adaptation of Buddhism in Early Medieval China* (Leiden: E. J. Brill, 1959), pp. 29–30; Kenneth Ch'en, *Buddhism in China: A Historical Survey* (Princeton: University of Princeton Press, 1964), pp. 29–36; Henri Maspero, *Taoism and Chinese Religion,* trans. Frank A. Kierman, Jr. (Amherst: University of Massachusetts Press, 1981), pp. 400–404; and Tsukamoto Zenryū, *A History of Early Chinese Buddhism from Its Introduction to the Death of Hui-yüan,* trans. Leon Hurvitz (Tokyo: Kodansha, 1985), vol. 1, pp. 41–50. For English translations of later editions of this scripture, see Samuel Beal, *A Catena of Buddhist Scriptures from the Chinese* (London: Trübner and Company, 1871), pp. 188–203; D. T. Suzuki, *Sermons of a Buddhist Abbot* (New York: Samuel Weiser, 1906), pp. 3–21; and John Blofeld, *The Sutra of 42 Sections and Two Other Scriptures of the Mahayana School* (London: The Buddhist Society, 1947), pp. 10–22.

The Scripture in Forty-two Sections

Translated in the Later Han dynasty by the śramaṇas Kāśyapa Mātaṅga and Dharmaratna of the Western Regions.

1. The Buddha said: "Those who leave their families and go forth from their homes to practice the Way are called śramaṇas (ascetics). Those who constantly

follow the 250 precepts in order to [realize] the four noble truths and progressively purify their intentions will become saints (*arhat*). A saint is able to fly and assume different forms; he lives a long life and can move Heaven and Earth. Next is the nonreturner (*anāgāmin*): at the end of his life the spirit of a nonreturner ascends the nineteen heavens and there attains sainthood. Next is the once-returner (*sakṛdāgāmin*): the once-returner ascends [to Heaven] once and returns once and then attains sainthood. Next is the stream-winner (*śrotāpanna*): the stream-winner dies and is reborn seven times and then attains sainthood. The severance of passion and desire is like the four limbs severed, they will never be used again."

2. The Buddha said: "Those who shave their heads and faces are *śramaṇas*. They receive the teaching, abandon worldly wealth and possessions, and beg, seeking only what is necessary. Taking a single meal at midday, and lodging a single night under a tree, they take care not to repeat either. That which makes men ignorant and derelict is passion and desire."

3. The Buddha said: "All beings consider ten things as good and ten things as evil. Three concern the body, four the mouth, and three the mind. The three [evil things] of the body are killing, stealing, and adultery. The four of the mouth are duplicity, slander, lying, and lewd speech. The three of the mind are envy, hatred, and delusion. He who lacks faith in the three honored ones [the Buddha, the teaching, and the community of monks], will mistake falsehood for truth. A lay disciple (*upāsaka*) who practices the five precepts [not to kill, to steal, to commit adultery, to speak falsely, or to drink alcohol], without becoming lax and backsliding, will arrive at the ten [good] things [i.e., the antitheses of the ten evil things] and will certainly attain the Way."

4. The Buddha said: "If a man commits multiple transgressions, yet does not repent and quickly quell the [evil] in his heart, his crimes will return to him as water returns to the sea, becoming ever deeper and wider. But should a man come to realize the error of his ways, correct his transgressions, and attain goodness, his days of wrongdoing will come to an end and in time he will attain the Way."

5. The Buddha said: "Should a man malign me and seek to do me harm, I counter with the four virtues of benevolence, [compassion, joy, and equanimity]. The more he approaches me with malice, the more I reach out with kindness. The forces (*qi*) of beneficent virtue lie always in this, while harmful forces and repeated misfortune will revert to the other."

6. Once a man heard that the Buddha's Way lies in persevering in benevolence and compassion, and meeting evil with goodness. He then came and cursed the Buddha. The Buddha, remaining silent, did not respond, but rather had pity for one whose ignorance and rage led to such an act. When his cursing abated the Buddha asked him: "If you offer a gift to someone who does not

accept it, what happens to the gift?" The man replied: "I would have to take it back." The Buddha said: "Now you have offered me curses but I do not accept them. They return to you, bringing harm to your own person. Like an echo responding to sound, or a shadow following an object, in the end there is no escaping it. Take heed of your evil ways."

7. The Buddha said: "An evil man trying to harm a worthy man is like looking toward Heaven and spitting; the spittle will not befoul Heaven but will return and befoul the one spitting. It is like throwing filth at someone while facing into the wind; the filth will not befoul anyone else but will return and befoul the one throwing. A worthy man cannot be harmed; a man's transgressions will surely destroy only himself."

8. The Buddha said: "The virtue of one who practices universal love, compassion, and generosity for the sake of the Way is not that of great generosity. But if he [further] guards his intentions and honors the Way, his merit is truly great. If you see someone practicing generosity and you joyfully assist him, you too will gain merit in return." Someone asked: "Would not the other person's merit be diminished thereby?" The Buddha said: "It is like the flame of a single torch that is approached by several hundred thousand men each bearing torches. Each lights his torch from the flame and departs, using it to cook food and dispel darkness, yet the original flame is ever the same. Merit is also like this."

9. The Buddha said: "Feeding one hundred common men is not as good as feeding one good man. Feeding one thousand good men is not as good as feeding one who observes the five precepts. Feeding ten thousand men who observe the five precepts is not as good as feeding one stream-winner. Feeding one million stream-winners is not as good as feeding one once-returner. Feeding ten million once-returners is not as good as feeding one nonreturner. Feeding one hundred million nonreturners is not as good as feeding one saint. Feeding one billion saints is not as good as feeding one solitary buddha (*pratyekabuddha*). Feeding ten billion solitary buddhas is not as good as liberating one's parents in this life by means of the teaching of the three honored ones. To teach one hundred billion parents is not as good as feeding one buddha, studying with the desire to attain buddhahood, and aspiring to liberate all beings. But the merit of feeding a good man is [still] very great. It is better for a common man to be filial to his parents than for him to serve the spirits of Heaven and Earth, for one's parents are the supreme spirits."

10. The Buddha said: "There are five difficult things under Heaven. It is difficult for the poor to give alms, it is difficult for the powerful and privileged to cultivate the Way, it is difficult to control fate and avoid death, it is difficult to attain a glimpse of the Buddha's scriptures, and it is difficult to be born at the time of a buddha."

11. There was a śramaṇa who asked the Buddha: "Through what causal factors does one attain the Way, and how does one come to know of one's previous lives?" The Buddha replied: "The Way is without form, and thus to know these things is of no benefit. What is important is to guard your intentions and actions. It is like polishing a mirror: as the dust is removed the underlying luminosity is revealed and you are able to see your own image. Eliminate desire and hold to emptiness and you will come to see the truth of the Way and know your past lives."

12. The Buddha said: "What is goodness? Goodness is the practice of the Way. What is supreme? A mind in accord with the Way is supreme. What has great power? Patience in the face of insult is strongest, for patience and the absence of anger is honored by all. What is supreme enlightenment? When mental impurities are uprooted, when evil conduct has ceased, when one is pure and free of blemish within, when there is nothing that is not known, seen, or heard—from the time when there was yet no Heaven and Earth down to the present day, including everything extant in the ten quarters as well as that which has yet to appear—when omniscience has been attained, this can indeed be called enlightenment."

13. The Buddha said: "A man who holds to passion and desire will not see the Way. It is as if one muddied water by throwing in five colored pigments and vigorously mixed them together. Many might approach the edge of the water, but they would be unable to see their own reflections on the surface. Passion and desire pollute the mind, leaving it murky, and thus the Way goes unseen. If the water is filtered and the filth removed, leaving it pure and free of dirt, one's own reflection will be seen. But if a kettle is placed over a hot flame bringing water to a rapid boil, or if water is covered with a cloth, then those who approach it will similarly not see their own reflections. The three fundamental poisons [of greed, hatred, and delusion] boil and bubble in the mind, while one is cloaked without by the five hindrances [of desire, hatred, sloth, agitation, and doubt]. In the end the Way goes unseen. When mental impurities are exhausted one knows whence the spirit comes and whither life and death go. The Way and its virtue are present in all buddha lands."

14. The Buddha said: "The practice of the Way is like holding a burning torch and entering a dark room: the darkness immediately vanishes and everything is illumined. Cultivate the Way and perceive the truth and evil and ignorance will both vanish, leaving nothing unseen."

15. The Buddha said: "What do I contemplate? I contemplate the Way. What do I practice? I practice the Way. Of what do I speak? I speak of the Way. I contemplate the true Way, never neglecting it for even an instant."

16. The Buddha said: "When gazing at Heaven and Earth contemplate their impermanence. When gazing at mountains and rivers contemplate their im-

permanence. When gazing at the tremendous variety of shapes and forms of the myriad things in the world contemplate their impermanence. If you keep your mind thus you will attain the Way in no time."

17. The Buddha said: "If for but a single day you continually contemplate and practice the Way you will attain the foundations of faith. Its blessings are incalculable."

18. The Buddha said: "Ardently contemplate the four primary elements that comprise the body. While each has a name, they are all devoid of self. The [sense of an] 'I' emerges from the aggregate, but it is not long lived and is really but an illusion."

19. The Buddha said: "For a person to follow his desires in search of fame is like putting fire to incense. Many may savor the smell of the incense, but the incense is all the while being consumed by the fire. The foolish, coveting worldly fame, hold not to the truth of the Way. Fame brings misfortune and harm, and one is sure to regret it later.

20. The Buddha said: "Riches and sex are to men what sweet honey on the blade of a knife is to a young child: before he has fully enjoyed a single bite he must suffer the pain of a cut tongue."

21. The Buddha said: "The misery of being shackled to wife, children, wealth, and home is greater than that of being shackled in chains and fetters and thrown in prison. In prison there is the possibility of pardon, but even though the desire for wife and children is as perilous as the mouth of a tiger, men throw themselves into it willingly. For this crime there is no pardon."

22. The Buddha said: "There is no desire more powerful than sex. Sexual desire looms so large that nothing stands outside of it. But luckily there is only one such desire, for were there yet another there would not be a single person in all the world capable of the Way."

23. The Buddha said: "Passion and desire are to man what a flaming torch is to one walking against the wind. Foolish ones who do not let go of the torch are sure to burn their hands. The poisons of craving and lust, anger and hatred, ignorance and delusion all reside in the body. He who does not quickly relinquish these perils by means of the Way will surely meet disaster, just as the foolish one who clings to his torch is sure to burn his hands."

24. A deity presented a woman of pleasure to the Buddha, wanting to test the Buddha's will and examine the Buddha's Way. The Buddha said: "Why have you come here bearing this leather sack of filth? Do you think to deceive me? It is difficult to stir [one possessed of] the six supernatural powers. Begone! I have no use for her." The deity, with increased respect for the Buddha, asked about the Way. The Buddha instructed him, whereupon he attained the stage of a stream-winner.

25. The Buddha said: "A man practicing the Way is like a piece of wood floating downstream with the current. As long as it avoids catching either the left or the right banks, as long as it is not picked up by someone or obstructed by some spirit, as long as it does not get stuck in a whirlpool or rot away, then I assure you it will eventually reach the sea. As long as a man practicing the Way is not deluded by passion or deceived by falsehood, as long as he energetically advances without doubt, then I assure you he will eventually attain the Way."

26. The Buddha told a śramaṇa: "Take care not to place faith in your own intentions. Ultimately intentions cannot be trusted. Take care not to wallow in sensuality, for wallowing in sensuality gives birth to misfortune. Only when you attain sainthood can you place faith in your own intentions."

27. The Buddha told a śramaṇa: "Take care not to look at women. If you meet one, look not, and take care not to converse with her. If you must converse, admonish the mind to right conduct by saying to yourself: 'As a śramaṇa I must live in this befouled world like a lotus, unsullied by mud.' Treat an old lady as if she were your mother, an elder woman as your elder sister, a younger woman as your younger sister, and a young girl as your own daughter. Show respect for them through your propriety. Remember that you see only the outside, but if you could peer into the body—from head to foot—what then? It is brimming with foulness. By exposing the impure aggregates [that comprise the body] one can free oneself from [impure] thoughts."

28. The Buddha said: "A man practicing the Way must eliminate sentiment and desire. It must be like grass encountering fire; by the time the fire arrives the grass is already gone. In encountering passion and desire the man of the Way must immediately distance himself."

29. The Buddha said: "Once a man was tormented by feelings of lust that would not cease, so he squatted down on the blade of an ax in order to castrate himself. The Buddha said to him: 'Severing the genitals is not as good as severing the mind, for the mind is chief. Put a stop to the chief and all his followers will cease. But if you do not put a stop to your depraved mind, what good will castration do? It will surely result in death.' " The Buddha said: "The vulgar and topsy-turvy views of the world are like those of this foolish man."

30. There was an adulterous young lady who made a pact with another man, but when the scheduled time arrived she did not come. The man repented and said to himself: "Desire, I know you! The initial intent is born with thought. If I did not think of you, you would not come into being." The Buddha was passing by and heard him. He said to the śramaṇa: "I recognize those words! It is a verse once uttered by Kāśyapa Buddha as he passed through this profane world."

31. The Buddha said: "From passion and desire arises sorrow. From sorrow arises dread. Without passion there is no sorrow, and without sorrow there is no dread."

32. The Buddha said: "A man practicing the Way is like a lone man in combat against ten thousand. Bearing armor and brandishing weapons, he charges through the gate eager to do battle, but if he is weakhearted and cowardly he will withdraw and flee. Some get halfway down the road before they retreat; some reach the battle and die; some are victorious and return to their kingdoms triumphantly. If a man is able to keep a firm grip on his wits and advance resolutely, without becoming deluded by worldly or deranged talk, then desire will disappear and evil will vanish, and he is certain to attain the Way."

33. There was a *śramaṇa* who mournfully chanted the scriptures at night, his spirit full of remorse as if wanting to return [to lay life]. The Buddha summoned the *śramaṇa* and asked him: "When you were a householder what did you do?" He answered, "I regularly played the lute." The Buddha asked: "What happened when the strings were too loose?" He replied: "It did not sound." "And when the strings were too taut, what then?" [The *śramaṇa*] replied: "The sound was cut short." "And when it was neither too loose nor too taught, what then?" "Then the tones all came into sympathetic accord." The Buddha told the *śramaṇa*: "The cultivation of the Way is just like that; keep the mind in tune and you can attain the Way."

34. The Buddha said: "Practicing the Way is like forging iron: if you gradually but thoroughly cast out impurities, the vessel is sure to come out well. If you cultivate the Way by gradually but thoroughly removing the impurities of mind, your advance will be steady. But when you are too harsh with yourself, the body becomes fatigued, and when the body is fatigued, the mind becomes frustrated. If the mind is frustrated, one's practice will lapse, and when practice lapses, one falls into wrongdoing."

35. The Buddha said: "Whether or not you practice the way you will certainly suffer. From birth to old age, from old age to sickness, from sickness to death, the misery of man is immeasurable. The distressed mind accumulates misdeeds, and life and death know no surcease. Such misery is beyond description."

36. The Buddha said: "It is difficult to free oneself from the three evil realms [the hells, the realm of hungry ghosts, and the realm of animals], and attain human birth. Even if one attains human birth it is difficult to be born a man rather than a woman. Even if one is born a man it is difficult to be born perfect in all six sense faculties. Even if the six faculties are perfect it is difficult to be born in the Middle Kingdom. Even if one lives in the Middle Kingdom it is difficult to be born at a time when the Buddha's Way is honored. Even if born when the Buddha's Way is honored it is difficult to encounter a noble man of the Way. [Moreover,] it is difficult to be born in the family of bodhisattvas.

Even if born in the family of bodhisattvas it is difficult to encounter the Buddha's presence in the world with a mind of faith in the three honored ones."

37. The Buddha asked a group of *śramaṇas*: "How should one measure the span of a man's life?" [One] replied: "By the span of a few days." The Buddha said: "You are not yet able to practice the Way." He asked another *śramaṇa*: "How should one measure the span of a man's life?" [The *śramaṇa*] replied: "By the space of a single meal." The Buddha said: "You are not yet able to practice the Way." He asked another *śramaṇa*: "How should one measure the span of a man's life?" [The *śramaṇa*] replied: "By the space of a single breath." The Buddha said: "Excellent! You can be called one who practices the Way."

38. The Buddha said: "Should one of my disciples venture several thousand miles from me yet remain mindful of my precepts, he is certain to attain the Way. However, should he stand immediately to my left yet harbor depraved thoughts, in the end he will not attain the Way. The gist lies in one's practice. If one is close to me but does not practice, of what benefit are the myriad divisions [of the path]?"

39. The Buddha said: "Practicing the Way is like eating honey, which is sweet all the way through. My scriptures are also like this: they are all about happiness, and those who practice [in accord with them] will attain the Way."

40. The Buddha said: "A man practicing the Way must be able to pluck up the roots of passion and desire, just as one would pluck a bead from a necklace. One by one they are removed until they are no more. When evil is no more the Way is attained."

41. The Buddha said: "A *śramaṇa* following the Way must be like an ox bearing a heavy burden treading through deep mud, so exhausted that he dares not glance left or right, yearning only to get out of the mud quickly so as to catch his breath. The *śramaṇa* regards his emotions and passions as more formidable than that mud. Mindful of the Way with a one-pointed mind, one is able to escape from myriad sufferings."

42. The Buddha said: "I regard the status of lords as a passing stranger. I regard treasures of gold and jade as gravel. I regard the beauty of fine silks as worn rags."

—— 29 ——

The Scripture on Perfect Wisdom for Humane Kings
Who Wish to Protect Their States

Charles Orzech

One of the most important dimensions of Buddhism in China, Korea, and Japan was its forging common cause with the state and its promotion of itself as the best religion for the protection of the state. State protection or, more prosaically, the promotion and use of Buddhism for the acumen of its prognosticators, the power of its thaumaturges to produce seasonable rains, or for its power to legitimate a rule by appeal to a grand cosmic vision and the ruler's place in it, has been more the norm than the exception in East Asia. The Chinese apocryphon *The Scripture on Perfect Wisdom for Humane Kings Who Wish to Protect Their States* (*Renwang hu guo banrou boluomiduo jing,* hereafter the *Scripture for Humane Kings*) was, for more than 1,500 years, the scriptural underpinning of what we might call "National Protection Buddhism." Indeed, the scripture was used to repulse invaders, both spiritual and military, from the eighth-century Tibetan invasion of the Chinese heartland to the twentieth-century American invasion of Japan.

The *Scripture for Humane Kings* was purportedly given by the Buddha to the Indian king Prasenajit for use in the future time of the decline of the teaching (*mofa*) and the disappearance of saints. Probably composed in Chinese in Central Asia or North China between 450 and 480, the scripture was based on ideas that flourished in Northwest India in Mahāyāna and proto-tantric circles. Two versions are extant, one from the fifth and one from the eighth century. Although the earliest catalogue notice of the *Scripture for Humane Kings* in *A Compilation of Notices on the Translation of the Tripiṭaka* (*Chu sangzan jiji*) of 515 lists it among texts for which the names of the "translator has been lost," the next catalogues, the *Catalogue of Scriptures* (*Chongjing mulu*) of 594 and the *Record of the Three Treasures throughout Successive Generations* (*Lidai sanbao ji*) of 597, mistakenly attribute it as the work of the famous translator Kumārajīva and list two other proported translations by Dharmarakṣa and Paramārtha.

The first recorded instance of the scripture's use in China was under Emperor

Chen Wudi in the year 559 C.E. when a great vegetarian banquet was ordered and, in accordance with the scripture, an altar with one hundred buddha images was constructed and one hundred teachers were called upon to expound its teachings. Probably composed in the aftermath of the persecution of Buddhism under the Northern Wei between 446 and 452, it apparently circulated anonymously until the last part of the century.

The shift from anonymous circulation to circulation under the names of Kumārajīva, Dharmarakṣa, and Paramārtha is linked to the fortunes of the Sui imperial house and the Tiantai founder Zhiyi. In 585 Zhiyi was coaxed down from his mountain retreat by the Chen emperor, and soon thereafter he was instructed to preach on the *Scripture for Humane Kings*. If his later "unofficial biography" (*bie zhuan*) is to be given credence, the lectures were attended by the emperor himself, and though two important clerics raised strenuous objections he overcame them. It is indeed significant that commentaries on the *Scripture for Humane Kings* are listed among the works of Guanding, Zhiyi's chief disciple and proponent. Correspondence between Guanding and the Sui rulers indicate a close link between the Tiantai school and the late Sui aristocracy.

The *Scripture for Humane Kings* quickly spread beyond China. The earliest notice of Japanese use of the *Scripture for Humane Kings* appears about a century after its first circulation in China, in the year 660, and the Korean *History of the Koryŏ* (*Koryŏ sa*) abounds in references to the scripture and its rites.

A second version, a new "translation" (765–766), was prepared by the monk Bukong jingang (Amoghavajra) at the request of Tang Emperor Daizong, and it became a key text in the propagation of the Zhenyan school (*mi jiao* or esoteric Buddhism) in eighth- and ninth-century China and of its descendant, Japanese Shingon Buddhism. Bukong had his first opportunity to celebrate the rite according to his new version in 765 during the Tibetan invasion of that year. The *Old Tang History* (*Jiu Tang shu*) notes that the rite was expressly ordered by Bukong's patron, Emperor Daizong, and it was carried out at the Shiming and Zesheng temples in the capital both for the repulsion of enemies and for the promotion of rain. In 767 Bukong requested an imperial edict to provide for the ordination of monks for the performance of the rite, which was to be used repeatedly as a centerpiece of Bukong's state cult. Thirty-seven monks (the number of the deities of the Vajradhātu maṇḍala) were ordained by imperial edict to chant the *Scripture for Humane Kings* and perform the rites on Mount Wutai, "to establish the state as a field of merit."

The *Scripture for Humane Kings* is a Perfect Wisdom scripture (*prajñāpāramitā*) extolling the path and salvific action of the bodhisattvas of Mahāyāna Buddhism. Large parts of the scripture are indistinguishable from Perfect Wisdom scriptures composed in Sanskrit, and it has strong affinities with the *Scripture of the Flower Garland* (*Avataṃsaka*, T 278), the *Scripture of the Ten Stages* (*Daśabhūmikasūtra*, T 286) and the *Nirvāṇa Scripture* (T 374–376). Scholars have linked the composition of the *Scripture for Humane Kings* with two other fifth-century Chinese scriptures, the *Scripture of Brahmā's Net* (*Brahmajālasūtra*, T 1484), which quotes the *Scripture for Humane Kings,* and the *Scripture of the Original Acts that Serve as Necklaces of the Bodhisattvas* (*Pusa yingluo benye jing,* T 1485), which is like it both in style and in the content of its bodhisattva path. Yet, unlike other Perfect Wisdom texts, the *Scripture for Humane Kings* is overtly addressed to rulers who, in this age of the decline of the teaching, have assumed roles indispensable for the pursuit of salvation.

The *Scripture for Humane Kings* reflected a broad range of concerns, from achieving enlightenment to attaining material wealth and security. In the *Scripture for Humane Kings* the Buddha, a renunciant, promised to help those who conquer or who wish to avoid conquest. Whether drought or pestilence, enemy armies or spiritual malaise threatened, the rituals prescribed in the text offered relief. If sufficient offerings and recitations were performed, then "the calamities shall be extinguished."

The two versions of the text that are extant are divided into an introduction and eight chapters. The introduction sets the scene of the preaching of the scripture as the Buddha's response to King Prasenajit's request for a teaching that "protects both the Buddha-fruit and the state." Chapters 2, 3, and 4 are in the classical mold of Perfect Wisdom scriptures: they present discourses on the three "gates" to liberation, (the empty, the signless, and the wishless), on the "perfections" of the bodhisattva path (rearranged into Fourteen Forbearances or *ren,* Sanskrit *kṣāntipāramitā*), and on the Two Truths. Chapter 5 directly addresses the problem of the protection of states, prescribing the following in response to a wide variety of disasters: In a gloriously adorned ritual arena, set up one hundred Buddha images, one hundred bodhisattva images, and one hundred lion thrones. Invite one hundred masters of the teaching to explicate this scripture, and before all of the thrones light different kinds of lamps, burn various incenses, scatter various flowers, and make vast and abundant offerings of clothing and utensils, drink and food, medicinal draughts, places of shelter and repose; all of the [appropriate] matters of offering. Twice each day [the masters] should expound and recite this scripture. Chapters 6, 7, and 8 reiterate and reinforce the relationship among the theological doctrine of Perfect Wisdom, the decline of the teaching, the bodhisattva path, and the role of kings.

Both versions of the scripture link the Perfect Wisdom teachings to the decline of the teaching, and the two versions are, in large part, identical word-for-word. Yet there are certain differences that bear noting. The fifth-century version of the text contains references to a favorite Six Dynasties (420–581) Chinese Buddhist apocalyptic figure, Prince Moonlight (Yueguang wang, Candraprabha). All references to him have been expunged from Bukong's version. In a more theological vein, the list of fourteen emptinesses in the fifth-century version owes more to a similar list in the *Nirvāṇa Scripture* than to any list in the Perfect Wisdom corpus. The inconsistency was cleaned up by Bukong. Both versions invoke Buddhist guardians to protect the state, but the eighth-century version supplements the earlier rite of setting up one hundred buddha images and so forth with an esoteric ritual (in chapter 7) to employ the kings of illumination (mingwang, Sanskrit vidyārāja) to assist in this task and appends there a long spell (tuo-luo-ni, Sanskrit dhāraṇī). These innovations were the subject of several ritual commentaries produced in the esoteric school in the late T'ang. Perhaps the most striking form of revisionism in Bukong's text is his substitution of the more common five hundred– and one thousand–based calculations of the decline in place of the Scripture for Humane Kings peculiar sequence of "eighty, eight hundred, and eight thousand" years.

Key to understanding the ideological and hermeneutic implications of the scripture is the linguistic and cosmological framework of the decline of the teaching and its relationship to the Perfect Wisdom teachings, a combination that brought together the two most widespread and influential Buddhist ideologies, one popular, the other theological. Both ideologies invoke ideas of emptiness and the unreliability of signs and referents. This combination of ideologies provided a compelling interpretive framework applicable to almost any situation.

The Scripture for Humane Kings is structured on an analogy between exterior rulers and interior rulers, between the conquerors of states and the conquerors of the self. Both sorts of conquerors must protect and nurture what they have attained. The deeper meaning of the analogy is grounded in the critique of language propounded by Nāgārjuna, the Indian author of the Mādhyamikakārikās, and embodied in the formula of the Two Truths. Just as worldly rulers are related to rulers of the self, so too conventional, everyday truth is related to absolute truth. Further, just as conventional truth is, finally, inseparable from absolute truth, so too are conventional rulers inseparable from rulers of the self. In the Scripture for Humane Kings these relationships are the object of a series of word plays, particularly the homophone ren, which means both "humane" (the virtue of the Confucian king) and "forbearing" (Sanskrit kṣānti, the virtue of the bodhisattva). According to reconstructions of ancient Chinese by Karlgren and others, these words were pronounced nzien and 'nzien, differing only in tone. The relationship between these words has been the starting point of nearly every traditional commentary, from those attributed to Zhiyi and Guiji to the modern Taiwanese productions. We find, for example, the following passage in the commentary attributed to Zhiyi:

Because the humane king is he who explicates the dharma and disseminates virtue here below, he is called "humane" (ren). Because he has transformed himself he is called "king." The humane king's ability is to protect. What is protected is the state. This is possible because the humane king uses the dharma to order the state. Now if we consider the prajñā [pāramitā], its ability is to protect. The humane king is he who is protected. Because he uses the prajñā [pāramitā], the humane king is tranquil and hidden. Thus, if he uses his ability to propagate the dharma, the king is able to protect [the state], and it is the prajñā [pāramitā] that is the [method of] protection. Moreover, one who is humane (ren) is forbearing (ren). Hearing of good he is not overjoyed, hearing of bad he is not angry. Because he is able to hold to forebearance in good and bad, therefore he is called forebearing (T 1705 253b28–253c4).

The *Scripture for Humane Kings* builds on this wordplay, as both "humane kings" and "kings of forbearance" are said to "transform" (*hua*) the people. Both "cultivate," "nurture," or "protect" (*hu*) their "states" (*guo, di,* Skt. *bhūmi*). Yet it is clear from the text that this linguistic play reflects a deep structural bond that is normally hidden or disguised. Thus, the *Scripture for Humane Kings* describes the hierarchy of cosmic authority as founded on a single underlying continuity and expressed in "geographic" terms, ranging up to lords of the highest trance-heavens:

> If a bodhisattva-mahāsattva dwells in one hundred buddha-fields he becomes a Wheel-turning King of Jambudvīpa. He cultivates one hundred brilliant gates of the teaching and uses the perfection of giving to abide in equinamity, and he transforms the beings of the four quarters of the world. If a bodhisattva-mahāsattva dwells in one thousand buddha-fields he becomes the celestial king of the Heaven of the Thirty-three. He cultivates one thousand brilliant gates of the teaching, and he discourses on the ten good paths [of virtue], transforming all living beings. . . . (T 246 8378a8–12)

The puns and analogies between conventional and absolute truth, conventional and interior rulers, are crucial to the *Scripture*'s popularity in China and Japan. They allow the text itself to inscribe and reproduce a crisis of referentiality that characterizes the onset of apocalyptic times. In these latter days the outward signs of authority (monastic robes, earlier canonical texts, etc.) no longer refer to inward realities. Indeed, in a key passage the decay of the teaching is signaled by the fact that "White-robed [commoners will occupy] high-seated 'bhikṣu' (monk) positions," a reference to lay officials in positions of power over monastic affairs and to the common topos that in the last age of the teaching monastic robes would of themselves turn white. In such a decayed world, surprising reversals and unusual connections are hidden amid the confusion of images. Rulers are, contrary to common understanding, bodhisattvas, and they are traversing the bodhisattva path.

The hermeneutic structure of the decline of the teaching was used not only by rulers to legitimate their reigns, but also by monks in a ritual triple entendre. For while the "humane kings" could point to the *Scripture for Humane Kings* to undergird their status, esoteric rites performed by monks—the "kings of forbearance"—upheld the "humane kings." Thus, the crisis of referentiality embodied in the decline of the teaching makes possible the puns of the *Scripture for Humane Kings* and the many uses to which the scripture was put.

The translation below includes the most distinctive part of chapter 5 and all of chapter 8 from the eighth-century version by Bukong, *Renwang huguo banruo boluomiduo jing,* T246, 8.840a–45a.

Further Reading

The best treatment of the theme of the "decline of the teaching" is Jan Nattier's *Once upon a Future Time* (San Francisco: Asian Humanities Press, 1991). Charles Orzech's "Puns on the Humane King: Analogy and Application in an East Asian Apocryphon," *Journal of the American Oriental Society* 109.1 (1989) explores some of the implications of the words "humane" and "forbearing." The role of the *Scripture of Brahmā's Net* and other apocrypha related to the *Scripture for Humane Kings* is covered in essays collected by Robert E. Buswell, Jr., in *Chinese Buddhist Apocrypha* (Honolulu: University of Hawaii Press, 1990). On the bodhisattva Moonlight (Candraprabha), see E. Zürcher, "Prince Moonlight: Messianism and Eschatology in Early Medieval Chinese Buddhism," *T'oung Pao* 68 (1982): 1–59. M. W. de Visser's *Ancient Buddhism in Japan: Sūtras and Ceremonies in Use in the Seventh and Eighth Centuries A.D. and Their History in Later Times* (Leiden: E. J. Brill, 1935), vol. 1, pp. 116–242 provides a summary translation of approximately one-third of the *Scripture for Humane Kings* as well as summaries of the important esoteric ritual commentaries. A complete study and translation is forthcoming in Charles Orzech, *Signs of Authority: The Scripture for Humane Kings and the Creation of National Protection Buddhism* (Pennsylvania State University Press).

The Perfect Wisdom (Prajñāpāramitā) Scripture for Humane Kings Who Wish to Protect Their States

CHAPTER 5: PROTECTING THE STATE (T 246, 8.840a9–29)

At that time the World-Honored One told King Prasenajit and all of the other kings of great states, "Listen carefully, listen carefully, and on your behalf I will explain the method for protecting states. In all states at times when [things are on] the point of disorder, and all of the disasters, difficulties, and bandits come to wreak havoc, you and all of the kings should receive and keep, read and recite this Perfect Wisdom [scripture]. In a gloriously adorned ritual arena set up one hundred buddha images, one hundred bodhisattva images, and one hundred lion thrones. Invite one hundred masters of the teaching (*fashi*) to explicate this scripture and before all of the thrones light different kinds of lamps, burn various incenses, scatter various flowers, and make vast and abundant offerings of clothing and utensils, drink and food, medicinal draughts, places of shelter and repose; all of the [appropriate] matters of offering. Twice each day [the masters] should expound and recite this scripture. If the king, the great officers, monks, nuns, and male and female lay devotees hear, receive, read, and recite and, according to [the prescribed] method, cultivate and practice it, the disorders and difficulties will then be eradicated.

"Great king! In every territory there are numberless spectres and spirits each of whom has countless minions. If they hear this scripture they will protect your territory. When a state is on the verge of disorder the spectres and spirits are first disorderly. Because of the chaos of the spectres and spirits the myriad people become disorderly, and in due course there are bandit uprisings and the one hundred surnames perish. The king, the heir apparent, the princes, and the one hundred officers engage in mutual recrimination.

"In Heaven and on Earth there are transformations and monstrosities, and the sun, the moon, and all the stars lose their proper times and appearances. There are holocausts, great floods, typhoons, and the like. When these difficulties arise everyone should receive and keep, read and recite this Perfect Wisdom [scripture]. If, as [stipulated] in the scripture, people receive and keep, read and recite, everything they seek—official position, abundant wealth, sons and daughters, wisdom and understanding—will come according to their wishes. Human and celestial rewards will all be attained and fulfilled. Illness and difficulty will be totally eradicated. [Those with] bonds and fetters, cangues and locks encumbering their bodies will all be liberated. [Those who have] broken the four most serious prohibitions, committed the five heinous crimes, or even violated all the prohibitions [will see their] limitless transgressions all be completely wiped out."

CHAPTER 8: THE CHARGE ("ENTRUSTING" THE SCRIPTURE) (T246, 8.844b6–845a1)

The Buddha told King Prasenajit, "Now let me caution you and the others. After my extinction the correct teaching (zheng fa, Sanskrit saddharma) will be on the point of extinction. After fifty, after five hundred, or after five thousand years there will be no buddha, teaching, or community, and this scripture and the three jewels will be committed to all the kings of states for establishment and protection. [I want to] tell all my disciples of the four categories and so on to receive and keep it, to read and recite it, to understand its meaning and principles, and to broadly expound the essentials of its teaching on behalf of beings and have [them] practice and cultivate it and [thereby] depart from birth and death (sheng si, Sanskrit saṃsāra).

"Great King, in the latter [part] of the five impure epochs (wu du shi, Sanskrit kasyaya) all the kings of states, the princes, and great officers will be haughty and hold themselves in great esteem and destroy my teaching. [They] will institute laws to restrain my disciples—the monks and nuns—and [they] will not permit people to leave the family to cultivate and practice the correct way (zheng dao), nor will they allow people to make Buddhist stūpas and images. White-robed [lay persons] will assume high seats [hitherto reserved for monks], while monks will stand on the ground. [Their position] will be no different from that [stipulated] in the regulations for soldiers and slaves. [You] should know that at that time the extinction of the teaching will not be long [off].

"Great king, the causes of the destruction of states all are of your own making: Trusting in your awesome power you regulate the fourfold assembly and will not permit the cultivation of blessings. All the evil monks receive preferential treatment (*shou bieqing*, contrary to the vinaya), while [in contrast] monks wise and learned in the teaching come together in a single-minded pursuit of fellowship, vegetarian feasts, and the quest for religious merit. (The passage seems to imply that learned monks are engaged in a selfish pursuit of merit rather than a selfless service to the ruler.) These heterodox rules are completely contrary to my teaching. [Thus,] the one hundred surnames sicken [and face] limitless sufferings and difficulties. [You] should know that at that time the state will be destroyed. Great king, during the teaching's final era (*famo shi*), kings of states, the great officers, and the four classes of disciples all will act contrary to the teaching and in contravention of Buddhist teaching. [They] will commit every transgression and, contrary to the teaching and to the discipline, bind monks and imprison them. [By this you] will know that the extinction of the teaching is not long [off].

"Great king! After my extinction the four classes of disciples, all the kings of states, the princes, and the one hundred officers and all those appointed to hold and protect the three jewels will themselves destroy [the teaching] like worms in a lion's body that consume his own flesh. [And these] are not the heterodox [teachers]! Those who ruin my teaching [are guilty of] a great transgression. When the correct teaching decays and weakens, the people are bereft of proper conduct. Every evil will gradually increase, and their fortunes will daily be diminished. There will no longer be filial sons, and the six relationships will be discordant. The heavenly dragons will not defend [them], and evil demons and evil dragons will daily become more injurious. Calamities and monstrosities will intertwine, causing misfortunes to multiply (lit., vertical and horizontal, criss-cross). As is fitting [they] will be suspended in hell and reborn as animals or hungry ghosts, and [even] if they should attain human birth they will be poor and destitute, and lowborn with faculties impaired or incomplete. Just as shadow follows form, as an echo follows a sound, as a person writes at night when the light has gone out yet the words remain [the next day], the fruit of the destruction of the teaching is just like this.

"Great king! In generations to come, all the kings of states, the princes, the great officers, together with my disciples will perversely establish registration [of monks] and institute overseers and great and small monk directors (*da xiao sengtong*), contravening the principle [forbidding] employment [of monks] as lackeys (lit., as servants). Then you should know that at that time the Buddhist teaching is not long [to survive].

"Great king! In generations to come all the kings of states and the four classes of disciples [will] correctly rely upon all the buddhas of the ten directions, and constantly [these will] practice the Way, establish and disseminate it. Nevertheless, evil monks seeking fame and profit will not rely on my teaching, and they will go before the kings of states and will themselves utter transgressions and evil, becoming the cause of the destruction of the teaching. These kings will not distinguish [between the good and evil monks], and believing and accepting these sayings will perversely establish regulation [of monastic communities] and not rely on the Buddhist prohibitions (vinaya). You should know that at that time the extinction of the teaching is not long [off].

"Great king! In generations to come all the kings of states and the four classes of disciples will themselves be the cause of the destruction of the teaching and the destruction of the state. They themselves will suffer from this, and it is not the Buddhist teaching that is to blame. The heavenly dragons will depart, the five turbidities will in turn increase. A full discussion of this would exhaust an aeon and would still be unfinished."

At that time, [when] the kings of the sixteen great states heard the exposition concerning what was yet to come and all such warnings, the sound of their wailing and crying shook the three thousand [worlds]. Heaven and Earth were darkened and no light shone. Then, all the kings and the others, each and every one, resolved to receive and keep the Buddha's words and [to forgo] regulation of the four classes [of disciples who] leave the family to study the way; [this] is in accordance with the Buddha's teaching.

At that time, these assemblies—numberless as the sands of the Ganges—sighed together, saying: "It would be fitting that at such a time the world would be empty; a world bereft of buddhas."

Then King Prasenajit said to the Buddha: "World-Honored One, what should we call this scripture? How am I and the others to receive and keep it?" The Buddha said: "Great king! This scripture is called *The Perfect Wisdom for Humane Kings Who Wish to Protect Their States*. It may also be called *The Sweet Dew Teaching Medicine* [because] it is like a remedy whose action is able to reduce all illness.

"Great king! The merit and virtue of this perfect wisdom, like [that of] the void, cannot be fathomed. If one receives and keeps it, reads and recites it, the merit and virtue obtained will be able to protect humane kings and even all beings, like walls, yea, like a city's walls. This is why you and the others should receive and keep it."

When the Buddha had finished expounding this scripture, Maitreya the lion-roarer and all the countless bodhisattva-mahāsattvas, Śāriputra, Subhūti, and so forth, the limitless auditors, and the numberless gods and men of the desire realm, the form realm, and the formless realm, the monks and nuns, the male and female lay devotees, the asuras ("demons" or "titans")—all of the great assemblies—heard what the Buddha had said and with great joy trusted [in it], accepted and received [it, and put it into] practice.

— 30 —

The Buddhism of the Cultured Elite

Peter N. Gregory

The Buddhist monk and scholar Zongmi (780–841) played an important role in the development of two of the major traditions of medieval Chinese Buddhism, Huayan and Chan, being honored as a "patriarch" in each. His writings are thus often portrayed as representing a blending of Huayan theory with Chan practice. Huayan was one of the principal scholastic traditions that developed during the Tang dynasty (618–907). It claimed that its teachings were based on the mystical vision of the infinite interpenetration of all things that the Buddha realized during his enlightenment as revealed in the *Huayan* (or *Avataṃsaka*) *Sūtra,* from which it took its name and spiritual warrant. Chan (or Zen) began to emerge as a self-conscious tradition at the end of the seventh century. Rejecting scriptural authority, it claimed to be based on a historical transmission of the Buddha's enlightened understanding down through an unbroken lineage of patriarchs.

Zongmi lived and wrote during a time when a number of radical movements were gaining currency within Chinese Chan. The iconoclastic rhetoric of these traditions could easily be misinterpreted in antinomian ways that denied the need for spiritual cultivation and moral discipline. Having grown up and received his early Chan training in Sichuan, an area in which the most extreme of these movements flourished in the late eighth and early ninth centuries, Zongmi was particularly sensitive to such ethical dangers. He accordingly adapted Huayan metaphysics as a buttress against the antinomian implications of these radical interpretations of Chan teachings.

In using Huayan to articulate the ontological basis and philosophical rationale for Chan practice, however, Zongmi also redirected the thrust of some of the central Huayan teachings. Most importantly, he shifted emphasis away from the *Huayan Sūtra* to the *Awakening of Faith in Mahāyāna* (*Dasheng qixin lun*). Although the Chinese tradition ascribes the *Awakening of Faith* to Aśvaghoṣa, modern scholarship has shown that it was not a translation of a work by that venerable Indian master but that it was instead an apocryphal text composed in Chinese during the third quarter of the sixth century. By extending the Indian Buddhist doctrine of the *tathāgatagarbha* (womb or embryo of the Tathāgata) to claim that all sentient beings are intrinsically enlightened to begin with, this treatise became the cornerstone for East Asian Buddhist theory and practice. In addition to offering an ontology that locates enlightenment within the original nature of all human beings, the *Awakening of Faith* also provides an explanation for how the process of delusion arises and perpetuates itself. Zongmi was thus able to use this text to furnish a cosmogony that he made serve as a map for Buddhist practice.

The two works translated below, Zongmi's *Response to a Question from Wen Zao* (*Da Wen Shangshu suowen*) and his *Response to Ten Questions from Shi Shanren* (*Da Shi Shanren shiwen*), are typical of the learned discourse that transpired between Zongmi and his literati disciples. Both exchanges reiterate a number of the major themes amplified in Zongmi's longer and more famous works, such as his *Inquiry into the Origin of Humanity* (*Yuanrenlun*) and *Preface to the Collected Writings on the Source of Chan* (*Chanyuan zhuquanji duxu*), as well as reveal some of the central issues that Chinese Buddhists debated in the second half of the eighth and first half of the ninth centuries.

Zongmi's response to Wen Zao was probably written sometime between 828 and 835 and was subsequently included in his *Collected Correspondence with Laity and Clergy* (*Daosu chouda wenji*), compiled by his disciples shortly after his death in 841. Wen Zao (767–836) was one of Zongmi's most prominent lay disciples. He was connected to the imperial line through marriage, and his devoted service to the Tang cause while on the staff of various provincial governors eventually earned him a prestigious appointment in the central government as minister in charge of the Board of Rites. Zongmi's response to Wen Zao answers his question about the fate of the enlightened person after death. Zongmi appended a short verse to his original letter and later, in response to a further entreaty from Wen Zao, added his own explanatory note to his essay and verse (the latter of which is not translated below). Here and elsewhere, Zongmi insisted that an initial experience of enlightenment did not obviate the need for further religious effort but had to be followed by an often protracted regimen of spiritual practice so that it could be thoroughly integrated into all of one's activities. Sudden enlightenment is made possible by the teaching that an intrinsically enlightened mind is inherent in all beings; the subsequent gradual cultivation is necessitated by the persistence of the habitual residue of past conditioning. As his explanatory note reveals, Zongmi's theory of sudden enlightenment followed by gradual cultivation is based on his understanding of the *Awakening of Faith*.

The second text, Zongmi's *Response to Ten Questions from Shi Shanren*, records an exchange that took place in 824. Each of Shi Shanren's questions and Zongmi's answers was originally composed as a separate letter; all ten were then collected together and subsequently included in Zongmi's *Collected Correspondence with Laity and Clergy*. Nothing is known about Shi Shanren, although both his name, Shanren ("mountain man"), and his historical obscurity suggest that he was a lay recluse, perhaps living in seclusion on Mount Zhongnan, the mountain where Zongmi passed much of the last two decades of his life. The sophistication of Shi

Shanren's questions indicates that he was a member of the cultured elite, and the ten questions and answers are characteristic of the learned discourse that Zongmi and his literati disciples engaged in.

The exchange is important for revealing some of the central issues that Chinese Buddhists debated in the eighth and early part of the ninth centuries. It begins with a discussion of the nature of the Way (*dao*), a term that here means both enlightenment and the path by which it is realized. If the Way is unconditioned, then the question naturally arises of how it could be achieved by practice, which is based on cause and effect and thus falls within the realm of the conditioned. How could a conditioned practice bring about an unconditioned result? This question had direct bearing on the nature of religious practice, and in the eighth century it was given paradigmatic expression in the sudden/gradual controversy.

The sudden/gradual controversy enfolded a complex set of issues, and the terms were used variously by different partisans in the debate. One of the primary meanings of "sudden" was direct or unmediated. The sudden teaching was thus the teaching in which the truth was revealed immediately without recourse to any expedients as exemplified by the *Huayan Sūtra*, in which the Buddha was believed to have fully revealed the content of his enlightenment without making any concessions to the limited ability of his audience to comprehend its meaning. In the gradual teaching, by contrast, the truth was mediated by expedient means (*upāya*) to make it accessible to the limited abilities of the Buddha's followers. Since many Chinese Buddhists regarded truth as a single, unitary principle, a further connotation of "sudden" was that truth could only be grasped all at once in its entirety—enlightenment, therefore, could only occur suddenly. Gradualists, on the other hand, assumed that enlightenment admitted of degrees, or at least that it could be approached in a graduated series of stages. In the *Platform Sūtra of the Sixth Patriarch,* which expressed the orthodox position for the later Chan tradition, gradualists were criticized for teaching that meditation practice was a means for attaining enlightenment. Subitists, however, held that there could be no duality between meditation and enlightenment. One way in which the two positions were often reconciled was to claim that they represented opposing, but interrelated, perspectives on practice and enlightenment: whereas the gradual position looked at practice from the point of view of the unenlightened, the sudden position looked at practice from the point of view of the enlightened. Thus the sudden position was often associated with ultimate truth (*paramārtha-satya*), and the gradual position, with conventional truth (*saṃvṛti-satya*). As a further corollary, the sudden teaching was frequently said to be appropriate for beings of the highest capacity, whereas the gradual teaching was appropriate for everyone else.

The *Platform Sūtra of the Sixth Patriarch* represented the sudden/gradual debate as the cause for a fundamental split that occurred within the Chan tradition during the eighth century, dividing the so-called northern line from the so-called southern line. Thus the southern line of Huineng (638–713) and Shenhui (684–758), which emerged as the orthodox tradition, claimed the ideological high ground over the northern line, which it pictured as espousing a gradualistic, and hence inferior, approach to enlightenment. In this way the sudden/gradual issue was related to the question of lineage, the subject of Shi Shanren's ninth question. Standing within the southern lineage of Shenhui, Zongmi was committed to upholding the sudden position but (as seen in his response to Wen Zao) moderated its radical implications by insisting that sudden enlightenment had to be followed by gradual practice.

Both Zongmi's *Response to a Question from Wen Zao* and *Response to Ten Questions from Shi Shanren* are appended to his biography in the *Transmission of the Flame Compiled during the Jingde Period* (*Jingde chuandeng lu*), compiled by Daoyuan in 1004 and published in the Taishō Tripiṭaka, vol. 51, pp. 307b3–308b16. A slightly different version of both exchanges appears in a manuscript discovered at Shinpuku-ji in Japan and published by Ishii Shūdō in *Zengaku kenkyū* 60 (1981):98–104. Zongmi's *Response to Ten Questions from Shi Shanren* is also appended to his biography in fascicle 6 of the *Chodang chip,* compiled in 952.

Further Reading

For a study of Zongmi's life and thought, see Peter N. Gregory, *Tsung-mi and the Sinification of Buddhism* (Princeton: Princeton University Press, 1991); see also Gregory, *Inquiry into the Origin of Humanity: An Annotated Translation of Tsung-mi's Yüan jen lun with a Modern Commentary* (Honolulu: University of Hawaii Press, 1995).

Response to a Question from Wen Zao (Da Wen Shangshu suowen)

[Wen Zao's question:] If one who has realized the truth and cut off delusion is not bound by karma, then what does his numinous nature depend on after his life has come to an end?

[Zongmi's reply:] There is not a single sentient being that is not fully endowed with an enlightened nature, which is numinous, bright, empty, and tranquil and which is no different from the Buddha. It is only because for aeons without beginning [sentient beings] have never realized it but have deludedly clung to their bodily existence as their selves that they give rise to feelings such as attraction and aversion and, in accord with those feelings, generate karma. Receiving retribution in accord with their karma, they experience birth, sickness, old age, and death and prolong the aeons in which they transmigrate.

Thus the enlightened nature within our bodily existence never is born nor dies. [Its presence within deluded beings] is like dreaming one is being driven away while one is safe at home. Or it is like water: although it turns to ice, its wet nature does not change. If one is able to realize that this very nature is the dharma body, which from the beginning is unborn, then how could there be anything to depend on? [This nature] is our numinous, unobscured, clear, and bright ever-present awareness. There is nowhere from which it comes and nowhere to which it goes.

Since over many lifetimes deluded attachments have become second nature, the subtle effects of delight, anger, grief, and joy continue to flow on so that even though the true principle is penetrated all at once, it is difficult to cut off these feelings suddenly. One must methodically become aware of them over a long time so as to reduce them and further reduce them [until there are none left]. [This process] is like the wind: although it suddenly ceases, the waves [it has stirred into motion] only gradually subside. How could the cultivation of a single lifetime equal the activity of the buddhas? Just take empty tranquility to be the self-essence. Do not acknowledge your physical body [as your self] but take your numinous awareness as your own mind. Do not acknowledge deluded thoughts [as real]; whenever deluded thoughts arise, do not follow any of them. Then at the time of death your karma will naturally not be able to bind you, and you may resort to the heavenly or human realms as you wish. If thoughts of attraction and aversion have been eliminated, then you will not receive a predestined bodily existence and will be able to alter the length of your life and physical appearance. When the flow of the subtle effects is altogether extinguished and just the great wisdom of perfect enlightenment shines forth alone, then, according to circumstances, you will be able to manifest billions of bodily forms to save sentient beings caught in conditions—that is what is meant by buddhahood.

[Zongmi's explanatory note:] Aśvaghoṣa bodhisattva gathered together the hundred books of the great vehicle and condensed their essential message in writing the *Awakening of Faith in Mahāyāna*. His treatise establishes the cardinal principle, explaining that the mind of all sentient beings has an enlightened and unenlightened aspect. Within the enlightened [aspect] there is also an intrinsically enlightened aspect and an experientially enlightened aspect. Even though what I wrote above was phrased in terms of illuminating the truth and contemplating the mind, its meaning is the same as [Aśvaghoṣa's] treatise. From the beginning to "no different from the Buddha" corresponds to intrinsic enlightenment. From "it is only because for aeons without beginning" corresponds to unenlightenment. From "if one is able to realize" corresponds to experiential enlightenment. Within experiential enlightenment there are also sudden enlightenment and gradual cultivation. From here ["if one is able to realize"] to "nowhere to which it goes" corresponds to sudden enlightenment. From "since over many lifetimes deluded attachments" corresponds to gradual cultivation. Within gradual cultivation from the time when one first generates the thought of enlightenment until one attains buddhahood there are three levels of freedom. From "you may resort [to the heavenly or human realms] as you wish" corresponds to freedom in receiving existence. From "if thoughts of attraction and aversion [have been eliminated]" corresponds to freedom in transformation. From "when the flow of the subtle effects [is altogether extinguished]" corresponds to ultimate freedom. Finally, from "just take empty tranquility as the self-essence" to "your karma will naturally not be able to bind you" truly is the way one who has realized the truth puts his mind into practice from dawn to dusk and corresponds to the essentials of the cultivation of calming and contemplation. (Zongmi's poem:)

> Doing what is right is the awakened mind;
> Doing what is wrong is the unruly mind.
> The unruly [mind] follows affective thoughts—when you meet your end you
>   will be pulled by your karma.
> The awakened [mind] does not follow feelings—when you meet your end you
>   will be able to transform your karma.

Response to Ten Questions from Shi Shanren
(Da Shi Shanren shiwen)

Q: What is the Way, and how is it cultivated? Must it be cultivated to be completed, or does it not depend on effort?

A: Being unobstructed is the Way; enlightening delusion is cultivation. Even though the Way is originally perfect, delusion arises, and [beings] become bound. When deluded thoughts are entirely exhausted, cultivation is complete.

Q: If the Way depends on cultivation to be completed, then it is conditioned and is the same as mundane dharmas, which are false and not true. If, being completed, it once again falls into decline, then how can it be called supermundane?

A: What is conditioned is tied up with karma and is called false and mundane. What is unconditioned is the practice of cultivation and is true and supermundane.

Q: Is the process of cultivation sudden or gradual? If it is gradual, then, in forgetting the past and letting go of the future, how are [past and future] brought together and completed? If it is sudden, then how can the myriad practices and numerous means be consummated at one time?

A: As soon as the true principle is realized, it is suddenly perfect, but the process of completely eliminating deluded feelings occurs gradually. Being suddenly perfect is like a newborn babe: in one day its limbs and body are completely intact. Gradual cultivation is like rearing, nurturing, and bringing a person to adulthood: only after many years does his personality become formed.

Q: In the cultivation of the teaching of the mind ground, does the realization of the mind take place all at once or is there a further practice to be undertaken? If there is a further practice, why is it called the sudden purport of the southern lineage? If on realization a person is the same as all buddhas, why does one not emit spiritually pervading light?

A: When you recognize that a frozen pond consists entirely of water, [you understand that] it will melt by means of the sun's heat; when you realize that the ordinary person is true reality, you will cultivate yourself assisted by the power of the dharma. When ice melts, water flows freely, immediately releasing its benefits of washing [impurities] away. When delusions are exhausted, the spiritual energy of the mind pervades [everywhere], and one for the first time emits the response of pervading light. There is no further practice beyond cultivating the mind.

Q: If one attains buddhahood only by cultivating one's mind, then why do various scriptures also preach that it is necessary to adorn buddha-lands and teach other beings and that only [fulfilling such practices] is what it means to complete the Way?

A: When a mirror is bright, it reflects images in thousands of variations; when the mind is pure, it spiritually pervades in myriads of responses. Reflected images represent adorning buddhalands; spiritually pervading means teaching other beings. The adornment is at once [adornment] and not adornment; the reflected images are both form and not form.

Q: The scriptures all preach liberating living beings and that, furthermore, living beings are not living beings. Why, then, should we strive to liberate them?

A: To truly liberate living beings takes effort. You have just said that they are not living beings; why did you not add that they are [both] liberated and not liberated?

Q: Some scriptures say that the Buddha is eternal, whereas others say that he passed into nirvāṇa. If he is eternal, then he is not deceased; if he is deceased, then he is not eternal. Is not there a contradiction here?

A: [Those who] transcend all phenomenal appearances are called buddhas—how could there be any reality to their appearing in the world and entering nirvāṇa? Manifesting his appearance and disappearance is a matter of exigency. In response to exigencies, he appears under the bodhi tree; when those exigencies have been completely met, he passes into nirvāṇa between the sāla trees. The mindlessness of clear water offers an analogy: there is no image that is not reflected in it. But images are not real existents, so how could the going and coming of external things be? Phenomenal appearances are not the Buddha's body, so how could the appearance and disappearance of the Tathāgata be?

Q: How is the Buddha born through transformation? Is it like my being reborn? Given that the Buddha is without birth, what meaning could birth have? If you say that dharmas are born when mind is born and that dharmas are extinguished when mind is extinguished, then how can the acceptance of the nonbirth of dharmas (anutpattikadharmakṣānti) be attained?

A: You just spoke of transformation. Since transformation is itself empty and emptiness is without birth, what need is there to inquire into the meaning of birth? When birth and death have been extinguished, tranquil extinction is true reality. Accepting that this dharma is without birth is what is called the acceptance of the nonbirth of dharmas.

Q: Buddhas complete the Way and preach the dharma solely for the sake of liberating living beings. Since living beings have six paths [of existence], why did the Buddha only manifest himself within the human [path]? Again, after the Buddha's demise, the dharma was passed down through a mind-to-mind transmission from Kāśyapa down to the seven Chinese patriarchs, and in each generation [the dharma] was only transmitted to a single person. Since you have said that all living beings without exception attain the stage of "the one son" (a phrase generally referring to buddhahood, where everyone is equally valued as one's only son, but here used by Shi Shanren with the further connotation of "sole heir"), why was the transmission not to everyone?

A: Although the sun and moon traverse the heavens, illuminating all directions, the blind do not see them. Shrouded in darkness, they do not know that it is not the sun and moon that do not reach everywhere; the fault lies in their [vision] being obscured. The case of the meaning of liberating and not liberating is like this. It is not that [out of the six paths] humans and gods were chosen over [hungry] ghosts and beasts. It is because only human beings are able to accumulate [experience] and pass it on [to successive generations] without interruption that we know that the Buddha appeared among humans. After his death, he entrusted [the dharma] to Kāśyapa, and the succession of one person [in each generation] continued in turn. Furthermore, it is like the principle of patrilineal organization in the present age: a country surely does not have two kings. It is not that those who are liberated are limited to that number.

Q: On what basis does one give rise to the thought of enlightenment (bodhicitta), and in emulation of what dharma does one renounce the world? Now, how should practice be cultivated, and how does one experience the taste of the dharma? What level will practice attain to? Should one abide in mind, or should one cultivate mind? If one abides in mind, that hinders the cultivation of mind; but if one cultivates mind, when thoughts stir one is not settled—how can that be called mastering the Way? If one settles the mind in a single meditative practice (samādhi), how does that differ from [what is practiced by] the adepts of meditation? I pray that you will be moved by your great compassion to explain each [of these matters] in turn for me in accord with the truth.

A: Giving rise to the thought of enlightenment involves mastering that the four great elements [of earth, water, fire, and wind] are as [unreal as] something conjured; penetrating that the six sense objects are as [illusory as] flowers in the sky; realizing that one's own mind is the mind of Buddha; and seeing that [one's] original nature is the dharma nature. Understanding that the mind does not abide is itself the practice of cultivation. That it does not abide and yet is aware is the taste of the dharma. If one clings to dharmas, that is stirring thoughts into motion, which is thus like when someone is shut in darkness, there is nothing that can be seen. Now if one does not abide [in anything], there is no defilement or clinging, which is thus like someone with eyes who, when he comes into the full light of the sun, sees the multitudinous dharmas. How could that be [like what is realized by] adepts of meditation? When there is no clinging, how can one talk about a level to be attained?

—31—

Buddhist Ritual and the State

Albert Welter

What role should Buddhist ritual have in Chinese state ceremonies? This question was asked with increasing frequency from the closing years of the Tang dynasty (618–907), as Confucians steadily began to reassert their claim over the Chinese tradition. Behind this concern lurked an even more serious one: Does a foreign religion like Buddhism have a legitimate role in China? Not since the early advances of Buddhism on Chinese soil had the presence of Buddhists and their institutions in Chinese society been so aggressively challenged. This challenge prompted a series of debates within the imperial bureaucracy over the legitimate role of Buddhist institutions within Chinese society.

The *Outline History of the Saṅgha* (*Seng shilue*) occupies a key position within these debates. It was written by the Buddhist scholar-monk Zanning (919–1001) at the request of Emperor Taizong in the early years of the Song dynasty (960–1279). As an expert on Buddhist monastic ritual and a highly respected member of the imperial bureaucracy, Zanning was in a strategically advantageous position to influence imperial opinion and advance the cause of Buddhism. In the *Outline History*, Zanning argues that Buddhism has a legitimate role in Chinese society and that it serves a useful function in state ceremonies. He thus calls for the continued sponsorship of Buddhist ceremonies by the Chinese state.

Arguably the most sensitive of all official rites in China were those associated with the imperial ancestors. On the surface, these rites were conducted for the purpose of showing filial respect to departed ancestors. In reality, they served a broader social and political function. Funeral and memorial rites affirmed the position of the emperor as the Son of Heaven (*tian zi*) by connecting the emperor with the ancestral founders of the dynasty in question. By implication, these rites helped to legitimize the current social and political order established under imperial authority. The performance of the rites themselves was sanctioned by ancient precedent veiled in the aura of hallowed tradition. Among the classic works of the Confucian tradition, the *Record of Rites* (*Liji*) and other classic ritual texts set the standard for ancestral worship. The model of the *Record of Rites* stipulated that respect for departed ancestors be provided through visits to the ancestral temple on appointed memorial days. At these memorials, the flesh of sacrificial animals, agricultural produce, and libations were to be offered to the spirits of the departed. Incense was not originally used in these ceremonies. Other aromatic substances, however, played an important part. The aroma produced by the blood and fat of the sacrificial victim and that produced by millet and artemisia were regularly offered to Heaven as a common feature of these ceremonies. The conclusion of the ceremony involved a banquet at which the descendants of the departed paid respects to their common ancestor and renewed their communal bonds with each other. This was the model adopted by the Confucian state for offerings to imperial ancestors.

Buddhist influence on Chinese beliefs and rituals, including funeral and memorial services for departed ancestors, is exhibited in the effect that it had on the ritual practices of the emperor. By the Tang dynasty, Buddhist memorial services were officially sanctioned on anniversaries of deceased emperors. These services accompanied the traditional Confucian rites. The Buddhist rites stemmed from the religious tradition of India and were based on notions of rebirth and the transmigration of souls after death. The belief in the transmigration of the soul of the deceased provided a compelling rationale for performing the Buddhist rites. Buddhist memorial services were established on the premise that the living could enlist the aid of the buddhas and Buddhist deities on behalf of the deceased. Central to this Buddhist practice was the belief that merit accumulated through the religious efforts of the living could be transferred to the transmigrating soul of the deceased. The accumulation of such merit called for the performance of specific Buddhist rites under the jurisdiction of the Buddhist clergy. The offering of incense was a central feature of these Buddhist rites. The incense-offering rite was typically followed by a vegetarian banquet sponsored for members of the Buddhist clergy by those seeking merit on behalf of the soul of the deceased. In the case of departed emperors, these rites and banquest were sponsored by the government and required the attendance and participation of government representatives.

Within this apparently harmonious solution to the popularity of Buddhism in China lay the seeds of potential conflict. Inherent in the dual structure of Confucian and Buddhist rites were two competing visions of the world and the position of the Chinese emperor. In the Confucian vision, the Chinese emperor was akin to the "north star" as the representative of Heaven on Earth, the pinnacle of the human order around which terrestrial bodies revolved. In this vision, the emperor served as the ultimate source of both political and spiritual authority on Earth. In the Buddhist vision, the emperor was a disciple of the Buddha, albeit a very important one, whose authority was ultimately subjected to the sanction of Buddhist teaching. As earthly ruler, the emperor was entrusted with supporting and promoting the Buddhist cause. This conception provided strong pretext for dividing political and spiritual authority between the imperial bureaucracy and the Buddhist clergy. The tension inherent in these two competing visions eventually resulted in a dramatic rupture. In the late Tang dynasty, the conflict surfaced in an official challenge to Buddhism that precipitated a campaign of massive restrictions placed on the institutions and activities of the Buddhist clergy, known as the Huichang Suppression (ca. 840–845). As part of this campaign, Buddhist memorial rites for departed emperors were ordered abolished by imperial decree. Although this decree was soon rescinded, subsequent imperial policy toward the performance of Buddhist rites at state memorial services was marked by a high degree of ambivalence.

In the following excerpt from the *Outline History,* Zanning argues that the Buddhist incense rite be continued at imperial services for a number of reasons, ranging from very practical concerns over the fate of the deceased to the inherent harmony between Buddhist teachings and Confucian virtues. Two basic points emerge from Zanning's comments that characterize his position throughout the *Outline History.* The first is that Buddhism represents a legitimate expression of Chinese religiosity. Buddhist scriptures are viable canonical sources on a par with the Confucian Classics. The implication is that Buddhism should be accepted as legitimate and not excluded on the basis of regarding it as foreign and incompatible with native Chinese sentiment. The second is that Buddhist teaching is harmonious with the native Chinese, Confucian-based system of virtue. As a result, Buddhist rites should be encouraged as promoting and enhancing the same virtues cherished by Confucianism.

The style and arrangement of materials included in the *Outline History* were aimed at a specific audience, the imperial bureaucracy. This group collectively deliberated over the policies of the state, arbitrating areas of dispute, ultimately determining the direction of Chinese culture. The Confucian orientation of the members of this group made them naturally sympathetic to arguments that supported a Confucian agenda. In addition, they were most easily persuaded by a specific mode of argumentation in which a position was substantiated through the citation of relevant precedents.

Finally, the names of three Buddhist figures are mentioned in important contexts in the following passage. Dao'an (312–385), an important figure in the early history of Buddhism in China, was responsible for establishing many of the lasting features of Chinese Buddhism, including the offering of incense as an expression of faith. Xuanzang (ca. 596–664) was the most famous of the Chinese pilgrims to visit India in search of Buddhist teachings. After an absence of sixteen years, Xuanzang was greeted in the capital with eager anticipation and imperial ceremony. Bukong (Amoghavajra) (705–774) was an influential foreign monk at the Tang imperial court who had a profound impact on the adoption of Buddhist ritual practices by the Chinese state.

The translation that follows is from *Dasong seng shilue, Taishō daizōkyō,* T 54:241b–42a.

Further Reading

Kenneth K. S. Ch'en, *The Chinese Transformation of Buddhism* (Princeton: Princeton University Press, 1973).

Justification for Buddhist Incense-Offering Rites

Incense clears away foul odor and spreads fragrant aroma, causing people to delight in their olfactory senses. The original impulse for this [in China is found in the *Record of Rites,* where it says], "the people of Zhou esteemed the pungent aroma [emanating from their sacrifices]." Unknowingly, they agreed with the high esteem placed on incense in India. The Buddha lived during the reign of the Ji family [the emperors of the Zhou dynasty]; although separated by great distance, both the Buddha and the Ji family were in implicit agreement [about the value of aroma].

According to a Buddhist scripture, [*The Book of Gradual Sayings*] (*Zhengyi jing/Anguttara Nikāya*), when a lay devotee of the Buddha climbed up into a tower in the middle of the night to pray to the Buddha, the devotee took a clump of incense and with it conveyed sincerity of faith. The Buddha appeared the following day at mealtime. From this we know that incense serves as an envoy for [conveying] the sincerity of one's faith to the Buddha.

The *Scripture Transmitting the Teaching of the Great Vehicle* (*Da yijiao jing*) says, "When monks are about to eat, they precede the meal by burning incense and chanting hymns of praise [to the Buddha]." Moreover, in the *Scripture [on Wisdom and Folly]* (*Xianyu jing*), a snake (Śāriputra in a previous life) paid a visit to Buddhist monks and explained why he had repeatedly been reborn as a snake, confessing the evil deeds he had committed in his past that caused him to become so. Along with this, the *Scripture* mentions someone (the Buddha in a previous life) coming with a special conveyance [to avoid being bitten by the snake] to take the snake to offer incense. (Confession of sins, followed by incense-offering as a rededication of one's faith, are standard procedures in the Buddhist repentance ritual.)

Here in China, even after Buddhist teaching had become widespread, the scriptures and monastic rules were scattered far and wide [i.e., knowledge of Buddhism was piecemeal and there was no comprehensive understanding]. For this reason, the first among Daoan's three sets of regulations governing the activities of the Buddhist faithful dealt with offering incense, sitting in meditation, and giving lectures. This marked the beginning of incense-offering ceremonies in China. The use of incense was held in high esteem both in the Northern Wei dynasty (386–534) and in southern China, but there is no record of it.

During the reign of Tang Emperor Gaozong (r. 649–683), the government ministers Xue Yuanchao and Li Yifu were ordered to offer incense at a vegetarian banquet sponsored by the heir apparent, the purpose of which was to honor the return of the Master of the Three Branches of Buddhist Learning, Xuanzang. Moreover, when Emperor Zhongzong (r. 684–710) sponsored a Great Assembly to demonstrate imperial support for Buddhism, he ordered government officials of the fifth rank and above to offer incense. [In this instance,] "incense-offering" referred to either fumigating the hands with the smoke of burning incense or walking in a circle holding a portion of incense.

Later in the Tang dynasty, the Master of the Three Branches of Buddhist Learning, Bukong (Amoghavajra), petitioned the throne to sponsor vegetarian banquets and incense-offering rites on the memorial days of the previous Tang emperors, from the founding emperors of the dynasty, Gaozu and Taizong, to the seventh sage-emperor of the dynasty (and father of the current emperor) Suzong. The petition was authorized by imperial decree. Owing to the great frequency of these memorial services, however, only incense-burning rites were carried out in the end, and the vegetarian banquets were not held.

In the reign of Emperor Wenzong (r. 827–839), the imperial secretary Cui Yuan petitioned the throne: "There is no authorization in the classic scriptures for [government] sponsorship of vegetarian banquets or for [participation in] incense-offering rites by government officials on national memorial days. I humbly request that these be abolished. An imperial decree concurred: "Cui Yuan's petition has succeeded in discerning the roots from the branches (the essentials from the peripheral). The ritual texts and stipulated rules of conduct clearly do not include any mention of it. This practice of offering incense at Buddhist and Daoist temples on national memorial days in the two capitals, Chang'an and Luoyang, and in the administrative districts of the empire shall hereafter be abolished."

I (Zanning) would like to comment on this. Cui Yuan said there was no authorization [for the incense-offering rite] in the classic scriptures, but isn't the reference to offering incense in the above episode involving the snake (Śāriputra in a previous life) from a classic scripture? Master Dao'an quoted from Buddhist teaching to establish the regulations for offering incense, so how can it be said to be without authorization? The imperial decree stated that Cui Yuan discerned the roots from the branches, and that the ritual texts and stipulated rules of conduct clearly do not include any mention of it, but how could the rituals of the ancient Chinese dynasties, the Xia, Shang, and Zhou, refer to sponsoring feasts for Buddhist monks and incense-offering rites? In any case, the stipulated rules of conduct are simply laws that change with the passing of the ages. How, for example, could regulations implemented after the reign of Emperor Daizong (r. 762–779) appear in the stipulated rules of conduct for the late Sui or early Tang dynasty [prior of Daizong's reign]? Doesn't it make much more sense to take Buddhist texts as evidence for rites that are beyond the purview of Confucians? It surely makes no sense to use the Confucian canon to authorize activities that originated with Buddhists. Judged in terms of their own criteria, the Buddhist rites would at once be said to be reasonable, but Confucians fail to allow this and instead cite Confucian texts [to deny their validity]. How do Buddhists differ from those facing criminal prosecution summoning relatives and colleagues to provide testimony? If the Confucians wish to dismiss the evidence supporting the incense rite in Buddhist scriptures, on what grounds is it defensible?

For the filial son, goodness is exclusively associated with paying respect to his departed forebears. [In this regard], the [Confucian sanctioned] practice of burning the living with the dead is of no benefit to the deceased in the realm of constant rebirth and must definitely be prohibited. The practice of offering incense, [on the other hand,] is beneficial to the deceased in [their journey through] the vast underworld. Filial sons know this and always act accordingly. If one reflects on the weakness of Emperor Wenzong in comparison to emperors Gaozu and Taizong, it is better to follow the example of the latter two [and encourage participation in the incense-offering rite].

Some question the need to perform the incense-offering rite. This is explained by comparing it with [the practice in China during] the Zhou period, when the aroma of blazing dried wood, the aroma of the blood and fat of the sacrificial victim, and the aroma of millet and artemisia were esteemed, and when it was said that Heaven accepts these aromas as offerings. How can Heaven consume the aroma of blood and fat, of millet and artemisia [as if Heaven were a person]? It is only because the people of Zhou esteemed these aromas that they served Heaven with them. If this is the case, how can one fault Buddhist teaching for the importance it places on incense? More significantly, when government officials offer incense, they are acting on behalf of their Lord [the emperor]. When government officials serve the imperial ancestors, they are also [acting as] subjects of the emperor. Before Confucians entertain even for a moment the idea of abolishing the Buddhist incense rite, they should consider the effect it could have on loyalty and filial piety.

When Xuanzong ascended the throne (r. 846–859), he revived Buddhist teachings. In the fifth year of the Dazhong era (851), he had it decreed in the capitals and major cities of the empire, as well as the distant provinces and garrisons, that incense-offering rites held on national memorial days should, in addition, be occasions where purity is observed; he prohibited taking wine and meat into temples to be heated up and fried. [These practices] deprive the heart of deep reverence [appropriate to the occasion] and completely contradict the way blessings are obtained for the deceased [according to Buddhist teaching]. From Emperor Xuanzong on, [all of the Tang emperors] down to the last one, Emperor Aizong (r. 904–907), sponsored Buddhist incense rites [at imperial memorial services] according to the old model.

When Zhu Quanzhong (r. 907–912), founder of the Liang dynasty (907–923), destroyed the Tang, [the practice of worshiping at] the shrines of the seven imperial ancestors of the Tang dynasty came to an end. But at the Festival of Great Illumination (*daming*) held in the third year of the Kaiping era (909), government officials entered Buddhist temples to offer incense and pray for the longevity of the emperor. Later on in the dynasty there was a return to the practice of seeking blessings for deceased imperial ancestors [through incense-offering rites]. These incense-offering ceremonies have continued unabated down to the present time.

During the Jin dynasty (937–946), in the fifth year of the Tianfu era (940), a government official, Dou Zhengu, petitioned the throne: "At national memorial services, the chief ministers of state kneel at incense burners while the remaining officials of the government are seated in rows. I humbly request that henceforth, while the chief ministers of state kneel at the incense burners, the officials of the government stand in the order determined by their normal rank." In addition, it was ordered that following the incense-offering ceremonies, vegetarian banquets for a hundred monks always be included as part of the normal procedure [on such occasions].

During the reign of the current Song Emperor Taizong (r. 976–997), an employee of the Bureau of Forestry and Crafts, Vice Director Li Zongna, petitioned the throne in the third year of the Chunhua era (992): "With regard to incense-offering rites at national memorial services, I request that those lower in rank than the chief ministers of state be prohibited from drinking wine and eating meat after the incense-offering rite as an expression of the purity of the occasion." An order was issued to the Censorate (the agency charged with the responsibility of maintaining disciplinary surveillance over the officialdom) to enforce the above request.

— 32 —

Biography of a Buddhist Layman

Alan J. Berkowitz

In traditional "Confucian" China, while the customary path to achievement was through service to the state, from the earliest times certain individuals have been acclaimed for doing just the opposite, for repudiating an official career in state governance. These men fit a dictum of the *Classic of Changes* (*Yijing*); "He does not serve a king or lord; he loftily esteems his own affairs." Through time, this characterization came to serve as the byword of voluntary withdrawal, the image of the man whose lofty resolve could not be humbled for service to a temporal ruler.

Throughout the history of traditional China, men who eschewed official appointments in favor of the pursuit of their personal, lofty ideals were known as "men in reclusion" (*yinshi*), "high-minded men" (*gaoshi*), "disengaged persons" (*yimin*), "scholars-at-home" (*chushi*), or the like. Regardless of the attractions or dangers of service, and regardless of the motivations for avoiding it, they strove to maintain their autonomy and self-reliance. The distinction of these men was a particular strength of character that underlay their conduct; they maintained their resolve, their mettle, their integrity—their moral and/or religious values—in the face of adversity, threat, or temptation, and for this they received approbation.

For most civilizations, reclusion usually has indicated withdrawal from the world into a life of seclusion, most often within a religious context. In China this was not always the case; reclusion was typically secular and usually meant withdrawal from active participation in an official career in state governance. Men who chose to live outside of the traditional path for worldly success were said to be in reclusion (*yin*, lit. hidden or in hiding), hiding the jewel of their virtue from appropriation by their rulers. However, while recluses and hermits certainly have been present in all ages, they were not the norm of reclusion in traditional China. The actualization of lofty ideals did not necessarily imply aloof behavior, nor did renunciation necessarily imply ascetic self-denial, and those who withdrew most often played active roles within the world of men. In fact, the descriptive terminology of reclusion in China most often describes a self-conscious, highly moral, well-educated elite that actively participated in some of the most engaging activities of the times. On the other hand, the fundamentally secular nature of reclusion notwithstanding, a sizable number of men who practiced reclusion were also ardent men of religion, and, at least since the suffusion of Buddhism into the Chinese intelligentsia during the fourth century, it is apparent that in certain cases religious motives were a factor in one's decision to remain outside of officialdom.

Since the early centuries of the common era, men who were esteemed above all for their lifelong lofty eschewal of positions in officialdom received biographical accounts in a special section of China's official dynastic histories, as well as in a host of separate biographical compilations. A number of such practitioners of reclusion achieved renown during the short-lived Qi dynasty, which lasted only twenty-three years from the fourth lunar month of 479 until the fourth month of 502, and Xiao Zixian (489–537) included their biographies in a section entitled "Lofty Disengagement" (Gaoyi) in his History of the Southern Qi (Nan Qi shu). Several of these practitioners of reclusion also were distinguished for their religious roles, being that they were instrumental in the formulation of Buddhist and Daoist theology, and in the propagation of those faiths. The biography of Ming Sengshao (d. 484), translated below, evinces a man whose family included generations of government officials and who himself was offered various occasions for success in worldly pursuits, but who chose instead to repudiate service to the state in favor of a life devoted to study and, especially, to his religion, Buddhism.

The biography is in many ways formulaic, reflecting the normative pattern of the worthy man in reclusion: the man's virtue and talent are noted by regional and state officials and he gains the esteem of the emperor himself, but he chooses to eschew honors and official appointments for the pursuit of his personal, lofty, ideals. A few factual situations are recounted in the biographical account, as well as several illustrations of conduct exemplifying the mettle of a man in reclusion. But much is left unsaid, perhaps because it was not deemed important, or perhaps because it was not seen as appropriate for inclusion in an official state history. Other sources can supply additional information about the man, further illuminating reasons for his esteem and providing a broader picture of his activities and legacy. Thus, in accordance with historiographical convention, the official portrayal of the life of Ming Sengshao depicts him primarily as a practitioner of reclusion; his own legacy, however, shows him foremost as a practitioner of religion.

Ming Sengshao's biography tells us that he was learned in the Confucian tradition and respected for his scholary acumen, so much so that the emperor wished him to take up official teaching duties in the capital. And we read that he was an ardent devotee of Buddhism, a layman (jushi, upāsaka in Sanskrit; a pious initiate who practices Buddhism at home, who has taken certain vows but has not taken the full priestly vows to enter the clergy) who spent his years, particularly his mature years, in the outskirts of the capital Jiankang (modern Nanjing, Jiangsu Province), in dedication to his faith. However, the biography does not mention the scope of his scholarship, nor does it inform us of the range of his religious activities. Through citation in other works we know of at least two of his writings on classical works that were transmitted for a number of centuries, of which only the briefest of excerpts now exist: his *Commentary on the "Great Appendix" of the Classic of Changes* (*Zhou Yi xici zhu*), and his *Commentary on the Classic of Filial Piety* (*Xiaojing zhu*). His religious activities are witnessed in much greater detail.

When Ming Sengshao took up residence on Qixia Mountain (also called She Mountain), approximately twenty kilometers northeast of the capital Jiankang, he gave his full attention to the precepts and practice of Buddhism. During this time there was a running scholarly debate on the relative merits of Buddhism and Daoism, and in particular on the origins of the faiths. Gu Huan (ca. 425–ca. 488), an eminent proponent of Daoism, had written a "Discussion on the Barbarians and the Chinese" (i.e., Buddhists vs. Daoists, "Yi Xia lun"), wherein he upheld Daoism as being superior to Buddhism. Among other arguments, he presented textual "evidence" that the two religions in fact were of a common origin, quoting a Daoist scripture that writes of the Buddha being none other than the venerable progenitor of Daoism, Laozi, who had gone west out of China to a miraculous rebirth as the Buddha. Ming Sengshao composed a "Treatise in Rectification of the Two Religions" ("Zheng er jiao lun") in rebuttal to Gu Huan, which has been preserved in full. In the treatise, Ming Sengshao addresses in refutation eight points of Gu Huan's discussion and adds a summary of his views on the relative merits of the two religions.

On the twenty-fifth day of the fourth month of 676 (June 11), the Tang emperor Gaozong (r. 649–683) had a stele erected at Ming Sengshao's former residence at Qixia Temple on Qixia Mountain in honor of Sengshao's sixth generation descendant, Ming Chongyan (d. 679). The stele, incised in beautiful running script and still to be seen today on the temple grounds as one of the earliest extant examples of this script, bears an epigraph composed personally by the emperor in commemoration of the life of Ming Sengshao. The epigraph tell us, among other things, that Ming Sengshao passed away in 484, a fact not recorded in any other account of Sengshao's life. The inscription also gives a literary recounting of the circumstances of the founding of the Qixia Temple, probably derived from an inscription written about the temple by Jiang Zong (519–594), who himself had spent considerable time at the temple. This latter text was inscribed on a stele erected at the temple; the original stele was destroyed in the mid-ninth century, but a number of reproductions were made throughout the years.

Jiang Zong's inscription tells us that when Ming Sengshao took up residence on the mountain (it says that Sengshao lived there for more than twenty years, but he did not move there until 480, just four years before his demise), it was known for its restorative herbs. Still, the local residents cautioned Sengshao against the ferocious tigers and poisonous snakes inhabiting the wild areas where Sengshao chose to reside. Sengshao answered that poisons were not as lethal as the Three Poisons of concupiscence, anger, and ignorance, and that a devoted believer would not find wild beasts menacing. He built his rustic residence and devoted himself to his religious pursuits, remaining detached from worldly affairs.

Sengshao often recited sūtras with a Buddhist monk called Fadu (d. 497 or 500 at age sixty-four), and once in the middle of the night when the two were chanting the *Sukhāvatīvyūha-sūtra* (*Wuliang shou jing, Sūtra of Boundless Life,* a central text of the Pure Land sect), a golden light suddenly illumined the room. The glow seemingly contained the image of a terraced pavilion, and for an instant the Human King shone on the incense burner cover, and streams and stones gleamed in the dark room (i.e., a representation of the contents of the sūtra, of the Amitābha Buddha and his Western Paradise). On account of this, the layman Sengshao donated his residence for the construction of the Qixia Temple, which was consecrated on February 18, 489. Sengshao also once saw in a dream the Tathāgata Buddha illumined on the cliff near his residence and wished to have religious statuary fashioned. His son Zhongzhang together with the monk Fadu later had sculpted into the cliff an imposing statue of the Amitābha Buddha accompanied by two slightly smaller statues of bodhisattvas. Many men of renown, including members of the imperial clan, donated pledges for further statuary to be carved into the cliff; the stone iconography, known as the "Cliff of the Thousand Buddhas" with its 515 Buddhist images sculpted into 294 hollows, still may be visited today.

The Qixia Temple, founded at the residence of Ming Sengshao through his religious ardor and the bequeathal of his estate, remains today as Sengshao's living legacy. Even when the armies of the Sui completely decimated the capital in 589, the temple was not harmed. Instead, in 601 the founder of the Sui, Emperor Wen, had erected on the grounds one of eighty-three wooden dagobas he had constructed throughout the empire to house Buddhist relics (the stone dagoba that today is the centerpiece of the temple dates from 945). The temple has been a center of Buddhist activity since its founding, as it still is today, but for several very brief periods. During the Tang it was one of the four greatest Buddhist temple complexes in China, and the temple halls have been continuously renovated through the centuries; the present halls date from early this century, after having burned down in 1856 during a battle between the imperial armies of the Qing and those of the Heavenly Kingdom of Great Peace (Taiping Tianguo, which had Nanjing as its capital from 1853 to 1864). In terms of the Buddhist faith, the Qixia Temple perhaps is most memorable for being the place where the Three Treatises (San lun) school, the Mahāyāna philosophical school (known as Mādhyamika, Middle Way, in Sanskrit) that flourished in medieval China and spread also to Korea and Japan, began to achieve prominence and formalization with the teachings of the monk Senglang. Senglang was, according to several medieval sources, a student of Ming Sengshao's companion in religion, Fadu.

Ming Sengshao's biography in the *History of the Southern Qi* was appropriated and revised during the Tang dynasty by Li Yanshou (fl. 625) and included in the official *History of the Southern Dynasties* (*Nan shi*). There it was no longer placed in the section of collective accounts of men in reclusion so that the biography of Sengshao's son Shanbin, who held a number of high official posts during the Liang dynasty (which followed the Southern Qi), could be appended to it.

The biography of Ming Sengshao translated below is that included in the *History of the Southern Dynasties,* with additions from the *History of the Southern Qi* included in double angle brackets ⟨⟨ ⟩⟩. Li Yanshou (fl. 625), comp., *Nan shi* (Beijing: Zhonghua shuju, 1975), 50.1241–44. Bracketed additions from Xiao Zixian (489–537), comp., *Nan Qi shu* (Beijing: Zhonghua shuju, 1972), 54.927–28.

Further Reading

On the special character of reclusion in China, see Alan J. Berkowitz, *Patterns of Disengagement: The Practice of Reclusion in Early Medieval China and Its Portrayal* (Stanford: Stanford University Press, forthcoming); Aat Vervoorn, *Men of the Cliffs and Caves: The Development of the Chinese Eremitic Tradition to the End of the Han Dynasty* (Hong Kong: Chinese University Press, 1990). On Buddhism and the Chinese gentry, see E. Zürcher, *The Buddhist Conquest of China: The Spread and Adaptation of Buddhism in Early Medieval China* (Leiden: E. J. Brill, 1959); Arthur F. Wright, "Buddhism in Chinese Culture: Phases of Interaction," *Journal of Asian Studies* 16.1 (1957): 17–42; reprinted in his *Studies in Chinese Buddhism,* ed. Robert M. Somers (New Haven: Yale University Press, 1990).

The Biography of Ming Sengshao

Ming Sengshao, whose byname was Xiulie, was a man of Li District (approximately seventy-five kilometers northeast of modern Jinan City, Shandong) in Pingyuan Commandery. One source gives his byname as Chenglie. His ancestor Mengming, son of Baili Xi of the lineage of Taibo of Wu (an ancestor of the Zhou), took his given name as his surname; Sengshao was his descendant. Sengshao's grandfather Wan was a Regional Retainer, and his father Lüe was a Supervising Secretary.

Sengshao was learned in the classics and proficient in the Confucian arts. During the Yuanjia period (424–453) of the Song dynasty he was repeatedly nominated as a "Flourishing Talent," and during the Yongguang period (465) the Garrison of the Commander of the North appointed him to its Personnel Evaluation Section; in no case did he accede. He lived in reclusion at Lao Mountain in Changguang Commandery (just northeast of modern Qingdao City, Shandong), where he assembled disciples and set up his practice of instruction. When the Wei [armies] overcame the area north of the Huai River (ca. late 466), he crossed the river [to the south].

⟨⟨During the sixth year of the Taishi reign-period of Emperor Ming (470) he was summoned for the position of Court Gentleman for Comprehensive Duty, but he did not accede.⟩⟩ During the Shenming period (477–479) when [Xiao Daocheng, who would shortly become] Emperor Gao of the Qi was acting as Grand Mentor, he instructed that appointment be granted to Sengshao along with [two other men in reclusion,] Gu Huan and Zang Rongxu. Sengshao was summoned for the position of Secretarial Aid with the ceremony of pennants and bestowal of silks but did not go. When Sengshao's younger brother Qingfu was [Regional Inspector] of Qing Province (he was appointed to this post in 477), Sengshao was lacking in grain and comestibles and followed Qingfu to Yuzhou (modern Lianyungang City, Jiangsu), where he resided at Yanyu Mountain, roosting in the clouds in a cottage for contemplation, delighting in the waters and rocks; in the end he never once entered the walls of the regional command.

Toward the end of the Taishi reign (465–471), when mountainslides occurred in Min and Yi (mountain locales around modern Chengdu, Sichuan), and the Huai River dried up in Qi Commandery (here meaning modern northeastern Jiangsu), Sengshao addressed his younger brother in confidence, saying, "The ethereal cosmic forces (qi) of Heaven and Earth do not deviate from their [natural] order. If the yang is being repressed and is not released, and the yin is pressing and is not given vent, then under these conditions occur the aberrations of mountains collapsing and rivers going dry. Of old, when the Yi and Luo rivers went dry, the Xia was lost. When the [Yellow] River went dry, the Yin was lost. When the Three Rivers went dry and Ji Mountain collapsed, the Zhou was lost. And when five mountains (actually three) collapsed, the Han was lost. Now, for a state to exist, it must rely on mountains and rivers for stability; when mountains and rivers produce aberrations, what could be attendant but demise? At present the virtue of the Song is comparable to that of the final years of the four eras [just mentioned]. Record my words, but do not divulge them." In the end, it was just as he had said [i.e., the Song soon demised].

In the winter of the inaugural year of the Jianyuan reign of the Qi (early 480), [the emperor] decreed: ⟨⟨"We are duly solicitous toward learned men of conscience, and hold in Our heart [those who] live beyond the mundane. Ming Sengshao of Qi Commandery manifests his resolve and stays loftily aloof, indulging his predilection for the worthy writings of the ancients; for his adherence to Remoteness and Inviolability, it is befitting to confer honorific adornments."⟩⟩ Sengshao was summoned for the position of Regular Gentleman Cavalier Attendant, but on the pretext of illness he did not accede. The emperor subsequently wrote to Cui Zusi, saying: ⟨⟨"Ming the lay Buddhist manifests his will with great measure; could it be that my former directive will not be successful? The minor and less priviledged wish to have the services of an Expositor, and you should have him arrive. State my aims fully, and order him to return [to the capital] together with [his brother] Qingfu."⟩⟩ The emperor further said, "Not to eat the grain of the Zhou, yet to eat the bracken of the Zhou (as had the two renowned brothers in reclusion Boyi and Shuqi of old): for this, criticism also was expressed in the past. In the present, how could it be that talk would cease? It is simply a matter for ridicule."

Qingfu left his post [in the third month of 480], and Sengshao accompanied him back [to the capital] where he took up lodging at She Mountain in Jiangcheng [just outside the capital]. Sengshao heard of the long-standing virtue of the Buddhist monk Sengyuan (414–484) and went to pay his respects to him at the Dinglin Temple [at Zhong Mountain, just east of the capital]. When Emperor Gao wished to go out to the temple to see him (Sengshao), Sengyuan asked Sengshao, "Should the Son of Heaven [i.e., the emperor] come, what would you, the lay Buddhist, have as response for him?" Sengshao said, "Men of the mountains and moors (i.e., men in reclusion) ought but bore a hole through the wall to escape [when faced with government service]. If I were to decline [appointment], I would not be able to secure my life; it would be better to follow the precedent of Master Dai." He then withdrew and returned to She Mountain, where he had the Qixia Temple constructed and took up residence. Emperor Gao was deeply regretful. In the past, Dai Yong had lain aloof below his window, his body dressed in the clothes of a man of the mountains; this is what was referred to by Sengshao.

Emperor Gao later addressed Qingfu, saying, "Your elder brother 'loftily esteems his own affairs' and might be counted among the 'extramundane officials' under Yao [who repudiated official service]. ⟨⟨Although We cannot meet with him, at times we meet in my dreams.⟩⟩ We think in Our dreams about that Remote One, and long have been ardently looking forward [to our meeting]. This is what is called 'paths and roadways cut off, but wind and rain pass through.' " He then bestowed Sengshao with a ruyi ("as-you-wish") scepter of bamboo root and a cap of bamboo shoot husks, things in which men in reclusion take honor. A certain Feng Yanbo of Bohai, a gentleman of lofty conduct, heard of this and sighed, "Ming the Buddhist layman keeps himself in the background, yet his reputation is always to the fore. He is rightly the Ruzhong (i.e., Wang Ba, a renowned practitioner of reclusion of the Later Han) of the Song and the Qi." ⟨⟨In the inaugural year of the Yongming reign (483), Shizu [i.e., Emperor Wu] issued Sengshao an imperial edict of summons, but pleading illness he (Sengshao) did not agree to go to an audience. Sengshao was summoned by imperial proclamation⟩⟩ for the position of Erudite of the National University, but he did not accede; he later demised.

Sengshao's eldest brother Sengyin was proficient in discussing the occult. When he served the Song as Adjutant to the King of Jiangxia, Liu Yigong, the king prepared a couch especially for him, comparing him to Xu Ruzi [i.e., Xu Zhi, a renowned practitioner of reclusion of the Later Han who was treated with special courtesy by the Grand Administrator of the commandery where he lived]. He rose to the rank of Regional Inspector of Ji zhou. During the Yuanhui reign-period (473–477), his (Sengyin's) son Huizhao served as Registrar for the Arbiter of the South under [Xiao Daocheng, who would shortly become] Emperor Gao of the Qi, whom he accompanied in the [successful] resistance campaign at Guiyang [in 474]. He accumulated official ranks, reaching Calvary Adjutant of the Inner Troops, where he was paired for concurrent duties with Xun Boyu (d. 483). In the inaugural year of the Jianyuan reign (479) he held the position of Regional Inspector of Ba zhou. He paid solicitous attention to the Man and Yan [minority peoples of the southwest], and the emperor approved his appointment as Regional Inspector of Yizhou; however, before he transferred he demised. . . .

Sengshao's own sons Yuanlin, ⟨⟨whose byname was⟩⟩ Zhongzhang, and Shanbin both continued the family undertakings; Shanbin received the most acclaim. . . . Although the Ming clan crossed to the south late, its members had both fame and position. From the Song through the Liang, six of them attained the office of Regional Inspector.

— 33 —

The Book of Good Deeds: A Scripture of the Ne People

Victor H. Mair

The present selection is unusual in a number of respects. In the first place, it was written in a non-Sinitic language called Ne. That being said, however, I must point out that it is based upon a well-known Chinese text entitled the *Tract of the Most Exalted on Action and Response (Taishang ganying pian)*. Yet this by no means implies that *The Book of Good Deeds (Nheh Muh Suh)* is a mere translation or reworking of the Chinese original, as we shall soon see.

The Ne formerly (from around the thirteenth century) were usually referred to as Lolo, but since this became a pejorative term in Chinese, it has now been replaced by Ne. Ne is the native pronunciation of the word that is pronounced in modern standard Mandarin as Yi (see chapter 26). The Ne, in different times and places, have also called themselves Rosu, Nasu, Lowu, Samibo, Sani, Axi, and other names. The center of Ne culture today is at Liang Mountain in southern Sichuan, but the Ne people are also located in Guizhou to the east and in the mountainous areas of Yunnan. There are also Ne speakers in Thailand, Burma, and Vietnam. In 1982 there were 5.5 million Ne living within the borders of China.

Although the Ne speak a Tibeto-Burman language, they are ethnically very difficult to type. Early reports from Western observers emphasized their somewhat Caucasoid features (especially their aquiline noses). The ethnology of the Ne is further complicated by the fact that they are divided into a Black division and a White division. The terms "Black" and "White" have nothing to do with skin color but rather respectively designate the more aristocratic rulers and their subjects. Indeed, the Ne practiced serfdom and slavery on a wide scale well into this century, and the White Ne are generally the descendants of Han Chinese slaves who have been enculturated by their former masters in spite of the fact that they outnumber them by a huge majority. The Ne were probably able to achieve this estimable feat through a combination of rigorous feudal administration and magnanimity. All food in a Black Ne household would be shared with the serfs and slaves, including their children. Furthermore, while the Black Ne looked down on farming, which they usually left to their Chinese slaves, they tended their flocks carefully and were excellent pastoralists. Their sensitivity to and familiarity with animals is abundantly apparent in *The Book of Good Deeds*.

Of the more than fifty minority nationalities living in China, the Ne arguably have the longest traceable history and richest cultural heritage. The Ne claim a continuity with the Shu state, which existed in Sichuan during the Eastern Zhou period and which has in the past few years been archaeologically attested by a series of stunning discoveries that demonstrate its high level and essential separateness from the culture of the Yellow River plain. The Ne have also made headlines around the world recently with the reconstruction of their ancient calendar, which shares remarkable similarities with that of the Maya.

During the eighth and ninth centuries, the people of the powerful Nanzhao kingdom in Yunnan posed a serious threat to the hegemony of the Tang rulers. The Nanzhao were the ancestors of the Ne and another Tibeto-Burman people called the Bai. This is evident from the close linguistic affiliation of Nanzhao words that survive in Chinese transcription with Ne and Bai words. Although the Nanzhao kingdom collapsed in 902, various groups of Ne continued to resist central government authority throughout the Song dynasty (960–1279) and were only subdued by the Mongols in 1253. After the Yuan dynasty (1280–1368), the Ne reasserted their fiercely independent nature, terrifying the Han Chinese population who lived in the regions they controlled. Although the lands occupied by the Ne have technically been a part of Chinese territory since the Yuan period, the Ne have never been fully subdued.

Another glory of the Ne is their unique script. The Ne script certainly existed already from the time of the Ming dynasty (1368–1644) because there are bronze and stone inscriptions that survive from that period. In addition, there is persuasive evidence that the Ne script may already have come into being as early as the Eastern Han period (25–220). Even more remarkable is the recent discovery of a hitherto unknown script in Sichuan that has been dubbed "silkworm writing" due to its curly shape. It certainly dates to the Zhou period (ca. 1027–256 B.C.E.), is completely unrelated to Chinese characters, and may conceivably be the forerunner of the Ne script. The Ne script is a large and unsystematic syllabary that has included as many as 8,000 distinct symbols. In 1975 this number was reduced by language reformers in the Chinese government who selected 819 symbols as a standard set. Since 1956 the Ne have also had an auxiliary romanized alphabet for learning the sound values of their syllabary.

Having possessed their own script for centuries, the Ne have not unexpectedly produced a considerable amount of literature. This may be broken down roughly into the following categories:

1. Sacrificial texts that tell of the origins and usages of the Ne people
2. Texts concerning divination, of which there are many different types and techniques
3. Calendrical texts

4. Genealogies
5. Poems (a famous one by a woman poet is entitled "Song against Marriage")
6. Ethics and etiquette
7. Histories that recount the achievements of the ancestors
8. Myths
9. Translations and explications of texts written in other languages

All of these categories, including the translations and explications, bear the unique stamp of the Ne people and their long-lasting civilization. Careful study of the entire corpus of Ne literature by qualified scholars is sure to be rewarded with interesting insights not only into Ne society and culture, but also into the relationship between the Chinese and the Ne throughout history.

The most important intellectual and religious leaders of Ne society are called soothsayers (*pimu*). The soothsayers function multifariously as chief priests, magicians, diviners, historians, teachers, and physicians. They are naturally the guardians of the sacred books and the Ne script, and every Ne village has at least one soothsayer.

The *Tract of the Most Exalted on Action and Response* was written by an unknown author sometime around the year 1164 (see chapters 34 and 35). It is a popular sermon or tract, ostensibly Daoist, that is extremely straightforward and down to earth. In this and in many other respects, it is quite unlike that other most widely circulated Daoist text, the *Classic on the Way and Its Power* (*Dao de jing*), with its abstruse metaphysical speculations. About the only things the two texts share are their supposed attribution to Laozi (the Old Master) and their great brevity. The expression Taishang (Most Exalted), which occurs in the full title of the *Tract* and at the very beginning of the text, is a reference to Laozi in his deified form (Taishang Laojun; "The Most Exalted Lord Lao").

When it comes to shortness, however, the *Tract* wins hands down since it consists of only 1,277 characters, whereas *The Way and Its Power* weighs in at over five thousand. The *Tract* has appeared in countless editions and in an incredible number of different formats. Some of them were quite simple and sold for next to nothing or were distributed free like Grolier Society New Testaments. The printing and distribution of the *Tract* were considered meritorious acts.

Written in relatively uncomplicated classical Chinese that could be understood fairly easily by those who were fortunate enough to have had several years of education, the *Tract* was nonetheless unreadable for the vast majority of those toward whom it was directed. Consequently, it was necessary for paraphrases of the text to be presented orally in one or another of the vernacular Sinitic languages. The *Tract* has thus often been issued together with hundreds of anecdotes and apologues, which narrate in a more leisurely fashion the terse pronouncements of the text itself. Such editions provided the basic materials for lecturers and others who presented lessons of the *Tract* before groups of auditors (see chapter 35). Another way in which the *Tract* was made more accessible to illiterate individuals was through the creation of elaborate versions of the text that not only were supplied with illustrative stories for each moral teaching but also came with woodblock prints on the upper portion of each page. Thus there was a visual impact even for those who were incapable of reading and an enhanced immediacy for those who could. An example of such an edition is the *Taishang ganying pian tushuo,* published by Zhao Hong in 1825. Furthermore, the mere physical possession of the *Tract* was considered to be morally uplifting, so that whether one actually read it oneself was not of the utmost importance. In any event, the printing and distribution of this text were held to be acts of merit. Consequently, the *Tract* was published in enormous numbers and became quite well known among Western Sinologists. Already by the early twentieth century it had been translated into European languages at least ten times, and two of these translations are still in print (those by Suzuki and Carus and by Legge).

As we have seen, the *Tract* itself is very short and can fit on just a few pages, but with all of its explanatory apparatus and eulogistic verse, it fills several large fascicles of the Daoist canon (vols. 834–839, Harvard-Yenching no. 1159). It is ironic that what began as an attempt to inculcate basic moral values in the population ended up as an object of scholarly commentaries and annotations that removed it even further from its targeted audience.

Naturally, if few Chinese were capable of reading the *Tract* by themselves, still fewer Ne individuals would have been able to, and even oral explanations in one of the Sinitic vernacular languages would have been of little relevance among the Ne. Consequently, if the teachings of the *Tract* were to be made available to the Ne people, it would be necessary to translate them into their language. This is precisely what happened with *The Book of Good Deeds,* but the author took advantage of the opportunity afforded by the translation to present his own views and to go far beyond what was contained in the *Tract.*

The *Tract* describes good and bad traits (with a naturally greater emphasis on the latter), exhorting men toward the former and warning them against the latter. In tandem with the ledgers of merit and demerit that have been studied in depth by Cynthia Brokaw (see chapter 34), it sets up a sort of accounting system for morality. A person was awarded so many points for each meritorious act and had points subtracted from the total for each demeritorious act. At the end of the person's life, the score would be added up and the person would receive his or her just desserts. *The Book of Good Deeds* has incorporated the concept of ledgers immediately at the conclusion of its treatment of the contents of the *Tract.*

The *Tract* is far less Daoistic than the implied authorship of Laozi in his deified form would seem to indicate. This is actually a highly eclectic work with obvious Confucian influence and an even stronger grounding in Buddhist precepts, including an unacknowledged quotation from the *Dhammapada* (*Verses on the Teachings*). (The very first sentence of the *Tract* is an unacknowledged quotation from the *Zuo Commentary* [*Zuozhuan*].) In the explications of *The Book of Good Deeds,* the eclecticism of the *Tract* is melded further with the native Ne ethos to create a most intriguing combination. When the author is explaining the importance of loyalty, a fundamental Confucian virtue, he strives to make it compatible with the slave structure of Ne society.

Most Ne texts are handwritten manuscripts, there being few woodblock prints. *The Book of Good Deeds* is the earliest extant woodblock-printed Ne text. It is also the longest extant Ne text and has the richest and most varied content. *The Book of Good Deeds* was probably written during the latter part of the fifteenth century when the Ne rulers maintained close relations with the Ming court.

The majority of texts written in the Ne language and script are religious scriptures, and *The Book of Good Deeds* is no exception in having religious instruction as its main purpose. But it is far more than a simple recounting of the lessons in the *Tract*. In addition it relates the customs and beliefs of the Ne people themselves in such a fashion that we may say the author has borrowed the *Tract* as a ready-made framework upon which to hang the ideas of himself and his own people. Although he obviously sees value in the moral teachings of the *Tract,* he is also eager to let it be known where the Ne differ from the Han people. For example, he stresses that the Ne do not eat dog meat, whereas the Han consider it a delicacy. The author also takes advantage of the opportunity to provide his audience with all sorts of useful information. In a sense, *The Book of Good Deeds* functioned as a handbook of practical wisdom. For instance, it offers quite detailed information on animal husbandry, expanding a tiny four-character phrase in the Chinese tractate into the largest portion of the Ne scripture. The genuine sensitivity and sympathy, indeed empathy, that the author displays toward animals is extraordinary and may well be unparalleled in world literature. While the springboard for the discussion of these matters is always some moral question, one senses that the author intended his work to serve as a sort of multipurpose volume of education on ecology, veterinary science, public health, and other fields of knowledge that were vital for the smooth functioning of society. A good example of this is his long discussion about leprosy (whether it is caused by fate, as the "ignorant" Han people believe, or by infection, as he insists), which has precious little to do with the phrase from the *Tract* concerning the setting of fire to underbrush that it is ostensibly meant to explicate. Here and elsewhere, the author displays an unusually rationalistic and critical cast of mind. In fact, he is so remarkably rationalistic and modernist in his orientation that one would suspect missionary (his antiabortion views seem almost Catholic) or other foreign influence were the date of *The Book of Good Deeds* not so early. The author's strictures against Ne soothsayers are also curious since a work such as this would normally have been written by a *pimu*.

Even those portions of *The Book of Good Deeds* that are meant to translate specific passages from the *Tract* are inevitably not identical to the Chinese original. Except when too close adherence to the Ne text would cause unwelcome dissonance with fundamental formulations of the *Tract* (as in the title and opening words where the Ne has "Heavenly Official" for "Most Exalted"), the Ne wording is given precedence over the Chinese. This is required because the annotations and explications of *The Book of Good Deeds* are keyed to the Ne version of the

Tract rather than to the Chinese. Readers should therefore be warned not to expect that the passages from the *Tract* cited in the English translation will always match the Chinese original perfectly, although they are generally very close.

The translation is from Ma Xueliang, et al. *Yiwen Quan Shan Jing yi zhu (Translation and Annotation of the Ne Scripture of Exhortation to Goodness)*, 2 vols. (Beijing: Zhongyang minzu xueyuan, 1986). This includes the text in the Ne syllabary, an IPA transcription, a literal word-for-word rendering into Chinese, and a free translation into Chinese. Passages translated in this selection are from pages 1–11, 31–34, 37–47, 52–58, 182–201, 290–92, 303–18, 362–68, 385–95, and 437–87 (excerpts).

Further Reading

Cynthia J. Brokaw, *The Ledgers of Merit and Demerit: Social Change and Moral Order in Late Imperial China* (Princeton: Princeton University Press, 1991), esp. pp. 35–43 for a detailed history of the *Tract* and for abundant scholarly notes concerning research on the subject in Chinese, Japanese, English, and French. Alain Y. Dessaint, *Minorities of Southwest China: An Introduction to the Yi (Lolo) and Related Peoples and an Annotated Bibliography* (New Haven: HRAF Press, 1980). For anyone who wishes to pursue research on any aspect of Ne culture and history, this bibliography with its hundreds of annotated entries is the place to begin. James Legge, trans., *The Thāi-Shang Tractate of Actions and Their Retributions,* pp. 233–46 in the translator's *The Texts of Taoism,* part 2, being vol. 40 of *The Sacred Books of the East* (New York: Dover, 1962); first published by Oxford University Press in 1891. Also see pp. 38–44 of part 1 of the *Texts of Taoism* (vol. 39; same publication data) for a brief introductory essay on the *Tract* that treats it strictly as a volume of popular Daoism. Leo J. Moser, *The Chinese Mosaic: The Peoples and Provinces of China* (Boulder: Westview, 1985), an excellent book for embarking on the study of the various Chinese nationalities. S. Robert Ramsey, *The Languages of China* (Princeton: Princeton University Press, 1987), esp. pp. 250–61 for a reliable and informative discussion of Ne (Yi) language and society. D. T. Suzuki and Paul Carus, trans. *Treatise on Response and Retribution by Lao Tze* (La Salle, Ill.: Open Court, 1973), 3rd ed.; 1st ed., 1906. This edition includes a character-by-character rendering of the *Tract* that makes the original Chinese text more or less available even to those who are not trained in Sinology. Herold J. Wiens, *China's March into the Tropics: A Discussion of the Southward Penetration of China's Culture, Peoples, and Political Control in Relation to the non-Han-Chinese Peoples of South China and in the Perspective of Historical and Cultural Geography* (Washington, D.C.: United States Navy Office of Naval Research, 1952) offers invaluable insights and information on the interaction between Sinitic and non-Sinitic peoples in South China.

The Book of Good Deeds

The Most Exalted Saith: "There are no gates leading us to fortune and misfortune; people bring these upon themselves."

Annotation. "Most Exalted" refers to the one who is in charge of the universe. "Fortune" refers to good fortune. "Misfortune" refers to bad fortune. "Gates" refers to doors and entrances generally. "Bring upon themselves" indicates that it is not a matter of predestination.

Explication. The meaning of this passage is as follows: The Most Exalted says that, in the world, there are no predestined gates leading to fortune and misfortune. If you practice evil, you will go through the gate of bad fortune. If you practice good, you will go through the gate of good fortune. If you practice evil, you will bring bad fortune upon yourself. If you practice good, you will bring good fortune upon yourself. Whether or not people find bad fortune or good fortune is completely dependent upon themselves.

"Requital for good and evil follows people like their shadows."

Annotation. "Evil" refers to a bad conscience and not doing good. "Good" refers to a good conscience and doing good. "Follows" refers to whatever comes after someone on a certain path. "Shadows" refers to people's shadows.

Explication. The meaning of this passage is as follows: Of all the people in the world, those who do evil will be followed and pursued by bad fortune; those who do good will be followed and pursued by good fortune. When people bend at the waist, their shadows follow along by bending at the waist; when people stand straight, their shadows follow along by standing straight; and so forth, no matter what they do. In other words, one who does evil will not have good fortune, just as one's shadow cannot be straight when one bends at the waist. One who does good will not have bad fortune, just as one's shadow cannot bend at the waist when one is standing straight.

"Therefore, Heaven and Earth above appoint spirits of the land who judge people's faults. Depending on the seriousness of the crimes, they snatch away time from people's lives."

Annotation. "Above" indicates a superior position. "Judge people's faults" refers to being in charge of the sins of those who do not do good. "Spirits" refers to the spirits who are in charge of people's sins. "Of the land" refers to all such spirits as mountain spirits, earth spirits, and village spirits.

Explication. The meaning of this passage is as follows: As for the people of the world who do not do good, the officials of Heaven and Earth establish spirits of the land to be over them. The spirits follow after them and watch them. When the bad things people do are great, their sins will be heavy and the calamities in their lives will be many. When the bad things people do are small, their sins will be light and the calamities in their lives will be few. Not only are there spirits appointed to judge the faults of people who do bad, there are also spirits of the good over those who do good. When the good things people do are great, their lives will be lengthened, their descendants will prosper, their livestock and grain will be plentiful, and they will succeed in everything they do. When the good things people do are small, they will not be involved in criminal cases, they will not lose their livestock, their grain will not diminish, but that is about it.

"Do not trod upon paths of depravity; do not cheat in a dark room."

Annotation. "Paths of depravity" refers to paths whereby one does evil. "A dark room" refers to a room that is pitch-black like a cave and where people can neither see nor hear anything. "Do not cheat" implies that in every room there is a spirit of the room. Even in a dark room where other people cannot hear or see you, if you think of doing something bad and then really go ahead and do it because you believe other people will not know about it, do not cheat the spirit of the room.

Explication. The meaning of this passage is as follows: "Do not trod upon paths of depravity" is to say that whenever one does something bad, such as being a thief or a robber, it harms others, so one should not follow such paths of depravity. "Do not cheat in a dark room" is to say that, even when you are in a pitch-black room like a cave where people can neither see nor hear anything and you believe that other people cannot see you, so you start to think wild thoughts about harming others or about being a thief or a robber, do not bring a curse upon your ancestors' graves and do not cheat the spirit of the room. The text tells us that this is how we should behave.

"Be loyal, filial, friendly, and fraternal."

Annotation. "Loyal" indicates being loyal toward one's ruler. "Filial" indicates being filial to one's parents. "Friendly" indicates deference among brothers. "Fraternal" indicates respect and love among brothers.

Explication. The meaning of this passage is as follows: Being loyal to one's ruler is to say that the person who rules over the slaves of the world is the ruler and the ruler of the common people is their lord. When the common people are disloyal to their lord, they do not pay taxes, do not pay levies, do not perform labor, do not dry out grain before they hand it in, and are rebellious. In such cases, their lord or king regards them as criminals. If slaves are disloyal to their masters, do not serve according to their wishes, do not listen to their commands, or talk back, contradict, and rebel their masters regard them as criminals. Heaven and Earth, too, will censure people who are disloyal to their ruler or who go against their masters. Therefore, the common people should be loyal to their lord or king by paying taxes and levies, by performing labor, by drying their grain before handing it in, by not causing trouble, and by not being rebellious. Slaves should be loyal to their masters by serving according to their wishes, by listening to their commands, and by not causing trouble. They should not talk back, contradict, or rebel. All this is being loyal to one's ruler.

Being filial to one's parents is to say that, from the time a person is born, from that day when he or she is just a tiny baby, his or her parents bring that person up—wiping away yellowy feces, worrying that a speck might get in an eye, carrying the child on their backs, holding him or her in their bosom, raising the child until he or she grows up. People should find warm clothes for their parents to wear and tasty food for them to eat. They should not talk back to them and contradict them. They should take good care of themselves and work diligently so that their parents will be happy and content. All this is being filial to one's parents. Whoever maltreats their parents will be punished by heavenly fire and thunderclaps. One who is unfilial to one's parents will have descendants who are unfilial to their parents. One who is unfilial to one's parents will have unworthy descendants. One who wishes to live a life of good deeds must first be filial to one's parents and love one's parents.

Being deferential to one's brothers is to say that all brothers who have inherited many productive fields from their ancestors and do not divide them up will have disputes and, if it should happen that they have inherited only a few productive fields from their ancestors and wish to divide them up, they should be deferential to each other and not be stirred up by believing their sisters-in-law, their slaves, or their neighbors, and thus remain friendly with each other.

Being fraternal with one's brothers and cousins is to say that when the brothers and cousins of a family see one of their members who is ruined, they should encourage him; when they see one of their members do something improper, they should counsel him with love; when they see one of their members who has no descendants to look after his parents, they should help him support his parents; when they see one of their members pass away and leave his children without any parents, they should help raise the orphans; when they see one of their members with a daughter that he cannot marry off, they should help him marry her off; when they see one of their members with a son who cannot find a wife, they should help him find a wife. If brothers and cousins wish to remain fraternal, they should behave this way.

"One should not harm even insects, grasses, and trees."

Annotation. "Insects" refers to bugs and ants.

Explication. The meaning of this passage is as follows: Without mentioning human beings, livestock, cultivated grains, wild animals, and flying birds, all of whose lives are of great significance, one should not carelessly harm bugs and ants whose lives are of little significance or grasses and trees that grow without any particular use. A person who moves a hornets' nest and then burns it to obtain the larvae so he may serve them as a delicacy to his guests, thereby destroying tens of thousands of lives by burning the hornets, does a bad deed. Because he does not possess hidden virtue, he will not prosper. When a person channels water to a place where there are ants and he encounters bugs or ants, he should scrape them up and move them to a dry place. If he digs in a place where there are ants and he encounters bugs or ants, he should scrape them up and send them to a place where there is no digging. If he is chopping a tree that has ants and comes across bugs or ants, he should shake them off.

In olden times, in the land of the Han there was a man named Song Jiao who saw an ants' nest that was being flooded, so he used a bamboo strip as a sort of bridge to let the ants get across to dry land, thereby rescuing tens of thousands of them. The Lord of Heaven, recognizing that he had done a good deed by rescuing the lives of so many ants, gave him blessings and grain and decided to make him the prime minister of the emperor. And indeed, before long he did become prime minister. For the rest of his life, no one was richer or more honored than him. Therefore, without mentioning such large creatures as human beings, cattle, and horses, even if you save the life of a single bug or ant, it will also be accounted a good deed.

"To slaughter and cook when not required by the rites."

Annotation. "Not required by the rites" indicates doing something that is not in accord with the rites.

Explication. The meaning of this passage is as follows: The uses of domestic animals should be in accordance with the rites. The ceremony of torches at the new year, sacrifices for one's deceased parents, at weddings, when friends and relatives come—in these instances one may kill an animal. The above are in accord with the rites, so one may kill an animal. One may not kill simply because one has a hankering for a delicious taste. One should not think that simply because one has domestic animals one may carelessly slaughter them. To harm the lives of many domestic animals is to do a bad deed.

Another thing, the domestic animals that may be raised for slaughter are the goat, sheep, pig, and chicken. Horses, cattle, and dogs may be raised, but it is unreasonable to kill them. Horses may be ridden or used to carry burdens uphill and downhill. As they climb slopes they save people's energy and they offer many other advantages to people, so to say that it is unreasonable to kill and eat horses refers to these things. The ox and the water buffalo provide food for people because of their plowing and harrowing of the land. By their cultivation of the crops, they nurture and benefit people. If a poverty-stricken orphan has only a single draft ox, he can rely on the ox to keep his stomach full, just as though he had a mother and father. Thus it is unreasonable to kill and eat a draft ox. If a wealthy family has a draft ox, they rely upon it to plant their crops just as though they had a slave. It is unreasonable to kill and eat such a draft ox.

Whenever a leader or a master dies, there must be a sacrifice in each case. The same holds for when one takes a wife or marries off a daughter. If we practice the rites of the Han people and kill a pig or a sheep on such occasions, rather than an ox, then the common people will have more than enough cattle to till the land and to keep in reserve.

Another thing, if you have a cow and kill its calf, you will cause the mother to go crying from the tops of the hills to the bottoms of the valleys in search of it, a most pathetic state of affairs.

The better people among the Han who do good deeds will not have eaten the meat of cattle or horses for thirty generations of their ancestors. When a Han person who kills lots of cattle to make beef jerky is about to die and thinks back on all of the cattle he has killed, he cannot help but cry out like all the cattle as they were dying. And when he dies, he will certainly turn into an ox or cow.

As for dogs, they are people's helpers. When people go out in open country, dogs drive off wild animals for their master. Around home, they protect the house and its surroundings day and night. That is why we call them "people's helpers" and what we are referring to when we say that it is unreasonable to eat dog meat.

We Ne people do not eat three kinds of meat: the meat of horses, the meat of cattle after they have fallen sick, and the meat of dogs.

If one does good, one will receive good. Nothing can be better than this.

There are common people who let their cattle and horses wallow in dung. One should not permit the dung in a cowshed to be too deep and watery. Though the dung may be deep and watery, they still let people ride upon them and use them for draft purposes. They do such good things and are without sin, so we should cherish them. How could one lock them up to soak in the ooze of watery dung? The Han people lock up those who have committed great crimes in watery prisons.

During the day, we ride our horses until they are exhausted and plow with our cattle until they are exhausted, affording them no opportunity to sleep or even to sit down. At night, when their labors finally cease and we bring them back, they cannot find a spot of dry ground upon which to sleep. Instead, they are forced to soak in urine and excrement, the water drenching them all the way to their bellies, standing thus all night long until the light of day. Sometimes colts and calves drown in the dungy muck. A person who would do this sort of thing is unprincipled. Few animals can survive being buried away in such conditions, so one should not do this sort of thing.

There should be a separate place for tramping on manure, and the cowshed should be well constructed. Dig a deep channel so that the urine of the cattle will drain away quickly. Bring in thick bundles of straw as pallets so that the cattle will only have to step on their urine and excrement in between them. This will make for handy fertilizer, and the cattle and horses will be able to sleep. If one does not harm them, the cattle and horses will be fecund.

The common people who raise draft cattle should ensure that there is sufficient hay and water for their animals when the tenth month comes and they run out of grain for fodder. They should always make sure that the animals are fed enough salt and that they actually eat it. If the cattle have sufficient hay and water, when the snow falls at the transition from the last month of the old year and the first month of the new year, they will remain warm in their sheds and will not die because they are too skinny. And when the rainy season comes, one will not have to worry about not having an ox for plowing.

Another thing, when there is a cattle epidemic or horse epidemic, one's cattle and horses should not be permitted to stand next to each other. If they do not smell each other's breath, even if they happen to look in each other's eyes, they will never be infected by the illness their whole lives. Therefore, when there is a cattle epidemic or a horse epidemic, you will have nothing to fear if you are very cautious about helping your animals avoid it.

Another thing, not only may diseases be transmitted among cattle and horses through their excrement, if people go to other places and come back after having eaten infected beef, or if they meet someone on the road who has eaten infected beef, or if they carry infected beef into their village, the vapors from the infected beef can transmit the disease to the local cattle. One must be very careful to seal out and to avoid infection. Only if one does so will everything be all right.

In a year when there is a cattle epidemic, we instruct the people to seal off their pastures and not let their cattle smell each other's breath. Then, even if the animals look in each other's eyes, there will be nothing to fear. Believe my words and be very careful about avoiding infection and keeping your animals separate. But if you do not believe my words and think that it is impossible to avoid infection and so do not take steps to avoid it, your cattle will be infected by the disease and die. Viewed from this perspective, how can you say that separation is impossible? These are the facts: if you avoid infection, everything will be all right. Whoever has cattle should keep this firmly in mind.

"To proclaim one's defamation of others to be straightforwardness; to proclaim one's abuse of the spirits to be rectitude."

Annotation. "Spirits" refers to the spirits of the community and the hills.

Explication. The meaning of this passage is as follows: "To proclaim one's defamation of others to be straightforwardness" is to say that we slander and impugn someone who is irreproachable by concocting stories behind his or her back and even claim that another person has blamed him or her when such is not the case. Or we may say that another person did something we ourselves did.

"To proclaim one's abuse of the spirits to be rectitude" is to say that one should not dare to abuse the bodhisattvas of the Han lands and the community spirits, hill spirits, and valley spirits of the Ne lands. We should not casually abuse them and proclaim that we are correct in doing so, without fear of the community spirits, benign spirits, and demons.

"To have excessive lewd desires; to have poison in one's heart and a kind countenance."

No *annotation* is necessary.

Explication. The meaning of this passage is as follows: "To have excessive lewd desires" is to say that, when they are driven by lewd desires, people will commit homicide and break the law.

Another thing, if you have excessive lewd desires, this is to say that you will have many illnesses and will not live long.

Another thing, if one is given to seducing other men's wives and daughters, this is to say that the wives and daughters of his descendants will be dissipated and have bad reputations. "To have poison in one's heart and a kind countenance" is to say that one's face may be covered with laughter and smiles, as though one has a good conscience, but one's heart actually may be dark as a cave, scheming to harm and damage others. You should not be like this.

"To give others unclean food; to delude the masses with sinister ways."

No *annotation* is necessary.

Explication. The meaning of this passage is as follows: "To give others unclean food" is to say that, when someone is hungry and we give that person filthy food to eat, it may not be obvious to the eye. But, although it may not be obvious, the heavenly father and mother can see it.

Another thing, if someone puts food in a filthy place and it becomes contaminated, heavenly fire and thunderclaps will pursue that person and burn him or her up.

"To delude the masses with sinister ways" is to say that the witch doctor may quite calmly tell us that behind him are demons who inform him that this-and-such is incorrect, that this-and-such is wrong, that such-and-such will haunt you, that such-and-such will harm you, that so-and-so will bury your soul, that such-and-such will poison you, that calamities and disasters are coming, and that you therefore must have a soothsayer make a determination. They concoct all sorts of horror stories to deceive people, causing people to be terrified of this and that. As a result, the people miss the right times for planting and pasturing, their grain and livestock production decreases, they fall into debt with others, and their sons and daughters are harmed. It is this sort of cheating and injury that is being referred to.

Because they have bodies, it is inevitable that the people of the world will sometimes fall ill. The weather is such that sometimes it rains, sometimes it is hot, sometimes it is cold, and sometimes the wind blows, which can cause people to become ill.

If you eat fancy foods that are sweet, bitter, and astringent, you may become ill and have diarrhea, then you will feel the pain of sickness. If you do not drink alcohol, do not work, and do not change the position of your sleeping mat, should the illness be light, it will last for a couple of weeks or so. Should the illness be serious, you must be abstemious for half a year before you will get better. If you are going to die, a doctor will not be able to cure you, and if you are going to get better, then you do not need a doctor; you will get better when the illness has run its course.

The Han people do not make presentations to ghosts, yet the Han race has not become extinct. Next are the Ne clans. The White Ne do not make presentations to ghosts, yet the White Ne race has not become extinct. The Lahu make presentations to ghosts, and some of them have died out while others have flourished. That is the way it is.

If you believe the calamitous stories concocted by the witch doctors, your fields will be damaged, your descendants harmed, and the path to prosperity will be no more.

Han people who practice sinister ways refers to those who have a method for pulling the wool over others' eyes, and it also refers to Han witch doctors. You should not be like this.

Another thing, in the treatment of illness, no matter whether of Ne or of Han women, the Han people will not get near them while they are pregnant and until a month after they have given birth. Consequently, many women die or become ill for this very reason, but they are not thought to befoul or infect other people. As for the soothsayers of the Ne people, they believe that women who die in pregnancy will befoul or infect other people, so no one dares get near to them. Instead, they invite a soothsayer to come and perform an exorcism of the infected house. The soothsayer carries off on his back all of the utensils used in the exorcism, and he demands a large payment of "spirit" grain. After he has finished his purifying incantations, he declares that people will no longer be infected.

Well, how did the woman who died in pregnancy become infected before she died in pregnancy? How can the Ne people be so foolish that they do not think and reflect but instead believe the stories concocted by others? These are the facts: this sort of death in pregnancy cannot really befoul and infect other people. In the future, it goes without saying that women who die in this manner should all receive sacrifice.

"To destroy young children and abort fetuses; to engage in many clandestine perversions."

No *annotation* is necessary.

Explication. The meaning of this passage is as follows: "To destroy young children and abort fetuses" is to say that human beings, cattle, horses, wild animals, and flying birds have animate life. We should not kill their offspring when we see them, nor should we cause them to miscarry when we see that they are fetate.

Another thing, if women who are jealous of each other use medicines to destroy each other's fetuses; or if a young girl has no husband but takes a lover and becomes pregnant and, fearing that they will be discovered, destroys her fetus, or should the infant be born and she kills it, later on when she has a husband she will not be able to have a baby because her baby was the life that she had already killed, or later on it may come back to reclaim the debt she owes and she will die from a difficult labor. Above all, one should not do this sort of thing.

"To engage in many clandestine perversions" is to say that, no matter how a man does things, he should always be reasonable, whether in his public or his private dealings. Unless one reflects on what sorts of things are clandestine perversions, one may be subject to nefarious intentions, such as being a thief or a robber, or ogling other men's wives and seducing their daughters-in-law. One should not dare go ahead with one's many clandestine perversions.

Another thing is when, having bad thoughts and a voracious appetite, you stealthily eat and drink, fearing that others will know. "To engage in many clandestine perversions" refers to this kind of person. One should not do this sort of thing.

"To burn off the underbrush for hunting in the spring months."

No *annotation* is necessary.

Explication. The meaning of this passage is as follows: when spring arrives, the wild animals are pregnant, birds lay their eggs, and so do bugs and ants. When we hunt wild animals or shoot flying birds, fires are set in the wilds to capture the animals. They burn in the hills and burn in the valleys, burning tens of thousands of bugs and ants. This should not be.

Therefore, it is said that those who set many fires in the wilds have no hidden virtue and their descendants will get leprosy. Yet there are no proven instances that the descendants of those who set many fires in the wilds will get leprosy.

People get leprosy because of mutual infection, so one must carefully avoid getting infected. The Han people ignorantly say that avoidance will not work, because whether or not one gets leprosy is determined by fate. But that is also untrue. Among the Han people, there is also infection of the disease. Those who get near lepers become leprous, while those who do not get near lepers will never catch leprosy their whole life long.

Certain people are possessed of strong constitutions from the day they are born. When they come in contact with lacquer, they do not have an allergic reaction; when they get near someone with boils, they do not develop boils; and when they get near lepers, they do not catch leprosy. The Han people's claim that someone is fated not to catch a disease actually refers to this sort of thing, but such people are exceedingly rare.

Certain people are possessed of weak constitutions from the day they are born. When they come in contact with lacquer, they have an allergic reaction; when they get near someone with boils, they develop boils; and when they get near lepers, they catch leprosy. The Han people's claim that someone is fated to catch a disease actually refers to this sort of thing, and such people are comparatively numerous. Therefore, those who are born with weak constitutions must pay attention to avoiding sources of disease. If they do not come in contact with lacquer, they will not have allergic reactions; if they do not get near someone with boils, they will not develop boils; and if they do not get near lepers, they will not catch leprosy.

Do not believe all that talk about being fated and not being fated, so there is no need for avoidance. As a matter of fact, one must carefully avoid a disease like leprosy. Leprosy can infect others after it becomes evident, but it more often happens that people are infected before it becomes evident. If a person has a poor appetite and is sluggish, you must be very careful to avoid that person. Among the common people, when someone's relative contracts leprosy, they take pity on that person and build a nice leper's house for him or her in a distant place. They send grain to eat and go to console the person, but they do not sleep where he or she sleeps, sit where he or she sits, walk where he or she walks, wear his or her clothes or shoes, or use his or her implements, being attentive to the avoidance of these things. By being careful to avoid contamination, their descendants will remain clean and free from leprosy.

The Book of Good Deeds is of the highest excellence. Written in the front part of the book are three pages giving the original text. All that "the Most Exalted saith" is to instruct the people of the world. All that is said in the tiny annotations and explications that come afterward is our own. All that comes after the main text of what "the Most Exalted saith" is a detailed exposition for the edification of the people.

This book must be kept in a clean place. You must put it in a high, clean place. After it disintegrates and there is no more use for it at home, it must be burned. If you carelessly let it become soiled by unclean things, put it in an unclean place, or throw it in an unclean place, that is a sin.

Preserve this book in a clean place. Take it out carefully, study it carefully, and read it carefully to instruct others. Recite it carefully so that others may hear and be benefited by it.

Examples of good deeds.
    Annotation. "Examples" refers to examples of all good deeds.

"One deed is worth a hundred."
    Annotation. If you do one extremely good deed, it is worth a hundred merits. Saving a person's life is worth a hundred merits. Not to insult a woman who is trying to preserve her chastity is worth a hundred merits. If a woman has extramarital relations with a man and, having become pregnant, wishes to destroy the fetus, or if a couple have too many children and wish to abandon one of their infants because they cannot support it, to persuade them not to do so is to save the life of a baby and is worth a hundred merits. Persuading someone to save the life of a fetus is worth a hundred merits.

"One deed is worth fifty."
    Annotation. If you do one very good deed, it is worth fifty merits. If you take

in a person who has no place to go and support him, it is worth fifty merits. To bury a person's skeleton is worth fifty merits.

"One deed is worth thirty."

Annotation. If you do one quite good deed, it is worth thirty merits. If you teach a wastrel to become good, it is worth thirty merits. If you give a family that has no burial plot a place to bury their deceased, it is worth thirty merits.

"One deed is worth ten."

Annotation. If you do one rather good deed, it is worth ten merits. If you introduce a person who practices good to an official who gives him employment, it is worth ten merits. To write a book that is useful to others is worth ten merits. To help remove from office someone who harms the people is worth ten merits.

"One deed is worth five."

Annotation. If you do one fairly good deed, it is worth five merits. To encourage people not to sue each other is worth five merits. To teach people the way to live long is worth five merits.

"One deed is worth three."

Annotation. If you do one pretty good deed, it is worth three merits. If you are willing to listen when others speak the truth, it is worth three merits. Not to deny a mistake is worth three merits. To praise a person who has done something good is worth three merits.

"One deed is worth one."

Annotation. If you do something minor, it is worth one merit. To cure someone's illness is worth one merit. If you instruct someone with *The Book of Good Deeds*, it is worth one merit. Giving a person who is hungry and thirsty something to eat and drink is worth one merit. Donating money for the making of a Buddhist image or the construction of a temple is worth one merit. Donating money for the digging of an irrigation ditch is worth one merit. Donating money for the paving of a road or the building of a bridge is worth one merit.

"One deed is worth a hundred."

Annotation. If you do one extremely bad deed, it counts as one hundred demerits. To harm one life is worth a hundred demerits. If you take liberties with a woman who is trying to preserve her chastity, or if you insult her and force her, it is worth one hundred demerits. To instruct someone to murder a fetus is worth a hundred demerits.

"One deed is worth fifty."

Annotation. If you do one very bad deed, it is worth fifty demerits. Breaking up a husband and wife is worth fifty demerits. Casting aside a skeleton is worth fifty demerits.

"One deed is worth thirty."

Annotation. If you do one quite bad deed, it is worth thirty demerits. To harm a person by spreading rumors is worth thirty demerits. If you see someone who is innocent and you do not speak out on his behalf, it is worth thirty demerits. Divulging a person's secrets and causing him to be punished is worth thirty demerits.

"One deed is worth ten."

Annotation. One rather bad deed is worth ten demerits. To vilify a person who does good deeds is worth ten demerits. Writing a book that teaches people to do evil is worth ten demerits. Throwing away a copy of *The Book of Good Deeds* is worth ten demerits.

"One deed is worth five."

Annotation. One fairly bad deed is worth five demerits. To incite people to sue each other is worth five demerits. To obstruct a road or break a bridge is worth five demerits.

"One deed is worth three."

Annotation. One pretty bad deed is worth three demerits. Sitting ahead of one's elders is worth three demerits. Injuring another person when you are drunk on liquor is worth three demerits.

"One deed is worth one."

Annotation. If you do something minor, it is worth one demerit. If you do not wait for a person with whom you have an appointment, it is worth one demerit. To be discourteous before others is worth one demerit. Taking a needle and thread from another person is worth one demerit. If you see someone who is sad and you do not comfort that person, it is worth one demerit. Not paying back your debts to others, even if it is one coin, is worth one demerit.

— 34 —

Supernatural Retribution and Human Destiny

Cynthia Brokaw

Yuan Huang (1533–1606), the author of "Determining Your Own Fate" (*Liming pian*), was born into a wealthy landowning family in Jiashan County, Zhejiang Province, one of the wealthiest regions of South China. The Yuans were well known as a family of distinguished physicians; Yuan Huang's father, grandfather, and great-grandfather had all practiced medicine. Though he studied medicine as a young man, Yuan Huang was the first to break with family tradition, abandoning his medical education for the study of the Confucian Classics and competition in the civil-service examination system. "Determining Your Own Fate" is, at one level, the story of this choice and its happy outcome: Yuan Huang succeeded in passing the last of the examinations in 1586, thereby earning an official post, a mark of high status in Chinese society.

But "Determining Your Own Fate" is more than simply a brief account of Yuan Huang's life. It also explains and defends a religious belief and method of moral practice that Yuan claimed had determined his success. Yuan believed in the operation of supernatural retribution—that is, that gods and spirits watched over the actions of men and women and rewarded their good deeds (often with this-worldly benefits like success in the examinations or the birth of sons) and punished their bad ones (with premature death, poverty, examination failure, and so forth).

Naturally, a man interested in earning rewards for himself and his family was supposed to practice good as assiduously and efficiently as possible. The method of merit accumulation, set forth in texts called ledgers of merit and demerit, offered practical assistance to this end: the ledgers listed good and bad deeds and assigned different points to each, thus providing a means of measuring precisely the magnitude and value of each deed. Ledger-users were able, then, to plan their moral behavior and calculate their moral worth (and thus the likelihood of reward) in specific, numerical terms. For example, the act of giving money to a poor man might be "worth" ten merit points, while that of gossiping about a neighbor might be assigned five demerit points. At the end of every day, ledger keepers were to record all the merit points they had earned in the course of the day and then to subtract from these all the demerit points they had accumulated. Keeping a running total, they would be able, at the end of every year, to know exactly where they stood with the gods—a large balance of merits assured them of reward, a considerable total of demerits, of punishment.

Yuan Huang was by no means the creator of either the belief in supernatural retribution or the method of merit accumulation. As a reading of the Song dynasty *Tract of the Most Exalted on Action and Response (Taishang ganying pian)* reveals, both the belief and the method had been around for centuries before Yuan Huang. What is interesting about Yuan Huang's treatment of the system is his effort to explain it in terms that would make it attractive to the highly educated elite. Although both the belief and the method seem to have been derived largely from "heterodox" Daoist and Buddhist sources, Yuan is eager to provide Confucian supports as well: hence his frequent references to the Classics (especially the *Book of Documents (Shangshu)*, the *Classic of Poetry (Shijing)*, the *Classic of Changes (Yijing)*, and *Mencius (Mengzi)*). His effort to justify the belief in supernatural retribution and the method of merit accumulation in Confucian terms is not always persuasive, as his distorted reading of Mencius makes clear. But that is, in a sense, beside the point. What is important here is Yuan's conviction that all of the Three Teachings support his practice.

In holding this conviction Yuan was very much a man of his times. The late Ming was a period when many thinkers developed systems of belief and methods of self-cultivation that drew eclectically on Confucian, Buddhism, and Daoism. Yuan's particular system enjoyed considerable popularity, however. Though "Determining Your Own Fate" was written originally as instructions to his sons, it soon began to circulate more widely, outside the Yuan family. An edition of the text was published in 1601, and thereafter the essay was frequently republished in collections of moral admonitions. (Indeed, it is still available today, on Taiwan and in the People's Republic of China). The ledgers of merit and demerit, as necessary tools of merit accumulation, also became quite popular, at least in part as a result of Yuan's efforts. The ledger appended here to "Determining Your Own Fate" is quite brief and summary; yet within decades of Yuan's death, long, twelve-volume ledgers, full of detailed instructions and illustrative stories, appeared as an aid to those interested in accumulating merit, reducing their demerits, and thus ensuring themselves of rewards from the gods.

"Determining Your Own Fate" is translated from the 1607 edition of *Liming pian,* 1a–8b. It was not until several years later, in 1618, that the ledger Yungu gave to Yuan Huang was published with "Determining Your Own Fate"; the autobiographical essay and "The Articles of the Ledger of Merit and Demerit" appeared at that time under the title *Instructions to My Sons (Xunzi yan)* in the collection *Baicheng.* (See the facsimile reproduction in *Baibu congshu jicheng,* no. 17.) Earlier versions of the translation here were published as part of "Yuan Huang (1533–1606) and the Ledgers of Merit and Demerit," *Harvard Journal of Asiatic Studies,*

47.1 (June 1987), pages 137–95, and in *The Ledgers of Merit and Demerit: Social Change and Moral Order in Late Imperial China* (Princeton: Princeton University Press, 1991).

Further Reading

For more on Yuan Huang, see Cynthia J. Brokaw, "Yuan Huang (1533–1606) and the Ledgers of Merit and Demerit," *Harvard Journal of Asiatic Studies* 47.1 (June 1987): 137–95. Brokaw, *The Ledgers of Merit and Demerit: Social Change and Moral Order in Late Imperial China* (Princeton: Princeton University Press, 1991), studies the ledgers and the system of merit accumulation in the context of the social and economic changes of the late Ming and early Qing. The reader might also want to consult Sakai Tadao's pioneering work on the morality books and Chinese society, *Chūgoku zensho no kenkyū* (Tokyo: Kōbundō, 1960); some of Sakai's arguments are summarized in his "Confucianism and Popular Educational Works," in *Self and Society in Ming Thought*, ed. Wm. Theodore de Bary (New York: Columbia University Press, 1970). Finally, for a discussion of the moral and religious implications of the system of merit and demerit, see Wolfram Eberhard's *Guilt and Sin in Traditional China* (Berkeley and Los Angeles: University of California Press, 1967).

"Determining Your Own Fate" by Yuan Huang

I lost my father when I was a child, and since my mother was old, I gave up my preparations for the civil service examinations and took up the study of medicine instead. My mother explained, "Then you can both preserve your own health and bring relief to others. And it was your father's wish that you earn a name for yourself by practicing some profession."

Later, when I was visiting Ziyun Monastery [in Beijing], I met an old man with a long beard, a striking countenance, and the airy grace of an immortal. I bowed reverently to him, and he said to me, "You are on the way to becoming an official. Next year you will pass the examination for the licentiate (*sheng-yuan*) degree. Why are you not studying?" I told him the reason. He said, "My name is Kong, and I come from Yunnan. I have mastered the orthodox transmission of Master Shao's prognosticatory computations. (Shao Yong was a Daoist thinker of the Song dynasty. One of his most famous works, *Supreme Principles that Rule the World [Huangji jingshi]*, developed a numerological method for explicating the past and predicting the future; this method was the basis of the prognosticatory computations referred to here.) They are to be passed on to you, and so I have traveled a great distance in search of you. Is there a place where I can stay?"

I took him home with me and explained to my mother that Kong was an eminent scholar who knew many miraculous techniques. She told me to treat him kindly. I tested the prognostications he had made, and when I found that they had all been fulfilled, I then thought of taking up my studies for the examinations again. I consulted with my cousin Shen Cheng and he said, "Master Yu Haigu is teaching at Shen Youfu's house. I will send you to study with him; it will work out well." I thereupon performed the appropriate ceremonies and Yu became my teacher.

Kong calculated my fortune as follows: in the district examination I would place fourteenth, in the prefectural examination, seventy-first, and in the qualifying examination for the licentiate degree, ninth. When I took these examinations the next year, the three rankings he had predicted were all correct. Then he foretold the good and bad fortune that I would have throughout the rest of my life, explaining when I would pass the examinations, and what place I would take each time. In such-and-such a year I would fill a vacancy as a stipend student, in another I would occupy tribute-student (*gongsheng*) status. Then in such-and-such a year I would be appointed magistrate of a district in Sichuan. After two and a half years in office, I should retire. At the age of fifty-three, in the early morning of the fourteenth day of the eighth month, I would die at home, unfortunately without an heir. I prepared a record of these predictions and carefully learned them all.

From this time on, whenever I took an examination, my rank, whether high or low, never deviated from Kong's predictions. The only exception seemed to be his calculation that after I had consumed ninety-one piculs, five bushels of rice as a stipend student, I would take the position of tribute student. For when I had received only a little more than seventy piculs, the prefectural director of education, Mr. Tu, endorsed my petition to fill a vacancy as a tribute student, and I began to doubt the accuracy of Kong's predictions. But in the end the petition was rejected by the acting director of education, Mr. Yang.

In 1567, however, the prefectural director of education Yin Qiuming saw me writing essays in the examination hall, and he commented sadly, "These five essays are equal to any five memorials submitted to the throne. How can I allow a scholar of such wide and penetrating knowledge to grow old in the study?" Then he approved my petition to fill a vacancy for tribute-student status. By that time I had actually received ninety-one piculs, five bushels of rice, including the amount that I had been given before. Because of this experience, I believed even more that success and failure were fated, and that the timing of events was appointed, so I placidly ceased to strive for success.

As a tribute student, I went to Beijing for a year. That whole year I practiced quiet sitting, without studying. Then I traveled back to Nanjing. Before entering the Directorate of Education, I paid a visit to the Chan master Yungu at the Qixia Monastery. We sat together in one room for three days and nights, without sleeping. Yungu, inquiring about my apparent calmness of mind, said, "The reason that men ordinarily cannot become sages is that they confuse themselves with deluded thoughts. You have sat with me for three days, and you have not had a single deluded thought." I explained, "My future has been calculated by Mr. Kong. Glory and disgrace, life and death all have fixed allotments; even if I wanted to have deluded thoughts, there would be no place for them."

Yungu laughed and said, "I considered you an exceptional man, yet you are really just an ordinary fellow." When I asked why, he explained, "In the end a man's mind is bound by the forces of yin and yang, so how can there be no allotment? ("Allotment" refers to the measure of fate given each individual at birth. It was believed that this allotment could be discovered through the use of certain methods of prognostication, such as the one Kong practiced on Yuan Huang.) But only the ordinary man has a fixed lot in life. The exceptionally good man is certainly not constrained by his lot; nor is the exceptionally bad man constrained by his. For the past twenty years you have never moved a hair's breadth because of Kong's predictions—how can you be anything but an ordinary fellow?"

I asked, "Then I can escape my lot?" He replied, "A man determines his fate himself, and secures good fortune himself—this is what the *Classic of Songs* and the *Book of Documents* say, and it is a brilliant teaching. Our Buddhist scriptures say that if you seek a good reputation, you will receive it; if you seek wealth, you will receive it; if you seek sons and daughters, you will receive them; if you seek long life, you will receive it. Now speaking falsely is a great prohibition among Buddhists—how could all these buddhas and bodhisattvas lie and trick people?"

I went on: "Mencius says, 'If we get by seeking, . . . then what we have been seeking is something within ourselves.' One can strive hard to be virtuous, good and righteous, but how can one be sure of securing good reputation, wealth and rank?"[1]

Yungu explained, "Mencius's statement is correct, but you have misunderstood it. The Sixth Patriarch of Chan Buddhism (Huineng, 638–713) said, 'The field for all blessings is simply the mind.' If your desire arises from the mind, there is no goal you cannot achieve. If you seek within yourself, you will attain not only virtue, goodness, and righteousness, but also a good reputation, wealth, and high status: you gain both internal and external benefits. This kind of seeking will be efficacious. If you do not turn within and examine yourself, but merely chase after things from the outside, then your search follows a fixed path, and you will receive what was fated for you: you lose both internal and external benefits. Therefore this kind of seeking is useless."[2]

Then he asked what Kong had calculated for my future. After I had told him, he asked, "Do you think that you deserve to pass the examinations? Or that you deserve to have a son?" I reflected for a while and replied, "I do not deserve either. The sort of man who passes the examinations possesses physiognomical signs of good fortune. (Yuan Huang is expressing here the common Chinese belief that a person's physical features, if "read" properly, will reveal his or her fate.) My good fortune is slight; moreover, I have not been able to build up merit or accumulate good deeds to increase my good fortune. And I have no patience with troublesome affairs, and am not tolerant of other people. At times I use my abilities and intelligence to override others. Or I believe things too easily, and speak carelessly. All these characteristics are signs of my lack of good fortune—how could it be right for me to pass the examinations?

"The dirtiest soil produces the most crops, while the purest water never contains fish. I favor purity—that is the first reason I should not have a son. A peaceful disposition can nourish all things. But I am easily angered—that is the second reason I should not have a son. Love is the source of production and reproduction, and continence is the root of childlessness. I am always concerned about my own reputation and cannot put aside my own interests to help others—this is the third reason I should not have a son. I talk too much and thus dissipate my substance—this is the fourth reason I should not have a son. I like to drink and so wear down my mental energy—this is the fifth reason I should not have a son. I like to sit up all night and do not know how to preserve my inborn virtue and nurture my spirit—this is the sixth reason I should not have a son. My other faults and evils are so many that I cannot enumerate them all."

Yungu said, "How can this principle—that those who succeed are those who deserve to succeed—apply to the examinations alone? Those who deserve a thousand taels worth of property are surely people who have a thousand taels. Those who deserve one hundred taels worth of property are surely people who have one hundred taels. Those who should starve to death are surely people who do starve to death. Heaven bestows favors simply according to a man's own quality. When did it ever add the slightest bit more than he deserves?

"Now, when it comes to having a son, if you have one hundred generations worth of virtue you will surely have one hundred generations of descendants to preserve it. If you have ten generations worth of virtue you will surely have ten generations of descendants to preserve it. If you have two or three generations worth of virtue you will surely have two or three generations of descendants to preserve it. If your line is cut off without descendants your virtue is extremely slight.

"You already know your faults, and you should do your best from now on to correct all the characteristics that have kept you from passing the examinations and fathering a son. You must do your best to build up virtue. You must do your best to be tolerant. You must do your best to be compassionate. You must do your best to conserve your mental energy. It will be as if the "you" of the past died yesterday, as if the "you" of the future has just been born today. In this way you become a man in whom moral principle has been revitalized, and a man of moral principle can model himself on Heaven.

"The 'Taijia' chapter of the *Book of Documents* says, 'Calamities sent by Heaven may be avoided, but from calamities brought on by oneself there is no escape' (James Legge, *The Chinese Classics* [Hong Kong: Hong Kong University Press, 1960], vol. 3, p. 207). Master Kong's prediction that you would not pass the examination for the provincial degree (*juren*) is a prediction of a calamity sent by Heaven; you can still avoid it. If you now extend the inborn goodness of your nature, exert yourself to do good deeds, and accumulate a large store of hidden virtue, this is good fortune you are making yourself. How can you not take advantage of it? The *Classic of Changes* tells the superior man to pursue good fortune and avoid calamity. But if you say that fate is fixed, how can good fortune be pursued and calamities avoided? In the first section of the *Classic of Changes* it is written: 'The family that accumulates goodness is sure to have superabundant happiness. The family that accumulates evil is sure to have superabundant misfortune' (Z. D. Sung, *The Text of the Yi King and Its Appendixes* [Shanghai: China Modern Education Company, 1935], p. 20). Do you believe that this is possible?"

I was impressed by what Yungu said, so I respectfully received his teaching. Then I confessed all my past sins before the Buddha. I wrote a petition, seeking first to pass the examination for the provincial degree, and pledging to perform three thousand good deeds to repay the goodness of Heaven and my ancestors if this petition were granted. Yungu took out a ledger of merit and demerit and showed me how to register there what I did that day—if good, then to record the merits, and if bad, to subtract the demerits. Then he taught me to chant an incantation to Zhunti, in the hope that my petition be granted. (Zhunti is most commonly associated with the Buddhist goddess Guanyin, but she [or, at times, he] functions as a god in the Daoist pantheon as well. In each teaching she/he appears as an agent of supernatural retribution, and thus a fitting object of Yuan's worship.)

He explained to me, "A Daoist writer of charms once told me, 'If you do not know how to draw charms, then the spirits will laugh at you. There is a secret tradition: it is simply to have a mind unmoved by intentions. When you grasp your brush to write a charm, first release all entanglements with worldly things from your mind, and do not let one speck [i.e., any conscious thought] arise in your mind. From the point where your mind is unmoved, draw the first dot. This is called establishing a foundation from chaos. Then from this beginning complete the charm in one movement of the brush, still without any conscious thought. If you do it this way, then the charm will be effective. All supplications to Heaven for the determination of your own fate must be made from a mind free of conscious thought and free of reflection in order to evoke a response.

"When Mencius discussed learning how to decide one's fate, he first said, '[For the man who knows Heaven,] there is no distinction between early death and long life.' Now early death and long life are opposites, but when the mind is unmoved, what is early death? What is long life? And so too, only after you see no distinction between abundance and deficiency can you determine your fate in regard to poverty or wealth. Only after you see no distinction between failure and success can you determine your own fate in regard to life or death. Only after you see no distinction between early death and long life can you determine your own fate in regard to life or death. Men, as creatures born into the world, consider only early death and long life to be important, so I speak of early death and long life, but all favorable and unfavorable circumstances are included in this argument.[3]

"As for 'awaiting whatever is to befall you with a perfected character,' this is the same thing as accumulating merit and praying to Heaven. When Mencius speaks of cultivation, it means that if a person has faults and evils, they should be controlled and eradicated. When he speaks of awaiting whatever befalls you, it means that even your slightest desires and even your slightest expectations for the future should be cut off. When you have reached this point, when the tiniest speck will not move your mind, then without leaving the realm of desires, right away you can create your condition at birth [i.e., your inborn goodness]. This, then, is true learning.

Originally my pen name was Xuehai, meaning "the hundred rivers study the sea and thereby attain it." That day I changed it to Liaofan, "putting an end to ordinariness." Now that I had been enlightened about the doctrine of deciding my own fate, I did not want to fall back into the ways of ordinary men.

From this point on I was anxious all day. I felt different from the way I had before. Previously I had discharged my duties only very lackadaisically, but now I was always apprehensive and fearful about my situation. When I was alone in my own courtyard, I was constantly afraid of offending the spirits of Heaven and Earth. When I met people who hated and slandered me, I could calmly tolerate them.

But when I performed righteous deeds I was still not sincere, and when I examined my conduct I found many errors. Sometimes, though I saw what was right, I did not act on it courageously. (This sentence is an allusion to the *Analects:* "To see what is right and not to do it is want of courage" [Legge, *The Chinese Classics,* vol. 1, p. 154].) Or, although I did help other people, at heart I often doubted my motives in doing so. Or, although I exerted myself to do good, I transgressed in speech. Or, although I resolved to do good when sober, I relaxed my resolution when drunk. These faults cancelled out my merits, and days frequently passed empty of merits. From the time I made the pledge in 1569, over ten years had passed until, in 1579, I finally completed the three thousand good deeds.

I had just gone to Guanzhong with Li Jian'an, and I had not yet transferred the merit I had earned from my deeds. In 1580 I returned south and for the first time I asked Xingkong, Huikong, and all the other monks of the Dongta Chan Temple (close to Yuan's ancestral home in Jiashan County) to transfer my merit. (A man could have the merit he had accumulated himself transferred to the merit-store of another [or simply to that of all people]; this act of generosity was a means of further increasing one's own store of merit.) Then, in seeking a son I set up an altar to the Buddha and again promised to perform three thousand good deeds. In 1581 my son Tianqi was born.

As soon as I performed a good deed, I would record it with a brush. Your mother could not write, so each time she performed a deed, she would use a goose quill to stamp a vermilion circle on the calendar. We might give relief to the poor, or buy fish and shellfish and set them free. One day there were as many as ten-odd circles on the calendar. By the eighth month of 1583, the three thousand had been filled in. Again I asked Xingkong and the other monks to come to our house to transfer the merit.

On the thirteenth day of the ninth month I set up an altar to Buddha, seeking the metropolitan (*jinshi*) degree, and pledged to perform ten thousand good deeds for it. I passed the examination in 1586 and was appointed magistrate of Baodi.

In Baodi I took an empty ledger and entitled it *Governing My Mind* (*Zhixin pian*). Early in the mornings when I rose to sit in court, servants brought the book to the yamen guards and placed it on the bench at which cases were heard, so that I could record whatever I did, good or evil, in minute detail. Then in the evenings I set a table up in the courtyard and, following the example of Zhao Yuedao, burned incense and reported my actions to Heaven. (Every evening, Zhao Yuedao [Zhao Bian], a Song dynasty official noted for his moral rectitude and integrity, would recount to Heaven his actions during the day, a practice designed to ensure that he never did anything he would be ashamed to mention in his report.)

Your mother, seeing that few deeds had been performed, frowned and said, "Before, when we were at home, we helped each other in doing good deeds, so that the three thousand could be completed. Now you have vowed to do ten thousand, but there are no good deeds that can be done in the yamen. When will you be able to complete them all?"

That night it happened that a god appeared to me in a dream. When I told him that it was difficult to complete the good deeds, he said, "By simply reducing the land tax you can with one stroke complete all of the ten thousand deeds." Now in Baodi the tax for each unit (*mu*) of cultivated land was two *fen*, three *li*, seven *hao*. My plan was to reduce the rate to one *fen*, four *li*, six *hao*. But at heart I was a little doubtful that this would really work.

Just at that time, the Chan master Huanyu from Mount Wutai came to Baodi. I told him about my dream and asked whether it was right to believe such a thing. He replied, "With a sincere mind, even one deed can be worth ten thousand good ones. Moreover, if you reduce the tax rate for the whole district, then will not ten thousand people enjoy good fortune?" I donated my salary to provide a vegetarian feast for the monks of Mount Wutai and to have the merit of the ten thousand deeds transferred.

Mr. Kong had predicted that I would die at the age of fifty-three. I have never yet prayed for long life, but this year, without ever having a serious illness, I am sixty-eight. The *Classic of Documents* says, "It is difficult to rely on Heaven—its appointments are not constant," and "Heaven's appointments are not constant" (Legge, *The Chinese Classics*, vol. 3, pp. 213–14, 397). Both these statements are true. Now I understand that what is called good or bad fortune is what a man seeks himself. *This* is the teaching of the sages and worthies; saying that good and bad fortune is fated by Heaven is vulgar talk.

Your fate is still unknown. Even if your fate should be glorious, always be dissatisfied with your achievements. Even if it should be favorable, always be doubtful. Even if you have enough food and clothing, always be anxious about poverty and distress. Even if your scholarship is relatively refined, be fearful of vulgarity.

Reflect on the past and praise the goodness of your ancestors; reflect on what is near at hand and conceal your father's errors. Reflect on what is above and repay the grace of the state; reflect on what is below and create good fortune for your family. Reflect on what is outside you and save others from distress; reflect on what is within you and defend yourself against depravity. Every day know your errors. Every day correct your faults. Each day you do not know your errors is a day you have been complacent in thinking yourself right. Each day you have no errors that can be corrected is a day when no progress is made. There are many clear-sighted and talented people in the world, and the only reason goodness is not more intensely cultivated and this instruction not more widely practiced rests in the one word "indolence"—because of this fault people put off correcting their faults throughout their lives.

The doctrine of determining one's own fate that I learned from the Chan master Yungu is the most brilliant, the most profound, the most accurate, and the most proper principle. Explore it fully, exert yourself to the practice of it, and do not waste your life.

ARTICLES OF THE LEDGER OF MERIT AND DEMERIT

Merit Ledger (50 items). Do not count any merit if you received a bribe for the deed.

Count 100 merits:
    Rescuing a person from death
    Preserving a woman's chastity
    Preventing someone from drowning a child or from having an abortion

Count 50 merits:
    Arranging for the adopting of an heir
    Raising an orphan
    Burying someone who has no one to care for his or her remains
    Preventing a person from becoming a vagabond

Count 30 merits:
    Helping a person to dedicate himself to Buddha [i.e., to become a monk]
    Urging a person who follows evil ways to change his or her conduct
    Saving a person from oppression
    Offering land for the burial of a person who has no one to care for his or her remains

Count 10 merits:

  Recommending a virtuous man

  Removing a cause of harm to the people

  Compiling a scripture that will aid the people

  Using your skill to cure a serious illness

Count 5 merits:

  Urging the cessation of a court case

  Transmitting to a person a method for improving his life

  Compiling a book that will tell people how to preserve or improve their lives

  Using your skill to cure a mild illness

  Saving the life of a creature capable of repaying human kindness

Count 3 merits:

  Accepting a wrong to yourself without anger

  Bearing slander without complaint

  Accepting an unpleasant truth

  Preventing the beating of a person who deserves it

  Saving the life of a creature that does not have the power to repay human kindness

Count 1 merit:

  Praising a person's goodness

  Concealing a person's evil deed

  Preventing a person from doing evil in one instance

  Preventing a person from fighting

  Helping to relieve a person's illness

  Collating and editing a moral work left after a person's death (1 merit for every 1,000 characters)

  Refusing an invitation to a feast or drinking party

  Rescuing a person from hunger

  Giving a person shelter for the night

  Persuading a person verbally to follow the way of virtue

  When your affairs are successful, extending the profit to another

  Helping a person or animal to rest when he or it is weary from labor (1 merit for one hour)

  Burying a bird or animal that has died

  Saving the life of a small insect

Count 1 merit for each 100 cash spent (whenever you spend money to do good deeds, record the amount; grain and cloth count also):

  Repairing roads, bridges, and ferries

  Channeling canals and digging wells for the benefit of the people

  Repairing sacred images and altars, and giving food as sacrifices to the gods (when you pay to have other people do the repairs, reduce the merit by half)

  Returning an article that someone had left behind (even if this takes less than 100 cash, it is worth 1 merit)

Releasing someone from debt

Distributing books that urge people to do good

Doing good deeds to extend the merit to the soul of someone who has died an untimely death

Showing eagerness to relieve the poor

Establishing granaries and keeping the price of grain steady

Giving things like tea, medicine, clothing, and coffins to the poor

Demerit Ledger (50 deeds). If done accidentally, do not count them.

Count 100 demerits:

Causing a person to die

Making a woman lose her chastity

Urging someone to drown a child or to have an abortion

Count 50 demerits:

Cutting off a family's line of succession

Preventing a marriage

Abandoning an unburied corpse

Causing a person to become a vagrant

Count 30 demerits:

Destroying a person's resolve not to do evil

Making up slanders about a person

Revealing a secret entrusted to you, one that ruins a business deal

Count 10 demerits:

Ostracizing a virtuous person

Recommending an evil man for employment

Having contact with a woman who has lost her chastity

Keeping a weapon that can kill

Count 5 demerits:

Destroying a scripture that would improve morals

Compiling a work injurious to the people

Unjustly allowing a person falsely accused of a crime to be thought a criminal

Refusing to aid a sick person who is seeking relief

Urging a person to start litigation

Creating slanders about and a bad name for a person

Harming a person through slander

Blocking a road or bridge, or preventing a ferry from passing

Killing an animal capable of repaying human kindness

Count 3 demerits:

Getting angry when you hear an unpleasant truth

Reversing the order of high and low, old and young

Harming someone when you are drunk

Beating a person who does not deserve it
Sowing discord among people by telling lies
Wearing clothing that is inappropriate for your position
Killing an animal not capable of repaying human kindness

Count 1 demerit:
Concealing a person's merit
Inciting a person to fight
Making a person's evil deeds known
Encouraging a person to do evil in one instance
Doing nothing to stop a thief in the act
Taking insignificant things from a person without asking permission
Cheating an ignorant person
Breaking a promise
Neglecting your manners
Neglecting to comfort a person who is grief-stricken
Refusing to allow your servants or animals to rest when they are tired
Killing a small and insignificant insect

Count 1 demerit for each 100 cash spent or gained:
Wasting food that someone else could be eating
Destroying another's success
Ignoring the good of people in making a profit
Using other people's money wastefully
Neglecting to pay debts
Embezzling an inheritance (count 1 demerit even if less than 100 cash is involved)
Extorting money with the excuse that you need it for public welfare
Intriguing to get people's money, possessions, labor, and so forth for yourself

Users of this ledger of merit and demerit should every evening record their merits and demerits under the ledger for that day. If you have performed deeds that do not appear in this ledger, then give an example of what you have done. At the end of the month compare the merits and demerits, and subtract the demerits from the merits. Having deducted the demerits, you will clearly see your score. At the end of the year do a comprehensive comparison, and you will know what good or bad fortune to expect.

Notes

1. The full passage from *Mencius* is: "Seek and you will get it; let go and you will lose it. If this is the case, then seeking is of use to getting and what is sought is within yourself. But if there is a proper way to seek it and whether you get it or not depends on fate, then seeking is of no use to getting and what is sought lies outside oneself." Mencius is saying that goodness is worth seeking only for its own sake; if a man thinks of goodness as a means of earning external rewards from Heaven, then he has lost goodness. Note that Yungu goes on to distort somewhat the point of this passage in his defense

of the system of merit accumulation. Citation from D. C. Lau, trans., *Mencius* (New York: Penguin Books, 1970), pp. 182–83.

2. Here Yungu is misinterpreting both Mencius and Huineng, each of whom is making a point rather different from the one Yungu is pressing. As note 1 explains, Mencius stated that if one does good in order to earn reward, all goodness (and all hope of reward) is lost. Huineng argued, similarly, that points earned from the performance of good deeds will *not* earn true merit. He explained, "Building temples, giving alms, and making offerings are simply means of seeking blessings. One cannot make blessings into merit. . . . Merit is created in the mind; blessings and merit are different" (Philip B. Yampolsky, *The Platform Sutra of the Sixth Patriarch* [New York: Columbia University Press, 1967], p. 156).

3. The full passage from *Mencius* is: "For a man to give full realization to his heart is for him to understand his own nature, and a man who knows his own nature will know Heaven. By retaining his heart and nurturing his nature he is serving Heaven. Whether he is going to die young or live to a ripe old age makes no difference to his steadfastness of purpose. It is through awaiting whatever is to befall him with a perfected character that he stands firm on his proper destiny" (Lau, *Mencius,* p. 182). It is difficult to see how Yungu can reconcile this passage with his suggestion that Yuan Huang do good deeds in order to accumulate merit points. See notes 1 and 2 above.

Stories from an Illustrated Explanation of the *Tract of the Most Exalted on Action and Response*

Catherine Bell

Late imperial China (1550–1911) saw a remarkable proliferation of religious books written for nonelite social classes, which were growing in strength and status in conjunction with the economic expansion of the period. The availability of inexpensive mass printing at this time also promoted both widespread literacy or near-literacy and the broad marketing of books. In many of these popular religious works, Daoist, Buddhist, and neo-Confucian ideas were woven into a type of nonsectarian, heavily moralistic message concerning virtue, universal laws of cause and effect, and systems for calculating merit and demerit. Such works are generally known as "morality books."

The oldest and most famous morality book is the twelfth-century *Tract of the Most Exalted on Action and Response (Taishang ganying pian)*. It is a relatively short work of about 1,200 characters that presents itself as the words of the Most Exalted, usually understood to be the Daoist deity, Laozi. His message is that good and bad fortune do not come into one's life without reason; rather, they follow as natural consequences of what people do, just as a shadow follows a form. Alluding to a complex cosmology in which a variety of deities oversee human behavior, the *Tract* teaches how the merit earned from good deeds will bring long life, wealth, and successful descendants, while the retribution that attends evil deeds ensures the eventual suffering of the wicked.

Within a century of its first published appearance in 1164, a Song dynasty emperor printed and distributed thousands of copies of the *Tract* in order to convey this message to his subjects, launching a long history of reprintings for didactic and meritorious purposes. The brief tract was republished with prefaces, commentaries, and stories to help illustrate its principles. Later editions added miracle tales, woodblock illustrations, proverbs, ledgers with which to calculate one's balance of merit and demerit, as well as lists of those who had donated to the printing of the text. In contrast to the direct message of the Most Exalted, which comprises the original short tract, many of these expanded editions began to call attention to the physical text itself, urging the reader to venerate the book and disseminate it in every way possible. Such piety and enthusiasm gave rise to innumerable large- and small-scale devotional projects to reprint the text. When D. T. Suzuki and Paul Carus published one of several English translations in 1906, they suggested that more copies of the *Tract* had been published in China than any other book in all history.

An "Illustrated Explanation" of the *Tract* compiled by Xu Zuanzeng in 1657 was the basis for an expanded edition published by Huang Zhengyuan (fl. 1713–1755) in 1755. Huang's edition stresses two themes. First, he argues that the *Tract* contains the eternal wisdom of the Confucian sages, but in a form that even the most simple-minded can understand. With the easy commentaries and the selection of appealing stories that he has provided, he goes on, everyone can now read, appreciate, and profit from the message of the *Tract*. Second, Huang repeatedly declares that the most meritorious deeds of all are those activities that help to make the *Tract* available to others. Doing one good deed, such as setting free a caged animal, is certainly laudable, but how can it compare to making others aware of the consequences of their own actions? Hence, in the stories and segment from one of Huang's prefaces that follow, distributing the *Tract* is the height of virtue and sure to bring to anyone the formulaic rewards of prosperity, official position, and filial children.

The ideas of virtue and retribution expressed in these excerpts reflect the neo-Confucian idea that anyone, not just the educated elite, could become a virtuous sage. However, scholars have noted that this idea appears to be highly nuanced by a somewhat mercantile perspective: actions count over intentions; good and bad deeds not only add up or cancel each other out, they are also investments that bear fruit and testify to one's true character; and a practical, this-worldly orientation locates the causes and effects of morality and immorality in the here and now. At the same time, the goals of moral action include not only material prosperity, but also the time-honored goals of social prestige through official recognition by the emperor and a position in the government. It has been suggested that this particular vision of moral action flowered in an era marked by heightened social mobility and the social restructuring that attended urbanization and the expansion of commercial activity. Certainly, morality books like the *Tract* appear to have worked out a simplified and generalized Confucian moral ethos readily appropriated by major segments of the population. This achievement has been linked to the unity and traditionalism of Chinese culture in the late imperial period, on the one hand, and to the emergence of a modern style of moral individualism, on the other.

Huang Zhengyuan, *Taishang ganying pian tushuo* (*Illustrated Explanation of the Tract of the Most Exalted on Action and Response*), also called *Taishang baofa tushuo* (*Illustrated Explanation of the Precious Raft of the Most Exalted*), 8 juan.

Further Reading

Catherine Bell, "Printing and Religion in China: Some Evidence from the *Taishang Ganying Pian," Journal of Chinese Religions* 20 (Fall 1992): 173–86; Judith A. Berling, "Religion and Popular Culture: The Management of Moral Capital in *The Romance of the Three Teachings,"* in *Popular Culture in Late Imperial China,* ed., David Johnson, Andrew J. Nathan, and Evelyn S. Rawski (Berkeley: University of California Press, 1985), pp. 188–218; Cynthia J. Brokaw, *The Ledgers of Merit and Demerit: Social Change and Moral Order in Late Imperial China* (Princeton: Princeton University Press, 1991); Evelyn S. Rawski, *Education and Popular Literacy in Ch'ing China* (Ann Arbor: Center for Chinese Studies of the University of Michigan, 1979); Sakai Tadao, "Confucianism and Popular Educational Works," in Wm. Theodore de Bary, *Self and Society in Ming Thought,* ed. (New York: Columbia University Press, 1970); D. T. Suzuki and Paul Carus, trans., *Treatise on Response and Retribution by Lao Tze* (La Salle: Open Court, 1973).

"On Distributing Morality Books" by Huang Zhengyuan

It is said that those who do good deeds will obtain good fortune, while those who are not virtuous will experience misfortune. This is the reason for the blessings or calamities that befall the moral and the immoral. How clear it is! There is more than one road to virtue, but none can compare to distributing morality books. By transforming one person, a morality book can go on to transform ten million people. Spreading its teachings through one city, it can spread them through ten million cities. By exhorting one generation to virtue, it can effectively exhort ten million generations. This is different from all other means of virtue, which do things one at a time in only one direction.

If people can make use of this book, they will develop a virtuous heart; then they can be taught how to calculate their merits and demerits, thereby gradually extending their moral character until their virtue is complete. They will come from the towns and villages to advance the nation. The intellectuals will teach the ignorant. Preserving "the way" in this world, they will reverse the degenerate customs of our day. All depends on this book!

Although the book has a philosophy that divides things up into cause and effect, this is the only way to teach people to act virtuously. There is an old saying, "With upper-class people, one talks philosophy; with lower-class people, one talks of cause and effect." Now, it is difficult to exchange talk about philosophy, but there are many who can talk about auspicious or calamitous retribution. And such talk is enough to influence people's hearts. Therefore, while it is appropriate to have books on philosophy, there should be at least as many books on cause and effect.

Those who have composed, compiled, published, or donated to the printing of morality books and were subsequently saved from calamity and danger, amassing blessings and years of long life, both in the past and the present—well, they are too numerous to count! . . . These forebears attained high positions, prosperity, prestige, and longevity because they distributed morality books. These are just some of the good effects that distributing morality books has on the world and on people's hearts. It is not a small thing and yet it does not burden people. Why then are there so few believers and so many unbelievers? People just do not know the truth within morality books. But if you want people to know the truth of morality books, you must first encourage them to be distributed. After they are disseminated, then one can hope that many will actually see the books. The greater the number of people who see it, then naturally the number who come to know its truth will also increase. Those who can sincerely grasp the truth in morality books will grow in virtue.

STORIES

A. Zhu Jiayou of the Qiantang District in Zhejiang Province was employed in the salt business and fond of doing good deeds. When Mr. Lin Shaomu was the General Surveillance Commissioner for Zhejiang, Zhu begged him to write out the two morality books, *Tract on Action and Response* and *Essay on Secret Merit* (*Yinzhi wen*), in handsome script in order to engrave the texts in stone. He also asked him to contribute more than ten thousand sheets of paper to make copies. All those who obtained a copy treasured the fine calligraphy. Night and day Zhu made copies. After a while, he gradually became able to understand the full meaning of the text, fortifying his body and soul. Both the one who wrote out the texts and the one who gave copies of them away received blessings in return. Zhu's son was given an eminent position in Anhui Province, while Lin was later appointed to an office with jurisdiction over the provinces of Hubei and Hunan. (Huang, 1:20b)

B. Once there was a man from the Wu Xi District in Jiangsu, named Zou Yigui, also called Xiaoshan (Little Mountain). At the time of the provincial examinations people were contributing to the printing of morality books and wanted him to donate also. Zou declined, saying, "It is not because I am unwilling to give money. Rather I fear that people will be disrespectful to the text and that would put me at fault." That night he dreamed that the god Guandi appeared to scold him, saying, "You study books and illuminate their basic principles, yet you also speak like this! If all people followed your example, virtue would practically disappear." Zou prostrated himself and begged forgiveness. He printed and circulated one thousand copies in order to atone for his fault. Moreover, by himself he painted a religious image on a board and devoutly chanted in front of it morning and night. Later, in the year 1727, he placed first in special examinations and entered the prestigious Hanlin Academy, where he held a series of official positions, culminating in an appointment as Vice Minister in the Ministry of Rites. Zou always said to people, "One word is enough to incur fault. And among evil doers, no one is worse than the person who hinders the virtue of others." This story demonstrates that anyone who impedes contributions to morality books is guilty of the greatest fault and will be punished by Heaven. (Huang, Zushi shanshu bian section, 1:20a–b)

C. Shan Yangzhu lived at a small Buddhist temple. When he was born, he was weak and often ill. His mother prayed for him, vowing that if her son were cured, he would be a vegetarian for his whole life. In addition, she nursed him at her breast for six full years until he began to eat rice at the age of seven. When his mother died, he continued to live at the temple for forty-one years, yet he was in constant pain and suffering for half his life. One day he read the *Tract on Action and Response* and, thinking about his parents, suddenly repented of all his bad deeds. Thereafter, he collected different editions of the *Tract* and amended them with his own understanding of its meaning—revising, distinguishing and analyzing point by point. Altogether his study came to 330,000 words, divided into eight volumes and entitled *An Exposition of the Tract of the Most Exalted on Action and Response.* He did this in order to made amends for all his misdeeds, but also as an attempt to repay some small part of the boundless loving kindness of his parents. In 1655 he organized people to donate the money for publishing it. Because of these activities, everything that was painful and unhappy in his life gradually improved. (Huang, 1:28b)

D. At the end of the Yuan dynasty (1280–1368) there was a man named Chu Shaoyi, who not only diligently practiced the teachings of the *Tract on Action and Response,* but also printed and distributed it. He set each phrase to music so that his wife and the women in their quarters could understand it and be enlightened.

At that time the country fell into strife caused by rival warlords. One of them was Chen Youliang. When Chen was young and very poor, Chu had once helped him. Many years later, after Youliang and his army had occupied the provinces of Hubei and Guangdong, Youliang falsely proclaimed himself emperor of the country. He summoned Chu to come work for him and frequently gave him gifts of gold and silk. Chu did not dare refuse the gifts, but stored them in a bamboo chest and used them only to aid hungry families. Although he himself needed firewood and rice, he was not willing to use any of the gifts.

After the Ming emperor Taizu quelled the chaos and ascended the throne (1368), he sought out retired scholars of virtue throughout the empire. Civil authorities communicated the proclamation and recommended Chu, who was summoned to the capital. The emperor asked him: "Dear sir, what would give you the most pleasure?" Chu replied: "As for me, I am just an ordinary man who is pleased to live now in an age of great peace and prosperity. I only want the strength and diligence to plow and plant my fields. Virtue comes naturally that way. In addition, I want to instruct my children in virtue and teach my grandchildren. Nothing can give me more pleasure than these things."

Taizu then said: "The day that Chen Youliang usurped the throne, you sir did not join his side. Youliang honored and respected you, so we can see that even though he was an evil man, he was capable of rewarding virtue and righteousness. Virtue can influence anyone—you can trust that. The *Book of Chu* says that only virtue should be treasured. You sir will be called 'the treasure of the nation.' " Then the emperor himself wrote out those four characters, "regard as the treasure of the nation," and bestowed it on him. In addition, the emperor gave him elegantly spun silk and a special one-horse chariot to take him back home. By imperial order, each month the civil authorities were to provide Chu with grain and meat for the rest of his life. His son was appointed a provincial governor in Yunnan and his grandson entered the national university to study. As soon as the grandson's studies were completed, he received an official post in accord with his abilities. (Huang 3:6a)

E. Zhou Guangpu developed an upset stomach and became so ill that for more than twenty days he could not eat or drink. He was so sick that two deputies from the underworld arrived, put him in chains, and led him out the door. When they had traveled approximately ten miles, he saw a man off in the woods calling his name. He quickly went over to him and saw that it was none other than his dear old friend Ji Yunhe. The two men clasped hands and wept, greatly moved to talk with each other again after such a long separation. Then Ji drew close to Zhou's ear and whispered: "While I was alive, I was without fault because of all my education. I am trusted by the chief officers and judge of the underworld beneath Mount Tai. The fates of all the living and dead pass through my hands, so I can help you in the other world. The most important thing is the *Tract on Action and Response*. In a little while, when you come before the court, just say that you once made a vow to recite it ten thousand times. Beg to be released and returned to life in order to complete the vow. If the judge has any questions, I will plead for you myself." When he finished speaking, he left.

The two deputies escorted Zhou to a huge government office where he saw lots of people coming and going. Some were welcomed or sent off with drum rolls in their honor. Some wandered about freely, while others, manacled with chains, were led to and from the hells. Suddenly he heard his name called out as his case was summoned before the court. Zhou went up to the desk and kneeled. The judge spoke: "You are said to have been well-behaved and devout, but you were fond of eating animals and birds—even catching insects for food. If you please, are they not living things too? It is appropriate for you to be sentenced to the hell of the hungry ghosts for punishment."

Weeping and pleading, Zhou repeated what Ji had told him. The judge asked his officers if the story was true or not. Ji, who had been waiting on the side, cried out "It is true!" and presented his record book to the judge. When he had examined it, the judge smiled and said: "Because of this virtuous vow, it is proper to return him." Ji then spoke up again, saying, "This person was very sick. You should order a heavenly doctor to cure him." So the judge issued a command that Zhou be attended by a heavenly physician. The same two deputies escorted Zhou back home where he saw his body lying on the bed. The deputies pushed his soul back into its place and Zhou immediately regained consciousness.

Thinking that the heavenly doctor would be one of the Daoist immortals, Tao [Hongjing] (456–536 C.E.) and Xu [Mi] (303–373 C.E.), Zhou made a great effort to get up and with a cane started off for the Tao and Xu Temple across the river to pray. By the time he got to the middle of the bridge, he was doubled over and stumbling. A traveler from Shanxi stopped to help him. "I can see from your fatigue and the look on your face that you are troubled by a sick stomach. If it is not cured, you will surely die. I have some small skill and can cure you immediately. Why not follow me?"

They went together to a small house where they found a stove. The traveler started a fire to boil water for tea. From his side he pulled out a silver needle. He inserted it approximately an inch into the right side of Zhou's heart, and then twice lit some herbs on the end of it. Zhou cried out with pain. The traveler immediately stopped the burning, pulled out the needle, and applied a medicated bandage.

By this time the tea was ready. The traveler filled a small cup and asked Zhou to drink. Zhou declined, saying, "For many days I have not been able to consume even small amounts." The traveler replied, "This tea is not the same. Please try it." Zhou then drank two cups without any trouble. He felt his energy suddenly renewed. The traveler advised him, saying: "When you return home, it is best to drink rice soup at first, then eat only diluted rice gruel. After seven days you can eat and drink normally."

Zhou did as he had been told, and as a result he recovered in several days. He went to find the traveler in order to thank him, but there was no trace of him—even the house was gone. Only then did he realize that the stranger must have been the heavenly physician sent to cure him. Throughout his life Zhou faithfully recited the *Tract on Action and Response,* acquiring success, blessings, and long life. (Huang, Lingyan section, 10a)

F. Li Dezhang was a middle-aged man whose wife had died. He had only one child, a fourteen-year-old son named Shouguan. Dezhang acquired some merchandise, one thousand carrying poles, and proceeded to the provinces of Hunan and Guangdong in order to sell them. Liyong, a man-servant with the household, accompanied the merchandise to keep an eye on it, while Li himself and Shouguan looked for a fast boat in order to take a trip on the Wujiang River. Father and son leisurely went ashore to visit the great royal temple there. Inside there was a Daoist priest with a book, who inquired of them, saying: "This temple prints the *Tract on Action and Response.* Would you be so kind as to make a contribution?" Dezhang hesitated without answering. Just then the boatman arrived to say that the wind was favorable and he wanted to set sail. So Li Dezhang put down the book and they hurried away to the depart in the boat.

When they came to the middle of the river, they suddenly encountered a storm that overturned the boat. Father and son both fell into the water, but the two were not able to find each other. Dezhang was rescued by a fishing boat, which let him off where he could meet his own cargo ship. He thanked and generously rewarded the fishermen. Then the master and his servant, Liyong, returned to the temple where they prayed for an explanation. The response was: "The *Tract on Action and Response* is a sacred text to save the world. Earlier you were not willing to make a contribution to it. Hence, you have come to this end." Dezhang replied: "If the Most Exalted has the divine power to enable my son and me to meet again, I will put up the whole cost of the project, and you will not have to use a cent that has been contributed." He ordered Liyong to fetch two hundred ounces of silver from the bank and hand it over to the temple as an offering.

Master and servant supervised the loading of the cargo on the ship and traveled to the city of Wuchang. On route they met an old traveling merchant named Fu Youcai who had lost money and was having trouble making his return trip home. This man was an engaging talker who could flatter people with his charm. Dezhang developed a close friendship with him. While they were traveling, the merchandise was greatly delayed, so Dezhang left half of it in Wuchang and half with Youcai. Liyong left them to go to Jingxiang. Less than a month later he received a letter from his master telling him that the merchandise had already been sold for two thousand ounces of silver. Since Liyong was in Jingxiang taking care of things and unable to get away, he arranged for the receipts to be given to Youcai, who would go to Wuchang and collect the money. When Youcai had the silver in his hands, however, he immediately rolled up his conscience and fled with the money. When Dezhang learned that Youcai had taken the money, he was grieved and depressed, losing all interest in returning home. He drifted for two years before he made any plans to go back. But Heaven helps virtuous people, and Dezhang had already contributed to the *Tract on Action and Response*. When there is virtue, there will be recompense.

When his son Shouguan fell into the water, he grabbed hold of a large piece of wood and floated to a village. There a widow took care of him as if he were her own son. He studied and entered school. Unexpectedly one day at the bank of a stream he saw a young woman throw herself into the water. He immediately dove in to rescue her. When he asked her why she had done it, she answered: "My father's name is Fu Youcai. Years ago he left on business and arranged for me to stay with the family of my maternal uncle, who has no scruples at all. He wanted to sell me into a house of prostitution, so I tried to commit suicide." Suddenly there were lots of people all around. One of them was an old man who asked the young woman in surprise, "You, why are you here?" The woman looked at him and saw that it was her father. Father and daughter were reunited; you can imagine their happiness. Youcai was moved to gratitude by Shouguan's righteousness, so he gave his daughter to the young man as a wife and also arranged that the thousand ounces of swindled silver be entirely turned over to him as well.

Shouguan missed his father, and his heart pressed him to try to find him. So with his father-in-law he bought a boat and went to the Wujiang River to search for clues to his father's whereabouts. Not far from the royal temple, he saw the back of a boat with its sails set in readiness to depart. At the prow stood a man who looked just like his father. When they came up to each other, both father and son rejoiced in wild excitement, stopping only to question the other about what had happened since they had been parted. Shouguan told how he had taken a wife and obtained so much silver, recounting his story detail by detail. Dezhang asked to meet his new in-laws and entered the other ship's hold. He noticed that his son's father-in-law lay in bed with his face covered, not rising to get up. Dezhang lifted the cover and saw that it was Youcai. He laughed and said: "Once we were good friends. Now we are relatives by marriage and the thousand ounces of silver you have given to my son. What harm has there been? Let us be friends as we were before."

Together they went to the royal temple to fulfill Dezhang's vow. The carving of the blocks was completed, so they contributed another three hundred pieces of silver to print one thousand copies and have them distributed widely to exhort people to virtue. Families that were separated are brought back together again—is this not a reward for printing the *Tract on Action and Response?* (Huang, Lingyan section, 14a)

— 36 —

Record of Occultists

Alan J. Berkowitz

In the formulation of a religious tradition, great attention is paid to the narration of the lives of the protagonists of the religion, both mortal and divine, the patriarchs and other individuals credited with the articulation and transmission of the tradition. For it is the lives of these personages that are as keystones in the edifice of the religion and witness the interweaving of the divine and the mundane. In many ways the *Record of Occultists* (*Xuan pin lu;* lit. *Categorized Record of the Occult*) is one of Daoism's analogues to the various *Lives of Saints* in the Western tradition; and it is a good representative of the hagiographic genre, being inspirational but not homiletic, instructive but not arcane, entertaining but not frivolous.

China has a rich tradition of biographical compilation, both secular and religious. Huijiao's (497–554) *Lives of Eminent Monks* (*Gaoseng zhuan*), the preeminent Buddhist example, greatly influenced religious hagiography, but Daoist hagiography is not entirely derivative, drawing also from Han and later traditions of compiling records of extraordinary people and strange events. Daoist hagiographical compilations proliferated as the Daoist religion pervaded Chinese society in a general sense and as sectarian movements and schools established their own particular traditions. Some hagiographies recount the life of one or more of the saints associated with particular cults, while others are collective accounts of a more general or comprehensive nature. One hagiography, compiled in the 1120s and called simply *A History of Transcendents,* supposedly contained accounts of 50,000 persons.

The *Record of Occultists* is a compilation of hagiographical notices of 144 adepts celebrated in the Daoist tradition, from early times through the Song (the latest entry is for the early thirteenth century). It was compiled by Zhang Yu (ca. 1280–ca. 1350), whose preface to the work is dated October 1, 1335. The notices are grouped within a general chronological framework according to dynasty and are categorized under eleven designative headings: Daoist Virtue (*Dao de pin*); Daoists (*Dao pin*); Daoist Political Influence (*Dao quan pin*); Daoist Transformative Influence (*Dao hua pin*); Daoist Scholarship (*Dao ru pin*); Daoist Arts (*Dao shu pin*); Daoist Reclusion (*Dao yin pin*); Daoist Obscurity (*Dao mo pin*); Daoist Eloquence (*Dao yan pin*); Daoist Nature (*Dao zhi pin*); and Daoist Efflorescence (*Dao hua pin*). While all of the entries concern persons of the Daoist persuasion, those in the category of Daoists (*Dao pin*) generally were particularly notable for their religious achievements.

The accounts are derived primarily from earlier hagiographical works, as well as from the standard histories. The inspirational work would have been directed to a wide audience and read also by initiates and scholars. The notices primarily concern men whose names and exploits would have been common knowledge to the general literate populace, as well as to the educated elite and adherents to the Daoist religion; many would have been known through oral legend as well. The work is found in the Daoist canon (HY 780), although it also achieved independent transmission for a time; it has an entry in the imperial catalogue compiled between 1773 and 1782 under the patronage of the Qianlong emperor (which says that there were accounts of 135 adepts in ten categories), but it was not included into the imperial collection itself.

Zhang Yu (also known as Zhang Tianyu) became a Daoist priest in his twenties, going to live at Mount Mao in Juqu (modern Jurong, Jiangsu). He chose for himself the appellation Unofficial Historian of Juqu (*Juqu waishi*), regarding his work on chronicling his chosen place of residence as his greatest achievement; still, he was acclaimed during his own time and later for his poetry and, especially, for his calligraphy. In addition to the *Record of Occultists,* he also compiled a *Gazetteer of Maoshan* (*Maoshan zhi*); his many other writings in prose and poetry were collected after his death and published in an independently circulated collection.

Zhang Yu explains in his preface to the *Record of Occultists* that he was moved by the summary of the Daoist school written by the historian Sima Tan (180–ca. 110 B.C.E.) to record the lives of Daoist exemplars from past to present, as a demonstration of their discernible presence in the world. Chosen for inclusion in his *Record* were those adepts of the Way who, in his view, best exemplified the tradition of Laozi, the patriarch of Daoism. As he reasoned that the highest form of veneration for the pater familias of a tradition would be a record of his legacy, he did not include Laozi himself in his hagiographical compilation. As Laozi was "the one most consummate in the occult" (*xuan zu zhe*), Zhang titled his work *History of the Occult* (*Xuan shi*); it is not known when the title was changed to the *Categorized Record of the Occult.* The word translated as "occult" has the basic meaning of black or very deep purple, with the common extended meanings of "dark, profound, abstruse"; it generally refers to the arcane unfathomable Mystery. Due to a taboo on the character *xuan*, the near homophone with analogous meaning *yuan* often was used as replacement; thus the *Xuan pin lu* sometimes is referred to as the *Yuan pin lu.*

Zhang Yu envisioned his hagiographical compilation as a testimonial to followers of the Way of Laozi, and biographies in the *Record of Occultists* display the full compass of adepts in the Dao, the Way. Accordingly, not only mortals-cum-divinities, priests, visionaries, and adepts of particular Daoist religious traditions are included, but also men whose lives exemplify the general secular precepts of pre-imperial "Daoist" texts. Thus we find biographies of Zhang Ling, the founder of the Five Pecks of Rice sect and First Patriarch of the Tianshi (Supernal Preceptor or Celestial Master) sect and the Zhengyi tradition, and of the Three Lords Mao, deities associated with Mount Mao. Yet we also find biographies of such diverse personalities as Zhuangzi (Zhuang Zhou), Tao Qian (Tao Yuanming), Li Bai, and a large number of medieval practitioners of reclusion. As the compiler's predilection and religious affiliation favored the traditions associated with Mount Mao, it is not surprising that a number of entries concern the Shangqing (Highest Clarity) tradition centered around Mount Mao.

Hagiographies are by nature not purely historical recountings of lives; the portrayal of individuals generally is subservient to the purport of the religious biographer, and aspects of the lives of individuals, especially in collective hagiographies, are selected as exemplifications of the tradition to which they belong. But while hagiographical accounts are by no means comprehensive biographies, often the compiler includes information that is not found in other, more traditional, sources. Some entries in the *Record of Occultists* are brief and ostensibly factual, while others are relatively lengthy and spiced with anecdote. In the sampling of entries chosen for inclusion below are accounts of adepts of the occult in both the religious and secular traditions of the Dao; sixteen accounts in eight of Zhang Yu's categories have been included.

Translations from the *Xuan pin lu* are according to the text established by Yan Yiping, as found in his *Daojiao yanjiu ziliao, di yi ji* (Taibei: Yiwen yinshuguan, 1974), with reference to the text in the *Daozang* (HY 780).

Further Reading

On the formation of China's most influential religious hagiography, see Arthur F. Wright, "Biography and Hagiography: Huichiao's *Lives of Eminent Monks*," in *Silver Jubilee Volume of the Jimbun-Kagaku-Kenkyusho* (Kyoto, 1954), pp. 383–432; reprinted in his *Studies in Chinese Buddhism*, ed. Robert M. Somers (New Haven: Yale University Press, 1990). On Daoist hagiography, see Judith M. Boltz, *A Survey of Taoist Literature, Tenth to Seventeenth Centuries* (Berkeley: Institute of East Asian Studies, University of California, 1987), pp. 54–99. For the extended treatment of one Daoist saint in history and hagiography, see Anna Seidel, "A Taoist Immortal of the Ming Dynasty: Chang San-feng," in *Self and Society in Ming Thought*, ed. Wm. Theodore de Bary (New York: Columbia University Press, 1970), pp. 483–531.

ACCOUNTS OF DAOIST ADEPTS, FROM THE RECORD OF OCCULTISTS (XUAN PIN LU)

THE ZHOU DYNASTY (ca. 1027–256 B.C.E.)

Daoist Virtue (Dao de pin)

Yin Xi was a grandee of Zhou. Adept at alchemical disciplines, he often ingested pure quintessence; concealing his innate virtue and refining his outward conduct, none of his time recognized his true nature. When Laozi traveled west, Xi noticed the aura [that preceded him] and knew that a perfected man was about to pass by. Recognizing one with the appropriate attributes, Xi blocked his passage and as a result came upon Laozi. Laozi for his part also recognized Xi as being uncommon and wrote for him *The Way and Its Power* (i.e., *Dao de jing*) in two fascicles, which he bestowed on him. Later Yin Xi went together with Laozi to the Land of the Flowing Sands (the great western desert), where he ingested the fruit of the Great Overcomer (either sesame or, perhaps, cannabis), and none know what became of him.

Xi also wrote a book in nine fascicles, which he called *Master Yin of the Pass*. Liu Xiang (77–6 B.C.E.) opined that the book was heterogeneous in nature, towering and tortuous, broad and boundless, highly expansive; yet as it contained patterns and norms [for conduct], it brought people to be dispassionate and calm and did not bring them to be wild. The *Zhuangzi* also quotes the following from the book: "He cleaves not to subjectivity, so form and materiality are manifest of themselves. In action he is as water, when still he is as a mirror; he is as an echo in his response [to externals]. He is indifferent as if oblivious, quiescent as if placid. Ones in concert with him find harmony; ones who would gain from him lose. He never places himself in precedence of others, but always follows them." What is described is the unbounded great Perfected Man of the past. Yin Xi originally had the epithet Master Wenshi.

Yin Gui's byname was Gongdu; a man of Taiyuan [in Shanxi], he was Wenshi's [i.e., Yin Xi's] nephew. He was broadly learned in the Five Classics, and especially astute in astrological charts and apocrypha; he ultimately passed down various Daoist scriptures in over a hundred fascicles. He often ingested cakes of deer bamboo. At first, when Wenshi met Laozi at the Hangu Pass (a strategic pass in Henan) during the time of the Zhou kings Kang and Zhao (ca. eleventh century B.C.E.), he (Yin Gui) constructed a rustic storied edifice at Mount Zhongnan (southwest of modern Xi'an, Shaanxi) in which to reside. When King Mu (ca. early tenth century B.C.E.) renovated his rustic edifice, reconstructing it into a storied academy in order to host men possessing the Way, Gongdu subsequently cultivated [his person] and refined [his arts] in this place along with the practitioner of reclusion Du Chong. Attaining the Way, he (Yin Gui) was deified as Perfected One of the Great Harmony (*Taihe zhenren*).

Du Chong of the capital city Hao (southwest of modern Xi'an) had the byname Xuanyi (Mysterious and Disengaged). When he heard that Wenshi (Yin Xi) had ascended to the realm of the Perfected during the year *dingsi* of King Zhao (ca. 964 B.C.E.), he studied the Way, abiding in the occult in a numinous lodging. At this time there were five recondite disengaged persons who arrived from afar, all of whom were receded in silence to vacuity and the ultramundane, whose arcane techniques and cultivated manners were lofty and pristine, who were engrossed to abstraction in their Daoist arts, who together promulgated the principle of "nonaggrandizement of oneself." King Mu had an academy constructed and a memorial temple set up for them, and he installed Chong as Daoist mentor there. When he was over 120 years old, he attained the Way and ascended; he was given the epithet Perfected One of the Great Ultimate (*Taiji zhenren*).

THE QIN DYNASTY (221–207 B.C.E.)

Daoists (Dao pin)

Guo Sizhao (third century B.C.E.) was a man from the state of Yan (central Hebei). Sizhao was the eldest of four brothers, all of whom attained the Way. He resided at Leiping Mountain in Huayang [i.e., at Mount Mao in Jiangsu], planting trees of the five fruits. This land was suitable also for planting the small sour apple, of which it is said, "the small sour apple of the Land of Fortune is good for ridding calamity and pestilence." In front of his residence Sizhao constructed a banked pool. Often he alighted a small skiff to sport about in, and each time he would strike the gunnels and sing [the following four poems]:

> The clear pool is skirted by numinous peaks,
> The deep forest dense with green vegetation.
> A dark crane soars over the remote outlands:
> We exchange words and I go out free and easy.
> Drumming the gunnels I ride a divine swell;
> Kowtowing, I wish for a morning breeze.
> Not yet free of my worldly form,
> I'll amble freely in the hills and forests.

> I loose my spirit beyond the Highest Heaven;
> Practiced in the Way, I keep perfection intact.
> I then fold these magic phoenix wings
> And tuck away my floriate dragon scales.
> My bit of a heart soars aloft,
> But below all is windblown, all dirt and dust.
> I look with pity on the short-lived mole cricket:
> Who'll finish you beneath a cart's wheel?

Roaming the void I descend a flying whirlwind,
And magically pace the formless realm.
As round moonlight glows in dawn's blush,
The Nine-headed Phoenix chants at the morning sun.
Waving its pinions, it screens the Heavenly Ford;
Overspreading the mists, it soars in variegated clouds.
I then come to the eaves of the Grand Tenuity stars,
And decant this Golden Pear Potion.
Ambling about beyond the Mystic Frontier,
Neither am I incarnate, nor am I deceased.

Harnessing a gust, I dance in divine nebulae;
Splitting roseate mists, I gird the Nine Suns.
The August One on High keeps pace in his dragon-drawn conveyance,
And now I reach the Northern Floriate Chamber.
The Divine Tiger penetrates the Carnelian Forest;
Wind and clouds blend into one.
I open apart the gates to the Profound Extramundane;
Magically transformed, I mystically extinguish my traces.

After obtaining the Way, Sizhao ascended to fill Zuo the Transcendent Lord's (Zuo Ci) position at the Ninth [Celestial] Palace and concurrently served as Attendant in Charge of Outings at the [Celestial] Jade Pavilion. During the Xuanhe reign of the Song (on September 12, 1124), an imperial edict proclaimed, "The Three Primordial Forces are obscurely numinous and thus cannot be fathomed by names or words. The myriad gods are consolidated in their transformations, and it is unavailing to seek to determine them through discussion. All are ranked in order in the Highest Perfection and are truly extensively arrayed in the Paramount Way. Guo the Perfected One, Gentleman-in-Attendance at the [Celestial] Jade Pavilion, in merit is commensurate to the Ten Supremacies, and in position is ranged in the Ninth [Celestial] Palace. Clenching numinous jade pendants he already is sallying in flight in the Ne-Plus-Ultra. Bracing the Floriate Matinal Baldachin, he acts as General Attendant for the Sovereign of Vacuity. As he now is in great eminence in the Primal Administration, it is fitting that he greatly prosper under an illustrious appellation. Hitherto he has attained to his rank and will forever further the Glorious [Celestial] Design. It is permitted to grant him the special [posthumous] title of Perfected One of the [Celestial] Grand Tenuity Who Hides His Brilliance (Taiwei baoguang zhenren)."

THE WESTERN HAN DYNASTY (206 B.C.E.–25 C.E.)

Daoist Political Influence (Dao quan pin)

Zhang Liang (d. 187 B.C.E.) was styled Zifang; his ancestors were men of the state of Han (in southern Shanxi). When [the state of] Qin destroyed Han,

Liang sought to use his patrimony to engage a retainer to assassinate the King of Qin (later to be known as the First August Emperor of China) to avenge Han, on the grounds that his (Liang's) family had served as Grand Councilor in Han for five reigns. Liang once studied ritual in Huaiyang (in eastern Henan); going east he met with the Lord of Canghai, from whom he gained the employ of a mighty bravo who fashioned an iron mallet weighing 120 catties. When the King of Qin traveled east and arrived at Boliangsha (near modern Kaifeng, Henan), Liang and his retainer attacked in ambush the King of Qin but mistakenly struck an attendant's vehicle. The King of Qin became enraged and sought out the offenders with great urgency. Liang then changed his name and escaped in hiding to Xiapi (southeast of Xuzhou, Jiangsu).

Liang once was ambling complacently on a bridge at Xiapi. There an elderly man dressed in homespun came to where Liang was standing and deliberately dropped his slipper over the bridge. Turning to Liang he said, "Budding lad, go down and fetch my slipper." Liang was astounded and wished to strike him, but he stifled his anger and went down to fetch the slipper, following which he presented it on his knees. The elderly one accepted it with his foot and said, "The budding lad can be instructed. Five days hence at the peak of dawn you shall meet with me here." Liang was perplexed on account of this but knelt, saying, "I consent." Liang went at the peak of dawn on the fifth day, but the elderly one was there first and said in anger, "Why is it that you've arrived after I?" Five days later Liang went at cockcrow; but the elderly one again was there first, and once again said in anger, "Why is it that you've arrived after I?" Five days later Liang went at midnight. After a short time the elderly one also came and, being pleased, said, "It ought to be like this." He took out a book in one fascicle, saying, "Read this and you will be a teacher to kings. Ten years hence you will prosper. In the thirteenth year you, budding lad, will see me north of the Ji River: the yellow stone at the foot of Gucheng Mountain (southwest of Jinan, Shandong) will be none other than me." Thereupon he left and was not to be seen. In the dawn light Liang looked at the elderly man's book: it was *The Patriarch's [Lü Shang's] Military Arts*. Liang consequently found the book extraordinary and studied it assiduously.

Living at Pixia, Liang acted as a trustworthy knight. He used [the book's strategies] in his persuasions to the Lord of Pei, Liu Bang (247–195 B.C.E.), who was pleased and constantly made use of his strategies, eventually winning the whole empire. Liang later followed Emperor Gao (Liu Bang) when he made his capital in Guanzhong (Within the Pass; referring here to Chang'an). As he was by constitution often ailing, Liang practiced yogic stretching and did not eat grain; closing his gate, he did not go out for more than a year. When the emperor wished to set aside the heir designate and set up in his place Ruyi the King of Zhao, his son by the Lady Ji, Empress Lü consulted with Liang. Liang accordingly occasioned the appearance of the [reclusive] Four Elderly Gentlemen of the Shangluo Mountains (to the southeast of the capital), who accompanied the heir designate as wine-attendants [at a banquet for his father the emperor]. When the banquet was finished, that the emperor in the end did not replace the heir designate was due to the influence of Liang's strategy of summoning the Four Gentlemen.

Liang subsequently declared, "My family served the Han state for generations. When Han came to be destroyed, I did not begrudge the sum of ten thousand in gold to avenge Han. Now with my three-inch tongue I am teacher to an emperor, have entitlement of ten thousand households, and am ranked among the lords. This is the utmost for the common-clothed, and for me, Liang, it is sufficient. I wish to rid myself of mundane affairs and go roaming in the company of [the Transcendent] Master Red Pine." He then took to studying the Way, wishing to float up [into transcendency]. When he demised he was given the posthumous appellation Lord of Cultured Accomplishment (Wencheng hou).

Initially Liang had met the elderly man of Pixia, and thirteen years later, when he accompanied Emperor Gao north across the Ji, he indeed did find the yellow stone at the base of Gucheng Mountain, which he took and worshipped as a treasure. When Liang died, the yellow stone was buried together with him. Each time one ascends his tumulus for the summer and winter sacrificial offerings, the yellow stone also is worshiped. The Temple of Celestial Bequeathal in Chenliu Prefecture is the locus for his (Liang's) worship; during the Zhenghe reign of the Song (1111–1118) he was granted the [posthumous] title Perfected One Who Ascends into Vacuity (Lingxu zhenren).

Daoist Arts (Dao shu pin)

Yan Zun (first century B.C.E.), styled Junping (Lordly and Imperturbable), was a man of Shu (Sichuan). Of refined nature, he was tranquil and unperturbed. His scholarly endeavors were particularly sublime; he was specialized and expert in the *Great [Classic of] Changes* and gave himself freely to [the writings] of Laozi and Zhuangzi. He regularly divined with stalks in the Chengdu market, maintaining that "One who divines has a lowly profession, yet is able thereby to benefit the multitudes. When there is a query about something perverse and unjust, then I address its advantages and harm according to divination with milfoil and tortoise. What I say to sons concerns filiality, to brothers I speak of deference, and to servitors loyalty. Each according to his particular circumstances, I direct them in the way of goodness, and already more than half have followed my words." He but in a day assessed for several persons, and when he had obtained a hundred cash, being sufficient for his self-maintenance, then he would close his stall, hang his curtain, and give instruction on the *Laozi*. He read widely, there being nothing he did not know thoroughly. Drawing on the ideas of Laozi and Zhuang Zhou (Zhuangzi), he wrote books totaling more than one hundred thousand words. Yang Xiong (53 B.C.E.–18 C.E.) when young went to study with him, and most of what he acquired concerned Junping's Daoist [teachings].

In Shu there was a certain wealthy man named Luo Chong. He asked Jun-

ping, "For what reason does m'lord not serve in office?" Junping replied, "I've
not the means to start off." When Chong collected for Junping a cart and horse,
clothing and food, Junping replied, "I'm simply ailing; it's not that I am lacking.
I have a surfeit and you, sir, not enough. How could it be that your insufficiency
could contribute to my surplus?" Chong said, "I've got ten thousand in gold
and you are lacking even a picul-weight. Now you say you've got a surfeit—is
that not erroneous?" Junping replied, "Not so. I stayed previously in your
home. When people should have turned in, still you hustled and bustled without rest. Morning and night you are all ahurry, never ever having enough. Now
I divine for a profession; I don't even get out of bed, yet money arrives by itself.
I still have several hundreds, with dust on it an inch thick, and do not know
what to do with it. Is this not my having a surfeit and you not enough?" Chong
was greatly mortified. Junping said with a sigh, "What increases my goods
harms my spirit; what makes my reputation destroys my self." In the end he
did not serve.

Over ninety years old, he died still in his profession. The people of Shu
respected and loved him, and to the present they still praise him. There is a
shrine to him at Mianju Prefecture in Hanzhou (northeast of Chengdu, Sichuan). During the Shaoxing reign of the Song (1131–1162), Junping was
granted the [posthumous] title Sublime and Penetrating Perfected One (Miao-
tong zhenren).

(Original commentary: He originally was surnamed Zhuang; during the time
of the Han emperors Zhang and He [75–144] when Ban Gu [32–92] was compiling the *History of the Han,* as a taboo on the personal name of Emperor Ming
[Liu Zhuang; r. 57–75], he [Ban Gu] changed it to Yan. The characters Zhuang
and Yan have likewise been interchangeable throughout the ages, therefore
Lao-Zhuang [i.e., the school of Laozi and Zhuangzi] also is called Lao-Yan.
Gushenzi [of the Tang] said, "Junping was born during the middle period of
the Western Han; when Wang Mang usurped the throne [January 10, 9 C.E.],
he [Junping] forthwith hid in seclusion, fearing to join [Wang Mang]. He
assumedly was a Perfected One of a former age.")

Daoists (Dao pin)

The Three Lords Mao. The Elder Lord was named Ying, styled Shushen, the
Second Lord was named Gu, styled Jiwei, and the Younger Lord named Zhong,
styled Sihe; they were from Nanguan in Xianyang (to the south of Chang'an).
The Elder Lord was born in the year *bingshen,* the fifth year of the Zhongyuan
reign of the Han emperor Jing (145 B.C.E.); his two brothers were born in the
years *wuxu* (143 B.C.E.) and *gengzi* (141 B.C.E.). When the Elder Lord was
eighteen, he abandoned his family and took leave of his relations, entering into
the Heng Mountains (the northern sacred peak, in northeastern Shanxi), where
he read the The *Classic on the Way and Its Power* (Dao de jing) and the *[Great]*
Treatise of the Zhou [Classic of] Changes (Zhou Yi zhuan), seeking the Way
through refined contemplation. Later he went to Xicheng (south of Chang'an

at modern Ankang Prefecture, Shaanxi), where he was graced by a visitation by Lord Wang, Chief of the Perfected, who entrusted him with overseeing [religious] vestments, books, charts, and registers. Subsequently he attained the Way and became a disciple of the Chief of the Perfected. Mao Ying returned home; at the time he was forty-nine. He could rise the dead and return life; his father and mother in their hearts thought him peculiar. He served his parents through the end of the mourning period [following their deaths], altogether remaining at home fifty-three years.

The Second Lord was nominated as Filial and Incorrupt (a category in the imperial recommendatory system) during the reign of Emperor Jing (sic; r. 157–141 B.C.E.) and in the inaugural year of the Yuanshuo reign (128 B.C.E.) was selected [in the category] Worthy and Excellent, taking office as Court Attendant for Miscellaneous Uses. In the second year of the Zhenghe reign (91 B.C.E.) he was transferred to Grand Mentor of the Heir Designate, and during the inaugural year of the Yuanfeng reign (80 B.C.E.) he was appointed as Governor of Wuwei (in Gansu), Commandant in Charge of Obliterating the Barbarians.

The Younger Lord when young gained renown through his principled conduct, living in reclusion in the Huayin Mountains (near Hua Shan, east of Chang'an in Shaanxi). During the third year of the Jianyuan reign of Emperor Wu (sic; 138 B.C.E.) he was nominated [in the category of] Straightforward and Upright but did not go. Moving to the state of Liang (at Shangqiu, in eastern Henan), he was retained as King Xiao's Superior Guest. During the second year of the Dijie reign of Emperor Yuan (68 B.C.E.) he was promoted to Prefect of Luoyang and transferred to [the post of] Commandant of Xicheng, Governor of Shangjun (northern Shaanxi). When Emperor Yuan ascended the throne (early in 48 B.C.E.), he was appointed as Fivefold Experienced Grandee and transferred to Governor of Xihe (on the northeastern border of Shaanxi, adjacent to Inner Mongolia).

At this time, the Second Lord had been appointed Chamberlain for the Imperial Insignia, and the brothers were to go together [to the capital] to take up office. Several hundred men of their district turned out to send them off [with a ceremony invoking luck on their journey]. The Elder Lord addressed the guests, "I may not be serving as high-salaried Minister or Grand Council to the state, yet I in turn am to have a posting among the divine gods. I have been selected by the Celestial Thearch (tiandi) to fill the position of Supreme Minister of the Eastern Sacred Peak, Lord Director of Destiny of the Huolin Mountains (in southeastern Fujian), to control initiates in the study of the Way, and to oversee the registers of the living and the dead in Wu and Yue [i.e., the southeast]. This is an important rank in the divine offices of the Ancestral Masters of the Superior Perfected Ones. On the third day of the fourth month of the coming year I am to ascend aloft; will you or will you not, m'lords, be able to come to pay respects as you are today? If it happens that you are reduced in number, a reduction in expenses nevertheless is not permitted, for it is necessary for you to have the wherewithal to provide offerings and accommodate me."

At the appointed time, welcoming [divine] officers did in fact descend, and Lord Mao left parting instructions to his ancestral clan. He addressed the sons and young men of the district, saying, "At this moment I take my leave and temporarily will stop in the mountains of Juqu [i.e., Mount Mao], east of the Yangzi River. Although [my brothers] Jiwei and Sihe shall perceive matters late, they are certain to be capable of personal regrets; they will forsake office and abandon their emolument in order to come and seek me out." When his words were finished, he took his leave of the people of the temporal world and departed. This most likely was in the year *dingchou,* the fifth year of the Chuyuan reign of Emperor Yuan (44 B.C.E.), when Lord Mao was 102 years old.

The two younger brothers were in their postings, but when they heard that their elder brother had become a divine Transcendent in broad day, they each abandoned their office and returned home. On the sixth day of the third month of year *renwu,* the fifth year of the Yongguang reign (39 B.C.E.), they crossed the [Yangzi] River south, seeking their brother in the Eastern Mountains. When they saw him, they shed tears in sadness and joy. The Elder Lord addressed his brothers, saying, "How late has come your illumination." Thereupon he bestowed on them divine powder and extramundane formulas to carry them across [to the other world], and they both became Perfected Ones, having jurisdiction over the caverns at Juqu Mountain [i.e., Mount Mao], the Heavens of the Golden Altar, and Huayang. He then styled the Second Lord as Divine Lord Who Adjudges the Registers (Dinglu shenjun), and the Younger Lord as Transcendent Lord Who Ensures Fate (Baoming xianjun); these both are heavenly ranks.

Coming to the year *gengshen,* the second year of the Yuanshou reign of Emperor Ai (1 B.C.E.), the Elder Lord was 145 years old. On the eighteenth day of the eighth month of this year he received the text of the Jade Slate of the Nine Bestowals [for achieved merit] and was transferred to assume duties over the Department of the Jade Grotto of the Vermilion Citadel, in the post of Perfected One of the Vermilion Inception, Supreme Minister of the Eastern Sacred Peak, Supreme Perfected One Who Directs Destiny (Siming shangzhen Dongyue shangqing Chiyuan zhenren). He announced to his brothers, "I now am leaving for intendant functionary responsibilities and will not be able to have frequent contact with you; I must serve for one year, after which I will once again come to this mountain. The eighteenth day of the third month and the second day of the twelfth month are arranged for my mentor Lord Chief of the Perfected (Zongzhenjun) and the Vermilion Perfected One of the Southern Sacred Peak and the Grand Vacuity (Nanyue Taixu Chizhenren) to journey here to appear at the locale of my two brothers, for the purpose of registering you and making your acquaintance. Those who are devoted to the Way will wait for me on this day and I shall personally make accommodations for them, for they can give instruction to the unenlightened."

With this, the two [younger] Lords remained behind, having jurisdiction over the interior of the caverns at Mount Mao, at the entrances of which they erected a temple and other structures. They brought the Way to the myriad things [of the phenomenal world], spread nurture to the world of nature, accorded benignity to the birds and beasts, and all things assumed their endowed character. There were divine attestations of good and bad fortune; crime and evil were certain to be discerned. As the immanent principle effused, the exoteric teaching became widely diffuse.

Then it was that wind and rain were timely, the five grains fully ripened; illness and pestilence did not arise, violence and harmfulness were not practiced, within the realm there were no disasters or calamities, and the cities were without criminals or troops. Patriarchs and elders sung and intoned,

> Mount Mao connects to Jinling,
> The rivers and lakes belong to the coastal flows.
> The three divinities are borne on white swans;
> Each rules a single mountain.
> They summon rains to water dry paddies,
> And land and field also soften again.
> Wives and children all are safe in their rooms,
> And we have no worry even till a hundred.
> White swans have soared in the azure heavens;
> When again will they come a'roaming?

When the Three Lords departed, they each once rode a white swan and alighted on three locations in the mountains. There were people who witnessed this, therefore it has come out in song. Further, in accordance with the locations where the swans alighted, they differentiated the mountains of Juqu into three mountains called Elder Lord Mao, Second Lord Mao, and Younger Lord Mao. But to speak in general terms, they actually are a single mountain in Juqu [i.e., Mao Shan], for which there are no variant names.

THE EASTERN HAN DYNASTY (25–220 C.E.)

Daoists (Dao pin)

Zhang Ling (34–156; original commentary: Daoist books give him the honorary name Zhang Daoling), styled Fu (Supporter), was a man of the Han dynasty who hailed from Feng Prefecture in the state of Pei (in the northwestern tip of Jiangsu) but was born on Tianmu Mountain in Yuhang (Zhejiang). Originally a student at the Imperial Academy who extensively studied the Five [Confucian] Classics, later in life he sighed, "This is of no benefit to one's longevity." He then took up studying the *Yellow Thearch's Cinnabar [Alchemical] Classic of the Nine Tripods* (*Huangdi jiu ding dan jing*) and performed alchemical transmutations on Fanyang Mountain (just northeast of Chengdu, Sichuan). Subsequently he discovered an occult book in a stone chamber on Mount Song (the Central Sacred Peak, Henan).

At this time the Middle Kingdom was disrupted in chaos, and the Han was coming to its downfall. Realizing that the Civil Way had fallen into desuetude and was no longer sufficient in alleviating danger and coming to the assistance of the world, he retired into seclusion in Yuhang for ten years. He then entered Shu (Sichuan) along with his disciples, where the common people came in unison to serve him as their teacher. He made it his practice to transform people through honesty and modesty, kindheartedness and compassion, and did not favor the use of punishments and penalties. He directed the ill and ailing to give a self-confession of the sins and transgressions they had committed throughout their entire lives and to give a sacred declaration before the gods, entering into a covenant binding their bodily death. Thus all reformed evil and followed goodness. He opened up salty springs [for refining salt] to benefit the common folk and drove away the great snakes.

He combatted demons, and twenty-four of them in defeat assumed the twenty-four [preternatural] administrative offices; he rid the people of Shu of bane. In sum, he was fully proficient in the art of controlling the destiny of the many spirits of the peaks and mountains, while his meritorious virtue was equally manifest. He was given the appellation Supernal Preceptor (or Celestial Master, Tianshi). His disciples Wang Zhang and Zhao Sheng had particular attainments in his Way.

Daoist Reclusion (Dao yin pin)

Liang Hong (pre-24–post-80 C.E.), styled Boluan (Elder Simurgh), was a man from Pingling in Fufeng (to the west of Chang'an). As his family was poor, he herded swine within the Shanglin Imperial Hunting Preserve. He once mistakenly left a fire unattended and it spread to another's hut. Hong repaid him fully in swine. When the proprietor still considered it insufficient, Hong was willing to work it off personally in residence.

Later he returned to his district, where the influential families admired his lofty integrity and many wished to marry him to their daughters. Hong refused them all and did not marry. The Meng family of the same commandery had a daughter who physically was fat and ugly and with dark skin, who was powerful enough to lift a stone mortar. Mates had been selected, but she would not marry, and her years had reached thirty. When her parents asked her reason, the daughter said, "I wish to get a worthy such as Liang Boluan." Hong heard of this and asked to marry her. The woman endeavored to make homespun clothing and hemp sandals [for her trousseau], and for weaving made a chest and utensils for spinning and reeling.

At the nuptials, she entered his gates adorned for the first time with cosmetics. For seven days Hong gave no response. His wife then knelt next to the bed and implored him, saying, "This humble one has heard that you, master, have lofty principles, and straightaway dismissed several [prospective] brides. Your wife also has rebuffed numerous men. Now that I have been selected, could I dare not ask what I have done wrong?" Hong said, "I sought someone who dressed in a greatcoat of fur and coarse attire, one together with whom I could seclude myself in the deep mountains. But now your clothes are of fine silk damask and you have applied cosmetic powder and kohl. How could this be what I wished for?" His wife said, "It was simply to observe my master's will. Your wife certainly has attire for dwelling in seclusion." She then changed her coiffure to a coiled bun, donned homespun clothing, and presented herself ready for manual labor. Hong was greatly pleased and said, "This verily is the wife of Liang Hong, capable of attending to me." He gave her the style Deyao (Virtuous Brilliance).

Together they entered into the Baling mountains [to the east of Chang'an] and made their living plowing and weaving. He recited the *Odes* and *Documents* and strummed the zither for his own amusement. He looked up to and admired the Lofty Gentlemen of former ages and composed eulogies for twenty-four of these men dating since the Four Hoaryheads [who once appeared at the court at the behest of Zhang Liang].

Because they passed through the capital going east out of the pass, he composed the "Song with Five Ai!s," which went:

> I climb Beimang Hill,
> Ai!
> And gaze back on the capital,
> Ai!
> The palace lodges loom loftily,
> Ai!
> The weary toil of the people,
> Ai!
> On and on, forever lasting,
> Ai!

The Xianzong emperor (r. 57–75) heard of it and censured him; he searched for Hong but did not catch him. Hong then changed his cognomen to Yunqi, his name to Yao, and his style to Houguang (Fine Brightness) and resided with his wife and children in the vicinity of Qi and Lu (modern Shandong).

He then left again, heading for Wu [in Jiangsu]. There he affiliated himself with the great householder Gao Botong, dwelling on the veranda and hiring out as a grain-huller. Each time he returned home and his wife presented his meal, she did not venture to lift her gaze in the presence of Hong, raising the food tray level with her eyebrows [while kneeling in respect]. Botong espied this and, finding it peculiar, said, "If that hireling can cause his wife to respect him like that, then he is no ordinary man." So, straightaway he lodged him in his home. When Hong became ill and in distress, he notified his host, "Take care not to allow my children to hold to funerary practices and return me home." When Hong came to his end, Botong and others chose a burial spot for him alongside the tomb of [the local hero] Yaoli of Wu. All said, "Yaoli was a man of distinction, while Boluan was pure and lofty. It should be that they be near one another." Hong's friend was Gao Hui.

Daoists (Dao pin)

Wei Boyang (second century C.E.) was a man of Wu (Jiangsu). Originally the scion of an esteemed family, as he by nature was fond of Daoist arts, he was not willing to serve in official capacity. He lived complacently, nurturing his spirit. No one of his time understood his doings, simply saying that he took care of people and nurtured his person. He entered the mountains and prepared divine cinnabar. When it was concocted he ingested it; he died but returned to life. As he departed into transcendency along with his disciple surnamed Yu, he met a woodcutter and sent along in a handwritten letter his departing words to the people of his district and to his two [other] disciples.

Boyang produced the [*Arcane Essentials of the*] *Correlative Categories of the Five Phases in the "Consonance of the Three"* (*Cantongqi wuxing xianglei* [*biyao*]) in three rolls altogether, where his doctrine is derivative of the *Zhou* [*Classic of*] *Changes* (*Zhou Yi*). In fact, he appropriated the Lines and Images [of the *Classic of Changes*] in discussion of the principles of alchemy par excellence; yet people of the profane world are not learned in alchemical affairs and often explain his book in terms of yin and yang, which greatly misses its purport. I [the compiler of this writing] comment: As for the book *Consonance of the Three,* the great Confucians Zhu Yuanhui (Zhu Xi, 1130–1200) and Cai Yuanding (1135–1198) both deeply grasped its significance and often addressed it in their discussions and treatises. If one does not understand with penetration the profound purport of the *Changes* and the *Laozi*, then one will not be able to apprehend it.

THE JIN DYNASTY (266–420)

Daoist Scholarship (Dao ru)

Huangfu Mi (215–282), styled Shi'an (Gentlemanly and Peaceful) and having the name Jing (Tranquil) as a child, was a man of Anding (northwest of Chang'an, in eastern Gansu). He was the great-grandson of Defender-in-chief Huangfu Song of the Han. At age twenty he was not fond of study, but later he went to receive instruction from Xi Tan, a man of his district. As he lived in poverty, he carried the *Classics* with him when he went farming. He subsequently comprehensively mastered the words of the classical writings and the hundred schools. He was steeped in quietude with few desires and early on held lofty and elevated aspirations; he considered composition and exegesis as his vocation. He gave himself the appellation Master Mystical and Serene

(Xuanyan xiansheng) and composed discourses on "Ritual and Music" and "Sagehood and Perfection." Later, he was afflicted with the malady arthritis, but his hands would not abandon the [written] rolls.

When someone urged him to cultivate a reputation and expand his relations, Mi composed a "Discourse on Abiding in the Mystery" ("Shouxuan lun") in response to him, in which he wrote, "Poverty is the constant state of the scholar; humbleness is the true nature of the Way." He subsequently did not serve in office. He abandoned himself with pleasure in the writings of antiquity, forgetting his malady and forgetting to take sustenance; people of his time referred to him as "abandoned to books." Someone admonished him for being excessively diligent, and that his energy and spirit would soon be depleted. Mi said, "If in the morning one hears of the Way, in the evening it is alright to die. How much the more as the allotment and determination of the longevity or brevity of one's life is hung from Heaven!"

He was nominated [in the imperial recommendatory system category] Filial and Incorrupt and was summoned to appointment by the Counsellor-in-chief, and further was nominated [in the category] Worthy and Excellent, Straightforward and Upright, but he did not once accede. When he personally memorialized to borrow books from Emperor Wu (r. 266–290), the emperor sent to him a cart full of books [as a gift]. Although emaciated and afflicted, he opened and examined them without fatigue. He was repeatedly summoned [to court], but to the end he did not serve. He demised in the second (sic) year of the Taikang reign (281; official sources give the year of his death as 282). The books he wrote, *Annals of the Generations of Emperors and Kings* (*Diwang shiji*) and the accounts of *Lofty Gentlemen* (*Gaoshi*), *Disengaged Gentlemen* (*Yishi*), and *Illustrious Women* (*Lienü*), all were acclaimed in his age.

THE HISTORY OF THE SOUTH (here: 420–589)

Daoists (Dao pin)

Tao Hongjing (452–536), styled Tongming, was a man of Moling (just outside the capital Jinling, modern Nanjing, Jiangsu). At age ten, when he obtained Ge Hong's (ca. 283–ca. 343) *Lives of Divine Transcendents* (*Shenxian zhuan*) and read it, he said to someone, "When I look up at the azure-hued clouds and gaze at the white sun, I don't feel that they are distant." His expression and bearing were radiant and refined, with bright eyes and wide brow, slender body, long forehead, and high ears. On his right knee there were several tens of black spots forming a design of seven star-clusters. He read more than ten thousand rolls of books, and if there was a single thing about which he was not knowledgeable, he considered it a deep shame. He was skilled at the zither and chess, and practiced in cursive and official script.

He had not yet been capped (at age twenty) when [the future] Emperor Gao of the Qi (Xiao Daocheng, 427–482), then acting as Grand Councilor, brought him in as Reader-in-waiting; he was selected as Master Audience Attendant, and often he was relied on for age-old matters [of etiquette]. As his family was poor, he sought appointment as his district's Magistrate, but he did not get his wish. In the tenth year of the Yongming reign (492) he shed his court attire, hanging it on the Shenwu Gate, and submitted a memorial resigning from his emolument; it was decreed that he be so allowed. He was bestowed bundled silks, and it was ordered that the jurisdiction where he resided monthly provide him fifty catties of China root and two *sheng* (at that time about six liters) of white honey to accommodate his macrobiotic ingestions. When he was to set off, dukes and ministers sent him off [with a ceremony invoking luck on his journey] at the Zhenglü Pavilion; it was said by all that "Through the Song and the Qi dynasties, never has there been anything like this."

Thereupon he went to stay at Juqu Mountain in Jurong (i.e., Mount Mao, about a day's ride from the capital), where he established a center for learning in the mountains. He gave himself the appellation Huayang's Dweller-in-Retirement (Huayang yinju), and he used *Yinju* instead of his name on correspondence in the mortal world. Earlier, he had received instruction on [Daoist] talismans, charts, and scriptures from [the Daoist master] Sun Youyue of Dongyang and had traveled extensively throughout the various famous mountains south of the [Yangzi] River, searching after the various traces of perfection of Yang (Yang Xi, 330–386) and the Xus (Xu Mi, 303–373, and his son Hui, 341– ca. 370). Once he told his disciples, "I have seen the vermilion gates and vast edifices [of the imperial palace], yet even though I know of their resplendence and pleasures, I have no wish in my heart to go. Yet after gazing at the high cliffs and viewing the great lowlands, knowing these it is hard to stay put, and straightaway I constantly wish to go to them. Moreover, during the Yongming reign I sought after emolument and promptly knew I was mistaken; if not so, then how could I be doing what I'm doing now?"

As a person, the Master was flexible and accommodating, modest and respectful; he understood intuitively when to issue forth [into the public world] and when to stay put. His mind was like a shiny mirror, and he comprehended things as soon as he encountered them. His words were never tedious or confused, and what he did say was invariably illuminating.

At the beginning of the Yongyuan reign (499), he further constructed a three-tiered pavilion, his disciples and guests living below him, and forthwith severed relations with the mundane. He especially loved the wind in the pines and listened to its reverberations with pleasure. At times he would tramp alone the stream-laden ridges, and those who saw him from afar thought he was a transcendent-immortal. By nature he was fond of composition and exegesis, and esteemed the peculiar and exceptional. He was particularly proficient in *yinyang* and the Five Phases; in augury according to the winds; in astrological reckoning; in the topology of mountains and waters; in the production of things of all types; in medical arts and pharmacology; in the consecution of rulers and the succession of the years. He once fashioned an armillary sphere some three feet tall in which the Earth was at the center and the heavens rotated while the Earth stood still; it was operated by a mechanism and completely corresponded with the heavens. He said that it was something necessary for cultivation in the Daoist way.

He deeply respected how Zhang Liang had conducted himself, saying that he was peerless among the worthies of the past. At the end of the Qi (ca. early 502), he prophesied: "Water, sword-blade, and wood form the character *liang* (bridge)." When the armies of [Xiao Yan (464–549), the future] Emperor Wu of the Liang reached Xincheng (just outside of the capital), he (Tao Hongjing) sent his disciple Dai Mengzhi to use the quickest route to memorialize [the prophecy]. When he heard of deliberations about the succession to the throne, the Master cited a number of specialists in diagram prognostication, who all had formulated the character *liang,* and had his disciple present these [to the court]. The emperor earlier had had associations with Tao, and when he took the throne his grace and courtesy were all the more generous.

The Master had already obtained sacred talismans and secret formularies; each time his marvelous elixirs were suspended [due to lack of ingredients] after repeated compounding, the emperor provided him medicinal substances. Moreover, as there were confirmatory verifications when he (the emperor) ingested the Sublimated Elixir that Tao had concocted, he increasingly honored and respected him. When he obtained writings submitted by Tao, he burned incense and received them with reverence. When the emperor had him compile a chronology, he (Tao) added a vermilion mark by the year *jisi,* which in truth was the third year of the Taiqing reign (549; the year in which the emperor would demise).

The emperor summoned him by handwritten decree and bestowed on him a deerskin headcovering (as worn by men in reclusion), and in response Tao but painted two bovines: one bovine was loosed free among the water plants, one wore a gold bridle and had a person holding its halter, driving it along with a staff. The emperor laughed, saying, "There is nothing this man will not do. As he wishes to imitate a tortoise dragging his tail [in the mud] (as in the example Zhuangzi had used for freedom from engagement in the government), how could there be reason for presuming he could be brought in [to serve]?" On great affairs of state, the emperor always first consulted with him, and in the space of a month there often were a number of letters exchanged; people of the time referred to him as Grand Councilor Mid the Mountains (Shanzhong zaixiang).

In the fourth year of the Tianjian reign (505), he moved his residence to the stream on the east of Accumulated Gold Ridge (Jijin shan, between the Greater and the Middle of the three Mount Mao peaks), in order to practice the highest Daoist arts. After living in reclusion some forty-odd years, when his years had passed eighty he still had a robust appearance. Books about transcendent-immortals say, "Those whose eyes are square have a thousand years of longevity." In the Master's later years, one eye at times was square.

As he was profoundly versed in arcane arts, he had foreknowledge that the imperial sovereignty of the Liang was soon to be overturned; he composed a prophetic poem, which went:

> Yifu gave reign to his unrestrained behavior;
> Pingshu but sat discoursing on the void.
> How would they answer at Zhaoyang Hall,
> When it transformed into a Shanyu's palace?

(Yifu is Wang Yan [256–311], a free soul and participant in arcane repartee who paid more attention to self-interest than the common good when in office; he was captured and put to death by a conquering chieftain. Pingshu is He Yan [ca. 190–249], a dandy given to dissipation, also known for his arcane discourse; when in office he placed his cohorts, all devotees to "pure conversation," in positions of power, and was executed when the clique to which he belonged fell. Shanyu refers to a non-Chinese chieftain.)

He secreted the poem in a trunk, and only after his departure due to transformation (i.e., death) did his disciples take it out. At the end of the Datong reign (ca. 544–546), scholars in office vied in discussion of arcane reasoning and did not prepare in military affairs. When Hou Jing usurped (at the end of 551), he indeed situated himself in the Zhaoyang Hall.

Foretelling the date, Tao knew in advance the day of his own demise and composed a "Composition Announcing My Departure." He died in the second year of the Datong reign (536) at eighty-one years of age (eighty by Western reckoning). He was granted [posthumously] the rank of Palace Attendant Grandee and was conferred the posthumous title Master Undefiled and Unsullied (Zhenbai xiansheng). A book he authored, *Document on the Mountain World* (i.e., monasteries; *Shanshi shu*), amounted to several hundreds of rolls, and disciples who received his instruction numbered more than three thousand.

His nephew Tao Yi wrote a *Record of the Essential Activities of Huayang's Dweller-in-Retirement Master Tao* (*Huayang yinju Tao xiansheng benqi lu*). Xie Yue (of the Liang?) of Wuxing wrote a *Concise Life of Master Tao* (*Tao xiansheng xiaozhuan*). Li Bo (of the Tang) wrote a *Life of Mao Shan's Master Undefiled and Unsullied of the Liang* (*Liang Maoshan Zhenbai xiansheng zhuan*). Jia Song (of the Tang) wrote a *Privied Biography of Tao the Perfected One, Supervisor of Waterways at Penglai* (*the Blessed Isles*) (*Penglai dushuijian Tao zhenren neizhuan*). And during the Xuanhe reign [of the Song] (on September 12, 1124), there was the "[Imperial] Declaration Granting [Posthumous] Entitlement as the Perfected One Who Reverences the Mystery and Furthers the Teachings" (*Feng zongyuan* [i.e., *zongxuan*] *yijiao zhenren gao*).

The words of the "Declaration" are: "We are recipient of the great mandate of the Jeweled Heavens and retain the precious register of the Primordial Kalpa (or Original Primogenitor). We now shall elaborate and diffuse the divine tidings, develop and promote transformation through the Way. We shall explain subtle words by the supreme teachings and shall commend extended destiny among the ranks of the Perfected. Supervisor of Waterways at Penglai, Tao the Dweller-in-Retirement galvanized his worldly acts in the net of renown, cleansed his rarefied nature among the splendid towers [of state]. He had divine associations and was free of encumbrances; his worldly legacy nonetheless was as a Councilor mid the mountains. His sincerity moved [the gods] to quick recognition, and he was granted transcendent-immortality out on the oceans [at the Blessed Isles]. When We consider the incomparability of his virtuous repute, how could the sublime sanctuary [of Our dominion] venture to disregard it? Would that he accrue the honor of an illustrious [posthumous] appellation, to forever intermediate blessings for all that has life."

THE TANG DYNASTY (618–907)

Daoist Efflorescence (Dao hua)

Wu Yun (d. 778), styled Zhenjie, was a man of Huayin Prefecture in Huazhou (just north of Mount Hua in eastern Shaanxi). When young he mastered the classics and was adept at composing writings; he was selected for the Advanced Scholar [examination] but did not place. By nature he was lofty and pure and had no patience for popular vogue. He went to Mount Song (the Central Sacred Peak, Henan), and affiliating himself with Revered Master Pan (Pan Shizheng, 585–682) he became a Daoist priest focusing on the Zhengyi ways. He painstakingly delved assiduously [into his master's teachings] and subsequently fully comprehended his arts. During the Kaiyuan reign (713–741) he traveled south to Jinling (modern Nanjing, Jiangsu), seeking after the Way at Mount Mao. After some time he traveled to the Tiantai Mountains (in eastern Zhejiang), where he went to gaze over the blue reaches of the sea and sported in pleasure with scholars of repute.

His writings and verse made their way to the capital, and when the Xuanzong Emperor (r. 712–756) heard of his reputation, he dispatched someone to summon him [to court]. When he arrived, he was beckoned to the Datong Hall, where [the emperor] was greatly pleased upon speaking with him. He was ordered [to the posting] Expectant Official at the Hanlin Academy. On one occasion, when he was asked about Daoist arts, he replied, "As for the quintessence of Daoist arts, there is nothing comparable to the five thousand words [of the Laozi]. The various other writings and versifications are prolix verbiage and simply waste writing paper." When further asked about the matters of divine transcendency and [alchemical] cultivation and refinement, he answered, "These are matters for people in the wilds. One must pursue them through skillful practice for years on end; they are not what should be asked about by the ruler of men." Each time Yun expounded, it always concerned preeminent doctrines and worldly duties; he gave indirect criticism with subtle words, and the Son of Heaven held him in high regard. He was bestowed the appellation Master Who Reverences the Mystery (Zongyuan [i.e., Zongxuan] xiansheng).

During the Tianbao reign (742–756), when Li Linfu (d. 752) and Yang Guozhong (d. 756) held authority, the mainstays of government were unraveling by the day. Yun sought insistently to return to Mount Song; he memorialized repeatedly [to be so allowed] but was not permitted. Finally [the emperor] decreed that a Daoist seminary be separately established [for him] at the Peak Monastery (on Mount Song). Just prior to the revolt of [An] Lushan (at the end of 755), Yun sought to return to Mount Mao and was so permitted. As it turned out, there were great vicissitudes in the central plains, and there were many bandits in the area between the Yangzi and Huai rivers (i.e., Anhui and Jiangsu), so he traveled [south]east to the Tiantai Mountains and the Shan locale (in eastern Zhejiang), where he enjoyed an extramundane association with Li Bai (699–762) and Kong Chaofu (d. 784).

Yun's collected writings are in twenty rolls, with a preface by Quan Deyu (759–818). His "Three Fascicles on the Mainstay of the Mystery" ("Xuangang sanpian") and "Discourse on 'Divine Transcendency Can Be Learned' " ("Shenxian ke xue lun") were acclaimed by scholars of penetrating understanding. When Yun was in the Hanlin Academy, he was especially favored. Gao Lishi (684–762) was partial to Buddhism and consequently once berated Yun in front of the emperor; Yun then inexorably pursued the extramundane. So it was that his phraseology and reasoning were magnificent and profound, and his literary talent shone forth. Each time he composed a fascicle of writing, people would vie to repeat and copy it. One [whose writings] could be on a par even with Li Bai's sublime unrestraint and Du Fu's (712–770) majestic elegance: would that not be but Yun?

THE SONG DYNASTY (960–1279)

Daoists (Dao pin)

Chen Tuan (872–989), styled Tunan, was a man from Qiao Commandery (in the northwestern corner of Anhui). When young he was playing by the Guo River (in Anhui) when [the divine] Lady Dressed in Green (Qingyi yu) held him in her arms and suckled him, saying, "This will cause you to forever be without cravings and desire." His intelligence and brilliance surpassed others. During the Changxing reign of the [Later or Southern] Tang (930–933) he was nominated as Advanced Scholar, however he failed [the examination]. He departed into seclusion in the Wudang Mountains (in northwestern Hubei), where he abstained from eating grains and practiced [yogic] breathing. He composed eighty-one stanzas of poetry, which he named "Fascicle Aiming at the Mystery" ("Zhi xuan pian"). The Mingzong emperor of the Later Tang (r. 926–933) gave him the title Pure and Vacuous Scholar-at-Home (Qingxu chushi).

Shortly thereafter he moved to the Cloud Pavilion Temple at Mount Hua (the western sacred peak, east of Chang'an in Shaanxi), where he often would close his door and lie down, not rising for months at a time. The Shizong emperor of the [Later] Zhou (r. 954–959) summoned him to the Forbidden Quarters [of the imperial palace]; he (the emperor) found him authentic upon examination. At the close of the Xiande reign (954–959), Tunan mounted a white mule and was about to enter the eastern capital when he heard that the Taizu emperor of the Song (r. 960–976) had ascended the throne. He laughed loudly, saying, "The empire now is stable." When he was summoned to court during the [first years of the Taiping xingguo] reign (976–984) of the Taizong emperor (r. 976–997), Tunan expressed the following words: "I, your servant, have a nature like that of an ape or a bird, and my mind is similar to dead ashes. I understand neither the shallow nor the deep points of 'humanity' and 'right conduct'; how could I comprehend what is appropriate or inappropriate of ritual and decorum? I break off lotus [leaves] for my clothing, and peel off bamboo skin for my cap. My body is covered by black hairs, and my feet lack [even] straw slippers. If I were to approach the railing and steps [of the palace], this would give occasion to ridiculing Your sagely wisdom."

Taizong again dispatched the Palace Receptionist to make certain of having him accede, and moreover conferred on him a poem, which went:

Once past in a former reign, you left the white clouds;
Later on you vanished away, sought without a trace.
Now at present should you deem, to follow this summons to court,
The Three Peaks one and all, I beg to bestow on you.

Having no recourse, Tunan paid a visit to the palace towers capped in a Huayang headpiece, treading in straw slippers, with plumed vestments and hanging sash, and [in this his outfit of a Daoist priest] was ceremoniously given audience as a guest. He was conferred the appellation Master Imperceptible and Imperceivable (Xiyi xiansheng). He was sent to call at the Hall of the Secretariat, where an aide addressed the Grand Councillor Song Qi (917–996) and others, saying, "Tuan but perfects his person and does not concern himself with power or gain. He entered into Mount Hua for forty years, and his years are reckoned as nearing a hundred. As the empire is ordered and at peace, he therefore has come for an audience at court. This can well be kept in mind." Qi and the others then asked of the Way of cultivating and nurturing, and Tunan replied, "The sagely emperor has physiognomic markings between his eyes and on his forehead (indicative of a great ruler of man). It is now just the time for lord and servant to harmonize their virtue and make plans for the rule. How could diligent practice of alchemical refinement add to this?" The scholars and grandees went to him daily begging for choice words, to which he always answered, "Do not dote long on sources of leisurely pleasures; do not again return to circumstances which fulfill your wishes." Those who understood approved.

Tunan had vast understanding of the many classics and was particularly proficient in the study of the [*Classic of*] *Changes*. It seems that he passed his instruction down to his disciple Mu Xiu (979–1032); Xiu transmitted it to Li Zhicai (d. 1045), and Zhicai transmitted it to Master Kangjie, Shao Yong (1012–1077). Moreover, he passed on his "Diagram of the Ne-Plus-Ultra (or, Great Ultimate)" to Chong Fang (955–1015); Fang transmitted it to Mu Xiu, and Mu Xiu transmitted it to Master Lianxi, Zhou Maoshu (Zhou Dunyi, 1017–1073). By means of ancient numerological arts Tunan gave prognostications [as quick as] firing a crossbow. Whereas later they turned out to be so, the hearsay of the time was that he had a mantic mirror of human relations.

Earlier, when the Taizu emperor once went out incognito and was traipsing through the Chang'an market together with Zhao Zhongxian (Zhao Pu, 921–991), Tunan met him on the road and said, "Would you have a drink?" Taizu said, "I'd like to, with Single Classic Specialist Zhao along." Tunan glanced at him (Zhao) obliquely, and said, "That's also all right." When they arrived at the tavern, Zhongxian, who suffered rheumatism of the foot, quickly went to sit on [the emperor's] right. Tunan reviled him, saying, "Just a little star in the Purple Tenuity Constellation (corresponding to the terrestrial imperial entourage)—dare you take the second best [seat]?" Zhongxian yielded, taking a seat of lesser importance [to that of Tunan].

When the Taizong emperor summoned Tunan, he directed him to pay audience to the [future heir designate and future] King of Shou (he was appointed King of Shou in 994, heir designate in 995). Tunan went to his door and returned, saying, "At the king's door the slaves and servants all are about to be assembled; why is it necessary for me go see the king?" Due to this, Taizong set his attentions on [the King of Shou, the future] Zhenzong emperor.

During the second year of the Duangong reign (989), Tunan foresaw his own death. He sent a memorial to that effect to the emperor, which read, "My great number of years are coming to their end; it shall not be possible to dote on my time with you, sagely emperor." He instructed his disciple Jia Desheng to tunnel out a chamber of stone at Zhang Chao Valley (on Lotus Flower [Lianhua] Peak at Mount Hua), and when the chamber was completed, he demised (on August 25, 989). For months multicolored clouds hid the mountain vale without dispersing.

Daoist Obscurity (Dao mo pin)

Shuai Zilian (d. 980) was a farmer in the Heng Mountains (the Southern Sacred Peak, in eastern Hunan). He was dull-witted and simple, and not complaisant. Everyone called him Shuai the Ox. Late in life he entered the Temple of the Southern Sacred Peak as a Daoist priest. Southwest of the temple was the Pavilion of Purple Vacuity, an ancient altar to [the goddess] Lady Wei. Because it was desolate and lonesome, none of the Daoist priests was willing to stay there. Zilian alone was happy to inhabit it; as he was nothing but grave and silent, no one observed his doings.

As it was, he was sorely fond of wine and regularly lay drunk amid the mountain forest. He was oblivious of great wind and rain, and tigers and wolves crossed before him without inflicting harm. Thus it was that when Vice Minister of Rites Wang Gonghu came to his post as Governor of Changsha and under imperial decree went to pray at the Southern Sacred Peak and pay respects at the altar to the Lady Wei, Zilian was just then lying drunk, unable to rise. He looked straight at the minister and said, "This Daoist priest of the village loves wine; as I cannot always get some, when I do at once I straightaway get drunk." The accompanying officials were incensed at him, but Lord Wang discerned that he was extraordinary and carried him home with him. For more than a month Zilian fell into silence, not speaking a word. Wang then sent him to return to the mountains, saying, "You, venerable teacher, conceal your luminescence but shine from within. This is what this old fellow did not fathom; it is appropriate that I should respectfully proffer poetry to you." As it turned out, Wang forgot about this. One day when he was sleeping in the morning he dreamt that Zilian came to claim the poetry. So he then composed two quatrains, which he wrote on a panel and set up above his office. The many Daoist priests said in surprise, "How did Shuai the Ox rate this?"

On the twenty-seventh day of the sixth month of the fifth year of the Taiping xingguo reign (August 10, 980), Zilian suddenly addressed the men of the temple, saying, "I am about to be off on a calling. The pavilion cannot be left unmanned, and you should quickly send someone to succeed me." All were even more startled and said, "With the weather hot like this, where is Shuai the Ox off to?" They looked at him perplexedly and [discovered that] he was dead. At first they greatly marveled at him, saying, "So, Shuai the Ox knew the day of his death!" And they proceeded to bury him beneath the mountain peak.

Not long after, Shoudeng, a [Buddhist] monk of the Temple of the Southern Terrace, was returning from the eastern capital and encountered Zilian outside the Nanxun Gate. Zilian had a divine air about him, serenely uplifted. When Shoudeng asked why he had left the mountains, Zilian laughed, saying, "I'm simply traipsing in leisure," and entrusted him with a letter to his cohorts in the mountains. When Deng returned home he learned that Zilian had died, and when he inspected the letter, it was [written] the day of his death. When his grave was opened, there was nothing but his walking stick and sandals.

Daoist Arts (Dao shu pin)

Liu Yongguang (ca. 1155–ca. 1224) was a man of Guixi in Xinzhou (modern Shangrao, northeastern Jiangxi). His appearance, strange and ancient, was swarthy. When he reached adulthood, he had no cause for renown. He went off to the Southern Sacred Peak (Heng Shan), and when he reached Linchuan Prefecture in Fuzhou (modern Fuzhou, Jiangxi), he met a man of the Way [i.e., a Daoist] on the road, who said he was Zhang Fuyuan and traveled on together with Yongguang. When traveling, Yongguang acted as Zhang's porter; when camped, he cooked for Zhang. When they stopped over at Changsha (in

Hunan), Zhang addressed him, saying, "You have attended to me with diligence and to your utmost. Always when I was rude to you, in order to observe your reaction, you were reverent all the more. As now I am going on to Shu (Sichuan), I have a fascicle [of writings] to bestow on you; you should keep it secret." He then departed. When Yongguang opened it for a look, it was the *Book of [the Method of] the Five Thunders* [for invoking rain] (*Wu lei [fa] shu*).

During the Qingyuan reign (1195–1200) there was drought in Quzhou (western Zhejiang). Commandery Governor Shen Zuoli dreamt one night of a black dragon coiled at the gates of the Temple to the City God, and when morning came he went to check it out: it was Yongguang lying there drunk. When he engaged Yongguang and charged him with invoking rain, it rained. The commandery reported the matter, and when Yongguang again invoked rain at court, it also rained. Yongguang was nearly forty in years and had not yet had occasion to be ordained as a Daoist priest. At this point, the emperor bestowed upon him cap and vestments and conferred the appellation Master Complaisant and Tranquil (Chongjing xiansheng).

The Ningzong emperor (r. 1194–1224) issued funds from the National Treasury on his behalf and entirely renovated and enlarged the Temple of the Highest Clarity. When the Lizong emperor took the throne (in 1224), Yongguang again was summoned. He said to the [imperial] emissary, "Return and memorialize to the Son of Heaven that for governing the empire the five thousand words of the [*Classic on*] *the Way and Its Power* are sufficient. If a rustic man of the mountain forests were to come [to court], how would that be to greater advantage?"

In the end he was transformed through liberation [from his body] in the Longhu Mountains (in northeastern Jiangxi). As for Zhang Fuyuan, the man he had met in the past, some say he was the Supernal Preceptor (Tianshi) of the Han [dynasty] [i.e., Zhiang Ling, or Zhang Daoling].

37

Imperial Guest Ritual

James L. Hevia

In the Qing dynasty (1644–1911), Guest ritual (*binli*) was a body of codified practices involving the procedures and protocols for dealing with an embassy from a foreign kingdom. Guest ritual was one of five categories of imperial rites, along with Auspicious rites (*jili*), Felicitous rites (*jiali*), Martial rites (*junli*), and Funerary rites (*xiongli*). Beginning in the Tang dynasty (618–907), the practice of the five types of rites constituted imperial rulership.

From the Grand Sacrifices to the Cosmos, Earth, Ancestors, and Soil and Grain, through the mundane routines of state such as Guest ritual, the Qing imperial order was continually reproduced in ritual action, intimately linking the world of human beings to the realm of the invisible. Moreover, higher-order rites, such as the winter solstice sacrifice to the Cosmos on the round altar outside the southern wall of Beijing, provided a pattern for the organization of other imperial rituals. For example, they embodied coherent logics governing the temporal sequences of rites and the spatial deployment of people and ritual objects. This was also the case for ancestral sacrifice or other forms of worship held in temples. Moreover, the physical structure of temples varied little from halls used for the many kinds and levels of imperial audience, of which Guest ritual was a part. Finally, Grand Sacrifice established principles of hierarchical precedence duplicated throughout imperial ritual: north was superior to south, east to west, and high to low.

The structural affinities and redundancies among the five rites place in the foreground the fact that it was in and through the performance of an annual ritual cycle that the emperor and his court solidified a dynasty's claim to the Mandate of Heaven (*tianming*) and produced imperial virtue (*de*). This virtue not only served to order the empire but emanated outward in the world, attracting other princes to the court of the emperor. It was the capacity to configure the world in this way, to connect the Cosmos to the local and the global, that formed the basis of an emperor's claim to be both Son of Heaven and supreme lord (*huangdi*). Because of the many connections, both metaphorical and metonymic, that can be discerned among the imperial rites, distinctions between sacred and secular seem somewhat misplaced for Chinese ritual practice. Instead, imperial guest ritual seems to have extended the link fashioned by emperors in Grand Sacrifice to other kingdoms, constituting a cosmo-moral order of global proportions.

Each dynasty tended to produce its own ritual manual, one that drew upon and altered the rites of previous dynasties. Such manuals were sometimes reedited several times during the reigning dynasty. The last imperial court in Chinese history, the Manchu conquest dynasty called the Qing, was no exception. Their ritual manual was entitled the *Comprehensive Rites of the Great Qing* (*Da Qing tongli*, hereafter cited as *Comprehensive Rites*) and was originally promulgated in 1756 during the reign of the Qianlong emperor and reedited in 1824. It is from the latter edition of the *Comprehensive Rites* that the following translation is made.

In the ritual manual of the Tang dynasty (*Da Tang Kaiyuan li* (c. 732), Guest rites were defined as the ceremonies appropriate to meetings between an emperor and a foreign prince. The rite included the reception of the prince and/or his embassy, the offering of local products by the prince to the emperor, and audiences, feasts, and rewards bestowed on the prince by the emperor. During the embassy, all the needs of the visitors were taken care of, including food, housing, entertainment, sight-seeing, and travel conveyances. Embassies were generally allowed to remain a certain amount of time in the imperial capital (usually a few weeks or months) and then were ordered to return to their own kingdoms.

Although Guest ritual in the Qing followed the general form of the Tang, a number of changes in procedure were made and, perhaps more importantly, the category itself was expanded. Apparently in accord with their understanding of guest ceremonies in the *Rites of Zhou* (*Zhouli*) (compiled in the third or second century B.C.E.) of the Zhou dynasty (ca. 1027–256 B.C.E.), Qing editors made a number of additions in the two chapters devoted to Guest ritual in the *Comprehensive Rites*. These included a section on the dispatching of an embassy to enfeoff a foreign prince; protocols for visits between imperial princes of the blood and foreign nobles graded into five ranks; visits among capital officials; and visits between capital officials and provincial officials, among provincial officials, and among commoners. These additions signified a general trend in the Qianlong reign to transcend the practices of previous dynasties and to recover the spirit, if not the exact form, of the rites of the Zhou dynasty.

Translated here is the first of the two chapters of Guest ritual, which itself is divided into two parts. The first deals with the reception of an ambassador from a foreign kingdom (*fanguo*); the second with the dispatching of imperial envoys to enfeoff the successor prince of a foreign kingdom. Throughout the translation I have placed headings and subheadings to aid the reader; some are actually in the manual. Subheadings are consistent with the more fully elaborated sections of imperial audience and feasting found in the Felicitous rites section of the *Comprehensive Rites*.

The first chapter of Guest ritual (chapter 45) is prefaced by comments about the rite, which help to locate both the editing project at work in the creation of this text and the context in which guest rites were placed. Referring to the *Rites of Zhou*, rather than the more elaborate ritual manuals of the Tang or Ming (*Ming jili*, 1530), the editors begin by noting that everything outside the nine provinces that made up the Zhou domain was considered foreign. The text does not explain what the relation between the Zhou kingdom and foreign lands might have been. It suggests, however, that for the Qing the relation being organized through imperial Guest ritual was one between the Manchu emperor as Huangdi, the "supreme lord" (the "lord of lords," the "paramount king") and the princes of foreign kingdoms (the multitude of lords in the world) as lesser or inferior lords. As such, the text indicates an imagining of the world in which the position of a paramount ruler or overlord was established through the submission of other princes to him. The paramount king received lesser lords in audience, and the latter brought the "most precious things" (*guibao*) of their kingdom and "offered" them up (*zhi*, *Comprehensive Rites* 45:1a) to their acknowledged superior.

Let us take up these two images in turn, the coming of foreign princes or their embassies to the court of Huangdi and their precious offerings. The Qing emperor was designated as Huangdi in a variety of court audience situations. Guest ritual is only one of these and, in part, appears to be organized with reference to other occasions of court assemblage. In the *Comprehensive Rites,* imperial assembly or audience is placed among the Felicitous rites (chapters 18 and 19), where it is divided into Grand audience (*dachao*) held on the first day of the year, the winter solstice, and the emperor's birthday; regular audience (*changchao*), held two or three times a month; and the rite for "attending to the affairs of the realm" (*tingzheng*), held several times a month for the purpose of presenting memorials to the court and for the dissemination of imperial edicts. In the case of Grand or Regular audiences, provisions were made for the participation of foreign princes or their ambassadors. Chapter 45 of the *Comprehensive Rites* frequently refers readers back to the Felicitous rites chapters for information about placements of people, regalia, and other necessary preparations for audience and feasting.

In all forms of audience, the emperor addresses the imperial domain and the world at large by instructing, admonishing, cherishing, and rewarding his servants, including foreign princes. All of these imperial attributes are associated with the emperor as the south-facing king. They derive their coherence from his prior act of facing north as the primary sacrificer to Heaven as the Son of Heaven and to his ancestors as a filial son.

By the end of the reign of the Qianlong emperor (1796), the foreign princes in question had come to include a vast host, many of whom received titles of noble rank from the Manchu court. First and foremost among those so entitled by the Qing were the many Mongol groups of northern and inner Asia. Also included were the various kingdoms located along the silk route through Xinjiang, Moslem kingdoms of Inner Asia, the kingdoms of Korea (which is distinguished from other kingdoms in the *Comprehensive Rites;* see especially the section on personnel designated imperial envoys to other courts), the Ryukyu Islands, Vietnam, Laos, Burma, Siam, Nepal, the island kingdoms of Southeast Asia, the kingdoms of Great Britain, Holland, Sweden, Portugal, and Spain, as well as the Papacy. As the preface indicates, for over one hundred years these domains had sent embassies at one time or another to the Qing court, and many returned in 1796 when the Qianlong emperor abdicated in favor of his son.

We might well ask why they came to the Qing court, why foreign kings sent embassies sometimes over great distances and at great risk and hardship. Why did they present valuable gifts to Qing emperors and presumably accept a position of inferiority to that of the Manchu overlord? The answer given in the preface is that foreign princes have heard and recorded the "enunciated teachings of the imperial family" (*guojia shengjiao*). While the text does not provide further elaboration on what these teachings might entail, I believe that they refer to the sagely and virtuous instructions of the current emperor and the extension through him of the virtuous attributes of previous Qing emperors. These enunciations move outward to encompass the whole world (*siyi*, the four directions), reorienting other lords and attracting them to the imperial court. Put another way, the powerful ideological formation implicit in this imagining of the world locates the Qing kingdom as the central domain (Zhongguo); all others ought to position themselves with respect to it. The princes of other kingdoms should, therefore, be desirous of submitting to the emperor by acknowledging his superiority. This desire is frequently presented in a variety of sources as "the sincerity of facing toward transformation" (*xianghua zhi cheng*). For their part, the emperor and his court are said to "cherish men from afar" (*huairou yuanren*), that is, to reward them for their sincerity.

The capacity of imperial enunciation to reorient lesser princes was made manifest through the presentation of offerings by these princes in a proper sequence at court. At the correct time of year (or in some cases every few years), the princes or their ambassadors come to court to present petitions and offer the most precious things of their domain to the emperor. These valuable offerings were further glossed in the *Comprehensive Rites* as local products (*fangwu*). They are, in other words, those things produced in the foreign kingdom and may be understood as things specific and unique to the kingdom of the prince who sends embassies to the imperial court. The court, in turn, incorporated the power of inferior princes into the rulership of the emperor by granting audience, bestowing precious things of its own on the embassies, and dispatching embassies to enfeoff successor princes.

The ideology of Guest ritual suggests, therefore, that Qing imperial sovereignty was constituted through the submission of foreign princes. The emperor accepted the sincere and humble prostrations of other powerful rulers and incorporated their strength into his own rulership. In turn, the emperor also accepted responsibility for the well-being of his loyal inferiors. Implicit in this version of sovereignty is an assertion that the lordship of the foreign prince is somehow linked to the moral authority of the Qing emperor as Huangdi. The proper way of establishing the relationship between the paramount king and the many lesser lords of the world was in and through imperial Guest ritual.

The translation of Qing Guest ritual provided here might best be read as a recipe rather than as stage directions, as the making of something rather than the acting out of a script. In this regard, a few general principles are useful in understanding the many references to placement, positioning, movement, and actions of participants. First and foremost, all directions are organized from the point of view of the emperor sitting on a throne at the north end of an audience hall facing south. Left and right are his left and right; high and low, closer and farther all relate to his position. Second, with the exception of the initial audience that takes place in the Board of Rites, the right or west side of halls, courtyards, and stairs are reserved for the guest. The west is also the martial or military side (wu), as opposed to the east or civil (wen) side of halls. In other words, the guest is placed among the Manchu Banners and other military officials of the Qing empire. Third, prostration in the form of kneeling and bowing the head to the ground occurs numerous times throughout the rite. Fourth, the center space of halls or courtyards running from the imperial throne south (and including the central space of other official halls as well) is reserved for the emperor and for tables upon which documents to or from the emperor are placed.

Finally, the Chinese language text of Guest ritual and the translation provided here understate the spectacular scope of ritual evident in some participant accounts and court pictures of imperial audience. More elaborate directions for the setting up of imperial regalia (banners, flags, chariots, and so on) and for the establishment of places for people and things can be found in the *Comprehensive Rites*, chapters 18 and 19; also see chapter 40 on banqueting. In addition, it is helpful to consult pictures or diagrams of audience halls (see the *Diagrams of the Collected Statutes of the Great Qing (Da Qing huidian tu)*, chapters 19–21). Since the emperor and his court arrayed themselves in robes appropriate to imperial audience, all such occasions would also have been a visual feast of color (the imperial regalia displayed in the paintings of the Guangxu emperor's wedding is similar to that found in Grand Audience).

Throughout the translation there are a number of offices and titles related to the Qing administrative structure. The text indicates that responsibilities for embassies were divided among the Board of Works, the Board of Revenue, and the Board of Rites, with the bulk of the duties falling on the last of these. The Department of Ceremonies, the Banqueting Department, the Reception Department, the Guest Hostel, as well as announcers, translators, and ushers were all affiliated with the Board of Rites. The Court of Ceremonial, a unit revived during the Qianlong reign and given various responsibilities for embassies, including the staffing of the Guest Hostel, was separate from the Board of Rites. Guard officers and guards were from the Imperial bodyguard.

The translation is from *Da Qing tongli* (*Comprehensive Rites of the Great Qing*) (Peking: Palace edition, 1883 reprint of 1824 reedited edition). Other sources cited are *Da Tang Kaiyuan li* (*The Rites of the Emperor Kaiyuan of the Great Tang Dynasty*), in *Siku quanshu* (*Complete Library in Four Branches of Literature*), series 8, vols. 99–108 (Taipei: Shengyu yinshuguan, 1978); *Da Qing huidian tu* (*Diagrams of the Collected Statutes of the Great Qing*), ed. Tuo Jin et al. (Peking: Palace edition, 1818); and *Ming jili* (*Collected Rights of the Ming Dynasty*), in *Siku quanshu* (*Complete Library in Four Branches of Literature*), series 8, vols. 113–24 (Taipei: Shengyu yinshuguan, 1978).

Further Reading

James L. Hevia, *Cherishing Men From Afar: Qing Guest Ritual and the Macartney Embassy of 1793* (Durham: Duke University Press, 1995); Christian Jochim, "The Imperial Audience Ceremonies of the Ch'ing Dynasty," *Bulletin of the Society for the Study of Chinese Religions* 7 (1979): 88–103; Richard D. Smith, *China's Cultural Heritage: The Qing Dynasty, 1644–1912* (Boulder: Westview Press, 1994), chaps. 6 and 7; and Angela Zito, "Re-presenting Sacrifice: Cosmology and the Editing of Texts," *Ch'ing-shih wen-t'i* 5.2: 47–78.

Guest Ritual, Chapter 45

PREFACE

In the *Rites of Zhou* the Grand Conductors of Affairs managed the rites and ceremonies of the guest. Kingdoms external to the nine provinces were called foreign kingdoms. Each of these kingdoms took its most precious things to be the offering [to the Zhou king].

In our time the enunciated teachings of the imperial family have reached the foreign peoples of the four directions who come as guests. The various kingdoms from beyond mountains and seas have recorded this. For over a hundred years, the Board of Rites, by Imperial Order, has feasted and rewarded them.

Various ceremonial and canonical works have been examined and combined, and thus compiled to make Guest ritual. Then the ceremonial usages for visits among the multitude of officials, the gentry, and the common people were appended afterward, each according to its correct category. In the ceremony of court audience and the presentation of offers, the foreign peoples of the four directions are classified as domains and order their offerings according to the proper season. [The princes] of these domains send their servants to present petitions and local products. They come to our court in the capital.

RECEIVING THE AMBASSADOR OF A FOREIGN PRINCE AT THE IMPERIAL COURT

GREETING THE VISITING EMBASSY

Greeting

When the ambassador is about to enter at the border, the Military Governor and the Governor-General of the province prepare a memorial and receive a response from the Board of Rites.

> *Internal note:* Korea crosses the Yalu River from Fenghuang City and enters via the Shanhai pass. Liuqiu crosses the sea and enters at Minganzhen, Fujian. Vietnam enters Pingxiangzhou, Guangxi, via the continental road and the Zhennan pass. Nanchang, going by way of the continental road, enters at Yongchangfu, Yunnan. Siam crosses the sea and enters via the Tiger Gate in Guangdong. Burma fords the river and enters at Pu'erfu, Yunnan, via the continental road. Sulu crosses the sea at the deepest point and enters at Amoy, Fujian. Holland crosses the sea to Guangdong. All other West Ocean domains enter at Macao, Guangdong.

The embassy is given postal credentials. Provincial officials select an escort of two or three civil and military officials to see them through each jurisdiction.

> *Internal note:* When the Korean embassy crosses the border, the prefect of Fenghuang City sends a captain of the guard to accompany them.

As they pass through each district, the responsible officials supply them with housing, food, boats, carts, and horses and send a staff of clerks and officials (civil and military) to protect and see them off through each jurisdiction until they reach the capital.

Preparation for Reception in the Capital

The Board of Rites notifies the Board of Works to make ready lodgings, prepare necessary implements, and lay fires; notifies the Board of Revenue to furnish millet, rice, and beans; and notifies the Court of Banqueting to furnish meat, fish, wine, spices, vegetables, and fruit.

Greeting

Upon their arrival, the embassy is met and watched over by the Subdirector of the Court of Ceremony. The Board of Rites instructs the embassy to enter the Guest Hostel where, for a time, they remain and are provided with food and drink.

PRESENTATION OF CREDENTIALS AND OFFERINGS OF LOCAL PRODUCTS

Preparation

The day after the ambassador has entered the Guest Hostel, the local products the embassy has brought, their credentials and petitions, and the retinue of the ambassador are all examined by court officials. Each member of the embassy dresses in the court dress of his domain and waits.

Establishing Places

At the Board of Rites, officials of the Department of Ceremonies set up a table for the credentials and petitions in the exact center of the upper part of the hall.

Taking Places

At the crack of dawn an official of the Court of Ceremony, in court dress, leads the ambassador to the Board of Rites. The ambassador enters via the left corner door and reverently waits at the foot of the left-hand stairs.

With credentials and petitions in hand, the ambassador stands in front of his retinue. The vice-ambassador stands behind him with the remainder of the retinue to his rear. One of the two vice directors of the Board of Rites enters and takes up a position to the left of the table. Two officials from the Department of Ceremonies stand to the south of the left and right pillars. All are attired in court dress. The official from the Court of Ceremony ascends the stair first and stands to the west of the left pillar.

Audience

One translator and one usher lead the ambassador up the stairs. The vice ambassador ascends a little to the rear of the main ambassador. The ambassador's retinue proceeds to its position according to rank. All kneel.

The ambassador holds in front him the credentials and petitions. The official from the Court of Ceremony reverently takes them and hands them to the vice director of the Board of Rites, who accepts them, places them in the exact center of the table, and returns to his position [to the left of the table]. The ambassador and his retinue perform three kneelings and nine bows. They rise and the usher leads them down the stairs. The official from the Court of Ceremony escorts them out.

Seeing Off

An official of the Department of Ceremonies sees off the petitions and credentials to the Inner Court and waits for an Imperial Order to be handed down. The Board of Rites divides up the local products and gives them to the appropriate officials (probably in the Imperial Household Department).

COURT AUDIENCE

When the ambassador has sent up his petitions and credentials, he may be fortunate to have arrived at the time of a Grand or Regular Court Audience.

Taking Places

The emperor proceeds to the Grand Harmony Hall for the rite of receiving the multitude of officials. At the proper time the usher leads the ambassador and his retinue to the outer courtyard of the Grand Harmony Hall, where they are ranked at the rear of the west side of the courtyard. They listen for the announcement to perform the rite, as in other ceremonies.

Internal note: See the Felicitous rites [section on Audiences].

If it is not the time for a Grand or Regular audience, then the Board of Rites memorializes requesting an audience. The Board of Rites receives an edict summoning the ambassador for viewing.

Preparation

The official of the Guest Hostel carries out the purification of the ambassador, and the translator conducts practice sessions in ritual protocol.

Taking Places

When the day of the audience arrives, the translator, attired in plain dress, leads the ambassador, who wears the court dress of his own domain, to a position outside the palace gate, where he respectfully waits.

Attired in regular court dress, the emperor takes his throne in the designated hall.

The Chamberlain of the Guards, the Chamberlain, and the Officers of the Guards take up their left and right in-waiting positions as they would in a regular audience ceremony. The director of the Board of Rites, in gold-thread boa constrictor robes, leads the ambassador in. The translator follows.

When they arrive at the west side of the courtyard, they perform of three kneelings and nine bows. At the completion of the rite, the ambassador is led to the west stairs and ascends. The translator follows him up the stairs. When they reach the door to the audience hall, they kneel.

Audience

The emperor asks the ambassador soothing questions.

The director of the Board of Rites transmits the imperial inquiries to the translator. The translator turns around and informs the ambassador.

The ambassador responds. The translator translates his words. The director of the Board of Rites molds the response and memorializes [to the emperor]. The rite is complete. All rise. The ambassador is led down the west stairs and out in retreat.

SPECIAL RITES

Taking Places

If there is to be a special rite, on the appointed day the emperor takes his throne in the designated hall.

The Officers of the Guard arrange themselves as before. The Great Officers of the Eight Banners, all attired in their usual gold-thread boa constrictor robes, enter the hall and take up their in-waiting positions on either side of the hall. The director of the Board of Rites leads the ambassador to the west side of the courtyard, where he performs three kneelings and nine bows and rises. He is led up the west stairs and enters the hall through the right [west] door to take up a position at the end of the line of the right [west] flank of the Great Officers of the Eight Banners. The translator enters and takes up a position a bit to the rear of the ambassador.

Audience

If the emperor has decided to bestow a seat, the Chamberlain of the Guards, the Chamberlain, the Officers of the Eight Banners, their deputies, and the director of the Board of Rites all go to their places, kneel and bow, and sit in ranked order. The ambassador follows, kneels, bows the head, and sits.

Then the emperor bestows tea. A special tea is brought forward. The emperor drinks the tea. All kneel and bow the head. The guards dispense the tea to the high officials and the ambassador, who kneel in acceptance, perform one bow, sit, and drink. When finished, all kneel and bow the head again.

The emperor asks soothing questions. The ambassador kneels, listens carefully, and responds. As in the previous ceremony, the director of the Board of Rites transmits the imperial inquiries and the translator conveys them to the ambassador. The rite is complete.

The director of the Board of Rites leads the ambassador to an antechamber of the audience hall. There the emperor bestows on the embassy food and drink like that from their homeland. When finished, an official from the Court of Ceremony escorts the ambassador in retreat.

GIVING THANKS FOR IMPERIAL BENEFICENCE

The next day at the crack of dawn the ambassador and his retinue appear outside the Meridian Gate to give thanks for the emperor's beneficence. An official of the Court of Ceremony transmits the announcement. An usher ranks them properly. The ambassador proceeds to the west side of courtyard before the Meridian Gate, faces north, and performs three kneelings and nine bows as in other rites. Then he retreats.

FEASTING AND REWARDS

Preparation

When the rites of presenting offerings and imperial audience are completed, the Board of Rites requests imperial bestowals for the kingdom and a feast for its ambassador and his retinue. When the Board of Rites obtains the Imperial Edict, it circulates it to the various responsible officials who will supply and make preparations for the appropriate day.

Establishing Places

Officials arrange the bestowal on the left [east] side of the Imperial Way outside the Meridian Gate. Bolts of silk, cloth, and gold are arranged on tables. Horses are arranged in the courtyard with complete equestrian outfitting.

Internal note: Only the Korean king and his ambassador are bestowed horses.

Taking Places

An official from the Guest Hostel, in court dress, escorts the ambassador and his retinue, each in their native court dress, through the east side of the Flourishing Peace Gate, the Heavenly Peace Gate, and the Upright Gate, to a position in front of the west antechamber in the forecourt of the Meridian Gate. Ranked in proper order, all face east and wait.

A vice director of the Board of Rites stands to the south of the table, facing west. The official in charge of the Reception Department follows him. Four censors and two announcers from the Court of Ceremony divide and stand to the left and right of the Imperial Way facing east and west. Two ushers stand to the north of the ambassador facing east. All are in court dress. The announcer tells them to take their places according to rank.

Audience

The usher leads the ambassador and his retinue into the west side of the courtyard [before the gate]. They stand according to rank facing north with the east position superior. The announcer intones "come forward." All move forward. The announcer intones "kneel, bow the head, and rise." All perform three kneelings and nine bows.

The official in charge of the Reception Department receives with both hands the enfeoffing document for the foreign prince. In front of the tables on which the imperial bestowal has been placed, he presents the document to the ambassador. The ambassador kneels in acceptance, turns, and passes it to a member of his retinue.

Then, in order of their rank, the ambassador, his officials, and his retinue receive the imperial bestowal. A clerk from the Reception Department takes these items in both hands and presents them to members of the embassy. Each kneels in acceptance. When the bestowal is complete, the announcer intones "bow the head and rise." The embassy again performs three kneelings and nine bows, rises, and is led in retreat. The official of the Guest Hostel escorts the ambassador and retinue out.

Feasting

A feast is then given at the Board of Rites according to feasting ceremony.

Internal note: See the Felicitous rites.

When the feast is over, the embassy returns to the Guest Hostel.

SEEING OFF THE EMBASSY

Preparation

When all affairs pertaining to the embassy are complete and the ambassador is about to return to his native domain, the Banqueting Court prepares [sacrificial] victims, wine, fruit, and vegetables.

Feasting

One of the vice-directors of the Board of Rites goes to the Guest Hostel and invites them to a feast. If the feast takes place in the Board of Rites, then the ceremony is as before.

Departure

The officials sent to accompany them in their departure protects and sees them off. On the embassy's departure from the imperial domain, the Board of Military Affairs returns their credentials.

Internal note: In the case of Korea, this is done at the Shanhai pass.

The Board of Rites sets out their itinerary and transmits it to each General and Governor-General [of the jurisdictions they will pass through]. Along their route, the embassy is supplied with lodging, boats and carts, food and drink, and a civil and military escort, as was done when it entered.

Imperial feasts may be bestowed at provincial capitals. One of the people responsible for their route hosts them. The ceremony is the same as in the Board of Rites feast. On the day that the ambassador crosses the border a report is transmitted to the emperor.

DISPATCHING IMPERIAL ENVOYS TO ENFEOFF A FOREIGN PRINCE

The rite of enfeoffing a foreign prince is performed for all domains that make offerings to our court. Whenever there is a succession to the throne, the successor takes up the affairs of the foreign kingdom and sends an officer to request an Imperial Order.

APPOINTING AND DISPATCHING IMPERIAL ENVOYS

Preparation

The Board of Rites presents the request to the emperor and receives an Imperial Edict. It then informs the Board of Works to prepare credentials and the Inner Court to draw up the enfeoffing documents.

Internal note: They print on this the lineage of the prince.

Once prepared the documents are sent to the Board of Rites. The Board of Rites memorializes for the appointment of a head envoy and vice envoy for enfeoffment, one being the bearer of credentials and the other the bearer of the enfeoffing document.

When going to enfeoff Korea, the enfeoffing envoys employed are the Chamberlain, Assistant Chamberlain, Guard Officer of the First Rank, the Manchu Subchancellor of the Inner Court, the Chancellor of the Hanlin Academy, or the vice director of the Board of Rites. They wear clothing of the ceremonial color appropriate to their ranks.

For Vietnam and Liuqiu the envoys employed are the Subreaders, the Subexpositors, the Compilers, or graduates of the Third Degree in the Hanlin Academy, Censors of the Six Boards, the Senior Secretary of the Board of Rites or his assistant; or an Assistant Secretary, recorders, or secretaries of the Inner Court.

If the emperor decides to bestow first rank unicorn dress for the envoys, all are looked upon as of the first rank in the ceremony that follows.

On the day the envoys are to depart, the Board of Works gives them a Dragon Banner, Imperial Staves, and an Umbrella. The Board of War provides them with transport and a protective guard.

Establishing Places

The civil and military officials all wait inside the Great Gate of the Board of Rites. An official from the Department of Ceremonies in the Board of Rites establishes a table in the exact center of the upper part of the hall and places the credentials on the left [east] side of the table and the enfeoffing document on the right [west].

Taking Places

The director of the Board of Rites stands to the left side of the table and the vice director on the right. Two officials from the Department of Ceremonies stand to their rear. All are in court dress.

Audience

The enfeoffing envoys arrive at the Board of Rites and proceed to the middle of the Hall, where they kneel. One official from the Department of Ceremonies holds the credentials in front of him; the other holds the enfeoffing document. Each conveys the document to the director and vice director, who in turn convey them to the head envoy and vice envoy. They reverently receive them, rise, and go out.

Departure

Outside the gate of the Board of Rites an officer of the military escort receives the documents. He covers the credentials and binds up the enfeoffing documents. The assemblage mounts and proceeds with the banner and staves to the front. The envoys change into traveling clothes, mount, and proceed together.

THE ENFEOFFMENT

Greeting the Imperial Envoys

When the enfeoffing envoys and their entourage enter the border of the kingdom in question, border officials supply food, prepare lodging, and provide transport, including horses. Along the route civil and military officials come out and kneel in receiving the imperial envoys, just as they do in the ceremony for greeting an Imperial Edict [see the Felicitous rites of the *DQTL*, 30:3b–4b].

When the envoys are about to reach the capital of the kingdom, the successor prince sends his officials to the environs of his city. They reverently greet the enfeoffing document by performing three kneelings and nine bows. The envoys honor them by performing one kneeling and three bows.

Preparation

Officials decorate the lodgings for the envoys and display outside the gates of the capital a properly prepared portable palace, an incense carrier, flags, staves, drums, and music, and respectfully await the arrival of the envoys. They greet the envoys when they arrive. The envoys reverently place the credentials and the enfeoffing document in the portable palace. They perform rites according to proper ceremonial usage. Officials of the prince visit the envoys and perform three bows. The envoys receive them.

Establishing Places

On the chosen day, there is an announcement of the reading of the enfeoffing document. Then it is displayed in the upper part of the prince's audience hall, where a table is established in the exact center. In front of it is placed an incense table. Both face south.

The position for the foreign prince to receive his investiture is to the south of the incense table. His bowing position is to the south of this. His officials' bowing position is established on the east and west sides of the courtyard, with all facing north. Positions for two announcers are established to the north of the prince's bowing position. Positions for two conductors who will lead the prince into the hall are to the south of the announcers. The positions for four people who will rank and lead officials of the prince into the courtyard are to the north of the positions for the prince's officials, facing east and west. An orchestra is placed within the gate. Ceremonial staves are placed in the middle of the courtyard, divided in two files on the left and right.

Taking Places

The prince leads his officials to the envoy's lodging. All are in the court dress of the domain. They solemnly perform the greeting rite. When finished, the prince and his officials take up a position outside the gate of the prince's audience hall. Then the portable palace is lifted up and set in motion. It is preceded by the incense carrier, flags, staves, drums, and music. The envoys follow on horseback.

The prince and those below him all kneel and wait. When the procession has passed, they rise. The portable palace is taken through the middle gate of the prince's audience hall and placed in the center of the courtyard. The envoys dismount.

The officer of the imperial military escort uncovers the credentials, raises them in front of himself, and conveys them to the head envoy, who proceeds alone to a forward position. Then the officer conveys the enfeoffing document to the vice envoy, who follows the head envoy in entering the prince's audience hall.

The envoys place the credentials and the enfeoffing document in the middle of the table. Both then retreat to stand to the east of the table. The reader of the imperial announcement stands behind them.

The conductors lead the prince to his bowing position where he faces north. Those who rank the prince's officials lead them to their bowing positions, where they stand facing north.

Audience

The announcer intones "kneel." The prince leads his officials in kneeling. The announcer intones "bow the head and rise." The prince and those below him perform three kneelings and nine bows, and rise.

The prince advances to the position where he will receive his investiture. The announcer intones "kneel." The prince kneels. The vice envoy comes forward and holds up the enfeoffing document. The reader faces west, opens, and reads the document. When finished, the vice envoy places it back on the table and returns to his position. The prince and those below him again perform three kneelings and nine bows and rise. The prince leads his officials out of the hall and they wait outside the gate.

The head envoy takes up the credentials and proceeds to the front of the portable palace. The officer of the imperial military escort places the cover on the credentials and puts it in the palace, which is then raised and carried out. The envoys follow it out.

Seeing Off

The prince and those below him kneel in seeing off the envoys. The envoys take the credentials to their lodging.

The prince then changes into regular dress and proceeds to the lodging. The envoys reward him by performing the rite of bowing and yielding precedence. When finished, the prince retreats.

Feasting

The prince feasts the envoys with animals slaughtered according to ceremonial usages and then returns to his hall. The prince sends his officers to wait and see off the envoys as was done previously in the greeting rite.

Return to the Imperial Court

The envoys return to the Imperial Court and report on the completion of the rite to the emperor. They return the Imperial Order and credentials and at the same time the emperor bestows clothing that accords with their management of the undertaking.

A FOREIGN PRINCE SENDS A PETITION GIVING THANKS FOR IMPERIAL BENEFICENCE

After the envoys have returned to the Imperial Court, the prince prepares a petition and local products. He sends his officers to the Imperial Court to give thanks for imperial beneficence. They are given the reward of a feast from the imperial granaries. All is conducted according to the ceremony for presenting offerings during a regular court audience [see above].

THE FIRST ENFEOFFMENT OF A FOREIGN KINGDOM

If foreign peoples express sincerity for the first time, the Court Order process begins. The Board of Rites memorializes requesting an Imperial Order. A head envoy and vice envoy are specially credentialed and presented with the enfeoffing document. The ceremony of enfeoffment is the same as in the previous case.

If, however, the domain is wild, far away, and difficult to reach, the enfeoffing document is conveyed to an ambassador who comes to the Imperial court and takes it back to his prince's domain.

The Ceremony

An official of the Department of Ceremonies in the Board of Rites sets up a table outside the Meridian Gate in the middle of the upper end of the Imperial Way and places the enfeoffing document on it. The director of the Board of Rites stands to the left of the table. The official from the Department of Ceremonies stands behind him. Two announcers from the Court of Ceremony stand to either side of the Imperial way. All are in court dress.

The head of the Guest Hostel escorts the ambassador, who is in court dress, to the west side of the forecourt in front of the Meridian Gate, where they wait.

The announcer intones "present the enfeoffment." An usher leads the ambassador in front of the table, facing north. The announcer intones "kneel" and the ambassador kneels. The official from the Department of Ceremonies takes the enfeoffing document and presents it to the director of the Board of Rites, who in turn presents it to the ambassador. The ambassador reverently receives it and gives it to one of his accompanying officials. He rises and retreats to the west side of the courtyard. Here he listens for the intoning of the order and then performs three kneelings and nine bows. When completed, he then reverently returns to his domain to present the document to his prince.

The prince dispatches an ambassador to the Imperial Court to give thanks for the Imperial Beneficence as in the previous case.

INDEX

This index covers the introductions to the translations only. It includes the names of historical figures, deities, titles of works, and technical terms. Place names and the names of historical periods are not generally included.

Abridged Codes for the Daoist Community. See Lu xiansheng daomen ke lue
actualization. *See cun*
Aisin-Gioro Wulaxichun, 225
alchemy, 11, 54
Almighty Sky Deity, 225
Amitāyus Buddha. *See* Amituo fo
Amituo fo (Amitāyus, Amitābha Buddha), 15, 20, 203, 205–211, 261, 264, 400
Amoghavajra. *See* Bukong jingang
An Shigao, 19
Analects (of Confucius). *See Lunyu*
Ānanda, 16, 278, 279
ancestor worship, 25, 26–27, 42–44, 107, 253, 269, 293, 390–391. *See also* sacrifices
anomalies. *See yi*
apocrypha: Buddhist, 98, 262, 372, 381; Han, 54–55
astrology, 52, 54, 241
Aśvaghoṣa, 381
Avalokiteśvara. *See* Guanyin
Avataṃsaka Sūtra. See Huayanjing
aw-ha (human soul, "counterpart"), 329
Awakening of Faith in Mahāyāna. See Dasheng qixin lun

Bailian jiao (Teaching of the White Lotus), 20, 206
Baimasi, 361
baixing (common people), 24
Baiyi Dabei wuyinxin tuoluoni jing (The Dhāraṇī Sūtra of the Five Mudrās of the Great Compassionate White-robed One), 98, 99–100
Baiyi Guanyin. *See* Guanyin
Bamboo Grove Monastery. *See* Zhulin si
banruo boluomiduo (Perfect Wisdom), 372–376
Banruo boluomiduo xin jing. See Heart Sūtra

banzhou sanmei (pratyutpanna samādhi, buddha-mindfulness sanctuary meditation), 207
Bao'en fengpen jing (Scripture for Offering Bowls to Repay Kindness), 278
Baopuzi (He Who Embraces Simplicity), 10, 54, 149
Beijing, City God of, 78–79
Bhaiṣajyaguru. *See* Yaoshiwang
bimo. See mediums
binli (Guest ritual), 471–488
Biography of Spirit Immortals (of Ge Hong). *See Shenxian zhuan*
Blofeld, John, 362
Bo Yi, 294
bodhisattva (*pusa*), 15–16, 28, 64, 211, 373, 376; images of, 261, 374. *See also* Bodhisattva Inexhaustible Mind, Dizang, Guanyin, Puxian, Wenshu, Yaoshiwang
Bodhisattva Inexhaustible Mind, 82
Book of Good Deeds. See Nheh Muh Suh
Brief Gazetteer of Phoenix Mountain Temple. See Fengshansi zhilue
Buddha (Fo), 13–15, 16, 20, 28, 56, 82–84, 205–211, 360, 361, 363, 372, 374, 381, 383, 391, 399; defined, 13, 15; images of, 261–264, 299, 373. *See also* Amituo fo, Mile fo
Buddhapāli, 208
Buddhism (Fojiao), 3, 7, 12, 13–20, 21, 82–86, 97–99, 203–211, 360–371, 381–384; and Daoism, 56, 269–270, 307, 310, 408, 424, 437; defined, 13; and early popular traditions, 242; icons of, 261–267; and kinship, 27–29; and Lahu ritual, 328; and miracle tales, 85; and reclusion, 397–404; and rites for the dead, 278–280, 284, 391–392; and state ceremonies, 391–396; and state protection, 372–380; tantric, 97–98, 372;